Encyclopedia of Literary Modernism

Encyclopedia of Literary Modernism

Edited by
PAUL POPLAWSKI

GREENWOOD PRESS
Westport, Connecticut • London

Library of Congress Cataloging-in-Publication Data

Encyclopedia of literary modernism / edited by Paul Poplawski.
    p. cm.
  Includes bibliographical references and index.
  ISBN 0-313-31017-3 (alk. paper)
  1. Modernism (Literature)—Encyclopedias. I. Poplawski, Paul.
PN56.M54E53   2003
809′.9112—dc21   2003040825

British Library Cataloguing in Publication Data is available.

Library of Congress Catalog Card Number: 2003040825
ISBN: 0-313-31017-3

First published in 2003

Greenwood Press, 88 Post Road West, Westport, CT 06881
An imprint of Greenwood Publishing Group, Inc.
www.greenwood.com

Printed in the United States of America

♾™

The paper used in this book complies with the
Permanent Paper Standard issued by the National
Information Standards Organization (Z39.48-1984).

10 9 8 7 6 5 4 3 2 1

Contents

Preface

Scope of This Book

Despite intense critical debate and disagreement over its very name, nature and scope, modernism continues to be widely acknowledged as probably the most important and influential artistic-cultural phenomenon of the twentieth century, whether it is considered primarily as a movement, a period, a genre, a style or an ideology. Within literature and literary studies especially, modernism looms large as an established canonical category, for publishers, readers, critics, students, and scholars alike.

It is surprising therefore to find a relative dearth of ready reference material devoted specifically to literary modernism, especially when there exists such a plethora of handbooks, companions and glossaries on literary topics generally, and a plethora, too, of developed critical scholarship on modernism in the shape of introductory overviews, scholarly monographs, edited essay collections, and anthologies of primary source materials. The classic survey of the field presented in Malcolm Bradbury's and James McFarlane's seminal essay collection, *Modernism 1890–1930* (Harmondsworth: Penguin, 1976; rptd. 1991), and the similar more recent collection edited by Michael Levenson, *The Cambridge Companion to Modernism* (Cambridge UP, 1999), are perhaps the nearest we have to the sort of reference guide I mean here. However, though these are both invaluable sources of information and critical insight, neither of them is specifically designed as a reference book and certainly not as a source of quick reference (though the former contains such elements as a detailed chronology of events, a hundred "Brief Biographies," and an extensive general bibliography).

The present volume, then, has been designed to fill the gap suggested above by providing a comprehensive and accessible source of quick reference to the key authors, works, movements, theories, places and events commonly associated with literary modernism. Written by expert scholars from around the world and covering hundreds of different topics in a clear, incisive and critically informed manner, this *Encyclopedia* presents a unique range of detailed entries—many in the form of mini-essays—mapping out the complex and variegated field of literary modernism in a fresh and original way from an early twenty-first century perspective.

Although the principal focus of the book is on English language literary modernism and the period 1890–1939, many entries extend substantially beyond these loose parameters to include important precursors and successors of modernism, as well as to cover the crucial European and interdisciplinary dimensions of modernism, and to provide complementary comparative perspectives from countries and regions not usually included in traditional accounts of the subject (thus there are entries, for example, on India, Southern Africa, and Hispanic America). Each entry includes a selected bibliography to guide the reader to essential primary and secondary sources, and a simple system of cross-referencing by means of bold type directs the reader to relevant related entries elsewhere in the book. There is also a selected bibliography of useful general works on modernism at the end of the *Encyclopedia,* as well as a comprehensive index. It should be noted that the index clearly highlights all main entries and may therefore be browsed to provide an initial overview of the book's contents. The index will also prove useful for locating discussions of significant authors, movements or topics that do not have their own main entries because of having been incorporated within some of the more substantial synoptic entries, such as those dealing with countries or regions (e.g., France, Spain, Russia), or with art movements (e.g., cubism, impressionism, surrealism), or with general topics (e.g., dance, feminism, film, music, psychoanalysis, thought).

Definitions of Modernism

As I suggested at the start, the field of modernism is a highly complex and hotly contested one, and there is no universal consensus on precisely what constitutes modernism. The name itself remains radically unstable, shifting in meaning according to who uses it, when, where and in what context—to the extent that several critics now prefer to talk of discrete and disparate "modernisms" rather than of one overarching "modernism." Whether or not this merely multiplies problems of definition is a moot point, but it certainly reflects the dynamically conflicted and heterogeneous nature of our current understanding of modernism.

In addition to its straightforward reference function, therefore, this book has been conceived and developed also to encourage critical reflection on established views of what the term "modernism" means or might mean. In compiling the book, I have taken a very catholic and pragmatic approach as to what falls within its purview, erring purposely on the side of inclusiveness in order implicitly to challenge any narrow or neatly programmatic views of modernism; and I have allowed contributors a free hand to develop their own ideas, in relation to their particular topics, as to what modernism means to them. In this way, I hope to have given clearer definition to shifting conceptions of modernism as they have evolved over time, place, and culture, and to have generated multiple and multifaceted perspectives on modernism which may suggest new ways of conceiving it in the future. The book's twofold aim overall, then, has been to provide comprehensive and reliable factual information on the people, places, principles, and texts normally identified with literary modernism, while also interrogating conventional, canonical conceptions of what, when, why, how and who modernism was (and/or is).

It should be clear from the above why a discrete entry on modernism itself is conspicuously—indeed constitutively—absent from the book; and, for similar reasons, it would be presumptuous of me (and not a little foolhardy) to try to present some sort of ready-made dictionary definition of the term here. Apart from inevitably belying the manifest complexity of modernism, such an attempt would sit uneasily with the intended open-endedness of what might be called the book's "rhizomatic" exploration of modernism—its intention of generating new and unplanned roots/routes of inquiry. However, notwithstanding the difficulties, some initial orientation on the subject may be helpful, if not in the form of a definition, then in that of a brief checklist of some of the key points commonly adduced in discussions of modernism (both within this book and elsewhere).

A certain protean indeterminacy may in fact be self-reflexively appropriate to a phenomenon tellingly described by Bradbury and McFarlane as "an appallingly explosive fusion" of many disparate and often contradictory trends (48). But several more determinate features of modernism can also be identified as part of a fairly common frame of reference within most critical discussions of the topic. To begin with, the emphasis on volatility in Bradbury's and McFarlane's formulation derives quite naturally from what has been probably the most prominent and constant element in definitions of modernism since the term came into regular literary-critical usage in the 1960s: that is, modernism's avant-garde experimentalism and its concern for radical innovation in artistic form, style, content and method. This emphasis, in turn, is linked to what is often seen as the revolutionary dynamic within modernism. On the one hand, we have modernism's literary-aesthetic and epistemological rejection of the conventions, assumptions, procedures, and perceptions of the classical and realist art of the eighteenth and nineteenth centuries—a rejection precipitated by a range of related art movements such as impressionism, imagism, symbolism, futurism, and expressionism. On the other hand, we have its ideological critique—variously radical or conservative—of modernity and of the complex social developments associated with industrialization, urbanization, and democratization. This sense of living through a period of momentous social, political and cultural upheaval can be seen as a key motivating factor in the modernist insistence on an equivalently momentous upheaval in aesthetic practice (itself often seen as fundamentally political).

It can also be seen to motivate another major nexus of modernism: its profound concern with themes of alienation, fragmentation, and the loss of shared values and meanings, and its concomitant search for alternative systems of belief in myth, mysticism, and primitivism—or in art itself, seen by many modernists as a privileged sphere of order and of heightened ephiphanic revelation. Linked to all this, depictions of modernism also typically draw attention to the self-conscious focus in modernist art on the very processes of making meaning and on the difficulties and complexities of representation and perception. Thus, questions of ambiguity, relativity, and subjectivity, along with linguistic experimentation and formal experiments in disordered chronology and shifting points of view, all feature prominently in most discussions of modernism, as does the fundamental importance to modernism of psychology and the elusive workings of the conscious and unconscious mind.

Anyone who comes to this book with little or no previous knowledge of modernism may well be surprised to find that this brief inventory of its commonly assumed features makes it sound remarkably familiar and contemporary. As Bradbury and McFarlane suggest, this is precisely because

> Modernism is still, in some fashion, a shaping art behind the art of our own times . . . it still remains integrally woven into our contemporary awareness, still possessing the power to startle and disturb. (12)

What better reason, then, to introduce modernism afresh with this *Encyclopedia* and to continue the task, so ably advanced by Bradbury and McFarlane themselves, of interrogating and reinterpreting for our own generation what they call in the same place "this most living of creative pasts"?

Acknowledgments

My first and main debt of gratitude must be to all the contributors to this volume for their enthusiasm for the project and for their superb professionalism and scholarship in carrying out their commissions—also, for their kind patience in the face of various delays to publication, and for their friendly support and cooperation over the several years it has taken to bring the project to completion. I would like to thank George Butler for commissioning and encouraging the project in the first place; Anne Thompson and the other support staff at Greenwood for their administrative and editorial work on the book; and the team at Impressions for keeping the final production process on such a tight leash. I am grateful to my sister, Alina, for help with the entry on Poland; and, as always, to my wife, Angie, for her unstinting support throughout.

A

Adler, Alfred (1870–1937)

Austrian doctor and originator of Individual Psychology.

See under **Psychoanalysis.**

Africa and the South

Has modernism any relevance to the South of the world? From the perspective of the rich North modernism is a Euro-American reaction to the bourgeois rationalism of urban life. The individual personality—the invention of enlightenment modernity—rebels against the middle-class habit, and the rebellion assumes paradoxical proportions: an avant-garde experimentalism of style, which is attracted to romantic freedom, finds itself checked, painfully, by intimations of a metaphysical abyss, in which the Greco-Roman inheritance sheds the sustenance of myth to be retrievable only in fragments shored against ruin. With glimpses that beneath the confidence of Empire lay a heart of darkness, the condition of Europe suggested both Western decline and revivification in the politics of blood and soil. The social imagination—often damaging in its modernist anti-democratic tendencies—is transmuted through an art religion into a psychological correlative according to which it is not so much Marx, as **Freud,** who lends Euro-American modernism of the years 1880 to 1930 the delineation of its high achieve-

ment. The achievement is embodied in the great art works of the period: artifacts that in a de-familiar style—a style that "makes strange"—signal their autonomy from social dependency.

Such works—**Eliot**'s *The Waste Land* (1922), for example—are, according to mythic predisposition, complex and comprehensive in their grasp of the modern urban scene. Conversely, the social conscience may identify a simplification of the scene. As **Brecht** might have put it, *The Waste Land* understands modernity as a politics of culture rather than a culture of politics. Simultaneously, however, Brecht complicated his own apparently anti-modernist aesthetic. In rejecting the hallmark of Euro-American modernism—romantic symbolism—as an obfuscation of material life, Brecht together with Hanns Eisler offered the *Lehrstücke* (c. 1929), in which the word is stripped of "bourgeois excrescence" in order to communicate meaning in plain speech. This is not entirely unconnected, though, to a key modernist maneuver: that of **imagism,** in which the writer avoids the superfluous word in the realization that the natural object is the adequate symbol. Where Brecht differs from the imagism of **Pound** and Eliot is in his skepticism, rather than nostalgia, for the master texts of Western civilization. In ironic modification of the mythic method, in which heritage yearns to be salvation, Brecht's modernism anticipates **postmodernism,** or at least one version of what is another paradoxical concept. While he might have undermined Western culture in forms of pastiche, Brecht would have been out of sympathy with an obverse, but a related, version of the postmodern: the celebration of superfluity in the consumer culture. Given the slipperiness of the definitions, modernism is probably both relevant and irrelevant to the hard life of the South.

It is instructive to consider Césaire's epic of exile and homecoming, *Return to My Native Land* (1939; tr. 1968). Subjecting his French literary education to the negritude mission of restoring identity and pride to the colonized person, Césaire created his poem out of the shards of late nineteenth-century European modernism. Where Césaire rejects the Euro-American model, however, is in his restoration of the African mask—the mask that Picasso had utilized in order to "distort" conventions of classical mimesis—to an African ontology. This is based not on the imitation of reason, but on the expression of vital forces intimately connecting physical and metaphysical aspects of being: an "undistorted" humanity. We are not in the company here of **Lawrence**'s dark gods. Rather, Césaire seeks beneath the surreal for a contract between artist and citizen. It is at this point of human community—usually represented by a gap of incomprehension in Euro-American modernism—that the modernist may begin to inhabit an *Africanicity.*

The Africanicity provides an analogy for a general adaptation of modernism to the condition of the South, whether in Africa, the Caribbean, Latin America, or indeed in African American culture. One may turn in illustration to South Africa, where for over 400 years economic and cultural production have experienced a to-and-fro between Africa and the West. A founding text, Van Riebeeck's *Dahgregister* (1652–61; *Journal*), has the Dutch commander at the Cape increasingly frustrated in dealing with a trickster Khoikhoi, or Hottentot, who refuses to respect European laws of boundaries and controls. In consolation Van Riebeeck gazes inland dreaming of riches in some mythical hinterland. To the imagination schooled in the modernist manner of unexpected or abrupt juxtaposition, it is almost as if Van Riebeeck had anticipated the hubris not only of Cecil John Rhodes but also a more contemporary buccaneer. Hotel magnate Sol Kerzner has set his extravaganza The Lost City—its kitsch is probably postmodernist rather than modernist—amid the poverty of one of apartheid's old dumping grounds, or "homelands." The point is that the very unevenness of South African modernization in sharp juxtapositions of systems, whether economic, religious, racial, or linguistic, has ensured that the characteristic virtually absent from the literary culture is the empirical **realism** against which Euro-American modernism launched its initial assault.

Instead, one encounters in South Africa simultaneous forms of traditional-oral and contemporary-oral expression. There are the syncretic Christian-African hymns of the early Xhosa convert Ntsikana (c.1820) alongside Thomas Pringle's attempts to transform Scottish border ballads into searing protests against settler encroachment on African ancestral land (1834). There are Olive Schreiner's late nineteenth-century amalgamations of allegory, dream, parody and social indictment as well as Sol T. Plaatje's mingling, in *Mhudi* (1930), of Shakespearean romance and historical prophecy. In *Cry, the Beloved Country* (1948) Alan Paton subjects the archetypal journey of innocence and experience to sociological necessity. The Afrikaans Sestigers (novelists of the Sixties) adapt the *nouveau roman* to their rebellions against the Father figures of Afrikaner State Calvinism. J. M. Coetzee has remained committed to the novel as allegory amid the iron laws of history. In search of a Black Consciousness voice, Soweto poets of the 1970s made impulsive raids on a miscellany of sources including Fanon, Biko, the **Harlem Renaissance,** the projective verse of the Beat generation, and the oral praises to the great Zulu kings. Finally, Nadine Gordimer lends to the Freudian family romance a dialectical political consciousness. If all of this may be characterized broadly as a modernist recognition, either period or single intention clearly cannot bind modernism.

One must be cautious, however, of turning an admittedly elusive concept into a portmanteau term. A salient feature of Euro-American modernism was its self-consciousness as high art. In the South, in contrast, art enclosures are thinly dispersed across societies of thin literary culture and, despite exceptions, writers and artists have not always responded to self-consciously artistic demands. To take the example of Olive Schreiner whose *The Story of an African Farm* (1883) yokes together apparently disparate forms of representation: stories-within-stories veer between realism and allegory while at key points in the narrative Schreiner deserts novelistic conventions altogether in favor of pamphleteering or lyrical-philosophical digressions. In defending the book—is novel the appropriate classification?— against the view that as realism the form is flawed, some critics have described *African Farm* as a proto-modernist work. The counter-argument, however, might refuse to regard Schreiner's plot of comings and goings, of sudden juxtapositions of different planes of experience, as primarily an aesthetic challenge. The style could, instead, reflect a condition of anxiety: in the colony nothing quite satisfies the metropolitan expectation. When one story, or convention, is dropped for another Schreiner is not so much pushing against the boundaries of realist art as registering her own psychic dislocation in colonial or— given the rude intrusion of early South Af-

rican industrialization—postcolonial time and space. Life in the South strikes one as a mutation of romance, even gothic, in which little credence is granted to the domestic middle-class manner.

One could argue here that in matters of style, expression in the South often appears to derive from Euro-American modernism. Accordingly, one might consider the rejection of realism for the fictive mode in a wide variety of writers including Breytenbach, Fugard, Douglas Livingstone, Marechera, Vieira, and Couto (southern Africa); Soyinka, Okigbo, and Okri (West Africa); several Latin American magical realists; Walcott and Harris (the Caribbean); Indian *émigrés* like Rushdie; and of course Achebe in both the parable-like *Things Fall Apart* (1958) and the more postmodern *Anthills of the Savannah* (1987). Yet—as in the case of Césaire and Schreiner—these writers are not so much derivative of, as distinct from, the Euro-American tradition. Generally, literary-cultural responses have been invoked by crises imposed from the outside. Individuals have not necessarily felt free to explore their social, let alone psychological choices; action, space, and time do not usually progress in the confidence of autonomous, even semi-autonomous destiny. The narrative may be curtailed, for example, in the episode that is both logically and temporally unrelated to a coherent chronology. Similarly, space may be refracted into multiple aspects that resist being assembled into a unifying picture. To use Eco's words, a "poetics of action" has been supplanted by a "poetics of cross-sections."

What has been described here would strike the South not as a modernist but a post-colonial dilemma. That is not to ignore certain common features. But, at the same time, one may return to the earlier point about human comprehension at the center of the work. Whereas Eliot almost paradoxically revels in impersonality and incompletion, Rushdie like Achebe and others searches the rim of the world for things that should not be permitted to fall apart. The modernist in the South—if modernism retains the authority of definition—requires the abundance of imagination in the reconstruction of a homeland.

The comparison suggests that one should avoid reducing modernism to a style without a content, or context. Rather, the form of the experience has to be restored to the form of the work. It is then possible, whether in South Africa, Latin America, in the diasporic expression of the Indian *émigré* or the Caribbean Creole, to connect Appiah's contention that Africa is about suffering before it is about the simulacrum to the great contribution of modernism: that beneath the prose of life the imagination explores our capacity for both cruelty and beauty, sin and redemption. Given the nature of such an exploration modernism in the North and modernism in the South refuse cross-cultural conversation at the risk of a mutual reduction of a common humanity. It is a danger not altogether unfamiliar to Euro-American modernism. Perhaps it is appropriate, therefore, that the warning be issued by the more vulnerable South.

Michael Chapman

Selected Bibliography
Achebe, Chinua. "An Image of Africa: Racism in Conrad's *Heart Of Darkness*." 1975. In his *Hopes And Impediments: Selected Essays 1965–87*. London: Heinemann, 1988. 1–13.
Ahmad, Aijaz. *In Theory: Classes, Nations, Literatures*. London: Verso, 1992.
Appiah, Kwame Anthony. *In My Father's House: Africa In The Philosophy Of Culture*. London: Methuen, 1992.
Arnold, James A. *Modernism And Negritude*. Cambridge, Mass.: Princeton UP, 1981.
Ashcroft, Bill, Gareth Griffiths and Helen Tiffin. *The Empire Writes Back: Theory and Practice In Post-Colonial Literatures*. London: Routledge, 1989.
Chapman, Michael. *Southern African Literatures*. London: Longman, 1996.
———. "The Aesthetics of Liberation: Reflections from a Southern Perspective." *Current Writing* 10.1 (1998): 1–16.
Fanon, Franz. *The Wretched Of The Earth*. New York: Grove Press, 1965.
Gilroy, Paul. *The Black Atlantic: Modernity And Double Consciousness*. London: Verso, 1993.
Mphahlele, Es'kia. *The African Image*. 1962. London: Faber & Faber, 1974.
Rushdie, Salman. *Imaginary Homelands*. London: Granta Books, 1991.
Soyinka, Wole. *Myth, Literature And The African World*. Cambridge: Cambridge UP, 1976.

Agee, James (1909–1955)

U.S. journalist, poet, novelist, critic and screenwriter. Pulitzer Prizewinner (1958) for posthumous novel *A Death in the Family* (1957).

Agee is best remembered for *Let Us Now Praise Famous Men* (published 1941, developed 1936–40), a prose account of eight months visiting poor Alabama families in 1936 with photographer Walker Evans, whose pictures are integral to the project. The "sharecropper book," part of a flowering of Southern literature, recalls **William Faulkner**'s novels in its dense rhetorical style—part **interior monologue**, part religious oratory—shiftings of chronology and perspective, tragic mood, and social observation (Evans's images almost uncannily illustrate *As I Lay Dying* [1930], a novel that espouses a similar philosophy of language).

Agee is as much concerned with his subjective reactions as he confronts the contradictions of his cultural roots after years in New York—he worked on the 52nd floor of the Chrysler Building—as with his ostensible topic, the daily oppression of dirt farmers. In 1929 Agee had reacted angrily to the unimaginative theatrical use of film soundtracks (see **Film and Modernism**), proposing instead a fusion of images and sounds that would fulfill the visions of William Blake— "great pictures, poetry, color and music"— and the verbal experimentation of **James**

Joyce (letter to Dwight Macdonald, April 24). Blake, in the transparently luminous figures inhabiting his engravings, as well as in his poetry, and Joyce, in his **epiphanies** —when something's "soul, its whatness leaps to us from the vestment of appearance" (*Stephen Hero*)—were both aware of ambiguities in language and appearance, yet convinced of an underlying mystical reality. Also from Joyce, Agee followed Stephen Dedalus's description of the "simplest epical form": "when the artist prolongs and broods upon himself as the centre of an epical event . . . till the centre of gravity is equidistant from the artist himself and from others" (*A Portrait of the Artist as a Young Man*). Having studied with I. A. Richards at Harvard, Agee understood the impossibility of transparent representation.

Agee makes the struggle for expression a major concern. The book has several false beginnings (in fact, never really reaches a beginning) and combines various styles, techniques and genres. The author's centrality as narrating consciousness, free-associating back and forth across his life (in a manner reminiscent of **Proust**), during both the events described and their later recollection, provides a unifying focus. Agee often implies comparisons between his vision and a camera (torn newspaper columns appear verbatim, as fractured poetry), to encourage awareness of the selection through which any account is filtered.

Fortune initially sponsored the project, but withdrew after Agee encountered problems shaping it into a magazine article. His unsuccessful second application for a Guggenheim Fellowship in 1937 listed nearly fifty ventures he wanted to tackle, including "An Alabama Record" to be an exhaustive "reproduction and analysis of personal experience, including the phases and problems of memory and recall and revisitation and the problems of writing and of communication . . . with constant bearing on two points: to tell everything possible as accurately as possible: and to invent nothing." Agee continued writing, but protracted wrangles over alleged obscenity made publication no longer commercially viable. Onset of war changed the political and economic circumstances that supported proletarian fiction which Agee's subject resembled (although not its form).

The book's comprehensiveness, ambiguity, abstract symphonic structure, epic scale, poetical language, idiosyncratic punctuation, mysticism, and ultimate grounding in naturalistic realism—in a word, its excess—have led some critics to liken it to Herman Melville's *Moby Dick* (1851). Others, especially early reviewers, have been affronted by its egocentricity, obliqueness, and complexity. It went out of print (remaindered, by some accounts) but enjoyed a revival in the 1960s when Agee, seen as both rebel-victim and champion of the dispossessed, became something of a cult figure.

Agee's influential film criticism, informed by the same attitudes toward realism, led to his writing seven screenplays including *The African Queen* (co-screenplay with director John Huston, 1951) and *The Night of the Hunter* (Charles Laughton, 1955). The film writings are collected in two volumes, *Agee on Film* (1958, 1960). Also published are a volume of poems, *Permit Me Voyage* (1934); the *Letters of James Agee to Father Flye* (1962), his former teacher; and another novel, *The Morning Watch* (1951). Controversy over the status of Agee's work continues. It has generated considerable academic attention, including over forty doctoral dissertations.

Nigel Morris

Selected Bibliography

Barson, Alfred T. *A Way of Seeing.* University of Massachusetts Press, 1972.

Huse, Nancy Lyman. *John Hersey and James Agee: A Reference Guide.* Boston: G.K. Hall & Co, 1978.

Kramer, Victor A. *James Agee.* Boston: Twayne Publishers, 1975.

———. *Agee and Actuality: Artistic Vision in His Work.* Troy, N.Y.: The Whitston Publishing Company, 1991.

———(ed.). *Agee: Selected Literary Documents.* Troy, N.Y.: The Whitston Publishing Company, 1996.

Larsen, Erling. *James Agee.* Minneapolis: University of Minnesota Pamphlets on American Writers, no.95, 1971.

Aldington, Richard (1892–1961)

English poet, novelist, biographer, translator, essayist and editor.

Born in Hampshire and educated at Dover College, Aldington grew up in a rural area near the sea, a geography he thoroughly enjoyed and sought throughout his life. He attended University College, London, for one year (1910–1911), but was forced to leave because of his father's financial misfortunes. Having resolved to be a poet, he refused to clerk in the city and supported himself briefly as a sports journalist. From 1912 through the 1920s, he earned a modest income from reviewing as well as from his more literary work, but except during the period of his military service, he lived entirely on the revenues of his writing.

In late 1911, Aldington met **Ezra Pound** and, through him, **Hilda Doolittle (H. D.),** whom he married in 1913. With a common interest in the ancient world, Aldington and H. D. worked together on translations from *The Greek Anthology.* During the summer of 1912, which they spent in Paris, they wrote poems jointly and separately in response to their reading of Greek sources. When they returned to London in the autumn of 1912, Pound was very impressed with the results. In order to launch the careers of his two friends, he sent their work to Harriet Monroe at *Poetry Magazine* in Chicago, hailing their poems as evidence of a new literary movement he now labeled "imagisme."

Through Pound, Aldington became literary editor of *The Egoist,* the small but influential literary journal edited by Dora Marsden and Harriet Shaw Weaver. Through his auspices and those of his friends (Pound, H. D., F. S. Flint, John Cournos, John Gould Fletcher, **Ford Madox Ford, Wyndham Lewis,** Amy Lowell, **D. H. Lawrence** and others), Aldington championed the cause of modernism by publishing the work of his avant-garde contemporaries (not only poetry and prose by his friends but also work by such writers as **James Joyce,** Remy de Gourmont and Storm Jameson). Aldington also fostered interest in modernism through reviews of books, musical and dramatic performances, and art exhibitions. His own poetry and essays, whether in the form of reviews or more broadly as reflections on contemporary art and culture, reveal his engagement with modernist ideas and his struggle to define a mode of modernism that, while contemporary, would preserve what he saw as the best elements of the past. A scholarly and independently educated man, Aldington's familiarity with classical and European languages (especially French and Italian) as well as his wide knowledge of European literature and history made him reluctant to follow Pound's interest in **vorticism** and other new movements. Like H. D., Aldington sought a modernism distinct from the immediate and conventional past, while he celebrated not only Greek literature but the literature and art particularly of the middle ages, the early renaissance and eighteenth-century **France.** His first collection of verse, *Images,* appeared in 1915.

Aldington enlisted in the British army in June of 1916, served as a corporal in a pioneer battalion in France, became a lieutenant in the Signal Corps in 1917, and was demobilized as an acting captain in February of 1919. Having shared editorial duties at *The Egoist* with H. D. during his first year in the army, he gave over this post to **T. S. Eliot** soon after his return to France as an officer in 1918. Aldington's marriage to H. D. did not survive the stresses of these years, and his next two volumes of poetry, *Images of War* and *Images of Desire,* both published in 1919, attest to the effects of the war on his life and imagination.

Aldington continued to write poetry during the 1920s, but he also turned to translations and took on the position of French Reviewer for *The Times Literary Supplement,* thus offering British readers a particular angle on modern French culture throughout the decade. His translation of Laclos' *Les Liaisons Dangereuses,* for example, appeared in 1924, followed by Voltaire's *Candide* in 1927. As well as his own long war poem *A Fool i' the Forest* (1924), this very productive period included Aldington's first biographical studies—of Voltaire (1925) and de Gourmont (1928).

In 1929, Aldington published *Death of a Hero,* his famous war novel, the first of a host of important war fictions by such writers as Robert Graves and Frederic Manning. Aldington called his modernist book a "jazz" novel, and its powerful blend of numerous genres (among them social satire, burlesque, memoir, and threnody) heralded a major shift in Aldington's career from poetry to fiction. He followed this best-selling book with two collections of short stories and six subsequent novels published between 1930 and 1939.

During World War II, Aldington, who had left England for the south of France in 1928, moved to the United States, first to Florida and then to California. He published his memoir *Life for Life's Sake* in 1941. In 1946 he returned to France, and his *Complete Poems* appeared in 1948. The 1950s were characterized chiefly by significant biographies: *Portrait of a Genius, But . . . ,* the first full-length biography of D. H. Lawrence, appeared in 1950, followed by *Pinorman* (1954), a biography

of Norman Douglas, and a controversial first biography of T. E. Lawrence, *Lawrence of Arabia: A Biographical Inquiry* (1955), in which Aldington revealed his subject's illegitimacy and questioned his status as a war hero. The furor which greeted this book even before its publication effectively ended Aldington's literary career, reducing him to penury as a result of legal fees and loss of reputation.

Unfairly branded as difficult, unkind, and angry, Aldington was a shy, sensitive, honest, and skeptical man who struggled with and was shaped by the intellectual movements and the traumas of his age. His writing in an impressive variety of genres bears re-reading not only for what it reveals about the development of literary modernism but in its own right as an eloquent, perceptive and neglected modernist voice.

Caroline Zilboorg

Selected Bibliography

Cecil, Hugh. *The Flower of Battle: British Fiction Writers of the First World War.* London: Secker and Warburg, 1995.

Crawford, Fred D. *Richard Aldington and Lawrence of Arabia: A Cautionary Tale.* Carbondale: Southern Illinois UP, 1998.

Doyle, Charles. *Richard Aldington: A Biography.* London: Macmillan, 1989.

Gates, Norman T., ed. *Richard Aldington: An Autobiography in Letters.* University Park: Pennsylvania State UP, 1992.

Gates, Norman T. *The Poetry of Richard Aldington: A Critical Evaluation and an Anthology of Uncollected Poems.* University Park: Pennsylvania State UP, 1974.

Gregory, Eileen. *H. D. and Hellenism: Classic Lines.* Cambridge: Cambridge UP, 1977.

Kershaw, Alister, and F.-J. Temple. *Richard Aldington: An Intimate Portrait.* Carbondale: Southern Illinois UP, 1965.

Laity, Cassandra. *H. D. and the Victorian Fin de Siècle: Gender, Modernism, Decadence.* Cambridge: Cambridge UP, 1996.

MacGreevy, Thomas. *Richard Aldington: An Englishman.* London: Chatto, 1931.

Zilboorg, Caroline, ed. *Richard Aldington and H. D.: The Early Years in Letters.* Bloomington: Indiana UP, 1992.

Zilboorg, Caroline, ed. *Richard Aldington and H. D.: The Later Years in Letters.* Manchester: Manchester UP, 1995.

Anderson, Sherwood (1876–1941)

Like Theodore Dreiser (1871–1945), Edgar Lee Masters (1869–1950), Carl Sandburg (1878–1967), Vachel Lindsay (1879–1931) and a little later **Ezra Pound** and **T. S. Eliot,** Sherwood Anderson was a child of the American Midwest. But his advent as a writer was particularly unpredictable. Born in the small town of Camden, Ohio, of parents who had little money and many children, he received limited formal education and worked from an early age, yet went on to become, at forty, a published author hailed by critics of the east coast like Waldo Frank as a new voice in American literature. Sherwood Anderson had first come to Chicago in early youth and had developed an interest in writing poetry and prose. Then, after running a small business in Elyria, Ohio, while he wrote, he broke down in 1912, dramatically left the town, his family and his firm, and fashioned his soon-to-be mythical image of the man who had sacrificed everything to his artistic calling.

He returned to Chicago in time to participate in the Chicago Renaissance, which began around 1912 and outlived World War I by a few years. In 1914, the first issue of *The Little Review* featured his call for a new sense of craft and greater artistic freedom entitled "The New Note." From then on, Sherwood Anderson was encouraged by magazine editors who published his stories, while influential east coast critics like Paul Rosenfeld, Van Wyck Brooks and Henry Mencken praised him. He made two trips to Paris, where he won the respect of Eugene Jolas, the founder of *transition,* and began a lifelong friendship with **Gertrude Stein,** whose passion for the word was illuminating to him and who advised

him and supported his work from then on. Sherwood Anderson also appeared in translation in French literary reviews, then in several books during the twenties. He was acknowledged by French critics, soon to be followed by Cesare Pavese in **Italy,** as a representative of the new American literature.

Although he shared a number of aesthetic reactions and strivings with some modernists, his work was intensely personal and local at the same time. He sought his own idiom experimentally and with reference to principles and ideals we can trace back to the British and American Romantics and forward to "the revolution of the word" (*transition* manifesto, June 1929), drawing also on Midwestern cadences of speech. The most distinctive "stories" of this self-proclaimed "storyteller" are about the difficulties of telling.

Between 1913 and 1941, Anderson published essays, poetry, short stories, a short-story cycle, a few plays, several novels (one autobiographical), and an autobiography of his youth. He left hundreds of letters, several unfinished novels, and unfinished memoirs.

His two volumes of verse bear significant titles: *Mid American Chants* (1918) and *A New Testament* (1927). Closer to **Whitman** and to Biblical **rhythm** and tone than to the work of the imagists, the poems of these collections are interesting to Anderson scholars because they bluntly reveal his obsessions, but they do not represent his breakthrough. His first two novels, *Windy McPherson's Son* (1916/1922) and *Marching Men* (1917), were bolder in their thematic development than in their writing. Both were rightly read as allegorical visions of America. Indeed, Anderson would always link the individual self with a reflection on America and its changes, for instance from a rural to an industrial society in *Poor White* (1920). His later novels are uneven. The most successful, *Dark Laughter* (1925), was the weakest. In his essays on the Depression, *Puzzled America* (1935), Anderson returns to the narrative posture of his short stories, with excellent results.

In the stories of *Winesburg, Ohio* (1919), *The Triumph of the Egg* (1921), *Horses and Men* (1923), and, later, *Death in the Woods* (1933), Anderson produced some of his best writing. *Winesburg, Ohio* has much in common with **Joyce**'s ***Dubliners*** (1914) and, closer to home, with Edgar Lee Masters' *Spoon River Anthology* (1915), but Anderson has here created his own version of the American grotesque as a way of seeing and a way of writing. *Grotesque* often becomes a noun rather than an adjective; people are or become grotesques. Yet, in this world, the grotesques are neither horrible nor ludicrous when one tries to understand them for what they are. Besides, they are not particularly exceptional, and often only exhibit deformations common to many of us in less exaggerated forms. They are, however, conditioned and sanctioned by social norms and expectations. Their grotesqueness is not always explained, but often results from frustration. Sexual frustrations are foregrounded, especially those endured by women, and Anderson, called a "Phallic Chekhov" by Rosenfeld, proclaims the centrality of sexual energy, somewhat like **D. H. Lawrence.**

The third person narrator, in his efforts to express what he perceives to be a character's "story," relies on selected details (the nervous hands which betray Wing Biddlebaum's tensions in "Hands," *Winesburg, Ohio*) and on an oblique approach, often through symbolic images ("the sweetness of twisted apples" defines Dr. Reefy and most other grotesques in *Winesburg, Ohio*). First-person stories may blend pathos with humor, as in "The Egg," which shows the destructiveness of the American myth of success. That narrative voice also serves to portray youthful desire and frustration in several stories of boys

growing up in the Midwest in the horse-and-buggy age. As they recall an episode in their adolescence, the narrators are uncertain both of what exactly happened and of whether they have since become grotesques in their turn or not.

The frustration of Anderson's characteristic narrators is inseparable from a proclaimed difficulty in telling, in "finding the word." A powerlessness which has social, class, and individual relevance becomes Anderson's best aesthetic stance, as witness his early poem "The Dumb Man" which exemplifies a way of telling that involves the reader in the narrator's doubts as to what he witnessed or experienced and how to express it. "Death in the Woods" is an excellent later story in which all these elements are combined.

Since his death, Anderson has been treated more fairly by writers acknowledging their debt, from **William Faulkner** to Raymond Carver (1938–1988) and Charles Bukowski (1920–1994), than by general criticism.

Claire Bruyère

Selected Bibliography

The *Complete Works of Sherwood Anderson* have been published in English in Japan (21 volumes, including the *Portable Sherwood Anderson*): Ed. K. Ohashi. Kyoto: Rinsen Book Co., 1982. Many individual works have now been separately reprinted in the United States and in the United Kingdom. Some hitherto unpublished stories have appeared in *Certain Things Last* (Ed. Charles Modlin. New York: Four Walls Eight Windows, 1992; reprinted as *The Egg and Other Stories*. Harmondsworth: Penguin, 1998).

Anderson, David D., ed. *Critical Essays on Sherwood Anderson*. Boston: GK Hall, 1981.

Anderson, Sherwood. *Letters of Sherwood Anderson*. Ed. H. Mumford Jones and Walter B. Rideout. Boston: Little, Brown, 1953.

———. *Sherwood Anderson: Selected Letters*. Ed. Charles Modlin. Knoxville: University of Tennessee Press, 1984.

———. *Sherwood Anderson's Memoirs: A Critical Edition*. Ed. Ray L. White. Chapel Hill: University of North Carolina Press, 1969.

Bruyère, Claire. *Sherwood Anderson: L'impuissance créatrice* [*Creative Powerlessness*]. Paris: Klincksieck 1985.

Rogers, Douglas F. *Sherwood Anderson: A Selective, Annotated Bibliography.* Metuchen: N.J.: Scarecrow Press, 1976.

Townsend, Kim. *Sherwood Anderson.* Boston: Houghton Mifflin, 1987.

White, R.L., ed. *The Achievement of Sherwood Anderson: Essays in Criticism.* Chapel Hill: University of North Carolina Press, 1966.

Andreas-Salomé, Lou (1861–1937)

Louisa von Salomé was born in St. Petersburg. She enjoyed an intellectual relationship with Nietzsche, until rejecting his proposal of marriage. In 1897 she met **Rilke,** and greatly influenced his artistic development as his lover and surrogate mother. From 1912 she studied under **Freud,** and practiced as a psychoanalyst. She wrote fiction, including the cycle *Im Zwischenland* (1902), *Das Haus* (1919) and *Rodinka* (1922), but her critical and biographical works have had a more enduring significance.

In *Friedrich Nietzsche in seinen Werken* (1894), she argued that the philosopher's thought was paradoxically energized by his suffering and disease, and by his loss of faith which he attempted to recoup by religiously creating new ideals. In *Rainer Maria Rilke* (1928), she criticized the poet for being hysterical and emotionally unbalanced. In *Mein Dank an Freud* (1931, *The Freud Journal of Lou Andreas-Salomé*), she describes the atmosphere of the psychoanalytic community during the crucial period of **Adler**'s and **Jung**'s break from it.

In recent years feminists have debated the literary value of Andreas-Salomé's writings, which were previously considered merely for their biographical interest. Emphasis has been placed on how her intimate, psychological insights, presented in a non-objective tone and style which Freud had admired, offer a unique perspective on her subjects which reveals the personal motives behind their achievements.

Andreas-Salomé's works are available in Insel Verlag, Frankfurt am Main, and Quartet Publications, London.

Carl Krockel

Selected Bibliography

Biddy, Martin. *Women and Modernity: The (Life)Styles of Lou Andreas-Salomé.* New York: Cornell UP, 1991.

Livingstone, Angela. *Lou Andreas-Salomé.* London: Gordon Fraser Gallery, 1984.

Pfeiffer, Ernst, ed. *Sigmund Freud and Lou Andreas-Salomé.* New York: Harcourt Brace Jovanovich, 1972.

Androgyny

Virginia Woolf's concept of androgyny is important in several of her novels. She most fully discusses androgyny in her book *A Room Of One's Own.* In these lectures, first given at Cambridge in 1928, Woolf wonders "whether there are two sexes in the mind corresponding to the two sexes in the body, and whether they also require to be united in order to get complete satisfaction and happiness . . . in each of us two powers reside, one male and one female. . . . It is fatal to be a man or woman pure and simple; one must be womanmanly or man-womanly" (Woolf 93). Androgyny has been further defined by Elaine Showalter as "full balance and command of an emotional range that includes male and female elements." While many more recent theorists have opposed themselves to all constructions of masculinity and femininity, of male or female behavior, Woolf's strategy appears to be to fuse them, to argue for a hybrid identity that is both male and female, like that of Orlando in Woolf's novel of that name (1928). In *Mrs. Dalloway,* to take another example, there is the description of Peter Walsh as a womanly man, while on the other hand, we hear of Clarissa's pleasure, which is like a man's, with Sally Seton.

Peter Childs

Selected Bibliography
Woolf, Virginia. *A Room Of One's Own*. London: Grafton, 1973.

Anthropology

Anthropology is often regarded as one of the modern sciences, fueled in the late nineteenth century by the rise of Darwinism and colonial expansion across the globe. Historians of the discipline, concerned to establish a longer lineage, point out that its roots go deep down into early studies of civilization. However, during the nineteenth century the very idea of civilization, especially civilization allied to progress, began to look more and more questionable. Enlightenment thinkers, such as Montesquieu in **France** and Adam Smith in **Scotland,** had already given a preliminary shake to the concept of progressive civilization by describing societies as natural systems in which everything is organically related to everything else. A little later, the German philosopher Herder made an important sideways move in his *Outlines of a Philosophy of the History of Man* (1784–91) by foregrounding the idea of culture as a way of looking at human organization. Culture (or "cultures," for the easy plural inflection is a key to the term's usefulness) proved to be a more adaptable and durable concept than civilization, and not just for anthropologists.

There was a strongly Romantic flavor about Herder's interest in German folklore and high regard for mythology in general, which was subsequently to become an important strand in the development of anthropology. Scholars in a number of different fields helped to further explorations of **myth:** philologists such as Jacob and Wilhelm Grimm wrote down orally-transmitted legends and folk-tales, and or-

ientalists (again, many of them German) translated and published ancient Sanskrit and Persian texts, thus paving the way for a broader view of human history and culture that drew on sources beyond the familiar classical texts of Europe and the Near East. Another addition to the nineteenth-century anthropologists' literary data-banks came in the form of contemporary travel accounts published by missionaries, colonial administrators, and various kinds of scientists; descriptions of peoples and societies from all quarters of the globe thus became available to European and North American anthropologists.

During the later nineteenth century, this mass of ethnographic material was partly organized along lines drawn from the existing "science of races," or ethnology, but more expansive theoretical possibilities were opened up once social anthropologists freed themselves from earlier ideas of racial determinism. A leading proponent of this new direction for anthropology was E. B. Tylor, keeper of Oxford University's Museum, with its important ethnological collection bestowed by General Pitt Rivers. Using a combination of ethnographic and archaeological data, Tylor rejected notions of cultural variation that depended on biological difference and posited instead a more uniform concept of human societies. He described universal processes of cultural development, placing contemporary "primitives" within the same framework as ancient "civilized" societies. Although the unilineal simple-to-complex development implied in this kind of progressivist approach was repudiated by later anthropologists, the general principle of social evolution gained wide currency and made it more difficult to keep ideas of the "savage" and the "civilized" in separate compartments.

One of the topics that particularly interested Tylor was the origin of religions. When J. G. Frazer, then a Cambridge classicist, read Tylor's book *Primitive Culture*

(1871), he began to shift his attention to the emergent science of anthropology and embarked on an evolutionary study of the transitions from magic to religion to science (the last stage demonstrating the triumph of reason). The outcome of this study was *The Golden Bough,* first published in 2 volumes in 1890, expanding to 3 in 1900, and then a monumental 12-volume edition in 1911–15. Frazer's work, which reached an extraordinarily wide readership, was intended to demonstrate the stages of progress in human belief, but its impact was sometimes unexpected: "in the era of World War I, disillusioned intellectuals found the objective correlatives to their feelings of despair in [Frazer's] eternal images of dying kings and parched fields. Hundreds of readers were moved to write to him. . . ." (Kuklick 9). Frazer's work continued to exert considerable literary influence even when twentieth-century anthropology had moved on into new fields of inquiry, using new methods.

Tylor and Frazer were essentially "armchair" scholars, but in the closing years of the nineteenth century anthropology moved from the study to the field. This development seems to have been prompted by the realization that, under the impact of **colonialism** and globalization, many "primitive" cultures were on the brink of disintegration, so anthropologists hurried to observe and analyze exotic peoples before their distinctive social and physical characteristics disappeared altogether. The decisive moment in British anthropology was 1898, when an interdisciplinary team from Cambridge University, led by a former zoologist, Alfred Haddon, spent several months amongst the islanders of the Torres Straits, between Australia and New Guinea. The Melanesian island societies that the expedition studied were small and, being numerous, offered ample scope for comparison. The expedition team included the psychologist W. H. R. Rivers, who took to the Torres Straits the brand-new techniques of experimental psychology for testing such things as color vision and reaction time; he allied the results of such experiments to genealogical surveys organized rather like late-Victorian surveys of the British poor. Although the precise methods of the Torres Straits expedition did not set a pattern for future research, the expedition was highly significant as, for the first time, anthropologists became not simply theorists but collectors of data too.

Fieldwork as it evolved in the early twentieth century meant that anthropologists became "participant observers" spending long periods in their chosen societies, in order to arrive at detailed, objective, scientifically-based descriptions of other cultures. The supreme exponent of this method was Bronislaw Malinowski, who also worked in Melanesia, but rejected the team approach of Haddon and Rivers. Malinowski was the first anthropologist to conduct his research in the native language, and his lengthy study of the Trobriand Islanders resulted in several books, most famously *Argonauts of the Western Pacific* (1922). For all its concern with groups and societies, anthropology as practiced by Malinowski and those he subsequently taught came to depend on an elevated sense of the individual's perception. Like the modernist artist, the anthropologist constructed and interpreted societies and selves from the point of view of a solitary eye-witness. Malinowski drew attention to the literary parallel himself when he famously claimed "[W. H. R.] Rivers is the Rider Haggard of Anthropology: I shall be the Conrad!"

Thus it is not only in its scope as a discipline, striving towards a world-picture with a built-in sense of strangeness, that anthropology offers parallels with modernism. The anthropologist, too, is a kind of modernist whose profession involves "a spiritual commitment like that of the creative artist or the adventurer or the psychoanalyst." This quotation comes from Susan Sontag's 1966 essay on Claude Lévi-Strauss, significantly titled "The Anthropologist as Hero." Lévi-Strauss's work, with its structural emphases, has had far-reaching effects on approaches to culture and communication in the second half of the twentieth century. But as well as recognizing the importance of his contribution to modern thought, Sontag also offers, through the example of Lévi-Strauss, a view of the anthropologist in the field as a model of twentieth-century consciousness. Her essay concludes: "The anthropologist is . . . not only the mourner of the cold world of the primitives, but its custodian as well. Lamenting among the shadows, struggling to distinguish the archaic from the pseudoarchaic, he acts out a heroic, diligent, and complex modern pessimism" (cited in Hayes 185, 196).

Lynda Prescott

Selected Bibliography

Hayes, E. Nelson and Tanya Hayes, eds. *Claude Lévi-Strauss: The Anthropologist as Hero.* Cambridge, Mass.: M.I.T. Press, 1970.

Kuklick, Henrika. *The Savage Within: The social history of British anthropology, 1885–1945.* Cambridge: Cambridge University Press, 1991.

Moore, Jerry D. *Visions of Culture: An Introduction to Anthropological Theories and Theorists.* Walnut Creek, Cal.: AltaMira Press, 1997.

Stocking, George W. *Victorian Anthropology.* New York: The Free Press, 1987.

The Armory Show

The Association of American Painters and Sculptors held an International Exhibition in 1913 in the Armory of the 69th Regiment in New York. Introducing fauvism, **cubism, futurism** and **expressionism** to America, the exhibition, comparable in importance to the London post-impressionist exhibitions of 1910 and 1912, revolutionized American art and criticism. Although Man Ray in *Self Portrait* (1963) indicates Alfred Stieglitz had shown Cé-

zannes even earlier in his gallery, the publicity attracted by the Armory Show opened the way in America for cubism and **dada;** these dislocations of tradition, producing assemblages rather than unity, radically influenced innovative poetry and prose in the United States from the 1920s, and encouraged the incorporation of cadences and rhythms from spoken American English. They clarified, for example, **Pound**'s distinction between lyric poetry, that transforms music into speech, and poetry that resembles painting and sculpture ("imagisme and England," 1915).

The Exhibition brought experimental American art and literature into the same project as the European avant-garde, at the same time as World War I, expatriation in the 1920s and economic globalization reawakened debates concerning American artistic separateness and autonomy. **Dos Passos** and **Cummings** were among those who visited.

Nigel Morris

Selected Bibliography

Brown, Milton W. *The Story of the Armory Show.* 2d ed. New York: Abbeville Press, 1988.

Green, Martin Burgess. *New York 1913: The Armory Show and the Paterson Strike Pageant.* New York: Scribner's, 1988.

Auden, W(ystan) H(ugh) (1907–1973)

Widely regarded as one of the pre-eminent poets of the twentieth century, W. H. Auden was also an accomplished essayist and critic, dramatist, editor, and librettist.

He was born in York and grew up in Birmingham, in the industrial midlands of England. He won a scholarship to Oxford to study science and engineering, but his interest in poetry caused him to change his subject to English. At Christ Church he became the central figure of a group of poets which included Stephen Spender, Cecil Day-Lewis, and Louis MacNeice: collectively, they became known as the "Oxford

Group" and, later, as the "Auden Generation." In the Oxford of the 1920s, Auden
inevitably fell under the spell of **T. S. Eliot,** whose poem *The Waste Land* appeared
to distill the post-war sense of fragmentation and loss of value. He also assimilated
the ideas of **Freud** and Marx: two of the
key influences on his early poetry. Auden's
poetry from the late 1920s through to the
end of the 1930s displays an increasing
search for political commitment. His first
collection of poems was published privately by Stephen Spender in 1928, after
which time he attracted the attention of
T. S. Eliot, who published his verse play
Paid on Both Sides in *Criterion* in 1930.
After Oxford, Auden spent some time with
his friend Christopher Isherwood in Berlin, where he came under the influence of
the work of **Bertolt Brecht.** On his return,
he took up teaching posts in England and
Scotland. During the 1930s, with the rise
of European fascism, Auden embraced
left-wing politics and a committed poetry
that, avoiding propaganda, would enable
its reader to make a rational and moral
choice in public affairs. *The Orators: An
English Study* (1932) employs modernist
techniques in satirizing and undermining
not only fascism but also the ossification
of British society. In 1935 he married Erika Mann (daughter of **Thomas Mann**) in
order to procure her a passport to escape
Nazi **Germany;** in 1937 he traveled to
Spain, where he made a number of broadcasts on behalf of the Republicans. The
poem he wrote on his return, entitled
"Spain," was famously criticized by
George Orwell for its description of a
"necessary" murder carried out by the Sta-
linists who fought for the Republican
cause. Auden subsequently altered the of-
fending line and for the remainder of his
life suppressed his more political poems of
this period.

In 1939, before the outbreak of the
Second World War, Auden left England

for America, becoming an official citizen
of the United States in 1946. Here, his poetry moved away from its earlier political
explicitness: a move indicated by his reference to poetry's inability to change the
world in the February 1939 poem "In
Memory of W. B. Yeats." In America he
met Chester Kallman, his lover and lifelong companion, with whom he would collaborate on libretti for works by Benjamin
Britten and **Igor Stravinsky,** among others. His re-conversion to Christianity accompanies the emergence of more
personal ethical dimensions in his poetry.
Significant influences on his later work are
the philosopher Søren Kierkegaard and the
theologian Reinhold Niebuhr. In 1956,
Auden became Professor of Poetry at Oxford for the statutory five years. He spent
the rest of his life moving between England, Austria, and the United States.

It has been said that Auden was the
first poet of the English language to feel at
home in the twentieth century, and that his
writings manage to capture the tone of his
age. His poetry is heavily anthologized.
Among his most famous poems are "Lay
Your Sleeping Head, My Love," "Musée
des Beaux Arts," "The Unknown Citizen,"
"September 1, 1939," and "The Night
Mail." *The Age of Anxiety: A Baroque Ec-
logue* (1947) won the Pulitzer Prize, and
in 1967 he was awarded the National
Medal for Literature.

Andrew Harrison

Selected Bibliography

Auden's works are published in England by Faber
    and Faber and in America by Random House.
    A bibliography of his works is contained in
    Smith (1997).
Hynes, Samuel. *The Auden Generation: Literature
    and Politics in England in the 1930s.* London:
    Bodley Head, 1976.
Page, Norman. *Auden and Isherwood: The Berlin
    Years.* London: Macmillan, 1998.
Smith, Stan. *W. H. Auden.* Plymouth: Northcote
    House Publishers, 1997.

B

Barnes, Djuna (1892–1982)

Djuna Barnes' experimental modernist works weave together a dense verbal style, grotesque plots and patterns of imagery, literary parodies, black humor, and wit to probe unconscious and tragic levels of human existence. Barnes' often dark vision emanates from intricate constellations of words that rarely intimate a naturalistic social world. Although she was a celebrated figure in the 1920s and '30s, Barnes' literary reputation has varied in the past decades, yet her works are generally appreciated for their verbal power, often compared to that of her friend **James Joyce.** Her works often treat sexuality in its many variations, but in general her grand theme is the underside of life; as the character Matthew O'Connor says toward the end of *Nightwood,* "Only the scorned and the ridiculous make good stories" (159).

Barnes was born on June 12, 1892 in Cornwall-on-Hudson, N.Y., into a highly unconventional family. Her father, Wald Barnes, a sometime musician, writer, and painter, and a perpetual schemer, created a home with three women: his mother, Zadel Barnes, a suffragist, spiritualist, and writer; his wife and the mother of Djuna, the English violinist Elizabeth (Chappell) Barnes; and a lover named Fanny Faulkner. Through her belief in "free love" and her economic support, Zadel encouraged Wald's polygamous tendencies; the two families under one roof produced eight children. The children were educated at home, largely in the arts, although Barnes later attended the Pratt Institute in Brooklyn (1911–12) and the Art Students' League of New York (1915). The family dynamics are rumored to have included sexual irregularities including perhaps incest between Barnes and her grandmother Zadel, but evidence is not definitive (Herring 54–58). At eighteen, Barnes was "married" in an informal and unsanctioned ceremony in her grandmother's room to fifty-two-year-old Percy Faulkner, brother of Fanny, but they lived together for only two months (Herring 60). When Wald divorced Elizabeth in favor of Fanny, Barnes began a career as a journalist to support her mother, younger brothers, and herself. Beginning in 1913, Barnes wrote for the *Brooklyn Daily Eagle;* Carl Van Vechten then hired her to write for the *New York Press.* She also worked for *New York World Magazine, New York Morning Telegraph, New York Tribune* and had articles and short stories published in *McCall's, Vanity Fair, Charm,* the *New Yorker,* the *Dial* and other magazines. Her articles included portraits of those on the fringes of life in New York, such as Coney Island performers and street people, prototypes of the odd characters who would people her fiction (Levine 27). Not a political activist, Barnes nevertheless used her journalism to call attention to particular social ills, for example famously subjecting herself to the pain of force-feeding to report on the plight of suffragists in England. Some of this journalism has been collected in the volumes *New York* and *Interviews* edited by Alyce Barry and published by Sun and Moon Press.

Barnes' first volume of poems and drawings, *The Book of Repulsive Women,* was published by Guido Bruno in Greenwich Village as a chapbook in 1915. This early work is often dismissed as being highly derivative of decadent precursors such as **Oscar Wilde** and Aubrey Beardsley, but one critic suggests that the ambiguity of these "repulsive" portraits forms a Dickinsonian "'twisting' of conventional literary forms" for the purpose of approaching lesbian sexuality (Galvin 87). Barnes lived with Courtenay Lemon, whom she called her "husband," from 1916 to 1919. They moved among artistic and political circles in Greenwich Village and developed connections to the Provincetown Players. Barnes wrote a significant number of short plays during these years, some influenced by her admiration for **John Millington Synge** and his "frank pessimism" (Herring 123). Three of her plays were staged by the Players during the 1919–20 season. Margaret Anderson and Jane Heap also began publishing Barnes' short stories in the *Little Review* during this period.

After leaving Lemon, Barnes moved to Paris in 1920, there to begin two decades of work and life in avant-garde circles. In Paris she came to know **Joyce, Gertrude Stein, Ezra Pound, T. S. Eliot,** Robert McAlmon, Mina Loy, and Peggy Guggenheim, among many others, and frequented the lesbian circle of Natalie Barney, which she satirized in the privately printed *Ladies' Almanack* (1928). This work parodies multiple literary forms—Biblical parables, myths, eighteenth-century fiction, the zodiac, melodrama, fairy tales, romance, sonnets—in addition to the form of the almanac, and includes witty drawings by Barnes. This pastiche of forms presents the adventures of Barney as Dame Evangeline Musset, who "had been developed in the Womb of her most gentle Mother to be a Boy, " but despite coming "forth an Inch or so less than this," she "took her Whip in hand, calling her Pups about her, and so set out upon the Road of Destiny" (7). On that road she encounters characters who represent Janet Flanner, Solita Solano, Radclyffe Hall, Una Troubridge, Romaine Brooks, and others of the circle. The tone of the book is largely comic, and *Ladies' Almanack* is most often read as an affectionate portrait of this salon. For example, the fate of Dame Musset is to live to ninety-nine years of age when she becomes "uprooted in the Path of Love, where she had so long flourished," and on her funeral pyre "all had burned but the Tongue, and this flamed," eventually bringing sexual pleasure to some of her mourners. Some readers, however, spy a more critical edge "verging on viciousness" in the work (Jay 185). Barnes' sombre tone about human existence is also apparent, for example in the following Biblical-Shakespearean passage: "We shake the Tree, till there be no Leaves, and cry out at the Sticks; we trouble the Earth awhile with our Fury; our Sorrow is flesh thick, and we shall not cease to eat of it until the easing Bone . . . we are not wise this side of *rigor mortis*" (59). While Barnes downplayed the importance of *Ladies' Almanack* to her oeuvre, it remains one of her most imaginative works.

Barnes became involved with her "great love," the artist Thelma Wood, in 1922, and their often unhappy relationship lasted for eight years. Later in life Barnes resisted the label "lesbian" by protesting that she had "just loved Thelma" (Herring 302), even though she had had multiple affairs with women before Thelma entered her life. She reported to a friend in 1935 that she could not be confined to the category "lesbian," speaking in terms that reveal the loneliness of many of Barnes' later years: "I might be anything, if a horse loved me, I might be that" (Herring xix). Barnes also preferred her work not to be judged by categories of identity: "Talk about, teach, preach—etc. *writers. Why women* writers?" (Herring 255).

Barnes had published a collection of stories in 1923 titled *A Book,* later revised and reissued as *A Night Among the Horses* (1929). Her literary reputation was enlarged by the publication of the "novel" *Ryder* in 1928, which was listed for a brief time on the best-seller list of *The New York Times.* The book is a fantastical account of a family much like her own, with little plot, and much literary parody. The text incorporates Chaucerian, Renaissance, and eighteenth-century language, with a hearty emphasis on bawdy and scatological puns and scenarios, some of which were censored. For all of its comedy, much of the book exposes and censures the heterosexual dynamics of a patriarchal culture. Numerous chapters return obsessively to the theme of a woman's virginity and her ruin due to unscrupulous and lying seducers; the sexual act leads inevitably to painful childbirth and a woman's further weakness. Chapter 5 is titled "Rape and Repining," and proceeds for eight pages in the following fashion: "A Girl is gone! A Girl is lost! A simple Rustic Maiden but Yesterday swung upon the Pasture Gate, with Knowledge nowhere, yet is now, to-day, no better than her Mother, and her Mother's Mother before her! Soiled! Despoiled! Handled! Mauled! Rumpled! Rummaged! Ransacked! No purer than Fish in Sea, no sweeter than Bird on Wing, no better than Beasts of Earth!" (21). The parody works to reveal the language used to denigrate women due to their sexuality, but the emphasis on violent action also underscores the oppressive conditions under which that sexuality was often exercised.

Later in the book Amelia and Kate-Careless argue viciously with one another over their plight of sharing the polygamist Wendell Ryder. Amelia wonders to Kate why she did not "thrust a spade into you when I first laid eyes on you" and realizes that she "spaded not because I judged [Wendell] greater than my judgment, honoured him above my honour, and loved him above my love; and I find . . . that he nests with vermin, that beneath the shadow of his wings, corruption breeds, that he moults bastards, and broods upon exceeding bad eggs!" (150). Romantic views of love have no chance in Barnes' fictional world. Yet the text includes glee, for Barnes revels in the "self-importance of language"; for her "a phrase no one else could have dreamed up is more precious than whole sequences of action or talk" (West 247–49). The chapter titled "The Psychology of Nicknames" provides an example of such; it is largely an inventive list of names Amelia "tossed" at Wendell during their courting. They include "Braggart-the-Britches," "All-Woman's Thumbs," "Pluck-of-my-Luck," "Try-Again-Thomas," "Hot-Put-and-Hurry-o," "Penny-Be-Priceless," "Wrench-Away-Willie," "The-Way-is-Dark-but-the-Way-is-Short," "Shaft-Pole-of-Cod's-Withers," and when she's pleased, "Sweet-Driller" and "Dear Damage." Wendell, however, is left at the end of the book among "the animals," his sexual philosophy no better than theirs, with the narrator repeating "Whom should he disappoint now?"

Barnes' most famous work and her most important contribution to modernism, *Nightwood* (1936), continues this theme of the animal nature of sexuality, the tragic inevitability of disappointment and pain in human life; it makes clear that these are by no means confined to the conventional heterosexual world. The book includes the stories of misfits, marginal figures whose tales are told in oblique fashion through grotesque descriptions and imagery, commentary by the outrageous but wise Doctor Matthew-Mighty-grain-of-salt-Dante-O'Connor, and sketches of inconclusive or truncated scenes. The first chapter includes an Italian Jew who hides his heritage in favor of a "pretence to a barony" (3) and his son Felix Volkbein; the Duchess of Broadback, a trapeze artist; Nikka, the black man covered head to foot in tattoos; and various other hard-drinking figures who establish the milieu of the book as that of the eccentric underworld, leading some critics to see *Nightwood* as a response to the increasingly intolerant Europe of the fascist 1930s (Marcus 229). The book's central drama is that of Nora Flood who falls in love with Robin Vote, a "beast turning human," and loses her to the brittle and hysterical Jenny Petherbridge, the "squatter." As with *Ryder,* however, the drama and the pleasure of the book are much more in the language than in the plot. The eight chapters compose a kind of mosaic rather than a linear plot, although cause-effect logic is not abandoned. Robin functions as an absence in the book, for the reader is never presented with her point of view. The narrative is one of loss and the tone that of tragic, inescapable sorrow and death: "Robin was an amputation that Nora could not renounce. As the wrist longs, so her heart longed, and dressing she would go out into the night that she might be 'beside herself,' skirting the cafe in which she could catch a glimpse of Robin" (59).

In the depths of her sorrow and confusion about Robin, Nora visits Dr. O'Connor at three in morning, finds him in a "narrow iron bed" with "heavy and dirty linen sheets" dressed in a "woman's flannel nightgown . . . a golden semi-circle of a wig . . . heavily rouged and his lashes painted," and she asks him to tell her "everything you know about the night" (79). His highly suggestive monologue advises that Nora do as the French do, and value both the night and the day "as one contin-ually," the dream life and the conscious life as of a piece. He fears, however, that Nora, Robin, and Jenny will end "like the poor beasts that get their antlers mixed and are found dead that way, their heads fattened with a knowledge of each other they never wanted, having had to contemplate each other, head-on and eye to eye, until death" (100). At the end of their conversation, Dr. O'Connor staggers out to a bar, and angrily muses about his garrulous contributions to those in misery: "I've not only lived my life for nothing, but I've told it for nothing—abominable among filthy people—I know, it's all over, everything's over . . . Now . . . the end—mark my words—now *nothing but wrath and weeping*" (166). The text then ends with the short and ambiguous chapter "The Possessed" in which Robin, in a chapel on Nora's property in New York state, acts out an encounter with a dog that is at once dreamlike, sexual, violent, poignant, and finally touching and peaceful. Whether she remains the "beast turning human," or reverts from human to beast is a matter of interpretation.

This disturbing text is an important example of anti-naturalistic, psychological modernism that uses a densely tortuous prose to allude to the unconscious life. The work was published with the help of Emily Coleman who told Barnes: "You make horror beautiful—it is your greatest gift" (Herring xvii). Coleman interceded with T. S. Eliot to get Faber & Faber to accept the manuscript. Eliot and Coleman both helped Barnes edit the draft to give it shape. Eliot wrote an introduction that concludes with the following summation: "What I would leave the reader prepared to find is the great achievement of a style, the beauty of phrasing, the brilliance of wit and characterisation, and a quality of horror and doom very nearly related to that of Elizabethan tragedy" (xvi).

In September 1940, Barnes moved into an apartment in Patchin Place in

Greenwich Village, and stayed there for the next forty-two years, until she died at the age of ninety in June, 1982. By most accounts she became increasingly hostile and depressed and struggled with alcoholism for many years. Her pessimistic view of human relations led her to prefer life as more or less a recluse. She continued to write, but did not publish much. Her last major published work, *The Antiphon* (1958), was a blank-verse play again bearing comparison to Elizabethan or Jacobean drama, and also to T. S. Eliot's *The Family Reunion* (1939). The plot rehearses some of Barnes' family resentments in the reunion of an extended and dysfunctional family. The play's menacing tone and eventually murderous plot suggest depths of fury even in the later Barnes for her family circumstances. The play also presents a conflict of values between the U.S. capitalist glorification of "success" and "trade" and the European preference for culture (Herring 262). While critical reactions to the play after publication were mixed, Dag Hammarskjold, United Nations Secretary General, facilitated interest in *The Antiphon* in Sweden where it was first performed in 1961.

Barnes' brand of modernism has roots in and connections to many forms of European culture. Her works have been compared not only to the writers and movements mentioned above, but also to Rabelais, the surrealists, the Metaphysical poets, the Bible's book of Lamentations, Flannery O'Connor, medieval morality plays, symbolist poetry, Nathanael West, the Gothic novel, Sartre, Gide, and many others. She also influenced equally diverse writers, many of whom Barnes felt should have acknowledged her work more directly. Some of those whose works bear her influence include John Hawkes, Anaïs Nin, Isak Dinesen, Angela Carter, and Truman Capote. Barnes, like Joyce, helped to develop the potentialities of parody during the modernist era, and her emphasis

on marginal figures and on women's experiences of sexuality and love expanded the themes of literary modernism.

Loretta Stec

Selected Bibliography

Barnes, Djuna. *Interviews.* Ed. Alyce Barry. Los Angeles: Sun & Moon Press, 1985.
———. [By a Lady of Fashion]. *Ladies' Almanack.* 1928. Normal, IL: Dalkey Archive Press, 1992.
———. *New York.* Ed. Alyce Barry. Los Angeles: Sun & Moon Press, 1989.
———. *Nightwood.* 1937. Norfolk, CT: New Directions, 1961.
———. *Ryder.* 1928. Normal, IL: Dalkey Archive Press, 1990.
Eliot, T. S. "Introduction." *Nightwood.* 1937. Norfolk, CT: New Directions, 1961.
Galvin, Mary E. *Queer Poetics: Five Modernist Women Writers.* Westport, CT: Praeger, 1999.
Herring, Philip. *Djuna: The Life and Work of Djuna Barnes.* New York: Viking, 1995.
Jay, Karla. "The Outsider among the Expatriates: Djuna Barnes' Satire on the Ladies of the *Almanack.*" In Mary Lynn Broe, ed. *Silence and Power: A Reevaluation of Djuna Barnes.* Carbondale: Southern Illinois University Press, 1991. 184–194.
Levine, Nancy J. "'Bringing Milkshakes to Bulldogs': The Early Journalism of Djuna Barnes." In Mary Lynn Broe, ed. *Silence and Power: A Reevaluation of Djuna Barnes.* Carbondale: Southern Illinois University Press, 1991. 27–36.
Marcus, Jane. "Laughing at Leviticus: *Nightwood* as Woman's Circus Epic." In Mary Lynn Broe, ed. *Silence and Power: A Reevaluation of Djuna Barnes.* Carbondale: Southern Illinois University Press, 1991. 221–251.
West, Paul. "Afterword." Djuna Barnes. *Ryder.* 1928. Normal, IL: Dalkey Archive Press, 1990. 243–250.

Beckett, Samuel Barclay (1906–1989)

Born in Dublin on Good Friday, 13 April 1906, Beckett, allegedly, meant to die on a Christmas Day; he fell short of Christmas 1989 by three days. In his work too, life and death often do not matter quite so much as half-comic theological and philosophical preoccupations, nor, indeed, as much as the imperatives of form, pattern and symmetry. Beckett was a poet, translator (of himself and others) and critic (of literature and painting) as well as a dramatist and prose writer ("novelist" is barely appropriate). Only *Dream of Fair to Middling Women* (written in 1932 but not published until 1993) and a book of short stories, *More Pricks Than Kicks* (1934), are easily recognizable as modernist works; with their verbosity and extravagant multilingual wordplay, they are more Joycean than Beckettian. But the scope and experimentation of Beckett's mature works are not contained within any modernist movement, whether symbolism, **futurism, expressionism, imagism, vorticism, dada,** or **surrealism.** Below, I refer to the English versions of a selection of Beckett's theatrical and prose works, written from 1943–1980.

Waiting for Godot (written in French 1948–49, first performed 1953, published in French 1952; English 1954). In Paris in 1950, the actor-director Roger Blin was offered two plays by Samuel Beckett for possible production. *Waiting for Godot* was preferred to its rival *Eleutheria* (written in French 1947, published in French 1995; English 1996), mainly because *Godot* required only five actors and a simple set— "A country road. A Tree" (Beckett, *Godot,* 11)—instead of *Eleutheria*'s seventeen characters and complicated split-stage set. *Godot* is proverbially the play where nothing happens, twice; Godot, assuredly, does not come. In its earliest days, however, its stasis and circularity provoked dramatic responses from its audience:

During a stormy interval, the most irate protesters came to blows with the play's supporters, then trooped back into the theater only to stomp noisily out again as the second act opened with the same two characters still waiting for Godot as they had been at the beginning of act one . . . As *Godot* became the talk of theatrical Paris, the character of the audiences

changed and it became the play that everyone simply had to see. (Knowlson 387)

As James Knowlson confirms, *Godot* "changed everything" for Beckett; "It marked both the end of his anonymity and the beginning of his theatrical and financial success" (Knowlson 387).

Endgame (written in French 1953–56, first performed 1957, published in French 1957; English 1958). Beckett wrote extensive production notebooks detailing the correct specifications for the practical production of *Endgame* but refused to engage in any form of explanation as to its meaning. Thus his instructions in a 1957 letter to Alan Schneider, the American director of *Endgame:*

when it comes to journalists I feel the only line is to refuse to be involved in exegesis of any kind. And to insist on the extreme simplicity of dramatic situation and issue. If that's not enough for them, and it obviously isn't, it's plenty for us, and we have no elucidations to offer of mysteries that are all of their making. My work is a matter of fundamental sounds (no joke intended) made as fully as possible, and I accept responsibility for nothing else. (Beckett, *Disjecta,* 109)

Endgame, like *Godot,* is replete with verbal patterning—repetitions, variations and oppositions recur in phrasing and through complex dialogue sequences; there is further elaborate patterning in staged movement. The play does indeed offer "plenty" for merely formal analysis. Both *Endgame* and *Godot,* however, have also proved irresistible to the "analogymongers" (Beckett, "Dante . . . Bruno," 4). Much critical effort has gone into determining the symbolic significance of locating Hamm's "Accursed progenitor[s]" (Beckett, *Endgame,* 96) in two dustbins. For Beckett, the ability of Nagg and Nell to appear from and retreat into their dustbins solved the merely technical problem of effecting the entrances and exits of two characters who had "crashed on our tandem and lost our shanks" (Beckett, *Endgame,* 100). The tone of *Endgame* is a mixture of such levity and cruelty; as Nell confirms, in what Beckett identified as the most important line in the play, "Nothing is funnier than unhappiness" (Beckett, *Endgame,* 101).

Quad (written in English 1980, first broadcast 1982, published in English 1984). The definitive version of *Quad* was recorded for television in **Germany** by Süddeutscher Rundfunk in 1982 under the title *Quadrat 1 + 2.* It is "A piece for four players, light and percussion" (Beckett, *Quad,* 451). It has no dialogue, only sound and movement. The players wear long gowns and cowls to hide their faces; player 1 is dressed in white, player 2 in yellow, player 3 in blue and player 4 in red. Each, entering and exiting in consecutive sequences, paces the sides and diagonals of a square according to set courses. The center of the square is "supposed a danger zone" (Beckett, *Quad,* 453): each player deviates on his diagonal path to avoid it. The combination of courses in *Quad* is potentially infinite; when Beckett transformed *Quad* into *Quadrat 1 + 2,* he supplemented his original conception with a second version performed at a much slower pace and with the colors of the players' costumes faded to gray. This, Beckett said, was *Quad* revisited ten thousand years later. *Quad* is based entirely around permutation and combination: it is about patterning, in a purer, clearer way than *Endgame* or *Waiting for Godot.* It exemplifies in stark terms what it means to analyze the internal formal constitution of a dramatic situation, rather than its conceptual "meanings." There is nothing outside itself that *Quad* might be about.

Watt (written in English 1943–44; published in English 1953). *Watt* was written while Beckett was in hiding in Roussillon in occupied **France** during the Second World War. Like *Quad,* permuta-

tion dominates its construction. *Watt* also has a spectacularly unreliable narrator:

> With regard to the so important matter of Mr. Knott's physical appearance, Watt had unfortunately little or nothing to say. For one day Mr. Knott would be tall, fat, pale and dark, and the next thin, small, flushed and fair, and the next sturdy, middle-sized, yellow and ginger, and the next small, fat, pale and fair, and the next middle-sized, flushed, thin and ginger, and the next tall, yellow, dark and sturdy, and the next fat, middle-sized, ginger and pale, and the next tall, thin, dark and flushed, and the next small, fair, sturdy and yellow, and the next tall, ginger, pale and fat, and the next thin, flushed, small and dark . . . (Beckett, *Watt,* 209)

Mentioning only "the figure, stature, skin and hair" (Beckett, *Watt,* 211), the narrator supplies two pages of such data while simultaneously proving to have, in terms of determinate information, "little or nothing to say" (Beckett, *Watt,* 209). Beckett would switch languages for his next prose work.

Molloy (written in French 1947, published in French 1951; English 1955). The narrative line of *Molloy* is deceptively simple. Molloy "resolved to go and see [his] mother" (Beckett, *Molloy,* 16), finds his bicycle (although he did not know he had one), and sets out. On the way, he runs over a dog called Teddy, as owned by a Mrs. Loy or Lousse or Sophie. They bury the dog, with Molloy unable to dig the hole, or lay Teddy within his grave. He thus doubts his contribution to the ceremony. He escapes Loy, Lousse, or Sophie, finds himself within a forest, then in a ditch, losing the use of his legs as he more and more slowly proceeds. When he comes to a final stop, we switch into Part II, the Moran half of the narrative. Moran's task, as set by the mysterious Gaber and Youdi, is to find Molloy; it is also to take over the narrative. Moran has little patience with his readers' inquiries and interests: "What . . . was the source of Ballyba's prosperity? I'll tell you. No, I'll tell you nothing. Nothing" (Beckett, *Molloy,* 135). He does tell us something despite himself: we are made aware by these narrative interventions that we are reading a fiction. We must be made to know that its narrators are inventing, lying, writing stories.

Malone Dies (written in French 1948, published in French 1951; English 1956). The title *Malone Dies* describes succinctly what happens during its narrative: by the end of the text, it seems, the narrator is dead and the narrative itself peters out to nothing. There are always two levels to Malone's narration: his stories and his metanarrative comments upon his own performance in telling them. He confesses to being unable to tell the story he envisages about Saposcat: "The peasants. His visits to. I can't" (Beckett, *Malone Dies,* 196). Sometimes descriptions of nature are too much trouble: "A stream at long intervals bestrid—but to hell with all this fucking scenery" (Beckett, *Malone Dies,* 279). The prospective scenery is no more; it cannot exist for us if Malone refuses to determine and state what it, fictionally, is. This narrator is self-reflexive; he can comment upon and cancel his own narrative statements. Prior to his own death, Malone organizes the murder of his last set of fictional characters, sending them back to the oblivion from which he originally distinguished them.

The Unnamable (written in French 1949–50, published in French 1953; English 1958). The narrator of *The Unnamable* struggles to make sense of who he is, where he is, what he is supposed to be doing, when his situation (whatever it is) might change and even whether he exists. The narrator, probably in common with the reader, is primarily conscious of a morass of confusion:

> I seem to speak, it is not I, about me, it is not about me . . . What am I to do, what shall I do, what should I do, in my situation, how proceed? By aporia pure and simple? Or by affirmations and negations invalidated as uttered, or sooner or later? Generally speaking. There must be other shifts. Otherwise it would be quite hopeless. But it is quite hopeless. I should mention before going any further, any further on, that I say aporia without knowing what it means. Can one be ephectic otherwise than unawares? I don't know. (Beckett, *The Unnamable,* 293)

The Unnamable is shot through with contradictions and inconsistencies. The narrator will put forward one hypothesis that might explain something about his situation, and just as quickly abandon it for an alternative explanation. There are no stable narrative facts in this text. The narrator might be legless and armless in a jar; or he might be advancing, merely one-legged, on crutches, in spirals, toward his family. Alternatively, a cast of Beckett's old characters, Molloy, Moran, Malone, and Murphy orbit around our narrator, like planets around the sun. We are also told, at regular intervals, that all such stories are lies. *The Unnamable* is not just self-reflexive, but self-defeating: if all the "affirmations and negations" contained within it are to be "invalidated as uttered, or sooner or later" (Beckett, *The Unnamable,* 293), then this affirmation must be subject itself, "sooner or later," to the general invalidation it commands. The Trilogy, *Molloy, Malone Dies* and *The Unnamable,* ends with this impasse unresolved. Its final words are "I can't go on, I'll go on" (Beckett, *The Unnamable,* 418): on this promise of continuation, the text ends.

Beckett criticism: modernism and the Theatre of the Absurd. Much Beckett criticism assumes that metaphysical insight constitutes the greater glory of the works of Samuel Beckett. Martin Esslin, author of *The Theatre of the Absurd* (1961), has been more influential than any other critic in this respect. For Esslin, a "sense of metaphysical anguish at the absurdity of the human condition is, broadly speaking, the theme of the plays of Beckett, Adamov, Ionesco, Genet" (Esslin 23–24). Critics writing from a cultural materialist perspective recommend impatience with Beckett precisely because of the essentialism, and pessimism, endemic in such criticism. *Molloy* thus has a role in Georg Lukács' diagnosis of the distortion of reality inherent in modernism, where "escape into neurosis as a protest against the evils of society" becomes in "modernist writers an immutable *condition humaine*"; for Lukács, "Beckett's *Molloy* is perhaps the *ne plus ultra* of this development" (Lukács 31). In *Molloy,* Lukács argues, a historically contingent situation is mistakenly elevated to the irremediable status of an eternal metaphysical condition. The distinction blurred had already been drawn by Nietzsche: "Modern pessimism is an expression of the uselessness of the *modern* world—not the world of existence" (Nietzsche §34, 23). Lukács castigates Beckett for presuming to cultivate a metaphysical dimension in his writing; Esslin celebrates the same. Yet the little expertise that Beckett's own narrators do possess, notwithstanding their contradictions, inconsistencies and paradoxes, is certainly not in metaphysical matters; as the narrator of *Enough* (published in French 1966; English 1967) complains, "What do I know of man's destiny? I could tell you more about radishes" (Beckett, *Enough,* 144). More recent postmodernist criticism frees Beckett's work from the weight of profundity that both the enemies and proponents of modernism insist upon.

Postmodernism

Beckett's work has become central to explorations of postmodern fiction and drama. Beckett has been identified as "a pioneer of postmodernism" (Brienza 257). Entering the 1990s, it could be argued that "any discussion of postmodernism which omits him seem pallid" (Mitchell 114). In this new orthodoxy, Beckett is amongst those writers "invariably classified as postmodern" (Hornung 177). Brian McHale cautions against treating Beckett "monolithically as *either* modernist or postmodernist":

> This effaces the differences between earlier and later Beckett: between the Beckett who is still preoccupied with modernist issues of reliability and unreliability of narrators, radical subjectivity, and multiplicity of perspectives, as in *Watt* and *Molloy,* and the Beckett who focuses instead on the status of fictional worlds, and the power (and impotence) of language to make and unmake worlds, and the relationship between fictional being and elusive "real" being, as in *Malone Dies, The Unnamable,* and many of the later short texts . . . (McHale, *Constructing Postmodernism,* 34)

McHale includes Beckett amongst those "writers who in the course of their careers travel the entire trajectory from modernist to postmodernist poetics" (McHale, *Postmodernist Fiction,* 11)—a transition completed by the end of the Trilogy. The prose works which follow recognize no injunctions against their own exploitation of the illogical or the impossible in the elaboration of their fictional worlds. *Texts for Nothing* (published in French 1954; English 1967), for example, is simply unconcerned with the logical impossibility of maintaining "it's true and it's not true":

> what has become of the wish to know, it is gone, the heart is gone, the head is gone, no one feels anything, asks anything, seeks anything, says anything, hears anything, there is only silence. It's not true, yes, it's true, it's true and it's not true, there is silence and there is not silence, there is no one and there is someone, nothing prevents anything. (Beckett, *Texts for Nothing,* 115)

That criticism of Beckett should endeavor to make sense of his texts is not commonly questioned. Coherence is a prerequisite in conceptual discourse. Dissent from this most basic cognitive presupposition is largely confined to documents such as Beckett's own works.

Sue Wilson

Selected Bibliography

(Except where noted, dates in brackets refer to the first English edition.)

Beckett, Samuel. "Dante . . . Bruno. Vico. Joyce." Samuel Beckett, *et al. Our Exagmination Round his Factification for Incamination of Work in Progress* (1929). London: Faber and Faber, 1961: 3–22.

———. *The Complete Dramatic Works.* London: Faber and Faber, 1986.

———. *Collected Shorter Prose 1945–1980.* London: John Calder, 1984.

———. *Disjecta: Miscellaneous Writings and a Dramatic Fragment.* Ed. Ruby Cohn. London: John Calder, 1983.

———. *Dream of Fair to Middling Women.* Ed. Eoin O'Brien and Edith Fournier. London: John Calder, 1993.

———. *Eleutheria.* Translated by Barbara Wright. London: Faber and Faber, 1996.

———. *Endgame* (1958). *Complete Dramatic Works.* 89–134.

———. *Enough* (1967). *Collected Shorter Prose.* 139–144.

———. *Molloy* (1955). *Malone Dies* (1956). *The Unnamable* (1958). *The Beckett Trilogy.* London: John Calder, 1959.

———. *More Pricks Than Kicks* (1934). London: Calder and Boyars, 1970.

———. *Quad* (1984). *Complete Dramatic Works.* 449–454.

———. *Texts for Nothing* (1967). *Collected Shorter Prose.* 71–115.

———. *Waiting for Godot* (1954). *Complete Dramatic Works.* 7–88.

———. *Watt* (1953). London: John Calder, 1976.

Brienza, Susan D. *Samuel Beckett's New Worlds: Style in Metafiction.* Norman: University of Oklahoma Press, 1987.

Esslin, Martin. *The Theatre of the Absurd* (1961). Revised 2nd ed. Harmondsworth: Penguin, 1968.

Hornung, Alfred. "Reading One/Self: Samuel Beckett, Thomas Bernhard, Peter Handke, John Barth, Alain Robbe-Grillet." In *Exploring Postmodernism.* Ed. Matei Calinescu and Douwe Fokkema. Amsterdam: John Benjamins Publishing Company, 1990. 175–198.

Knowlson, James. *Damned to Fame: The Life of Samuel Beckett.* London: Bloomsbury, 1996.

Lukács, Georg. *The Meaning of Contemporary Realism* (German 1957). Trans. John and Necke Mander. London: Merlin Press, 1963.

McHale, Brian. *Postmodernist Fiction.* London: Routledge, 1987.

McHale, Brian. *Constructing Postmodernism.* London: Routledge, 1992.

Mitchell, Breon. "Samuel Beckett and the Postmodernism Controversy." *Exploring Postmodernism.* Ed. Matei Calinescu and Douwe Fokkema. Amsterdam: John Benjamins Publishing Company, 1990. 109–121.

Nietzsche, Friedrich. *The Will to Power* (German 1901). Ed. Walter Kaufmann. Trans. Walter Kaufmann and R. J. Hollingdale. London: Weidenfeld and Nicolson, 1968.

Benn, Gottfried (1886–1956)

A poet and essayist, Benn also retained a career as a physician. His expressionist works appropriate his scientific terminology for a ruthlessly unromantic style, in which he paradoxically rejects optimistic notions of empirical progress for a romantic mythology. *Morgue,* his first collection of poems from 1912, includes "Happy Youth," whose title refers to the nest of young rats in a girl's corpse. In "Songs I and II" he calls for a return to the "primeval dawning," where "life and death, impregnation and spawning / Could be left to our mindless slime." In "Ithaca," from his prose collection *Brains* (1916), a professor who believes he can understand "the vast complex of forces which control the universe" in his laboratory experiments, is killed by his student who uses his mind to head-butt him.

The later part of Benn's career is partly significant for his adherence to the Nazi regime. In his essays, which include "To the Literary Emigrés: a Reply" and "Confession of Faith in Expressionism" he attempted to reconcile **expressionism** with Nazism as anti-rationalist and sympathetic to the "Volk"; he declared that expressionism is only irrelevant, "now that the great national movement is at work creating new realities." Ironically, after the war he enjoyed great public acclaim, providing an understanding to the post-War generation of how Nazism had developed from German culture, in essays and autobiographical works, such as *Doppelleben* (1950, *Double Life*), and *Über mich selbst* (1956, *On Myself*).

Benn's works are available in Stuttgarter Ausgabe, and Marion Boyars Publishing, New York.

Carl Krockel

Selected Bibliography

Adams, Marion. *Gottfried Benn's Critique of Substance*. N. V.: Van Gorcum & Company, 1969.

Alter, Reinhard. *Gottfried Benn: The Artist and Politics (1910–1934)*. Bern: Herbert Lang, 1976.

Ritchie, J. M. *Gottfried Benn: The Unreconstructed Expressionist*. London: Oswald Wolff, 1972.

Bloomsbury

The "Bloomsbury group" was the name given to an informal network of twentieth-century writers and artists, who met regularly in the Bloomsbury district of London. The origins of the group can be traced to the turn of the century and a circle of friends—Lytton Strachey, Desmond MacCarthy, Clive Bell, Leonard Woolf and Thoby Stephen (brother of Vanessa Bell and **Virginia Woolf**)—who came under the influence of the moral philosopher, G. E. Moore, at Trinity College, Cambridge. According to Leonard Woolf, it was Moore's Socratic virtues of "clarity, integrity, tenacity and passion" and his advocacy (in the oft-quoted remark from Moore's magnum opus *Principia Ethica*, 1903) of "the pleasures of human intercourse and the enjoyment of beautiful objects," that led to the group's deification of personal relationships.

After the death of Leslie Stephen in 1904, the Stephen children moved to 46 Gordon Square in Bloomsbury, a Georgian terraced house close to the British Museum. The house quickly became the venue for a series of Thursday evening parties devoted to the discussion of the arts. Among habitués of these evenings, overseen by Thoby Stephen (until his death in 1906), were Clive and Vanessa Bell, Leonard and Virginia Woolf, Desmond and Molly MacCarthy, Lytton Strachey, Roger Fry, **E. M. Forster,** John Maynard Keynes and Duncan Grant—a by no means exhaustive list of pre-war "Old Bloomsbury"—whose interests ranged broadly over the subject-matter of the visual arts, literature, theater, history, economics and political philosophy.

Bloomsbury was never a self-conscious artistic "movement," although it did have significant points of overlap with avant-garde currents in European modernism. In 1910, the year in which Virginia Woolf hyperbolically claimed "human character changed," Roger Fry (with Desmond MacCarthy's assistance) organized the ground-breaking "Manet and the post-impressionists" exhibition at the Grafton Galleries in London. Progressive Liberals in politics and mildly, if daringly, louche, bohemian and hedonistic in taste, Bloomsbury defined itself in opposition to the piety, patriotism and sexual propriety of their Victorian forebears (many members of the group were agnostic, pacifist, or homosexual). Lytton Strachey's *Eminent Victorians* (1918), for instance, sought to debunk the popular reputations of Cardinal Manning, Florence Nightingale, Thomas Arnold and General Gordon; while Virginia Woolf's conversational, if slightly mannered, essay "Modern Novels" (1919) delineated the contemporary writer's struggle to evade the stylistic conventions of the nineteenth-century "realist" novel in order to capture heightened, quasi-symbolist, states of consciousness.

During the 1920s, Bloomsbury assumed a central place in literary London, buttressed by the cultural means of production afforded by the Woolfs' Hogarth Press (which published **T. S. Eliot**'s *The Waste Land* in 1923) and by Leonard Woolf's and Desmond MacCarthy's respective literary editorships of the influential intellectual weeklies, *The Nation and Athenaeum* and *The New Statesman* (when the two magazines merged in the 1930s, the Bloomsbury torch was taken up by the new literary editor, Raymond Mortimer). Moreover, during the inter-war period Bloomsbury had an outpost at King's College, Cambridge ("Bloomsbury-by-the-Cam" as John Lehmann called it), the *alma mater* of Fry, Forster, Keynes, the theater director George "Dadie" Rylands and the undergraduate poet Julian Bell (son of Clive and Vanessa Bell and Bloomsbury's *heir apparent* until his death in the Spanish Civil War aged 29). Indeed, Bloomsbury's pre-eminence in English cultural life—a sort of intellectual aristocracy—could lead to delusions of grandeur, not least Clive Bell's equation of "civilization" with "a lunch party at Gordon Square."

However, by the 1930s Bloomsbury's star had begun to wane. **Wyndham Lewis**'s savage attack in *The Apes of God* (1930) branded the group as moneyed, talentless, dilettanti—"a select and snobbish group." The war-cry was taken up in Cambridge by F. R. Leavis and his quarterly magazine, *Scrutiny,* which portrayed Bloomsbury as the rotten core of a supposedly corrupt metropolitan literary elite prone to "clique-puffery." *Scrutiny*'s growing influence in the academy did lasting damage to the image of Bloomsbury, such that the suicide of Virginia Woolf in 1941 appeared to mark the final demise of "Old Bloomsbury." Nonetheless, in the more permissive intellectual climate of the late 1960s, Michael Holroyd's candid two-volume biography of Lytton Strachey (1967–8), together with Quentin Bell's 1972 life of his aunt, Virginia Woolf, re-vived the group's flagging fortunes and unleashed a torrent of gossipy memoirs, published diaries, collected letters, biographies, critical studies, and even films, dealing with the phenomenon of Bloomsbury. Assessment of the place of Bloomsbury in the intellectual history of twentieth-century Britain can still excite strong emotions: ranging from Lewisite-Leavisite denunciations of a self-absorbed and self-promoting upper-middle-class clique, to Stephen Spender's generous acknowledgment of the group as "the most constructive and creative influence on English taste between the two wars."

Jason Harding

Selected Bibliography

Avery, Todd. *Close Affectionate Friends: Desmond and Molly MacCarthy and the Bloomsbury Group.* Bloomington, Ind., 1999.

Bell, Quentin. *Bloomsbury.* London, 1968.

Caws, Mary Ann. *Women of Bloomsbury: Virginia, Vanessa and Carrington.* New York, 1990.

Edel, Leon. *Bloomsbury: A House of Lions.* London, 1979.

Holroyd, Michael. *Lytton Strachey: A Biography.* Rptd. London, 1979.

Luckhurst, Nicola. *Bloomsbury in Vogue.* London, 1998.

Palmer, Alan and Veronica. *Who's Who in Bloomsbury.* Brighton, 1987.

Rosenbaum, S. P. *Aspects of Bloomsbury: Studies in Modern English Literary and Intellectual History.* London: Macmillan, 1998.

Stansky, Peter. *On or about December 1910: Early Bloomsbury and its Intimate World.* Cambridge, Mass., 1996.

Todd, Pamela. *Bloomsbury at Home.* London, 1999.

Bowen, Elizabeth (1899–1973)

The Anglo-Irish novelist and short story writer Elizabeth Bowen was born in Dublin in 1899, the inheritor of an estate or "Big House" in North Cork, **Ireland.** Her writing is significant both in terms of Twentieth-Century English modernist fiction and also within the context of the Anglo-Irish Ascendancy novel. Bowen divided her working life between North Cork and London, publishing her work between 1923 and 1969; she died in 1973. About this divided sense of self, she once wrote that she felt English in Ireland, Irish in England and at home on the Irish Sea— her fictions turn on from this divided, fractured sense of identity. Her biographer, Victoria Glendinning, argues that Bowen is "the link which connects **Virginia Woolf** with Iris Murdoch and Muriel Spark." During her writing life, she produced ten novels and seven collections of short stories. Her themes were modernist (Sean O'Faolain once told her that her novels were "exquisitely composed of logs of disaster"): the betrayal of passion, the burden of tradition, the elusive nature of selfhood, the flimsy gap between past and present.

Bowen once defined the novel as "the non poetic statement of a poetic truth" and her fictions dramatize the gap between interior self and external reality. Her early novels are narratives of social observation with Bowen using a detached, ironic authorial voice to comic effect. Works like *The Hotel* (1927) and *Friends and Relations* (1931) are situated firmly within the genre of the English Comedy of Manners novel—"Life with the Lid On" as she termed it herself. With Bowen's 1929 *The Last September,* a different note is struck. This novel is based in Ireland during the Irish War of Independence and charts the demise of the Anglo-Irish, Bowen's own class. In *The Last September,* Bowen employed the wartime experiences of her family in Bowen's Court (remade as the fictional Danielstown) to represent the divided nature of Anglo-Irish identity and the resentment of the young protagonist, Lois, against her class and her heritage. Bowen's imaginative interest in this work is in the imminent collapse of this whole social world in the face of war and destruction. The novel concludes with an archetypal Bowen image, the murder of a house:

"Then the first wave of a silence that was to be ultimate flowed back, confidant, to the steps. Above the steps, the door stood open hospitably upon a furnace."

Her most popular novel, *The Death of the Heart,* published in 1938, deals with familiar themes of emotional dispossession and betrayal, but it was during World War II that Bowen's imagination was energized by what she called the "lucid Abnormality" in life in wartime London. The sudden realization of the fragility of buildings, of lives, of an entire city, ennervated Bowen's writing and released her into fictive meditations on the fragility of selfhood. Her writing during this period is alive with the empowering sense of cracks beneath the surface, of fissures deep within the experiences of her protagonists. This experience of living under possible sentence of death inspired her to write some of her most vivid short stories, ghost stories like *The Demon Lover* and *The Happy Autumn Fields,* and she also produced *The Heat of the Day* (1949), a novel about the conflicting claims of private affection and public loyalty. After the war, Bowen continued to publish novels and short fiction and her final novel *Eva Trout* is a masterly and poignant account of the destructive illusion of a self constructed as a result of isolation and neglect. As Graham Greene wrote of Bowen's success as a novelist: "She has dramatised ignorance." Critically, Bowen has been accounted an important figure in the development of the English novel during the middle of the twentieth century and her achievement has been, as Bennett and Royle identify, "an affirmation of the undecidability of identity and towards the ethics and erotics of such an affirmation."

Eibhear Walshe

Selected Bibliography

Bennett, Andrew, and Nicholas Royle. *Elizabeth Bowen and the Dissolution of the Novel.* MacMillan Press: London 1995.

Glendinning, Victoria. *Elizabeth Bowen: Portrait of a Writer.* Phoenix: London 1977.

Jordan, Heather. *How Will the Heart Endure?* Michigan: University of Michigan, 1992.

Lee, Hermione. *Elizabeth Bowen*. Vintage: London 1999.

Walshe, Eibhear. *Elizabeth Bowen Remembered*. Four Courts: London 1998.

Brecht, Bertolt (1898–1956)

Brecht's plays emerged alongside his poetry while he was still in Augsburg, his birth place. The hero of his first play *Baal* (1918) is a fictionalized account of the poet hero to whom he aspired; his vitality leads him to breaking society's conventions by committing murder and becoming a vagabond. Brecht's first poetry, collected in *Bertolt Brechts Hauspostille* (1927, *Manual of Piety*), was aggressive and nihilistic. "Vom ertrunkenen Mädchen" ("On the drowned Girl"), recounts how God gradually forgets a girl while her corpse rots away.

From 1928 Brecht studied Marxist theory and the "Proletarian Theater" of Erwin Piscator, developing a radical dramaturgy of "epic theater." It resisted **naturalism**'s urge to elicit empathy from the audience through mimesis and catharsis. Instead, the audience was "alienated" from the action, so that it could objectify the reification of capitalist society as it was represented on stage, and could also imagine an alternative. To achieve this, the action consisted of the *gestus*, attitudes communicated by the actors which contradicted and relativized each other; they were unlike the expressions of symbolism which tended to dissolve into a whole atmospheric effect, or the naturalist gestures which attempted to convey coherent patterns of behavior for their characters in a concrete environment.

The first fruits of Brecht's new ideological perspective were his collaborations with the composer Kurt Weill. They revolutionized traditional, "culinary" opera into "didactic" opera, where the libretto and music independently play against each other in a dialogue instead of merging into an organic whole, and scenes are juxtaposed in a montage effect without linear narrative. The criminal and protagonist of *Die Dreigroschen Oper* (1929, *The Threepenny Opera*), Mac the Knife, parodies bourgeois conventions to reveal their underlying brutality. In *Aufstieg und Fall der Stadt Mahagonny* (1929, *Rise and Fall of the City of Mahagonny*) characters become mouthpieces of different ideological positions to reveal the workings of the capitalist city. Women and the "Here-You-May-Do-Anything Inn" are available to those who can pay:

> Jimmy is executed
> On account of lack of money,
> which is the greatest crime,
> that exists on the face of the earth.

Yet these works occasionally invite us to empathize with the characters, and with the social structures they inhabit, unlike Brecht's greatest plays which were composed throughout his exile from **Germany** to Switzerland in 1933, and to the USA until 1947. Following from his study of Marxist dialectics, Brecht explores the double-nature of modern society, of its morality and its brutality, and incites his audience to criticize it.

Mutter Courage und ihre Kinder (1941, *Mother Courage and her Children*) is set in the Thirty Years War. Mother Courage earns her living through a canteen wagon which serves the troops; she is dependent on the continuation of the war, yet over the course of the play it causes the deaths of her three children. *Der Gute Mensch von Sezuan* (1943, *The Good Person of Szechwan*), explores the conflict between the individual's ethical and economic interests. Shen Teh can only protect her business from people demanding charity from her, by dressing up as her ruthless male "cousin" Shui Ta who abides by capitalist frugality. In *Der Kaukasische Krei-*

dekreis (1954, *The Caucasian Chalk Circle*), the judge Azdak allows the servant girl Grusha to keep the child which she saved during a rebellion, because she resents having to risk its well-being by fighting for it against the original mother; Azdak's former career as a village rogue qualifies him as the ideal judge, who understands the necessary pragmatic considerations when dealing out justice.

In 1949 Brecht returned to East Berlin, repudiated by the McCarthyism rife in the United States. He concentrated less on composition, and more on establishing his approach theoretically in his *Kleines Organon für das Theater*, (1948, *Little Organon for the Theater*), and in practice through productions at the Berliner Ensemble, which was supported by the designer Caspar Nehar, and the composers Hanns Eisler and Paul Dessau.

Although acknowledged as the foremost playwright of the period, internationally as well as nationally, Brecht's stature as a representative of the political Left has remained a subject of controversy. His friend Walter Benjamin regarded his epic theater as the only viable guide for the proletariat in exposing its historical situation; Theodor Adorno, on the other hand, criticized the didacticism resulting from Brecht's direct political commitments as a corruption of his artistic integrity.

Brecht's works are available in Suhrkamp Verlag, Penguin, and Methuen, London.

Carl Krockel

Selected Bibliography

Benjamin, Walter. *Understanding Brecht.* London: NLB, 1973.

Brooker, Peter. *Bertolt Brecht: Dialectics, Poetry, Politics.* New York: Croom Helm, 1988.

Thomson, Peter, and Glendyr Sacks, eds. *The Cambridge Companion to Brecht.* Cambridge: Cambridge UP, 1994.

Wright, Elizabeth. *Postmodern Brecht.* London: Routledge, 1989.

Broch, Hermann (1886–1951)

Broch first wrote essays on philosophy, aesthetics and politics, while running a textile factory. His career as a novelist began in 1929 with *Die Schlafwandler* (1930–1932, *The Sleepwalkers*), while studying mathematics, physics and philosophy at Vienna, the place of his birth.

In *Die Schlafwandler,* like *Die Schuldlosen* (1950, *The Guiltless*), Broch attempts to capture, and criticize the fractured "zeitgeist" of his time by treating his characters in the varying literary styles which are historically appropriate to them. The novel is divided into three parts: the first is in the realist tradition of Fontane, describing a young landowner in 1888 who is unaware of the possible alternatives to his conventional life; the second part, set in 1903, borrows from **expressionism** in its depiction of a book-keeper embroiled in the anarchy of his environment; finally, in a heterogeneous style which incorporates philosophy and poetry, Broch describes how an army deserter in 1918 destroys the two previous heroes to achieve power in a nihilistic society.

In America, where he emigrated in 1940, Broch completed *Der Tod des Vergil* (1945, *The Death of Virgil*). In this extremely complex and poetic work on the Ancient Roman poet, Broch attempted to grasp the problems of the artist in his own time. Virgil agonizes over the *Aeneid,* that its beauty lacks truth and morality because it is detached from a reality which he cannot grasp; he concludes that Orpheus was "the enchanter, but not the savior of mankind," and that he must "burn the Aeneid." His friends and his patron Augustus try to justify to him the significance of his poem as immortalizing Rome, but Virgil is skeptical about whether this constitutes the "truth" of his "perception"; he believes that he must understand death to find truth in love. He entrusts the *Aeneid* to Augustus through reconciling himself to its failings, and anticipates a future savior in whose "being the world will be redeemed to truth." Like Virgil, Broch accepted his limits as an artist and hoped for a future savior of the modernist age.

Broch's works are available in Verlag, Frankfurt am Main, and Quartet Publications, London, and Cambridge University Press.

Carl Krockel

Selected Bibliography

Dowden, Stephen D., ed. *Hermann Broch: Literature, Philosophy, Politics.* Columbia: Camden House, 1988.

Schlant, Ernestine. *Hermann Broch.* Chicago: University of Chicago Press, 1986.

Simpson, Malcolm R. *The Novels of Hermann Broch.* Bern: Peter Lang, 1977.

Burdekin, Katharine Penelope (1896–1963)

As the events of the twentieth century became increasingly horrific, Katharine Burdekin, among many other writers of the modernist era, turned to the genres of utopian and dystopian fiction to critique European society. In ten published and an equal number of unpublished novels (Patai "Afterword" 166), Burdekin specialized in creating imaginative worlds her readers could compare to their own, using the technique of defamiliarization to effect satiric ends. Her work can be seen in the utopian/dystopian line of fiction which in the modernist era stretched from Charlotte Perkins Gilman's *Herland* (1915) to George Orwell's *1984* (1949), the latter a work Burdekin may well have influenced (see Bonifas and Croft). Instances of dystopian fiction increased in the interwar period due to an intensified pessimism about the Enlightenment-inspired belief in human progress (Booker 14); despite the vehemence of Burdekin's critiques of modernity, she did maintain a vision of progress that would result in a society of members who had become fully "human,"

who had evolved beyond the "misery" of their "partially conscious brains" (*Proud Man* 24). Burdekin's highly discursive and didactic tales are notable for their foregrounding of gendered social structures; she chose to emphasize that much of the "misery" of modernity was rooted in "sex privilege, sex dominance [and] sex antagonism" (*Proud Man* 25). She insisted that a better future would result if humans could transcend gender altogether, her ideas thereby intersecting with some of **Virginia Woolf**'s on **androgyny,** and anticipating feminist theory of later in the century.

Burdekin was born Katharine Penelope Cade in Derbyshire, England, in 1896 to upper-middle-class parents Charles James Cade and Mary Casterton Cade. After she completed her studies at Cheltenham Ladies' College at the age of 17, she requested that her parents send her to Oxford where her brothers were studying; they refused. During World War I Burdekin served as a nurse in the Voluntary Aid Detachment in an army hospital, and this experience fueled the anti-war sentiments found throughout many of her works. In 1920, she and her husband of five years, Australian barrister Beaufort Burdekin, relocated to Sydney where she began writing fiction. By 1922 Burdekin had left her husband and returned to England with their two daughters. Several years later, she began a life with a female companion; together they led a quiet country existence until the end of Burdekin's life (Patai "Afterword" 161–163).

During these years, Burdekin came to know numerous writers, some of whom wrote to her about her work. Radclyffe Hall sent a letter praising Burdekin's *The Burning Ring* (1927); **H. D.** wrote praising *Proud Man* (1934) (Patai "Afterword" 164). Burdekin and her companion maintained aquaintances with Leonard and Virginia Woolf, Bertrand and Dora Russell, Margaret Goldsmith, Norah James, and others, but they lived removed from the literary life of London, reading and writing in comparative solitude (Patai "Afterword" 165). Burdekin's place in the literary history of the modernist era was also complicated by her choice to use the pseudonym Murray Constantine for four of her published novels. The reasons she chose a pseudonym are obscure, but she may have understood that the radical gender critiques of her novels would gain authority if published under a male name. Crossley suggests she knew of the **censorship** of Naomi Mitchison's fiction on female sexuality, and responded with this pseudonym (96). It was not until the 1980s that the indefatigable scholar Daphne Patai established that Burdekin and Constantine were the same person; Patai tracked down Burdekin's companion and manuscripts in England, and has begun to republish her novels, and publish her manuscripts through The Feminist Press.

The first of Burdekin's "mature" works, *The Rebel Passion,* published in 1929 (Patai "Afterword" 164), provides an abbreviated history of the Western world in the visions of a twelfth-century monk with a woman's soul, which contributed to his compassion and pity for other living beings. This positive merging of gender characteristics appears in most of Burdekin's works, including an unpublished novel whose protagonist is a "young woman with a 'masculine soul'" (Patai "Afterword" 182). Her next published novel, *Quiet Ways* (1930) is a more conventionally realist work set in the World War I era among an unconventional family friendly to pacifism and **feminism,** and skeptical of religion. The novel tells the story of a volunteer nurse, a reluctant soldier, and other characters "discontented with the way humanity orders itself" (175); they rebel against rigid gender and class stereotypes, heterosexuality, and war. Like many writers, Burdekin distanced herself from pacifism when confronted

with fascism, but her keen critique of the masculine culture of war continued through her significant utopian and dystopian works.

Proud Man, published under the name Murray Constantine in 1934, was the first of these. The narrator of this novel is a "Person" who has achieved full humanity in a utopian world thousands of years in the future; its attributes include being utterly unselfish, telepathic, and self-fertilizing. This narrator travels backwards in time in a kind of dreamstate to the England of the 1930s, and experiences two years among creatures the "Person" considers "subhumans," "neither animal nor human, but in a transition state between the two" (14). Burdekin uses the form of a fictional anthropological report to defamiliarize and criticize many aspects of her society that her readers may have assumed were natural or inevitable; one reviewer compares the book's satire to that of Swift (Patai "Foreword" xi). The "Person" critiques industrial modernity as do many modernist writers, for example complaining of London as "vast and filthy and noisy," full of machines and pollution (155). The utopian possibilities of the novel lie with the "subhumans" developing the germs of "humanity" the "Person" spies—honesty, unselfishness and courage—while doing away with the hierarchies of gender and class that impede positive progress.

Swastika Night (1937) continues these themes, but in a much darker vision. As a Left Book Club selection—one of the only works of fiction in that series—this was Burdekin's most widely read novel (Patai "Introduction" vii). It presents a gruesome dystopian future created by seven centuries of "Hitlerian" rule. Like Virginia Woolf in *Three Guineas,* Burdekin explores the similarities between the patriarchal worlds of England and **Germany** in the 1930s, and the future fascism projects. Both writers posit that cultures rooted in phallic power (*Proud Man* 29) can grow into militaristic nightmares, especially for women, as they are based on the subordination and "reduction" of women. In Burdekin's novel, women live in communal cages and have lost all sexual and personal autonomy. This novel anticipates themes of Orwell's *1984,* published a dozen years later, and Bonifas has made a case for its influence on this much more famous dystopia. Burdekin's plot remains somewhat skeletal; here and in her other works of this type, Burdekin's fictional mode tends to be expository, theoretical, and didactic rather than dramatic or focused on psychology in a modernist manner. The only glimmer of hope in this dystopia is through textual salvation. One book of pre-Hitlerian history has survived the centuries, and its alternative vision of political and social functioning could spur resistance to Hitlerian rule. While Burdekin did not fashion her works with the intricacy and attention to verbal nuance of the high modernist writers, she, like them, postulated a kind of salvation through the word.

The End of This Day's Business (written 1930s, pub. 1989) reverses the gender coding of *Swastika Night* by presenting a feminist utopia in which women are dominant in a happy, but hierarchical order that constrains men. The rebel in this novel is an artist who sees that the perfection of humanity can only take place if society moves beyond hierarchy, and she must die for her traitorous vision. Burdekin here critiques feminism rooted in difference, and her analysis of power anticipates later feminist theories.

Burdekin continued to write after World War II, but stopped publishing her works. She moved away from directly political fiction, and returned to concerns with religion and spirituality that had made their appearance in earlier novels. Burdekin's philosophical use of utopian and dystopian fictional forms to probe questions of politics, epistemology, evolution, spirituality and many other themes

broadens our understanding of the functions of writing in the modernist era.

Loretta Stec

Selected Bibliography

Bonifas, Gilbert. "Nineteen Eighty-Four and Swastika Night." *Notes and Queries* (March 1987): 59.

Booker, M. Keith. *The Dystopian Impulse in Modern Literature.* Westport: Greenwood, 1994.

Burdekin, Katharine. *The End of This Day's Business.* New York: The Feminist Press, 1989.

———. *Proud Man.* 1934 Murray Constantine. New York: The Feminist Press, 1993.

———. *Swastika Night.* London: Victor Gollancz, 1937 Murray Constantine. New York: The Feminist Press, 1985.

Croft, Andy. "Worlds Without End Foisted Upon the Future—Some Antecedents of Nineteen Eighty-Four." *Inside the Myth: Orwell, Views from the Left.* Ed. Christopher Norris. London: Lawrence and Wishart, 1984. 183–216.

Crossley, Robert. "Dystopian Nights." *Science Fiction Studies* 14 (1987): 93–98.

Patai, Daphne. "Afterword" to Burdekin's *The End of This Day's Business.* 159–190.

———. "Introduction" to Burdekin's *Swastika Night* (1985): iii–xv.

———. "Foreword" to Burdekin's *Proud Man* (1993).

Butts, Mary Franeis (1890–1937)

Mary Franeis Butts was born in Poole in Dorset on 13 December 1890 to an upper-middle-class English family. Butts's great-grandfather, Thomas Butts, had been William Blake's patron and a substantial collection of Blake's works were housed in Salterns, her family home and birthplace. The elder child of Captain Frederick Butts and his wife Mary (née Briggs), Mary Butts grew up in late Victorian England with a nanny and—unusual even for privileged middle-class girls—had a school education, first locally and then at St Leonard's School for Girls in St Andrew's, **Scotland.** By the time she went there in 1905, the central elements of her imaginative education had been established: a love of classical **myth** (taught her by her father, who died in 1905), a deep-seated sense of belonging to the countryside of her native Dorset and a visionary quality—"the kind of seeing there is in Blake"—which she used to evoke her childhood and adolescence in her autobiography *The Crystal Cabinet* (1937). After St Leonard's she returned to Salterns for a short time before it was sold and then she left her childhood "temenos" (sacred enclosure) "where the trees toss / to look for Gods at Charing Cross." In London she attended Westfield College as a General Student (1909–12) but left without completing her degree. She then trained at the London School of Economics (1912–14) to acquire the equivalent of a modern diploma in social work.

On reaching twenty-one in 1911 she received a small annuity from her father's will which would have enabled her to live comfortably, had she so wished. However she rebelled against the restrictive middle-class conventionality of her mother, becoming a socialist and pacifist, working on the Children's Care Committee in the East End of London when the Great War (see **The War**) broke out and then for the first National Council for Civil Liberties. She married the poet and publisher John Rodker (1894–55) in May 1918. She partly funded and was involved in working on Rodker's Ovid Press (1919–20) which published poetry by **Ezra Pound** and **T. S. Eliot,** both of whom thought highly of her writing.

A sensitive and precocious child, Butts published her first poem at fifteen and wrote continually and prolifically throughout her life. From her twenties onwards she published poems, novels, stories, essays, reviews, and historical narratives as well as keeping an extensive diary. She also read voraciously. In and out of various literary scenes of the 1910s and '20s, she discussed art and literature with Roger Fry, **Ford Madox Ford,** May Sinclair and **H. D.,** had her portrait painted by Nina

Hamnett and Cedric Morris, explored magic and the supernatural at Aleister Crowley's Abbey of Thelema, partied with Evelyn Waugh, **Dorothy Richardson,** Glenway Wescott, **Djuna Barnes** and Paul Robeson and was lampooned by **Wyndham Lewis** in his satirical *The Apes of God* (1930). Butts' ebullient sociability often belied the fact that she wrote on almost a daily basis. She perfected her style by the early 1920s and its high quality is attested by her inclusion in most of the little magazines of the period (e.g., *The Egoist, The Dial, The Athenaeum, The Little Review, Calendar, the transatlantic review*). **Marianne Moore** was one of the first of her contemporaries to recognize the originality and power of Butts' arresting prose and along with H. D. and Bryher reviewed her work and acclaimed her significance to modern letters.

Butts and Rodker had one child, Camilla, born in 1920, but the marriage soon foundered and they separated in 1921 and divorced a few years later. 1923 saw the appearance of her first book-length publication, *Speed the Plough and other Stories* (two further story collections were *Several Occasions* (1932) and *Last Stories* (1938)). Her first novel, *Ashe of Rings,* written and set during the Great War (see the war) and described by Butts as a "War-fairy-tale," was published by Robert McAlmon's Contact Editions in 1925 (Boni & Co brought out an American edition a year later). Two very different novels followed. *Armed with Madness* (1928) illustrates Butts' startling command of modernist experimentation and lyrical prose (Marianne Moore praised it for its chamois agility), and her fine ear for dialogue as it probes the consequences of scientific materialism, **psychoanalysis** and the breakdown of religious faith in a modern rewriting of the Grail myth. Less overtly experimental in form, *Death of Felicity Taverner* (1932) is an ecological detective story which presents with disquieting prophetic insight the impact of a proposed commercial redevelopment (i.e. destruction) of the Dorset coastline for a theme park.

The 1920s were restless years for Butts, spent mainly in Paris with lengthy stays in Villefranche and London, where like so many of her artistic contemporaries she lived at a turbulent pace, experimenting with automatic writing, occultism, and opium, alcohol, and other drugs. She had a series of passionate but difficult relationships with, amongst others, the French artist and writer Jean Cocteau (1889–1963) who illustrated several of her works; the American composer, Virgil Thomson, who called her his "Storm Goddess" and the French writer, Mireille Havet (1898–1932), whose life she saved at one point. In October 1930 she married the English painter and illustrator, Gabriel Atkin/Aitken (1897–1937) and in 1932 they settled in Sennen Cove, Cornwall—the most westerly inhabited village in England. During the 1930s Butts published a range of essays (on Aldous Huxley (1931), Baron Corvo (1934), M. R. James (1934)), as well as *Traps for Unbelievers and Warning to Hikers* (1932), a study of supernatural fiction, "Ghosties and Ghoulies" (1933), and over a hundred stories and reviews (in *Life and Letters To-day, The Manchester Guardian, The Bookman, The Sunday Times, The Cornhill*).

Butts gazed out across the Atlantic from her bungalow "perched on the top of Sennen cliffs [from where] you can only see the sea and the sky full of gulls" and over that "Aphrodite Sea" she wrote historical narratives about Alexander the Great, *The Macedonian* (1933), and Cleopatra, *Scenes from the Life of Cleopatra* (1935), which were acclaimed for their accuracy, magnificence and originality. The second marriage was not successful and, from 1934, Butts lived alone in Sennen, where she became an anglo-catholic. She

died suddenly from appendicitis and a perforated ulcer on 5 March 1937. She was forty-six years old. Describing her as "a historian of twenty years and poet of them," Bryher provided her most lasting memorial to Mary Butts by publishing her posthumous *Last Stories*.

The significance and brilliance of Butts' contribution to literature is now recognized as she features in most encyclopedias of twentieth-century literature and an increasing number of critical texts. Her published works are now all in print, together with a range of her previously unpublished writing.

Nathalie Blondel

Selected Bibliography

Works by Mary Butts (in print)

The Crystal Cabinet. Foreword by Camilla Bagg and Afterword by Barbara O'Brien Wagstaff. 2nd expanded ed. Manchester: Carcanet, 1988; Boston: Beacon Press, 1988.

With and Without Buttons and other Stories. Selected with an Afterword by Nathalie Blondel. Manchester: Carcanet, 1991.

From Altar to Chimney-Piece: Selected Stories of Mary Butts. Preface by John Ashbery. Kingston, NY: McPherson & Co, 1992.

The Taverner Novels: Armed with Madness and Death of Felicity Taverner. Preface by Paul West and Afterword by Barbara O'Brien Wagstaff. Kingston, NY: McPherson & Co, 1992.

The Classical Novels: The Macedonian/Scenes from the Life of Cleopatra. Foreword by Thomas McEvilley. Kingston, NY: McPherson & Co, 1994.

A Sacred Quest: The Life and the Writings of Mary Butts. Ed. Christopher Wagstaff. Kingston, NY: McPherson & Co, 1995.

Ashe of Rings and Other Writings. Preface by Nathalie Blondel. Kingston, NY: McPherson & Co, 1998.

Secondary Works (1980s and 1990s)

Blondel, Nathalie. *Mary Butts: Scenes from the Life.* Kingston, NY: McPherson & Co, 1998. (Biography and extensive bibliography.)

Hamer, Mary. "Mary Butts, Mothers and War." *Women's Fiction and the Great War.* Ed. Suzanne Raitt and Trudi Tate. Oxford: Oxford UP, 1997. 219–240.

Hanscombe, G., and V. Smyers. "Mary Butts, Mina Loy and the dead language of Amor." *Writing for their Lives.* London: Women's Press, 1987. 109–27.

Hoberman, Ruth. "When Mana meets Woman: Mary Butts and Cleopatra." *Gendering Classicism: The Ancient World in Twentieth-Century Fiction.* Albany, NY: SUNY, 1997. 137–149.

Wright, Patrick. "Coming Back to the Shores of Albion: The Secret England of Mary Butts (1890–1937)." *On Living in an Old Country: The National Past in Contemporary Britain.* London: Verso, 1985. 93–134.

C

Canada, English

One of the Grand Old Men of Canadian literature, Charles G. D. Roberts (1860–1945), declared "to Canada, modernism has come more slowly and less violently than elsewhere" (298). The question of belatedness has continued to beleaguer critical discussions of Canadian modernism with charges of colonial prejudice being variously bandied about. Nonetheless, most recently Brian Treherne has submitted that "although Victoria had died in 1901, Victorian Canada lived on, a fact upon which memoirists, historians, and literary critics are in essential agreement" (315). Indeed, literary critics continue to sift through the wealth of material from the early decades of the twentieth century indicating the varied dialogue which Canadian poets maintained with nineteenth-century literary movements (e.g., late romanticism, symbolism, decadence, and aestheticism). The models exploited by these poets were most frequently emanating from *Old Europe.* Remembering this period, the poet Leon Edel confided: "We lived among belated Victorians; we were touched with Victorianism ourselves" ("When McGill Modernized" 113).

There is a critical willingness to locate the Canadian modernist moment in the 1930s: W. J. Keith, for example, contends that "until the 1930s Canada saw little of the artistic challenge and achievement of the modernist movement that had transformed literary attitudes in other parts of the English-speaking world" (58). Nonetheless, it is becoming increasingly apparent that the genealogy of modernist thinking can be traced in earlier decades through some isolated productions by individuals and groups of writers. Most frequently, these productions focused upon the need for technical experimentation. In their ground-breaking study published in the 1960s, Louis Dudek and Michael Gnarowski drew particular attention to Arthur Stringer's poetry collection *Open Water* (1914) declaring it to be "a turning point in Canadian writing if only for the importance of the ideas advanced by Stringer in his preface" (3). Stringer's preface stressed most importantly the significance of free verse and the abandonment of literary proprieties for the development of a modern poetic in Canada: "No necrophiliac regard for its established conventions must blind the lover of beautiful verse to the fact that the primary function of poetry is both to intellectualize sensation and to elucidate emotional experience. If man must worship beauty only as he has known it in the past, man must be satisfied with worshipping that which has lived and now is dead" (see in Dudek and Gnarowski 8–9). Such a call to arms would take over two decades to be fully heard in Canada. In these early years, however, the most significant achievement in terms of modernist influence would be focused on the theorizing rather than the practice of new poetics. In "Rhymes With and Without Reason" (1919) for example, J. M. Gibbon insisted that "Rhyme is the natural refuge of the minor poet. . . . How can the spirit of a half-tamed new continent be expressed in a courtly seventeenth-century jingle? . . . It would be a great thing for Canadian literature if it kept pace with the times instead of lingering in the drawing rooms of the early Victorians. The times are moving. Dynasties are falling, are being swept away" (see in Dudek and Gnarowski 15, 19, 20).

In 1920, the preface to F. O. Call's poetry collection, *Acanthus and Wild Grape,* voiced a very similar message to that of Stringer's in appealing for greater technical creativity: "So in this little book will be found some poems in the old conventional forms and some others in free rhythms, in which the author has tried in a humble way, to mingle elements of thought, emotion and beauty" (see in Dudek and Gnarowski 23). Call (1878–1956) would ultimately treat his reading public to an increasingly large measure of "Acanthus" (traditional poetics) as his career unfolded, rather than the more challenging "Wild Grape" variety. Indeed, even in this early collection, conventional poetic voices are inflected with more frequency than might be expected from the preface.

However, by the 1920s other Canadian poets were hearing **Ezra Pound**'s challenge to *make it new.* The influence of **imagism,** for example, upon the work of such figures as W. W. E. Ross (1894–1966) and Raymond Knister (1899–1932) has been widely documented. The Poundian emphasis (upon doing away with poetic clutter; attending to the musicality of language rather than metrical conformity; stressing the presentation of the experiential moment in its most pared-down, revelatory form which requires no intrusive poetic commentary) had a sustained influence on these two figures, amongst others (see, for example, Knister's most famous poem, "The Hawk," where imagist influences are most clearly in evidence). However, it would be wrong to suggest the aesthetics of imagism wholly dominated the writing of Knister or Ross (or even Pound!). Indeed, Treherne argues persuasively that much Canadian poetry "from 1900 to 1925 was simply late romanticism" (13). Nonetheless, like the voice in Knister's poem "The Plowman," isolated poets in Canada were now starting to emerge who were more willing to "Look backward/Ever with discontent" in at least some of their writing. From 1923, imagist-influenced work by Ross and R. G. Everson was appearing in Chicago's *Poetry* and **Marianne Moore**'s *The Dial;* and *vers libre* poetry by Dorothy Livesay, for example, was being published in *Saturday Night* and Boston's *Voices* in the mid 1920s. A strategic development in the debate over contemporary Canadian poetics would now focus on the activities of poets in and around Montreal. The need was for a platform for discussion and the *McGill Fortnightly Review* (1925–7) attempted to secure this—although (like the other so-called "little magazines" which were later established) it was never to attract the attention of a large readership. The *Review* was associated with the names of A. J. M. Smith, F. R. Scott, A. M. Klein, Leo Kennedy, and Leon Edel who later confided that "Like Bloomsbury—and why not compare ourselves with it?—our main delight was in needling the stuffed shirts, the Victorians" ("When McGill Modernized" 115). Deeply influenced by a host of different international cultural traditions and most recently by the work of **Eliot** and Pound, for example, these poets wished to explore new kinds of intellectual and experimental poetics.

However, it should be underlined that these poets were simultaneously still attempting to formulate their responses to the prevailing poetic traditions in Canada;

as Treherne points out, "in November 1925, it still seemed natural to Smith to quote from Symons, Verlaine, Moréas and **Yeats**" (254). Similarly, Scott had begun the decade promoting Tennyson as his poetic role model (Djwa 19); and in his reminiscences, Edel confesses, "I had soaked myself in every form of European culture which, as a student, I could find and afford; I bought the Oxford editions of the English poets in their collected volumes, bound in proper dark blue; I knew something of the Georgians from the little anthology called *Poems of Today,* whose second series came out as late as 1922; but I had not read a word of Frost or **Williams** or Pound or Eliot, or even heard of *Poetry* (Chicago)" ("A. J. M. Smith" 78). The circumstances surrounding the modernist re-alignment in Smith's poetic career, for example, have been linked by critics to the meeting in 1926 with Lancelot Hogben, a young mathematics professor at McGill University, who seems at one time to have lingered on the margins of the **Bloomsbury** circle. As time went on, Smith emerged as the leading spokesperson and theoretician of the Montreal group and he stressed the need for Canadian writing to respond dynamically to the challenges posed by the international scene of modernism. Indeed, much of Smith's and Scott's work in this period was imitative of American and British modernist verse.

Later other magazines, such as *Canadian Forum,* would participate in this debate on contemporary poetics; and *much later,* Edel would confide that the *McGill Fortnightly Review* "was, of course, a characteristic product of that decade—down to its menckenisms, its eliot-poundism, its proustian self-examination and its james joyceing; above all in its serene belief in the sanctity of art and literature divorced from all life, and the unimportance of everything except the editors, the review and the university, in the order named" ("The McGill" 19). In a similar mode, remembering the "*McGill Fortnightly* days" in a letter of July 30, 1966 to the poet Raymond Souster, Scott conceded that "we were not as revolutionary as we thought. Styles and conceits in verse—dropped lines, wiggly lines, no punctuation, verbal abbreviations, breath pauses, coughs and sneezes etc.—come and go like bustles and bikinis. Ultimately, as every child knows, there is only good poetry and bad poetry." Clearly, the *Review* did not, as has sometimes been thought, single-handedly herald the arrival of modernism in Canada, nor indeed did modernist theorizing and verse dominate its issues: "While Smith's and Scott's modernism certainly did sketch its first principles in those pages, there was a good deal published which had nothing whatsoever to do with modernism . . . " (Treherne 254). Nevertheless, this campus-oriented, modest periodical was clearly instrumental in diffusing knowledge *a little* more widely of contemporary thinking in poetics, as the following words from Smith's essay on "Contemporary Poetry" (December 15, 1926) suggest:

> Our universe is a different one from that of our grandfathers, nor can our religious beliefs be the same. The whole movement, indeed, is a movement away from an erroneous but comfortable stability, towards a more truthful and sincere but certainly less comfortable state of flux. . . . Poetry today must be the result of the impingement of modern conditions upon the personality and temperament of the poet. Some have been awakened to a burning enthusiasm by the spectacle of a new era; others are deeply disturbed by the civilization of a machine-made age. Some have heard music in the factory whistle; others have turned aside into solitude that they might the better hearken to the still small voice. (see in Dudek and Gnarowski 28)

It should be stressed, once again, that the reading public for the *Review* and later "little magazines" was very small and, as so often in the early stages of the development of modernism, the writers involved felt that they were under siege in a society hostile to change and given over to a fayre of mass publications and mediocre journalism. The *Review* and subsequent productions of a similar nature were often energetic responses to an unsympathetic Establishment, most notably the publishing industry, unwilling to take risks with more challenging writers. Given the context of such (familiar modernist) cultural perceptions, these poets felt that they were writing primarily for other "modern" writers.

Highly influenced by his reading of Eliot, for example, Smith promoted vigorously the exploitation of literary traditions by modern writers in order to re-configure cultural links with the past, to expose the difficulties of maintaining seamless relations with previous generations of writers, and to generate new poetic possibilities. Like Smith and Scott, poets such as Kennedy and Klein were also responding to the renewal in interest of classical and metaphysical poetry in addition to a host of different poetic legacies. However, Smith was to be most vocal in his avowed rejection of the Romantic legacy in Canadian poetry—a commitment never wholly realized by Smith himself, nor uniformly felt by many other poets. He was also particularly associated with the Eliotian promotion of impersonality and/or detachment in the formulation of textual voices—"I am not I, but a generation/ Communicant with trickling sand . . ." ("Testament"). (Again, such an emphasis was to be noticeably absent from the work of other poets such as Dorothy Livesay and Earle Birney.) Nageswara Rao proposes that "a modernist is one who finds fault with his/her predecessors and declares war on the received, the bourgeois, and the sentimental" (3). Unsurprisingly, such a "modernist" war could never be won con-

clusively and indeed the commitment of the poets under analysis to such a mission would waver considerably as the years progressed.

To what extent these poets exploited rather than submitted to literary traditions and waged war on "the sentimental," for example, remains a subject of continuing critical debate. The high-flown rhetoric emanating from Smith and his circle cannot disguise a persistent poetic traditionalism in their work in terms of technical and thematic emphasis. Whatever the nature of his poetic practice, Smith was keen to be seen scorning what he viewed as the exhausted Romantic modes of an earlier generation of Canadian poets born in the 1860s: Charles G. D. Roberts, Bliss Carmen, Archibald Lampman, Wilfred Campbell, Duncan Campbell Scott—the so-called "Confederation Poets." Smith believed that poetry could only survive by responding to the disorienting technological environment being experienced at the beginning of the twentieth century, and this particular clarion call was to be taken up by other poets, such as Kennedy:

> The pot-bellied, serene protestantism of Victorian England which still flourished in Canada during the spruce youth of Edward, and which underlay Lampman's spiritual make-up, causes us [the moderns] to chafe. We are impatient of reading into the face of nature the conservative policies of an Anglican omnipotence. We are principally concerned with the poetry of ideas and emotional conflicts. We have detected . . . that all is decidedly not right with the world; we suspect that God is not in his Heaven. Uncertain of ourselves, distressed by our inability to clarify our relationship to these and comparative issues, we do not feel superior to circumstances at all. (*Canadian Forum* 13 (May1933): 301–3; see in Treherne 128)

Instead of a nostalgic, nationalistic romanticism identified in the "Confederation poets," Smith and many of his circle proposed an Eliotian classicism of restraint, irony and erudition: "Modernity and tradition alike demand that the contemporary artist who survives adolescence shall be an intellectual. Sensibility is no longer enough, intelligence is also required. Even in Canada" (Smith in *Canadian Forum* (April 1928); see in Dudek and Gnarowski 33).

So the poetic debate which emerged in these inter-war years (and most particularly associated with the McGill group) centered upon technical experiment and the eclectic exploitation of past literatures in order to express the fractured identities compelled upon the modern subject by the experience of new technologies and bodies of knowledge. Increasingly, Canadian poets would privilege satirical and ironic textual voices in order to access new possibilities of cultural critique.

Despite the immense difficulties of publication of poetry during the years of the Depression, the change in poetic direction would gather its fullest momentum in the 1930s. This decade would produce, for George Woodcock (74), "the first actual Canadian book of modernist verse": Ross's *Laconics* (1930). Kennedy's 1933 collection, *The Shrouding,* was also to demonstrate clear modernist emphases (most notably in drawing creatively upon the poetics of Donne and Eliot) in its formulation of "contemporary" textual voices.

However, the most frequently cited collection in the development of Canadian modernism for this decade is a collaborative project of 1936, *New Provinces: Poems of Several Authors*—what Treherne views as "the landmark publication which signaled the demise of the old school of Canadian poetry" (115). Smith, Scott, Kennedy, Klein, Robert Finch and E. J. Pratt (a poet particularly associated with the modern Canadian epic, but whose collection *Newfoundland Verse* [1923] had shown signs of modernist influence) brought out a collection which was in many ways an attempt to imitate contemporary British examples, such as *New Writing* and *New Signatures.* (However, Woodcock (51) is timely in his reminder that "not many people noticed it at the time; not many people bought it or read it.") Smith's original prefatory remarks to the collection were focused once again on the poetic legacy of sentimentality and the need to break away from stifling parochialism in Canadian poetic attitudes: "We do not pretend that this volume contains any verse that might not have been written in the United States or in Great Britain. There is certainly nothing specially Canadian about more than one or two poems. Why should there be? Poetry today is written for the most part by people whose emotional and intellectual heritage is not a national one; it is either cosmopolitan or provincial, and, for good or evil, the forces of civilization are rapidly making the latter scarce" (see in Dudek and Gnarowski 40). The attacks upon previous generations of Canadian poets in his preface were particularly objected to by the more traditional poets Finch and Pratt and this led to a milder version being penned subsequently by Scott: "What has been described as the 'new poetry' is now a quarter of a century old. Its two main achievements have been a development of new techniques and a widening of poetic interest beyond the narrow range of the late Romantic and early Georgian poets. Equipped with a freer diction and more elastic forms, the modernists sought a content which would more vividly express the world about them. This search for new content was less successful than had been the search for new techniques, and by the end of the last decade the modernist movement was frustrated for want of direction. In this, poetry was reflecting the aimlessness of its social environment" (see in Dudek and Gnarowski 38).

As the 1930s unfolded, apart from isolated figures like E. J. Pratt, three groups came to have a significant influence over the complexion of the Canadian poetic scene: the imagist-influenced poets such as Ross and Knister; the Montreal poets; and the "Western" group which initially had responded to imagist influences, comprising of figures such as Dorothy Livesay, Anne Marriott and Earle Birney. In the later 30s, the Depression and the influence of English Marxists such as **Auden** and Spender caused this poetic map to disintegrate and increasingly poets turned to the business of social and political critique (see, for example, Livesay's "Autumn 1939").

In the 1940s and 1950s, the phenomenon of the "little magazine" (e.g., *First Statement, Preview, Northern Review, Contemporary Verse*) acted as an enabling device for a second generation of modernist poetic interrogations to emerge in Canada at the hands of Louis Dudek, Jay McPherson, Margaret Avison, Irving Layton and Ralph Gustafson, for example. These magazines were modest, amateur productions which often relied solely upon help from volunteers, but they were clearly important in offering platforms for new poets. Nevertheless, if these magazines voiced a poetic need for change in an aggressive and idealistic fashion, declaring their mission to be the reform of prevailing concepts of literary "taste," they failed in general to attract the notice of the wider public. The *McGill Fortnightly Review* was clearly significant as a role model for later little magazines, as were European publications such as *Blast, The Little Review* and Chicago's *Poetry,* for example. *First Statement* (Layton, Dudek, John Sutherland, Souster) and *Preview* (P. K. Page, Patrick Anderson, Scott, Klein) first appeared in 1942; and the emphasis of debate on contemporary poetics in the magazines of this time centered not only upon technical experimentation but also political *en-*

gagement and thematic diversification. Contemporary literary movements in the United States had a much greater attraction than before for the emerging generation of writers and the model of Pound's contemplative verse, for example, would have a dominant influence on the work of Souster and Dudek—most especially in his long poems such as *En México, Atlantis* and *Europe.*

Clearly, the 1940s saw the emergence of a new generation of Canadian poets wishing to extend and complicate the existing cultural dialogue with modernism. Woodcock contends that "modernism in Canada was international modernism located in a new environment, but, as happens in all immigrations, its offspring was native, the authentically Canadian literature that began to take shape during the 1940s and especially the 1950s" (58). Indeed, increasingly, scholars of Canadian literature are promoting the notion of two modernist generations: "Anyone glancing at the poets of the 1920s, and at those of the 1940s, will be able to make certain immediate comparisons: whereas the earlier poets show a tendency to subject matter drawn from myth, landscape, ritual, and 'objective experience,' the later poets tend towards a poetry of ironic **realism,** urban life, and class-conscious historicity; whereas the earlier poets tend strongly towards traditional forms and seem to have elaborated few of the modernist formal breakthroughs, the later poets welcomed more openly the formal revolution and shaped their verse accordingly" (Treherne 313). In the final years of the decade, many critics locate a watershed moment in the development of Canadian poetry. Dudek and Gnarowski, for example, propose 1948 as a critical year in the narrative of Canadian poetics, a year of "self-doubt and reorientation" (113). In the previous year, in his introduction to the anthology *Other Canadians: An Anthology of the New Poetry in Canada 1940–46,* John

Sutherland (editor of the *Northern Review*) voiced a vigorous repudiation of the international modernist creed of Smith and his disciples and brought to a head the ongoing critical debate surrounding "cosmopolitanism v. nationalism": "Why this Eliotian stand is so harmful today can only be understood if we consider the persistent colonialism of Canadian poetry in the light of new developments of the forties. . . . No amount of gabbling about 'European masters' can remove that pressure which focuses Canada's attention on her North American future, and which must draw Canadian literature willy-nilly in its train. Mr. Smith's oxygen tent with its tap to the spirit will keep a few remnants breathing for a while, but can hardly impede the growth of socialism in Canada, or prevent the radical consequences which must follow for the Canadian writer" (see in Dudek and Gnarowski 53, 61). In that same year, he objected publicly to Finch receiving the 1946 Governor General's Award for poetry and, as a result, Smith, Scott, and Klein amongst others, resigned from the editorial board of the *Northern Review*. More generally in this period, Montreal was having to make way for Toronto to emerge as a major cultural center of poetic activity and this revision in the poetic geography of Canada was compounded by growing regionalist sympathies amongst writers of the period. Cultural fragmentation/diversification and a re-interrogation of traditional poetics from the late 1940s onwards heralded a new age of Canadian literary creativity no longer dominated necessarily by modernist concerns—but it could not be left untouched by them.

Andrew Hiscock

Selected Bibliography

Djwa, Sandra. "F. R. Scott: A Canadian in his Twenties." *Papers of the Bibliographical Society of Canada* 19 (1980): 19.
Dudek, Louis, and Michael Gnarowski, eds. *The Making of Modern Poetry in Canada: Essential Articles on Contemporary Canadian Poetry in English*. Toronto: Ryerson, 1967.
Edel, Leon. "The *McGill Fortnightly Review*: A Casual Reminiscence." *McGill News* 21.1 (Autumn 1939): 19.
———. "When McGill Modernized Canadian Literature: Literary Revolution—The Montreal Group." *The McGill You Knew: An Anthology of Memories 1920–1960*. Ed. Edgar A. Collard and Don Mills. Ontario: Longmans, 1975.
———. "A. J. M. Smith: A Personal Memoir." *Canadian Poetry: Studies, Documents, Reviews* 11 (Fall–Winter 1982): 78.
Keith, W. J. *Canadian Literature in English*. London: Longman, 1985.
Nageswara Rao, T. *Inviolable Air: Canadian Poetic Modernism in Perspective*. Delhi: B. R. Publishing Corp, 1994.
New, W. H. *A History of Canadian Literature*. Toronto: Macmillan, 1991.
Norris, Ken. "The Beginnings of Canadian Modernism." *Canadian Poetry: Studies, Documents, Reviews* 11 (Fall–Winter 1982): 56–66.
"A Note on Modernism." *Charles G. D. Roberts: Selected Poetry and Critical Prose*. Ed. W. J. Keith. 1974. 298.
Stevens, Peter. *The McGill Movement*. Toronto: Ryerson, 1969.
Treherne, Brian. *Aestheticism and the Canadian Modernists*. Montreal: McGill Queens UP, 1989.
Woodcock, George. *George Woodcock's Introduction to Canadian Poetry*. Toronto: ECW, 1993.

Canada, French

For much of the first half of the twentieth century, an incipient French Canadian modernism—and this, essentially, equates with Québécois modernism—was embattled with a monolithic, conservative ideology propagated by the catholic clergy and certain social elites. This all-powerful ideology sought to safeguard a traditional way of life steeped in the supposed values of the rural milieu, and eschewed all thinking that proposed other values or other remedies for what were considered the ills of industrialization and urbanization. It found its most effective literary expression in the *roman du terroir*, a genre epitomized by Louis Hémon's *Maria Chapdelaine* of 1914 that notoriously asserted that "au

Québec, rien ne doit mourir et rien ne doit changer." A succession of authors wrote novels that idealized the rural existence and consequently celebrated and legitimized a sentimental nationalism. Others, however, did adopt a more critical stance and, while working within the genre, mocked and deflated the rural idyll whose mystique was eventually to be extinguished with Ringuet's *Trente arpents* (1938) and Germaine Guèvremont's *Le Survenant* (1945). But the espousal and promotion of modernism as such were more evident in other literary spheres, notably the review and poetry. With the outbreak of the Great War (see **the war**), a number of French Canadian writers and artists living in **France** returned home. They included the writers Marcel Dugas and Jean-Aubert Loranger, the painter Ozias Leduc, and the concert pianist and music critic Léo-Pol Morin. Familiar with contemporary cosmopolitan artistic trends, they were resolutely opposed to the restrictive hegemonic ethos they encountered upon their return to Quebec, as is brought out by their nickname *les exotiques* (in contrast to their opponents, *les régionalistes*). In 1918 they founded an avant-garde review, *Le Nigog,* to spread their modernist ideas. *Le Nigog,* which did not enjoy the sort of financial support and approbation that its opponents could count on, was inevitably short-lived—several of its founders returned to France for good after the war—but undoubtedly influential. Another review that would subsequently take up arms against the traditional discourse was *La Relève,* founded in 1934 by a group of young Jesuit-trained intellectuals, and renamed *La Nouvelle Relève* in 1941. Inspired by French writers such as Péguy, Bernanos, and Mauriac, *La Relève* was significant because it recognized the fact that the dominant ideology had no answers to the urgent questions of an industrialized, urbanized society in the grips of the Depression. The spirit of *La Relève* is also apparent in a generation of poets whose work is compellingly modernist in its themes (solitude, inner exile, failure) and its formal qualities: especially Hector de Saint-Denys Garneau and Alain Grandbois. Garneau's early work, clearly influenced by Baudelaire, was written in alexandrines. However, in 1937 he published a collection, *Regards et jeux dans l'espace,* written in free verse which, inevitably, met with hostility from a majority of critics for whom such modernist tendencies were synonymous with an attack on authority and inimical to a national literature. In time, however, the rhythmical freedom of Garneau's poetry, together with its spiritual introspection, was to be immensely influential. As was the work, influenced by **surrealism** (he was in touch with the Port-Cros group of French poets) and Christian existentialism, of Alain Grandbois. Grandbois was to mark in particular a group of modernist poets associated with the Hexagone publishing house founded in 1953. The most celebrated of these is Gaston Miron. If Miron's early poetry owes much to fifties' existentialism, the collection which made his name, *L'Homme rapaillé* (1970) is characterized by a political militancy—assumed by more and more writers as the so-called Quiet Revolution of the sixties unleashed a new nationalism—that urgently explores the linguistic and cultural alienation provoked by the dominance of Anglo-Saxon capitalism.

But the defining moment of Québécois modernism was the publication in 1948 of the manifesto *Refus Global,* a document of social, political and cultural revolt conceived by the *automatiste* artist Paul-Emile Borduas. *Refus Global* was, among other things, a fierce denunciation of the hegemony of the Catholic Church that had fostered fear, guilt, and inferiority complexes, and stifled originality and creativity. It also analyzed the causes of change in Quebec that were heralding the end of the old orthodoxy: the recent war, travel abroad, the influx of gifted refugees, the influence of the *La Relève* poets. Finally, it championed personal and collective freedom and the liberation of the self through unfettered spontaneity. *Refus Global* was a significant intellectual enterprise and a courageous one—Borduas was instantly dismissed from his teaching post for his audacity—but it gave fresh impetus to changes that were already afoot rather than prompting them. Those changes would culminate in the transformation of Quebec's society during the aforementioned Quiet Revolution and in the emergence of a literature which, while thoroughly Québécois in many of its concerns (debate over the status of Québécois French, questions of collective identity, nationalism) is unmistakably modernist. Significantly, the novel was transformed, notably by Anne Hébert, Marie-Claire Blais, Hubert Aquin and Réjean Ducharme. Aquin, who committed suicide in 1977, was inspired by authors such as **Joyce,** Nabokov and Borges; he eschews the conventional linear narrative and plays with illusion, paradox, metamorphosis. The major themes of his aesthetic are failure, ambiguity, madness, violence, incoherence. In certain regards, in its self-reflexiveness and use of anamorphosis for example, his work possesses postmodern tendencies. Ducharme's novels are characterized by their striking verbal playfulness, unbridled imagination, and a nostalgia for childhood. His use of pastiche, parody, and intertextuality mean that he, too, may be considered postmodern. Meanwhile, with Michel Tremblay, Quebec possesses a truly great modernist playwright, one who has been compared to **Beckett,** Franz Kroetz, and Dario Fo, whose *Misterio Buffo* he has translated into *joual,* the Québécois vernacular he insists on using in all his own plays.

So a literature that began the twentieth century entrenched in insularity ended

it receptive to every trend. Feminist writing—in particular, the works of France Théoret, Nicole Brossard, Louky Bersianik, Denise Boucher—had further subverted old orthodoxies and former certainties. The experimental theater of the eighties, led by Robert Lepage and Jean-Pierre Ronfard and groups such as Opéra-Fête and L'Eskabel had "désacralisé" the text. Science fiction and magic realism had left their mark. And immigrant writers—Emile Ollivier, Dany Laferrière, Ying Chen, Marco Micone, and others—had brought the exile's perspective to the traditional themes of identity and belonging and further transformed a literature that was going from strength to strength.

Christopher Rolfe

Selected Bibliography

Filteau, Claude. *Poétiques de la modernité au Québec, 1895–1948.* Montreal: L'Hexagone, 1994.

Harel, Simon. *Le Voleur de parcours, identité et cosmopolitisme dans la littérature québécoise contemporaine,* Montreal: Le Préambule, 1989.

Lamonde, Y. and Trépanier, E. *L'Avènement de la modernité culturelle au Québec.* Quebec: I.Q.R.C., 1986.

Lapierre, René. *Hubert Aquin. L'Imaginaire captif.* Montreal: Quinze, 1981.

Lapointe, Gilles. *L'Envol des signes. Borduas et ses lettres.* Montreal: Fides, 1996.

Laurent, Françoise. *L'Œuvre romanesque de Ducharme.* Montreal: Fides, 1988.

Magnan, L. M. and Morin, C. *Lectures du postmodernisme dans le roman québécois.* Quebec: Nuit blanche, 1997.

Nepveu, Pierre. *Les Mots à l'écoute. Poésie et silence chez Fernand Ouellette, Gaston Miron et Paul-Marie Lapointe.* Quebec: Presses de l'Université Laval, 1979.

Censorship 1890–1940

Sexual explicitness and political radicalism have often been integral to literary modernism. The Nazis burned modernist texts, artwork, and music, and displayed relics as "degenerate art." Franco purged many "disgraceful writers" (Haight 37,

47). In England, **Ireland,** and America, attempts to suppress such texts were common, either before attempts at publication (by outright rejection, bowdlerization, or less officious editing of MSS), through their being slighted or ignored by media or a writer's colleagues, or officially, through the actions of the police, vigilant anti-vice societies, and the courts. **Lawrence, Joyce,** and Henry Miller were the most renowned victims, but the list includes Balzac, Zola, **Shaw,** Havelock Ellis, **Arthur Schnitzler,** Theodore Dreiser, James Branch Cabell, Radclyffe Hall, **Richard Aldington, Eugene O'Neill,** Lillian Hellman, Norah James, Erich Maria Remarque, **Hemingway, Faulkner,** Edmund Wilson—and of course Frank Harris. Those in whom experimental writing generated extreme moral indignation saw its practitioners not only as obscurantists and dilettantes, but as foreigners, atheists, and pornographers.

The business of publishing was undergoing many changes after World War I, especially in America. Some of these were encouraging to modernists. Owners of new concerns (Horace Liveright, Thomas Seltzer, Ben Huebsch, Max Schuster, Alfred Knopf) had begun to specialize in presenting European writers to an American audience curious about their sexual frankness and Marxist ideas. However, the opportunities these young publishers offered had to be balanced against the attitudes of the established houses. Their executives felt that books from the parvenus' presses constantly crossed into those regions where the degenerate influences of licentious sensuality flourished. Amy Lowell, with her connections among the Boston literati, warned Lawrence not to publish with Thomas Seltzer, for he had begun to develop a reputation as "rather an erotic publisher." And New York's "town censor," head of the city's Society for the Suppression of Vice, told Dreiser in 1916 that "the people of this country. . . . need to

uphold our standards of decency more than ever in face of this foreign and imitation foreign invasion" of European novelists (Gertzman 113–17, 139–40). This attitude was shared by established writers such as Hamlin Garland, Edwin Markham, Booth Tarkington, and Mary Austin (Boyer 110–12).

The law of obscenity in England and America through most of the modernist period was based on an 1868 definition in *Regina* v. *Hicklin:* a work was obscene if it tended "to deprave and corrupt those whose minds are open to such immoral influences and into whose hands [it] may fall." The federal Comstock statutes passed by Congress in 1872 similarly made the most impressionable and immature minds in a community the standard for determining obscenity. In England, liberalization came with a reformed Obscene Publications Act in 1959. Allen Lane of Penguin Books took full advantage a year later, when an Old Bailey jury cleared his paperback unexpurgated edition of *Lady Chatterley's Lover* for publication. The previous year, Barney Rosset had won the right to send *Chatterley* through the American mails. His Grove Press imprint became the medium through which Americans discovered writers such as Henry Miller, Burroughs, **Beckett,** Alexander Trocchi, Ionesco, Genet, and "Pauline Réage." Rosset impressed the presiding judge with the scholarly introduction to his *Lady Chatterley,* and the lack of any prurient advertising ("pandering"). The liberation of the Grove Press edition was a final indication that the "into whose hands" doctrine was outmoded. In 1913, Learned Hand had written that it would "reduce our treatment of sex to the standard of a child's library," not the average intelligent adult, thus anticipating by 21 years the convictions made explicit by the defeat of the customs interdiction of **Ulysses.** The *Ulysses* decision set no constitutional precedent, however, and the post office and local magistrates ignored it for decades. Was it just as well? The implications of this case were that the sexual content of "literature" was "frank," not indecent or obscene, part of a responsible writer's artistic intentions, which were neither subversive nor mercenary. The average intelligent adult would regard the artist or novelist as morally right and emotionally pure; s/he would not be corrupted. Henry Miller, for one, preferred his works remained banned than accept such premises, which liberal lawyers and judges, necessarily advocates of the values of their culture, idealistically put forward.

Obscenity is a subset of "indecency," which may include scatological language, violence, and radical (especially communist) doctrine. In the United States, various municipalities banned works of Hemingway, Steinbeck, Sinclair Lewis, and Faulkner as indecent. In the latter three cases, political implications were relevant, as was the case in England, most notably with Shaw, **Yeats,** and Lawrence. The twenties produced two renownedly puritanical British public officials. Archibald Bodkin prosecuted *A Young Girl's Diary* (as did the New York Society for the Suppression of Vice). Bodkin called the work "filth" (Craig 80). It had been recommended by the quintessentially "foreign" **Freud,** and the growing awareness after **World War I** among non-academics of his ideas made authorities, who believed implicitly in the "into whose hands" criteria, uncomfortable on both sides of the Atlantic. Freudianism seemed not only to be sexually explicit, but to make people focus "indecently" on the pathological and bizarre. Home Secretary William Joynson-Hicks pursued *The Well of Loneliness* and *Lady Chatterley's Lover* assiduously. Subjects such as "inversion" and the primacy of a woman's passion over her wifely obligations were deeply subversive.

In the latter part of the nineteenth and first half of the twentieth centuries, literary works available only at high prices in limited editions often were not interdicted, for their tendency to deprave and corrupt the general population was not an issue. Modernism disdained the literary conventions and social values which would lead to a large reading public. However, its sexual explicitness and frank language stirred the moral entrepreneurs: clergy, politicians, postal inspectors, and reformist societies. Publishers who knew that censorship stimulates curiosity and that sex sells made texts challenged as obscene or indecent widely available, either by fighting for them in the courts or by making them available under-the-counter. Ironically, the censors helped popularize modernism as much as did the dedicated and opportunistic publishers. One of the most important "bookleggers" was Jack Kahane of the Obelisk Press in Paris. He issued *Tropic of Cancer,* and other books unpublishable in England or America by Miller, Radclyffe Hall, Anaïs Nin, Peter Neagoe, Cyril Connolly, and Lawrence Durrell. Other important bookleggers were bookstore owners: Sylvia Beach in Paris, Frances Steloff in New York, Ben Abramson in Chicago, Jake Zeitlin in California, and Frank Groves and Charles Lahr in London. Both the publishing houses and the bookstores were not only targets of harassment from Lawrence's "censor morons"—they, as much as the writers themselves, benefited ideologically and materially from the publicity. Modernism, due to its alienation from the conventional zeitgeist, got under the skin of the most censorious of the guardians of morals. Therefore, by them, it was dragged into the public gaze. Not a few artists and writers, knowing the notoriety that would come, recognized and appreciated the accruing benefits.

Jay A. Gertzman

Selected Bibliography

Boyer, Paul. *Purity in Print: The Vice Society Movement and Book Censorship in America.* NY: Scribner's, 1968.

Craig, Alec. *The Banned Books of England and Other Countries. 1962.* Westport, Ct.: Greenwood Press, 1977.

de Grazia, Edward. *Girls Lean Back Everywhere: The Law of Obscenity and the Assault on Genius.* NY: Random House, 1992.

Gaipa, Mark. "The Avant-Garde as Erotica: Kiki and Samuel Roth at the Margins of Modern Art." *Modernity: Critiques of Visual Culture* 1.1 (Fall 1997): <http://www.ux1.eiu.edu/cfsje1/gaipa.html> (May 18 1998).

Gertzman, Jay A. *Bookleggers and Smuthounds: The Trade in Erotica, 1920–1940.* Phila.: U. of Pennsylvania Press, 1999.

Haight, Ann Lyon. *Banned Books.* NY: Bowker, 1970.

Journal of Modern Literature. Special Gotham Book Mart Issue 4.4 (April 1975).

Laufe, Abe. *The Wicked Stage: A History of Theater Censorship and Harassment in the United States.* NY: Ungar, 1978.

Lewis, Felice F. *Literature, Obscenity, and Law.* Carbondale: So. Illinois U. Press, 1976.

McDermott, John Francis, and Kendall Taft, eds. *Sex in the Arts: A Symposium.* NY: Harper, 1932.

The Review of Contemporary Fiction. Grove Press Number 10.3 (Fall 1990).

Slade, Joseph W. "Pornography." *Handbook of American Popular Culture.* Rev. Ed. Westport, CT: Greenwood, 1989. 2: 957–1010.

Vanderham, Paul. *James Joyce and Censorship: The Trials of Ulysses.* NY: New York University Press, 1998.

Willison, Ian, Warwick Gould, and Warren Chernaik, eds. *Modernist Writers and the Marketplace.* NY: St. Martin's Press, 1996.

Cinema and Modernism

See under **Film and Modernism.**

Coffey, Brian (1905–1995)

Brian Coffey's poetry was praised by **Samuel Beckett,** in a 1934 survey of Irish contemporary poetry, for qualities Beckett saw as rare in Irish verse—as being alive to "the breakdown of the object, whether current historical or spook," and as posited on an awareness of a "rupture of the lines of communication" (70). Beckett's comments serve to identify in Coffey's early poetry the influence of early modernism; and Beckett is keen to distinguish Coffey's poetry, alongside that of **Denis Devlin** and, to a degree, **Thomas MacGreevy,** from what he views as the ossifying conventionality of Irish poetry in the wake of the Irish Literary Revival. In the same year as Beckett's essay appeared, Coffey had congratulated MacGreevy on the appearance of his *Poems,* optimistically claiming that "I think . . . you have, in practice, distinguished between the AngloIrish [*sic*] school of writers and the hypothetical poets of **Ireland** who are to come after you." Coffey's *Poems* (1930), which collected his and Devlin's undergraduate verse, was followed by a chapbook, *Three Poems* (1933). Both volumes show Coffey's formative interest in Anglo-American and European modernism, though *Three Poems,* owes too much, perhaps, to **Eliot**'s *Prufrock and Other Observations* and *The Waste Land.* By way of contrast, his 1938 lyric sequence, *Third Person,* explores the complexity of human and divine love in a style utterly Coffey's own, and introduces the richly ambiguous texture, and hypnotic rhythms, central to his mature poetry.

Third Person also demonstrates the importance to Coffey of Thomism, and the late 1930s would see him at the Institut Catholique de Paris, working under the neo-Thomist philosopher, Jacques Maritain, research which would bear fruit in his doctoral thesis on the idea of order in the thought of Aquinas (presented in 1947). Whether Maritain's speculations on the difficulty for the artist in conjoining catholicism and modernism had any impact on Coffey is difficult to ascertain, but Coffey ceased publishing poetry (though not philosophical papers and reviews in *The Modern Schoolman*) at the end of the '30s. He returned to print at the beginning of the 1960s with a number of poems published in the *University Review* (Dublin), including his 1962 work, *Missouri Sequence,* which he had begun composing nearly a decade before. The composition of *Missouri Sequence* overlaps with Coffey's translation of Stéphane Mallarmé's *Un Coup de dés,* which, as *Dice Thrown Never Will Annul Chance,* was published in 1965. Dónal Moriarty has persuasively argued that Coffey's translation of Mallarmé's poem should be read as as much a reply to the French poet's original text, as it constitutes its rendering into English; and, in this respect, *Dice Thrown* dovetails with *Missouri Sequence,* some of the preoccupations of which can be read as a Thomistic rejoinder to aspects of Mallarmé's atheistical poetic.

The Christian existentialism of Coffey's musings on the issues of grace and choice in *Missouri Sequence* lead him to invoke the American poet, Laura (Riding) Jackson: "One poet I admire has written: / *wherever the soul gives in to flesh / without a struggle is home.*" The italicized lines are a quotation from (Riding) Jackson's "Laura and Francisca," a poem in which the "home" inhabited by her and Robert Graves in Deyá, on the island of Mallorca, becomes the starting-point for a series of reflections on the manifold totality in which the human exists, the "truth" of which her poetry, she came to believe, failed to deliver. On several occasions *Missouri Sequence* associates poetry with truth ("No servant, the muse / abides in truth"); Coffey's concern with quite literally maintaining the poet's house, in a difficult period as Assistant Professor of Philosophy at Saint Louis University (1947–52), is an extended metaphor for the relevance of the poetic vocation to the human condition. While (Riding) Jackson's concern with those universals that unify humanity led her to conclude that poetry occluded such truth through its basis in a unique mode of perception, Coffey's sequence makes the claim that "Poetry becomes humankind" precisely because "without [it] nothing exact is said." From his particular experience as an emigrant, Coffey extrapolates the truth of humanity's existential plight, in which "we face a testing / based on other grounds than nature's."

Subsequent to *Missouri Sequence,* Coffey published *Advent* (1975), a long poem that recalls *Third Person* in its reflections on God and love, but which extends its speculations into the fields of beauty, ethics, and environmental issues, to name but a few. *Advent*'s is a large canvas; but linking its many frames of reference is an emphasis on humanity's existential plight, this universal given grounded throughout the sequence in the particularities of the poet's life (including the death of his mother and one of his sons). *Death of Hektor* (1980), arguably Coffey's finest poem, reflects upon Homer's treatment of the Trojan hero, and upon the heroism of war in general, in the light of the potential for nuclear conflict at the time of its writing. Like *Advent,* the later sequence develops its case not through logical argument, but through an associational accretion of images and motifs. Both sequences deploy remarkably various rhythmic units, in contrast to the conversational tone of *Missouri Sequence;* and, in a fashion reminiscent of *Un Coup de dés,* make use of typographical layout to underscore their semantic content. The "visuality" of these two poems is a feature they share with other poems by Coffey, some of which have a "concrete" poetic form, while others (such as *Leo,* 1968) are the fruit of collaboration with visual artists.

The most restlessly experimental of modern Irish poets, Coffey is perhaps the most unjustly neglected.

Alex Davis

Selected Bibliography

Beckett, Samuel. *Disjecta: Miscellaneous Writings and a Dramatic Fragment.* Edited by Ruby Cohn. London: John Calder, 1983.

Coffey, Brian. *Poems and Versions 1929–1990.* Dublin: Dedalus, 1991.

Davis, Alex. "'Poetry is Ontology': Brian Coffey's Poetics." In *Modernism and Ireland: The Poetry of the 1930s.* Edited by Patricia Coughlan and Alex Davis. Cork: Cork University Press, 1995.

Irish University Review. Brian Coffey Special Issue. Edited by J. C. C. Mays. 5.1 (1975).

Mays, J. C. C. "Passivity and Openness in Two Long Poems of Brian Coffey." *Irish University Review* 13.1 (1983): 67–82.

Moriarty, Dónal. *The Art of Brian Coffey.* Dublin: University College Dublin Press, 2000.

Smith, Stan. "On Other Grounds: The Poetry of Brian Coffey." In *Two Decades of Irish Writing: A Critical Survey.* Edited by Douglas Dunne. Manchester: Carcanet, 1975.

Colonialism and Postcolonialism

The rise of modernism in the late nineteenth century coincided with the dawn of what was called the "new imperialism," from the 1880s onwards. The colonization of large parts of the world by various European powers had been proceeding for centuries, with some fluctuations such as the loss of the American colonies at the end of the eighteenth century. What was new about the new imperialism was chiefly the pace of European expansion, particularly into **Africa,** the far East, and the Pacific. The frenetic speed of the "scramble for Africa" was symptomatic. Fifteen European nations participated in a conference at Berlin in 1884–85 to establish some principles that would govern the "scramble": essentially, the colonization worked inwards from occupied coastal areas to massive hinterlands that were defined as "spheres of influence." By this process of often violent invasion (and commercial exploitation) virtually the whole continent was quickly brought under European control. Another feature of the new imperialism could be illustrated in The United States' acquisition of the Philippines, its first south-east Asian colony, in 1898, during the Spanish-American War. Within the space of little more than a century the United States had gone from being a colony itself to wresting an important territory from a former imperial giant, **Spain.** By the turn of the century, then, not only was most of the globe divided up into several European or American empires, but subsequent redivisions, which were the only possible form of expansion for the future, were also underway.

At one level, these European and American conquests represented the triumph of Western science and technology. From the rapid-fire maxim guns that were used to subdue resistance to the colonizers' advances into Africa, to the railways that moved people and goods across continents with unprecedented speed and efficiency, the products of industrialized economies played a crucial part in the expansion of Western influence. In the rhetoric of the new imperialism, science was generally equated with "progress" and "civilization." But at another level, colonial expansion brought to the surface anxieties about the latter qualities. The "White Man's Burden," as articulated by Kipling, was an exhausting responsibility; perhaps worse still was the fear of atavism expressed in numerous late-Victorian romances and most famously depicted in the character of Kurtz in **Conrad**'s *Heart of Darkness* (1899).

For some writers, however, the prospect of tapping into "primitive" energies signaled a means of renewal rather than decline or destruction. Those who could no longer have faith in the progressive march of reason took encouragement from anthropological studies of tribal people that seemed to propose an alternative, prescientific worldview. Travel was not always a pre-requisite for this kind of inspiration: the art-markets of Europe and America were flooded with artifacts from remote colonies, so, for example, in **D. H. Lawrence**'s *Women In Love* (1921) Bohemian drawing-rooms in London are furnished with African sculptures. The relationship between metropolitan and other cultures, though, fitted into a largely predictable pattern. "In modernism," says Elleke Boehmer, "the colonial world was confirmed in its status as province to the Western city. *There* was the place that the artefacts came from. *Here* was where the definitions that counted were still made" (Boehmer 130). In some respects this situation, and the trade in cultural products, continued after the end of the colonial era; in *A Bend in the River* (1979) V. S. Naipaul has a collection of masks from a newly-independent African country being clandestinely shipped to the United States by a young American who had paraded his readiness to put on African clothes and dance African dances; the pillaged collection would form the nucleus of a profitable gallery of primitive art.

Despite these continuities, the travels of Lawrence and Naipaul themselves indicate some key differences between the colonial and the postcolonial periods. Leaving behind the English Midlands, Lawrence embarked on a series of journeys in the 1920s that took him beyond Europe to Ceylon, Australia, New Zealand, Tahiti, and Mexico, in search of societies that could be considered more organic than industrialized Britain's. Naipaul, a third-generation Indian from Trinidad, moved to Britain in 1950 and later traveled back to the Caribbean and to other newly-independent countries, finding much the same disorder and malaise all over the neo-colonial world. Naipaul has been described as a late twentieth-century modernist, attempting to hold together through writing what has been unraveled through history. Certainly the sense of rootlessness that runs through much of his work can be seen as a continuation of the alienated condition of many modernist artists and is also indicative of the transnational quality of late twentieth-century "migrant writing."

Cultural expatriation is almost a defining feature of postcolonial writing, but the phenomenon of migrant writers crisscrossing the world and evolving hybrid literatures actually predates postcolonialism. Neat divisions between periods and between cultures prove difficult to sustain, especially when interactions between the West and the colonial "other" are viewed through the long lens of what was called orientalism. Despite the political inequalities, cultural traffic between Europe and the Orient from the late eighteenth century onwards had profound effects on Western arts and philosophy. During the early twentieth century the movement of people around the world accelerated this process and fostered possibilities of cross-fertilization. For example, the Bengali poet, novelist and mystic Rabindranath Tagore traveled widely in Europe and America and translated his own poetry, grounded in Bengali forms, into English. Tagore's work was enthusiastically received, partly because his mysticism appealed to a wide readership in the years immediately before **World War I,** but partly also because his use of Indian legend and myth suggested a valid way of transforming history and tradition. **W. B. Yeats,** who promoted Tagore's work in Britain, found many parallels between his own poetry and Tagore's, as products of colonial cultures that were able to draw on deep sources of national literature. Both **Ireland** and **India** were, of course, engaged in anti-imperialist resistance at this period, and Tagore's lectures on nationalism, published in 1917, could be seen as a contribution to this struggle, as could Yeats's great poem "Easter 1916."

The presence of colonial writers in European and American cities in the early decades of the twentieth century was part of the evolution of a new relationship between "center" and "periphery." On the one hand, a sense of nationalism, literary and political, was making itself felt both in the colonies and in the centers of empire; on the other hand, "colonial writers like **Katherine Mansfield,** Claude Mc-

Kay, Mulk Raj Anand, **Jean Rhys,** C. L. R. James . . . came to form part of the 'complex and open milieu' of the new cosmopolitan city; . . . they helped constitute the cultural collage that was the modernist urban avant-garde" (Boehmer 124). In the later twentieth century, as displacement and rootlessness became increasingly common elements in human experience, the marks of modernism continued to show in postcolonial writing. The Indian-born British writer Salman Rushdie describes in his essay "Imaginary Homelands" (1982) the sense of loss experienced by writers who are "out-of-country" and even "out-of-language" and for whom perceptions are necessarily fractured and meanings shaky: "those of us who have been forced by cultural displacement to accept the provisional nature of all truths, all certainties, have perhaps had modernism forced upon us" (Rushdie 12).

Lynda Prescott

Selected Bibliography
Boehmer, Elleke. *Colonial and Postcolonial Literature.* Oxford: Oxford UP, 1995.
Rushdie, Salman. *Imaginary Homelands.* Harmondsworth: Penguin, 1992.
Said, Edward. *Culture and Imperialism.* London: Vintage, 1994.

Conrad, Joseph (1857–1924)

If modernist writers are marked by their experience of cultural dislocation and sense of language as substance, then Joseph Conrad has a head start. In a letter of 1897 to a new Polish acquaintance he gave a brief account of his troubled childhood in the part of Poland that had been annexed by **Russia** at the end of the eighteenth century. "In 1856 my Father, Apollo, married Ewelina Bobrowski, the daughter of a squire in the Ukraine . . . I was born in the country but my parents went to Warsaw (at the end of the year 1860) where my Father intended to start a literary fortnightly." Innocuous though this sounds, Apollo's own writings were patriotic and therefore subversive, and, once in Warsaw, he devoted himself to politics. He joined the resistance movement against the Russians and, during a period of what Conrad describes as "social unrest and demonstrations (caused by the recruitment)," he was arrested:

> my Father was imprisoned in the Warsaw Citadel, and in the courtyard of this Citadel—characteristically for our nation—my childhood memories begin. In 1862 we were moved to Perm and later to Vologda. Then, as an act of mercy, we were allowed to settle in Czernigow. My Mother died there. My father, who became seriously ill, received a permit to leave for Algiers in 1868 . . . [He] died in Cracow in 1869. (Karl & Davies, I, 357–58)

Although Apollo and his son had lived in Cracow only a few months, so were hardly known personally in the city, the funeral turned into a massive patriotic demonstration, and Apollo's gravestone was inscribed "Victim of Muscovy's tyranny" (Najder 36).

After his father's death, Conrad was cared for by his mother's brother, Tadeusz Bobrowski, who continued in his role of guardian and source of financial support until Conrad was 29. The boy's so far patchy education continued for a few years in Cracow, then in 1874 he left for Marseilles and joined the French merchant navy. His late teenage years were as full of drama as his childhood had been, including voyages to the West Indies and South America in which arms smuggling may have featured; there was also much spending and some gambling, and an apparent suicide attempt. The twenty-year-old Conrad's despair seems to have arisen, at least in part, from his realization that as a Russian subject, under an existing Franco-Russian agreement he was liable for military service in Russia, and his position in the French navy was thus very precarious. His way out of this dilemma was to turn to Britain, which had no comparable agreement with Russia, so he began working as an Ordinary Seaman in the British Merchant Navy in 1878, his meager income supplemented by Uncle Tadeusz's allowance. It was only at this stage that Conrad began to learn English, his third language. Nearly thirty years later, after publishing half a dozen novels and numerous short stories, he told a Polish correspondent: "English is still to me a foreign language whose handling demands a fearful effort" (Karl & Davies, III, 401). Nevertheless, in the Author's Note to his later volume of reminiscences, *A Personal Record,* he declared that "English was for me neither a matter of choice nor adoption . . . it was I who was adopted by the genius of the language." In other respects, too, Conrad became a committed Anglophile: by 1886 he had qualified as a Master Mariner and became a naturalized British citizen, changing his name from Josef Teodor Konrad Korzeniowski to Joseph Conrad. He did not see much of England itself, however, until he effectively retired from the sea in 1894. But he had seen a great deal of the rest of the world, his voyages having taken him many times across the globe, from Europe to **India** and Australia, around the islands of the Malay archipelago, and once, disastrously but significantly, into the interior of **Africa** as captain of a river-steamer in the Congo Free State.

Writing was thus Conrad's second career—he was 37 years old when his first novel, *Almayer's Folly,* was published in 1895. But even in the early stages of this career he saw himself following the difficult path that led away from popularity into the more rarified terrain that would later be identified with modernism. In another letter of 1897 (written in French) he describes his literary future as "anything but certain":

I am not a popular author and probably I never shall be. That does not sadden me at all, for I have never had the ambition to write for the all-powerful masses. . . . I have gained the appreciation of a few select spirits, and I do not doubt I shall be able to create a public for myself, limited it is true, but one which will permit me to earn my bread. (Karl & Davies, I, 390)

In fact one of his earliest attempts at writing for publication seems to have been in a competition run by the popular magazine *Tit-Bits,* which in 1886 offered twenty guineas for the best article on "My experiences as a Sailor." Conrad did not win the twenty guineas, but his experiences as a seaman did provide him with much of the material for his early fiction, and in the first phase of his writing career many of his readers might have described him as a "sea writer."

Almayer's Folly and *An Outcast of the Islands* (1896) both drew on Conrad's visits to islands of the Malay archipelago as first mate on the steamer *Vidar* during 1887 and 1888, and an earlier voyage, in 1884, on a ship called the *Narcissus,* was the stimulus for his third novel, *The Nigger of the "Narcissus"* (1897). The American title of this work, *The Children of the Sea,* reflects the novel's concern with the crew of the ship and their collective psychology, and perhaps there is an American parallel, too, with Stephen Crane's *The Red Badge of Courage* (1895), which Conrad admired, although it is not certain when he read it. A close friendship between the two writers began in October 1897, and Conrad praised the fresh, impressionistic quality of Crane's writing. Conrad's own concentration on sensory impressions began to be linked with a declaration of artistic purpose in the often-quoted Preface to *The Nigger of the "Narcissus."* Famously, he tells his readers that his task is, "by the power of the written word to make you hear, to make you feel—it is, before all, to make you see. That—and no more, and it is everything." In terms that recall his friend **Henry James**'s essay "On the Art of Fiction" (1884), and anticipate **Virginia Woolf**'s "Modern Fiction" (1919), Conrad continues:

> To snatch in a moment of courage, from the remorseless rush of time, a passing phase of life, is only the beginning of the task. The task approached in tenderness and faith is to hold up unquestioningly, without choice and without fear, the rescued fragment before all eyes in the light of a sincere mood. It is to show its vibration, its colour, its form; and through its movement, its form and its colour, reveal the substance of its truth—disclose its inspiring secret: the stress and passion within the core of each convincing moment.

Unlike James, however, Conrad also dwells on the artist's need to descend within himself, into "that lonely region of stress and strife," to find enduring meanings. The sense of struggle and ensuing pessimism, detectable in much of Conrad's fiction, is perhaps not purely attributable to his own temperament, but is characteristic of much late nineteenth-century thinking.

The struggles that Conrad's characters are engaged in often center around individual moral choices. In this sense his fiction continues the Victorian novel's concern with decisive moments of moral testing and analysis of the wider effects of a character's decisions. Looked at one way, Conrad's views on the truth-value of fiction and its capacity for minute examination of individual actions and the consequences of those actions might accord quite closely with those of, say, George Eliot. But Conrad's fiction is also deeply scored with a skepticism that belongs more to the *fin de siècle* than to the age of George Eliot. In a world without order, a human being is (to quote yet another of Conrad's letters from 1897), "less than a shadow, more insignificant than a drop of water in the ocean, more fleeting than the illusion of a dream" (Karl & Davies, I, 423), and simple principles of loyalty, honor, and so on, are inadequate props. If Conrad's fiction does ultimately suggest that such principles are worth maintaining, it is because human actions must be underpinned by ideas, one way or another, and the ideas might as well be old, tested ones such as fidelity; there is no sense of righteousness or optimism in such adherence, and Conrad is unflinching in his delineation of the failures of ideals.

Such a program requires a high degree of detachment in terms of narrative method. Conrad found his models in French literature, in the work of Anatole France, Guy de Maupassant and, especially, Maupassant's master, Gustave Flaubert. Flaubert carefully cultivated objectivity and precision of language in pursuit of a dispassionate **realism** that would transform the nineteenth-century novel; in his fiction the author is elusive, and style becomes of primary importance as a way of seeing the world. Conrad was rereading Flaubert, with "respectful admiration" (Karl & Davies, I, 111) at the time he was writing *Almayer's Folly*. In this novel and *The Outcast of the Islands* he was still struggling to achieve tautness of narrative, but within a few years he had developed an additional strategy that would supplement Flaubertian concentration and detachment and enable him to create an ironic distance between the events narrated and the person narrating them. He appropriated the traditional device of a tale-within-a-tale and gave it his own particular slant by making his narrator an experienced sailor who tells of his own earlier experiences. The most developed of these protagonist-narrators is Charles Marlow, who first made his appearance in a story Conrad wrote for *Blackwood's Magazine* in 1898.

Blackwood's was a fairly conservative monthly magazine, publishing both fiction and nonfiction, with an emphasis on travel and exploration. Conrad, who at this stage still tended to be labelled as a "sea writer," published a short story with a Malaysian setting in *Blackwood's* in 1897; this was "Karain: A Memory," which, as the title suggests, has a retrospective tale-within-a-tale structure. But his next *Blackwood's* story, *Youth,* introduced the middle-aged Captain Charles Marlow as a narrator who would tell some of his greatest tales, *Heart of Darkness* (1899) and *Lord Jim* (1900), both published serially in *Blackwood's,* as well as the later and much more popular *Chance* (1912). The readers of *Blackwood's,* like the publisher William Blackwood himself, would have recognized much that was familiar and comfortable about *Youth* with its nostalgic, sometimes comic recollection of a disaster at sea that tests youthful ideals. But they can hardly have expected the amazing change of gear that came, a few months later, with *Heart of Darkness,* a narrative so despairing, suggestive, and richly layered that it would become one of the founding texts of modernism.

Conrad had drawn on his disastrous African experience of 1890 in an earlier story, "An Outpost of Progress" (1897, published in *Cosmopolis* and collected with "Karain" and several other stories in the 1898 volume *Tales of Unrest*). "Progress" here is unmistakably ironic, for the two Europeans left in charge of a remote African trading post very soon find their "civilized nerves" severely jangled and their sustaining beliefs (such as they are) evaporating in their unwonted solitude. The tale is a scathing criticism of Belgian imperialism—for although the country is not named, there are enough clues for the reader to infer that this is the Congo under King Leopold II's notorious regime—but it has a more general thrust, too, as it ex-poses the insubstantial nature of so-called civilized values. Conrad continues and develops this double attack in *Heart of Darkness,* building in further complexities that have sustained generations of literary critics in an immense variety of re-readings. In *Heart of Darkness* Africa is again the crucible in which the supposed superiority of European civilization is tested, but this time the story is narrated by Marlow, who evokes a long upriver journey, like Conrad's own journey up the Congo in 1890, a journey that would take him to "the farthest point of navigation and the culminating point of [his] experiences." The trope of the journey into the unknown allows Conrad to present the reader with the spectacle of Kurtz, the once-idealistic white man who has plumbed unimaginable depths of depravity, from the point of view of a narrator who finds himself increasingly identified with Kurtz as he draws nearer to him physically. Marlow's journey forces him into "a choice of nightmares"—one nightmare being the hypocrisy of the rapacious colonizers scrambling for loot, and the other "the inconceivable mystery of a soul that knew no restraint, no faith and no fear." The sense of inconceivable mystery is not reserved exclusively for Kurtz: it floats oppressively over the landscape and the African people, so that Marlow's narrative, which progresses unevenly, with many shifts of tone, has at times the air of a dream. Indeed, before he is very far into the tale, Marlow asks his listeners:

> Do you see the story? Do you see anything? It seems to me I am trying to tell you a dream—making a vain attempt, because no relation of a dream can convey the dream-sensation, that commingling of absurdity, surprise and bewilderment in a tremor of struggling revolt, that notion of being captured by the incredible which is of the very essence of dreams. . . .

Contemporary responses to *Heart of Darkness* tended to emphasize Conrad's psychological penetration in his depiction of the "infinite shades of the white man's uneasy, disconcerted, and fantastic relations with the exploited barbarism of Africa" (Garnett, quoted in Sherry, 132). A few critics also drew attention to the subtlety of Conrad's narrative method, but it was only later that the novella's metaphoric richness would be explored using the techniques of close reading associated with New Criticism. By then *Heart of Darkness* had acquired extra modernist significance through its connection with the poetry of **T. S. Eliot.** Some readers have found echoes of *Heart of Darkness* in Eliot's *The Waste Land* (1922), but Eliot himself offered an uequivocal link when he quoted "Mistah Kurtz—he dead" as the epigraph to *The Hollow Men* (1925), a poem of modern despair and futility.

One of the main advantages of having a sea-captain like Marlow as his main narrator in *Heart of Darkness* is that it allows Conrad to transpose an adventure tale into a new idiom marked by ambiguity and indirectness. The "dream" quotation above shows how, in *Heart of Darkness,* Marlow is able to comment plausibly on the difficulty of communicating one's experience to others. The next Marlow-narration, *Lord Jim,* is at one level another adventure tale, set in Malaysia and using a real-life nautical incident as the springboard for its plot, although in this instance Marlow is more of an observer than he was in *Heart of Darkness.* Here again the suppression of any omniscient authorial voice gives Marlow room to express the difficulties that beset us when we try to understand others, and this leads him into reflections on the solitariness of every human soul:

> It is when we try to grapple with another man's intimate need that we perceive how incomprehensible, wavering and misty are the beings that share with us the sight of the stars and the warmth of the sun. It is as if loneliness were a hard and absolute condition of existence; the envelope of flesh and blood on which our eyes are fixed melts before the outstretched hand, and there remains only the capricious, unconsolable, and elusive spirit that no eye can follow, no hand can grasp. (Chapter 16)

Lord Jim, another examination of failed ideals, was originally planned as a third short story to complete the *Youth* and *Heart of Darkness* triptych, but, typically for Conrad, it outgrew its initial conception, and after serialization in *Blackwood's* it appeared in volume form in 1900, while *Youth* and *Heart of Darkness* were collected with another (Marlow-less) *Blackwood's* tale, "The End of the Tether," and published under the title *Youth* in 1902. It was with these two titles that Conrad's critical reputation became firmly established. Sensitive reviews, such as those by Edward Garnett, did much to encourage Conrad; his name began to be linked with that of Henry James, and comparisons were also made with the supremely popular Kipling.

Admiring reviews, however, did not necessarily lead to high sales, but from 1900 onwards Conrad's career was assisted by the energetic literary agent, J. B. Pinker, who also acted for Stephen Crane, H. G. Wells, and Arnold Bennett. For the next fourteen years Pinker's astute business sense and confidence in Conrad's ability would serve as "a life-line which guided Conrad from a financial quagmire into the haven of affluence" (Watts, 85). Conrad had married in 1896, and the first of his two sons was born in 1898. With a family to support as well as the habit of a gentlemanly life-style to maintain, Conrad's propensity for getting into debt became a more pressing problem than ever and added to the strain under which he wrote, so Pinker's assistance was probably a life-line in several respects. Conrad first turned to Pinker when trying to find a publisher for the novel *Romance* which he had written in collaboration with his younger friend and neighbor, **Ford Madox Hueffer** (later Ford). The collaboration with Ford resulted in three novels: *The Inheritors* (1901), *Romance* (begun in 1898 but not published until 1903), and *The Nature of a Crime* (published under a pseudonym in the *English Review* in 1909, then as a book under the names of Conrad and Ford in 1924). Conrad in fact referred to his collaborative work with Ford as "our partnership—in crime" (Karl & Davies, II, 334), implying that these ventures did not satisfy his artistic conscience. The main aim of the partnership was commercial, but although these would-be popular novels failed to make their authors' fortunes, the collaboration helped to sustain Conrad during a difficult period while he wrote further short stories drawing largely on his experiences as a sailor (his next collection was *Typhoon and Other Stories,* 1903) and, most importantly for his subsequent reputation, *Nostromo* (1904).

Nostromo is often grouped with *The Secret Agent* (1907) and *Under Western Eyes* (1911) as one of Conrad's great "political fictions." This is not to suggest that his other works necessarily lack a political dimension—questions about **colonialism** and imperialism, for example, surface almost everywhere in his fiction, and have helped to generate a multiplicity of new readings by postcolonial critics—but the politics in these three novels is an overt strand in the subject-matter, all of them dealing with revolutions and the complex human motivations underlying violent actions. *Nostromo* is set in South America, which Conrad had visited only very briefly during his time in the French merchant navy, so his imaginary republic of Costaguana is pieced together largely from books and newspaper articles. In addition

to a detailed and utterly convincing geography, Conrad invents a history of dictatorship, revolt, and political intrigue spanning half a century. This history, however, emerges in discontinuous scenes that baffle chronology; further fracturing arises from the differing viewpoints of characters who take up the narrative at various points. *Nostromo,* then, although it was billed on the dust-jacket of a 1918 five-shilling edition as "a moving tale of high adventure, of revolution, romance, hidden treasure, and a hero of the most vivid personality" (Batchelor 131), offers a bewildering reading experience. Like most modernist texts, it discloses its meanings only gradually, with rereading. It met with mixed reviews, and despite some appreciative responses (from the ever-perceptive Garnett, and from Arnold Bennett) Conrad was disappointed in the initial reception of this epic novel that had cost him so much creative effort. In an Author's Note prefacing a 1917 edition of the novel he described *Nostromo* as "the most anxiously meditated of the longer novels which belong to the period following upon the publication of the *Typhoon* volume . . . " Interestingly, this preface also baffles the reader all over again by including amongst the supposed sources for the novel a history of Costaguana by one of the novel's fictional characters; blurring the boundaries between fiction and history in this joking manner might be seen as a foretaste of postmodernist strategies.

The proliferating later editions of *Nostromo* indicate how, after the popularity of *Chance* in 1913, Conrad's earlier novels reached new and wider readerships. But in 1907 popular success still seemed out of reach, and the nearly fifty-year-old Conrad was growing more hungry for such success. In a letter to his agent, Pinker, he wrote: "my mind runs much on popularity now. I would try to reach it not by sensationalism but by means of taking a widely discussed subject for the *text* of my novel"

(Karl & Davies, III, 439). He had just completed *The Secret Agent,* a novel based on a recent and bizarre event in British history, the Greenwich Bomb Outrage of 1894, in which an anarchist named Bourdin blew himself up as he was approaching the Observatory. For the first time, Conrad was writing about London, a monstrous place that could accommodate all kinds of paradoxes, and for the first time he was employing a mixture of genres that included detective fiction as well as the political thriller. This sensational material was sealed within an all-pervading irony that allowed Conrad to manipulate his characters with "ruthless precision and aesthetic economy" (Erdinast-Vulcan 5). The novel's subtitle, "A Simple Tale," is both a further ironic touch and, perhaps, an appeal to a broad readership (it was first published, as a shortened and copiously-illustrated serial, in a down-market magazine called *Ridgway's: A Militant Weekly for God and Country*). But sales of the full-length novel were, once again, disappointing; it was only much later that *The Secret Agent* was hailed as a modernist masterpiece.

The London of *The Secret Agent* is partly colored, Conrad says in the Author's Note to the novel, by memories of his own lonely nocturnal walks through the city in his younger days; the reader easily feels this shadowy influence, for the bustling surface of Verloc's city is a veneer over a dark, menacing and hollow core. If the city is deceptive—"unreal," in Eliot's phrase—so are the anarchist-revolutionary characters in *The Secret Agent:* there is nothing significant about their politics and they themselves are grotesques whose characterization pulls the novel in the direction of macabre satire. The revolutionaries in *Under Western Eyes* are not so homogenous: there is idealism as well as cynicism amongst them, but the mixture can only be viewed with pessimism. The uncommitted student Razumov, caught up in the political ferment, defines revolutionary success as "hopes grotesquely betrayed, ideals caricatured." Here again, politics is, morally speaking, a sham, offering only alternating varieties of destructiveness.

The first part of *Under Western Eyes* is set in Russia, and the influence of Russian fiction, particularly Dostoyevsky's, is detectable, although Conrad expressed hostility to Dostoyevsky's work ("too Russian for me"). But the "western eyes" of the title are those of the narrator, an elderly British teacher of languages in Geneva, a city of exiles, who warns the reader at the outset of the novel that words "are the great foes of reality." The narrator strains for impartiality as he retells Razumov's Russian story, but his perspective is limited, so the sense of foreignness remains. As Edward Garnett had remarked in an earlier appreciation of Conrad's fiction, "Mr. Conrad's art seems to be on the line that divides East from West" (Sherry 107).

Conrad suffered a breakdown after writing *Under Western Eyes,* perhaps partly because writing about Russia re-opened old emotional wounds. His subsequent novels are generally considered to be less intense, although among his later works are some impressive short stories, notably "The Secret Sharer," first published in 1910 and collected in *'Twixt Land and Sea* (1912). But after his next novel, *Chance,* was serialized, with prominent publicity, in the *New York Herald* in 1912, Conrad found his literary fortunes transformed. His later novels, *Victory* (1915), *The Shadow-Line* (1917), *The Arrow of Gold* (1919), *The Rescue* (1920) and *The Rover* (1923), pleased contemporary readers but not later critics. "Once he had marched in the vanguard of literary innovation; but now, as a new generation of innovators emerged . . . Conrad seemed to be retreating from the battleground of ideas" (Watts 125). Even before his death in 1924 the inevitable critical reaction had set in, and his reputation did not begin to recover until the 1940s. But once he was installed in Leavis's "Great Tradition" scholarly attention gathered momentum and has continued unabated. Conrad's influence on other writers has also been profound, and echoes of his work can be found in all kinds of unlikely as well as likely places. Although he has been described as a modernist whose deepest affinities are with the past, even with romanticism, his deeply felt skepticism and ability to express that skepticism in the very fabric of his fiction are still impressively relevant.

Lynda Prescott

Selected Bibliography

Batchelor, John. *The Life of Joseph Conrad.* Oxford: Blackwell, 1994.

Brooks, Peter. *Reading for the Plot.* Oxford: Clarendon Press, 1984.

Erdinast-Vulcan, Daphna. *Joseph Conrad and the Modern Temper.* Oxford: Clarendon Press, 1991

Fincham, Gail and Myrtle Hooper, eds. *Under Postcolonial Eyes: Joseph Conrad After Empire.* Rondebosch, S.A.: UCT Press, 1996

Karl, Frederick R. and Laurence Davies, eds. *The Collected Letters of Joseph Conrad,* 4 vols. Cambridge: Cambridge UP, 1983–1990.

Najder, Zdzislaw. *Conrad in Perspective.* Cambridge: Cambridge UP, 1997.

Roberts, Andrew Michael, ed. *Joseph Conrad.* London: Longman, 1998.

Sherry, Norman, ed. *Conrad: The Critical Heritage.* London: Routledge & Kegan Paul, 1973.

Spittles, Brian. *Joseph Conrad.* Basingstoke: Macmillan, 1992.

Stape, J. H., ed. *The Cambridge Companion to Joseph Conrad.* Cambridge: Cambridge UP, 1996.

Tredell, Nicolas. *Joseph Conrad: Heart of Darkness.* Cambridge: Icon Books, 1998.

Watt, Ian, *Conrad in the Nineteenth Century.* London: Chatto & Windus, 1980.

Watts, Cedric. *Joseph Conrad: A Literary Life.* Basingstoke: Macmillan, 1989.

Cubism

The *cubist* revolution rejected "illusionistic" space, privileged conception over perception, and emphasized geometrical analysis of three-dimensional objects on a two-dimensional plane. Cubists, who asserted that painting constitutes its own reality, rearranged facets of the motif according to mental and structural principles. The material world was represented in the cubist grid with a density and complexity that had little to do with visual surfaces: the canvas was no longer a window onto a world in which space was organized by illusory Renaissance perspective. The intellectual austerity of early cubist works called for a near monochromatic palette that enabled the painters to handle the intersection of planes undistracted by color.

In 1906 Matisse and Derain discovered African art; when Pablo Picasso (1881–1973) repainted two faces as African masks in *Les Demoiselles d'Avignon* (1907), he was making a total break with mimetic tradition. The *heroic* period of analytic cubism spans the years 1907–12, with Picasso joining Georges Braque (1882–1963) in 1908. They collaborated as closely as "mountain climbers roped together," Braque later said, and their experimental work was so similar that the period 1910–12 has been called "the lookalike years." The second wave, synthetic cubism, spans 1912–14, with important contributions from Juan Gris (1887–1927) and Fernand Léger (1881–1955). While an academic school of cubism flourished in Paris from 1911–14, with Albert Gleizes (1881–1953), Jean Metzinger (1883–1957), Roger de la Fresnaye (1885–1925), Henri le Fauconnier (1881–1946), and the pre-orphist Robert Delaunay (1885–1941), Picasso and Braque remained aloof; when cubism made its public bow in 1911, they did not exhibit with the others.

Analytic cubism broke the motif into interlocking facets; synthetic cubism reintroduced color and synthesized objects in flattened patterns, retaining a "tactile" quality through overlapping planes. Braque saw beauty "in terms of volume, line, mass, and weight" (see Daix 39), which he analyzed in familiar objects; Gris's sensuous representation of volumes and planes combined conceptualization with aesthetics. Guillaume Apollinaire, in *The Cubist Painters* (1913), defined "authentic cubism" as "the art of depicting new wholes with formal elements borrowed not from the reality of vision, but from that of conception" (see Fry 112). But the pioneers of cubism, unlike some later innovators, never crossed the line into total abstraction. Two main sources were Cézanne's geometric distortions and the plastic volumes of African and Iberian art. Cézanne's interlocking planes showed Picasso the way to an autonomous picture space, while the simplified forms of primitive art struck him as "rational." But his drive toward cubism came from inner necessity rather than conscious intention— "We wanted simply to express what was in us," he said in 1935 (Picasso 273). The theories were constructed by imitators such as Gleizes and Metzinger in *Du Cubisme* (1912).

Reacting against the floating light of the impressionists, cubists wanted to articulate the material structure of reality. In Matisse's words, "[they] forced on the spectator's imagination a rigorously defined space between each object" (see Daix 44); or as Roger Allard (1912) put it, "cubism feels space as a complex of lines, units of space, quadratic and cubic equations and ratios" (in Fry 71). Picasso's *Les Demoiselles,* which was left unfinished, launched the revolution, although it is pre-cubist in form. A mordant answer to Cézanne's *Great Bathers,* it led to the fracturing and reassembling of forms. The poet André Salmon described the masklike features of the two women on the right as "naked problems, white numbers on the blackboard" and noted the "dynamic decomposition of light values" and the "geometry that was both infinitesimal and cinematic" (in Fry 82, 83). Picasso's ana-

lytic experiments had begun with a vengeance. After **World War I,** he reinvented classicism and moved on to a variety of styles, while Braque and Gris developed their painterly aesthetics. Picasso's *The Three Musicians* (1921), which has been called "the crowning masterpiece" of synthetic cubism (Fry 34), may be said to mark the end of the cubist epoch.

Apollinaire pointed out in 1912 that "cubism . . . is not an art of imitation but an art of conception" and that it is "more cerebral than sensual"; Maurice Raynal contrasted conception, which "makes us aware of the object in all its forms," with perception which gives only a partial view of it" (in Fry 116, 95). Cubist analysis dissects in order to reconstruct and challenges the viewer with a novel conception of reality. Picasso himself declared in 1935: "In my case a picture is a sum of destructions. . . . In each destroying of a beautiful discovery, the artist does not really suppress it, but rather transforms it, condenses it, makes it more substantial. . . . Art is not the application of a canon of beauty but what the instinct and the brain can conceive beyond any canon" (272, 273).

Cubism revolutionized materials as well as forms: the paraphernalia of café tables and studios provided motifs (guitars, cups, bottles), while human figures were anatomized into rhomboids, rectangles, triangles, and cubes. Cubism emphasizes materiality over appearance, Locke's "primary qualities" of form and extension over sensation (Kahnweiler 12). The aim was to reconstruct reality "in a self-sufficing, non-imitative art-form"; to do this, cubists abandoned conventional ways of seeing and "established the artist's right to look at things from several viewpoints simultaneously" (Cooper 49, 264). Cubist vision is analytical while cubist geometry is the structural basis for multiple perceptions of reality. According to Charles Lacoste (1913), cubist form "will show the sides we do not see together with the side we do see. It will depict the object as one knows it is—that is, from several angles at one time . . . " (in Fry 11). The cubist grid relates to an aesthetic of "clarity" that highlights "the substance and texture of the objects" (Berger, *Success* 48). Multiple viewpoints demand fragmentation and crystallize into new structures. Objects are dissected into facets and planes, faces into angular forms and serially superimposed segments. In Picasso's portraits of Vollard, Uhde, and Kahnweiler (1910), the sitter's personality gradually emerges from a dense network of shapes and lines. While Picasso exploited asymmetry, Braque (in his still-lifes) modeled space and connected forms with more nuanced transitions. Gris used mathematical calculations, synthesizing forms in "abstract geometric substructures: squares, golden sections and the diagonals which bisect them" (Golding 95). Cubist language developed stereometrically, freeing painting from fixed viewpoints.

The cubist inherited Cézanne's problem of representing solid volumes on a flat surface. At first, Picasso's and Braque's efforts (1909) produced "a shallow and ambiguous pictorial space, one that both recedes from the surface of the canvas and extends outward from it" (Kelder 284). The overall spatial conception became a priority for Braque, with "the space that surrounds and separates objects becom[ing] as important, as palpable, as the objects themselves" (Golding 69). Cubist space is only nominally static: reading a cubist painting is an active process. While Picasso "created his dynamic space essentially by means of volumes, filling his pictures with them till they overflowed," Braque's brushwork retained "vibrant inflexions . . . [that] set the planes turning and the volumes moving" (Daix 43). As Daix notes, "cubism draws us . . . into a shifting, quivering space which tends to include the spectator himself" (43).

Cubist "syntax" radically changed the possibilities of painting. As the canvas came to represent an autonomous reality, plasticity and planar structure became all-important. While minor painters orchestrated planes and forms, Picasso "penetrate[d] to the inner structure of things" (Cooper 48). The cubists practiced fragmentation and distortion, which Kahnweiler traces to "the conflict between representation and structure" (9). Picasso adapted distortion and geometric codification from tribal art and with these means unleashed "an irreducible discontinuity" (Daix 55).

Experimenting with the dialectics of inside and outside, virtual space and material substance, Picasso and Braque introduced letters, words, and numbers into their paintings, turning out collages, *papiers collés,* and assemblages. Braque painted a *trompe l'oeil* nail with attendant shadows near the top of his *Violin and Palette* (1909–10) and used stenciled lettering in *The Portuguese* (1911). Illusory unity gave way to hybridity, as print and paper were stamped or stuck to painted surfaces. Braque made the first *papier collé* in 1912, when he pasted strips of "oak-panelled" wallpaper onto canvas, then painted over and around the shapes, grafting them into a plastic design. Collage violates the integrity of the picture space, supplementing the artist's design with readymade materials. Picasso's *Still-Life with Chair Caning* (1912) is the first cubist collage: he glued a piece of oilcloth, printed like caning, to the surface of an oval canvas, superimposing the letters "JOU" (for "Journal") above it. A painting is now seen as an object that can assimilate other objects, affirming the interaction of all materials on a single level of reality.

The discovery of mixed media techniques signaled the shift from analytic to synthetic cubism. Gris collaged a fragment of mirror to a still-life, *The Washstand* (1912), using a piece of actual glass instead of simulating it with paint. Picasso "transformed his compositions into assemblages of plastic, coloured and conceptual elements permitting an overall grasp of the object, a synthesis" (Daix 99). His *Still-life with Violin and Fruit* (1913) shows many artful uses of cut-out and glued papers. He also constructed mixed media works such as *Guitar* (1912), in sheet metal and wire, and introduced a variety of materials into his canvases, including sand, lacquer, glass, plaster, sawdust, and beads. In these ways, cubism affirmed the object status of the artwork; it was more concerned with internal structure than with expression or interpretation. Real objects add clarity and relief to the plastic design, setting up an interplay between material and abstract, things and signs. Cubism is a non-mimetic art that constructs its own reality; as Wendy Steiner notes, with an eye to literary parallels, it is "definitionally self-reflexive" (181).

Picasso's and Braque's innovations extended the scope of painting, but were not easily grasped by their followers. They revolutionized the picture-space by combining surface and depth and eliminating optical illusion. Thanks to their bold experiments, cubist influence pervades twentieth-century art, extending to sculpture, architecture, music, applied arts, textiles, camouflage, theater, and **film.**

Picasso's interest in plastic volumes led him to try his hand at sculpture, an outstanding example being *Woman's Head* in bronze (1909–10). Other notable cubist sculptors were Raymond Duchamp-Villon (1876–1918), Alexander Archipenko (1887–1964), Otto Gutfreund (1889–1927), and Jacques Lipchitz (1891–1973). But given the difficulty of translating a two-dimensional painterly aesthetic into solid volumes, much cubist sculpture remained experimental.

Cubism had a direct impact on theater, ballet, and stage-design, through Picasso's sets and costumes for the Diaghilev ballet, *Parade* (1917), as well as on commercial art and poster-design. Postwar cubism was instinctively in touch with modernity, as in Léger's cult of speed, travel, work, and industry. His paintings, with their gleaming tubular forms—see *The Card Party* (1917) and *The City* (1919–20)—and his film, *Ballet Mécanique* (1924), offer aesthetic equivalents of industrial/mechanical reality. Léger connected the multiple perspectives of cubism with the fragmented perceptions of city life. Like the futurists, he wanted "to use basic pictorial elements to evoke the throbbing intensity, the opposing rhythms, the dynamism and the human involvement of modern civilization" (Cooper 93). Some contemporary critics linked cubism with the "fourth dimension," on the grounds that it combined space and time, presenting successive views of the object simultaneously. Notions of Einsteinian relativity were widely applied to cubism, as to the writings of **Gertrude Stein,** Apollinaire, Max Jacob, Pierre Reverdy, and Blaise Cendrars.

Cubist painters and poets lived and worked together, as did Picasso, Gris, Jacob, and Salmon at the Bateau Lavoir in Montmartre. Golding compares the poems of Reverdy, Apollinaire, and Jacob to cubist painting "in that they are beautifully constructed and coherent entities made up of overlaid, often seemingly fractured or dislocated parts" (94). Reverdy's metaphors, with their surprising conjunctions, can be compared with "the 'rhyming' shapes in Gris's work" (Golding 95), just as Mallarmé's self-referential use of the verbal medium can be compared with the autonomy of cubist picture-space. Gertrude Stein's cubist prose, as illustrated by her description of Picasso in *Camera Work* (1912), builds up a portrait of the subject from overlapping statements. Steiner adds **W. C. Williams** to the "canon" of cubist writers and finds cubist elements in the writings of **Ezra Pound, Wallace Stevens, E. E. Cummings,** André Gide, and Alain Robbe-Grillet. Her criteria for comparison are "actual contact between certain writers and the cubist painters" and/or "stylistic parallelism"—for example, the relation of "multiple perspective" and fragmentation in painting to the use of point-of-view and "polyperspectivalism" in poetry (Steiner 178–80). Hugh Kenner outlines cubist strategies for a metonymic literary style: "lay out . . . the elements all on one plane, each sharp, each bright, each of comparable importance; disregard their syntactic liaisons; make a selection, and arrange them anew, as the cubists arranged visual elements so that one cannot say what is theme, what is detail . . . " (140).

Cubism has been described as "a combination of vision, of understanding, of veracity, of modernism and of a will to represent a contemporary reality" (Cooper 263). It was committed to innovation and authenticity, dissection and reconstruction. All subsequent movements have had to contend with the cubist revolution in space, geometry, and perspective. Delaunay's path to orphism passed through cubism, as did Léger's to machinism. Expressionist, futurist, and vorticist dynamism were indebted to cubist splitting of forms, as were non-objectivist movements like rayonnism and suprematism. Cubism was intuitively in touch with the modernist zeitgeist, shaping it for the first two decades of the twentieth century. Its strength lies in its radical revisioning of forms, its mixture of clarity and ambiguity, and its dialectical relation with reality.

Jack Stewart

Selected Bibliography

Apollinaire, Guillaume. *The Cubist Painters: Aesthetic Meditations*. 1913. Trans. Lionel Abel. New York: Wittenborn, 1949.

Barr, Alfred. *Cubism and Abstract Art*. New York: Museum of Modern Art, 1936.

———. *Picasso: Fifty Years of his Art*. New York: Museum of Modern Art, 1946.

Berger, John. *The Moment of Cubism and Other Essays*. London: Weidenfeld, 1969.

———. *The Success and Failure of Picasso*. New York: Pantheon, 1965.

Cooper, Douglas. *The Cubist Epoch*. Oxford: Phaidon, 1970.

Daix, Pierre. *Cubists and Cubism*. Trans. R. F. M. Dexter. New York: Skira-Rizzoli, 1982.

Fry, Edward F. *Cubism*. New York: Oxford UP, 1966.

Gamwell, Lynn, ed. *Cubist Criticism*. Ann Arbor: UMI Research P, 1980.

Gleizes, Albert and Jean Metzinger. *Cubism*. London: Unwin, 1913.

Golding, John. *Visions of the Modern*. Berkeley: U of California P, 1994.

Gray, Christopher. *Cubist Aesthetic Theories*. Baltimore: Johns Hopkins P, 1953.

Kahnweiler, Daniel-Henry. *The Rise of Cubism*. 1920. Trans. Henry Aronson. New York: Wittenborn, 1949.

Kelder, Diane. "Cubism: Toward an Absolute Reality." *The Great Book of Post-Impressionism*. New York: Abbeville, n.d. Chap. 7. 269–309.

Kenner, Hugh. *The Pound Era*. Berkeley: U of California P, 1971.

Kozloff, Max. *Cubism/Futurism*. New York: Charterhouse, 1973.

———. "The Esthetic Valence of Cubism." *Art News* 70 (1971): 34–37, 78–82.

Mullins, Edwin. *The Art of Georges Braque*. New York: Abrams, n.d.

Picasso, Pablo. "Statement by Picasso: 1923." "Statement by Picasso: 1935." Barr, *Picasso* 270–71, 272–74.

Rosenblum, Robert. *Cubism and Twentieth-Century Art*. New York: Abrams, n.d.

Rubin, William, ed. *Pablo Picasso: A Retrospective*. New York: Museum of Modern Art, 1980.

Scobie, Stephen. *Earthquakes and Explorations: Language and Painting from Cubism to Concrete Poetry*. Toronto: U of Toronto P, 1997.

Steiner, Wendy. "A Cubist Historiography." *The Colors of Rhetoric: Problems in the Relation between Modern Literature and Painting*. Chicago: U of Chicago P, 1980. 175–219.

Cummings, E. E. (1894–1962)

E. E. Cummings is perhaps the most problematic of the modernist American poets of the 1920s generation. Stylistically he is one of the most audacious (and recognizable) of poetic innovators. The signature eccentricities of his style—idiosyncratic typography, capitalization, punctuation, and diction (including frequent coinages)—instantly identify him as a modern poet. Cummings speaks in many voices but always sounds like himself. His poems are bold, self-assertive, earthy, clever, playful, lyrical, sentimental, and aggressively iconoclastic.

The fractured language found throughout Cummings's poems seems to mirror and express the fragmentation of twentieth-century life. But at the same time there is no mistaking that beneath the seemingly experimental surfaces of his poetry is an oddly traditional, even old-fashioned poet. Cummings the in-your-face poetic innovator is also Cummings the sonneteer who sings uncomplicatedly of the joys of love, spring, and beauty. A New England individualist in the tradition of Emerson and Thoreau, he is always the avowed enemy of the establishment and "mostpeople." What other modernist asserts an unshakable belief that "love is the every only god"? At the beginning of the new millennium Cummings remains a poet of widespread popular appeal, but his academic status is at best uncertain.

Edward Estlin Cummings was born in Cambridge, Massachusetts, in 1894. His father was a sociology professor at Harvard who resigned to become pastor of the Old South Church in Boston. In 1915 Cummings graduated from Harvard "*magna cum laude* in Literature, especially in Greek and English"; he delivered a Commencement address on "The New Art." The next year he received his MA from Harvard. His famous early sonnet on the "Cambridge ladies who live in furnished souls" demonstrates his eagerness to distance himself from his Boston Brahmin background.

In May 1917 Cummings joined an ambulance corps attached to the French army. Charged with espionage because of letters his friend William Slater Brown had written back to the States, Cummings and Brown were arrested and sent to a detention center. Cummings's four months at La Ferté-Macé led to *The Enormous Room* (1922), his idiosyncratic memoir in which he condemns the French government and bureaucracy and celebrates the uniqueness of his highly marginal fellow prisoners. The young Cummings was already a romantic individualist and an enemy of authority before he entered the detention camp. But this experience confirmed attitudes that became the stuff of his poetry.

Cummings published four collections of poetry in the 1920s, most notably *Tulips and Chimneys* (1923). This flashy though uneven debut volume is notable for its diversity. In *Tulips and Chimneys*—and all the poetry that came afterwards—he celebrates spring and young love while recognizing that flesh must turn to dust. Such poems as the well-known *faux* pre-Raphaelite "All in green went my love riding" and the conventionally romantic "i spoke to thee / with a smile" and "my love / thy hair is one kingdom" are nineteenth-century throwbacks. The volume also features a good deal of self-conscious poeticizing (e. g., "the sky a silver / dissonance"). But such anthology pieces as the exuberant "in Just- / spring" (one of his "chansons innocentes") and the brashly vernacular "Buffalo Bill's / defunct" are understandably beloved.

Tulips and Chimneys becomes stronger as Cummings moves, as it were, from tulips to chimneys: from poems on standard poetic topics to grittier poems such as several set in a brothel ("when you rang at Dick Mid's Place" and the haunting " 'kitty'. sixteen, 5' 1", white, prostitute.") and also poems about his affair with Elaine Thayer (to whom he was later briefly married). These bold poems communicate the excitement of entering realms of experience that had been forbidden to the minister's son. In fact Cummings's publisher refused to include a number of sonnets that are sexually frank even by today's standards. Cummings published the twenty-two "sonnets-realities" and the twenty-four "sonnets-actualities" in the privately printed & (1925). Powerfully erotic sonnets like "her careful distinct sex whose sharp lips comb," "my girl's tall with hard long eyes," "if i should sleep with a lady called death," "my naked lady framed," and "i like my body when it is with your / body" are among his finest poems.

From early on Cummings was attuned to modernist developments in painting, sculpture, and music. He saw the **Armory Show** when it came to Boston, and he knew the music of Debussy and **Stravinsky** and the paintings of Cézanne, the Fauves, and the cubists well before the three years he lived in Paris between 1921 and 1924. (In an early poem addressed to Picasso, Cummings tells the painter, "you hew form truly.") Poems like the love poem "i will be / M o ving in the Street / of her body" emulate cubist effects of fragmentation and rearrangement, partly for expressive purposes, and the deciphering necessary to understand such a poem is akin to solving a puzzle or playing a verbal game. Readers must judge for themselves whether such experiments are successful. But once you have granted Cummings the right to such perversities, he somehow becomes safe from criticism. The sympathetic reader gives assent and goes along for the ride. (Often the eccentric presentation of a Cummings poem seems to depend as much on visual, painterly concerns as it does on strictly verbal considerations. This is especially true of his poetry of the 1930s.)

An expressive intention is almost always discernible in Cummings's verbal and typographical distortions, fragmentations, and other eccentricities, though it's not always easy to decide exactly what he's trying to express. For example, "sunset)edges become swiftly," a mood piece about the city in twilight as the office workers "spill lazily" at the end of the workday "out of final / towers" closes with a focus on "feet(fEEt/f-e-e-t-noWheregoingaLwaYS." Surely the lack of spaces between the words here aims to express the never-ending, grinding routine

of these lives. But why does Cummings capitalize the six letters he chooses to capitalize? Some of Cummings' assaults on verbal convention seem like amusing stunts. This is true of "r-p-o-p-h-e-s-s-a-g-r," the famous poem that captures (or imitates) a leaping, whirring grasshopper. The grasshopper also appears in the poem as "PPEGORHRASS" and "gRrEaPsPhOs" until in the last line, reintegrated and no doubt at rest, it thankfully becomes ", grasshopper;." The closing semi-colon suggests that the grasshopper is about to leap again.

Throughout his career Cummings raised his voice against the values and attitudes of twentieth-century mass society, sometimes satirically, sometimes angrily. Two anti-war poems are among his masterpieces: "i sing of Olaf glad and big" (which celebrates an abused conscientious objector) and "my sweet old etcetera / aunt lucy" (a droll account of the contrast between how a soldier in the trenches and his relatives back home experienced **World War I**). Elsewhere Cummings criticizes the deification of science ("space being(don't forget to remember) Curved"), civilization's blind belief in progress ("pity this busy monster, manunkind, / not"), the debasement of language by an advertising culture ("Poem.or Beauty Hurts Mr. Vinal"), false patriotism ("next to of course god / america i love you"), and a society in which everyone from the President down is trying to sell you something ("a salesman is an it that stinks"). It's no wonder that in the 1960s and early 1970s all Americans who had ever taken an English course seemed to own and treasure a copy of *100 Selected Poems* (1959—selected by Cummings himself).

Cummings's poetry is regularly highfalutin in its own idiosyncratic way ("morsel miraculous and meaningless / secret on luminous whose selves and lives / imperishably feast all timeless souls"). But like many other American modernist poets, Cummings also embraced the vernacular, almost always to telling effect. Poems like "Jimmie's got a goil / goil / goil," and "buncha hardboil guys from duh A.C." attempt no timeless truth. Instead they seem to intend no more than to communicate the poet's delight in the street language of the Northeastern USA (also cf. such Cummingsesque locutions as "yoozwidduhpoimnuntwaiv"). In the World War II poem "ygUDuh / udoan / yunnuhstan" Cummings presents a dialect argument between two barbaric Americans, one of whom insists on the need to "SIVILEYEz" the "lidl yelluh bas / tuds." But even this poem seems to communicate the poet's joy in the American vernacular as much as his message. In "let's start a magazine / to hell with literature" Cummings captures a rather different American idiom. These are among the many poems in which Cummings shines through, rather endearingly, as the eternal wiseguy.

One of the constant criticisms of Cummings's poetry has been its lack of development over the course of his career. Some patterns are discernible. His verbal and typographical eccentricities became more exaggerated in his middle years, less exaggerated later on. The appealing earthiness and sexuality of much of his early poetry disappeared from the work of his last two decades. Always a poet with a sentimental streak, he became more insistently sentimental in his last volumes. But from beginning to end he remained the lyric singer of love, innocence, and nature in his own off-center language, a poet who would rather learn to sing from one bird "than teach ten thousand stars how not to dance." From beginning to end he also sustained his contempt for authority.

It's not as if every modern poet is required to be **W. B. Yeats** and regularly to reinvent himself or herself. But the charge against Cummings is that he remained unquestioningly true to a set of beliefs insufficient to the age in which he lived. He dug in his poetic heels and wrote the same sorts of poems over and over again.

Two of Cummings's most cherished poems, "anyone lived in a pretty how town" and "my father moved through dooms of love," his elegy for his father, both appeared in *50 Poems* (1940). The lifelong love story of "anyone" and "noone" is set against the seasons ("spring summer autumn winter") and the cosmos ("sun moon stars rain"). Other people "sowed their isn't" and "reaped their same," but not "anyone" and "noone." The poem is easily parodied, but what does it matter that a "how town" is undefinable? The poem succeeds through Cummings's musicalization of language and the delicately restrained feeling. Meanwhile Cummings's father must move not only "through dooms of love" but also "through sames of am," "haves of give," "griefs of joy," "dooms of feel," and "theys of we" for seventeen quatrains until Cummings can ringingly affirm that because his father "lived his soul, love is the whole and more than all." Like "anyone lived in a pretty how town," this is a mannerist poem, but once again the feeling—here quite powerful and expressed in an unusual, self-contained rhetoric—makes the poem a success. And after all, this is a poet who insists that "feeling is first." Indeed one measure of the success of a Cummings love poem is whether the feeling seems authentic or fabricated.

Painting was Cummings's second talent; he was a conservative portraitist and landscape painter. He lived the life he believed in, dedicated full-time to his poetry and painting, living a rather bohemian existence in Greenwich Village and on the family farm in New Hampshire. He published new volumes of poetry periodically, a *Collected Poems* in 1938, and *Poems 1923–1954*. Other important works include *Him* (1927), an unplayable expressionist drama, and *Eimi* (Greek for "I am"—1933), a difficult, idiosyncratic account of his 1931 visit to the "unworld" of Soviet totalitarianism. In 1952–53 Cummings returned to Harvard as the Charles Eliot Norton Professor, delivering six lectures that mixed autobiographical reminiscence with new articulations of his familiar beliefs. These were published as *i: six nonlectures* in 1953. From 1955 until his death in 1962 he supplemented his income with memorable poetry readings on college campuses. His most prestigious honors were the Bollingen Prize (1958) and a two-year Ford Foundation grant of $15,000 (1957–58). Married and divorced twice, he lived with Marion Morehouse from 1932 until his death.

E. E. Cummings has always had a few fervent admirers within the academic community, but most critics of modern poetry hardly take him seriously. Nevertheless, readers of modern poetry, who care little or nothing about the opinions of critics of modern poetry, continue to provide a substantial audience for Cummings's poetry. In my estimation only Frost among twentieth-century American poets has a larger following.

Cummings is an indisputable modernist, determined to write a new kind of poetry to express a new century—and also determined to thumb his nose at the old kind of poetry. He is more accessible than he looks. Though he plays the lifelong role of *enfant terrible,* he is more congenial than

he sometimes seems. Cummings is clever, Cummings is humorous, Cummings is refreshing (though perhaps not in large doses). Most people (mostpeople?) like love poems, and Cummings can offer plenty of those. There may be "a hell of a good universe next door," but meanwhile E. E. Cummings—for all his limitations— makes the one we live in much more enjoyable.

Keith Cushman

Selected Bibliography

Blackmur, R. P. "Notes on E. E. Cummings' Language." *Hound & Horn* 4 (January–March 1931): 163–92.

Friedman, Norman. *E. E. Cummings: The Art of His Poetry.* Baltimore: Johns Hopkins UP, 1960.

Kennedy, Richard S. *Dreams in the Mirror: A Biography of E. E. Cummings.* New York: Liveright, 1980.

Kennedy, Richard S. *E. E. Cummings Revisited.* New York: Twayne, 1994.

Kidder, Rushworth. "Cummings and Cubism: The Influence of the Visual Arts on Cummings' Early Poetry." *Journal of Modern Literature* 7 (April 1979): 255–91.

Perkins, David. "E. E. Cummings." In *A History of Modern Poetry: Modernism and After.* Cambridge: Harvard UP, 1987. 38–47.

Rotella, Guy, ed. *Critical Essays on E. E. Cummings.* Boston: G. K. Hall, 1984.

D

Dada

The dada movement was born in February 1916 in neutral Zurich, out of disgust for the obscene slaughter on the battlefields of Europe and the rabid nationalisms that had caused and were perpetuating the so-called Great War (see **The War**). In founding the satirical Cabaret Voltaire (named after the eighteenth-century French *philosophe* who symbolizes intellectual tolerance and the fight against all forms of "superstition," including religion), the aim of German poet Hugo Ball (1886–1927) was to "remind the world that there are people of independent minds—beyond war and nationalism—who live for different ideals" (*Dada Zurich Paris 1916–1922*, 21). The Cabaret quickly became a meeting-ground for disenchanted, often pacifist or draft-dodging radical intellectuals from many countries and of many political persuasions, including Richard Huelsenbeck (1892–1874) from **Germany,** and Rumanians Marcel Janco (1895–1984) and Tristan Tzara (1896–1963), who grouped themselves under the name Dada, chosen because it meant nothing (or nothing significant) in many languages. The dadaists did not regard themselves as artists; instead, they wanted to change Western civilization by means of violent provocation calculated to expose the bankrupt values of a decadent and sclerotic society.

With the approaching end of the war the dadaists left Switzerland and dispersed around Europe. Amid the social chaos of a defeated Berlin, Huelsenbeck and others joined up with the lingering expressionist fringe to form an overtly political movement in unstable alliance with the Far Left. Part of Berlin was declared an independent Dada Republic, ephemeral publications (*Club Dada, Der Dada, Jedermann sein eigner Fussball* (*Everyman His Own Football*), *Dada Almanach*) came and went, while the hard-hitting caricatures of Georg Grosz (1893–1959) and photomontages of John Heartfield (1891–1968) and Raoul Hausmann (1886–1971) satirized the decadent foibles of Weimar society. When the revolution fomented by the spartakist (communist) movement was put down in 1919, some Berlin dadaists adopted more orthodox types of political action while the rest moved on to alternative pursuits. Meanwhile in Hanover, **Kurt Schwitters** (1887–1948) was making visual and verbal collages out of everyday ephemera (buttons, scraps of newspaper text, tram tickets, etc.); rejected by Berlin dadaists for having a bourgeois face, he created a one-man movement which he called Merz (an ironic fragment of the word "Kommerzbank," commercial bank), and set about turning his whole life (including successive residences in Germany and abroad, which he gradually filled with proliferating sculptural installations largely made of junk) into a Merz work. In Cologne, Alsatian-born artist and sculptor Hans (Jean) Arp (1887–1966), Johannes Baargeld (1892–1927: pseudonymously, "Johnny Cash") and future arch-surrealist Max Ernst (1891–1976) exhibited deliberately shocking constructions, some of which the public were cordially invited to destroy.

Another group of quasi-dadaist refugees from the war had fled to New York and grouped their subversive activities around the gallery of photographer Alfred Stieglitz (1864–1946). Notable among them were Francis Picabia (1879–1953) and Marcel Duchamp (1887–1968), inventor of the "readymade," in which a commonplace object was sarcastically elevated to the "dignity" of art simply by virtue of having been chosen by the "artist" (the most scandalous of these objects was his *Fountain* of 1917, a urinal which he signed "R. Mutt"). Duchamp also edited the proto-dadaist reviews *The Blind Man* and *Rongwrong*. At the end of the war he and Picabia returned to Europe to add their energies to the burgeoning dada movement, and were soon joined by American artist and photographer Man Ray (1890–1976). But it was the arrival of Tristan Tzara in Paris in 1920 that had the most explosive impact. Tzara was greeted as an anarchist messiah by a group of young French writers, André Breton (1896–1966), Louis Aragon (1897–1982), Philippe Soupault (1897–1990) and Paul Eluard (1895–1952), who had already founded their own review, *Littérature* (published 1919–24), and were looking for a radical new approach to the avant-garde agenda. Together, they set out to scandalize the Parisian bourgeoisie by their zany, unpredictable and not infrequently offensive performances, and for two years or so they succeeded in maintaining their notoriety in the press and the social life of the capital.

Born Samuel Rosenstock in Moinesti, Romania, Tristan Tzara was the author of many of the most challenging and original dada texts, from *La Première aventure céleste de Monsieur Antipyrine* (*The First Heavenly Adventure of Mr. Aspirin*) in 1916 and *Vingt-cinq poémes* (*Twenty-Five Poems*) in 1918, to the *Sept Manifestes* (*Seven Manifestos*) by which he remains best known today. Disagreements over the handling of the mock trial of right-wing author and ideologue Maurice Barrès in 1921 led to a cooling of relations with Breton and his friends and links were finally severed in 1923, when they decided to go their own way and found the surrealist movement on the ruins of dada's self-destruction. A reconciliation took place in 1930 when Tzara himself became a surrealist, then strove to bring about a *rapprochement* between **surrealism** and the Parti Communiste Français. In response to the growing extremism of European politics in the 1930s, he joined the PCF in 1936, and during World War II he was active in the Resistance. His later writings, including *L'Homme approximatif* (*The Approximate Man*) of 1931, *Parler seul* (*Speaking Alone*) of 1950 and *Le Fruit permis* (*The Permitted Fruit*) of 1956 are more lyrical in tone and humanistic in inspiration than his dada productions. He left the PCF in 1956 and devoted his last years to preserving documentary evidence of the dada period.

The most important exposition of dadaist principles is undoubtedly to be found in Tzara's *Manifeste Dada 1918,* published in French in the third issue of the *Dada* review (*Dada Zurich Paris,* 142–4; Tzara/Wright 3–13). Though superficially rambling and full of spelling mistakes, the 1918 manifesto contains a clear message about the strategic value of contradiction and the irrational, above all in the struggle to subvert bourgeois language:

I'm writing this manifesto to show that you can perform contrary actions at the same time, in one single, fresh breath; I am against action; as for continual contradiction, and affirmation too, I am neither for nor against them, and I won't explain myself because I hate common sense. (4)

Common sense, claims Tzara, also legitimizes the binary logic underlying accepted philosophical and social values, so logic too becomes a target for dada's anarchism:

Logic is a complication. Logic is always false. It draws the superficial threads of concepts and words towards illusory conclusions and centres. Its chains kill, an enormous myriapod that asphyxiates independence. (11)

Logic's tentacles ensnare the mind, confining and channeling thought and inhibiting the free expression of mental associations, which can only be released by the systematic application of contradiction (an article of faith soon to become a founding principle of surrealism).

Directly analogous to logic, for Tzara, is bourgeois morality, which also works to repress the disorderly freedom of the mind—"how can anyone hope to order the chaos that constitutes that infinite, formless variation: man?" (5)—by categorization and systematization:

Morals have an atrophying effect, like every other pestilential product of the intelligence. Being governed by morals and logic has made it impossible for us to be anything other than impassive towards policemen . . . (12)

The cause of bourgeois social conformism is therefore, in his analysis, an adherence to conceptual systems which have become fossilized and perverted; by attacking those systems of thought, dada will simultaneously undermine the social order:

I destroy the drawers of the brain, and those of social organisation: to sow de-

moralisation everywhere, and throw heaven's hand into hell, hell's eyes into heaven, to reinstate the fertile wheel of a universal circus in the Powers of reality, and the fantasy of every individual. (8)

Smashing the conceptual "drawers" into which the bourgeois mind classifies things and ideas (in clear anticipation of the surrealists' fascination with the context-free "found object") fundamentally means dismantling consensual language itself, for as Tzara realized—following (probably unwittingly) in the footsteps of the founder of structural linguistics, Ferdinand de Saussure (1857–1913)—a society's mental categories are determined by its language. Dada would therefore exploit verbal incoherence to perform acts of social "demoralisation" (in both senses: taking away society's *morale,* and destroying the hold *morality* has over it), replacing Manichean, binary oppositions with a life-enhancing "fertile wheel" of liberated meanings and values.

The message of Tzara's *Manifeste Dada 1918* is therefore not just a nihilistic one of universal subversion, as is often claimed, but an idealistic plea for individual freedom and a re-founded ethics: "after the carnage we are left with the hope of a purified humanity" (5). Dada's attack on society and its language was an attempt to *cleanse* the world of an accumulated mental pollution which had culminated in the collective insanity of the war:

Every man must shout: there is great destructive, negative work to be done. To sweep, to clean. The cleanliness of the individual materialises after we've gone through folly, the aggressive, complete folly of a world left in the hands of bandits who have demolished and destroyed the centuries. (12)

This act of linguistic purification through destruction is equated, in the text's climactic closing sentence, with the conviction of a new vitality whose promise was realized, in the end, less by dada than by surrealism: "Liberty: *DADA DADA DADA;*—the roar of contorted pains, the interweaving of contraries and of all contradictions, freaks and irrelevancies: LIFE" (13).

After decades of occlusion by its ideologically-dominant successor surrealism, which sought to minimize the importance of the movement from which it itself had sprung, dada has now come to be recognized as one of the most influential (anti-) cultural initiatives of the twentieth century. While its immediate socio-political antecedents lie in turn of the century European anarchism, a violent reaction to the impasse and cycle of decadence in which the institutions of Belle Epoque society seemed locked, its form of "cultural terrorism" goes back further, to the social and political satire practiced by the subversive young French poet Arthur Rimbaud (1854–1891) in the late 1860s and early 1870s (his famous principle of "dérèglement de tous les sens" implying not only *sensory* disorientation but also, in a double meaning impossible to reproduce in English, the disarticulation of *meaning*). Equally, although Tzara's manifesto expresses contempt for the avant-garde— "We've had enough of the cubist and futurist academies: laboratories of formal ideas" (5)—dada verbal and visual praxis had clearly assimilated all the latest techniques and themes pioneered by its immediate modernist precursors in their drive to discredit and supplant nineteenth-century **realism,** with its assumptions of a non-problematic representational relationship between the external world, social structures, and the work of art.

Such assumptions had already been ruined by the spatial and tonal distortions of **expressionism,** the liberation of color by the Fauves, and the "destruction" of the pictorial object wrought by **cubism** and **futurism.** The centuries-old ideal of a polished, impeccably crafted work of eternal, illusionistic beauty had been replaced by a fascination with transient, everyday reality and the disturbing power of non-western, so-called "primitive" modes of representation, shockingly pioneered by Pablo Picasso (1881–1973) in his unfinished painting *Les Demoiselles d'Avignon* (1907), which set mask-like heads on angular female nudes to represent the inhabitants of a Barcelona brothel. From 1909 **Italian futurism,** notably in the person of its leader **Filippo Tommaso Marinetti** (1876–1944), had launched the avant-garde's attack on the structures of language itself, with its "parole in libertà" and a-semantic bruitist poems, anticipating dada in its program of linking verbal liberation with the demolition of cultural values and artifacts from the past; while in the years immediately before the war the experimental poetry of Blaise Cendrars (1887–1961) and Guillaume Apollinaire (1880–1918) had fragmented the human subject into multiple simultaneous perceptions and identities. Moreover, these different avant-garde practitioners not only knew each other's work, they also published in the same reviews as the dadaists. Thus for instance the single issue of *Cabaret Voltaire* contains, in addition to contributions from dadaists Ball, Huelsenbeck, Arp, Tzara (the simultaneous multilingual/multivoiced performance-poem "L'Amiral cherche une maison à louer"), Janco and others, one of Marinetti's *parole in libertà* (in Italian), modernist poems by Cendrars and Apollinaire, and a cubist drawing by Picasso. Dada was, in its early stages at least, clearly part of a wider, eclectically-cosmopolitan avant-garde continuum: "Dada in Zurich . . . mixed irrationalist libertarian and anarchist incongruity with a generally welcoming attitude to other types of avant-gardist activity" (Butler 266).

However, dada rapidly came to stand out both for the rigor and the virulence of its attack on the language of art and the art of language, perhaps its most lasting legacy to the later twentieth century, as well as for the inventiveness of its satirical performance techniques. Beyond surrealism, which adopted many of dada's positions wholesale, the influence of its Nietzschean critique of language continued to be felt in many subsequent avant-garde movements, from lettrism to Conceptual Art and minimalism, and found a further substantial echo in continental philosophy and critical theory of the late 1950s, '60s and '70s, from the *nouveau roman* and structuralism to *Tel Quel* and deconstruction. At the same time, the anarchistic performance tradition that it inaugurated was perpetuated by the Internationale Situationniste of Guy Debord (1931–1994), as well as giving rise to the destructive concerts of the Fluxus movement ("MUSICIANS SMASH YOUR BLIND INSTRUMENTS on the stage" [Tzara/Wright 16], commanded Tzara in his "Unpretentious Proclamation" of 1919) and the "happenings" of Jean-Jacques Lebel (1936–)—in their turn intimately bound up with the revolutionary events of Spring 1968. Modern advertising techniques too owe much to dadaist experiments with collage and typography, while the movement's libertarian humor exerted a seminal influence on the wacky weltanschauung of cult television show *Monty Python's Flying Circus.* Even at the dawn of the twenty-first century the dada spirit continues to flourish in the form of neo-dadaist groups around the world (see for instance the *Neumerz Manifesto* of Victor Zygonov), often using the Internet to express their alienation from the established social order, their search for personal authenticity and their continuing allegiance to the irrational as an agent of social change.

Andrew Rothwell

Selected Bibliography

Arp, Hans (Jean). *Jours effeuillés: Poèmes, essais, souvenirs 1920–1965.* Paris: 1966.

Butler, Christopher. *Early Modernism. Literature, Music and Painting in Europe 1900–1916.* Oxford: Clarendon Press, 1994.

Dada Zurich Paris 1916–1922. Paris: Editions Jean-Michel Place, 1981. (Facsimile reprint of dada reviews including *Cabaret Voltaire, Der Zeltweg, Dada, Le Cœur à barbe*).

International Dada Archive. http://www.lib.uiowa.edu/dada/index.html

Motherwell, Robert. *The Dada Poets and Painters.* 2nd ed. Boston: G. K. Hall, 1981.

Picabia, Francis. *Ecrits I (1913–1920), II (1921–1953).* 2 vols. Paris: Pierre Belfond, 1975, 1978.

Richter, Hans. *Dada: Art and Anti-Art.* London: Thames and Hudson, 1965.

Sanouillet, Michel. *Dada à Paris.* Paris: Flammarion, 1965 (nouvelle édition revue et corrigée établie par Anne Sanouillet, 1993).

Sheppard, Richard, ed. *Dada: Studies of a Movement.* Chalfont St. Giles: Alpha Academic, 1980.

———. *Modernism, Dada, Postmodernism.* Evanston, Ill.: North Western University Press; London: Turnaround, 2000.

Short, Robert. *Dada and Surrealism.* London: Octopus, 1980.

Tzara, Tristan. [Lecture on Dada at Weimar.] 23 September 1922. In Merz, Hanover, January 1924. http://www.subsitu.com/kr/tzara.htm.

———. *L'Homme Approximatif.* Paris: Gallimard, 1977.

———. *Sept Manifestes Dada.* Paris: Jean-Jacques Pauvert, 1963. Transl. by Barbara Wright as Seven Dada Manifestos and Lampisteries. London: Calder Publications / New York: Riverrun Press, 1977 (4th impression 1992).

Young, Alan. *Dada and After: Extremist Modernism and English Literature.* Manchester: Manchester University Press, c. 1981.

Zygonov, Victor. *Neumerz Manifesto (2000).* http://www.smalltime.com/nowhere/neumerz/manifesto.html

Dance and Literary Modernism 1890–1940

Dance and literature may seem like odd bedfellows. One produces timeless, unchanging artifacts, while the other exists only at the ephemeral vanishing point. One is the silent art of the body, the other a verbal art of the mind. Yet dance in the first quarter of the century helped fertilize the shape of literary modernism by influencing several of its leading practitioners. These writers were particularly attracted to the dance's "primitive" subjects and themes and its formal properties, like the ability to express impersonality in art and to tap the unconscious.

Modernists on both sides of the Atlantic flocked to concert halls, entranced by the innovations of Diaghilev's Ballets Russes and the solo performances of modern dance precursors: Ruth St. Denis, Loïe Fuller, and Isadora Duncan. The diaries and memoirs of the **Bloomsbury** circle, for example, are full of notations about attending performances to see Nijinsky and Karsavina, to hear the music of **Stravinsky** and Prokofiev, and later to see the sets and costumes of Picasso and Matisse. Leonard Woolf called the Russian company a "revelation" and perceived it was at the forefront of the "profound changes" taking place in London in 1911 (37). **E. M. Forster** vividly recalled forty years after the event "Nijinsky's leap in *Le Spectre de la rose,* the first London performance of *Le Sacre du printemps,* and the drop curtain of *Schéhérazade*" (4). **Virginia Woolf,** Lytton Strachey, and Rupert Brooke all caught ballet fever and John Maynard Keynes married Lydia Lopokova, one of Ballets Russes' prima ballerinas.

Other modernists, like **Yeats** and **Eliot,** were even more profoundly affected by what they saw. The prevalent image of the dancer in Yeats's poetry, who appears most often as a beautiful woman with a perfectly proportioned body and a Mona Lisa smile, was modeled on a mixture of Ruth St Denis's mystical interpretations of Eastern deities, symbolist dancer Loïe Fuller's metamorphosis into abstract, surrealistic shapes, and eurythmic-trained Michio Ito's immobile expression while performing. T. S. Eliot was influenced by

two male stars of the Ballets Russes: Vaslav Nijinsky and Léonide Massine. Nijinsky subliminally inspired several images in Eliot's verse, like the martyr-figure in "The Death of Saint Narcissus," who performs a *danse macabre* in the desert while burning arrows pierce his flesh. Massine was a catalyst behind many of Eliot's aesthetic speculations, like the notion of impersonality in art. And although Eliot missed Nijinsky's original choreographic score for *Le Sacre du printemps,* there is an uncanny resemblance between the ballet's atavistic, dehumanized masses and Eliot's hordes of automatons blindly participating in *The Waste Land*'s debased rituals.

Another group of modernists, which included **John Dos Passos, E. E. Cummings,** Hart Crane, and **William Carlos Williams,** found a more congenial muse in fellow American Isadora Duncan. Duncan enjoyed taunting audiences with her freer, uninhibited movement, her scanty costumes, and blatant sexuality. Her independence and freedom became a sort of symbolic reference. Even before the public saw her perform, they were aware of her well-publicized, scandalous lifestyle, which included two children born out-of-wedlock, bouts of alcoholism, and a lengthy flirtation with Russian communism. **Dos Passos** would write a brief biographical segment on her in his trilogy *U.S.A.,* in which the dancer personified art in an era of big money and crass commercialism (Ludington 306). Crane paid homage to Duncan's steadfast adherence to artistic ideals in the "Quaker Hill" section of *The Bridge.* And where Eliot had lauded ballet's tradition and discipline, Williams found in Duncan's rebellion against a confining European ballet, an analog for his desire to forge a new, American poetry (Mariani 67).

"Male-dominated" modernism was also drawn to the subjects of the new dance, which consisted of "primitive" myths and rituals, like the portrayal of the Racial Other and Eternal Feminine. Included in this category are Duncan's *Mother,* St. Denis's *Radha,* all of Mikhail Fokine's Oriental ballets for the Ballets Russes like *Schéhérazade* and, later in the thirties, any of Martha Graham, Mary Wigman, or Doris Humphrey's archetypal dances like *Primitive Mysteries, Sacrifice* and *With My Red Fire.* Nijinsky's *Le Sacre du printemps,* in its sacrifice of a chosen maiden and primeval evocation of prehistoric **Russia,** was unquestionably the most famous dance in this genre and became virtually synonymous with the idea of modernity. Who is not familiar with its legendary Paris premiere in 1913, which caused one of the greatest furors in French theatrical history? Fighting broke out and the music was all but drowned in the hubbub.

The original ballet, unfortunately, was a casualty of dance's inherent ephemerality and vanished after eight performances. Nijinsky's impersonal form and profound innovations in movement were lost to posterity when his erstwhile lover Diaghilev fired him from the Ballets Russes for marrying the Hungarian ballerina Romola de Pulska. When the company revived the ballet after **World War I,** Diaghilev replaced Nijinsky's modernist choreography with Massine's conventionally romantic movement.

Reports, however, indicate that Nijinsky's original ballet resembled the involuntary condition of trance: the dancers shook, trembled, shivered, and stamped convulsively on the stage. Lincoln Kirstein likened it to an "apocalyptic epilepsy hypnotizing a community of ecstatic spastics" (144). The French critic Jacques Rivière described the horror of the depersonalized mass depicted in the ballet:

We find ourselves in the presence of man's movements at a time when he did not yet exist as an individual. Living be-ings still cling to each other; they exist in groups, in colonies, in shoals; they are lost among the horrible indifference of society. . . . Their faces are devoid of any individuality. (qt. in Kirstein)

Interestingly, *Le Sacre*'s graphic depiction of a ritualized female sacrifice had no precedent in either Slavic mythology or ballet tradition. Even in Frazer's descriptions of universal vegetation rites, it is always the male gods, like Attis and Osiris, who are slain and sacrificed. And while nineteenth-century romantic ballets like *Swan Lake* and *Giselle* conclude with a female sprite's death, she is a sacrifice to love rather than the prevailing social order and her demise occurs quietly, decorously offstage.

Nijinsky's ballet, however, did set a precedent for modernist literary texts. Eliot's *Sweeney Agonistes* hints at dark, secret connections between sex and sacrifice, **Thomas Mann**'s *Death in Venice* envisions an orgiastic dance fusing Eros and Thanatos, and **Lawrence**'s novella "The Woman Who Rode Away" concludes with an eroticized scene of ritualized female sacrifice. More generally, *Le Sacre*'s dark vision of a primal past, like *The Waste Land,* was a figure for modern life, especially its barbarism and savagery. It anticipated the evils of war and a depersonalized society ruled by the machine, and was a harbinger of the dark, Dionysian forces bubbling and ready to erupt under the surface, whether they were called **Freud**'s unconscious, Lawrence's dark gods or Yeats's Sidhe.

In addition to converging themes and aspirations, the dance's formal properties suggested several paradigms for modernists wishing to "make it new." They saw, for instance, in the dancer's endless struggle to achieve perfection of line, an analog for their own emphasis on the hard, dry presentation of the poetic image. They read in the dancer's blank, enigmatic expression while performing, an ideal of impersonality in art. As verbal artists growing increasingly conscious of the "prison-house of language," they perceived the dance's ability to tap the unconscious and express the uncanny. And as a result, several modernists, like D. H. Lawrence, turned to the study of non-theatrical, primordial dance rituals in an attempt to recover something they thought lost to the modern world.

Several modernists followed the lead of French symbolist poet Stéphane Mallarmé, who was the first to notice that the dancer epitomized "impersonality" in art. The dance's raw material—the human form—could, paradoxically, transcend the human in content. The doctrine of impersonality is perhaps best understood as a variant of what José Ortega y Gasset described as dehumanization in art; that is, the tendency in modern art to purify itself by a conscious deformation of reality. In discourse, according to Roland Barthes, "it is language which speaks, not the author; to write is, through a prerequisite impersonality . . . to reach that point where only language acts, 'performs' and not 'me.' Mallarmé's entire poetics, according to Barthes, "consists in suppressing the author in the interests of writing" (115). To Gasset, Mallarmé disappeared in his verse as a "pure, nameless voice." His poetry need not be felt and contains nothing human. "When a woman is mentioned it is 'the woman no one'" (29).

Interestingly, Mallarmé found his model of impersonality, the "woman no one" in the ballerinas at the Paris Opéra and in the American dancer Loïe Fuller, who concealed and transformed her body into abstract shapes created by the play of lights refracted off billowing folds of fabric, which she manipulated with long sticks hidden up her sleeves. For Mallarmé, Fuller was not a woman dancing, because she wasn't a woman and she did not dance. She was an otherworldly crea-ture who wrote poems with her body and who appeared before us as a totally impersonal vessel teeming with abstract, preliterate suggestions. Her "signature" was her ability to summon up elemental, fleeting visions of "a sword, a cup, a flower, etc.," which resonated with indefinite, mysterious meanings ("Ballets" 112). Paul Valéry, Mallarmé's disciple, added later that the dancer's world was "an almost inhuman state," discontinuous from nature. He referred to the dancer as an "it," whose gaze turned inward and seemed "to hearken to itself and only to itself, to see nothing as though its eyes were jewels, unknown jewels like those of which Baudelaire speaks" (61).

Nor is the dancer a woman to Yeats: as he says in one poem, she is "dead, yet flesh and bone." Yeats formulated his theory of impersonality watching Michio Ito, his collaborator in the Noh play *At the Hawk's Well*. Ito deliberately held his face immobile while performing, so that his personality was repressed and the idea enhanced. Impersonality for Yeats was synonymous with the wearing of masks—both the literal ones he used in his plays and the figural ones he assumed in the poetry. The impersonality of the mask meant for the poet a measure of personal, existential freedom in a deterministic universe.

In "Tradition and the Individual Talent," Eliot isolated impersonality in the poet who has "not a 'personality' to express, but a particular medium." His progress as an artist is "a continual self-sacrifice, a continual extinction of personality" (*Selected Essays* 7–9). Like Yeats, Eliot found his paradigm in a dancer. According to him, Léonide Massine extinguished his personality within an international, four hundred-year-old tradition of ballet. In "Dramatis Personae" (1923), Eliot called Massine the "greatest actor in London . . . the most completely unhuman, impersonal and abstract" (*Cri-

terion 303–06). In "Four Elizabethan Dramatists," Eliot was still thinking of Massine when he wrote:

> Any one who has observed one of the great dancers of the Russian school will have observed that the man or the woman whom we admire is a being who exists only during the performances, that it is a personality, a vital flame which appears from nowhere, disappears into nothing and is complete and sufficient in its appearance. . . . The differences between a great dancer and a merely competent dancer is in the vital flame, that impersonal, and, if you like, inhuman force which transpires between each of the great dancer's movements. (*Selected Essays* 7–9)

Besides impersonality, modernists were attracted to another formal property of dance which would reinforce their radical skepticism about language. Mallarmé again was the first to notice that dance was a semiotic system. The dancer's gestures, like words or Saussure's "sound-images," were signifiers standing for a larger meaning which could not be fully given in perceptual experience. But since words, according to Mallarmé, obstinately clung to the things they signified in the outside world, poetry was less spiritual than dance as an incantatory medium for evoking a transcendent reality. The dancer, on the other hand, could "suggest things which the written word could only express in several paragraphs of dialogue or descriptive prose" ("Ballets" 112). The "illiterate dancer," according to Mallarmé, was an "unwritten body writing" and what she wrote was a "sacred rite," which he defined as a "mysterious and holy interpretation" of universal life and of our inmost being (*Selected Prose Poems* 63).

Like Mallarmé, several modernists saw that dance tapped the unconscious and signified some deeply felt experience which eluded verbal utterance. Yeats, for example, felt dance's trance-like rhythms altered daytime consciousness into a twilight realm between sleeping and awaking. Being swept up into the rhythms of a collective dance made him forget his isolation as an "old scarecrow." Eliot felt the rhythms of dance traveled to the brain through the neurological system, what he called elsewhere the "dance along the arteries," and evoked the spiritual by tapping latent religious archetypes residing in the psychological unconscious. Lawrence also felt dance was experienced in the blood (moving in the opposite direction), and that it constituted (to the horror of feminists) "phallic consciousness," defined as both man and woman's sympathetic, intuitive awareness of all living things. Williams, on the other hand, envisioned dance as a numinous, pre-reflective state anterior to language, which was capable of loosening the mind of its inhibitions. He called dance "the thing-in-itself." Eliot labeled it the "stillpoint." To Lawrence, dance brought back a sense of awe and mystery missing in the modern age. And Eliot, echoing Mallarmé's sentiments, commended Diaghilev's ballets for their simplicity and concluded that what was needed in all art was "a simplification of current life into something rich and strange" ("London Letter" 214).

Nor does the interfusing of dance and modernism end here; the vectors of influence traveled the other way as well. Martha Graham's expressive, symbolist dance theater drew on Yeats's Noh-inspired plays and the next generation of post-modernist choreographers led by Merce Cunningham translated in dance terms the objective, formal and indeterminate poetics of William Carlos Williams. Even Eliot left his imprint on the dance world, when his *Book of Practical Cats* and a segment of the poem "Rhapsody on a Windy Night" were transformed into the exuberant feline dancing of Andrew Lloyd Weber's musical *Cats*.

Terri Mester

Selected Bibliography

Barthes, Roland. "The Death of the Author." *Modern Literary Theory.* Ed. Philip Rice and Patricia Waugh. London: Edward Arnold, 1992. 114–118.

Eliot, T. S. *Selected Essays.* New York: Harcourt, 1950.

———. *Criterion: A Quarterly Review.* (Apr. 1923): 303–06.

———. "London Letter." *The Dial.* (July 1921): 214.

Forster, E. M. "A Shrine for Diaghilev." *Observer* 25 (Dec. 1955): 4.

Kirstein, Lincoln. *Nijinsky Dancing.* New York: Knopf, 1975.

Ludington, Townsend. *John Dos Passos: A Twentieth Century Odyssey.* New York: Dutton, 1980.

Mallarmé, Stéphane. "Ballets." In *What Is Dance?* Ed. by Roger Copeland and Marshall Cohen. New York: Oxford UP, 1983. 111–115.

———. *Selected Prose Poems, Essays, & Letters.* Translated by Bradford Cook. Baltimore: John Hopkins UP, 1956.

Mariani, Paul. *William Carlos Williams: A New World Naked.* New York: McGraw, 1982.

Ortega y Gasset, José. *The Dehumanization of Art, and Other Writings on Art and Culture.* New York: Doubleday, 1956.

Valéry, Paul. "Philosophy of the Dance." In *What Is Dance?* Ed. Roger Copeland and Marshall Cohen. New York: Oxford UP, 1983. 55–65.

Woolf, Leonard. *Beginning Again: An Autobiography of the Years 1911–1918.* New York: Harcourt, 1963.

Devlin, Denis (1908–1959)

Denis Devlin's first publication, *Poems* (1930)—with **Brian Coffey**—appeared the same year as **Samuel Beckett**'s *Whoroscope,* and its disjunctive poetic procedures exhibit a related interest in avant-garde techniques to that of his friend and fellow Irishman. Beckett's 1934 appraisal of "Recent Irish Poetry" for the *Bookman* emphasized the importance of the *surréalistes,* **T. S. Eliot** and **Ezra Pound** to Devlin's early poetry, the essay situating Devlin, and Coffey, as members of a "nucleus" of Irish modernist poetry opposed to the ruralism and cultural nationalism of those Irish poets dubbed—and damned—by Beckett as "the antiquarians." Beckett astutely singled out for especial praise Devlin's "Est Prodest," a poem which frantically probes for religious certainty in the midst of the political and economic disarray of the 1930s. The titular allusion to Horace's dictum that poetry exists in order to be beneficial is a pointer to Devlin's anxious preoccupation with justice in many of the poems collected in *Intercessions* (1937); and in this respect his early poetry, while more surrealist than *engagé,* is colored by the debate over the nature of "committed" literature central to this decade.

The dream-logic of the longest poem collected in *Intercessions,* "Communication from the Eiffel Tower," for instance, owes much to the poetic procedures of André Breton; yet its deployment of a central futurist icon of technological modernity is in the service of a critique of totalitarianism not unrelated to that of the pylon-poetry of Devlin's British contemporaries, **W. H. Auden,** Cecil Day Lewis and Stephen Spender. In the course of Devlin's disorientating poem, the identity of the persona leaches into that of François-Nöel Babeuf, the French Revolutionary, whose radical egalitarianism is brought to bear upon the racist ideas of the French ethnologist Joseph-Arthur de Gobineau. The topicality of the latter's racial theories are brought home to the reader through the Dalí-like transformation of de Gobineau into the Germanic "Gobethau"; the Frenchman's *Essai sue l'inégalitie des races humaines* melting ("*tauen*") and mutating into contemporary fascist notions of Aryan supremacy.

Devlin's poetry of the 1940s—collected with earlier pieces in *Lough Derg and Other Poems* (1946)—continues to demonstrate his intense concern for the human detritus of a world in which, with the Second World War, "mullioned Europe [is] shattered" ("Lough Derg"), and to whom a Pascalian God remains withdrawn and indifferent. Formally, the poems of this period, and for the remainder of his career, have largely dispensed with the heady avant-garde mannerisms of Devlin's previous work. In their place, one finds in the main symbolic, densely-patterned poems in various stanzaic forms which, recalling the example of Eliot in *Poems* (1920), accord with the poetic principles laid down by the American New Criticism. Many of Devlin's poems of this period were published in New Critical journals, including the *Southern Review* and the *Sewanee Review;* and following his diplomatic posting to New York in 1939 and Washington in 1940, as a member of **Ireland**'s Department of External Affairs, Devlin formed friendships with the influential poet-critics Allen Tate and Robert Penn Warren (who were to edit a *Selected Poems* [1963] after Devlin's death). The New Critical autotelism of these poems is at one with the isolation experienced by Devlin's Jansenist persona in such notable works as "Lough Derg" and "Jansenist Journey." The possible functionlessness of poetry in the face of total war finds a parallel in "the form of prayer without content," as "Lough Derg" punningly, and movingly, phrases it. That is, a high modernist detachment from praxis, as evinced in the elevation of formal devices to fill a space once occupied by a social content, finds its spiritual corollary in a prayer the religious significance of which has drained away, leaving only its "form" as solace.

A similar predicament confronts the speakers of Devlin's love poetry, the concerns of which—after the example of San Juan de la Cruz—overlap with those of his religious poetry. The erotic poems frequently address an absent beloved, whose ontological status is shown to be as much the product of the desiring male poet's imagination as it is rooted in a referential woman. The latter's potential to allay the lover's solitariness is, therefore, highly problematic; and Devlin's personae are all too painfully aware that the lovers they recollect are consoling images, desperately spun out of their poetic entrails in an attempt to overcome their sense of privation. In "Farewell and Good," to take a representative instance, the speaker is forced to acknowledge the fact that the loved one will not appear again, except in imaginary form, as the poet "in phantasms of sleep assembl[es] her form." But such an idealized love-object is necessarily a wish-fulfilling poetic construct, and thus meager compensation for the literal, and now lost, object of desire.

In Devlin's late masterpiece, *The Heavenly Foreigner* (first published in 1950, and subsequently revised), the sequestered self of the love poems is equally the Jansenist subject of his religious lyrics. Based in part on Devlin's reading of Maurice Scève's *canzonerie* of love poems *Délie* (1544), and drawing upon Occitan poetry of *fin'amor*, *The Heavenly Foreigner* is constructed around memories of a lover in whose finite beauty the speaker hopes to discern the atemporal deity of the title. His recollections of the woman constitute nuclei around which he weaves imaginative conjectures, making the remembered woman his emblem, "the absolute woman of a moment." Yet in the process of idealizing the female, her sentient being vanishes, and with her recedes any hope of grasping the essence of the Heavenly Foreigner. For not the least of the paradoxes of the poem is its lushly metaphorical argument that the images denoting the woman constitute a fetishistic symbolism. "How she stood, hypothetical-eyed and metaphor-breasted," exclaims the persona, describing how the woman weaves his vision from his sight; yet the vision unravels leaving "only a light smoke" in his hands. It is precisely because of her figurative status that the female figure can never symbolize that which is perceived as existing beyond language, "God's Son," in the words of another late poem, "The Passion Of Christ," "foreign to our moor."

Alex Davis

Selected Bibliography

Advent VI. Denis Devlin Special Issue. Southampton: Advent Books, 1976.

Beckett, Samuel. *Disjecta: Miscellaneous Writings and a Dramatic Fragment.* Edited by Ruby Cohn. London: John Calder, 1983.

Coffey, Brian. "Of Denis Devlin: Vestiges, Sentences, Presages." *University Review* (Dublin) 2.11 (1963): 3–18.

Davis, Alex. *A Broken Line: Denis Devlin and Irish Poetic Modernism.* Dublin: University College Dublin Press, 2000.

Devlin, Denis. *Collected Poems.* Edited by J. C. C. Mays. Dublin: Dedalus, 1989.

Fogarty, Anne. "Gender, Irish Modernism and the Poetry of Denis Devlin." In *Modernism and Ireland: The Poetry of the 1930s.* Edited by Patricia Coughlan and Alex Davis. Cork: Cork UP, 1995, pp. 209–31.

Goodby, John. *From Stillness into History: Irish Poetry since 1950.* Manchester: Manchester UP, 2000.

Johnston, Dillon. *Irish Poetry after Joyce.* 2nd ed. Syracuse: Syracuse UP, 1997.

Smith, Stan. "'Precarious Guest': The Poetry of Denis Devlin." In *Modernism and Ireland: The Poetry of the 1930s.* Edited by Patricia Coughlan and Alex Davis. Cork: Cork UP, 1995, pp. 232–48.

Döblin, Alfred (1878–1957)

Döblin was born to a lower-middle-class Jewish mercantile family. At the age of ten he moved to Berlin, which was to become the setting of most of his important novels. He also wrote about distant countries and ages to free his imagination from the tendency to **naturalism,** such as his first successful novel *Die drei Sprünge des Wang-Lun* (1915, *The Three Leaps of Wang-Lun*), about a revolutionary who relies on his individual resources against the brutal force of the state. As a psychiatrist and doctor of internal medicine he was more critical of positivism than Zola and

the German naturalists had been. Döblin's novels, also including *Wallenstein* (1920), had been committed to the Left, until he became disillusioned in politics and resigned from the Social Democratic Party in 1928. He turned to speculative natural philosophy; in *Berge, Meere und Giganten* (1924, *Mountains, Seas and Giants*), he philosophized on nature's relationship to scientific and industrial progress, which was to become the theme of man's possible reconciliation to his urban environment in the city novels. In the essay "Der Bau des epischen Werks" (1928, "The Structure of the Epic Work"), he outlined his stylistic approach which would depict a "supra-reality" of "exemplary actions and figures" in an eclectic and open form developing half-formed ideas, without a predetermined plot.

In *Berlin Alexanderplatz* (1929, *Alexanderplatz*), Döblin used his knowledge as a physician in the slums of Berlin to explore the psychological experience of urban life, and borrowed heavily from **Joyce's** *Ulysses* to express it. Juxtaposed with anecdotal events is a biblical mythology which offers the hero possible salvation. From his "terrible" moment of freedom in which "He turned his head back towards the red wall, but the tram went racing on, and only his head was left looking towards the prison," Franz Biberkopf is spiritually and physically disorientated in Berlin, as he oscillates between various jobs, political groups, women, and crimes. He attempts to find a spiritual center through alcohol, his lover Mieze who supports him through prostitution, then death. Finally, he is "reborn," but the end of the novel remains ambiguous about his future fate, and of man's possible future relationship to the metropolis. Döblin's later urban novel *Pardon wird nicht Gegeben* (1935, *Men without Mercy*), is more uncompromisingly pessimistic in its depiction of the individual destroyed by conflicting social forces.

After fleeing **Germany** in 1933 Döblin constantly moved between **France,** the United States, and then West Germany after the war. His essays and novels in this period meditated on Germany's history since the First World War, which included the trilogy *November 1918* (1948–1950).

Döblin's works are available in Walter-Verlag, Olten and Freiburg im Breisgau, and Penguin, London.

Carl Krockel

Selected Bibliography

Dollenmayer, David B. *The Berlin Novels of Alfred Döblin.* Berkeley: University of California Press, 1988.

Kort, Wolfgang. *Alfred Döblin.* New York: Twayne Publishers, 1974.

Doolittle, Hilda (H. D.) (1886–1961)

Hilda Doolittle was born in Bethlehem, Pennsylvania in 1886. She married the English writer **Richard Aldington** in 1913, and until recently, her work has often been read in relation to male modernists, notably **Ezra Pound** and **D. H. Lawrence.** In fact, famously, it was Pound who, in 1913, in the British Museum Tearoom, re-named her H. D. Imagiste and *End To Torment* (1979) is a memoir of him. Her connection with Lawrence, with whom she had what has been termed a "scribbling sibling rivalry" (Gilbert and Gubar), is more tenuous, but his presence as the character of Rico in her autobiographical novel *Bid Me To Live* (1960) has been acknowledged. Her reputation, then, appropriately in a writer so concerned with the boundaries between land and sea, has ebbed and flowed in a literary career which spanned forty-five years, from the publication of *Sea Garden* in 1916 to *Helen in Egypt* in 1961, the year of her death.

Her early poetry was highly acclaimed and the publication of *Collected Poems Of H. D.* (1925) established her reputation. She was a crucial figure in the imagist movement and *Sea Garden* (1916), her first collection, follows its principles, which together with Pound and Aldington, she set out in 1916: brevity and concision where every word is essential; "direct treatment of the thing whether subjective or objective"; rhythms based on musical phrasing, and, centrally, the power of the image, defined by Pound as "that which presents an intellectual and emotional complex in an instant of time." "Sea Rose," which epitomizes these principles, has been frequently anthologized. Yet this example of modernist experimentation is shot through with **feminism,** as Dekoven suggests. Such a reading is signaled by the title which links a conventional poetic representation of female beauty with the power of the (female) sea and where words like "marred," "meagre" and "thin" seem to undermine such representations. In the final stanza the "hardened" leaf "is a further reminder "of the sea rose's empowered difference from the soft rose petals of feminine subservience" (Dekoven).

"Oread" too combines an encapsulation of imagist principles with an interrogation of a female consciousness. This poem rests on a single unified complex which presents and unites in musical free verse a sexually charged image of the sea with an evocation of Oread, a Greek mountain nymph. This early evocation of a figure from Greek **myth** anticipates H. D.'s continued use of the classical world in her work. Such allusion resonates through her poetry from Sea Garden through *Hymen* (1921), *Helidora And Other Poems* (1924), *Red Roses For Bronze* (1931) to *Helen In Egypt* (1961). In "Hymen," the title piece of her second volume, the scene is set for a musical masque with the entry of "sixteen matrons from the temple of Hera" who "pass before the curtain—a dark purple hung between Ionic columns." In *Heliodora* the Greek poet Sappho is invoked in both Fragment 113, "Neither honey nor bee for me"; and in Fragment 36, "I know not what to do: my mind is divided." These poems grapple with the tensions between commitment to passion and commitment to poetry. Perhaps the best known poem in *Heliodora,* however, is "Helen" whom "All Greece hates" and "All Greece reviles" yet whom "Greece sees unmoved." *Red Roses For Bronze* contains Choros translations and sequences.

Given the strength of this classical thrust in H. D.'s poetry it is fitting that her engagement with the Helen story began early in her career and persisted through her life. *Helen In Egypt,* a long, complex, tripartite poem was conceived in1918, begun in 1936 but not published until 1961, after her death. Helen's voice in dramatic monologue dominates the poem and recounts her experiences during the Trojan War, her seduction by Paris and her relationship with Achilles. This monologue is interspersed with comments in prose which anticipate and direct reader response. This is a poem which blurs borders and interrogates the nature of (her) reality where the formidable Helen can be read as H. D.'s alter-ego, strengthening her through illness and enabling her to construct a myth about herself. In this sense this poem is a ground-breaking work. Not only does it take on the epic, a conventionally male poetic form, but also, within this form, H. D. depicts a mythic female protagonist and informs this depiction with her own biography, addressing her emotional and sexual anxieties and her intellectual concerns.

Helen and the other female figures who inhabit H. D.'s poetry—mothers like Demeter and Thetis, lovers like Cassandra and Circe, and Phedra, the mother as lover are seen to suffer because of their relationships with men. They are misused by male lovers within a system which privileges beauty and associates it with possession. However it is a mistake to view such women as inevitable victims. Gilbert and Gubar refer to H. D.'s "depictions of quasi-feminist autonomy and retribution" and cite "Eurydice" (1917) who insists that even in death she is more alive than Orpheus is in life.

H. D.'s version of *Euripides Ion* (1937) demonstrates her continued interest in the classical world, yet this was the only poem published between 1931 and 1944. Then came *Trilogy,* written in London between 1942–1944 in response to the Second World War. The first part, "The Walls Do Not Fall," evokes the experience of bombing within an all-embracing, spiritual and mythological response. This eclecticism develops through "Tribute to the Angels," where the poet, boldly, is both prophet and witness, to the ending of "The Flowering of the Rod" with its redemption implications of the anointing of Christ's feet by Mary Magdalene. The poem is both a spiritual meditation and a linguistic experiment where, according to Gilbert and Gubar, H. D. "constitutes a new language through a magical, alchemical process." Certainly she probes and plays with words, hence "a word most bitter, marah" changes into "mer, mere, mater, Maia, Mary/Star of the Sea/Mother" and this star changes into "Venus, Aphrodite, Astarte,/star of the east/star of the west."

H. D.'s poetry, at its best, is characterized by elusive layerings of meanings and allusion, a style she associates with the notion of a palimpsest (a parchment from which one writing has been erased to make room for another). *Palimpsest* (1926), her first published novel, was written in three parts, "Hipparchia," "Murex," and "Secret Name." It is dedicated to Bryher, the woman with whom she had an emotionally and materially supportive partnership for forty two years. In this text familiar preoccupations emerge: the concern with female consciousness; an exploration within spiritual, sexual and aesthetic relationships; and a fascination with the contradictions of time and place. Hipparchia rejects two Roman lovers, Marius Decius, whom she describes as "a rather bulbous vegetable" and the dilettante scholar Quitus Verrus, and is seemingly rescued by Julia, a female friend, who admires her "Hellenic spirit." The next section is more overtly autobiographical. Here an American poet, Raymonde Ransome, tries to assuage the pain of her husband's past infidelities by writing poetry. Helen, the protagonist of "Secret Name," shares Hipparchia's love of Greek culture and Raymonde's failed love affairs, but this section, set in Egypt where H. D. and Bryher had visited, contains traces of cultural comment and social comedy.

The autobiographical *Bid Me To Live* (1960) is characterized by reworkings and layerings and *Palimpsest* can be viewed as one of these layers. This later novel, not published until 1960, can be viewed as the prose equivalent of *Helen in Eygpt* in that it originated many years earlier. Begun in 1918 its other "layers" include *Paint it Today* (1921) and *Hedylus* (1928), and, as H. D. wrote the 1939 draft after completing her period of **psychoanalysis,** her *Tribute to Freud* (1956), which as Kenneth Field has suggested is more a presentation of her own "psychic personage" than an account of Freud's interpretations. As suggested earlier it is because of *Bid Me to Live* that H. D. is viewed in relation to Lawrence. In fact she readily admitted that the book is a *roman à clef* based on the time when Lawrence and Frieda stayed in the flat she shared with Richard Aldington in Mecklenburgh Square in London. Yet it reveals not only insights into H. D.'s emotional and spiritual life but also into her creative process in its experimentation with polyphony and stream of consciousness.

An overview of her literary career indicates that there is more to this writer than the reductive "H. D." suggests and Hilda Doolittle's subsequent oeuvre, the longer poems and experiments with prose fiction, moved beyond the confines of Pound's "imagiste" label. She was awarded the Harriet Monroe Memorial Prize in 1958, the Brandeis Award in 1959 and the poetry award of the American Academy of Arts and Letters in 1960. More recently feminist critics have reclaimed her from associations with her male contemporaries and have assessed her poetry and prose in its own right. There have been autobiographies and posthumous autobiographical publications, *HERmione* (1981), *The Gift* (1982) and *Asphodel* (1992). *Hermetic Definition,* a collection of late arcane and spiritual poems was published in 1972 and *Collected Poems 1912–1944* in 1983.

Ann Hurford

Selected Bibliography

Gilbert, Sandra, and Susan Gubar. *No Man's Land Volume One.* Yale: Yale UP, 1988.

Dekoven, Marianne. "Modernism and Gender." *The Cambridge Companion to Modernism.* Ed. Michael Levinson. Cambridge: Cambridge UP, 1999.

Field, Kenneth. "Introduction." *Tribute to Freud by H. D.* Boston: David R Goldine, 1974.

Dos Passos, John (Roderigo) (1896–1970)

U.S. novelist, playwright, journalist, painter, poet, and political activist.

Best known for the politically and artistically radical satires *Manhattan Transfer* (1925) and the *U.S.A.* trilogy (1938; *The 42nd Parallel* [1930]; *Nineteen Nineteen* [1932]; *The Big Money* [1936]), Dos Passos was acclaimed by Sartre "the greatest writer of our time." His life experiences through to the late 1930s, even without these writings, would qualify him as a key figure in international modernism.

Born illegitimate in a Chicago hotel to a lawyer who rose from office boy to command an unprecedented fee for establishing the Sugar Trust (controlling 98% of U.S. refining), Dos Passos was raised by his mother in Europe as a foundling. He assumed his name when his parents married in 1910 following his father's first wife's death. At private schools in England and the United States his accent, name and background rendered him foreign. He thus began extensive transatlantic traveling during childhood, was close to the workings of corporate capitalism that recurrently emerge in his work, had access through wealth and education to the most influential figures of the era, yet remained perpetually an outsider.

He toured Europe and the Near East, where his personal aesthetic germinated in realizing that Greek statuary was originally adorned with painted surface detail rather than, as classicism taught, consisting of pure form. Entering Harvard, Dos Passos befriended **E. E. Cummings,** joined the Poetry Society, visited the **Armory Show** in 1913, and became involved with *Harvard Monthly.* He began his third published novel *Streets of Night* (1924), and published an essay, "Against American Literature," in *New Republic.*

Dos Passos's father stopped him joining the ambulance corps and sent him to **Spain** to study architecture. On his father's death in 1917 he joined the Norton-Harjes Ambulance Unit and served in **France.** He was gas-bombed in **Italy,** but also encountered Italian art and met **Hemingway.** Having joined the Red Cross he was sent home for criticizing **the war.** Enlisted in the United States Army Medical Corps, he returned to France.

In peacetime, Dos Passos studied at the Sorbonne, published (after accepting bowdlerization) in London his first novel, *One Man's Initiation–1917* (1920; reissued uncut, 1969) and traveled in Spain. He studied art in New York, contributed to journals including *The Dial* and *The Nation,* and worked for the Red Cross in the Near East. 1922 saw publication of a book on Spanish culture (involving personal Iberian introspection), a poetry volume,

and the novel that brought fame, *Three Soldiers,* which indicted wartime futility, absurdity, and suffering.

In New York Dos Passos knew the **Fitzgerald**s, Edmund Wilson, and **Sherwood Anderson;** exhibited his art; and published *Manhattan Transfer.* He met Léger, Cendrars and other modernists in Paris, attended **Stein**'s salon, and celebrated a Spanish fiesta with Hemingway.

In 1925 Dos Passos co-founded the socialist magazine *New Masses* and reported the murder trial of the anarchist Sacco and his associate Vanzetti, whose defense he assisted, and in 1927 published a poem protesting their execution; this event prompted international demonstrations, during which Dos Passos was imprisoned. The same year, *Orient Express* (spontaneous travel writings) praised poems by Cendrars that Dos Passos later translated and illustrated (*"Panama or the Adventures of My Seven Uncles" and Other Poems* [1931]).

Visiting Hemingway in Florida in 1928 Dos Passos met his future wife. During a long stay in **Russia** he discussed **film** with **Eisenstein,** Pudovkin, and others. After honeymooning in Europe and Mexico, Dos Passos settled on Cape Cod but continued to travel. Although disappointed with leftist politics, he joined the National Committee for the Defense of Political Prisoners in 1931, visited striking Kentucky coal miners, and voted communist in the 1932 presidential election. *New Masses* criticized him for condemning communist disruption of a 1934 Socialist Party rally in New York. In Hollywood, he scripted von Sternberg's *The Devil Is a Woman* (1935).

Dos Passos graced the cover of *Time* when *The Big Money* was published. Leftists judged the book pessimistic. He supported Roosevelt's 1936 presidential campaign, then joined Hemingway, Hellmann, MacLeish and others to produce a Spanish Civil War documentary (*The*

Spanish Earth) in 1937. In Spain to assist Hemingway and director Ivens, he lost faith when communist "allies" executed his Republican friend José Robles. Hemingway counseled silence to protect the cause and his reputation: they became estranged. Dos Passos published "Farewell to Europe!" in *Common Sense,* praising "Anglo-Saxon democracy" as "the best political method." He mounted a one-man show of drawings in New York, and published *Adventures of a Young Man,* about a leftist fighting for Franco after harsh treatment in the American labor movement. This inaugurated a second trilogy, *District of Columbia* (1939–49, 1952), which despaired that America would never cultivate individual liberty and self-determination.

Later prolific writings, including patriotic, sentimental biographies and histories, damaged Dos Passos's reputation. Increasingly conservative both as social commentary and artistically, they abandoned condemnation of free enterprise while attacking financiers, labor leaders and younger generations with equal severity. Dos Passos defended McCarthyism in the 1950s and attended the 1964 Republican National Convention, supporting Goldwater's presidential nomination, yet insisted his views remained consistent: his first *Harvard Monthly* essay had praised technocracy while questioning its effect on individualism.

Manhattan Transfer and *U.S.A.* deploy modernism as a revolutionary restructuring of culture. Wartime juxtapositions of horror and classical beauty demanded comprehensiveness that a cubist approach provided. The title *Manhattan Transfer,* alluding to a commuter interchange, appositely summarizes its form and strategies. Variegated citizens traverse multiple narratives, spanning forty years and combining history and fiction, as the city becomes a metropolis, finance center, immigrants' haven, and embarkation point for troops

and wealthy tourists. Dos Passos reputedly drafted each character's linear narrative before literally cutting and intersplicing them like film, incorporating incidental trolley accidents, speeding fire engines, accounts of kidnappings, and unexpected acts of violence—characteristic city sensations from tabloids and cinema. The fragmentation and energy of the writing, together with its embracing of low-life **naturalism,** led one critic to call it "an explosion in a cesspool." Objective descriptions, coldly scrutinizing urban existence, intertwine with variations on **interior monologue** and stream of consciousness, such as this synesthetic representation of drunkenness:

> Bars yawned bright to them at the corners of rainseething streets. Yellow light off mirrors and brass rails and gilt frames around pictures of pink naked women was looped and slopped into whiskyglasses guzzled fiery with tipped back head, oozed bright through the blood, popped bubbly out of ears and eyes, dripped spluttering off fingertips. (93; Penguin, 1987)

(Dos Passos's celebrated cinematic style in fact is well in advance of 1920s film, evoking sound as well as smells and physical sensations, and creating painterly patterns of color, in ways unavailable to filmmakers at the time.) Although more concerned with political, economic, and social forces than individualism, Dos Passos sympathizes with his characters. In line with his refusal to join the Communist Party, rejected as dogmatic and inflexible, his Marxism is humanist, intuitive rather than scientific. Human perception refracts the abstract ideals and shortcomings of the United States' emergence as a world power. Authenticating detail such as a piece of grit between a character's teeth receives equal attention to the rise of bolshevism. The individual narratives, seemingly arbitrary as characters are introduced gradually, impressionistically, and inconsistently, follow success and decline, achievement and disillusionment, fulfillment and personal tragedy: epic ingredients, insignificant against the impersonal dazzle and magnitude of burgeoning skyscrapers. The opening image, "broken boxes, orangerinds, spoiled cabbage heads" bobbing in the harbor, anticipates 1930s social **realism,** but its symbolism also parallels **Eliot**'s *The Waste Land* (Dos Passos's worldview is equally sterile), just as the commuters disembarking from a ferry recall Eliot's hordes crossing London Bridge. The imagist-like intensity of the first sustained metaphor—passengers "crushed and jostling like apples fed down a chute into a press"—evokes the wider background of mass immigration as well as daily commerce. The individualized characters, *typical* rather than average, are visionaries, decision makers, parasites, and victims—or cogs, loose parts, raw materials, and by-products of an environment repeatedly described in hard, metallic imagery: this includes natural phenomena, such as clouds "bright and white like tinfoil."

U.S.A., likewise a machine to fight an oppressive machine, covers similar events but now encompasses the entire continent, America's emergent military and industrial dominance (much of the action occurs abroad), and the Depression. Again the structure is primarily interlinked personal narratives ("U.S.A. is the speech of the people"), but this time lives are increasingly determined less by abstract forces and more by characters' propensity to greed, selfishness and pettiness: human weakness compromises the system. Transatlantic voyages and endless train journeys, across Europe and Central and South America as well as the States, reinforce the epic inexorability of modernity, restless and random. Drunken driving, airplane flights, and subjectively-described fatal crashes create a negatively futurist vision of unconstrained energies. **The war,** rather than a noble cause, is a public-relations exercise whipped up for political and industrial advantage, providing most characters opportunities not for service, which is hardly mentioned (perhaps too traumatic to recall), but relentless drinking and fornication. Prominent movers in technology, marketing, politics and the arts—makers of the twentieth century—are by the end dead from heart attacks, alcoholism, or suicide occasioned by ennui. Interpolated between these fictional lives are "Newsreels": snippets of actual headlines, reports and popular songs reminiscent of *The Waste Land,* concurrent with the narratives and relating their individual concerns to the collective life of the nation. Autobiographical sections titled "The Camera Eye" provide fragmented, first-hand impressions of unfolding events. Potted biographies of eminent modern Americans (Edison, Ford, Hearst, and so on) complete the picture; simply written, parodying Horatio Alger success parables, many are subtly scathing. Most striking is "The Body of an American," an obscenely graphic, cynical prose-poem about the Unknown Soldier, presented as a collective protagonist sold out by the peace settlement; its frankness and horror convey modernist disgust with abuse of language, confirmed as advertising and propaganda displace headlines in the "Newsreels" and presentation supplants concern with product in businesses run by several characters. Juxtaposed sections contrast and conflict, confirm, contradict, and ironize, forging new meanings through interaction according to Eisensteinian montage principles.

These novels, eclipsed by **Joyce** (whose methods Dos Passos virtually single-handedly introduced to America), became an embarrassment as political fiction lost favor and the author's writing grew irascible and dull. Yet they were highly influential in their day, as witness a sidewalk scene in *Manhattan Transfer* that presages **Lawrence**'s description of Lady Chatterley's alienated drive through Tevershall: "Aloof, as if looking through thick glass into an aquarium, she watched faces, fruit in store-windows, cans of vegetables, jars of olives, redhotpokerplants in a florist's, newspapers, electric signs drifting by." The achievement of *U.S.A.* is in combining painterly description—often dismissed as formalist experimentation—with free indirect discourse, intertextuality and image structures, rendering inner lives more vividly and judgmentally, as in Joyce's *Dubliners,* than is often recognized. A hyper-romantic art student's existence, for example, under a "very-pale blue sky" with "piles of dovegray fluffy clouds," utilizes the stark monotones of Whistler (her mother even dies of "pernicious anaemia"); another moves into a smart set whose bored conversation explicitly evokes Eliot's "Prufrock," before going to New Mexico to lose her virginity in a passionate affair with a Spanish artist named O'Riely: an affectionate parody of Lawrence. Understated intense experiences—"They ate fritto misto and drank a lot of fine gold Frascati wine at the restaurant above the waterfall"; "She was trembling when he came to her on the bed. It was all right, but she bled a good deal and they didn't have a very good time"—unmistakably recall Hemingway. Attention to heteroglossia and dialogism could advance an overdue critical rehabilitation.

Nigel Morris

Selected Bibliography

Nanney, Lisa. *John Dos Passos.* New York: Twayne Publishers, 1998.

Sartre, Jean-Paul. "John Dos Passos and *1919.*" In *Literary and Philosophical Essays.* Translated by Annette Michelson. London: Rider, 1955.

Schloss, Carol. *In Visible Light: Photography and the American Writer, 1840–1940.* New York: Oxford University Press, 1987.

Dubliners (1914)

Written between 1904 and 1907, **James Joyce**'s *Dubliners* is a collection of fifteen short stories later arranged as a thematically integrated and chronologically ordered series. The mostly lower-middle-class characters in the apparently undramatic stories illustrate the disabling effects of family, religion, and nationality.

Joyce had great difficulty finding a publisher as he refused to alter passages considered objectionable (see "Gas from a Burner" for Joyce's sarcastic reaction to the publication squabbles). During 1906 he described the governing idea of the collection in letters to the English publisher Grant Richards: "My intention was to write a chapter of the moral history of my country and I chose Dublin for the scene because that city seemed to me the centre of paralysis. I have tried to present it to the indifferent public under four of its aspects: childhood, adolescence, maturity and public life. The stories are arranged in this order. I have written it for the most part in a style of scrupulous meanness and with the conviction that he is a very bold man who dares to alter in the presentment, still more to deform, whatever he has seen or heard."

Joyce declared that "I believe that in composing my chapter of moral history in exactly the way I have composed it I have taken the first step towards the spiritual liberation of my country," and, defending *Dubliners* against possible charges of indecency, emphasized that "It is not my fault that the odour of ashpits and old weeds and offal hangs round my stories. I seriously believe that you will retard the course of civilisation in Ireland by preventing the Irish people from having one good look at themselves in my nicely polished looking-glass." The collection was eventually published by Grant Richards in 1914.

The stories add up to a complex portrait of the city and its inhabitants, and they illustrate the pervasive theme of paralysis in various forms—physical, emotional, intellectual, or social. Irish catholicism is in the background and a major underlying cause. Joyce employed that "style of scrupulous meanness" to show how the customary behavior of the citizens of Dublin is ruled by convention and inertia. The protagonists' moral limitations are subtly disclosed as their own phrases intersperse the third person narratives. The significant part reveals the whole. The stories abstain from intrusive authorial judgment, though they are varyingly suffused by irony and sarcasm.

Dubliners are open in structure, meticulous in detail, and mostly written in an apparently realistic style, with commonplace diction and descriptions. As for plot, what little is happening seems to be trivial. The childhood stories are retrospective unnamed first person narratives, while the remaining twelve stories are narrated in the third person. Shifts in focus and style are subtle. Joyce abhorred inverted commas, or "perverted commas" as he called them, using dashes instead to introduce dialogue. This typographically innovative technique blurs the conventional distinction between direct speech and narration.

The stories display Joyce's concern with words and their order as well as the total structure of a work. The collection foreshadows various techniques amplified in *A Portrait of the Artist as a Young Man, Ulysses,* and *Finnegans Wake.* Many of the characters from *Dubliners* reappear in *Ulysses,* and each of the titles of the short stories is parodied in *Finnegans Wake* (186–87).

Christine O'Neill

Selected Bibliography

Beja, Morris, ed. *James Joyce: Dubliners and A Portrait of the Artist as a Young Man: A Selection of Critical Essays.* London: Macmillan, 1985.

Benstock, Bernard. *Narrative Con/Texts in Dubliners.* London: Macmillan, 1994.

Bollettieri Bosinelli, Rosa Maria and Harold F. Mosher, Jr., eds. *ReJoycing: New Readings of Dubliners.* Lexington: UP of Kentucky, 1998.

Gifford, Don. *Joyce Annotated: Notes for Dubliners and A Portrait of the Artist as a Young Man.* 2nd ed. Berkeley, Los Angeles and London: U of California P, 1982.

Hart, Clive, ed. James Joyce's Dubliners: *Critical Essays.* London: Faber and Faber, 1969.

Jackson, John Wyse and Bernard McGinley. *James Joyce's Dubliners: An Annotated Edition.* London: Sinclair-Stevenson, 1993.

Power, Mary and Ulrich Schneider, eds. *New Perspectives on Dubliners.* Amsterdam and Atlanta: Rodopi, 1997.

E

Eisenstein, Sergei Mikhaelovich (1898–1948)

Russian filmmaker, theorist, and teacher. Exponent of montage.

See under **Film and Modernism.**

Ekelöf, Gunnar (1907–1968)

Swedish poet, critic and prose-writer.

His first collection of verse, *sent på jorden* (1932, *Late Arrival on Earth*), represents, with its new and daring imagery, a radical break with literary tradition, finding its affinities in movements within international modernism, such as **surrealism** and **dada**. *Dedikation* (1934) is headed by a motto from Rimbaud, indicating Ekelöf's relationship with the symbolist and surrealist tradition. In the following collections *Sorgen och stjärnan* (1936, *The Sorrow and the Star*) and *Köp den blindes sång* (1938, *Buy the Blind Man's Song*) the language is logically clearer and more direct. Here the poet adopts a romantic role but can also engage in social themes. *Färjesång* (1941, *Ferry Song*), characterized by the poet himself as his personal breakthrough, represents another renewal of style and content; a mystical view of life is expressed in an analytical and intellectual language, a mysticism which is continued in *Non serviam* (1945), a title furthermore indicating Ekelöf's role as a modernist outsider, declining fixed ideologies and clear-cut standpoints. *Om hösten* (1951, *In the Autumn*) is a varied and retrospective collection containing poems from a period of twenty-two years.

The next phase consists of the three collections *Strountes* (1955, *Nonsense*), *Opus incertum* (1959) and *En natt i Otoĉac* (1961, *A Night in Otoĉac*), described by Ekelöf as anti-aesthetic and anti-poetic, making use of the nonsensical, the absurd, the grotesque. *En Mölna-Elegi* (1960, *A Mölna Elegy*) is a poem dealing with the experience of time, using a highly allusive technique and reaching back all the way to ancient Latin graffiti. Ekelöf's last project was the trilogy *Diwan över fursten av Emgión* (1965, *Diwan About the Prince of Emgión*), *Sagan om Fatumeh* (1966, *The Tale of Fatumeh*) and *Vägvisare till underjorden* (1967, Eng. tr. *Guide to the Underworld,* 1980) where the Virgin becomes a central symbol for Ekelöf's universal mysticism.

Ekelöf's prose is comprised of the essay collections *Promenader* (1941, *Promenades*), *Utflykter* (1947, *Excursions*), *Blandade kort* (1957, *Shuffled Cards*) and, posthumously edited, *Lägga patience* (1969, *Playing Solitaire*). A critical edition of Ekelöf's complete works, *Skrifter* (1991–93), is edited in eight volumes by Reidar Ekner. A selection of Ekelöf's poetry has been translated by Robert Bly and Christina Paulston under the title *Late Arrival on Earth* (1967). Muriel Rukseyer and Leif Sjöberg have translated the *Selected Poems of Gunnar Ekelöf* (1967).

Mats Jansson

Selected Bibliography

Hellström, Per. *Livskänsla och självutplåning. Studier kring framväxten av Gunnar Ekelöfs Strountesdiktning.* Uppsala: Skrifter utgivna av Litteraturvetenskapliga institutionen vid Uppsala universitet, 1976.

Landgren, Bengt. *Ensamheten, döden och drömmarna. Studier över ett motivkomplex I Gunnar Ekelöfs diktning.* Stockholm et al: Scandinavian University Books,1971.

———. *Den poetiska världen. Strukturanalytiska studier i den unge Gunnar Ekelöfs lyrik.* Uppsala: Acta Universitatis Upsaliensis, 1982.

———. *Polyederns gåta. En introduktion till Gunnar Ekelöfs Färjesång.* Uppsala: Acta Universitatis Upsaliensis, 1998.

Olsson, Anders. *Ekelöfs nej.* Stockholm: Bonniers, 1983.

Thygesen, Erik G. *Gunnar Ekelöf's Open-Form Poem A Mölna Elegy. Problems of Genesis, Structure and Influence.* Uppsala: Acta Universitatis Upsaliensis, 1985.

Eliot, T(homas) S(tearns) (1888–1965)

Poet, critic, and dramatist, he became the most influential figure in Anglo-American poetry of the last century, a status which grew as much from his early critical writings, collected in *The Sacred Wood* (1920), as it did from his highly allusive modernist poetry which is generally held to concern modern futility and spiritual decay, of which *The Waste Land* (1922) is his most sustained expression.

Eliot was born in the latter part of a decade which now reads like a modernist nursery, with the births of **Lewis, Joyce, Woolf, Kafka, Lawrence,** and **Pound** all also falling within its temporal compass. Whatever other conclusions this might lead us to, the contemporaneity of these historical accidents should at least remind us that the minds of some of the most important writers of the twentieth century were being formed at the end of the nineteenth. Although born and raised in St. Louis, Missouri, Eliot was very much a product of a New England family which had made its name in the then coterminous spheres of religion and education, his grandfather having migrated to St. Louis in the 1830s, where he founded a Unitarian ministry and had a hand in the setting up of several schools. The young Eliot vacationed with his family in New England, but it was 1905 before he became a more permanent fixture there, spending a year at Milton College, Boston before his matriculation at Harvard, which was to remain his base until 1914, latterly as an assistant in the philosophy department. Eliot's parents hoped that his relationship with the famous university would continue well into his professional career, but the pull of Europe and especially its literatures proved too strong. Having already visited Europe and spent time in Paris on completion of his master's degree in 1911, where he attended a series of lectures given by the philosopher Henri Bergson and wrote early drafts of poems which were later published, Eliot secured a traveling fellowship which once again allowed him to cross the Atlantic. His destination was the University of Marburg, **Germany,** but the threats of war prompted a swift move to England, where, apart from brief trips abroad, he remained for the rest of his life.

One of the most important dates in British modernism involves the meeting of two Americans. Eliot was introduced to Ezra Pound on September 22, 1914, at the latter's flat in Kensington, London. Since his arrival in London in 1908, Pound had become a prominent figure of the literary avant-garde, both in terms of his own output and his assiduous promotion of new talents. Eliot's brilliance did not escape Pound, who worked hard to find a publisher for his latest find. Pound eventually succeeded: "The Love Song of J. Alfred Prufrock" appeared in the June 1915 edition of Harriet Weaver's American publication *Poetry,* and "Preludes" and "Rhapsody on a Windy Night" appeared a month later in the second, and final, edition of *Blast;* all three of which, together with nine other poems, were published in 1917 by Egoist Press, in Eliot's first collection, *Prufrock and Other Observations.*

The exhilarating opening lines of "Prufrock" invited its initial readership to leave behind the ferny lanes of Georgianism and make a journey through the insidious half-deserted streets of modernism. It was a journey for which many weren't prepared. Prufrock is one of the great antiheroes of modern literature. Diffident to the point of paralysis, thoroughly incapable of bringing the moment to its crisis, his overwhelming question is never answered precisely because it is never asked, and his muttering retreats lead nowhere but to his own drowning. But Prufrock is no more Ophelia than he is prince Hamlet. It is his inability to do anything but self-psychologize which drowns him; his love song proves a death knell.

If Prufrock invites us on a journey, then so does Eliot; the poem contains all of the modernist obsessions to which its author will continually return: thwarted erotic love, personal failure, death, the impossibility to say just what one means, and modern decay. Eliot's world is one of smoke and fog, of grimy scraps and broken blinds, where midnight shakes the memory as a madman shakes a dead geranium. It is the world of the *flâneur,* the street-idler, who, though apt to be moved by his observation of some infinitely suffering thing, is ever alert to the artificiality of his own expression in a glass.

Writing in 1930, Eliot said of Baudelaire that he had given poetry "a new stock of imagery of contemporary life": "It is not merely in the use of imagery of common life, not merely in the use of imagery of the sordid life of a great metropolis, but in the elevation of such imagery to the *first intensity*—presenting it as it is, and yet making it represent something much more than itself—that Baudelaire has created a mode of release and expression for other men." Men such as Eliot. But Eliot's modernist symbolism rejects epiphanic truths; there is no sense sublime for the speaker, only a stultifying inwardness that borders on schizothymia. Indeed, there is often such a proliferation of pronouns that all possibility of subjective stability is shattered, with I, You, and We merging into a kind of polyphonic soliloquy.

It is precisely this dialogic quality that gives Eliot's best poetry its tremendous energy. From "Prufrock" onwards, a multiplicity of discourses is evident, which meet and cut across each other at various levels, not simply in terms of a poem's protagonists ("Portrait of a Lady," for example), or in the interaction (explicit and implicit) with works of past writers, but also in Eliot's echoing of his own work (so that the "dying fall" of "Portrait" urges the reader back to "the voices dying with a dying fall" of "Prufrock"). These three strands, textual, intertextual, and intratextual, inform Eliot's poetry in complex ways. They are not decorative, but the very substance of his modernism.

In his essay "Tradition and the Individual Talent" (1917), Eliot suggests that the best and most individual parts of an artist's work are often those in which "dead poets, his ancestors, assert their immortality most vigorously." Consequently, any writer with serious intentions must develop what Eliot terms "the historical sense," which "involves a perception, not only of the pastness of the past, but of its presence," and which "compels a man to write not merely with his own generation in his bones, but with a feeling that the whole of the literature of Europe from Homer and within it the whole of the literature of his own country has a simultaneous existence and composes a simultaneous order."

Eliot's second collection of poems was published in 1920. *Ara Vos Prec,* taking its title from Dante, contains several poems written in French, and half a dozen or so written in strictly metered quatrains, which, informed by Gautier, was the result of a combined decision taken by Pound and Eliot to counterbalance the proliferation of second-rate *vers libre.* Despite these striking "experiments," which gave the world Burbank and the mytho-modern simian Sweeney, the collection's real triumph is the perplexing, free-versed "Gerontion," in which a wealth of allusions operate within a context of post-war deracination and spiritual decay. Like Prufrock, the dull-headed old man of "Gerontion" is characterized by inaction; doomed to live out his life in the tortuous passages and corridors of his dry brain, he waits to stiffen in a decayed house which deceitful history has tenanted. In many ways, the poem is a milestone: its use of allusion, the aridity and sterility of the setting, the references to the cycles of life, and the mixing of memory and desire, all preempt *The Waste Land.* Eliot was moving towards his modernist masterpiece.

The Waste Land was first published in the October 1922 edition of *Criterion,* a literary review which Eliot himself founded and which he edited throughout its lifetime. The reception of the poem was mixed to say the least, with Amy Lowell describing it as "tripe," and many reviewers suspecting it an elaborate joke. There were, however, those who acclaimed the poem, Edmund Wilson and Conrad Aiken being among the first. As Hugh Kenner reminds us, the poem was written during a particularly bleak period for Eliot, with the pressures of work and a demanding marriage contributing to what appears to have been a breakdown. As literary folklore has it, Eliot gave the "finished" poem to Pound, who in turn removed a significant amount of material and shaped the poem into what was to be its published format. There is evidence also that Eliot's wife made changes to the original text. These

origins of the poem have fascinated critics for decades, hardly surprising in a climate marked by Roland Barthes's post-structuralist essay "The Death of the Author." In "Tradition and the Individual Talent" Eliot had written: "The progress of the artist is a continual self-sacrifice, a continual extinction of personality." In light of this, one wonders whether the intensity of the biographical circumstances surrounding *The Waste Land* encouraged its author to surrender his poem to other authorities in order to effect its depersonalization. It would seem that Eliot was either unwilling or unable to at least put his lines in order.

If this is the case, then we should not find it surprising. Throughout Eliot's critical writings can be found a mindset which is particularly fluid on the issue of authorial control, and in this respect Eliot has more in common with certain post-structuralist thought than we might expect from one so unbending in other areas. For example, in a lecture given on "The Music of Poetry" (1942), Eliot notes that while the suggestion that poetry is beyond paraphrase is not unusual, it is "not quite so commonplace to observe that the meaning of a poem may be something larger than its author's conscious purpose," and he proceeds to add the following: "A poem may appear to mean very different things to different readers, and all of these readings may be different from what the author thought he meant. . . . The reader's interpretation may differ from the author's and be equally valid—it may even be better. There may be much more in a poem than the author was aware of." To fuse Eliot and Barthes, the extinction of personality means the birth of the reader.

The Waste Land's working-title was "He Do the Police in Different Voices," with an allusion being made to Dickens's *Our Mutual Friend.* Whatever other significance the preliminary title may have, its emphasis on the poem's "different voices" highlights the finished text's most striking feature, if not its organizing prin-ciple, with the equivocality of its author-ship becoming particularly apposite. As the final lines of the poem testify, *The Waste Land* is essentially a collection of fragments, many of which owe their exis-tence directly to other texts, appropriated by Eliot in such a way as to form a new whole.

The text is saturated by the present-ness of the past. From the epigraph (which is in itself polyglot) to the shantih, Eliot's historical sense (here ranging beyond Europe) establishes and maintains a sub-stantial intertextual network. Such an abundance of allusion has tended to pro-voke one of two responses from readers, who either bask in the glory of their eru-dition or despair in the wake of their ig-norance. Perhaps partly in self-defense, a conviction has grown in response to the poem that its meaning lies in its very dif-ficulty; that far from being written for an educated elite, as some argue, *The Waste Land* encodes a conscious effort to bewil-der its readership. The view is not without authority. In an essay entitled "The Meta-physical Poets" (1921), Eliot declares that "it appears likely that poets in our civili-zation, as it exists at present, must be *dif-ficult*. Our civilization comprehends great variety and complexity, and this variety and complexity, playing upon a refined sensibility, must produce various and com-plex results. The poet must become more comprehensive, more allusive, more indi-rect, in order to force, to dislocate if nec-essary, language into his meaning." The question remains one of whether or not there is meaning beyond "difficulty"; here Eliot seems to hover between the two pos-sibilities, which as we have noted is not altogether uncharacteristic of him.

Of course, a reader's response to *The Waste Land* must be personal. One only has to glance at the vast catalogue of ex-egetical materials concerning the poem to understand the futility of hoping for more.

Is the Waste Land a place of barrenness or fertility? Does the shantih forge a redemp-tive bond with Christian theology and the cycles of paganism, or does it assert a su-periority that passeth all understanding? Why is erotic love impossible? Does the polyglot city suggest multicultural har-mony or Babel? How adequately has the speaker shored his ruins? These questions, and numberless others of equal validity, are for each reader to identify and answer, or ignore.

Indeed, one need not go as far as the library shelf to comprehend the absurdity of imposing a totalizing reading on *The Waste Land.* Eliot's infamous notes are all that are required for such a realization. Variously regarded as a joke, a valuable index, a shameless piece of money-driven padding, an exercise in deception, and an attempt to ward off accusations of plagia-rism, Eliot's acknowledgement of his sources is of ambiguous worth, not simply because he is far from exhaustive and not always accurate, but because the notes' mode of reference serves to deconstruct the very reading process they aim to fa-cilitate. Even the reader (if there ever has been one) familiar with all of Eliot's ac-knowledged sources is encouraged to re-turn to them, and anyone who is not is faced with the dizzying, if not impossible, task of tackling an extensive reading pro-gram, from the *Satyricon* to the *Upani-shads.* Furthermore, there is the problem of the nature of this process, which is ret-rospective; that is it must take place in the light of Eliot, which is akin to reading the text in reverse. Eliot was aware of this, having noted that the past is "altered by the present as much as the present is di-rected by the past." Or as Borges puts it, "every writer creates his own precursors." Thus *The Waste Land,* with its inclusion of an exegetical supplement, makes a genuine claim to be the first self-consciously hy-pertextual work of art in Western litera-ture. And as with any hypertext, the movement away from the primary source occasions a deferment of meaning, or rather a continuous reappraisal in the light of secondary material.

Given this, perhaps the most sensible initial reading of *The Waste Land* for mere mortals, if not the final one, is a reading which attends to what in *Principles of Literary Criticism* (1926) I. A. Richards has called its "music of ideas": "The ideas are of all kinds: abstract and concrete, general and particular; and, like the musician's phrases, they are arranged, not that they may tell us something, but that their effects in us may combine into a coherent whole of feeling and attitude and produce a peculiar liberation of the will." This should not be rebuked for its simplicity. It is Eliot himself who introduced the term "auditory imagination," by which he meant "the feeling for syllable and rhythm, penetrating far below the conscious levels of thought."

In the same critique, Richards suggested that for some *The Waste Land* represented "the plight of a whole generation." Eliot always denied that this was his intention, though he would have perhaps been the first to recognize that the matter was out of his control. In the introduction to *Poems of Tennyson* (1936), Eliot writes: "It happens now and then that a poet by some strange accident expresses the mood of his generation, at the same time that he is expressing a mood of his own which is quite remote from that of his generation."

Be that as it may, there is certainly an inclusive tone to the poem that is said to have grown from *The Waste Land,* namely *The Hollow Men* (1925). The emphatic, repeated "We" of the poem's opening lines implicates us in what is surely Eliot's bleakest creation. Sightless, and with voices that are quiet and meaningless, the Hollow Men exist in a state of tortured paralysis, somewhere between a living death and death's other kingdom. It is a darkly sinister poem, drawing its terrible energy from the very sadism that remains latent in the child's burning of the guy. We are a long way from the shantih.

The Hollow Men is arguably Eliot's final modernist statement. It is evident that its creation was followed by an adjustment in the poet's life and thinking, which is perhaps best seen in his religious conversion. In a ceremony of suggestive secrecy, Eliot was received into the Anglican Church in 1927, and, as if to cement his decision, in the same year he took British citizenship. Significantly, 1927 was also the year when Eliot's "Journey of the Magi" appeared, one in a sequence of "Ariel" poems, and his first since *The Hollow Men.* The poem is central to Eliot's later work. Gone is Gerontion's stagnant bitterness, the arid futility of the Waste Land, and the Hollow Men's hopeless perdition, and in their stead is a very real sense of awakening, of spiritual rebirth, of life in death, rather than the death in life of the early output. This is perhaps to make too fine a point, but Eliot had certainly moved on. In his collection of essays *For Lancelot Andrewes* (1928), Eliot declared himself to be "classicist in literature, royalist in politics, and anglo-catholic in religion"; his "Waste Land phase" was clearly behind him.

Ash-Wednesday confirmed Eliot's new dispensation in 1930, though parts of it had appeared in print before being incorporated into a longer poem. In many ways it is a disturbing work, recording the speaker's struggle between the world and the Word, between the salt savor of the sandy earth and the ivory gates. Essentially the poem is a plea for divine forgiveness and a cry for spiritual strength. The speaker does not hope to turn from his journey to the garden where all love ends, that is where earthly love terminates and divine love finds its end, but his salvation is never assured, with the poem's repetition of "I do not hope" establishing a mind wavering on the edge of distraction and highlighting the tension between dying and birth. The poem is richly symbolic and strongly allusive, though with less of an emphasis on the *play* of allusion than in Eliot's earlier poetry.

Following *Ash-Wednesday,* Eliot began gradually to move away from writing poetry, and became instead interested in the possibilities of the theater, being drawn particularly to its communal nature. As Eliot said in 1933: "The most useful poetry, socially, would be one which could cut across all the present stratifications of public taste—stratifications which are perhaps a sign of social disintegration. The ideal medium for poetry, to my mind, and the most direct means of social 'usefulness' for poetry, is the theatre." Eliot had already experimented with verse drama after *The Hollow Men,* creating the fragments that were eventually brought together under the title *Sweeney Agonistes,* and in 1934 *The Rock* was performed. This was followed by *Murder in the Cathedral* (1935), perhaps Eliot's most successful play, written for the Canterbury Festival, and dealing with the martyrdom of Thomas à Becket, and *The Family Reunion* (1939), concerning the uxoricidal Lord "Harry" Monchensey's flight from the "Furies" and his coming to terms with his heredity ("We all felt like failures, before we had begun."). Perhaps owing to its complexity and the pre-war climate, the latter was not a commercial success, and almost a decade passed before Eliot looked again to the stage.

Eliot instead turned to poetry, writing *East Coker* (1940), a sequel to *Burnt Norton,* which had appeared in his *Collected Poems 1909–1935.* It is said that it was during Eliot's writing of *East Coker* that he determined to make it the second poem in a sequence of four, which he realized with *The Dry Salvages* (1941) and *Little Gidding* (1942). All four poems were eventually brought together in 1943 and given the title *Four Quartets.*

As with *Ash-Wednesday* before it, taken as a whole, there is a strong sense of the personal in *Four Quartets.* The persona hasn't the constructedness of a Prufrock, or a Gerontion, or a Magus, being instead a voice which at times is almost confessional in its tone and mood. However mistakenly, we feel we are somehow closer to Eliot, not simply in the biographical relevance of the quartets' titles, but in the poetry itself. Ostensibly, the sequence is a meditation on time, past, present, and future, and man's relationship with it, moving from a contemplation of missed directions in *Burnt Norton*—"Down the passages we did not take"—to *Little Gidding*'s history of "timeless moments." It is a movement from the self to the social, a situating of the self in the social, with poetry endeavoring to bring the "complete consort dancing together." Thus themes, images, sounds and rhythms are woven together in *Four Quartets* to produce an astonishingly complex poetic music.

Eliot went on to write three more plays—*The Cocktail Party* (1949), *The Confidential Clerk* (1953), and *The Elder Statesman* (1958)—but *Four Quartets* is regarded by many to have been the summit of his achievements. It was, in effect, his valediction to poetry; and, though not without its critics, confirmed his status as the major English language poet of his generation. It was in recognition of this and his other attainments, that in 1948 Eliot was awarded both the Order of Merit and the Nobel Prize for Literature. He died in January 1965, and his ashes were later interred at St. Michael's Church, East Coker.

Timothy Dobson

Selected Bibliography

Cox, C. B. and Hinchliffe, A. P., eds. *Casebook Series: "The Waste Land."* London and Basingstoke: Macmillan Press Ltd., 1972.

Davies, T. and Wood, N., eds. *The Waste Land.* Buckingham: Open UP, 1994.

Eliot, T. S. *Selected Prose.* Ed. John Hayward. Harmondsworth: Penguin Books, 1958.

———. *The Complete Poems and Plays.* London: Faber and Faber Ltd., 1990.

Gardner, H. *The Art of T. S. Eliot.* London: Faber and Faber Ltd., 1972.

Kenner, H. *The Invisible Poet: T. S. Eliot.* London: Metheun & Co Ltd., 1974.

Moody, A., ed. *The Cambridge Companion to T. S. Eliot.* Cambridge: Cambridge UP, 1994.

Sharpe, T. *T. S. Eliot: A Literary Life.* Basingstoke and London: Macmillan Press Ltd., 1991.

Williamson, G. *A Reader's Guide to T. S. Eliot.* London: Thames and Hudson, 1974.

Epiphany

In his youth, **James Joyce** wrote epiphanies, similar to prose poems, as an artistic exercise. He took the term from the Bible, where it refers to a divine revelation: the appearance of Jesus to the Magi or the manifestation of an angel. For Joyce, however, an epiphany was the "revelation of the whatness of the thing," the point at which "the soul of the commonest object . . . seems to us radiant." He felt there was an obligation on the artist to discover a spiritual truth "in the vulgarity of speech or of gesture or in a memorable phase of the mind itself" (Joyce 188). This is the description Joyce gives in **Stephen Hero,** but cut from its reworked version as *A Portrait of the Artist as a Young Man.* However, each of the chapters of *A Portrait,* which is in many ways a search for identity, ends with an epiphany, as Stephen sees in himself aspects of love, religion, art, or understanding. Here, each epiphany is a synthesis of triumph which the next chapter destroys. In some ways, Joyce's "epiphany" is a similar concept to **Woolf**'s idea of "The Moment [of Being]" (as in *Mrs. Dalloway*), but Joyce's interest is more in the spiritual and Woolf's in the physical.

Peter Childs

Selected Bibliography

Ellmann, Richard. *James Joyce.* Oxford: Oxford University Press, 1959.

Joyce, James. *Stephen Hero.* London: Jonathan Cape, 1944.

Evans, (David) Caradoc (1878–1945)

Short-story writer, novelist, and playwright.

He was brought up in poverty in the Cardiganshire village of Rhydlewis which, in distorted and fictionalized form, provided the setting for his first, notorious collection of short stories, *My People* (1915). Evans developed a strong sense of resentment against Welsh rural society, in which he felt his widowed mother and he had been persecuted and discriminated against by richer relatives, by the Chapel, and by the education system. Having failed to gain a place as a pupil-teacher in Rhydlewis school, Evans spent an unhappy period as a draper's assistant in Carmarthen, Cardiff, and finally London. Having arrived in the capital, he attended evening classes to gain command of English, his second language. Finally managing to free himself from the drapery trade, he established himself as a popular journalist and editor in London and then began publishing his short stories which purported to be accurate depictions of Welsh rural life.

What is most remarkable about Caradoc Evans and what distinguishes him as a modernist writer is his peculiar literary style. He employs a language which is bizarre in its strange combination of Biblical cadence and music hall vernacular, with a strong influence from the Welsh language which was his mother tongue. Similar to **Joyce**'s *Dubliners,* a contemporary work, Evans's *My People* displayed strong vestiges of **naturalism** in its willfully unpleasant depiction of peasant life but at the same time showed the modernist mixing of modes and the linguistic experimentalism which was also characteristic of Joyce. Evans excelled at Swiftian satire which immediately offended and outraged his compatriots, who soon came to regard him as a traitor to **Wales,** to the Welsh language, and, above all, to the Welsh nonconformist chapel tradition which he mercilessly lampooned.

Evans relishes the depiction of extremes: grotesque ugliness, physical decay, domestic abuse, incest, exploitation, and, above all, nauseating hypocrisy. There is a Gothic quality to his stories which is not dissimilar to the early prose tales of **Dylan Thomas** or Glyn Jones. *Capel Sion* (1916) continues in exactly the same vein of vicious and outrageously humorous satire as *My People,* focusing on the same targets in rural Welsh society, namely the nonconformist chapel, its ministers and deacons, immoral and cultureless farmers, and physically repulsive, browbeaten women. Although it is difficult to empathize with any of Evans's repellent characters, it is certainly true that he exposed the tyrannically patriarchal nature of Welsh nonconformist society, signaling continually the oppression of women within the system; for this reason, he has been regarded by some as a proto-feminist writer.

My Neighbours (1919) retains the same targets as his earlier stories but broadens its scope to include the shifty materialism of the London Welsh. *Taffy* (1923) is a play with similar themes, while *Nothing to Pay* (1930) explores Evans's characteristic obsessions in the form of a lurid and unforgettable novel, drawing upon his unhappy experiences as a draper's assistant. He went a little too far in his 1933 novel, *Wasps,* which was withdrawn because of its libelous portrayal of Evans's fellow-novelist, Edith Nepean, a woman who had dedicated her first distinctly unmodernist romance, *Gwyneth of the Welsh Hills,* to him when it appeared in 1917.

His later stories do move away both in style and mood from his early work, becoming a good deal mellower and increasingly abandoning the naturalistic mode in favor of the symbolic and allegorical. The stories in the volumes *Pilgrims in a Foreign Land* (1942) and the posthumous *The Earth Gives All and Takes All* (1946) reflect these changes. By the 1940s Evans had moved back to live in rural West Wales with his second wife, the popular novelist known as Oliver Sandys. The embittered exile returned to Wales in later life, then, and seems to have been somewhat reconciled to his native land, though he was said to have cherished his title as "the best hated man in Wales."

Evans's influence on other Anglo-Welsh writers was an important one. Arguably, he established a tradition of the defamiliarization and distortion of English as a literary language, a tradition which later embraced the work of otherwise dissimilar Anglo-Welsh modernist writers, such as Glyn Jones, Rhys Davies, and Dylan Thomas.

Katie Gramich

Selected Bibliography
Barnie, John. "Caradoc Evans: The Impious Artist." *Planet* 53 (Oct/Nov, 1985): 64–9.
Harris, John. "The Devil in Eden: Caradoc Evans and his Wales." *The New Welsh Review* 19 (Winter, 1992–3): 10–18.
Jones, Glyn. *The Dragon Has Two Tongues.* London: Dent, 1968.
Jones, Gwyn. "A Mighty Man in Sion: Caradoc Evans 1878–1945." In *Background to Dylan Thomas and Other Explorations* (1992)
Rees, W. J. "Inequalities: Caradoc Evans and D. J. Williams." *Planet* 81 (June/July, 1990): 69–80.
Weingärtner, Regina. "The Fight Against Sentimentalism: A Comparison of Caradoc Evans and George Douglas Brown." *Planet* 75 (June/July, 1989): 86–92.
Williams, Trevor L. *Caradoc Evans.* Cardiff: University of Wales Press, 1970.

Expressionism

Expressionism (1905–20) is associated with two pre-**World War I** groups, *Die Brücke* in Dresden (1905–10) and Berlin (1910–13) and *Der Blaue Reiter* in Munich (1908–14). Expressionism was an attitude of revolt with a desire to externalize inner experience, rather than a movement. Its precursors include tribal art, medieval woodcuts, Dürer's engravings, van Gogh, and the Norwegian artist Edvard Munch (1863–1944).

Ernst Ludwig Kirchner (1880–1938), in his manifesto for *Die Brücke* ("The Bridge"), proclaimed: "Whoever renders directly and sincerely what impels him to create belongs with us" (see Dube 11). Fellow members of *Die Brücke* were Erich Heckel (1883–1970), Karl Schmidt-Rottluff (1884–1976), Emil Nolde (1867–1956), Otto Mueller (1874–1930), and Max Pechstein (1881–1955). *Der Blaue Reiter* ("The Blue Rider") grew from the association of Russian expatriates Wassily Kandinsky (1866–1944) and Alexey von Jawlensky (1864–1941) in Munich; Kandinsky and Gabriele Munter (1877–1962) painted in Murnau, before Franz Marc (1880–1916), August Macke (1887–1914), Heinrich Campendonk (1889–1951), and Lyonel Feininger (1871–1956) joined the group; Swiss artist Paul Klee (1879–1940) was independently associated. Northern expressionism is characterized by force, angularity, distortion, and raw expressiveness, Southern by lyricism, plasticity, harmony, and abstraction. Key texts are Wilhelm Worringer's *Abstraction and Empathy* (1908), Kandinsky's *Concerning the Spiritual in Art* (1911), and Kandinsky's and Marc's *The "Blaue Reiter" Almanac* (1912). Key concepts include *Aufbruch* (breaking away from one pattern of existence to embrace another), *Vergeistigung* (spiritualization), *Kunstwollen* (artistic drive), and *innere Notwendigkeit* (inner necessity).

The Vienna Secession was the background of Austrian expressionists, Oskar Kokoschka (1886–1980) and Egon Schiele (1890–1918). Kokoschka was associated with Herwarth Walden's *Der Sturm* in Berlin from 1910, wrote plays on the battle of the sexes like *Mörder Hoffnung der Frauen* (1908), and was wounded on the Eastern front in 1916; his psychological portraits aim to reveal the sitter's inner life, often focusing on the hands. Schiele, influenced by Gustav Klimt and Jugendstil ("Youth Style" or Art Nouveau), painted agonized and erotic nudes and self-portraits. Ludwig Meidner (1884–1966), a member of *Die Pathetiker,* painted "Apocalyptic Landscapes" (1912–13). *Die Brücke* disbanded in 1913 when Kirchner attempted to define their aims; Macke and Marc were killed in World War I and Kirchner, after suffering a breakdown in the army, sought refuge in the Swiss Alps. The original impulse of expressionism did not survive the horrors of war and postwar social corruption; it was succeeded by *Neue Sachlichkeit* (New Objectivity), associated with the grotesque satire of Otto Dix (1891–1969) and Georg Grosz (1893–1959) and (marginally) with the nightmare realism, crossed with **myth,** of Max Beckmann (1884–1950).

Die Brücke projected a creative urge into the motif, with expressive distortion; following van Gogh and the Fauves, they explored the powers of color, laid on in thick impasto or broad flat areas. Nolde and Kirchner were inspired by the ecstatic rhythms of modern **dance** (Mary Wigman, Loïe Fuller) to heighten color contrasts and exaggerate gesture: Nolde attacked the canvas with a rapturous excitement that matched the waves of force in his *Candle Dancers* (1912). The desire to find a form-language to express inner states led to "entanglement of planes," "flames," "waves," "crystallizations," or "nervous vibrations" (Hadermann 131). Opposites collide with jarring force, as expressionists strive "to mate the abstract with the concrete, soul with body, and spirit with matter" (Weisstein, "Expressionism" 38).

The expressionists took what **D. H. Lawrence** calls a "curve of return" to the primordial, exemplified by motifs such as nudes in sunlight, gypsy lovers (Mueller), or tribal masks. Nolde, who visited the

South Seas in 1914, looked for the "pristine unspoiledness of nature" and felt an "intense, often grotesque expression of strength and life" in tribal art (see Vogt 58). Just as Franz Marc longed to break through the outer husk and grasp an inner core of reality or young artists like Wilhelm Morgner (1891–1917) "[strove] to break through the barriers to the 'universe of the inner man'" (see Vogt 116), so Lawrence strove "to break a way through the walls of the prison" in order to express "the profoundest experiences in the self" (*Women in Love* [1920; Cambridge UP, 1987]: 186, 485). Expressionists wanted to recover a pristine source of human experience, a wellspring of feeling too often repressed or corrupted by society. They sought to recuperate spontaneous expression from primitive man and, at the same time, championed progressive and humanitarian action intended to clear a way to the future.

Die Brücke's **primitivism** drew inspiration from African and Oceanic art and found its sharpest expression in the woodcut. With radical simplifications of line and stark contrasts of black and white, woodcuts reveal the profile of an emotion. Carving into the resistant substance of the woodblock, the artist exposes his original impulse to view, while using the most economic of plastic means intensifies expression. The prints of Munch, Kirchner, Heckel, and Schmidt-Rottluff generally surpass their paintings in expressive power, being marked by force, angularity, and boldness of line; their sensory impact clarifies a basic concept, "mak[ing] the invisible visible" (Klee). Impetuous execution and strength of statement make the woodcut "a miniature sculpture," in which the "fluid of existence" coagulates "into hard stagnant masses" (**Wyndham Lewis;** see Weisstein, "Expressionism" 38). Actual expressionist sculpture by Ernst Barlach (1870–1938) and Käthe Kollwitz (1867–1945) displays intensity in the modeling of mass and monumentalizes emotions such as rage or grief in stark postures or gestures.

The expressionist artist inscribes the unconscious symbolism of his spirit in the artwork. Expressionists were driven to self-exploration and sought emotional truth: "I explore within myself," Franz Marc declares, "and seek what it is that lives in me that can embody the rhythm of my blood" (see Vogt 92). Lawrence expresses a similar credo in his "Foreword to *Women in Love*" (1920): "The creative, spontaneous soul sends forth its promptings of desire and aspiration in us. . . . Man struggles with his unborn needs and fulfilment. . . . *It is the passionate struggle into conscious being*" (Cambridge UP, 1987: 485–86). Expressionism does not aim to reproduce surfaces, but to lay bare "the deep passional soul" (Lawrence). Munch declared that he was interested only in "live human beings, breathing, feeling, suffering and loving" (see Hadermann 114).

Die Brücke, who inherited their "fury for color" from the Fauves, undertook "[a] return to the primitive, shattering of form, intoxication with color"; they "[broke] down the subject by means of activized color, by brushwork at fever pitch, and by a dramatic conception" (Vogt 62, 64). In their early canvases, color virtually swamps form; Schmidt-Rottluff, for instance, was content with "monumental and unbroken color sonorities" (Vogt 68). In Nolde's paintings, "[all] color values were intensified to utmost brilliance and urgent expressive power" (Vogt 56), the only formal principle being contrast. As for *Der Blaue Reiter,* Kandinsky and Jawlensky first aimed at color harmonies derived from Russian folk-art; their emblematic color then became more purely expressive. Klee, visiting Tunis in 1914, exulted: "I and color are one, I am a painter" (see Vogt 106). Jawlensky experienced a similar ecstasy: "Apples, trees, human faces are for me no more than references to . . . the life of colour" (see Dube 46). Expressing feeling through colors, the painters "heightened the emotional potential or the symbolic value of these colors" (Hadermann 132), as Kokoschka does with the muted blues and mauves of *The Bride of the Wind* (1914), which celebrates his love for Alma Mahler.

Spatial distortion is characteristic of Northern expressionism. Kasimir Edschmid writes: "The space of the expressionist artist, then, becomes vision. He does not see, he looks. He does not describe, he experiences. He does not reproduce, he forms" (see Furness 36). Kirchner's *Red Tower in Halle* (1915) combines internal and external viewpoints, upsetting perspective and proportion (see Vogt 74–75). The high angle of vision discloses a nightmarish space, with planes tilted towards the foreground. The dizzying effect is reinforced by color contrasts of warm reds and cold blues, symbolizing the viewer's tension. As Hadermann notes, "[the] expressionist space, scarred with vibrations, trepidations, spasms, or a grand lyric breath, is that of the encounter of the total self with the entire world" (134). Kirchner expresses *angst* through the sheer angularity of his forms, as in his pictures of Berlin streetwalkers (1912–13). He studied motion, which gave him "[a] heightened sense of life": "A body in motion shows me many distinct features, and these fuse together in my mind into a total form, the inner image" (Kirchner; see Dube 76).

After the first outburst of spontaneity, expressionists, especially *Der Blaue Reiter,* sought life in form as well as color. For Macke, "[to] understand the language of forms means: to be closer to the secret, to live" ("Masks" 85). Marc's "animalization of art" involved "a combination of animal and landscape forms so closely and organically knit together as to set up a cosmic rhythm governed by the pure expressive

power of color" (Dube 52). Searching for forms to express a primal unity, Marc gravitated towards abstraction: his *Foxes* (1913) is a vivid hieroglyph of the animals' essence. As he "intensif[ied] [his] ability to sense the organic rhythm that beats in all things" (see Dube 50), his "pantheistic sympathy" became theriomorphic. In Marc's more abstract *Tyrol* (1914), the "color radiation" of densely packed crystalline forms symbolizes "[the] world as dynamic movement" (Vogt 94). Rebridging the gap between self and cosmos, expressionists reinvented natural forms: this urge to give shape to inner feelings, that Macke saw in the art of children and "savages," is a key to their art.

Die Brücke aimed at emotional intensification; *Der Blaue Reiter* at expressive form—which, for Kandinsky, must be derived from "*inner need*" (26). Attempting to balance overall organization of picture space with configuration of separate forms, Kandinsky arrived at total abstraction. Marc's tightly interlocking designs and Feininger's crystalline structures show the impact of **cubism** and **futurism** on expressionism; Heckel also adapted cubism in the transparent planes and facets of *The Glassy Day* (1913). Feininger's inner perspective drew on "concentration to the absolute limit of [his] capacity to see," while Nolde, seeking "absolute primeval originality" (see Vogt 102, 60), *experienced* the seas or sunsets he painted, in all their splendor. Expressionist mysticism took various forms, ranging from the spiritual vibration of pure color, through lyrical pantheism, to transcendent geometry and abstraction.

The expressionist emphasis on essence and archetype was transferred from painting to the other arts. Kokoschka's and Barlach's plays, Kandinsky's writing, and Klee's poetry are the work of "doubly gifted" artists. According to Weisstein, literary and visual expressionism share the following characteristics: (i) "anti-mimetic[ism]"; (ii) making the invisible visible; (iii) expressing "soul states"; (iv) extremism; (v) being "content-oriented"; (vi) springing from "inner need"; (vii) espousing humanism; (viii) relating to a "collective or metaphysical sphere"; (ix) aiming at essences; (x) combining subjective and objective; (xi) manifesting primitivism and impersonality ("Introduction" 23–25). The expressionist poetry of **Georg Trakl, Georg Heym,** Ernst Stadler, August Stramm, **Else Lasker-Schüler, Gottfried Benn,** and **Franz Werfel** is marked by rapturous or staccato imagery. Expressionist theater strips characters of personality to disclose the core, type, or archetype: its themes include revolt, oppression, and conflict between fathers and sons. Major dramatists are Georg Kaiser, **Ernst Toller,** and Carl Steinheim. Expressionist elements are also found in plays of **Frank Wedekind,** August Strindberg, **Eugene O'Neill,** and Tennessee Williams, and in novels such as Lawrence's *Women in Love* (1920), **Virginia Woolf**'s *The Waves* (1931), and **James Joyce**'s *Finnegans Wake* (1939).

Jack Stewart

Selected Bibliography

Buchheim, Lothar-Günther. *The Graphic Art of German Expressionism.* New York: Universe, 1960.

Dube, Wolf-Dieter. *Expressionists and Expressionism.* Trans. James Emmons. Geneva: Skira, 1983.

Elger, Dietmar. *Expressionism: A Revolution in German Art.* Trans. Hugh Beyer. Cologne: Benedikt, 1994.

Expressionism: A German Intuition 1905–1920. New York: Guggenheim Foundation, 1980.

Furness, R. S. *Expressionism.* London: Methuen, 1973.

Grohmann, Will. *Ernst Ludwig Kirchner.* Trans. Ilse Falk. New York: Arts, 1961.

Hadermann, Paul. "Expressionist Literature and Painting." Weisstein 111–39.

Haftmann, Werner. *Emil Nolde.* Trans. Norbert Guterman. New York: Abrams, n.d.

Kandinsky, Wassily. *Concerning the Spiritual in Art.* Trans. M. T. H. Sadler. New York: Dover, 1977.

——— and Franz Marc, ed. *The "Blaue Reiter" Almanac.* The Documents of 20th-Century Art. Ed. Klaus Lankheit. New York: Viking, 1974.

Selz, Peter. *German Expressionist Painting.* Berkeley: U of California P, 1974.

Sokel, Walter H. *The Writer in Extremis: Expressionism in Twentieth-Century German Literature.* New York: McGraw-Hill, 1964.

Stewart, Jack. "Expressionism in *Women in Love*." *The Vital Art of D. H. Lawrence: Vision and Expression.* Carbondale: Southern Illinois UP, 1999. 73–93. Illustrated.

Vogt, Paul. *Expressionism: German Painting 1905–1920.* Trans. Antony Vivis and Robert Erich Wolf. New York: Abrams, 1980.

Weisstein, Ulrich, ed. *Expressionism as an International Literary Phenomenon.* Paris: Didier, 1973.

———. "Introduction." Weisstein 15–28.

———. "Expressionism: Style or Weltanschauung?" Weisstein 29–44.

Worringer, Wilhelm. *Abstraction and Empathy: A Contribution to the Psychology of Style.* 1908. Trans. Michael Bullock. London: Routledge, 1953.

Expressionism, German Literary

The term **expressionism** has been used in various ways, in a technical sense of the German romantic tradition confronting European modernist trends, or in a historical sense of communities of artists. It does not form a movement, since the expressionists lacked a common goal, being separate from each other both geographically and over time, from Berlin to Vienna, and from 1910 to the 1930s. The only means of unity were provided by the publications *Die Aktion* (1911–1932), edited by Hans Pfempfert, and *Der Sturm* (1911–1932), edited by Herwarth Walden until 1919 (he also organized the *Sturm-Galerie, Sturm-Verlag, Sturmbühne,* and *Sturmschulen*). As a consequence of its diffuse history, literary expressionism also lacks central defining traits. One of its most important tendencies, though, is its confrontation of opposing romantic and naturalist, subjective and objective, realist and idealist perspectives, as polarities which are irreconcilable, yet whose tension generates an intense creative vitality.

Expressionism emerged from the nineteenth century tradition of romantic, sentimental nature poetry. **Georg Heym** and **Georg Trakl,** and even **Kurt Schwitters,** first wrote poetry in this style, expressing their subjective feelings in relation to love and nature. Yet this style had become inadequate after the rapid industrialization and urbanization since **Germany**'s unification in 1871. Writers were attracted to the dynamism of the city, yet had become alienated from nature, and from their own subjectivity which had become reified and fragmented. The driving force behind much of expressionist poetry is the attempt to regain an organic experience of a dislocated reality.

The philosopher Friedrich Nietzsche and art historian Wilhelm Worringer suggested possibilities of a new aesthetic to the expressionists. Nietzsche rejected late romanticism in the form of Arthur Schopenhauer's and Richard Wagner's nihilism; his vision of Greek tragedy as the Dionysian expression of instincts through **music** and **dance,** countered by Apollonian representation, inspired expressionists with a starkly dualistic vision of their art. This dualism was given further elaboration by Worringer's book *Abstraktion und Einfühlung* (1906, *Abstraction and Empathy*), which contrasted the Greeks' expression of harmony within reality in their plastic arts (Nietzsche's Apollonian), with the primitive individual's need to protect himself from a hostile reality through abstract markings on his body; the expressionists attempted to protect themselves from their own hostile environment, the city, through their art, so that they could ultimately regain a direct experience of it.

Heym and Trakl, who were unaware of each other, nevertheless follow parallel developments during early expressionism. Transplanting nature poetry into the city,

their work of 1910 to 1912 consists of impressions of urban features whose relationship to each other rests on the formal unity of each poem, which holds them together as a simultaneous experience in the act of reading. To achieve direct experience of this subject, metaphysical imagery is replaced by vivid and tactile description; for example, the word "darkness," with its connotations of unconsciousness and death, is replaced with "black," alongside other vivid colors which resemble the palette of the expressionist painter. Instead of merely connoting emotions, these colors have a physical significance, including violence, terror and sexual desire. **Gottfried Benn**'s poetry from the same period is related to this trend; through its vivid and grotesque descriptions of dead bodies it aims to thrust onto the reader an understanding of the processes of death—and ultimately of life as well.

This earliest phase of expressionism soon gave way to a style which reintegrated spiritual concerns into its visceral style. Heym died too young to enter this phase although his elegies look towards it. Trakl mastered it in the last three years of his life, creating a poetry which attempted to envisage a spiritual redemption for a shattered physical reality. **Franz Werfel**'s optimistic poetry describes epiphanic moments of understanding between individuals who are remote from each other in their physical circumstances. **Else Lasker-Schüler** used the extravagance of her imagery to transcend her sense of isolation from other women and from the rest of her Jewish race.

The process of life and death became a central theme to expressionist poets, as they envisaged the regeneration of a decadent present through its future apocalyptic destruction and rebirth. **World War One** was momentarily anticipated as this apocalypse, but instead its destruction of individuals through machines signified the absolute alienation of modern man from nature, and the antithesis of the expressionist ethos. Trakl was destroyed by his experiences in the war, and Werfel's optimism collapsed. Yet **Ernst Toller** attempted to justify the necessity of violence for a revolution to transform society; in his plays his realistic scenes are disrupted by "dream" scenes which envisage possible alternatives to them.

Toller's plays belong to the last phase of expressionism, from the end of the war to the rise of Nazism. This turned away from the personal, introspective path of nature, towards the wider political effort of overcoming the processes of reification in society. Although not aligned to any political party, Kurt Schwitters attempted to envisage a new wholeness in social experience after the war by incorporating fragments of everyday discourse into expressionist poetry. The aggression of **Brecht**'s early plays and poetry exposed the callousness of society. **Alfred Döblin**'s novels of the thirties explore the individual's personal experience of the city and his possible redemption in it.

Yet this period saw the decline of expressionism, since in many eyes it was regarded as an essentially anti-political movement, whose apocalyptic naïveté had fueled the war hysteria. The dadaists, towards the end of the war, deflated emotional pretensions, believing only in direct political action. New Objectivity of the twenties favored a realistic depiction of social experience, although this limited its potentiality for changing society. Perhaps, though, the historical importance of expressionism was confirmed by Hitler when he denounced it as "degenerate art" in the thirties.

Carl Krockel

Selected Bibliography

Allen, Roy F. *Literary Life in German Expressionism and the Berlin Circles.* Göppingen: Kümmerle Verlag, 1974.

Hill, Claude, and Ralph Ley, eds. *The Drama of German Expressionism.* Chapel Hill: University of North Carolina Press, 1960.

Pascal, Roy. *From Naturalism to Expressionism: German Literature and Society 1880–1918.* London: Weidenfeld and Nicolson, 1973.

Taylor, Seth. *Left-Wing Nietzscheans: The Politics of German Expressionism.* Berlin: Walter de Gruyter, 1990.

Weisstein, Ulrich, ed. *Expressionism as an International Literary Phenomenon.* Paris: Libraire Marcel Didier; Budapest: Akadémiai Kiadó, 1973.

F

Faulkner, William (1897–1962)

William Faulkner is best known as a novelist who exposes the U.S. South's racial and gendered conflicts within a fictional framework which simultaneously embodies strong links with international modernism. In many of his works Faulkner makes use of a variety of literary modernist techniques. The **formal experimentation** within Faulkner's novels can also be tied in with his interest in modernist art and **cinema.** Also, the radical aesthetic innovations which characterize Faulkner's own works have become a potent influence upon the international literary and cultural scene, particularly in Latin America.

Faulkner was born at a crucial point within U.S. history. The legacy of the defeat of the South in the Civil War was still recent enough to be strongly ingrained within the consciousness of many Southerners. The ongoing racial divisions between blacks and whites were strongly apparent within the Mississippi in which Faulkner grew up, thereby further contributing towards the sense of a region divided both against the North and within itself. At the same time, the early decades of the twentieth century witnessed a period of economic and social modernization which was also affected by the advent of **World War I.** It is in this turbulent context that Faulkner developed as a modernist writer, exploring the traumas experienced by his community within narrative forms which redefine traditional modes of perceiving reality.

Faulkner's early influences included novelists such as Balzac, Dickens, and French symbolist poetry. The assimilation of a wide range of writers whose work derived from diverse cultures laid important groundwork for Faulkner. His first significant published work was *The Marble Faun* (1924), a long poem written in octosyllabic couplets which owes much to the influence of the French poet Verlaine and also reveals echoes of Keats' *Ode on a Grecian Urn.* The poem focuses upon a marble faun who realizes that his status as an object of art ensures his immortality. However, this self-conscious knowledge of static artistic form is also a cause of pain, because it means that he can never experience the transitory joys and sorrows which constitute man's brief existence. Despite the derivative nature of the poem, there are already signs of tension here between a romantic and a modernist aesthetic in Faulkner's implicit critique of the very pastoral form he employs.

A vital influence on Faulkner's development as a modernist came when he traveled to Europe in 1925 and encountered the avant-garde artistic milieu of Paris (see **France**). During his time there, Faulkner was particularly struck by the new modes of visual representation he saw at the various art galleries he visited, and one might trace some of his later fictional techniques back to these experiences—his subtle use of color back to the impressionists, for example, and his distinctive swirling imagery back to Cézanne.

Faulkner's first novel, *Soldier's Pay* (1926), focuses on the postwar disillusionment experienced by Donald Mahon, a soldier who returns from active service to live an impaired physical and mental life. Faulkner's preoccupation with the chaos of a fragmented world and its psychological impact upon the individual is typically modernist. Yet, in many ways the novel occupies a transitional space between nineteenth-century **realism** and twentieth-century modernism. There is a clear sense of linearity in the plot development and characterization, but at the same time there are the surreal dream sequences and strikingly unconventional image patterns which characterize much of Faulkner's later work.

The Sound and the Fury (1929) was the first of Faulkner's works to reveal a decisive break with realist narrative forms in favor of a completely new approach. The story focuses on three brothers, Quentin, Jason, and Benjy, who all share the same incestuous obsession with their sister, Caddy, and with the decline of the old aristocratic South. The narrative is presented through four character monologues in a manner strongly resembling that of **James Joyce.** The style of each monologue closely mirrors the typical thought processes and voice style of the particular character in question and Faulkner here clearly adopts the modernist move away from omniscient narration and towards subjective viewpoints. The section attributed to Benjy, the mentally retarded brother, for example, uses short sentences and a very limited range of vocabulary, whereas Quentin, the suicidal intellectual, is given a much more complex linguistic style.

Faulkner followed up the success of *The Sound and the Fury* with *As I Lay Dy-*

ing (1930), another example of high modernist art. The novel centers on Addie Bundren, the dead mother, whose dying wish was that her coffin should be carried to Jefferson by her family and buried there. Accordingly, her family undertake a perilous journey, passing through fire, flood, and physical injury, until they finally reach their destination. Like *The Sound and the Fury,* the novel is divided into separate monologues, but in this case there are 59 rather than 4. Some of the visual descriptions within *As I Lay Dying* can be likened to developments within cubist painting, with three-dimensional objects often represented in two-dimensional form. The structure of the journey itself has strong mythic overtones and this attempt by Faulkner to fuse chaotic narrative form with the mythic pattern of the quest can be likened to other canonical modernist works such as **T. S. Eliot's** *The Wasteland.*

The "sensational" aspects of Faulkner's next novel, *Sanctuary* (1931), caused an adverse reaction amongst some critics when it was first published, and in many ways this novel represented a complete contrast to the highly experimental novels that had preceded it. Nevertheless, *Sanctuary* also exposes a different facet of Faulkner's modernist interests. The plot focuses on Temple Drake, a well-off white girl who becomes drawn into a Memphis underworld of violence and prostitution. Much of the shocked critical reaction to the novel was caused by the inclusion of a scene in which Temple is raped with a corn cob, but, arguably, this is an example of Faulkner's concern to strip off the respectable veneer of a certain stratum of middle class society and expose disturbing areas of experience in ways which would defamiliarize the reader's perceptions. Although the overall form of *Sanctuary* may not be as innovative as *The Sound and the Fury* or *As I Lay Dying,* some of its visual descriptions are still strikingly expressionistic.

Light in August (1932) tackles the subject of racial prejudice in the South. The central character, Joe Christmas, is of mixed race, and he has had an unhappy childhood, first in an orphanage and then in an extremely strict religious household. In later life he kills his ex-lover and is finally hounded to a violent death. Juxtaposed against this story is the ongoing journey of Lena Grove, a pregnant woman who sets off in search of the lover who has deserted her. Faulkner here evokes an acute sense of the injustices done to the individual within a specific social context, and within a larger framework of deeply resonant religious imagery—though in typically modernist fashion, Faulkner evokes Biblical parallels only to invert them. For example, Joe Christmas's lynching symbolizes a kind of crucifixion; but there is no sense in which his death represents a divine sacrifice or renewal for the community, as he himself is guilty of the crime that he commits, and the men who kill him have fixed racist views.

Faulkner's next novel, *Absalom, Absalom!* (1936) shares some thematic parallels with his preceding one. The story is set against the background of the Civil War, and it traces the life of Thomas Sutpen, a character who, despite humble origins, builds up a powerful estate. Sutpen abandons his first wife in Haiti, and she subsequently gives birth to a son, Charles Bon, who later reappears to haunt Sutpen. Faulkner's modernist interest in exploring extreme states of mind and sexual taboos is strongly in evidence here in the exploration of the South's concern with miscegenation, which Faulkner exposes as a locus of paradoxical desire and repulsion. *Absalom, Absalom!* is again narrated from different viewpoints, with rapid shifts backwards and forwards in time, and the instability of spatial form is interestingly represented by the destruction of the house which Sutpen builds.

The Wild Palms (1939) deals more directly with romantic love than any of Faulkner's previous novels, although the form and content of the novel is no less modernist in its orientation. Faulkner dramatizes two juxtaposed stories. One concentrates on a convict and explores the way popular literature has given him romantic notions of the life of a train robber. The other focuses on Harry and Charlotte, a couple who flee the constrictions of modern civilization in search of an ideal romantic love. Faulkner's allusion to and denigration of other forms of pulp fiction displays his self-reflexivity as a modernist artist, and shows him self-consciously interrogating the craft of fiction by challenging the parameters of particular genres.

The novel *Intruder in the Dust* (1948) marks the end of Faulkner's great period as a modernist writer. Although he continued writing into the next decade, subsequent works such as *A Fable* (1954) move away from the typical concerns of modernism in both form and content. *Intruder in the Dust,* however, deals with Lucas Beauchamp, a black man accused of murder, and again reveals Faulkner's interest in taking an established genre—here, the detective story—and using it as a vehicle to expose deeply paradoxical attitudes towards issues such as race. Faulkner is not concerned to follow "the rules of the game" of the detective novel, but rather to violate them, systematically challenging the familiar generic distinctions between the roles of villain, victim, and detective.

Faulkner's most highly experimental group of short stories is *Go Down, Moses* (1942), an interlinked collection centering on the McCaslin family. The most famous of the stories in this group is "The Bear," which tells of the attempt to shoot the elusive bear called Old Ben. Faulkner here explores how new technological developments, symbolized by the railway, threaten to destroy ancient rural ways of life such as those associated with the forest; but, as with *Absalom, Absalom!,* he is also deeply critical of the legacy of the white slaveholding society which, unable to emancipate itself from the specter of miscegenation, resists social change.

Another aspect to Faulkner's relationship with modernism is his interest in cinema. In 1933, Faulkner worked at MGM on a **film** entitled *Today We Live,* based on his short story "Turn About." He also collaborated with Howard Hawks at 20th Century Fox from 1935–1936 on another film called *A Road to Glory.* The screenplay for this film was written at the same time as *Absalom, Absalom!* and *Today We Live* contains resonances of *The Sound and the Fury.* The films concentrate upon a blind male protagonist who undertakes a suicidal journey in the pursuit of love. Although the actual form of these films was not radically avant-garde in the manner of Faulkner's novels, the themes of alienation of the individual, self-destruction, and existential angst are typical modernist tropes which dominate both the fiction and the films. Faulkner's relationship with Hollywood is most famous for the work he produced with Warner Brothers, from 1942–1945. He made a considerable impact on the genre of film noir through his collaborations on *The Big Sleep* and *To Have and Have Not.* Although much of his most experimental writing did not materialize on to screen, the fact that Faulkner was exposed to the process of film making for extended periods gave him opportunities to observe alternative ways of rendering visual effects. The rapid shifts from scene to scene which are common within his novels, for example, have affinities with film montage techniques.

Faulkner's legacy as a modernist writer has had a profound impact upon the broader international scene, and has influenced the development of modernism within countries outside the United States. The French were the first to exhibit an interest in translating and publishing Faulkner's works in the 1930s and 1940s. Critics such as Maurice Edgar Coindreau played

an important role in providing a certain kind of critical reception of Faulkner which stressed the modernist aesthetic qualities of his work rather than his Southern regionalism. Faulkner was also appropriated into a tradition of French existentialism by writers such as Jean-Paul Sartre.

A subject of intense debate in recent Faulkner scholarship has also been his impact upon **Hispanic American** writing. Contemporary writers such as the Colombian Gabriel García Márquez, the Mexican Carlos Fuentes, and the Peruvian Mario Vargas Llosa, have readily admitted to having been impressed by Faulkner's work. The reason often cited for Faulkner's continuing appeal in Latin America partly derives from his modernist credentials. Latin American novelists were trying to break free of constraining indigenous and Spanish models, and Faulkner's innovations in form and technique breathed fresh life into stultifying literary traditions.

Faulkner first appeared on the Latin American scene in the 1930s, partly as a result of the influence of the French reception of Faulkner. Several articles by Coindreau were published and translated in the Argentine journal *Sur.* In the 1940s articles and translations of Faulkner's works also began to appear in the Uruguayan journal *Marcha,* which like *Sur,* was keen to assimilate new modernist writers and artists from the international scene. In the 1950s in Mexico Faulkner began to be translated and reviewed, although his impact here was not as great as in Uruguay or Argentina, part of the reason being Mexico's resistance to U.S. cultural influences, which were often inextricably linked with forms of imperialism.

The number of translations and reviews of Faulkner soared dramatically in the 1950s throughout much of Latin America. It was also during this period that Faulkner himself took several trips abroad as a kind of cultural ambassador for the

United States In 1954, he attended an international writers' conference in São Paulo, Brazil, and in 1961 he made an appearance in Venezuela. Both visits ensured his reputation as a modernist writer who was capable of injecting fresh impetus into the literary traditions of foreign nations, a process which is still continuing today.

Helen Oakley

Selected Bibliography

Blotner, Joseph. *Faulkner: A Biography.* London: Chatto and Windus, 1974.

Gray, Richard. *The Life of William Faulkner: A Critical Biography.* Oxford: Blackwells, 1996.

Harrington, Evans, and Abadie, Ann J., eds. *Faulkner, Modernism and Film: Faulkner and Yoknapatawpha, 1978.* Jackson: Mississippi UP, 1979.

Minter, David. *William Faulkner: His Life and Work.* Baltimore and London: Johns Hopkins UP, 1980.

Moreland, Richard C. *Faulkner and Modernism: Re-reading and Rewriting.* Wisconsin: Wisconsin UP, 1990.

Singal, Daniel J. *William Faulkner: the Making of a Modernist.* Chapel Hill and London: Carolina UP, 1997.

Feminism 1890–1940

The movement to extend the role of women in society that we now term *feminism* derived from the Enlightenment concept of natural rights, which produced various forms of egalitarian ideas in the French Revolution. During the nineteenth century British feminism gathered strength from Owenite socialism on the left. But it also benefited from the way evangelical women had entered the public sphere at a time of religious revivalism. Throwing themselves into voluntary social work as an extension of woman's conventional maternal role, women had become the backbone of numerous philanthropic causes. Feminists could therefore draw upon a wide spectrum of support in campaigns to reform the property and divorce laws; to crusade against state-regulated prostitution; to demand entry into higher education and the professions and even call for voting rights.

By the 1880s women's organizations had become an important element in the Labor movement. Working-class activists became particularly prominent in the Women's Cooperative Guild (founded in 1883), and went on to form the Women's Trade Union League, Women's Industrial Council, Women's Labour League and Fabian Women's Group. In the 1890s there was a massive surge in cross-class and cross-party feminist campaigns for full citizenship. By 1897 coordination of these organizations produced a federation, the National Union of Women's Suffrage Societies. The constitutionalists, under the leadership of Millicent Garrett Fawcett were termed "suffragists." More militant "suffragettes," willing to take direct action, looked to Emmeline Pankhurst, who in 1903 founded the Women's Social and Political Union in Manchester. Fiction at the end of the century became preoccupied with controversy over the "new woman" or "feminist" as she was beginning to be called (Caine 135–47). This younger generation of firebrands, it was feared, might reject marriage and motherhood altogether. Novels featuring **The New Woman** included Sarah Grand's *The Beth Book* (1897), George Gissing's *The Odd Women* (1893), Thomas Hardy's *Jude the Obscure* (1896), and Emma Brooke's *The Superfluous Woman.*

World War I brought a lessening of suffragist activism because some feminists divided their time with supporting the peace campaign, while many concentrated on working for the war effort. In recognition of female patriotic support, on February 30, 1918, British women over thirty with a property qualification were enfranchised. This partial success contributed to some lessening of urgency and the relative disunity over priorities which characterized the postwar women's movement. It faced an uphill task, for there was a strongly antifeminist backlash. Despite the 1919 Sex Disqualification Removal Act, a marriage bar was introduced in many professions to rid the workplace of the women who had replaced men during the war. Women were now expected to choose between a career and marriage. Demobilized soldiers resented the feminists' demands for the right to work and for equal pay, and the "surplus" of unmarried women was perceived as a burden. Sexologists like Havelock Ellis proclaimed what Queen Victoria had refused to believe—the existence of homosexuality in women—so single women were also suspected as possible "inverts."

Though some Western states pioneered equal suffrage, feminism had initially progressed more slowly in the United States than Britain, for the nineteenth-century domestic ideal of "the angel in the house" was even more highly idealized in the republic, and its labor movement weaker and less interested in women's rights. But American women were quicker in breaking into higher education, and had a higher profile leading consumers' leagues and temperance societies. By World War I, the American women's movement had become a dynamic broadly-based alliance addressing many issues as well as the emancipation of women. Suffragist militancy increased after correspondence and visits from the British feminists. This and the political clout of women's moral crusades eventually prevailed and American women achieved suffrage parity with men in 1920.

By the mid-1920s it was apparent that there was a clear divergence in the British women's movement between old equal rights feminism and new welfare feminism (Law 161). The former, led by Lady Rhondda (Margaret Haig), the novelist Winifred Holtby and the "Six Point Group," concentrated on political emancipation and entry to the professions. But the National

Union of Women's Suffrage Societies now changed its name to the National Union of Societies for Equal Citizenship and, led by Eleanor Rathbone, aimed for a broader appeal by focusing on women's particular needs in their domestic role. This could be criticized as endorsing conventional femininity. But many "new" feminists also wanted to improve the lives of working-class women. They campaigned for family allowances, birth control advice, and the raising of the age of consent. Achievements of the decade included the Equal Franchise Act (1928), the Matrimonial Causes Act (1923) which equalized divorce, and the Guardianship of Infants Act (1925) which allowed divorced women custody of their children.

The thirties would see a diminution of feminist political activity but the debates on different strategies and emphases within the movement produced a proliferation of theoretical publications from the mid-twenties on (Caine 209). These included Eleanor Rathbone's *The Disinherited Family* (1924), greeted by *Time and Tide* as "perhaps the most important feminist text since Mill's *Subjection of Women*"; "Ray" Strachey's "*The Cause*" (1928), a classic history of British feminism; Winifred Holtby's *Women in a Changing Civilisation* (1935); **Virginia Woolf**'s *A Room of One's Own* (1928) which many placed alongside Mary Wollstonecraft's *Vindication of the Rights of Woman* (1792) in importance to the movement; and Woolf's even more radical *Three Guineas* (1938).

Like most modernist writers, Woolf maintained a certain distance from political activism. She presented herself as giving an individual perspective in her journalism and in the lectures to women's groups and colleges in which she worked out the ideas later embodied in her feminist books. Nevertheless she was closely involved with the Women's Cooperative Guild, wrote for Lady Rhondda's *Time and*

Tide and moved among feminist circles: Pippa and Ray Strachey, and Margaret Llewellyn Davies were close friends. Woolf's texts were particularly important for the direction of late twentieth-century feminism in that they argue for "new" or "difference" feminism (a separate tradition of women's writing and aesthetics in *A Room of One's Own,* the identification of women with peace and men with war and fascism in *Three Guineas*) yet imbue this supposedly "softer" feminism with a radical edge. *A Room of One's Own* takes a materialist stance: arguing that economic equality is necessary to give women the ideological independence from men that would establish their own distinct literary tradition as a primary source of cultural authority. *Three Guineas* is a refusal of female patriotism in the face of impending war, in its angry indictment of the militarism and tendency towards fascism of patriarchy.

It is apparent from the above account that the "first wave" of feminism coincided with the rise of literary modernism. Indeed, a repudiation of the perceived effeminacy of Victorian sentimentalism and yet a revulsion against the empowered New Woman gave a distinctly masculinist character to modernism, which prized aesthetic innovation over accessibility and objective precision over sensibility. Unsurprisingly, the Anglo-American canon of high modernist writers which held sway for forty years was entirely male: **James Joyce, T. S. Eliot, Ezra Pound, D. H. Lawrence, W. B. Yeats, Joseph Conrad.** Avant-garde modernists, however, have been accused of elitism in their fetishization of Art and their withdrawal from political or social engagement. Misogyny, racism, and anti-Semitism may be found in many modernist texts, generated by fear of the social upheaval which followed the World War I: the triumph of the Bolsheviks in Russia, and the rise of democracy and feminism throughout Europe.

Reaction against the rise of feminism was a prime factor in the crisis of masculinity, coinciding as it did with the demise of the cult of martial heroism in the carnage of Flanders, the first mass war after industrialization. This shows itself in the depiction by male modernists of weak male protagonists at the mercy of complex external forces, ironized or ridiculed as incapable of the romantic heroism of the past (Joyce's Bloom in **Ulysses,** T. S. Eliot's J. Alfred Prufrock, Lawrence's Clifford Chatterley in *Lady Chatterley's Lover,* Chaplin's tramp, **Kafka**'s K, **Beckett**'s Hamm in *Endgame*). Sexually inadequate protagonists may be juxtaposed with sexually experienced women who are sometimes feminists (Molly Bloom in *Ulysses,* Clara and Mrs. Morel in Lawrence's *Sons and Lovers*). The feminine is thus ambivalently portrayed and Marianne DeKoven (25) has interpreted this as prompted by an unresolved contradiction between fear of and desire for empowered women.

Since the "second wave" of feminism began in the 1970s, feminist critics have recuperated many female modernist writers, crucial to the founding and development of the movement, but marginalized by the mid-twentieth-century New Critics who shared the masculinist tendency of the modernists. These include **H. D. (Hilda Doolittle), Gertrude Stein, Djuna Barnes, Marianne Moore, Dorothy Richardson, Katherine Mansfield,** Mina Loy, Kate Chopin, Amy Lowell, Nancy Cunard, Rose Macaulay, Charlotte Mew, May Sinclair, **Rebecca West, Jean Rhys,** Anaïs Nin, Stevie Smith, **Zora Neale Hurston,** and Willa Cather. Virginia Woolf, who had been the one exception of a female modernist allowed into the canon, had been patronized as lightweight and solely concerned with ahistorical subjectivity within the private world of memories and sensations. But late twentieth-century feminist critics revalued Woolf by contextualizing her work in the female literary tradition and by recognizing that not only her feminist polemics and journalism but also her fiction emanate from her intense engagement with the feminist movement. For Woolf's feminist politics may be apprehended not merely through her subject matter (sapphism, the woman artist, lives of women) but, most importantly, in her literary style itself. Her disruption of linear plotting, foregrounding of fictionality, and dispersal of the authority of the omniscient author into multiple points of view, her fragmentation of stable social identity, may all be seen as intimately connected with her desire to find a specifically feminine sentence and style. Contemporary feminist critics have found much in common between Woolf's subversive and parodic repudiation of the conventions of realism and the ideas of French feminists like Hélène Cixous and Julia Kristeva, in their association of the semiotic with the feminine in its disruption of the Symbolic in writing. Linear plotting, an omniscient author, traditional realist techniques and closure, on the other hand, have been seen as reflecting and therefore validating patriarchal law.

Gilbert and Gubar (*The Female Imagination* 2–3) have posited not only male and female modernisms but even masculinist and feminist modernisms. They suggest that many female-authored texts express exuberance at the breakdown of traditional structures rather than the anxiety and fear of male canonical authors. It may even be, they continue, that women writers broke with their nineteenth-century precursors precisely because they were inspired by the prospect that feminism offered release from confinement. While such a polemical argument forcefully expresses the revision of literary history that second wave feminism necessitates, its generalizing tendency has the disadvantage of eliding somewhat the important differences between female modernist writers. Hanscombe and Smyers

(and see also Benstock) provide a historicist and contextual, rather than thematic, approach to female modernists, uncovering networks of women writers and publishers, and exploring the way their texts were circulated and published. These women can be seen to have rejected patriarchal norms in their lives and their writing simultaneously.

The extent and importance of female modernist writing has now been firmly established—not just as a separate enclave but as central to the movement. Moreover, the rise and subsequent decline of the feminist movement between 1890 and 1940 can be seen as one of the most important catalysts for literary modernism, whether male or female authored. The questioning of conventional gender roles which ensued inspired frank literary explorations of diverse forms of sexuality. Disillusion with traditional categories of stable, fixed identity also generated artistic experimentation in representing subjectivity as fragmented and fluid. Revisioning the dynamics of gender offered new insights into the ideologies of war and imperialism. Feminist thought during the period also acted as an important critique of the modernist guru, **Sigmund Freud,** questioning the male-centered nature of the Oedipal family romance at the heart of **psychoanalysis.** The ongoing political agenda of feminism, even after suffrage had been achieved, continued to provoke ambivalent reactions to social change: both fear and exhilaration at the prospect of the dissolution of the primary patriarchal institutions of marriage and the family.

Caroline Franklin

Selected Bibliography

Benstock, Shari. *Women of the Left Bank: Paris, 1900–1940.* London: Virago, 1987.

Bolt, Christine. *The Women's Movements in the United States and Britain from the 1790s to the 1920s.* Amherst, MA: U of Massachusetts P, 1993.

Caine, Barbara. *English Feminism 1780–1980.* Oxford: Oxford UP, 1997.

DeKoven, Marianne. *Rich and Strange: Gender, History, Modernism.* Princeton, Princeton UP, 1991.

DuPlessis, Rachel Blau. *Writing Beyond the Ending: Narrative Strategies of Twentieth-Century Women Writers.* Bloomington: Indiana UP, 1985.

Elliott, Bridget and Wallace, Jo-Ann. *Women Artists and Writers: Modernist (Im)Positionings.* London and New York: Routledge, 1994.

Felski, Rita. *The Gender of Modernity.* Cambridge, MA: Harvard UP, 1996.

Friedman, Ellen and Fuchs, Miriam, eds. *Breaking the Sequence: Women's Experimental Fiction.* Princeton: Princeton UP, 1989.

Gambrell, Alice. *Women Intellectuals, Modernism, and Difference: Transatlantic Culture, 1919–1945.* Cambridge: Cambridge UP, 1997.

Gilbert, Sandra and Gubar, Susan. *No Man's Land: The Place of the Woman Writer in the Twentieth Century.* 3 vols. New Haven: Yale UP, 1988; 1989, 1994.

———. *The Female Imagination and the Modernist Aesthetic.* 1986.

Hanscombe, Gillian and Smyers, Virginia L. *Writing for their Lives: The Modernist Women 1910–1940.* London: The Women's Press, 1987.

Harrison, Brian. *Prudent Revolutionaries: Portraits of British Feminists between the Wars.* Oxford: Oxford UP, 1987.

Law, Cheryl. *Suffrage and Power: The Woman's Movement 1918–1928.* London and New York: I. B. Tauris, 1997.

Scott, Bonnie K. *Refiguring Modernism.* 2 vols. Bloomington: Indiana UP, 1995.

———, ed. *The Gender of Modernism.* Bloomington: Indiana UP, 1990.

Film and Modernism

If "Make it new!" was modernism's rallying cry, cinema, product of the machine age, would seem an inherently modernist creation. First projected publicly in 1895, the medium advanced rapidly. Worldwide screenings of Queen Victoria's funeral (1901), the first truly mass event, displayed unprecedented immediacy. Alongside electricity, railways, telegraphy, and associated developments such as time zones, films irrevocably altered individuals' relationships to space, time, and society. Until sound erected linguistic barriers in 1928, film promised to fulfill modernism's internationalist aspirations. Yet film also facilitated national ideologies. Cameras occasioned imperialist spectacles such as the first public British royal wedding (1911), to popularize the monarchy, widely perceived as German, in preparation for war. United States immigrants were addressed as Americans and warned, by commercial interests, against "decadent" French films.

Many modernists embraced film enthusiastically. **James Joyce** in 1909 returned briefly from exile to establish **Ireland**'s first permanent cinema. Pablo Picasso, a keen moviegoer, in 1912 investigated film to animate artworks, but concentrated instead on cubism: imposition of multiple perspectives—like camera angles—to fragment and re-present a scene. **Ezra Pound** wrote passionately about films, and persuaded cinematographer Dudley Murphy to collaborate with composer George Antheil on *Ballet mécanique* (1924), directed by Fernand Léger. Pound increasingly elaborated interest in Oriental ideograms, which forge concepts through simultaneity and juxtaposition. Soviet filmmaker Sergei Eisenstein traversed a similar route, developing montage (editing) techniques in which splicing separate shots struck a third meaning from collision of existing meanings. Pound had earlier launched **imagism** (1912), a poetic tendency characterized by directness and juxtaposition; he particularly promoted **H. D.**, who later co-founded the film journal *Close Up* (1927–33), which first published Eisenstein's seminal theories in English. H. D. herself performed in avant-garde productions. **Surrealists** sought chance and stimulation by transporting a picnic between movie theaters during screenings, to maintain the distance, the hallucinatory otherness, of the images, rather than surrender to involvement. Salvador Dalí, with Luis Buñuel, was received into **surrealism** for their film *Un Chien Andalou* (1929)—not his paintings. Joyce discussed with Eisenstein filming ***Ulysses*** (1922); and the cyclical structure of ***Finnegans Wake*** (1939), often explained by reference to organic rhythms or models of history, may equally derive from the erstwhile normal experience of entering a cinema during a continuous performance and leaving at the same point in the program. **Samuel Beckett** intended to study with Eisenstein; his absurdist sensibility is indebted to slapstick comedy, apparent in his bowler-hatted tramps, amalgams of Charlie Chaplin and Laurel and Hardy, in *Waiting for Godot* (1952); he cast Buster Keaton for his experimental *Film* (1964).

Relationships between film and modernism, vital as these connections demonstrate, remain problematic. Modernism is rarely mentioned in film studies, except in comparisons with art or literature, otherwise in relation to countercinema in the 1960s. Earlier cinema, still evolving, lacked tradition; there were not yet tired forms to repudiate. A further complication is whether film modernism is synonymous with avant-garde, self-defined as an autonomous artistic practice.

Though film initially administered a shock of the new, audiences soon adapted: witness comedies such as *The Countryman's First Sight of the Animated Pictures* (R. W. Paul, U.K., 1901) and its American remake, *Uncle Josh at the Moving Pictures* (Edwin S. Porter, 1901), which ridiculed, on behalf of less credulous spectators, the bumpkin's attempts to expose reality "behind" the screen. Cinematic modernism as alternative practice arrives only after film achieves maturity, decades behind established arts, and not always self-consciously part of a movement. Earlier modernist disruptions were peripheral to mainstream practice unless, like Soviet montage, they could be incorporated into **realism.** Film is an expensive medium, largely determined by commer-cial pressures that discourage free experimentation. *Uncle Josh,* like the patent theatricality of fantasies by magician Georges Méliès, makes clear too that early film routinely flaunted its textuality and was a long way yet from the transparent realism that modernism in other arts contested.

Despite involvement of key personalities, influences are hard to determine. Did writers described, at the time or subsequently, as utilizing cinematic technique (these include Joyce, according to Eisenstein, and **Joseph Conrad** and **D. H. Lawrence**) consciously employ filmic style (as **John Dos Passos** did) or was this mere synchronicity? Or had modes of perception changed generally under the pervasive influence of movies? Conversely, were such parallels consequent upon writers responding to the same modernity that also, independently, attracted the camera's gaze?

Some high modernists, particularly in the 1920s, regarded cinema as symptomatic of debased popular values, severed from tradition. This was not entirely snobbery: most early filmmakers had no conception of their work having anything to do with expression, communication or, least of all, art. The freshness of single-shot studies by the Lumière brothers, the first public exhibitors, lies in close observation of the familiar (workers leaving the factory, baby being fed), combined with the makers' care to demonstrate the fidelity of their system as a scientific device. The charm of Méliès' fantasies resides in ingenuity and imagination, their unbounded enthusiasm for the potential of magic and illusion. Most early films, however, were produced merely to sell equipment. Rival systems competed to supply traveling shows and music halls. Nobody would buy a projector without a regular film supply, and when permanent movie theaters became established after 1905 demand for new titles soared as showmen could no longer travel to find new audiences for the same entertainment. Movies, frequently directed by whichever actor happened to be not in front of the camera, became a commodity, sold by the foot.

These conditions nevertheless fostered ways of seeing that spread quickly. (In 1903 the first purpose-built cinema opened, in Tokyo; by 1908 the United States had 8,000 nickelodeons.) Yet film was not entirely new; commercial viability evolved out of existing ambitions. Optical toys and automata had long fascinated scientific societies and exhibition visitors. Waxworks, lantern shows, camera obscuras, simulators, panoramas, dioramas, folk museums, and panoramic novels all sought to appropriate or imitate reality. Convoluted exhibition layouts suggested spatial or temporal movement, or created oblique viewpoints, anticipating camera angles. They involved spectators by encouraging identification with characters, represented by mannequins, and by appealing to voyeurism, integral to cinema from the start. The only utilitarian function of the Eiffel Tower was its novel view. (Visitors to the Musée Grévin observed a tableau of M. Eiffel on the unfinished edifice, their perspective shared with wax workmen in a structured relay of the gaze that cinematic editing would take two decades to formulate.)

The *flâneur* (Charles Baudelaire's dandy or idler) observed city attractions anonymously, like filmgoers in the dark. Life itself became a show. Arcades resembled exhibition halls; store windows displayed wonders of production. Posters vied for attention, thrusting exoticism, sexuality, and conspicuous consumption into everyday commerce. Streetcars, perceived through the filter of dramatic headlines, threatened public safety, stirring a frisson of excitement as they passed. Train journeys heightened visual sensation through a rectangle from a seated perspective. Uncoincidentally, a popular early film

genre was the Phantom Ride, taken from the front of a train to replicate forward motion. To some extent then, film was just another facet of modernity.

Yet film did bestow a distinct mode of vision, partly by the present absence of events depicted, partly by manipulating time. The Lumières' first screening spawned the urban legend about viewers fleeing to escape from an approaching train (a scene recreated in *Uncle Josh*). If true, this was not repeated; audiences learned quickly to distinguish illusion from reality. If false—although prompting a good publicity story, people may have been play-acting, participating—then they were aware of the mediation, never totally in thrall. The image was, after all, monochrome, flickering; and a feature of showmanship, until brighter, hotter lamps ended the practice, was to begin the image with unremarkable still projection before cranking it into life. *Baby's Breakfast* (Lumière, France, 1895)—from the same program—impressed audiences less with its predictable main action than with leaves blowing on a tree. This was quite outside the repertoire of artifice, and shows too that audiences did not yet expect foregrounded, centered compositions but scanned the entire image. Thus began the alternation, central to cinematic pleasure, between suspended disbelief, implying critical separation, and imaginative involvement. Later spectators identified with Uncle Josh even while mocking him.

Méliès was first to separate screen time from real time, by introducing editing. This freed filmmakers from events as they occurred before the camera and permitted a different ordering, according to narrative demands. Other manipulations of time also became common. Shortage of new films caused exhibitors to appeal to jaded tastes by projecting backwards, at high speed, or in slow motion, desperate to squeeze more profit from existing stock. Scientific films included speeded up recordings of plants growing, which were immensely popular along with micro-cinematography of bacteria and insects, X-ray images and, less elevatedly, pirated copies of surgical operations, including the 1902 separation of Siamese twins, that circulated in mobile freak shows. R. W. Paul in 1895, after reading H. G. Wells's "The Time Machine," had started patenting a simulator to transport audiences through history and the future; he instead became the first British film exhibitor.

Time, which the new century symbolized, was a major fascination, commodified in industrial production and transport schedules. Messages from **India** that once took up to two years, depending on sea conditions, could be telegraphed to London in minutes. Wireless telegraphy enabled instantaneous transatlantic communication. If time was money, leisure had value. Movies became one way of spending it. Time was understood in terms of space. The two combined in motion, which movies exemplified.

Trains featured prominently. Chases were immensely popular. While cinema expressed admiration for railroad efficiency, the destruction, absurdism and anti-authoritarianism of slapstick, a carnivalesque confrontation with mechanization, manifested a certain unease. Critic Siegfried Kracauer and many avant-gardists, including Léger, the surrealists, and theorist Walter Benjamin, noted this explicitly in the 1920s. For intellectuals, Chaplin embodied alienation.

While audiences delighted in the Lumières' *Demolition of a Wall* (France, 1895)—or, rather, the reverse-projection with which even these serious documentarists followed it, so that masonry defied gravity and soared into place—Henri Bergson was developing the philosophy of time central to **Marcel Proust**'s *Remembrance of Things Past* (1913–27). **Sigmund Freud** was examining memory and exploring rifts in identity that cinema itself

unconsciously exploited. Albert Einstein was on the verge of his theory of relativity (which in the 1920s he suggested should be animated by Dave and Max Fleischer, creators of *Popeye*). Accounts of modernism rightly emphasize the subjectivity and fluidity of perception common to these world views. Correspondences occur in early films: many incorporate keyhole-shaped apertures for overtly voyeuristic shots; others build jokes around waking and sleeping (*The Dream of a Rarebit Fiend,* Porter, U.S., 1906); in *How It Feels To Be Run Over* (Hepworth, U.K., 1900), a rapidly approaching automobile gives way to blackness bursting with exclamation marks and a fragment of the disembodied victim's stream of consciousness: "Oh dear, mother will be pleased."

Social commentators, whether in sensational newspapers, academic journals, or aesthetic manifestos, became obsessed with modernity as pervasive hyperstimulus and danger. Workers left noisy, hazardous factories to ride deafening, terrifying machines at fairgrounds, where they would also watch films of fire engines rushing to blazing apartments. Contemporary observers, and later Benjamin, believed shocks were attractive, even addictive, antidotes to exhaustion and torpor, a principle Eisenstein was to embrace positively in using montage for political agitation. **Filippo Marinetti** and the Italian futurists (from 1909) embraced such excitement with glee. (Intriguingly, at least one cinema, in Birmingham, England, was called The Futurist.) Perhaps the Joycean **epiphany,** encountered also in Lawrence, was—like **T. S. Eliot**'s return to **myth**—an attempt to see through transitoriness to something enduring and permanent, to escape Bergson's universe as flux.

Avant-gardists reveled in melodramatic cliffhanger serials, emblematic of fractured experience and speed. Even before **dada** and surrealism, Philippe Soupault and Jean Epstein hyperbolically praised Pearl White's smile in *The Exploits of Elaine* (Pathé, U.S., 1915) as "announcing the upheavals of the new world" and declared cinema to be no mere mechanical toy but "the terrible and magnificent flag of life." René Magritte featured the mysterious masked criminal *Fantômas* (Louis Feuillade, France, 1913–14) in a later painting to represent urban anxieties.

That some modernists, notably Eliot, took an elitist view of popular culture had much to do with its anarchic disruption of tradition. Before war and revolution made refugees of European aristocrats, circuses and fairs were already mistrusted for the social mobility they represented: rumors abounded of dukes working as clowns; many performers (particularly boxers, several of whom became film actors) achieved fortune despite humble origins; and violent outrage over a motion picture showing the first black heavyweight boxer, Jack Johnson, defeating his white opponent prompted a United States ban in 1910.

As novelty faded, educated people saw film as an industry, not an art. Many became disenchanted. Fires, exacerbated by flammable film, cost a number of lives, renewing memories of 140 deaths when a projector exploded in Paris in 1897. Adult illiteracy, poor eyesight, and, in the United States, lack of linguistic fluency among immigrants, combined with cheap admission, meant theaters were full of children brought in to read the intertitles, increasingly common as narratives gained length and complexity. Rowdy infantilism ensued. Concerns for morality joined those for safety, especially given the armed robberies and passionate embraces represented on screen. What kind of people anyway, when electricity validated technological triumphalism, *chose* to congregate in darkness?

Around 1908 the industry hit upon literary adaptations and historical dramas to woo back middle-class audiences. Luxurious cinemas, high-quality projection and,

in time, expensive epic films, with original orchestral accompaniments, justified inflated ticket prices that excluded riff-raff and lined the owners' coffers.

Cultural pedigree failed to impress some intellectuals, however. Wordless, pantomimic treatment of classics could be seen as risible and pandering to bourgeois tastes. Conscious alternatives evolved, committed to releasing the potential of "pure" cinema, sometimes situating this in the excitements of popular attractions.

Léopold Survage, who exhibited with the cubists in 1912, filmed *Colored Rhythm* to explore analogies between music and visual movement. Wholly abstract, neither illustration nor interpretation of music, this showed awareness of editing in establishing relationships between shapes, treating hues as notes. Wassily Kandinsky and Robert Delaunay also based abstractions on music, but the expense of color aborted this development. Others saw cinema as translating reality into dreamlike fantasies, eerily devoid of sound and color. Literary theorist Georgy Lukács, usually remembered for commitment to realism, extolled as cinema's "essential characteristic" a paradoxical present tense that unrolls elsewhere. Kandinsky too was attracted to film as fantasy: he planned collaboration with Arnold Schoenberg on a celluloid opera for which the composer, who desired "utmost unreality," proposed Kandinsky or Oskar Kokoschka as production designer.

Cubist analyses of the visual experience of motion and futurist impressions of its physical sensation derive directly from Jules-Etienne Marey's multiple exposures of moving figures in the 1880s, part of cinematic prehistory in that they attempted to capture duration. These were known to important painters and poets. Marcel Duchamp's *Nude Descending a Staircase* (1912), pays overt homage: the swirls of white dots at its center resemble reference points on the suits worn by Marey's models. Bergson, whose philosophy of form and perception influenced cubists, stated in 1911: "the mechanism of our ordinary knowledge is of a cinematographical kind."

Avant-garde film became discernible as a movement in the 1920s, led by poets and painters rather than experienced filmmakers. Non-commercial, typically non-narrative, it rendered inner vision rather than objective reality. The strands already established paralleled modern painting, ranging from rigorous abstract geometry (De Stijl, Bauhaus) to surrealism.

Hans Richter joined Dada after association with several movements, and worked on abstracted black and white studies in figure/ground relationships. These, a futurist ally observed, resembled musical counterpoint, an idea developed in his film *Rhythm 21* (1921), in which black, gray and white rectangles relate to each other and the frame on a screen treated as flat canvas rather than a window onto anything else. Richter was influenced also by Viking Eggeling, who investigated linear forms. The two together produced long scroll drawings, in which elements interacted and evolved in time and space. These culminated in a submission, supported by referees including Einstein, to UFA, the German conglomerate, which granted animation facilities. Although unsuccessful, the project taught that film is different from painting, that temporal is as important as pictorial form, and that mechanical graphics were required as projection magnified imprecisions in hand drawing and coloring. Both artists continued to make films, some of which survive, including Eggeling's adaptation of the scroll drawings, *Diagonal Symphony* (1921–23).

Abel Gance, a commercial director, was mistrusted by producers for constantly experimenting; his close ups and tracking shots were considered disorienting. *La Folie du Dr Tube* (1915), a magical fantasy in the manner of Méliès, employed dis-

torting mirrors to convey drug-induced hallucinations. Never publicly released, the film shows close affinities to later surrealism and **German expressionism.** Poet Blaise Cendrars, who had written a novella in the style of a film treatment (numbered scenes and single sentence descriptions), assisted on, and appears in, Gance's *J'Accuse* (France, 1919). Here rapid cutting is employed, a technique perfected in Gance's *La Roue* (1922) and his masterpiece *Napoléon* (1927) which was to influence Eisenstein and Soviet colleagues. *La Roue,* though largely conventional, dramatizes locomotive power. Léger would claim he abandoned painting and conceived *Ballet mécanique* after seeing a sequence, edited by Cendrars, in which Gance's face is superimposed on blurred shots of tracks, locomotives hurtling toward camera, spinning wheels, and reciprocating connecting rods: simultaneously external vision and psychological expression. The compositions of wheels and rods—machinery as aesthetics—strikingly resemble Léger's paintings at the time. Another montage portraying a crash incorporates abstracted forms and familiar elements presented too rapidly for recognition, dizzying camera movements and intercut negative shots. To Léger this extended the field of vision, presenting not objects but spectacle.

Pound, though he damned *La Roue* as "the usual drivelling idiocy," conceded these sequences were "essentially cinematographic," not derivative from existing arts. Film societies, such as *Club des Amis du 7me Art* (Casa, founded in Paris 1921), demonstrated that outside English-speaking culture cinema was taken seriously. (American poet Vachel Lindsay's *The Art of the Moving Picture* (1915) made little impact.) The expatriate American *Little Review* had carried poetry and articles about film since 1914 and French journals contained influential criticism for a literary intelligentsia; these were as likely to celebrate Keystone Comedies or Cecil B. DeMille epics as to philosophize over film aesthetics. Dadaists used movie imagery in many media. "The cinema saturates modern literature," Epstein insisted in 1921: René Clair, Germaine Dulac, Marcel L'Herbier, and Louis Delluc were among writers who became significant filmmakers; Desnos, Cendrars, Goll, Soupault, Artaud, Colette, Aragon, Apollinaire, and Cocteau all wrote screenplays or criticism.

L'Herbier's *L'Inhumaine* (France, 1924) opens on a Léger construction of a rotating wheel and rods, similar to his paintings and the close ups in *La Roue*. Although a narrative, it contains fast editing and split-screen techniques to convey exhilarating motion. Inventions such as radio and television feature in a laboratory, comprising fantastic, stylized machines, constructed from flat, black and white geometric shapes, oriented toward camera and defying perspective—designed by Léger in the style of his paintings, but influenced also by the set of Karel Capek's robot play *R.U.R.* (1920). (L'Herbier reportedly instigated a concert hall riot to obtain documentary footage when he fell behind schedule; Erik Satie, Joyce, Picasso, Man Ray, Pound, the Prince of Monaco and several surrealists are supposedly glimpsed among those brawling, provoked by avant-garde music from Antheil.)

Ballet mécanique is cinematic experimentation, not extension of painting. Time, determined by rhythm and duration, is divorced from narrative. Representation drains away: an extended shot of a woman on a swing gradually becomes a rhythmic pattern as no new information intrudes. Rhythm within shots complements rhythm imposed through editing: a shot of a washerwoman climbing steps is continually repeated, like a loop. As in poetry, juxtapositions and parallels create metaphors, tensions between stasis and movement, rhymes. Objects are anthropomorphized,

humans mechanized. (Recall Lawrence's characterization of Clifford Chatterley as man-machine.) A newspaper headline, filmed as letters separated in space and time, recalls the sandwich board men in *Ulysses*. Absence of color and context, for example a close-up eye, achieve defamiliarization. Dodgem rides, games of fortune, and an animated construction representing Chaplin, whom Léger, George Grosz and others had been drawing for years, embrace modernity, chance, motion and popular culture in an avant-garde alliance with "authentic" experience against bourgeois decorum. Prismatic fragmentations derive from **vorticism,** via Pound, of whom a "vortoscope" photograph had been exhibited in 1916. Twice *Ballet mécanique* cuts from eyes to whirling machinery: compare "Doctor T. J. Eckleburg" and speeding automobiles in *The Great Gatsby* (1925) or the vision of Tiresias and the "throbbing taxi cab" in *The Waste Land* (1922).

Richter situated *Ballet mécanique,* Clair's *Entr'acte* (France, 1924) and his own work in a movement, consolidated through *ciné-clubs* that developed an audience and provided discussion and influence. Initially better received in the German-speaking art world than Paris, *Ballet mécanique* was shown in 1926 at the new London *Film Society* (Alfred Hitchcock was a member) and many times with *L'Inhumaine* in New York.

In 1926 novelist Ilya Ehrenburg took avant-garde films to **Russia.** Here Eisenstein may have seen *La Roue* or *Ballet mécanique* as his *Old and New* (1929) contains experimental abstractions, such as a spinning bicycle wheel edited in to the famous cream separator scene in order to create light patterns, a technique employed by Léger using kitchen utensils.

Fritz Lang's *Metropolis* (Germany, 1927) incorporated the latest cinematographic devices as well as art direction based on sculptures by Walter Gropius and a vision of city planning inspired by architects such as Mies van der Rohe, presented in faceted, cubist style. This belated excursion of expressionism viewed mechanization pessimistically and, in its critique of Taylorism and fascination with the city, evidently based on Manhattan, confirmed the shift from Paris to New York as center of modernity.

In 1929 *Un Chien Andalou* shocked audiences with nightmare images, including an eye slit by a razor and a severed hand covered in ants, presented in what appears a realist mode but without apparent logic. Here, as in other avant-garde productions, such as *Entr'acte,* which includes a chase after a runaway hearse modeled on a Mack Sennett comedy, the modern unconscious is suffused with cinema: at one point the protagonist, who resembles Keaton, suffers a pratfall while hauling across his girlfriend's room two supine priests attached to pianos containing flayed horses. The ephemeral, involving, kinesthetic directness of cinema, allowing no time for contemplation, was the sensation modern art and stream-of-consciousness literature strove for. Dulac's *The Seashell and the Clergyman* (1927), a study in sexual frustration involving distorted images, double exposures, and slow motion, although denounced by its writer, Antonin Artaud, can be counted the first surrealist film.

Close Up confirms the centrality of film to modernism. Edited by filmmaker Kenneth Macpherson, novelist Bryher, and H. D., it published over twenty articles by **Dorothy Richardson.** Richardson persuaded Wells to contribute and obtained promises of articles from Aldous Huxley and Havelock Ellis and would have solicited a piece from Lawrence had his health permitted. ("You know Lawrence loathes films? *Foams* about them. I'm sure he'd foam for you," she wrote to Bryher, although evidence suggests Lawrence was a keen filmgoer, incensed, like *Close Up*

generally, by mediocrity rather than opposed to movies outright.) **Gertrude Stein,** Arnold Bennett, and **Marianne Moore** contributed, as did psychoanalysts Barbara Low and Hanns Sachs, who introduced H. D. to Freud for analysis in the 1930s. H. D. especially was enormously excited about P. W. Pabst, whose *Secrets of a Soul* (Germany, 1926) dramatized **psychoanalysis** with the help of Freud's assistants. Osbert Sitwell and André Gide were advertised as future contributors in early issues. Documentarist John Grierson and communist activist Ralph Bond developed key ideas in the journal's pages, while its importance in publishing Soviet theorists cannot be overstated, particularly as they became restricted by anti-formalist dogma. *Close Up* admired Russian and German films, but respected elements of Chaplin and the epic qualities of westerns as compatible with "film for film's sake." The editors initially despaired of sound as an end to internationalism (they were early champions of Japanese cinema, for example) and because they feared theatrical and literary contamination. They publicized artists such as Man Ray and the surrealists and supported "the Negro viewpoint"; Macpherson and H. D. made an avant-garde film with Paul Robeson, *Borderline,* in 1930.

Close Up cultivated a modernist, sometimes difficult, style, blending and dialogizing theory and journalism, poetry, impressionistic literary description, technical advice, and politicized manifesto. It strikingly pre-echoed 1970s theory in opposing ideological mechanisms of mainstream film, supporting "third cinema," theorizing spectatorship, advocating avant-gardism, fighting **censorship,** and arguing for alternatives in distribution and exhibition. The imbrication between cinematic and literary modernism—and their status as elite practices—is underlined by *Close Up* being financed by Bryher (pseudonym of shipping heiress Winifred Ellerman, whose father was the wealthiest man in Britain after the King), who also was patron of Joyce and Richardson and sponsored the Parisian publisher of **Ernest Hemingway,** Stein, H. D., and Mina Loy.

Close Up is interesting too for involving so many women and because it examined female spectatorship as a positive social phenomenon, especially given that modernism is frequently understood as masculine, with low culture its denigrated feminine counterpart. Lawrence, in several novels and essays, and poems in *Pansies* and *Nettles* (1929) in which he condemns hysteria over Rudolph Valentino, was guilty as anyone in propagating this attitude, although his views were selectively appropriated to justify conservatism and insularity: in contrast to the rigorous explorations in *Close Up,* the first issue of F. R. Leavis's *Scrutiny* (1932) pontificated: "No film yet produced can justify the serious critical approach demanded (for instance) by a good novel or poem."

In the late 1920s, then, cross-fertilization of talent and energy secured film briefly in a matrix of experimentation involving all the arts. The First International Congress of Independent Cinematography in Zurich (1929) attracted filmmakers from as far as Japan, and established a distribution network for film clubs. A lively and positive event, over which Eisenstein's presence had a galvanizing influence, the congress wrangled inconclusively over definitions of "independent" and "avant-garde." H. D. in *Close Up* used the newly-coined term "modernism" in describing such cinema as "mechanical efficiency, modernity and curiosity allied with pure creative impulse" and saw as its function "to shock weary sensibilities."

Talkies stopped the momentum dead. Enclosing cameras in soundproof booths and staging shots for hidden microphones ended the delirious mobility that in *Napoléon* permitted a point-of-view shot

from a speeding snowball. Absence of sound became noticeable, rendering silent films immediately old-fashioned. Costs rose. Non-commercial and artisanal production became difficult, especially after the 1929 crash. Totalitarian regimes in Russia and **Germany** discouraged experimentation, and Anglo-American documentary-making took a social democratic turn under Grierson. The Second Congress of independents in Brussels (1930) liquidated the aesthetic avant-garde in light of changing political imperatives. Refugees found Hollywood unconducive to individual creativity, although German directors relegated to 'B' pictures enjoyed relative non-interference and revived expressionist style and modernist themes of urban paranoia in *film noir* thrillers in the 1940s and 50s.

Eisenstein and colleagues had predicted in *Close Up* that exciting experiments with sound would give way to subordination of film to theatricality. Hitchcock, in *Blackmail* (1929), the first British talkie, was unusual in recognizing immediately the expressive possibilities of sound, used contrapuntally to the image, in montage. His subsequent career weaves an intermittent modernist thread into popular cinema: *The Man Who Knew Too Much* (two versions: U.K., 1934 & U.S., 1956), employs music to build suspense *within* the action; *Spellbound* (1945), foregrounding the psychoanalytic concerns of many Hitchcock films, incorporates a dream sequence by Dalí; *Rope* (1948), comprising ten-minute shots joined invisibly, dispenses with editing; *Rear Window* (1954), by contrast, makes brilliant use of editing principles established by Eisenstein's teacher, Lev Kuleshov; *Vertigo* (1958) is an exercise in point of view; and *Psycho* (1960) employs Eisensteinian montage to devastating effect. Another arguably modernist Hollywood film is *Citizen Kane* (U.S., 1941): Orson Welles, granted unusual freedom, constructs multiple points of view within a flashback structure reminiscent of **William Faulkner**'s novels, fluid chronological shifts, expressionist deep-focus camerawork, sound bridges between scenes, extended shots, and montage sequences, always flamboyantly flaunting technique.

Cinematic experimentation consists of isolated phenomena after 1930: Len Lye's drawings directly onto film, followed by semi-abstract propaganda shorts for the General Post Office (U.K.) in the late 1930s; rhythmic editing to match accompaniment by a **W. H. Auden** poem in *Night Mail* (Basil Wright, U.K., 1936), also for Grierson's G.P.O. Film Unit; dreamlike, poetic images in silent films by Maya Deren (U.S., 1940s); lurid fantasies by Kenneth Anger, mostly made in **France** but screened within the New York underground, starting with *Fireworks* (1947).

Art Cinema, a marketing niche for feature films, consciously defined against Hollywood and closely associated with national cinema, emerged after World War II when the studios broke up. In the 1950s and 60s international filmmakers, functioning as brand names, enjoyed considerable freedom. Typically they employed devices originating in national film industries of the silent era—which had sought to break the synthesis of entertainment, experiment, and art characteristic of the best American product, to compete on different terms—and in literary and theatrical modernism. They explored subjective states, often involving ambiguous narration, passive protagonists, heavy emphasis on flashbacks, and foregrounded enunciation.

The American underground revived filmmaking by poets and painters, using cheap equipment developed for military use. Refugees such as Richter, who had continued filming in collaboration with other artists into the 1960s, enjoyed revived interest. Usually silent for financial reasons, avant-garde film was more likely to be encountered in a gallery than a cinema. Andy Warhol's films, accompanied by avant-garde rock music, to some extent initiated a gradual, sexploitation-driven crossover into Art Cinema.

Shared language encouraged British producers to try competing with Hollywood within the United States. While this held back British national cinema, compared with government-subsidized "quality" productions elsewhere, it excluded independent production from all but political and avant-garde practices which complemented radical academic theory and criticism. Art Cinema occupied a distinctly alternative position in Britain, associated with cinema clubs, the only places where surrealist films or Soviet political films had been seen because of censorship. (Eisenstein's *Battleship Potemkin* (1925) was forbidden to public audiences until 1958). The result was a highly politicized countercinema. This gave vent in the English-speaking world, particularly North American campuses where film studies had become institutionalized, to energies sweeping across Europe, especially after the 1968 uprisings.

Meanwhile the French New Wave (inaugurated 1959) refreshed, interrogated and, in the Brechtian work of Jean-Luc Godard, politicized both Art Cinema and serious criticism of Hollywood by challenging realist assumptions and again highlighting the materiality of the text. In the modernist tradition, it made reading difficult, involving the spectator consciously and actively in producing meaning, challenging the transparency that appears inherent in photographic media.

As in the 1920s, a split was perceived between the artistic avant-garde, represented now by the North American Co-op movement, and political modernism. At the 1929 Independent Congress Eisenstein and Richter had made a comic short together—ironically the end, rather than instigation, of a dialogue. Now, again, circumstances changed. **Postmodernism** (especially appropriation of experimental techniques and intertextuality into television advertising and pop videos) normalized practices previously considered modernist. The rise of the New Right curtailed funding for innovation. Increasing permissiveness in film and television regulation reduced the political and artistic potential of shock. Video ownership changed the textual status and reception of films and offered easy access to production. The context within which modernism was meaningful had shifted.

Nigel Morris

Selected Bibliography

Bergson, Henri. *Creative Evolution*. New York, 1911.

Chanan, Michael. *The Dream That Kicks: The Prehistory and Early Years of Cinema in Britain*, 2nd edition. London and New York: Routledge, 1996.

Charney, Leo, and Vanessa R. Schwartz, eds. *Cinema and the Invention of Modern Life*. Berkeley, Los Angeles and London: University of California Press, 1995.

Christie, Ian. *The Last Machine: Early Cinema and the Birth of the Modern World*. London: BBC Education and British Film Institute, 1994.

Donald, James, Anne Friedberg, and Laura Marcus, eds. *Close Up 1927–1933: Cinema and Modernism*. London: Cassell, 1998.

Lawder, Standish D. *The Cubist Cinema*. New York: New York University Press, 1975.

Morris, Nigel. "Lawrence's Response to Film." In *D. H. Lawrence: A Reference Companion*. Edited by Paul Poplawski. Westport, CT: Greenwood Press, 1996, pp. 591–603.

Neale, Steve. "Art Cinema as Institution." *Screen* 22, no. 1 (1981): 11–39.

Smith, Murray. "Modernism and the Avant-gardes." In *The Oxford Guide to Film Studies*. Edited by John Hill and Pamela Church Gibson. Oxford and New York, 1998, pp. 395–412.

Soupault, Phillipe. "Cinema, U.S.A." (1923). In *The Shadow and Its Shadow: Surrealist Writings on Cinema*, 2nd edition. Edited by Paul Hammond. London: British Film Institute, 1991, pp. 60–61.

Wollen, Peter. "The Two Avant Gardes." In his *Readings and Writings: Semiotic Counterstrategies*. London: Verso Editions and New Left Books, 1982, pp. 92–104.

Finnegans Wake (1939)

James Joyce's last prose work is written in an uncompromisingly innovative narrative style intended to suggest the nocturnal dream world. Joyce wrote to Harriet Shaw Weaver in November 1926 that a "great part of every human experience is passed in a state which cannot be rendered sensible by the use of wideawake language, cutanddry grammar and goahead plot." He took the title from an Irish-American ballad which recounts the fall and resurrection of Tim Finnegan, a drunken hod-carrier who dies in a fall from his ladder but at his wake is revived by a splash of whiskey. The title also alludes to Fionn mac Cumhaill, the hero of ancient Irish legend, suggesting that having died ("Macool, Macool, orra whyi deed ye diie?"), he will surely return ("Mister Finn, you're going to be Mister Finnagain!") to be chastised again ("Mister Funn, you're going to be fined again!"). But "Finnegans" also suggests that an end is denied, as exemplified by the book's ending in mid-sentence ("A way a lone a last a loved a long the")—to be merged with its opening ("riverrun, past Eve and Adam's, from swerve of shore to bend of bay, brings us by a commodius vicus of recirculation back to Howth Castle and Environs"). Thus the "Wake" of the title refers both to a vigil held over a dead person's body, accompanied by drinking, and to a rising or resurrection. *Finnegans Wake* typically reconciles the polarity of opposites. Allusions to the title recur throughout the book (e.g., "to Finnegan, to sin again and to make grim grandma grunt and grin again," 580: 19–20).

The *Wake* is an all-inclusive ever-elusive non-linear narrative with cyclical patterns ("Teems of times and happy returns. The seim anew. Ordovico or viricordo. Anna was, Livia is, Plurabelle's to be," 215:22–24). According to the book, essential human experience recurs throughout history: birth and death, sexuality and family, guilt and judgment. For an accommodating structure Joyce used the Italian philosopher Giambattista Vico's cyclical theory of history which postulates three ages, divine, heroic, and human. He added to this a "ricorso," a period of transition and renewal. Joyce also made use of Giordano Bruno's theory that everything in nature is realized through interaction with its opposite (e.g., mourning and resurrection). He wove scores of languages into the *Wake's* pseudo-English, producing paradoxical meanings and limitless scope for associations. Yet if that multi-lingual work attempts to approach the Creation in its elaborate structure, its elusive meaning, and its universality, it is also profoundly comic in its conflation of laughter and sadness. *Finnegans Wake* abounds with allusions to literature and popular culture, history, mythology, religion, geography and folklore. If Joyce's encyclopedic tendency is obvious in *Ulysses,* it is everywhere in *Finnegans Wake.*

The central figures of the book's nocturnal world are Humphrey Chimpden Earwicker (HCE) and his family: his wife Anna Livia Plurabelle (ALP), their twin sons Shem the Penman and Shaun the Post, and their daughter Issy. The family live at the Mullingar Inn in Chapelizod, Co. Dublin. Rather than being particular individuals, however, these characters are archetypes representative of a kinship system which keeps repeating itself irrespective of time and place. As in a dream, they undergo numerous transformations. The identity of the dreamer remains a mystery; plausible guesses include HCE, Fionn mac Cumhaill, Joyce himself, and the reader, or any combination of them. The dream technique he developed gave Joyce the freedom to entwine archetypal and historical themes while enacting in language the actual processes of the sleeping mind. Freudian slips and puns, transferences and sublimations are omnipresent in the *Wake.*

Joyce also comes close to modern psychology in his treatment of Issy ("jung and easily freudened") whose split personality recalls his daughter Lucia.

Joyce began collecting material for *Finnegans Wake* and started composing in a fragmentary way late in 1922. Between March and October 1923 he began drafting short mock-heroic pieces that he was to alter and distribute throughout the book: "King Roderick O'Connor" (in II.3, 380–82), "Tristan and Isolde" (in II.4, 383–99), "St Patrick and the Druid" (in IV, 611–12), "St Kevin" (in IV, 604–6), "Mamalujo" (in II.4, 383–99, interpolated into "Tristan and Isolde"), and "Here Comes Everybody" (I.2, 30–4). It was during this period that Joyce began to form a clearer picture of the direction his avant-garde work was taking, and he gave it all his creative attention until it was published in spring 1939. During the book's composition Joyce referred to it as *Work in Progress* as suggested by **Ford Madox Ford** in 1924.

Studies of the drafts and notebooks held at the British Library and at Buffalo have revealed that *Finnegans Wake* came about less through multitudinous revisions than through a literary method based on systematic accretion. Joyce continued to revise and reorganize parts of the *Wake* even after they had appeared in various journals between 1924 and 1938. He was sharply criticized by some former admirers, including **Pound,** who thought he was engaging in substantially meaningless if stylistically complex exercises. Joyce encouraged a group of friends, **Samuel Beckett** and Frank Budgen among them, to compile a collection of essays justifying *Work in Progress.* The volume appeared as *Our Exagmination round his Factification for Incamination of Work in Progress* in 1929. Virtually all of *Finnegans Wake* was in print by 1938, either serialized in the Paris journal *transition* or as individual booklets. Joyce's failing eyesight made him rely on friends to read books and make lists of words and allusions; and he retained any dictational or transcriptional errors he thought interesting.

The *Wake*'s linguistic complexity and multidimensional narrative strategies make a concise meaningful plot summary virtually impossible. However, there is a kind of narrative line involving the Earwicker family in a number of situations. In the beginning HCE commits some sexual misdemeanor in the Phoenix Park, either with two girls or three soldiers. In the ensuing scandal ALP defends him in a "litter" written by Shem and carried by Shaun which is lost but retrieved by a hen scratching in a midden. The sons compete for Issy's favors. HCE grows old and impotent, but after death and burial revives. Completing the cycle old ALP prepares to reappear as Issy, and so attract HCE again.

In composing the work Joyce designated the main characters and aspects of their identity by the little signs or "sigla." In a footnote on page 299 several sigla appear together as the "Doodles family," and Joyce included some of the sigla throughout the book. Their role became increasingly complex as Joyce's work proceeded. HCE and ALP appear under many guises as various encodings of their initials are used as well as an elaborate series of numerological devices. Their metamorphoses range from the mythological to the geographical; they are aspects of the Dublin landscape, with the river Liffey and the hill of Howth serving as symbols for female and male in a world of flux. Joyce told Frank Budgen that "Time and the river and the mountain are the real heroes of my book." Other recurrent figures in the book are the four old men who are modeled on the four evangelists and collectively called Mamalujo; but they also represent the Irish annalists known as the Four Masters. There is an apostolic group of twelve who appear as clients in the pub or members of a jury. It is often difficult to attribute the narrating voice to any one figure, particu-

larly so since Joyce's stylistic parodies encompass the Bible and *The Egyptian Book of the Dead* as well as nursery rhymes and the banter of comic-strip characters such as Mutt and Jeff, referred to as Mutt and Jute or Muta and Juva.

The Wake contains seventeen chapters divided into four Books: Book I contains eight chapters; Book II four; Book III four; and Book IV one. Most editions of the *Wake* have the same pagination and line spacing, and critics customarily use Arabic numerals to refer to pages and lines, and Roman numerals to designate the Books.

Joyce himself liked to compare the *Wake* to the intricately illuminated *Book of Kells,* and indeed, the *Wake* is built on numerous complex symmetries. However, upon reading the Shaun chapter, Ezra Pound wrote to Joyce in November 1926 that "nothing short of divine vision or a new cure for the clapp can possibly be worth all the circumambient peripherization." The book's unequaled plenitude and forbidding impenetrability remain a matter of taste: *Finnegans Wake* remains elusive. As Samuel Beckett wrote, "the *Wake* is not *about* something; *it is that something itself.*"

Christine O'Neill

Selected Bibliography

Atherton, James S. *The Books at the Wake: A Study of Literary Allusions in James Joyce's Finnegans Wake.* Expanded and corrected ed. Mamoroneck, N.Y.: Paul P. Appel, 1974.

Bishop, John. *Joyce's Book of the Dark.* Madison, Wisconsin: U of Wisconsin P, 1986.

Campbell, Joseph and Henry Morton Robinson. *A Skeleton Key to Finnegans Wake.* London: Faber, 1947.

Devlin, Kimberley J. *Wandering and Return in Finnegans Wake: An Integrative Approach to Joyce's Fictions.* Princeton, N.J.: Princeton UP, 1991.

Glasheen, Adaline. *Third Census of Finnegans Wake: An Index of the Characters and Their Roles.* Berkeley: U of California P, 1977.

Hart, Clive. *Structure and Motif in Finnegans Wake.* London: Faber, 1962.

McHugh, Roland. *Annotations to Finnegans Wake.* London: Routledge & Kegan Paul, 1980.

Norris, Margot. *The Decentered Universe of Finnegans Wake: A Structuralist Analysis.* Baltimore and London: Johns Hopkins UP, 1976.

Rose, Danis and John O'Hanlon. *Understanding Finnegans Wake: A Guide to the Narrative of James Joyce's Masterpiece.* New York and London: Garland, 1982.

Fitzgerald, F. Scott (1896–1940)

The fiction of F. Scott Fitzgerald is often associated with the decade of the 1920s known as the Jazz Age. It has come to embody the perceived spirit of that post-war period of brittle excitement and potential disillusion, which was, in some senses, an invention of the author himself. This is particularly evident in the short stories which punctuated and, to an extent, funded Fitzgerald's oeuvre. As the titles of the collections *Flappers and Philosophers* (1920) and *Tales of The Jazz Age* (1922) suggest the stories they contain, first published in *The Saturday Evening Post* and *Scribner's,* resonate with the fashions and moods of the time. Yet even in these early stories, such as "The Diamond As Big As The Ritz," where the pursuit of the precious glitter which informs wealth ends in disaster, the underside of glitz and glamour is suggested. This is reinforced in the later collection, *Taps at Reveille* (1930) where the central theme of "One Trip Abroad" is the corruption of innocence. By this time, after the Wall Street crash of 1929, the bubble of the twenties' prosperity had burst; hence Fitzgerald's assertion in a letter to his editor Maxwell Perkins in May 1931, "The Jazz Age is over . . . I claim credit for naming it and that it extended from the suppression of the riots on May Day 1919 to the crash of the stock market in 1929—almost one decade" (*Letters*).

Fitzgerald was born in 1896 in the midwest city of St Paul, Minnesota. He moved east in 1913 where his experience at Princeton proved to be a formative one. Although he withdrew because of ill-health and a bad academic record, and even after re-entry failed to complete the course, the dangerous attractions of its world provided him with the context of *This Side of Paradise* (1920). This was a popular success because the concerns of its hero, the "romantic egoist" Amory Blaine, struck a chord for post-war youth. Blaine's quest for an image of self and his hunger for experience propels the text. He pursues fame, wealth, romance and amusement and is attracted by literary and religious thought. Yet this pursuit of pleasure and fulfillment is shot through with his sense of an evil presence. However he seems to succeed in accommodating this presence, which is associated with flawed romantic entanglements with a succession of young women, and the novel ends with the suggestion that he has achieved some self-knowledge.

Critical responses have pointed up the shortcomings of *This Side of Paradise,* citing literary borrowings, under-developed incidents and unconvincing characterization. Fitzgerald, too, in a letter of 1938 to Perkins dismissed the novel: "looking it over, I think it is now one of the funniest books since *Dorian Gray* in its utter spuriousness" (*Letters*). However, although immature, this text is significant in that it evokes not only the stylish preoccupations of the post-war generation but also Fitzgerald's developing engagement with the potent nexus of female beauty, evil, and wealth.

This nexus is suggested in the title of Fitzgerald's second novel *The Beautiful and the Damned* (1922) where Gloria and Anthony Patch relentlessly pursue an extravagant, leisured and destructive lifestyle believing that they will inherit even more wealth when Anthony's grandfather dies. This text is informed by a sense of both the sterility of life and the consequent vulnerability to evil which stems from the privileging of wealth and beauty. Ultimately Anthony's alcoholism alienates his friends and Gloria's beauty not only fades but, significantly, becomes *unclean.* According to Edmund Wilson, Fitzgerald's friend from Princeton, this novel is better written than *This Side of Paradise* but he still felt that Fitzgerald's imagination "suffers badly from lack of discipline and poverty of aesthetic ideas." Other critics have suggested that other flaws in the novel, such as a lack of authorial distance, stem from similarities between the Patch marriage and that between Scott and Zelda. However this line of argument, though valid, can be over-stated given Fitzgerald's satire of the conduct and snobbery of the upper-class characters.

Fitzgerald's fourth novel *Tender Is the Night* (1934) has also been read biographically, and certainly Fitzgerald's alcoholism and Zelda's psychological problems have resonances in a text which concerns the emotionally complicated relationship, played out within the fashionable expatriate life of the French Riviera and Paris, between Dick Diver, a Freudian psychiatrist and Nicole his wealthy and beautiful wife/patient. Yet Fitzgerald is also concerned here with larger and more public issues, with the tainting of innocence, with the dissipation of professional and personal integrity and with society's responsibility in this process. The novel was neither a commercial nor a critical success. The post-war fashionable life of the 1920s was no longer popular as subject matter in the depression of the 1930s. Furthermore the focus seems uncertain, evidence of this is the fact that it can be read in two versions and Fitzgerald continued to amend it after publication.

Lack of focus and uncertain structure are certainly not criticisms to be leveled against his third novel *The Great Gatsby* (1925). Although sales were poor, it was acknowledged at the time as a modern classic by **T. S. Eliot** and referred to recently by the critic Malcolm Bradbury as Fitzgerald's masterwork. Again the text is firmly rooted in the Jazz Age and it demonstrates the author's understanding of the doubleness of this era. This is a time when the liberated hedonism of wild parties coexists with Prohibition and the right-wing views voiced by Tom Buchanan; when his old money coexists with Gatsby's new and probably criminal money and when a leisured society coexists with a working class urban wasteland watched over by an advertising hoarding. The consumerism which informs this hoarding leads to a sense of the "vast meretricious beauty" embodied by Daisy Buchanan, whose "voice is full of money." Again a combination of female beauty and wealth prove to be destructive.

The plot can be simply summarized: it is the story of Jay Gatsby's failed attempt to recreate the love affair he once had with Daisy Fay, now the wife of Tom Buchanan. Such an attempt ends in death where Myrtle Wilson, Tom's mistress, is run down by Daisy driving Gatsby's car. After being told by Tom that the car was driven by Gatsby, Myrtle's husband kills Gatsby and then himself. Now the cultural specificity and historical reference which indicate Fitzgerald's concern for verisimilitude and which resonate through this plot, might suggest that the text can be placed within the conventions of **realism,** but this is not the case. This is not a linear narrative and Gatsby's story emerges through the retellings and interconnections associated with modernism. As Fitzgerald wrote to Perkins in 1922: "I want to write something new, something extraordinary and beautiful and simple and beautifully patterned" (*Letters*).

Yet the story is not "simple" in the telling. Nick Carraway is an unreliable narrator, revealing this from the outset where he follows a pronouncement that he is non-judgmental with a judgment. He distorts Gatsby's story; amplifying, omitting and ignoring in an attempt, which verges on the voyeuristic, to reconcile his fascination and repulsion with the subject. As Tony Tanner has suggested, "Fitzgerald's book is Nick's book, but Nick is not Fitzgerald . . . while Nick is trying to write Gatsby we are also reading Nick." Significantly, in a modernist text, the reader is made aware of the writing itself. In a further doubleness, Nick is both within and without the text, in both past and future. This alerts the reader to the fact of the artifact, that his telling is a narration in the process of being written.

Through Nick's narrative, Fitzgerald is not only satirizing the flawed priorities and snobbery of a section of twenties moneyed society, he is interrogating the American Dream. Gatsby as dreamer and vulgarian is its embodiment, his "heightened sensitivity to the promises of life" is undercut by his self-inventings and gesturings. The ending suggests the failure of the Dream, and the impossibility of a belief in "a fresh green breast of the New World," given not only the corrupt wealth of the Buchanans but "the valley of ashes" where the Wilsons live. That this failure can be read as mutilation is suggested in a letter of 1924 from Fitzgerald to Perkins: "I want Myrtle Wilson's breast ripped off—it's exactly the thing, I think" (*Letters* or Tanner?).

Fitzgerald was exercised by the ambiguities of the Dream until the end of his life. Evidence of this is the fact that his final novel, *The Last Tycoon* (1941), is set in Hollywood, the "dream factory" of America. This text is fueled by his experiences as a screen writer and informed with the confused nature of his domestic and professional life which is revealed in the essays of 1936 and 1937 "The Crack Up" and "Early Success." He explores similar tensions in the life of Monroe Stahr, a film producer. This novel was left incomplete because of Fitzgerald's sudden death in 1940 but edited by Edmund Wilson and published posthumously in 1941. After his death, Fitzgerald's reputation, diminished by accusations of sentimentality and superficiality, continued to decline, but a resurgence of popularity has led to the republishing of his novels and short stories and a wealth of critical material.

Ann Hurford

Selected Bibliography

Fitzgerald, F. Scott. *The Letters of F. Scott Fitzgerald.* Ed. Andrew Turnball. Harmondsworth: Penguin, 1968.

Tanner, Tony. "Introduction." *The Great Gatsby* by F. Scott Fitzgerald. Harmondsworth: Penguin, 1990.

Wilson, Edmund. *The Shores of Light.* New York: Farrar, Straus, 1952.

Ford, Ford Madox (1873–1939)

Ford's engagements with modernism are so extensive and diverse that they tend to have been seen neither steadily nor whole. He was born in 1873, the son of Francis Hueffer, a free-thinking German émigré who became **music** critic of the *Times,* and Catherine Madox Brown, the daughter of the painter Ford Madox Brown. Christened Ford Hermann Hueffer, he changed his name to Ford Madox Ford in 1919. He is a transitional figure, evolving from his Pre-Raphaelite origins, through turn-of-the-century **impressionism,** into the early modernism of Edwardian London, and later transatlantic modernist developments in Paris in the 1920s.

Ford was at the center of the three most innovative groups of writers in English in the first half of the twentieth century. His friends **Henry James,** Stephen Crane, and **Joseph Conrad,** formed what he imagined another friend, H. G. Wells, calling "a ring of foreign conspirators plotting against British letters." All these men lived near Rye, where Ford conspired with them about the plotting of novels. He collaborated with Conrad intermittently from

1898 to 1908. Though the resulting works are inferior to both men's own best work, the experience of collaboration was the making of Ford as a writer, furnishing him with material and technical confidence.

In Edwardian London he gathered the best writers together to contribute to his *English Review,* in which he published **D. H. Lawrence, Wyndham Lewis,** and **Pound** for the first time in London, next to James, Conrad, Bennett, Wells, and Hardy. After the Great War (see **The War**), in which he served, and was shell-shocked, Ford moved to Paris. There he founded the *transatlantic review,* bringing together the work of **Joyce, Gertrude Stein, William Carlos Williams, E. E. Cummings, Jean Rhys** and **Ernest Hemingway.**

From the late 1920s he divided his time between Paris, Provence, and America, especially New York. He died in **France** in 1939. His earliest fiction now seems dated: historical novels, romances, political and literary *romans à clef.* But his chief contributions as a modernist are the superb novels *The Good Soldier* (1915) and the tetralogy known collectively as *Parade's End* (1924–28).

The Good Soldier: A Tale of Passion explores the tensions and hypocrisies of upper-middle-class British and American society on the eve of World War I. The American narrator, John Dowell, tells of his friendship with the English couple Edward and Leonora Ashburnham. He recounts how Edward kills himself for love of his young ward Nancy, and how he later discovers that Ashburnham was having an affair with his wife Florence, who has also committed suicide. The milieu is that of Henry James's fiction. The story is redolent of Edwardian sentimentality. But the treatment is influentially modernist. The cunning shifts of time, place, tone, and psychology foreground the form and the telling, and raise questions about the narrator's reliability and motivation.

Like most of Ford's fiction, *Parade's End* pursues these questions of passion, knowledge, deceit, class, and power. But this time the setting is the war, and English life before, during, and after it. In *Some Do Not . . .* (1924), the eccentrically brilliant protagonist, the mathematician Christopher Tietjens, is separated from his society wife Sylvia, and meets the suffragette Valentine Wannop. When he is on leave in London, suffering from shell-shock and amnesia, he and Valentine almost become lovers. The second and third volumes are set mainly on the western front. *No More Parades* (1925) deals with the mental strains of Tietjens' life in the army: his experiences under bombardment; his concern for his men; his mortification when Sylvia pursues him to France to torment him more effectively. Most of *A Man Could Stand Up* (1926) concerns Tietjens waiting for and then surviving a German attack. It is framed by two scenes from the day of the Armistice: first Valentine trying to retain her authority in a girls' school; then a hallucinatory reunion between her and Tietjens. Some critics follow Graham Greene in thinking the sequence should have ended there. But Ford added the *Last Post* in 1928, detailing Valentine's and Christopher's life at Groby, the family estate, after the war, with his dying brother Mark and his French mistress.

Parade's End doesn't have Joyce's display of artifice, or Wyndham Lewis' cruel modernity. Its panoramic scale, tracing of history, preoccupations with love and honor, give it continuities with Victorian fiction. Yet it also continues Ford's experiments in modernism: the exact rendering of experience, in all its instability, evanescence, and bafflement. The techniques develop throughout the sequence, so that *Last Post* is structured entirely by streams of consciousness. The emphasis on the psychological effects of war, together with Ford's determination to see the war in relation to questions of society and sexuality, make the tetralogy seem ahead of its time:

a precursor of Pat Barker's *Ghost Road* trilogy, and of the post-psychoanalytic approach to war as trauma. It has become increasingly recognized as the best English fiction about the war.

Ford published 26 other novels, nearly fifty further books, and over five hundred periodical pieces, including reminiscences, poetry, criticism, and travel writing. His creative prose is often characterized by a generic hybridity that is perhaps more familiar in **postmodernism**. His memoirs incorporate a high degree of fictionalization. The best are *Return to Yesterday* (1931), recounting his pre-war literary recollections, and thus covering the period of *The Good Soldier; No Enemy* (1929), reworking some of his war reminiscences; and *It Was the Nightingale* (1934), dealing with his recuperation after the war, and the writing of *Parade's End*. The excellent memoir *Joseph Conrad: A Personal Remembrance* (1924), which Ford himself provocatively described as a novel, has more recently been seen as metafictional, for its accounts of the two men's theoretical thinking about the novel.

Ford's other contributions to modernism can perhaps best be analyzed under the related headings of poetry and criticism. As a poet his primary instinct was lyric. His earlier verse is strongly influenced by the expressive modesty of his aunt Christina Rossetti. His Edwardian poems become more ironic, testing traditional modes against modern urban experience. His best war poem, "Antwerp," describes Belgian refugees arriving in London. After the war he experimented with modernist parody in *Mister Bosphorus and the Muses* (1923), a work drawing on his knowledge of music hall as well as the history of poetry, and showing striking similarities with both *The Waste Land* and *Ulysses*. His verse of the 1920s and 1930s aspires to the more relaxed, conversational aesthetic that he had always advocated.

If much of Ford's poetry now seems dated, quaint even, besides the work of other modernists, it is in part because of the lessons they were able to learn from him. This is particularly true of Pound, whom Ford "discovered," befriended, published, took on as a secretary, and corresponded with for the rest of his life. The high value Pound placed on Ford's verse was due as much to its critical example as to its achievement. Pound called Ford the best critic in England, and repeatedly acknowledged Ford as one of his significant mentors. Two principles receive particular emphasis: that "poetry should be as well-written as prose"—a view that, thanks to Pound's mediation, was to influence **T. S. Eliot;** and the idea that poetry should be conversational, should not include anything that could not actually be said. Pound later felt that the increasingly conversational style of **Yeats**'s later poems owed much to Ford (again via the mediation of Pound, who acted as Yeats's secretary too). After Conrad and James, Pound was Ford's most significant literary contact: their writing to and about each other was crucial in establishing modernist poetics.

Ford was a prolific critic throughout his career, and of prose as well as verse. His phases of most intense critical activity coincide with the writing of his best fiction, and his activities as a literary editor. His editorials for the *English Review,* published selectively as *The Critical Attitude* (1911), have been seen as necessary preliminaries to the development of modernism. He wrote weekly "Literary Portraits" for the *Outlook* from 1913 to 1915—the period of *The Good Soldier.* Here, as in much of his writing about literature, reminiscences and biography are combined with criticism. He consistently advocates what he calls "impressionism." While this remains fundamentally a post-romantic theory of expression, attaching a high value to the personality of the artist, it paradoxically moves towards modernist theories of impersonality, in its emphases on self-effacement, the aloofness of the author, the rendering of concrete particularity to convey emotion rather than by authorial statements of feeling, and the presentation of intense perceptual experience with a minimum of discursive or narrative connection. Ford's activities as an editor represent a critical intelligence at work in another sense, of course. He has been described as the best literary editor of the twentieth century, unparalleled in his gift for discovering and encouraging new talents.

Max Saunders

Selected Bibliography

Cassell, Richard A., ed. *Critical Essays on Ford Madox Ford.* Boston: G. K. Hall, 1987.

Ford, Ford Madox. *Critical Writings of Ford Madox Ford.* Ed. Frank MacShane. Lincoln: U of Nebraska P, 1964.

———. *Letters of Ford Madox Ford.* Ed. Richard M. Ludwig. Princeton, New Jersey: Princeton UP, 1965.

———. *The Ford Madox Ford Reader.* Ed. Sondra J. Stang. Manchester: Carcanet, 1986.

———. *Selected Poems.* Ed. Max Saunders. Manchester: Carcanet, 1997.

———. *War Prose.* Ed. Max Saunders. Manchester: Carcanet, 1999.

Harvey, David Dow. *Ford Madox Ford. 1873–1939. A Bibliography of Works and Criticism.* Princeton: Princeton UP, 1962.

Judd, Alan. *Ford Madox Ford.* London: Collins, 1990.

MacShane, Frank, ed. *Ford Madox Ford: The Critical Heritage.* London: Routledge and Kegan Paul, 1972.

———. *The Life and Work of Ford Madox Ford.* New York: Horizon, 1965.

Mizener, Arthur. *The Saddest Story: A Biography of Ford Madox Ford.* London: The Bodley Head, 1972.

Saunders, Max, ed. Special double Ford issue of *Agenda* 27:4/29:1 (Winter 1989/Spring 1990), 1–169.

———. *Ford Madox Ford: A Dual Life.* 2 vols. Oxford: Oxford UP, 1996.

———. "Ford Madox Ford: Further Bibliographies." *English Literature in Transition* 43:2 (2000): 131–205.

Stang, Sondra J. ed. *The Presence of Ford Madox Ford.* Philadelphia: University of Pennsylvania Press, 1981.

Formal Experimentation

The period from 1890–1930 was characterized in literature by "a complex of inventive gestures, daring performances" (Levenson 2). Experimentation was in part the consequence of artistic attempts to engage with and assimilate aspects of social and cultural disintegration. Writers of this period wrestled with the complexities of new forms while confronted by an unpredictable, dislocating society that they aimed to assimilate and even revolutionize through art—broadening into the vast realms of politics. Literary innovation became a way of attempting to redress social breakdown: "A way of happening, a mouth" (Auden 82). Paradoxically, while engaging with and even relying on social modernization for much of its content and form, literature (along with the other arts) also provided a means of transcending social failure, offering an area of conviction and cultural pride.

It is crucial to recognize that while the modernist period was characterized by formal experimentation, the experiments were localized and resulted in a multiplicity of styles, impossible to quantify or explore exhaustively. *Modernism* as a term cannot be used (like *romanticism*) as a broad stylistic description. It is possible, however, to identify recurrent trends which are prevalent in many of the most significant writers of the period, and which facilitate a contrast with the preceding nineteenth-century literature.

The nineteenth-century realist novel was characterized by a past-tense, third-person narrative in which the presence of an omniscient narrator (indicating an external context or reality) was always implicitly or explicitly in evidence. Modernist fiction deviated from such pre-existing modes of discourse: its form was dictated instead by its preoccupation with the psychological workings of the conscious or unconscious mind. Structures relating to external events were therefore diminished or presented highly selectively, and replaced by **interior monologue** concerned with reflection and analysis rather than representation. The stream of consciousness method of **Virginia Woolf** exemplifies this technique, in which the conventional structure involving a beginning, middle, and end is entirely broken down, and replaced by a *flowing* stream of association through which experience is gradually conveyed. Expressionist drama from Strindberg's *A Dream Play* to **Eliot**'s *Sweeney Agonistes* analogously sought to avoid cause-and-effect narrative, employing dream-logic rather than conventional sequencing.

Chronological dislocation and the breaking down of conventional structural coherence often results in a sense of irresolution, and modernist writers frequently aimed to counteract both structural and linguistic closure through the use of open endings. **D. H. Lawrence,** for example, "ends" his novel *Women in Love* (1920) with an inconclusive argument between the protagonist-lovers, Birkin and Ursula, concluding with " 'I don't believe that', he answered" (Lawrence 481). The debate—about whether or not it is necessary for Birkin to supplement his relationship with Ursula with "another kind of love" is left unresolved, as the characters' perspectives are antithetical, and hence irresolvable without the intervention of an objective narrative voice.

The "end" of **James Joyce's** *Ulysses* exemplifies a radically different kind of resistance to closure. Here, Molly Bloom's monologue, which slides into a flow of words representing her unrestricted stream of thought, results in an abandonment of orthodox sentence structure and punctuation. This conclusion is, of course, characteristic of perhaps the most strikingly original and stylistically experimental novel of the modernist period. As well as grafting his novel onto a precursive literary text (Homer's *Odyssey*) and creating episodes which directly correspond to specific chapters in Homer, Joyce illustrates in *Ulysses* the way in which multiple styles and forms can coexist within a single book with great success and originality. From a combination of third-person, past-tense portrayal of events with first-person, present-tense depiction of the thoughts of the two protagonists, Joyce shifts to a preoccupation with symbolism and elaboration, incorporating musical structures and parodies of literary and other styles. Joyce referred to this promiscuous appropriation and rejection of multiple styles as a "scorching" method, in which "each successive episode, dealing with some province of artistic culture (rhetoric or music or dialectic), leaves behind it a burnt-up field" (Joyce 129). *Ulysses* is characteristic of modernist texts in its self-consciously allusive methodology, in which it appropriates both styles and intertexts.

Stylistic variety, as well as allusion to multiple myths and intertexts, is also characteristic of modernist poetry, such as Eliot's *The Waste Land* (initially entitled "He Do the Police in Different Voices"). Poetry of this period shifted away from conventional rhyming and rhythmic structures towards the use of free verse, which facilitated new flexibility and experimentation. Rejecting extended narrative or epic verse, poets such as **Yeats, Pound,** and Eliot turned to symbolism or **imagism** in their creation of a more self-consciously aesthetic method. Pound's "In a Station of the Metro" is perhaps the purest and most renowned exemplification of imagism. Pound's method, like Yeats's symbolism, was concerned with the creation of "the beautiful image." Yet imagism's terse minimalist method seemed to many modernist writers limiting at the time of a sociological cataclysm on the scale of **World War I.** New poetic experiments were necessary—resulting in more substantial poetic works such as *The Cantos, Spring and All, Observations,* and *The Tower.*

Pound's "Hugh Selwyn Mauberley" (1920)—the product of a close collaboration between Pound and Eliot—revealed the way in which a long poem could be constructed through juxtaposing shorter poems and fragments. In this respect it paved the way for *The Waste Land,* and the long poems of **Williams** and **Stevens.** "Mauberley" is also significant through being written in rhymed quatrains, thus constituting a "counter-current" or corrective to free-verse imagism, which Eliot and Pound felt had been pushed to its limit.

It is necessary to recognize that the formal experimentation evident in the work of key modernist writers did not necessarily constitute a linear development. Rather, it entailed a constantly shifting process of assimilation, revision, and rejection, in the attempt to establish a negotiation between the (often conflicting) demands of sociological awareness and modern aesthetics. James Longenbach rightly asserts that "reading the moderns, we need to remain open to their variousness, their duplicities, their contradictions" (Longenbach 125).

Bethan Jones

Selected Bibliography

Auden, W. H. "In Memory of W. B. Yeats." In his *Selected Poems.* Ed. Edward Mendelson. London: Faber and Faber, 1988.

Butler, Christopher. *Early Modernism.* Oxford: Oxford UP, 1994.

Joyce, James. *Letters.* Ed. Stuart Gilbert and Richard Ellmann. 3 vols. London: Faber and Faber, 1957–66. Vol. I.

Lawrence, D. H. *Women in Love.* Ed. David Farmer, Lindeth Vasey and John Worthen. Cambridge: Cambridge UP, 1987.

Levenson, Michael. "Introduction." *The Cambridge Companion to Modernism.* Ed. Michael Levenson. Cambridge: Cambridge UP, 1999.

Longenbach, James. "Modern poetry." In Levenson.

Pound, Ezra. *Personae.* Ed. Lea Baechler and A. Walton Litz. New York: New Directions, 1990.

Williams, William Carlos. "America, Whitman, and the Art of Poetry." *The Poetry Journal* 8 (November 1917).

Forster, E(dward) M(organ) (1879–1970)

English novelist, short story writer, essayist, critic, travel writer, biographer, and librettist.

His father having died nine months after his birth, E. M. Forster spent his happiest childhood years with his mother at "Rooksnest," a house near Stevenage that he would later immortalize as "Howards End." In 1893 he moved with his mother to Tonbridge, where he attended Tonbridge School as a day boy: he hated the experience and later wrote passionately about public school brutality. His education and his subsequent travels were funded by the trust money left for him by his great aunt, Marianne Thornton, on her death in 1887. At King's College, Cambridge, he studied first classics, then history. The friendships he forged at Cambridge underpinned the liberal humanist values of his upbringing: in 1901 he was elected to the *Apostles,* a diverse group of artists and intellectuals devoted to the polite social and intellectual ideals advocated by the Cambridge philosopher G. E. Moore. The Apostles group included such luminaries as Bertrand Russell, Lytton Strachey, and John Maynard Keynes, and its members would soon form the backbone of the **Bloomsbury** group, fronted by **Virginia Woolf.** Under the Cambridge influence, Forster shed the oppressive Christianity of his childhood and was able to confront his own homosexuality.

After Cambridge, Forster re-joined his mother for tours of **Italy** and **Greece.** During 1903 he contributed articles to the *Independent Review,* run by his Cambridge friends. His first short story, "Story of a Panic," was published in 1904. In 1905 he became tutor to the children of the Countess von Arnim at Nassenheide in Pomerania. He returned to England for the publication of his first novel, *Where Angels*

Fear to Tread, in October 1905. The following year he went to live with his mother in Weybridge, where he would stay for the next twenty years of his life. Here, he became tutor to the Muslim patriot Syed Ross Masood, with whom he would develop an intense friendship. Three more novels followed in quick succession: *The Longest Journey* (1907), *A Room with a View* (1908), and the novel that truly established his reputation, *Howards End* (1910). Forster's first three novels are concerned to show the effects of the repressive forms of English middle-class life. In *Where Angels Fear to Tread,* Lilia Herriton visits Italy to recover from the death of her husband, only to start a relationship with an Italian. When Lilia dies giving birth to a son, her outraged family scheme to snatch the child away and bring it up in England. In a tragic finale, the scheme fails and the child is killed. In *A Room with a View,* Lucy Honeychurch finds love with George Emerson in Florence only after finding the strength to reject Cecil Vyse, the "proper" young man who threatens to crush her. *Howards End* is concerned with the future of England: it looks for ways to *connect* culture and industry, sympathy and opportunism. Forster's novels are often compared to those of Jane Austen for their comedy and their concern with social manners, those of Samuel Butler for their liberalism, and those of **Proust** for their structural use of the leitmotif.

In the immediate pre-war years Forster made two important visits. One was to **India** in 1912, where he struck up a friendship with the Maharajah of Dewas Senior; the other was to Edward Carpenter at his house near Chesterfield in England. The meeting with Carpenter inspired Forster to write *Maurice,* his homosexual novel, published posthumously in 1971. During **the war,** he worked as a cataloguer in the National Gallery, before leaving for Alexandria to work for the International Red Cross. In Alexandria he became close friends with the Greek poet Constantin Cavafy, whose work he promoted in England. He stayed in Alexandria until 1919. After the war he became editor of the left-wing paper, the *Daily Herald,* but went back to India in 1921 to become secretary and companion to the Maharajah of Dewas Senior. In 1922 he published *Alexandria: A History and a Guide,* and in 1924 his last and most celebrated novel, *A Passage to India.* This novel reveals the oppressive nature of British colonial rule in India: it also shows the British tourists Adela Quested and Mrs. Moore falling under the spell of the country's strangeness. At the center of the novel is the mystery of the happenings at the Marabar Caves: the Indian Doctor Aziz is said to have raped the young English girl Adela Quested, but is acquitted at the trial after Adela realizes that the proceedings are being rigged.

Forster was to write no more novels after *A Passage to India.* Instead, he turned to journalism and criticism. He delivered a series of lectures on the novel at Cambridge University in 1927 that were subsequently published as *Aspects of the Novel* (1927); he wrote a biography of his friend, Goldsworthy Lowes Dickinson (1934); and he published a collection of essays entitled *Abinger Harvest* (1936) after the village in Surrey where he inherited a house in 1924. In 1946, a year after his mother's death, he was offered an honorary fellowship at Cambridge and a permanent home at King's College. In 1949 he worked with Eric Crozier on the libretto for Benjamin Britten's opera *Billy Budd.* *Two Cheers for Democracy* was published in 1951, and *The Hill of Devi,* his book on India comprising letters and commentary, appeared in 1953. Forster worked in his own time to uphold the rights of the individual and to oppose the **censorship** of literary works. He became the first president of the National Council for Civil Liberties in 1934, he campaigned against the suppression of Radclyffe Hall's novel *The Well* *of Loneliness,* and, in 1960, he appeared for the defense in the trial of *Lady Chatterley's Lover* at the Old Bailey. He was awarded the Order of Merit in 1969. *The Life to Come,* a collection of short stories dealing with homosexuality, was published posthumously the year after *Maurice,* in 1972. In 1980 his unfinished fictional works were collected in a volume entitled *Arctic Summer and Other Fiction.*

Andrew Harrison

Selected Bibliography

The standard Abinger Edition of Forster's works is published by Edward Arnold and André Deutsch. The standard bibliography of his works has been prepared by B. J. Kirkpatrick: *A Bibliography of E. M. Forster.* Oxford: Clarendon Press, 2nd edition, 1985. An acclaimed biography by P. N. Furbank was published in two volumes: *Volume I: The Growth of the Novelist (1879–1914).* London: Secker and Warburg, 1977. and *Volume II: Polycrates' Ring (1914–1970).* London: Secker and Warburg, 1978.

Gardner, Philip, ed. *E. M. Forster: The Critical Heritage.* London: Routledge and Kegan Paul, 1973.

Hertz, Judith Scherer, and Martin, Robert K. *E. M. Forster: Centenary Revaluations.* London: Macmillan, 1982.

Page, Norman. *E. M. Forster.* London: Macmillan, 1987.

Stone, Wilfred. *The Cave and the Mountain: A Study of E. M. Forster.* London: Oxford University Press, 1966.

France

Culture, Politics, and Society 1895–1939

As they visited the international pavilions, many in the sinuous *Art Nouveau* style, as they admired the banks of the Seine transformed to resemble the palaces of the Grand Canal in Venice, as they rode on the Big wheel, ascended the ten-year old Eiffel Tower (for many years the tallest structure in the world), or watched with amazement Sarah Bernhardt on **film** with synchronized phonograph sound, visitors to the Paris *Exposition Universelle* of 1900 might have been forgiven for thinking that this spectacularly beautiful and vibrantly cosmopolitan city was the capital of a confident world power whose stable government and united people were resolutely looking forward to the new century. In many ways they would have been mistaken. Closer to reality was the assessment of the journalist Adolphe Retté who wrote in 1898, "The dominant characteristic of an epoch of transition like ours is spiritual anxiety. It is not surprising we are living in a storm where a hundred contradictory elements collide; debris from the past, scraps of the present, seeds of the future, swirling, combining, separating under the imperious wind of destiny." Indeed for a time in the 1890s a wave of anarchist bombs had seemed to threaten the very fabric of the bourgeois society which the thirty-year old Third Republic had striven to consolidate but which remained deeply divided in matters of politics, religion, and culture. Potently symbolic of these divisions were two visual icons today universally synonymous with *Gay Paree,* but then both new and charged with conflicting messages: to the left, the Eiffel Tower, and to the right, the basilica of Sacré-Coeur. The Eiffel Tower (1889) was erected in two years to celebrate the centenary of the Revolution of 1789 and the triumph of Republican ideals; Sacré-Coeur was conceived in the 1870s as an act of reparation for the fratricidal massacres (including the Archbishop of Paris) by the *Communards* of 1871, in the miniature civil war which followed the defeat by Prussia of Napoleon III's Second Empire. The monumental pseudo-Romanesque edifice on the appropriately-named hill of Montmartre (Mont des Martyrs) took forty years to complete and was still unfinished in 1900.

On the left, Republicans and socialists led by Jean Jaurès, favored a modern secular state with no established church and no clerical involvement in education. They were the inheritors of the proto-socialist movements of the nineteenth century and the theories of positivist thinkers such as Auguste Comte (1798–1857), Ernest Renan (1823–92) and Hippolyte Taine (1828–93), for whom science and reason were the new religion of progress. On the right, an extreme form of nationalism was evolving, fueled by the defeat of 1870 and the loss of the provinces of Alsace and Lorraine; this championed the power of the army, the Catholic Church and the religious orders, fostered (in its worst manifestations) xenophobia and anti-Semitism, and campaigned for the restoration of the monarchy. The long-simmering hostility between these two factions erupted violently into the open over the Dreyfus Affair.

In 1895, Alfred Dreyfus, a captain in the French army (who happened to be Jewish) was tried and convicted by court-martial of spying for **Germany** and exiled to the notorious Devil's Island prison. As evidence of a gross miscarriage of justice, compounded by prejudice and cover-up began to emerge, public figures from all walks of life, not least men of letters, were drawn into a protracted and at times violent controversy which only partly abated with the complete exoneration and rehabilitation of Dreyfus in 1906. The most famous episode of the affair was the open letter "J'accuse!" from Émile Zola to the President of the Republic Félix Faure, published in 1898 in the newspaper *L'Aurore.* Zola accused the generals, the War Office, the courts and the right-wing press of conspiracy, cover-up, and prejudice. Zola was tried and convicted of libel and fled briefly to England to avoid arrest. An impressive list of major writers sided with the *pro-Dreyfusards* and they were backed by the radical republicans and socialists who now gained the upper hand in the Assemblée Nationale. Ranged against Dreyfus and, by

association, against the political left, were several influential authors now chiefly remembered for their politics; Léon Daudet, Maurice Barrès, and Charles Maurras. Edouard Drumont, the author of *La France Juive,* propagated anti-Semitism in his journal *La Libre Parole* and in 1899 Charles Maurras set up the nationalist and anti-Semitic movement and journal *L'Action Française.* This crucial event marks the beginning of French fascism. Maurras claimed that France was overrun with Jews, Protestants, Freemasons, and half-breeds and called for the restoration of a catholic monarchy. Maurras's journal was only suppressed in 1944 and he was imprisoned for Nazi collaboration. The polarization of political and cultural attitudes persisted long after the Dreyfus affair; the virus of anti-Semitism resurfaces in French society and literature in the Thirties, with the vitriolic outpourings of Céline, Drieu de la Rochelle, and Robert Bresillach. To the end of the twentieth century France was still coming to terms with the sinister history of its Nazi collaborators.

The involvement of the Catholic Church with reactionary forces undoubtedly hastened further the secularization of the state already undertaken by successive governments and, by 1906, the Church was completely disestablished, religious orders were disbanded and Church property was nationalized. But catholicism was not entirely tainted with extremism. A growing disillusion with positivist materialism in the last decades of the old century had led to a resurgence of catholic belief and practice, represented in literature first by Verlaine, then at the turn of the century by the former naturalist novelist J.-K. Huysmans and the poets Charles Péguy, Paul Claudel, and Francis Jammes. Catholic philosophy was revitalized in the 1920s by the convert Jacques Maritain and by Etienne Gilson and the catholic existentialism of Gabriel Marcel (1889–1973) predates Sartre and

Camus by twenty years; indeed much of the vocabulary of existentialism as popularized by Sartre can first be heard in the catholic philosophy of action propounded as early as 1893 by Maurice Blondel (1861–1949). A number of France's leading musicians were also inspired by their profound catholic faith; Gabriel Fauré, Francis Poulenc, and Olivier Messiean.

Unlike the flowering of "War Poets" to be found in British literature, the horror of **World War I** is recorded principally in the works of French novelists, of which Henri Barbusse's *Le Feu* remains a most powerful example. **Dada** and **surrealism** may be seen as a belated literary pendant of the bomb-happy anarchist idealists of the 1890s, all of whom seem to say "a plague on both your houses" to the feuding factions of the old political and cultural order. A telling example of this was the surrealist pamphlet "A Corpse," denigrating Anatole France and issued on the very day of his funeral, in which Aragon asked "Have you slapped a corpse yet?" The 1920s were known in France as *les années folles,* and there is perhaps, in the more frivolous excesses of surrealist happenings, in the craze for popular music and dancing, even in the newly liberated and uncorsetted women's fashions pioneered by Coco Chanel, a desperate desire to shake off the memory of a generation exterminated in the fields of Picardy and Flanders, and a sense that, after the false dawn of 1900, the new century was at last under way. Pacifism was widely advocated in politics and literature and this mood persists until the beginning of the 1930s when a sea-change is heralded by Louis Aragon's commitment to the communist party and his expulsion from the surrealist movement. The thirties see the rapid re-politicization of cultural life as writers and intellectuals attempt to come to terms with the challenge of Soviet communism in the wake of Stalin's overtures to European socialists. The *front populaire* brought an alliance of socialists and communists to government in 1936, the year which saw André Gide's trip to Moscow and subsequent rejection of Stalin. That same year, intellectuals were again forced to take sides for or against fascism in the Spanish Civil War; Georges Bernanos denounced the Falangists in his *Les Grands Cimetières sous la Lune* (1938), and Céline countered with his anti-Semitic and pacifist *Bagatelles pour un Massacre* and *L'Ecole des Cadavres* (1937–38). Drieu de la Rochelle took over as editor of *La Nouvelle Revue Française,* alienating all its seasoned contributors (including Gide and Valéry) as he steered it toward collaboration. Charles de Gaulle, a member of the last legitimate government of the Third Republic, warned in his writings of the futility of relying on the Maginot line to defend France's eastern border and the urgent need to replace cavalry with tanks.

Throughout these turbulent years, Paris remained the cultural mecca for artists and writers from around the world and virtually every major new movement in art and literature was born out of the coming together of so many original and innovative talents in the studios of the *Bateau Lavoir,* in the bohemian cafés of Montmartre, or the intellectual salons of Montparnasse, or in the pages of innumerable literary reviews of which *La Nouvelle Revue Française* was the most illustrious and influential. **James Joyce** and **T. S. Eliot** were early visitors and **Samuel Beckett** came and stayed. Pablo Picasso was the first of a whole host of foreign painters who either settled in Paris or created their most important works there. Serge Diaghilev brought his *ballets russes* and Nijinsky. **Gertrude Stein** led the invasion of "Americans in Paris," escaping from prohibition and a less than open attitude to artistic innovation. From America too came jazz and the much-admired cabaret artiste Josephine Baker. Paris's place at the center of the modernist movements of the early twentieth century is, quite simply, unique.

The Novel

Many major novelists writing in the first thirty or so years of the century contributed to the genre of the *roman-fleuve*. The term was coined by Romain Rolland, but saga or chronicle novels which trace the fate of recurring family members and social groups go back to Honoré de Balzac's *La Comédie humaine* and, above all, to the champion of **naturalism,** Émile Zola (1840–1902) and his twenty-volume cycle *Les Rougon-Macquart* (1871–93) which traces in meticulously realistic detail the public and private history of a family under the Second Empire, the regime which collapsed with France's defeat by Prussia in the war of 1870. Zola elaborated his theory and method in *Le Roman expérimental* (1880) and he researched his work with all the zeal of a modern campaigning journalist, denouncing poverty, corruption, and the exploitation of the proletariat. His involvement in the Dreyfus affair at the turn of the century was a fitting climax to a literary career constantly in the service of humane social causes.

Romain Rolland (1866–1944) published the ten volumes of his *roman-fleuve, Jean-Christophe,* between 1903 and 1912 and won the Grand Prix de L'Académie Française in 1913, the year in which **Proust** was obliged to publish *Du Côté de chez Swann* at his own expense. The central character Jean-Christophe is a German musician ("Beethoven in today's world") and Rolland traces his passionate life and loves and evokes the "divine exaltation" of his music. In spite of many fine passages on childhood, love, music, and an idealized and exalted sense of human fraternity, and in spite of the award of the Nobel prize in 1916, Rolland's position above hatred and above the fray of war was ill-understood by a country gripped by a virulent hatred

of Germany. Rolland remained a distinguished left-wing literary figure, in touch with public figures from around the world (Tolstoy, Gorky, Ghandi), seeking to promote pacifism and reconciliation. In 1933, with painfully accurate foresight, he refused the Goethe medal from Hitler's Germany.

Jules Romains (Louis Farigoule, 1855–1972) is remembered above all for his vast 27 volume *roman-fleuve, Les Hommes de bonne volonté* (1932–46), but his first distinctive contribution to the new century began when, one evening in October 1903, on his way home from the Lycée Condorcet, he experienced what he later called "l'illumination de la rue d'Amsterdam." Romains had a vision of the teeming population of the busy Paris streets not as depersonalized and alienated but somehow humanely interconnected as if sharing one interrelated soul or spirit. This was the origin of his doctrine of *unanisme* which was to influence a number of writers, some of whom gathered briefly as a literary commune known as *l'Abbaye* in honor of Rabelais' *Thélème*. Romains' poetry, especially *La Vie Unanime* (1908), contains many fine examples of his theory which clearly influenced Guillaume Apollinaire in whose poetry can be heard more than an echo of this sense of fraternity in the big city as a counterpoint to the more prevailing mood of melancholy isolation (one feels obliged to point out that most of this is already present in Baudelaire's verse and prose poems of the 1850s and 60s).

Romains' highly regarded first novel *Mort de quelqu'un* (1911) demonstrates how the apparent nobody of the title is subtly interconnected, if only in death, to the bustling life of the city, in a way reminiscent of John Donne's "No man is an island. . . ." In the Twenties, in his trilogy *Psyché* (1921–29), Romains explored conjugal bliss and a quasi-mystical eroticism at times reminiscent of his British contemporary **D. H. Lawrence.** However, in the eyes of many critics, the sheer vastness of the novel cycle *Les Hommes de bonne volonté* which charts the quarter-century between 1908 and 1933, ultimately dilutes and weakens its undeniably powerful moments, not to mention the fact that the later volumes concerning the 1920s and 30s were written in exile in America during World War II. Apart from unfolding the careers of two principal male characters, Romains presents an almost bewildering cavalcade of major and minor characters who lack the continuity and credibility of such characters in Zola or Proust. With the benefit of hindsight, the two most effective and poignantly affecting volumes are the detailed accounts of the Great War, *Prélude à Verdun* and *Verdun,* (both 1938) written on the eve of France's humiliating capitulation to Nazi Germany and the establishment of a collaborationist regime led by, of all people, Maréchal Pétain, "the victor of Verdun."

Few of his successors, though emulating many of his techniques and his concern for social justice, could equal him in style or energy. The novels of the socialist Anatole France (1844–1924) are more satirical, ironic and, ultimately pessimistic in spite of many comic touches. *La Rôtisserie de la Reine Pédauque* and *Les Opinions de Jérôme Coignard* (both 1893) were long admired for their witty irreverence and *L'Ile des Pingouins* (1908) and *La Révolte des Anges,* (1914), were compared to Voltaire. France was widely admired for the purity of his style and well into the 1920s he was internationally considered as the single most important voice in French literature, receiving the Nobel prize in 1921.

Georges Duhamel (1844–1966) after training as a doctor, began his literary career as a poet and playwright under the benign influence of *unanisme* and the *Abbaye* group. In his first novels *Vie des Martyrs* and *Civilisation* (1917–18) he writes movingly and with bitter immediacy of his experiences in wartime hospitals. In a more ambitious cycle *Salavin* (five vols. 1920–32), he charts the neurotic misadventures of the eponymous anti-hero, a hopelessly ineffectual and at times self-deluded creature (clear echoes of Dostoyevsky) who succeeds only *in extremis,* when he saves the life of a child at the cost of his own; Salavin in some ways prefigures the impotent or dilatory characters of mid-century fiction. Duhamel felt his greatest claim to fame was his ten-volume *roman-fleuve, Chronique des Pasquier* (1933–45), which follows the fortunes and misfortunes of an extended family based on Duhamel's own through the 1880s to the 1920s. While there is much of anecdotal and historical interest, and while Duhamel was an elegant and readable stylist, he does not have the dramatic sweep and vision of Balzac and Zola before him, nor, unlike Zola or Proust, is his work underpinned by a truly gripping ideological or aesthetic *idée-maîtresse* other than a vague humanitarianism, with the result that the overall effect is somewhat inconclusive and certainly inspired no real emulators.

Roger Martin du Gard (1881–1958) made a powerful contribution to the literature surrounding the Dreyfus affair in his second novel *Jean Barois* (1913) chronicling not only its repercussions in the intellectual and social life of the nation but also the rifts at the heart of families torn apart by conflicting religious and political attitudes. Alongside the heroic stand of Zola and his fictional transposition of the affair in his novel *Vérité* (1903), Anatole France's *Monsieur Bergeret à Paris* (1901), passages in Proust's *Le Côté de Guermantes* and his earlier *Jean Santeuil,* du Gard's novel is further evidence of the depth to which the Dreyfus affair had polarized French public life and letters and forced writers to take a stand which a later generation would admire and emulate as a model of *engagement.*

Du Gard's contribution to the *roman-fleuve* is the family saga *Les Thibault* (7 vols 1922–40, Nobel prize 1937). In this ambitious work, minutely documented contemporary details, objectivity and **realism** and a degree of deterministic behaviorism all betray a debt to Zola but there is also a personal and private sensibility haunted by the enigma of existence and the mystery of death which the author's agnosticism could not assuage. Thibault *père* believes all answers are to be found in his catholic faith whereas his two very different sons, Antoine and Jacques, embrace the faith of science on the one hand, revolt and humanitarianism on the other. Ironically the father dies a lingering death still plagued by doubt and fear and his sons both die as a result of the war. Only Jacques' illegitimate son is left to confront an uncertain future in the post-1918 world (an epilogue made doubly bleak by its publication in 1940). *Les Thibault* offers many fascinating glimpses into the private lives and public events, the mood and mentality of the years up to the Armistice but artistically and emotionally the work seems to chart an end rather than point to new beginnings.

From the time of his co-founding, with the theater director Jacques Copeau and the critic Jacques Rivière, of the influential *Nouvelle Revue Française* (1909) up to his death, André Gide (1869–1951, Nobel prize 1947) was widely regarded alongside Proust, Claudel, and Valéry (all published by NRF-Gallimard), as one of the truly great writers and innovators of the half-century; indeed in the thirties he was, in the words of one critic, "our most important contemporary." Like Proust, Gide was born into the well-to-do *haute bourgeoisie.* He was (again like Proust) a sensitive child but one whose strict protestant upbringing within an at least nominally catholic culture left him with a profound adolescent sense of guilt and difference. His early friendship with Paul Valéry and Pierre Louÿs and his meeting with Mallarmé made him familiar with the symbolist

themes and preoccupations which pervade his earliest works, *Le Cahier d'André Walter* and *Poésies d'André Walter* (1891–2) in which a fairly naïve adolescent conflict between the flesh and the spirit ends in the evasion of madness and death. However, in 1893, in the course of a visit to Tunisia, Gide experienced an emotional and sensual liberation which allowed him to come to terms with his unorthodox sexuality (in late twentieth-century terms he *came out*) and after rejecting his earlier persona and the sterility of a dreamy literature divorced from life (*Paludes,* 1895) he begins to find the unmistakable Gidean voice in *Les Nourritures Terrestres* (1897). At the same time he apparently bowed to convention by marrying his cousin Madeleine. The ensuing prose works which deal with this period of awakening and self-discovery may be considered as the first stirrings (in prose at least) of a genuinely modern literary aesthetic and one which was profoundly to mark many French writers up to and beyond Camus and Sartre. *Les Nourritures Terrestres* reveals many of the themes and attitudes which run like a leitmotif throughout his multifaceted literary career, namely, a throwing off of all conventions and received ideas, a quest for authentic personal experience, freed from the shackles of any pre-existent moral or social order ("Families, I hate you"), a commitment to openness (*disponibilité*) to self, others and new experiences ("every new thing must find us totally open to it"), a burning need for sincerity in all domains including sexuality, and, since such desiderata do not come easily, an abiding awareness of the conflicts and caprices inherent in the psyche of a lucidly narcissistic individual ("Throw away this book . . . find your own attitudes [to life]"). The somewhat breathless and ejaculatory style and tone of *Nourritures,* part diary, part prose poem, part sermon, are disciplined in the next three prose works, which Gide entitled *récits* not novels, but all of which are fictionalized narratives of aspects of personal experience. Thus, in *L'Immoraliste* (1902), the narrator, after a bout of tuberculosis, undergoes a physical and sensual reawakening in North Africa but when, having nursed him to health, his wife also falls ill and they return to Africa, he neglects her for hedonistic self-indulgence as she lies dying, and he is subsequently filled with a sense of impotence and remorse in the face of his ill-gained freedom. In *La Porte Etroite* (1909) Gide deals with the conflict between divine and earthly love. Here, puritan self-abnegation on the part of Alissa (whose diaries eventually form an important element of the *récit*) blots out all hope of fulfillment in love for the narrator Jérôme. The later *récit, La Symphonie Pastorale* (1919), written in journal form, along with the autobiographical *Si le Grain ne meurt* (1926) complete Gide's treatment of material essentially derived from his own early experiences. The first three of these works seem to be polar extremes of aspects of Gide's own inner life but for more than half a century, partly due to their subject and partly to their experiments with narrative form they caught the imagination of a younger generation of would-be writers for whom Gide offered (but very loosely as he would have wished) a model in life and art.

In 1914 Gide described what was in effect his first novel *Les Caves du Vatican* as a *sotie,* a form blending humor, irony, suspense, and something of the detective story. In this extremely funny story of the timid provincial bourgeois Amadée Fleurissoire's attempt to rescue the Pope from a supposed kidnapping, the debonair young Lafcadio commits the famous Gidean *acte gratuit* (an impulsive action without cause, premeditation or motive), when he pushes Fleurissoire to his death from a speeding train. In a typically Gidean paradox in which life imitates art, Lafcadio's novelist half-brother has hit upon the idea of the very same *acte gra-*

tuit; when he reads to Lafcadio the newspaper account of Fleurissoire's death he reveals that the dead man was his brother-in-law. As so often with Gide the precursor of modern literary experiment, there is no definitive closure at the end of the story. Lafcadio cannot flee from his own self-knowledge but Gide's sympathy clearly lies with this free individual (symbolized by his illegitimacy) rather than the conventional bourgeois characters who are mocked and lampooned.

In his Socratic dialogue *Corydon* (1924) Gide took the extremely daring step of openly discussing homosexuality, including his own. He had disapproved of Proust's disguising of male homosexual experience except for the more salacious or grotesque aspects embodied by the baron Charlus. From now on Gide was notorious as well as famous, attracting vehement criticism as a corrupter of youth, from conservative and religious quarters (virtually all his works were placed on the Catholic Church's index of banned books). Gide's courage in the climate of his time cannot be denied and was another source of admiration for younger generations. The much later emergence of lesbian, gay, and gender themes as a valid area of literary inquiry owes much to Gide, the pioneer of *coming out*. In 1927 Gide published the only work he described as a novel, *Les Faux Monnayeurs,* but this very label may be a playful irony as there are two novels, one taking place inside the other in the journal of the novelist-protagonist Edouard, a classic example of the *mise en abyme*. The counterfeiters of the title are for Gide not just the wayward students passing fake money but all those young or old who live in what Sartre would later call *mauvaise foi,* deceiving themselves and others. Gide's sympathies lie with Edouard who is trying to strip his novel (within the novel) of all that is superfluous, incidental, in an attempt to capture the essentials of the lived consciousness and experience of those who are "pure, honest, authentic." Like Proust, Gide jettisons the traditional adherence to chronological time with flashback, interpolations, and elements of simultaneity and *monologue intérieur.* When Edouard (often Gide's mouthpiece) admits he will never finish the novel, he is affirming Gide's view that a single closed work of art can never hope to capture once and for all the flux of personality or the kaleidoscopic continuum of duration. Here, in embryo, are the seeds of the post-1945 *nouveau roman.* The self-conscious questioning of literary forms and structures, coupled with an at times flamboyant rejection of social and moral norms remain at the center of much of Gide's best work and were widely admired and emulated by the next generation. In the 1930s, his intellectual curiosity led him to flirt with communism which he publicly rejected after a trip to the USSR, and his final posthumous memoir, revealing the suffering he had caused his wife, was one last example of his need for honesty, however painful. Critics in the second half of the century have underlined the internal inconsistencies in Gide's thought and the at times gratuitous complexity of his modes of expression, claiming also that many of his characters are not nearly as emancipated as they at first appear. Be that as it may, Gide's presence as a very public man of letters (including his journals, his correspondence and his involvement with NRF-Gallimard) did in its own day exert enormous influence, and his legacy is still palpable well into the second half of the century.

In the annals of twentieth-century literature, **Marcel Proust** (1871–1922) stands alone. Literally, because in his relatively short life he was often perceived as an aloof and snobbish dilettante, adhering to no school or movement and moving only in the closed and privileged world of Parisian aristocracy and the *haute bour-*

geoisie, eccentric, fastidious and, at the end, a sickly and obsessive recluse. But behind this façade, one of the most lucid and acutely perceptive minds of the century, coupled with a poetic sensibility of the highest order, was tirelessly sifting, recording and re-ordering the minutiae of everyday existence and simultaneously examining the mental processes by means of which the individual psyche evaluates, transforms, and interprets the given material of the outside world. Proust did in fact have a degree in literature and had attended the lectures of Henri Bergson which undoubtedly inspired or clarified his own reflections on the nature of consciousness, the role and functions of memory and, above all, the distinction between *le temps* and *la durée* which were to become cornerstones of his work. *A la recherche du temps perdu* occupied the second half of his life so completely that his life and work became coterminous in a way only dreamt of by artists of the romantic period; indeed, if Proust has a predecessor it must surely be Baudelaire whose obsession with time and fascination with memory and the past is encapsulated in lines which uncannily sum up Proust's quest for "l'enfance retrouvée à volonté": "Charme profond, magique dont nous grise/Dans le présent le passé restauré!" This is not to say that Proust did not share a wider literary inheritance. At the most banal level *A la recherche* is a *roman-fleuve* which traces the lives and loves, the fortunes and misfortunes of a number of inter-related families against the instantly recognizable and sharply delineated social and political background of, for instance, the Dreyfus affair and the First World War. Its wealth of minutely observed detail would be unthinkable without the example of Zola and realism. Its sense of the mystery immanent in the most mundane of material objects which thereby become symbols, would not have been so sharp without the poetic model of the symbolists. Its sustained meditation on the nature and power of art harks back to Proust's close reading of Ruskin. One could go on but there is a sense in which all of this is irrelevant because *A la recherche* transcends all its sources and, like its reclusive author, stands alone as a kind of universe of its own which, almost a century on, has not ceased to attract readers, critics, film-makers and even philosophers (see Raul Ruiz's critically acclaimed film *Time Regained* [1998] and Alain de Botton's *How Proust Can Change Your Life* [Picador, 1998]). The twentieth century's growing fascination with Proust seems to stem from the curious fact that the further its contemporary historical and social milieu fades into the shadowy pages of history, the more its real power and intentions become apparent. Above and beyond the specific characters and the convoluted interaction of their finite lives, Proust elaborated a sustained meditation on the very nature of consciousness, personality, friendship (or its impossibility), sexual desire and its unattainable goals, the delusions of romantic love, the subjective and intermittent nature of memory within which, for Proust, there lay a secret fullness of all past selves which could only be retrieved and restored through art, and even then, only through the elusive agency of involuntary memory. The work evolves in, and is crowned by, an understanding of time which is not linear or chronological, but suffused and illuminated by a purely Proustian inner sense of a temporality which embraces past and present, moments and durations, flashback, digression, inner monologue, juxtaposition, and simultaneity. The culmination, in *Le Temps retrouvé,* is an **epiphany** in which the fullness and value of one transient mortal is asserted within a Herculean work of art from which *le temps,* in its hideously contingent Baudelairean sense, has been triumphantly banished. And yet, without a trace of piousness or self-indulgence, the work is by turns witty, amusing and profoundly touching. Its linguistic and syntactical complexities perfectly mirror the complexities of its content and while demanding, never feel over-contrived. Proust once compared himself to Noah in his ark, "enclosed, and darkness covering the earth," who was yet able to see before him the whole world. From his ark on the Boulevard Haussman and finally at 44 rue Hamelin, Marcel Proust repopulated the world of twentieth-century fiction.

Another world apart, which within its own terms bears comparison with that of Proust, was the creation of the only woman writer of real stature in the first half century. [Sidonie-Gabrielle] Colette (1873–1954) served her literary apprenticeship ghost-writing the *Claudine* novels (1900–1903) which appeared under her husband's pen name Willy and were an instant success, partly for their frank and spicy attitude to adolescent sex. After her divorce and during a period in music-hall and cabaret, Colette began a highly successful career as a novelist which was to last forty years and bring her both popularity and serious critical acclaim with such well-known titles as *La Retraite sentimentale* (1907), *Les Vrilles de la Vigne* (1908), *La Vagabonde* (1910), *Chéri* and *La Fin de Chéri* (1920–26), *Le Blé en Herbe* (1923). In *La Maison de Claudine* (1922), *La Naissance du Jour* (1928) and *Sido* (1929), Colette drew on memories of her Burgundian childhood and schooldays, and her intense and observant love of nature. Of her later successes, *Gigi* (1943) brought her world fame through the musical and film. Colette's novels succinctly evoke the consolation of profound and affectionate friendships, the torment of adolescent love and of adult jealousy. She minutely but pithily details the pleasure and pain of sensual relationships and celebrates the plenitude of aesthetic enjoyment to be derived from the real world of places, people, her cherished pets, houses, and things. Her prose style was, and still is, considered a model of freshness, elegance, and minutely observed detail. In the post-feminist age, the praise Colette has received for her "woman's world" writing may seem dated and patronizing. Her works have an acuity and freshness found only in the very best writers of either/any gender. That hers is unmistakably the beautifully modulated voice of a self-possessed woman in a male-dominated milieu and moment, is in itself a remarkable achievement.

The catholic revival of the turn of the century had a profound influence on the two young men who perhaps best embody the most elevated and non-partisan aspects of what one might loosely call the catholic novel or novel of conscience. Both François Mauriac (1885–1970, Nobel prize 1952) and Georges Bernanos (1888–1998) were influenced by the vehemently nationalist and anti-Dreyfusard Maurice Barrès and the less doctrinaire but equally catholic and nationalist Charles Péguy. This brought them dangerously close to the virulent anti-Semitic and monarchist catholic tendency of the Action française movement around Léon Bloy and Charles Maurras and the virulently prejudiced author of *La France juive*, Edouard Drumont. Bernanos succumbed for a time but was later to use his inside knowledge to attack them all the more effectively. Mauriac's novels, often set in the rather bleak countryside of his native Bordeaux region, are heavily preoccupied with the sins of the flesh and the torments of souls torn between good and evil, between the presence of temptation and the apparent absence of God. The pre-1939 novels on which his later fame remained firmly established are *Le Désert de l'Amour* (1925), *Thérèse Desqueyroux* (1927), *Le Noeud de Vipères* (1932), *Le Mystère Frontenac* (1933) and *La Fin de la Nuit* (1935). Mauriac's style was much praised for its detached classicism even when dealing with passionate or tormented themes, as was his ability to recreate the

brooding and claustrophobic atmosphere of the provinces which mirrors the spiritual entrapment of his characters (notably Thérèse). While Mauriac's creations are often powerful and convincing and he is a compelling narrator, a later generation, in the person of Jean-Paul Sartre, accused Mauriac's characters of being trapped and predestined in a quasi-Calvinist universe with none of the authentic freedom of choice which was a pre-requisite of the existentialist view of the human condition.

Whereas Mauriac refused the label "catholic novelist," underlining his independence as a man of letters, Georges Bernanos's novels are more narrowly concerned with the Church through the somewhat melodramatic and tormented or humdrum and apparently unfulfilled lives of the priests who appear in many of his works from *Sous le Soleil de Satan* (1926) a steamy tale of seduction, murder, diabolic possession, and ultimate salvation through grace, to his masterpiece *Journal d'un Curé de Campagne* (1936), the story of a humble and pious country priest's struggle to serve the needs of his recalcitrant, devious, or anguished parishioners, at the end of which he dies exhausted but still convinced of the efficacy of divine grace. In spite of his earlier anti-Semitism, Bernanos, like Mauriac, rallied to the cause of anti-fascism and in the 1930s shocked the world with his forthright denunciation of the Spanish Church's support for Franco and his massacres during the Civil War (*Les Grand Cimetières sous la Lune*, 1937).

While for some, the horror of World War I may have reinforced the need for a theological worldview which at least offered the hope of meaning beyond evil and suffering, in other, slightly younger, novelists it may have contributed to a desire to flee from discredited Eurocentric cultural values. Henri de Montherlant (1896–1972), after describing his war experiences in his first novel *Le Songe* (1922) turned

verse and versets which echo the poetry of the psalms and of the Old Testament and of classical antiquity. The variety of images and moods (far greater than in Péguy) and the overarching sense of structure and purpose (far clearer than in Péguy) made his *Cinq Grandes Odes* (1904–10) a unique example of a catholic poet's response to the visionary aspects of Rimbaud's *Illuminations* and *Une Saison en Enfer,* a response which, in Claudel's own words, did not peter out in what he saw as the spiritual defeat of "poor" Verlaine and Mallarmé.

Saint-John Perse (Marie-René Alexis Saint-Léger Léger, 1887–1975, Nobel prize 1960) was a distinguished diplomat like his friend Claudel and was influenced by Claudel's use of the long, rhythmic line of free verse now known as the verset claudélien. His *Eloges* (1911) are filled with the sensual natural imagery of his native Guadeloupe couched in a style at times reminiscent of Rimbaud or Claudel. His *Anabase* (1924), a sweeping epic in which the conqueror-poet roams through torrid eastern landscapes and celebrates the richness and diversity of individual human experience, was translated into English by T. S. Eliot who clearly recognized a fellow "classical in literature."

Paul Valéry (1871–1945) had also sat at the feet of Mallarmé but moved on to become one of the most prominent secular intellectuals of the first half of the century. His early prose works, *Introduction à la méthode de Leonardo da Vinci* (1895) and the parodic *La Soirée avec Monsieur Teste* (1896) were reflections on the nature of mind and the limits of intellectual activity. In 1913, encouraged by Gide to return to poetry he began what eventually became *La Jeune Parque* (1917), a long reflective poem on the awakening of a youthful consciousness to a fuller awareness of the processes of solipsistic thought and, at the end, an embracing of the sensual world in a lucid spirit of intellectual enquiry. This poem is also noteworthy for the classical, almost Racinian, elegance of its diction and the studied musicality of its language, making it one of the great examples of traditional French lyricism alongside Lamartine, Baudelaire, Verlaine, and Mallarmé. This gift for mellifluous assonance, coupled with meditations on art and consciousness are to be found again in the masterly *Le Cimetière Marin* (1920) which ends with the life-enhancing cry, "Le vent se lève! . . . Il faut tenter de vivre!" and the studied elegance of *Charmes* (1922), all published by NRF-Gallimard. In the rigorous classicism of his verse forms, the careful musicality of his language and the lucidity of his themes, Valéry was a resolutely traditional poet but many French critics maintain that *La Jeune Parque* and *Le Cimetière Marin* are among the greatest French poems of the twentieth century. Valéry remained a central figure in French intellectual life largely because of his prolific output over twenty years of intellectual essays on many aspects of literature, politics, and philosophy: *Variétés, Tel Quel* and *Regards sur le monde actuel.*

In his excellent study of the origins of the avant-garde in France up to 1914 (*The Banquet Years*), Roger Shattuck called Guillaume Apollinaire (Guillaume Albert Wladimir Alexandre Apollinaire de Kostrowitsky, 1880–1918) "the impresario of the avant-garde." Until his premature death in the great flu epidemic of 1918, Apollinaire certainly seemed to be a common denominator between many of the poets, painters, and musicians who saw themselves as innovators and iconoclasts, rejecting (in loosely Nietzschean terms) Apollonian order (evolution within certain classical norms), in favor of Dionysiac adventure (modernist rupture and discontinuity). Indeed, in one of his last poems "La Jolie Rousse," which is something of a credo for all his fellow-artists, Apollinaire speaks of resolving "cette longue querelle . . . de l'ordre et l'aventure" but then takes up and restates the challenge which Rimbaud had abandoned over forty years earlier, and in so doing also provides a kind of pre-manifesto for surrealism (a word he himself invented);

> Nous voulons vous donner de vastes et
>   d'étranges domaines
> Où le mystère en fleurs s'offre à qui
>   veut le ceuillir
> Il y a là des feux nouveaux des
>   couleurs jamais vues
> Mille phantasmes impondérables
> Auxquels il faut donner de la réalité

Apollinaire had met Alfred Jarry and was influenced by the bizarre and outlandish techniques of his play *Ubu Roi* and his "science of imaginary solutions," *la Pataphysique,* but he was equally familiar with the mood and language of the symbolists and the poetry of Baudelaire, Rimbaud, and Verlaine. Apollinaire edited several short-lived magazines, *Le Festin d'Esope* (1903), *La Revue Immoraliste,* and *Les Soirées de Paris* (1912). In 1903 he met the painters Picasso, Derain, and Vlaminck, Marie Laurencin (with whom he had a long affair), and the poet Max Jacob. With his intense curiosity for all things new, and his raucous good humor, Apollinaire participated in the artistic and poetic ferment of the inhabitants of the Bateau Lavoir, a ramshackle old building in Montmartre which housed many poets and painters and witnessed the birth of **cubism,** which Apollinaire celebrated and publicized in his essay *Les Peintres Cubistes* (1913) when the movement was at the forefront of avant-garde art. In the same year, he wrote his influential *Antitradition futuriste,* which incorporated some of the ideas of **Marinetti** and the Italian futurists whose preoccupations with speed and the machine age also delighted him (compare with *Calligrammes,* "Allons plus vite nom de Dieu"). Since the turn of the century Apollinaire had published poems in various journals, the earliest of which, inspired by a stay in the Rhineland and his ill-fated affair with the English governess Annie Playden, still showed a debt to symbolism in spite of some daring images and syntax. Others reveal the influence of cubism in terms of discontinuity and juxtaposition of images. All of these were to be assembled in his first major collection *Alcools* (Mercure de France, 1913) from which punctuation was entirely banished and which begins with one of his latest and most resolutely modernist poems "Zone." The poem is a kaleidoscopic series of autobiographical flashbacks as the poet wanders alone and dispirited across Paris, and the urgent *simultanéisme* of its structure seems almost at odds with its themes of alienation and loss, culminating in a symbolic suicide at sunrise. But as the rest of the volume makes clear, Apollinaire's sense of a stable identity is precarious at the best of times and he continually recreates and destroys tentative personae in order to discover his true voice and identity. This fragmentation or multiplication of personality in the maelstrom of historical events and rapidly evolving artistic movements is to be found again in his last collection *Calligrammes* (1918). Apollinaire distilled into many of these poems his experiences at the battlefront which becomes a bizarre theater of war from which horror and pathos are not absent but buffered by verbal and visual fantasy, bittersweet humor, and an aching eroticism. Elsewhere, in "Lundi Rue Christine" one finds the first real *poème-conversation* made up of overheard scraps of conversation. The poem "Les Fenêtres," written for the catalogue of an exhibition of the paintings of Robert Delaunay, is a daring transposition into words of the swirling, highly colored near-abstractions of the original. In the *calligrammes* of the title (or *idéogrammes-lyriques,* as he also called them) Apollinaire "paints" with words just as the cubists had painted with letters (including collage of newsprint) in many of their most famous works. Thus "Pluies" is written in streams of letters falling like rain across the page. In "La Colombe poignardée et le Jet d'eau" the disposition of letters depicts the dove and the fountain. When one reads the dove, it is made up of the names of women the poet had loved, while the fountain weeps the names of his artist friends, separated by the war. At the base, the letters form a watchful eye which speaks of nightfall on the northern battle-front which is now a sea of blood. In the moving poem "La Petite Auto," which enthusiastically evokes Apollinaire's return to Paris at the outbreak of war and also more ominously prophesies the end of an old age and a brutal rebirth, the normal typographical layout gives way at one point to a depiction of the little car. These experiments were novel, playful, and at times touchingly effective. They also provided the surrealist poets and painters with an example of what Pierre Reverdy called "[the renewal of] the facade of words." Apollinaire had also prefigured the surrealists' preoccupation with dreams in his fantastical prose-poem "Onirocritique" (in *L'Enchanteur Pourrissant* 1908) and above all with his *drame sur-réaliste* (a term he first applied to Diaghilev's and Cocteau's *Parade*), *Les Mamelles de Tirésias* performed in 1917. The influence of Jarry is evident but so too is that of the *esprit nouveau* on which he had given a lecture in the same year. In the preface to *Mamelles,* Apollinaire called for an alliance of "sounds, gestures, colors, shouts, noises, music, dance, acrobatics, painting, actions and multiple décors. . . ." In his advocacy of effects of shock and surprise not least in the realm of imagery and metaphor, his exploitation of techniques of simultaneity and juxtaposition (see the poem "Il y a" in *Calligrammes*), and his voracious appetite for novelty and humorous fantasy, Apollinaire's life and work may be seen as a meeting place (like Paris itself) for much of the modernist experimentation of his time. His work is also a bridge between the end of symbolism and the first stirrings of surrealism.

Max Jacob (1876–1944) was one of Picasso's first friends in Paris and, although he never achieved the popular acclaim of Apollinaire, he exerted a profound influence on many of his contemporaries including Apollinaire, Reverdy, Cocteau, and the young surrealists, not only through his poetry, novels, and illustrations but through his zany and bohemian lifestyle in Montmartre and at the Bateau Lavoir where he lived for a time among the painters. He was fascinated by Jewish mysticism to which, after his vision of Christ and conversion in 1915, he added his own idiosyncratic blend of catholic piety, in which his friends didn't quite believe, thinking it to be the by-product of his addiction to ether-sniffing! He was a scholarly autodidact who half-seemed to live within his outlandish semi-autobiographical first novels, *Saint Matorel* (1909) and *Oeuvres mystiques et burlesques du Frère Matorel* (1911). He revitalized the form of the prose-poem with his prophetically presurrealist *Le Cornet à dés* (1916), whose very title implies the aleatory freedom of later surrealist techniques of composition and he continued to publish, treading his own original and idiosyncratic path, until his death from pneumonia in the notorious transit camp for French Jews at Drancy. The inimitable Max was a fervent proselytizer for modernism and, as his *Art Poétique* of 1922 and his voluminous correspondence reveal, saw his vocation partly as a mentor to the younger generation of poets.

Blaise Cendrars (Fréderic-Louis Sauser, 1887–1961) also deliberately blurred the distinction between life and art, truth and fiction in his influential early poems and his later novels. Fascinated by a sense of almost mystical self-discovery through real (or imaginary) travels, Cendrars' first success was with *Pâques à New York* (1912). This, and especially his *Prose du Transsibérien* (1913) clearly influenced the style, themes and language of Apollinaire's "Zone" as did his removal of much punctuation. *Prose* is a "railroad" poem in which impressions and images sweep past in quasi-simultaneous litany. The original edition was remarkable for being a two-meter long *dépliant,* advertised as "nearly as tall as the Eiffel tower," and illuminated with *couleurs simultanées* by Sonia Delaunay. In the period leading up to surrealism, Cendrars also published *Du Monde entier* and *Dix-neuf poèmes élastiques* (both 1919).

Pierre Reverdy (1889–1960) arrived in Paris from his native Narbonne in 1910 and with the friendship and guidance of Apollinaire, Jacob, and the cubist painters, quickly established himself as an unmistakably modern poetic presence in *Poèmes en Prose* (1915), *La Lucarne Ovale* (1916), the *roman poétique Le Voleur de Talan* (1917), and *Les Ardoises du Toit* (1918). Of all the modern poets writing around this time, Reverdy seems to possess a mood, tone, and style which appear to owe little to anything or anyone beyond his own creation of a poetic world of simplicity, sobriety, and a deep sense of the mysterious power of language to transform everyday objects into signs of a complex and haunted inner life via the juxtaposition of apparently banal images which create the "sparks" of which Breton later spoke as an essential ingredient of surrealist poetics. Aware of Mallarmé's experiments with typographical layout and emulating Apollinaire's suppression of punctuation (but not his *calligrammes*), Reverdy (especially in *Les Ardoises du Toit*) produced brief poems which by their manipulation of space and type on the page become objects (*le poème-objet*) for the eye as well as the ear. Reverdy creates a new mood of strangeness and expectancy at times not unlike the paintings of Giorgio de Chirico.

Reverdy's other claim to fame at this time was the launching of his short-lived but crucial review *NORD-SUD* (1917–18; facsimile edition published in 1980 by Jean-Michel Place) in which he offers an important definition of the modern poetic image taken up by the surrealists Breton, Eluard, Soupault, and Aragon, whom he befriended and whose first poems appeared here, alongside new poems by Apollinaire, Jacob, Tzara, and Cocteau among others, and illustrations by Braque and Léger. His reflections on poetry and imagery collected in *Self-Defence* (1919) also influenced the surrealists although, converted to catholicism in 1921, Reverdy never actively participated in the movement. A more personal and spiritually anguished tone is to be heard in his poetry from the late thirties, notably *Ferraille* (1937). His early volumes were corrected and collectively republished in *Plupart du Temps* (1945) and his later work (along with much that really belongs to his first period) in *Main-d'oeuvre* (1945). The modern Flammarion edition of his works brings together his valuable essays on poetry and reveals how fine an art critic he was, his friends' names reading like a roll-call of the greatest modern painters of the twentieth century to 1945.

Poetry was merely an element, and not the most important, of dada, the movement founded in Zurich in 1916 by Tristan Tzara (1896–1963) with Hugo Ball and the artist Hans Arp. Disgusted by what they saw as the bankruptcy of a culture which allowed the carnage of war, they defied logic and reason with madness and chaos and mocked conventional art through riotous anti-art events which prefigured the *Happenings* and certain other anti-establishment aspects of the American hippie scene of the 1960s, and, perhaps, the provocative *performance art* of the end of the twentieth century. From 1918 to 1921, the dadaist ranks included the avant-garde artists Francis Picabia and

Marcel Duchamp, as well as the poets André Breton, Louis Aragon, Paul Eluard, and Philippe Soupault. Innovation, iconoclasm, and provocation were the order of the day. In 1919 the four poets founded a review ironically entitled *Littérature* (from Verlaine's poem "L'Art poétique" of 1872 in which, after listing all that is desirable in a poetic work, he dismisses everything else as mere literature, "Et tout le reste est littérature"). They broke with dada in 1924 when they changed the name of the review to *La Révolution surréaliste,* officially inaugurating the surrealist movement. After Tzara's ground-breaking innovation he continued to write poetry in a more surrealist vein and is also important for his theoretical writings on poetry.

Moving effortlessly in and out of the various literary and artistic coteries of the period, Jean Cocteau (1889–1963) was a remarkably multi-talented and protean figure whose contribution (resented perhaps for its very versatility) has never quite been given the weight it deserves. Cocteau was fascinated by the **myth** of Orpheus and saw all his creative activity as poetic: *"poésie de théâtre, poésie de roman"* a reminder that all artistic activity is *poesis.* Profoundly galvanized by **Stravinsky**'s *Le Sacre du Printemps* (1912) and the impresario Serge Diaghilev's famous injunction "Etonnez-moi!," he threw himself into the melting-pot of modernism, briefly interrupted by his ambulance service in the war, which inspired his first novel, *Thomas l'Imposteur.* His early collections, *Le Potomak,* (published belatedly in 1919), *Ode à Picasso* (1919), *Le Cap de Bonne Espérance* (1919), *Poésies* (1920), *Vocabulaire* (1922), *Plain-Chant* (1923), *L'Ange Heurtebise* (1925) reveal a strikingly classical facility and flexibility of language and a thematic content rich in dreams, fantasy, humor, and paradox: "the poet is a lie who always tells the truth." At the same time, for Diaghilev's company he produced the ballet *Parade* (1917), with music by Erik Satie and décors by Picasso, *Le Boeuf sur le Toit* (1920) with music by Darius Milhaud and décors by Raoul Dufy, and the wickedly satirical *Les Mariées de la Tour Eiffel* (1921) with music by the composers known as *les six.* He was a gifted and original filmmaker, adapting his own works, and his surrealistic *Le Sang d'un Poète* is an early and influential example of cinema as a modern art form. He had a genuine talent as an artist and illustrator, with an economic and almost Picasso-like sense of line which may be admired in his frescoes for the Church of Notre-Dame de France, off Leicester Square in London, and for his own chapel at Milly-la-Forêt (as well as, in less edifying mode, in his erotic sketches, which speak for themselves!).

Apart from Marcel Proust's *magnum opus,* France's other major and, in many ways more obviously far-reaching contribution to modernism in art and literature is the surrealist movement, a movement whose genuinely revolutionary ideas and techniques can be seen to have permeated vast areas of both high and popular cultural activity right down to the end of the twentieth century. Suffice it to say that its roots (apart from the Swiss origins of its violent but short-lived precursor dada and the universal nightmare of war) are clearly to be found in the particularly French, and largely poetic, quarrel between order and adventure which was already present in the works of Apollinaire, Jacob, Cendrars, and Reverdy. While on the one hand refusing all tradition and ancestry in their "definitive clearout of the literary stable," the first surrealists, Breton, Soupault, Eluard, and Aragon (all poets), acknowledged this debt but also claimed to be the inheritors of a select band of largely marginal literary figures (the Marquis de Sade, Rimbaud, Lautréamont, and Jarry), as well as being the champions of the new theories of the unconscious expounded by **Freud,** with whom Breton exchanged letters. The central place they accorded to the drug-like power of *l'image,* is a key element in their quest for a new language, more profoundly in touch with the deepest recesses of the psychic and spiritual self, which had haunted the best of French poetry since Baudelaire. In their determination to make artistic endeavor more vibrantly relevant to the complexities of the modern age, they rejected Mallarmé's quest for a purer and more abstruse poetic diction ("donner un sens plus pur aux mots de la tribu"), and the linguistically traditional lyricism of his intellectual heir Paul Valéry. Their earliest experiments with dreams, automatic writing, aleatory juxtapositions, and the suppression of decipherable links between the poles of traditional metaphor, led at first to their denunciation as sensationalist charlatans and barbarian iconoclasts; indeed their most provocative public manifestations were often calculated to *épater le bourgeois.* But the early surrealists have left an immensely challenging and vibrant poetic legacy in French. André Breton in particular was a subtle theorist and the manifestoes of surrealism from 1924 onwards became the blueprints for a range of experimentation and refreshingly original creations in all the arts, not least the cinema (Buñuel's *Un Chien andalou,* 1928, and Cocteau's *Le Sang d'un poète,* 1931), all corresponding to the surrealist desire for *révolution permanente.* The post-1945 theater of the absurd owed much to their resolute anti-realism and in many ways surrealism realized Freud's dream of releasing the deeper voice of the id from the restrictive prisons of the ego. The influence of the surrealists continued to be felt to the end of the century in areas as diverse as new-wave French cinema, Sixties hippie culture (the student revolt of May 1968 in France provoked a wave of neo-surrealist verbal protest), advertising, pop videos, and stand-up comedy.

Theater

Theatrical activity in France was so profoundly influenced after 1945 by the emergence of the generation loosely known as the *theater of the absurd* that many earlier playwrights were eclipsed or seemed dated in their preoccupation with realistic plots, sets, and psychological verisimilitude. Nevertheless, the first half of the century offers a rich variety of plays reflecting many aspects of contemporary politics and society. Edmond Rostand achieved popular success with his neo-romantic verse drama *Cyrano de Bergerac* (1898). The novelist Jules Romains also had a highly successful career as a dramatist with a number of powerfully prophetic plays in which he evokes the dangers of dictatorship and the gullibility of **the masses:** *L'Armee dans la ville* (1911), *Cromedeyre-le-vieil* (1920), *Knock* (1923), *Le Dictateur* (1926). In the theater of pure entertainment, Georges Feydeau (1862–1921) was the supremely polished purveyor of the French farce which has enjoyed undimmed success throughout the century.

At this time the poet Paul Claudel was also writing his highly personal and passionately lyrical dramas which explore the conflict between human and divine love in historical settings: *Partage de Midi, L'Otage, Le Pain dur, l'Annonce faite à Marie, Le Soulier de Satin.* Although these plays were written between 1906 and 1923, many were not produced until after 1940 and it was only then that, thanks to the director Jean-Louis Barrault, Claudel came to be seen in retrospect as one of the major theatrical voices of the century.

Alfred Jarry's *Ubu Roi* (1896) is clearly the ancestor of a very different form of theater which seeks to break with the tradition of the theater of ideas and *the well-made play* in favor of a liberating world of fantasy, absurdity and anti-realism. The direct inheritors of this vision are Apollinaire in his surrealist *Les Mamelles de Tirésias* and Jean Cocteau, in his ballet *Parade* (both 1917). Cocteau developed his own vein of surreal fantasy and personal mythology in his first play *Orphée* (1926), a modern dress version of the myth, including a talking horse and the mysterious angel Heurtebise whose name Cocteau claims to have invented (from the brand-name of the elevator OTIS-PIFRE) while under the influence of opium. Mythical themes were the starting point for his highly original *Antigone* (1928, with music by Arthur Honneger) and *La Machine infernale* (1934). *Les Parents terribles* (1938), dealing with psychologically complex amorous liaisons caused, like most of his productions, a scandal at its first performance. After 1945, Cocteau made films of several of his earlier works and seemed to be one of the last representatives of the inter-war spirit of playful experimentation.

Wit, fantasy, and myth are also hallmarks of the theater of Jean Giraudoux (1882–1944) but these are allied to an almost classical elegance and lucidity of expression and a sustained humane reflection on pacifism and love. His first play *Siegfried* (1928), adapted from his own novel, was a sympathetic study of Franco-German relations and accurately reflected the need for reconciliation which was widely felt and expressed by large sections of the French intelligentsia. Its most powerful expression was to be found in Giraudoux's masterpiece *La Guerre de Troie n'aura pas lieu* (1935), in which mythological characters embody the desperately topical debate on war and peace. In 1929 his first mythological play *Amphytrion 38* had celebrated the joys of faithful human love in the face of which a rather less than omnipotent Jupiter was forced to bow out gracefully. Giraudoux's tone becomes darker throughout the thirties but in his *Impromptu de Paris* (1937) he defends refined language as a vehicle for refined and original thought, which was the hallmark of his entire career. Nevertheless, some critics have seen his work as too whimsical and precious. For all his love of verbal wit, fantasy, and paradox, Giraudoux was not tempted by surrealism but remained firmly in the camp of those who believed that "tout ce qui n'est pas clair n'est pas français."

In this he exercised a powerful influence on the young Jean Anouilh (1910–87) whose skillfully crafted historical and modern plays on both light and dark themes continued to hold the stage from the thirties until long after 1945, providing an antidote to what some critics saw as the muddier or more pessimistic extremes of the theater of the absurd.

While mainstream French playwrights remained fairly conservative in the first half of the century, they were well-served by a number of directors who actively sought to modernize production techniques and to train a new and more flexible breed of actors. Lugné-Poë had welcomed Jarry to his Théâtre de l'Oeuvre. Jacques Copeau ran his Théâtre du Vieux-Colombier from 1913 to 1924 and one of his actors, Charles Dullin, founded the avant-garde Théâtre de l'Atelier in 1921; Louis Jouvet, Georges Pitoëff, and Gustav Baty complete the list of innovative directors whose influence only fully begins to be felt as events tragically move once again from the theater of ideas to the theater of war.

Robert V. Kenny

Selected Bibliography.

Birkett, Jennifer, and James Kearns. *A Guide to French Literature*. London: Macmillan, 1997.

Connon, Derek, and Michael Cardy. *Aspects of Twentieth-Century Theatre in French*. New York: Peter Lang, 2000

Fletcher, John, ed. *Forces in Modern French Drama*. London: U of London P, 1972.

France, Peter, ed. *The New Companion to Literature in French*. Oxford: Oxford UP, 1995.

Guicharnaud, Jacques. *Modern French Theatre*. 1967.

Littérature française: Le XXe siècle, Pierre-Olivier Walzer, *vol 1 1896–1920,* 1975; Germaine

Brée, *vol 2 1920–1970,* 1978 (vol 2 also available in English).

Little, Roger. *The Shaping of Modern French Poetry.* Manchester: Carcanet Press 1995.

Nadeau, Maurice. *Histoire du Surréalisme.* 2 vols. 1945–48 (English translation, London: Jonathan Cape, 1965).

Potts, D.C., and D. G. Charlton. *French Thought Since 1600.* London: Methuen 1974

Raymond, Marcel. *De Baudelaire au Surréalisme.* Corti, édition nouvelle, 1969 (English translation 1970).

Sartori, Eva Martin. *The Feminist Encyclopaedia of French Literature.* Westport, CT: Greenwood, 1999.

Shattuck, Roger. *The Banquet Years: The Origins of the Avant-Garde in France; 1885 To World War I.* London: Jonathan Cape, 1969.

Unwin, Timothy. *The Cambridge Companion to The French Novel.* Cambridge: Cambridge UP, 1997.

Freud, Sigmund (1856–1939)

Viennese neurologist and originator of psychoanalysis.

See under **Psychoanalysis.**

Futurism

Futurism (1909–15) rebelled against past culture and attempted to express the dynamism of the machine age. Italian futurists proposed a new worship of speed, electricity, and machines. They were iconoclastic and provocative, commanding attention through shock and outrage. Led by **F. T. Marinetti** (1876–1944), a poet with a genius for publicity, they poured forth highly charged manifestoes. Marinetti chose the term *futurism* over *electricism* or *dynamism* to appeal to the younger generation. His founding manifesto, which appeared in *Le Figaro,* Paris, February 20, 1909, trumpets a new ideology: "We affirm that the world's magnificence has been enriched by a new beauty: the beauty of speed. A racing car whose hood is adorned with great pipes, like serpents of explosive breath . . . is more beautiful than

the *Victory of Samothrace*" (see Apollonio 21). Marinetti's proposals culminate in a dithyramb to dynamism:

> We will sing of great crowds excited by work, by pleasure, and by riot . . . of the multicoloured, polyphonic tides of revolution . . . of the vibrant nightly fervour of arsenals and shipyards blazing with violent electric moons . . . [of] deep-chested locomotives whose wheels paw the tracks like the hooves of enormous steel horses . . . (see Apollonio 22)

Marinetti's dazzling cluster of images opens up a panoptic futurist vision of industrial energy.

As the movement gathered force, it spawned statements, including *Manifesto of the Futurist Painters* (1910); *Futurist Painting: Technical Manifesto* (1910); Boccioni's *Technical Manifesto of Futurist Sculpture* (1912); Russolo's *The Art of Noises* (1913); Carrà's *The Painting of Sounds, Noises, and Smells* (1913); Marinetti's *Destruction of Syntax—Imagination without Strings—Words-in-Freedom* (1913), *The Variety Theatre* (1913), and *Geometrical and Mechanical Splendor* (1914); and Sant'Elia's *Manifesto of Futurist Architecture* (1914). There were manifestos on **music** (Pratella, 1910), photodynamism (Bragaglia, 1911), and **cinema** (Corra, 1912), culminating in a proposal for *The Futurist Reconstruction of the Universe* (Balla and Depero, 1915).

Futurists transposed Bergson's *élan vital* and Nietzsche's will-to-power into *universal dynamism,* in which disruption, asymmetry, and aggression galvanize consciousness. Science and poetry joined hands: Marinetti claimed that "[p]rofound intuitions of life added one to the other, word by word, according to their illogical conception, will give us the general outlines of an intuitive physiology of matter" (see Clough 195). Fusing vitalism and mechanism, he described mechanical forces as "vast nets of nerve impulses or electric currents, veritable systems of arteries and veins" (see Clough 136). The futurists "were seeking a mechanical pantheism in which the machine acquires a soul and the mind becomes a motor" (Clough 136). Anticipating science fiction and cybernetics, Marinetti envisaged " 'the mechanical kingdom' supplanting 'the animal kingdom' " and "an immortal superman who will be mechanized . . . with replaceable parts" (Martin 130).

The futurist painters, Umberto Boccioni (1882–1916), Carlo Carrà (1881–1966), Giacomo Balla (1871–1958), Gino Severini (1883–1965), and Luigi Russolo (1885–1947) were "inspired by the tangible miracles of contemporary life, by the iron net of velocity which envelops the earth . . . and by the anguished struggle for the conquest of the unknown" (see Carrieri 28). They exalted "the uproar [of great cities], the scientific division of work in the factories, the whistle of the trains . . . the pulsation of the motors; the cadenced beating of the transmission belts" (see Carrieri 33). As illustrated by Boccioni's *Dynamism[s] of a Human Body,* a *Footballer,* and a *Cyclist* (1913), they wanted to penetrate to "[the] dynamic waves which constituted the object's inner reality" and to achieve "the plastic expression of reality conceived as motion" (Clough 83, 80).

The concept of speed is vital to futurism: for Boccioni, "Velocity is an absolute," for Marinetti, "[it] creates the universe" (see Clough 87, 15). Marinetti's "reformed typesetting allows [him] to treat words like torpedoes and to hurl them forth at all speeds: at the velocity of stars, clouds, aeroplanes, trains, waves, explosives, molecules, atoms" (see Clough 52). Balla's *Abstract Velocity* (1913) is an attempt to render the "Plasticity of Light x Speed." Even architecture, as Antonio Sant'Elia (1888–1916) saw it, should reflect a new sense of lightness and swiftness in glass and steel.

To a futurist eye like Boccioni's, "moving objects constantly multiply themselves; their form changes like rapid vibrations . . . Thus a running horse has not four legs but twenty, and their movements are triangular" (see Apollonio 28). Antonio Bragaglia's photodynamism recorded light-traces of actions as swift as a slap, but Boccioni rejected the technique as merely automatic. Balla's *Leash in Motion* and *Rhythms of a Bow* (1912) borrow their analysis from chronophotography, but in *Study of Paths of Movements (Swifts)* (1913) he creates lyrical graphs of impulses. As Carrà explains, the futurist goal is not to paint a leaping figure or its trajectory, but the leap itself. Boccioni translated expansion and contraction into formal principles in *Muscles in Velocity* and *Spiral Expansion of Muscles in Movement* (1913). The plastic sense of movement in his *Elasticity* (1912) had its counterpart in architecture, where materials were to have a modern "elasticity and lightness" (Tisdall 130). Marinetti was fascinated by "the solidity of a sheet of steel . . . the incomprehensible and inhuman alliance of its molecules or of its electrons"; his anti-anthropomorphism and misogyny appear, when he adds: "The warmth of a piece of iron or of wood is now more attractive to us than the smile or the tears of a woman" (see Carrieri 80).

Rejecting human sentiment and psychology, futurists wanted to dramatize forces in matter. Marinetti proposed in 1912 "[to] capture unawares, by means of freely moving objects and capricious motors, the respiration, the sensitivity and the instincts of metals, rocks, wood, etc. Substitute the psychology of man, now depleted, with the LYRICAL OBSESSION OF MATTER" (see Carrieri 80). The futurists sought transcendence in physical forces which, for Marinetti, are "movements of matter, beyond the laws of intelligence" (see Carrieri 80). Boccioni aimed at "Physical Transcendentalism" in sculptures like *Unique Forms of Continuity in Space* (1913), a superhuman image of "muscular dynamism" with a surging sense of movement.

For the futurists, *mechanolatry* was the key to *modernolatry*. As early as 1907, Boccioni declared: "I want to paint the new, the fruit of our industrial time" (see Taylor 35). He explored construction sites on the outskirts of Milan and, in *The City Rises* (1910–11), aimed at "a great synthesis of labor, light, and movement" (see Taylor 35). Marinetti urged poets "to express the life of the motor" and the spiritual dynamism of the machine, "[which] is the symbol of the 'mysterious force' of the infinite" (Clough 136). The futurists tried to subject human life and rhythms to the machine, a cult that led to the glorification of industry, conquest, and war. Carrà wrote in 1915: "The war is creating in man a really new love for machinism and metallism, which inspire an entire new art . . ." (see Carrieri 165). Futurist war paintings include Carrà's *Interventionist Manifesto* (1914), a brightly colored collage of headlines, flags, and words or letters signifying shouts or noises; Boccioni's *The Charge of the Lancers* (1915); and Severini's *Armored Train* (1915). Marinetti bombastically called war "the only hygiene of the world" and Walter Benjamin justly criticizes the futurist aesthetics of war, machinery, power, and destruction.

Electricity was a prolific generator of futurist imagery. Marinetti exulted in electricity, speed, and power. "Nothing is more beautiful," he wrote in 1914, "than a great humming central electric station . . ." (Apollonio 155). Electricity might seem to defy plastic expression, but the futurists "[thought] of the picture zone as a flickering network of multiple stresses, charged with magnets and electric currents" (Kozloff 40). Balla mastered the scintillation of electric light in *Street Lamp* (1909), in which a shower of red, gold, and green chevrons outshines a crescent moon. "Ir-

radiation and the various types of geometrical optical illusions" (Martin 51), along with transparency and simultaneity, are integral to the futurist vision. The painters declared in 1910: "Space no longer exists: the street pavement, soaked by rain beneath the glare of electric lamps, becomes immensely deep . . . Thousands of miles divide us from the sun; yet the house in front of us fits into the solar disk" (Apollonio 28). Capturing simultaneity required decomposition of light in painting and deformation of mass in sculpture. Futurist dynamism and lines of force were translated into optical effects by Balla in *Thicknesses of Atmosphere* (1913) and *Mercury Passing in Front of the Sun* (1914) and by Severini in *Spherical Expansion of Centrifugal Light* (1914).

Futurists "saw the object as a nucleus of radiating forces" (Martin 169) and aimed to synthesize opposing or diverging lines of force in ways that would dramatize interaction. For Boccioni, "simultaneity is a lyrical exaltation, a plastic manifestation of a new absolute, speed; a new and marvellous spectacle, modern life . . ." (Apollonio 178).

Futurism expressed rhythm, vibration, and interpenetration rather than visual appearance. Boccioni proposes: "LET'S SPLIT OPEN OUR FIGURES AND PLACE THE ENVIRONMENT INSIDE THEM" and maintains: "Our bodies penetrate the sofas on which we sit, and the sofas penetrate us in the same way as the passing tram enters the houses and the houses, in turn, fling themselves on the tram . . ." (see Apollonio 63; Carrieri 32). The spectator is to be placed at the center of converging forces, as in *Simultaneous Visions* (1911) and *The Street Enters the House* (1912). Planes, forms, and colors intersect. The titles of futurist paintings allude to these principles—see for example Boccioni's *The Noise of the Street Penetrates the House* (1911) and Russolo's *Interpenetration of Light + House + Sky* (1913).

Boccioni's study of movement attracted him to "the poetry of the straight line and the mathematical calculation" (see Carrieri 25). He identified vitality with linear form: "Our straight line will be alive and palpitating . . . and its fundamental, naked severity will be the iron-severe symbol of the lines of modern machinery" (see Carrieri 74). The futurist vision of energy depicts *lines of force* radiating out from a nucleus, as in Carrà's *Centrifugal Forces* (1914). Boccioni insists that "[the] opening and closing of a valve creates a rhythm which is just as beautiful to look at as the movements of an eyelid, and infinitely more modern" (Apollonio 64). He introduced "spiral structure" and rhythmic interaction of convex and concave forms into his sculpture *Development of a Bottle in Space* (1912–13). Meanwhile, Russolo experimented with the "Art of Noises" and gave concerts with a battery of "Noise Intoners." His compositions, *The Awakening of a City* and *Meeting of Automobiles and Aeroplanes,* are soundscapes that relate to the futurist music of Balilla Pratella (1880–1955) and to later experiments with sound and silence by John Cage.

Futurist painters aimed at *pure plastic rhythm* through linear, spiral, overlapping, transparent, and wavelike forms, or through kaleidoscopic fragmentation as in Severini's *Dynamic Hieroglyphic of the Bal Tabarin* (1912). Boccioni represented psychological forces by directional lines in *States of Mind: The Farewells, Those Who Go,* and *Those Who Stay* (1911), fusing abstraction with lyricism. "Emotion in modern painting and sculpture," he wrote, "sings of gravitation, displacement, reciprocal attraction of forms, of masses and colors, sings of *movement,* the interpenetration of forces" (Apollonio 174).

Futurism evoked the dynamic rhythms of the modern city, its work, traffic, bustle, and entertainment. Boccioni acclaimed clowns, acrobats, circuses, fairs, cafés, streets, and workshops, while Marinetti celebrated the anarchic energy of the Variety Theater. Marinetti's "Futurist Evenings," staged in theaters and music halls in Milan, Paris, Moscow, and London, used aggressive tactics of "speed, brevity, absurdity, disruption, and audience involvement" (Tisdall 108) to provoke reaction. Futurist theatrics mixed songs, speeches, and stunts with mechanical noisemakers and films, breaking ground for dadaism in 1917 and Ionesco's theater of the absurd in the 1960s. Marinetti proclaimed that futurist poetry should consist of "perpetual dynamism of thought, an uninterrupted stream of images and sounds," stemming from an "elastic consciousness" (see Martin 91). Futurist poets—including Paolo Buzzi, Enrico Cavacchioli, Armando Mazza, and Aldo Palazzeschi—wrote hymns to industry and the machine, such as Mazza's ode to a futurist Venice, with roaring shipyards, "erect chimneys," and blazing furnaces. Marinetti, inventor of Words-in-Freedom, advocated the use of concrete images untied to logical structure. His inventive typography set words in expressive patterns, while the verbal designs of Francesco Cangiullo and Corrado Govoni anticipate concrete poetry.

Ardengo Soffici (1879–1964), Florentine editor of *Lacerba,* compared futurism with cubism, provoking a fist-fight with Marinetti's Milanese contingent. Carrà used cubist planar structure "[to tighten] up his composition," while Severini adapted it more loosely in the "shifting planes" of *The Obsessive Dancer* (1911) and "kaleidoscopic facets" of *Pan-Pan at the Monico* (1910–12) (Tisdall 44, 53). Despite their formal affinities with **cubism,** futurists were emotionally closer to "aggressive, expressionist vitalism" (Martin 55). They sought to intensify sensation and animate the image of contemporary reality by "opening up" objects to reveal the interplay of internal and external forces. Boccioni claimed that "[the]

Italian futurists [were] the only primitives of [a] completely transformed European sensibility," but their **primitivism** was the outcome of modern *complexity* rather than classical *simplicity* (see Clough 18, Kozloff 128).

Futurism and dadaism were the most violent of twentieth-century avant-gardes, but where dada was anti-art and anti-war, futurism heralded the new art of the Machine Age. Thanks to his powerful personality, Marinetti spread futurist ideology to a variety of fields and countries. Even in England, futurism had its impact on artists of the Rebel Art Centre, such as **Wyndham Lewis,** Christopher Nevinson, David Bomberg, and Edward Wadsworth—although Lewis fiercely defended the originality of his and **Ezra Pound**'s **vorticism.** Futurist theories sprang up ahead of practice, with the artists struggling to embody them. Dynamism was the motive force: for Boccioni, the outward shell of things was to be broken open to reveal "the lines and masses which form the internal arabesque" (see Tisdall 74). While futurists' attempts to express movement in the static media of painting and sculpture were sometimes incoherent, their explosive energy and cult of innovation left their mark on much of twentieth-century art.

Jack Stewart

Selected Bibliography

Apollonio, Umberto, ed. *Futurist Manifestos.* London: Thames, 1973.

Banham, Reyner. *Theory and Design in the First Machine Age.* New York: Architectural, 1960.

Benjamin, Walter. "The Work of Art in the Age of Mechanical Reproduction." 1936. *Illuminations.* Ed. Hannah Arendt. Trans. Harry Zohn. New York: Schocken, 1969. 217–51.

Carrieri, Raffaele. *Futurism.* Trans. Leslie van Rensselaer White. Milan: Edizioni del Milione, n.d.

Clough, Rosa Trillo. *Futurism: The Story of a Modern Art Movement. A New Appraisal.* New York: Greenwood, 1969.

Kozloff, Max. *Cubism/Futurism.* New York: Charterhouse, 1973.

Martin, Marianne W. *Futurist Art and Theory, 1909–1915.* New York: Hacker, 1978.

Poggioli, Renato. *The Theory of the Avant-Garde.* Trans. Gerald Fitzgerald. Cambridge: Harvard UP, 1968.

Taylor, Joshua C. *Futurism.* New York: Museum of Modern Art, 1961.

Tisdall, Caroline and Angelo Bozzola. *Futurism.* London: Thames, 1977.

Futurism, Italian

A movement which was launched by the publication on February 20, 1909 in the Parisian newspaper *Le Figaro* of Filippo Tommaso **Marinetti**'s "Fondazione e manifesto del Futurismo" ("The Founding and Manifesto of Futurism"). The atmosphere and the central tenets of Italian futurism are wholly evident in this first manifesto. The tone is brash and iconoclastic; there is a strike against the traditional humane forms and pieties of art, including conventional grammatical structures; there is a celebration of machinery, speed, youthfulness, and the irrational; and there is the promotion of alternative literary forms intended to capture the accelerated consciousness of the modern city (analogy; mathematical symbols to replace connective grammar). The emphasis of the founding manifesto is essentially literary, but the movement would swiftly expand to include painting, sculpture, architecture, music, theater, photography, cinema, politics, and even, in its later stages, cookery.

Italian futurism had its home in Milan, in the industrial north of **Italy** (a country which underwent a late and rapid process of industrialization). Its zealous celebration of industry reflects its support for the emergence of a new and independent Italy, and for its break from an artistic heritage which, it was felt, threatened to turn the country into a museum for foreign tourists. The movement's background helps to account for its strident attack on "passéisme" (a love of the past) and for its pronounced nationalism.

The tone and content of the Italian futurist manifestos represent a collage of popular influences, the most significant of which derive philosophically from Nietzsche and Bergson, politically from Georges Sorel, and in artistic terms from Zola, **Whitman,** Emile Verhaeren, and Alfred Jarry. Although Marinetti had, in his pre-futurist days, been immersed in the works of the symbolist poets, he soon came to define futurist literature in opposition to symbolism, which he represented as wallowing in "passéisme," singling out Gabriele D'Annunzio for particular criticism on this score.

In painting, the Italian futurists borrowed heavily from **impressionism** and **cubism,** but they wanted in particular to stress movement in their work, and often represented animate and inanimate subjects merging with their environments, conjuring up the bustle of modernity and the subject's loss of a stable identity. Key words for the Italian futurist painters are "compenetrazione" (interpenetration) and "scomposizione" (deconstruction). Umberto Boccioni's paintings, and his sculptures of the human form in movement, notably exemplify the exploration of these preoccupations.

Boccioni, arguably the most talented of the Italian futurist artists, died in 1915, a casualty of the First World War, and the most influential phase of **futurism** died with him. Although a new group of poets collected around Marinetti after the war, the impact of the movement waned and its previous revolutionary vigor was lost in its merger with Mussolini's fascist regime.

Nonetheless, Italian futurism must be afforded a considerable place in any construction of modernism. It was the first avant-garde movement, and its influence spread across Europe, and to America and Japan. In England, it exercised a particular fascination for **D. H. Lawrence,** and it lay behind the formation of the vorticist movement; in America, its influence is strongly felt in Hart Crane's important poem, "The Bridge."

Andrew Harrison

Selected Bibliography

Apollonio, Umberto, ed. *Futurist Manifestos.* London: Thames and Hudson, 1973.

Perloff, Marjorie. *The Futurist Moment: Avant-Garde, Avant Guerre, and the Language of Rupture.* London: University of Chicago Press, 1986.

Rye, Jane. *Futurism.* London: Studio Vista, 1972.

White, John J. *Literary Futurism: Aspects of the First Avant Garde.* Oxford: Clarendon Press, 1990.

G

George, Stefan (1868–1933)

From the 1890s onwards, George attempted to revive the German lyric tradition, which had long since dwindled into imitations of romantic poetry. His poetry is associated with the Jugendstil art movement, from 1895 to 1905, which valued a functional, linear ornamentation. He envisaged an alternative to the materialism of Wilhelmine society through his symbolist poetry which excluded everyday discourse, and through the "George-Circle" of his male disciples, with whom he published the *Blätter für Kunst* (1892–1919, *Papers for Art*), a journal of their work.

George's collections of the 1890s, such as *Hymnen* (1890, *Hymns*), *Pilgerfahrten* (1891, *Pilgrimages*), and *Der Teppich des Lebens* (1899, *The Carpet of Life*), are a series of attempts to overcome the *world suffering* of the poet's alienation from society and nature, in a style which rejected romantic subjectivity. His poetic heroes include the beautiful and hedonistic Roman emperor of the collection *Algabal* (1892), who tragically imposes his aestheticism on the world, destroyed by the mob which represents a vulgar reality. Also, in *Die Bücher der Hirten—und Preisgedichte der Sagen und Sänge und der Hängenden Gärten* (1895, *The Books of Shepherds—and Prize Poetry of Speeches and Songs and the Hanging Gardens*), a poet-king is split between his desires for political power and the power to create beauty. These figures represent George's concern with the incongruity between aesthetic and social realities. He suggests a solution to this problem in *Das Jahr der Seele* (1897, *The Year of the Soul*), in which the poet addresses himself as a Christ figure who can redeem the world through "The lights that shine from your wounds;" he acknowledges the death of his "youth in all its freshness," and rejects his feelings of social alienation, to embrace his role as a "seer" and "guide" for his disciples.

George's poetry after the turn of the century attempted to inspire his disciples with a sense of beauty, and guidance in action. Perhaps the most significant event of his life was meeting Maximilian Kronberger, a physically beautiful, aspiring poet who died at the age of sixteen years. George immortalized him as "Maximin" in *Der siebente Ring* (1907, *The Seventh Ring*), as the Greek ideal of harmonious mind and body, and potential savior for modern society. Maximin remains an important figure throughout the rest of George's poetry, symbolizing the younger generation of a possible Hellenic future in *Der Stern des Bundes* (1914, *The Leagues of the Star*). Yet the First World War destroyed George's cultural optimism, and his career as a poet ended in 1920.

George's works are available in Dr. Ernst Hauswedell and Co., Hamburg, and Schocken Books.

Carl Krockel

Selected Bibliography

Goldsmith, Ulrich K. *Stefan George: A Study of his Early Work.* University of Colorado Press: 1959.

Metzger, Michael M., and A. Erika Metzger. *Stefan George.* New York: Twayne Publishers, 1972.

Urban, G. R. *Kinesis and Stasis: A Study in the Attitude of Stefan George and His Circle to the Musical Arts.* The Hague: Mouton Publishers, 1962.

Germany

Modernist German literature drew its sources from a rich indigenous tradition since the late eighteenth century, as well as from the upheaval of contemporary events. A third source was French literature, which set an example to writers of the positions they would aspire to: the socially committed **naturalism** of Zola, the spiritually aspiring symbolism of Mallarmé, and the iconoclasm of Rimbaud.

The advent of modernism in Germany occurred with the sensational premiere of **Gerhart Hauptmann**'s starkly naturalistic play *Vor Sonnenaufgang* in 1889. Hauptmann became the most important representative of German naturalism, which was the dominant literary style throughout the 1890s. However, other writers such as **Frank Wedekind** and **Stefan George** felt inhibited by its limitations. Even Hauptmann diversified into symbolist, historical, and later, neoclassical forms. Wedekind had been attracted to naturalism's concern with social injustice, but felt that it could not envisage any alternatives. Opposed to Hauptmann's "Secondstyle" which accurately reproduced time and space in the narrative, the extravagance and exaggeration of the *Wedekind-Style* would provide inspiration for the later generations of expressionists

and dadaists, as well as for **Bertolt Brecht.** Stefan George aligned naturalist poetry with the materialism of industrializing German society, and upheld the symbolists Mallarmé and Verlaine as his "masters." He avoided everyday speech for a language which could transform the everyday world into poetry. The relative positions of these three German writers is evident in their relationships to the seminal German philosopher Friedrich Nietzsche. While fascinated by Nietzsche's affirmation of the individual's "will to power," Hauptmann still suffocates his tragic heroes under social conventions. Against Hauptmann, Wedekind believed that the liberation of the individual's will to power could revolutionize society; he encourages his audience to identify unconditionally with the Dionysian vitality of his heroes. George modeled himself on Nietzsche's aristocratic "superman" who could transcend society in poetry through his power over language.

The most important Austrian writers in the 1890s, **Hugo von Hofmannsthal** and **Arthur Schnitzler,** formed the "Young Vienna" movement, also in opposition to German naturalism. George feted Hofmannsthal as his Austrian counterpart, publishing his verse and introducing him to Mallarmé. Although emulating George in his poetry, Hofmannsthal denounced the attempt to transcend reality in his verse dramas; at the turn of the century, reaching out to a wider audience, he rejected George's purity of form for a fusion of literature with other arts in performance. Against naturalism, Schnitzler concentrated on the psychology of his characters in their social context; he used brief stage directions to denote their social level, instead of the longer directions more typical of naturalist drama.

The tensions among the different positions touched on above can be seen most clearly in the relationship between the brothers **Heinrich Mann** and **Thomas**

Mann. In the first decade of the century both of them explored the themes of decadence, borrowing heavily from Nietzsche. In 1910 Heinrich rejected Nietzsche, and on the outbreak of the First World War declared his affiliation with Zola. Thomas branded him as a "literateur of civilization" opposed to the German culture of **music.** Although Thomas abandoned his exclusive affiliation with German culture after the war, he retained the influence of Richard Wagner and Nietzsche; he also emulated the founder of German literature in the nineteenth century, Johann Wolfgang von Goethe, in his awareness of political extremes inherent in certain cultural positions. In his consciousness of Germany's national problems, Thomas superseded Hauptmann as the modern reincarnation of Goethe, and representative voice of the Weimar Republic, a position which, as we shall see, was vied for by many other writers. Heinrich had rejected Goethe for his lack of political involvement.

Friedrich Hölderlin, romantic poet and contemporary of Goethe, was revered by the generation of poets associated with **expressionism** in the first two decades of the century. **Georg Heym,** who satirized Goethe's Olympian calm, and **Georg Trakl,** both admired Hölderlin's expression of extreme emotions in an impersonal, almost classical, style. They found encouragement in Nietzsche's disdain for convention, and in Rimbaud's free verse which freed their style to express their particular visions. Heym and Trakl abandoned their romantic sentimentality by attempting to capture a tactile, visual sense of reality as a series of simultaneous, explosive images. Similarly, **Gottfried Benn**'s poetry depicted images of corpses in remorseless detail. These poets' styles emulated the romantic longing to regain immanent experience of nature, and with it, a spiritual transcendence. To express these longings they used a mythological language, but un-

like the romantics, it was uncomfortably juxtaposed with stark images of social reality, to express the tragic incongruity between the two levels of experience. **Franz Werfel**'s poetry concentrates on spiritual epiphanies between human beings in bleak circumstances. Together, these poets formed the core of German literary expressionism.

Else Lasker-Schüler was a central member of the community of expressionists in Berlin, but her style seems to be more a product of her experience as a woman with a diffuse sense of identity as wife, mother, and daughter, which freed her imagination, and of her identity as a Jew, which provided her with an objective reference point for her poetry. Another female writer, **Ricarda Huch,** wrote romantic fiction in the 1890s about the triumph of love over death and poverty; she later became more objective in her historical fiction and essays. **Lou Andreas-Salomé** fascinated her brilliant male companions for her subjective incisiveness, and in turn was attracted by their intellectual sophistication which she recorded, although she encouraged **Rainer Maria Rilke** out of his tendency toward sentimentality.

Rilke's poetry is not associated with expressionism, yet his development shares its concerns. He called his mature style "thing poetry," in which objects are depicted as they are perceived, but also in terms of their symbolic significance; his later poetry is concerned with the difficult relationship between humans and the "angels" of the spiritual realm. Perhaps the most individual of German writers, who was affected by the trends of his time nonetheless, is **Franz Kafka.** His restrained, classical style delineates the structures of an expressionist world of guilt and alienation, a world which in turn inserts disturbing connotations into his language, threatening to overwhelm its apparent rationality.

Towards the end of the First World War artists attempted to reconcile the inwardness of expressionism with their need to confront the problems of Germany on the verge of collapse—though also potentially on the brink of a new age. In his "Merz" work, derived from the word "Kommerz," **Kurt Schwitters** incorporated fragmentary quotations from everyday life which contradicted his expressionist concentration on a particular feeling. **Hermann Hesse**'s romantic sensibility had been shattered by the war; throughout his later career he attempted to salvage some reconciliation for his age. He attempted to combine the wisdom of Goethe, whose classical order not only enabled him to survive his age but also his unstable sensibility, with that of Hölderlin, whose close friend's name was borrowed for Demian's disciple, Emil Sinclair. **Ernst Toller** reflected that "in 1917 the drama was a leaflet for me;" he dialectically countered realism with expressionistic visionary scenes to inspire his audience to imagine a socialist future. Yet like Werfel, his transition to new objectivity in the 1920s signified an inability to imagine an alternative society to the Weimar Republic. This was left to the national socialists on one side, and to writers like Bertolt Brecht and **Alfred Döblin** on the other.

Brecht's development was a reversal of Toller's. From a nihilistic form of expressionism in his early work, Brecht moved toward an objective analysis of capitalist society that was designed to raise the consciousness of his audience to encourage it to promote change. With Döblin he opposed Thomas Mann's conservatism, as the left-wing voices of Weimar culture; Döblin perceived in both of the Manns' work a mere continuation of naturalism, declaring that "You can also write about Berlin without imitating Zola." The respective styles of Brecht and Döblin's "epic theater" and "epic novel" were characterized, according to Walter Benjamin, by their use of "montage" to combine an open form with documentary authority.

Brecht and Döblin, among the other surviving German writers, failed in their attempts to save Germany from Nazism; they could only save themselves by emigrating, mainly to the United States where they enjoyed varying fortunes. The last decades of German modernism, throughout the upheaval of the thirties and forties, included attempts to survey its historical and cultural past. **Robert Musil** and **Hermann Broch** incorporated philosophy in novels which encyclopedically incorporate the spectrum of German modernism's style and ideas, partly in a desperate hope of holding back its impending destruction. Other surviving writers, such as the Manns, Döblin, Benn, Werfel, and Huch used novels and essays to reflect on Germany after its destruction and the advent of "Year Zero," in an effort to provide the next generation with a possible way forward.

See also **Expressionism, German Literary.**

Carl Krockel

Selected Bibliography

Böschenstein, Hermann. *A History of Modern German Literature.* Bern: Lang, 1990.

Denham, Scott D. *Ideologies and Images of War in German Literature before and after the Great War.* Bern: Lang, 1992.

Gay, Peter. *Weimar Culture: The Outsider as Insider.* London: Penguin,

Heller, Erich. *The Disinherited Mind.* London: Bowes and Bowes, 1975.

Ritchie, James MacPherson. *German Literature under National Socialism.* London: Croom Helm, 1983.

Gibbon, Lewis Grassic (James Leslie Mitchell) (1901–1935)

Gibbon was born and grew up in the farming country of Aberdeenshire. Becoming fascinated by archaeology and evolutionary theory, he enlisted in the Royal Air Force and traveled to Egypt. H. G. Wells and Leonard Huxley introduced his first collection of stories, *The Calends of Cairo* (1931) but even in his first short book, *Hanno: or, the Future of Exploration* (1928), the prospect of what the future holds animates his vision.

His interests in archaeology and **myth** clearly relate him to J. G. Frazer, Jessie Weston, and Friedrich Schliemann, and so to **Eliot** and **Joyce.** He was equally concerned with contemporary possibilities and oppressions most keenly experienced by women, suggesting comparisons with **D. H. Lawrence** and Catherine Carswell. In his first, deeply troubled, frustrated, and unsatisfactory novel, *Stained Radiance* (1930), the central character, Thea Mayven, shares a London flat with two other women, one promiscuous, one more conventional. The urban world is depicted in startling juxtapositions similar to Joyce's Dublin or **Dos Passos**'s Manhattan.

Gibbon's other works are fascinating in their own right. The most effectively realized are the science fiction novels, *Three Go Back* (1932) and *Gay Hunter* (1933), where again the principal characters are women. In the biography *Niger,* the life of Mungo Park unfolds with the strangely Brechtian sense that it all might have happened differently. Political priority runs through *Spartacus* (1933), where the slave rebellion against imperial Rome in 73–71 B.C. is a potent symbol prefiguring modern socialism.

Scottish Scene (1934), Gibbon's most controversial book, a miscellany contradictorily co-authored with **Hugh Mac-Diarmid,** includes the essay "The Land" alongside provocative portraits of people and cities and the finest of Gibbon's short stories, "Greenden," "Smeddum," and "Clay." In "Clay" Gibbon's writing is close to Joyce's in "The Dead" in its poised revaluation of singular perspectives in the sympathetic and helpless knowledge of others. The technical accomplishment of the stories is expansively developed in *A Scots Quair* ("quair" means "book"). The achievement of his trilogy of novels, *Sunset Song* (1932), *Cloud Howe* (1933), and *Grey Granite* (1934), is a late but characteristic triumph of the modern movement.

The central character, Chris Guthrie, begins as a farm-girl, growing up among the seasonal cycles, increasingly aware of the political changes the twentieth century is visiting upon her people. She grows into womanhood, marriage, motherhood, and widowhood, when her husband is killed in **World War I.** *Sunset Song* takes us up to the end of that war. In *Cloud Howe,* Chris is married again, to a minister. Their life in a small town exposes her to a world of vicious petty-bourgeois rivalries. She survives the death of her second husband, when he is thwarted in his attempts to deliver a better life to his parishioners. In *Grey Granite,* Chris has moved to the city and her son, now a man, is immersed in the work of political activism, jailed for his hopes. Ewan is located in an international scene, locked into history as his mother is locked into her identity with the land.

A bare outline of the plot gives little indication of its distinction among the radical prose fiction of modernism. The narrative structure ambitiously encompasses the social and economic spectrum of Scottish life. The trilogy's triumph also resides in its language, effectively linking Gibbon's political thrust with a vernacular idiom immediately appealing to senses of humor and moral propriety exactly analogous to Joyce's reinstatement of the body as a measure of value. Gibbon's characterization is deft, vivid, and sharp, but frequently sketched: the characters are memorable, but less deeply realized, more emblematic, than Joyce's. This quality is crucial in the trilogy's overall design.

By the end of *Grey Granite,* Chris is dialectically posed against her son. Chris is identified with her native land (as opposed to the education she might have had at university), while Ewan identifies with the political struggle to achieve communism which, in the future, might portend a "golden age" to match the one Gibbon imagined in the past. But that crude dichotomy belies the sophisticated narrative tension which is at the heart of the trilogy, leaving readers with a fine, Brechtian resolution, demanding their own engagement and choice.

Alan Riach

Selected Bibliography

Gibbon, Lewis Grassic. *A Scots Hairst: Essays & Short Stories.* Ed. Ian S. Munro. London: Hutchinson, 1983.

Katin, Louis. "Author of 'Sunset Song.'" [Interview with Lewis Grassic Gibbon]. *Glasgow Evening News* (16 February 1933): 6.

[Mitchell, Rhea]. "So Well Remembered: Lewis Grassic Gibbon by His Wife." *New Scot* 4:6 (June 1948): 16–17.

Morgan, Edwin. "Lewis Grassic Gibbon and Science Fiction." Introduction to *Gay Hunter* by J. Leslie Mitchell (Lewis Grassic Gibbon). Edinburgh: Polygon, 1989.

Munro, Ian S. *Leslie Mitchell: Lewis Grassic Gibbon.* Edinburgh & London: Oliver & Boyd, 1966.

Thomson, Mary. "My Friend Lewis Grassic Gibbon." *The Scots Magazine* (September 1989): 602–607

Ginzburg, Natalia (1916–1991)

Novelist, short story writer, essayist, biographer, and dramatist, Ginzburg, together with **Elsa Morante,** is considered the most important modern Italian female writer. Ginzburg's central concern is with the problems involved in developing and sustaining relationships in the modern world. She touches upon the frustrated lives of her characters with a deceptively simple style that dwells upon apparently extraneous details in order to reveal complex psychologies: her work has been compared to that of Anton Chekhov.

Ginzburg published her first short stories in 1934 in the avant-garde Florentine journal *Solaria.* Her first novel was *La strada che va in città* (1943, *The Road to the City*), which was published under a pseudonym. Her other novels are *È stato così* (1946, *The Dry Heart*), *Tutti i nostri ieri* (1952, *A Light for Fools*), *Le voci della sera* (1961, *Voices in the Evening*), *Caro Michele* (1973, *No Way*), and *La città e la casa* (1984, *The City and the House*). *È stato così,* the story of the disintegration of a marriage ending in murder, helped to establish her popular and critical reputation, whilst *Tutti i nostri ieri,* perhaps her most ambitious novel, concerns itself with the experiences of fascism, the war, and the Italian Resistance.

Ginzburg has also written an autobiographical work, *Lessico famigliare* (1963, *Family Sayings*), which won the prestigious Strega Prize in 1964, a number of plays, including *L'inserzione* (1965, *The Advertisement*), several collections of critical essays, including *Mai devi domandarmi* (1970, *Never Must You Ask Me*), and a fictional biography tracing the family history of the eighteenth-century Italian poet Alessandro Manzoni and entitled *La famiglia Manzoni* (1983, *The Manzoni Family*). In 1946 she was responsible for an Italian translation of **Proust.**

Ginzburg's complete works are published in **Italy** by Mondadori. English translations have been published in England by Carcanet (Manchester). A bibliography of her works and details of the translations are contained in Bullock (1991).

Andrew Harrison

Selected Bibliography

Bullock, Alan. *Natalia Ginzburg: Human Relationships in a Changing World.* Oxford: Berg Publishers, 1991.

O'Healy, Anne-Marie. "Natalia Ginzburg and the Family." *Canadian Journal of Italian Studies* 9.32 (Spring 1986): 21–36.

Various Writers. "Natalia Ginzburg: July 5, 1916–October 7, 1991." *Contemporary Literary Criticism* 70 (Yearbook 1991): 279–84.

Greece

According to George Theotokas (1905–1966), one of the leading figures of Greek modernism, "the nineteenth century in Greece ended in 1922" with the defeat of the Greek troops in Asia Minor and the collapse of what remained the *grand* narrative of the Greek nation throughout the nineteenth century: the belief in the possibility of retrieving its long-lost Ionian homeland (Vitti 27). Between 1880 and 1912 the newly-founded modern Greek state had expanded its borders to more or less where they are at present. Marking the end of this period of optimism and national self-confidence, the Asia Minor disaster constituted for young intellectuals like Theotokas the last of a series of deceptions since **World War I;** these had left the older generations numb and had intensified the desire for renewal amongst the young. It is significant, in this light, that in 1929 Theotokas (then a student in Paris) published an essay which is now considered the manifesto of Greek modernism. The essay, titled *Elefthero Pnevma* (*Free Spirit*), condemned the literature of the past for its provincialism and failure to claim for itself a dynamic role in contemporary literary developments. It called for a "new" Greek literature, one that would be better able to capture the complexities of modern reality and would have the power to reciprocate in its contact with other, "stronger" literatures. Furthermore, it invited young Greek writers to turn to the West, thus departing from the long-held conviction that had led to the Asia Minor disaster, namely, that the (re)construction of the nation's identity could only be effectuated *within* the Christian Orthodox tradition and the East.

In Greece, then, the desire for a break with the past which has been associated with the modernist predicament took the form of a letting go of the nineteenth-century nostalgia for a Greekness felt to have been lost with the fall of the Byzantine Empire in 1453. As Dimitris Tziovas suggests, the crisis in the Greek aesthetic tradition witnessed at the beginning of the 1930s needs to be seen as inextricable from a crisis in the understanding of Greek identity (2). Hence the tension, pointed out by most scholars of Greek modernism, between the movement's cosmopolitan and Hellenocentric concerns. In many ways, this tension mirrors the wider debates around tradition and modernity which lie at the heart of most modernist movements in Europe and the United States. At the same time, however, it throws into relief the distinctive character of Greek modernism, the impetus of which needs to be sought less in the anti-bourgeois sentiment that has determined the nature of the modernist revolution elsewhere and more in the need experienced by a long-subjugated people to invent an independent identity for themselves.

In its advocacy of a "new" literature, Theotokas's essay marks the beginning of Greek literary modernism. Although it covered a time span of about thirty years, it is the 1930s which is considered the period of "high modernism" in Greece. Indeed, it was between 1930 and 1940 that the major European modernists were first translated into Greek—for example, Louis Aragon, **T. S. Eliot,** Paul Eluard, André Gide, **James Joyce, Ezra Pound,** and **Virginia Woolf.** A number of periodicals which openly supported and became the vehicles for Greek literary modernism were launched, the most important being *Ta Nea Grammata* (1935–40, 1944–45), *To 3o Mati* (1935–37) and *Makedonikes Imeres* (1932–39, 1952–53). Critical essays on **surrealism, futurism, imagism,** and the use of new narrative techniques in modern European fiction were published, while in all areas of literary production conscious attempts were made to take up the challenges issued by the new discourses and practices in literature.

More specifically, in the area of prose, the shift away from the realistic depiction of rural life (what is known as *ethographia*) had already started at the beginning of the century with novelists' increasing interest in urban settings and their growing dissatisfaction with what Theotokas would later call the "photographic" depiction of reality (Vitti 38). By the 1930s the novel had become more metropolitan and had displaced the short story in popularity, the latter having been the dominant prose genre throughout the nineteenth century. After 1930 Greek novelists increasingly start to experiment with European modernist techniques—**interior monologue,** free association, plotless structure, musical composition, shifting viewpoints—producing novels that were more self-reflexive and "poetic" in nature. The novelists most associated with modernist experimentation are those affiliated to the periodical *Makedonikes Imeres:* Melpo Axioti (1905–73), Yiannis Beratis (1904–68), N. G. Pentzikis (1908–92), Yiannis Skarimbas (1893–1984), and Stelios Xefloudas (1902–84) are among the best representatives of what came to be known as the "School of Thessaloniki." These writers followed European literary developments much earlier than their colleagues based in Athens (i.e., Theotokas, Angelos Terzakis, Kosmas Politis, Michalis Karayatsis), whose experimentation was considerably more limited in power and scope. Their aim was to move beyond the representation of a material, visible reality, seeking to do justice to what, in their view, remains unnamable, inexpressible in human existence; hence their focus on their characters' highly subjective, fragmented, and, at times, primarily textual realities.

Although the "School of Thessaloniki" challenged the established conventions in the writing of fiction and prepared the ground for more significant changes after World War II, the innovations it introduced do not appear as extensive or radical when compared to the developments taking place during the same period in the area of poetry. This is one of the reasons why poetry is widely accepted as the dominant literary genre in the period of high modernism in Greece. The two most important events that set the scene for the crisis in/of modern Greek poetry were the "discovery" and re-evaluation of C. P. Cavafy (1863–1933) after the 1920s and the publication in 1927 of *Elegeia ke Satires* by Kostas Karyotakis (1896–1928). In their rejection of romantic lyricism and their eccentric (ab)use of conventional metric systems, both these poets marked the limits of the established poetic tradition, prefiguring the revolution in poetic subject-matter and form that was to take place in the 1930s. The "new" poetry announced itself in a half-serious, half-joking gesture on the part of a poet who called himself Theodoros Dorros whose first (and only) collection of poetry, published in 1930 in Paris (*Stou Glitomou to Hazi*), threw the poetic establishment (literally) into a *racket* (this is one of the meanings of the word "doros" in Greek). This challenge was taken up by Nikitas Randos (also known as Nicolas Calas, 1907–88) who further spread the *dissonance* in the Greek poetic scene with the publication of his *Poems* in 1933. However, the definitive year for modern Greek poetry is 1935, when George Seferis's (1900–71) groundbreaking second collection *Mythistorema* appeared, written entirely in free verse. In the same year a work by Andreas Embeirikos (1901–75), *Ypsikaminos* (the first attempt to adopt the surrealist principle of automatic writing in Greece), became a sensational event, while Odysseus Elytis (one of the major exponents and practitioners of Greek modernism, 1911–97) made his first appearance as a poet in the periodical *Ta Nea Grammata*. What all these events seemed to attest to at the time was a desire on the part of the younger generation of Greek poets to break from traditional poetic forms and the romantic determination of poetry as "emotion recollected in [the] tranquillity" of a safely posited "I." By producing poetry that remained opaque to familiar processes of understanding or interpretation, and refused to unfold as the narrative thread that keeps the romantic "I" together, the poetic generation of the 1930s put forward its claim to the right of creating "difficult" poetry. Paradoxically enough, the "new" poetry was difficult because it insisted on being simple, "purified" of anything extrinsic or superfluous to its nature and medium. In many ways, then, the "new" Greek poetry (like its European counterparts) was a beginning via a re-turn to basics—to the *image* as the "raw," sensory experience of the thing, the *word* as the primitive sound/cry and, finally, to *life* as the instinctive *movement* of *eros* and *praxis,* a movement which was seen as inextricable from the act of *poiesis* itself. It is no wonder, in this light, that the two major influences on modern Greek poetry have been the Anglo-American movement of imagism and French surrealism. Seferis (who translated Eliot's *Waste Land* in 1936) was, undoubtedly, the best representative of the former, while, apart from Embeirikos and the poet/painter Nikos Engonopoulos (1910–85), who were the self-confessed surrealists, most significant poets of the generation such as Calas, Elytis, and Nikos Gatsos placed themselves in the tradition of surrealism.

The renewal that took place in the areas of modern Greek fiction and poetry brought about the revival and strengthening of the critical essay. Practiced mostly by the writers themselves who, as specialists, undertook to speak in the name of (their) art, the essay flourished in the decade of the 1930s in Greece, claiming for itself the status and value of an independent literary genre. The essays of Elytis, Seferis, and Terzakis are worthy of note here being, along with Theotokas's *Elefth-*

ero Pnevma, among the seminal documents of Greek modernism.

By contrast, developments in the areas of drama and the theater were considerably smaller in scale. On the level of performance, theater practitioners such as Fotos Politis (1890–1934) and Karolos Koun (1908–87) made conscious attempts to introduce new theatrical approaches and include in their repertory the latest experiments in the European theatrical scene. Despite these efforts, however, **naturalism** remained dominant on the Greek stage until 1951, when what is considered the first Greek modernist play was published (Skarimbas, *O Ichos tou Kodonos*). In this context, the contribution of Angelos Sikelianos (1884–1951) and Nikos Kazantzakis (1883–1957) who, due to the versatility of their work, are not always included in the canon of Greek modernist writers, deserves to be mentioned. In their effort to move beyond naturalism toward the creation of a *poetic* drama (now comparable to that of T. S. Eliot and **W. B. Yeats**), these two writers prefigured trends that were to take over the Greek theatrical scene much later.

The politics of Greek modernism remains today a major subject of debate. On the one hand, the insistence of Greek modernists on using European innovative principles and techniques in the service of a quest for national identity is considered a proof of the movement's *independence.* According to Roderick Beaton, for example, Greek modernism was not a passive transplantation of European aesthetic and cultural developments in Greece, but the adaptation of these developments to the specific needs of the nation at the time (19–24). On the other hand, this very concern with the production of a *national modernism* has repeatedly been discussed as a reflection of the *conservative character* of the movement since, as Vassilis Lambropoulos argues, it did not allow for those manifestations of European modernism "which might threaten the credibility and respectability of literature as a national institution" (64). Attempts to introduce a distinction between an avant-garde and a more conservative modernist movement in Greece (Tziovas 5–6) are still highly controversial mainly because even writers considered avant-garde (e.g., the surrealist poets Embeirikos and Engonopoulos) seem to have been readier to adopt formal techniques of experimentation than the avant-garde ideology that was associated with it. As Theotokas's *Elefthero Pnevma* betrays (despite its polemical tone), the outlook of Greek modernist writers in the 1930s was consciously individualistic, determined by a view of the artist as belonging to a species above the average human being. This was, in fact, the nature of the critique directed at the "all-too-soon" canonized high modernists by their postwar successors (especially, those affiliated to the periodical *Pali,* 1963–67). In this light, the terms of the debate around the politics of Greek modernism during the 1930s may need to be re-articulated.

Thus, rather than trace the *conservatism* of Greek modernism in the writers' quest for a re-definition of Greek national identity, we should, perhaps, look at the ways in which this quest was *itself* compromised by a formal radicalism which, in its dominant manifestations, proclaimed its independence from/superiority over politics. It is, indeed, no coincidence that, as Tziovas points out (37), in the period of high modernism in Greece, Greekness came to be defined "as a style" (i.e., as line, light, color, space). This, admittedly, facilitated its *exportation,* for Tziovas is right when he argues that the Greek modernists' concern with Greekness in the interwar period was part of their "attempt to show Europe that a genuine modern Greek culture exists" (37). It did not, however, protect it from the dangers of becoming *exotic* both in Europe and in the context of the patriotic ethnocentrism imposed by the

Metaxas dictatorship (1936–40). Therefore, rather than a reaction against such ethnocentrism, the modernist definition of Greek national identity, even if other, remained *tame,* precisely because its alterity was sublimated and aestheticized.

Maria Margaroni

Selected Bibliography

Beaton, Roderick. *An Introduction to Modern Greek Literature.* 2nd rev. ed. Oxford: Oxford UP, 1999.

Calas, Nicolas. *Transfiguration: Art Critical Essays on the Modern Period.* Ann Arbor: UMI Research Press, 1985.

Cavafy, C. P. *The Complete Poems of Cavafy.* Trans. Rae Dalven. Burlington, MA: Harcourt Brace, 1983.

———. *Collected Poems.* Trans. Edmund Keeley and Philip Sherrard. Ed. George Savidis. Princeton: Princeton UP, 1993.

Elytis, Odysseus. *Open Papers: Selected Essays.* Trans. Olga Broumas and T. Begley. Port Townsend, WA: Copper Canyon Press, 1994.

———. *The Collected Poems of Odysseus Elytis.* Trans. Jeffrey Carson and Nikos Sarris. Baltimore: Johns Hopkins UP, 1997.

———. *Eros, Eros, Eros: Selected and Last Poems.* Trans. Olga Broumas. Port Townsend, WA: Copper Canyon Press, 1998.

Jusdanis, Gregory. *Belated Modernity and Aesthetic Culture: Inventing National Literature.* Minneapolis: U of Minnesota P, 1991.

Lambropoulos, Vassilis. *Literature as National Institution: Studies in the Politics of Modern Greek Criticism.* Princeton: Princeton UP, 1988.

Layoun, Mary, ed. *Modernism in Greece?: Essays on the Critical and Literary Margins of a Movement.* New York: Pella, 1990.

Leontis, Artemis. *Topographies of Hellenism: Mapping the Homeland.* Ithaca: Cornell UP, 1995.

Mackridge, Peter. "European Influences on the Greek Novel during the 1930s." *Journal of Modern Greek Studies* 3 (1985): 1–20.

Politis, Linos. *A History of Modern Greek Literature.* Oxford: Oxford UP, 1973.

Seferis, George. *On the Greek Style: Selected Essays on Poetry and Hellenism.* Trans. Rex Warner and T. D. Frangopoulos. Athens: Denise Harvey and Company, 1992.

———. *Collected Poems.* Ed. Edmund Keeley and Philip Sherrard. Princeton: Princeton UP, 1995.

Sherrard, Philip. *The Marble Threshing Floor: Studies in Modern Greek Poetry.* Athens: Denise Harvey, 1982.

Theotokas, George. "Free Spirit." Trans. Soterios G. Stavrou. *Modern Greek Studies Yearbook* 2 (1986): 153–200.

Tziovas, Dimitris, ed. *Greek Modernism and Beyond: Essays in Honor of Peter Bien.* Lanham, Maryland: Rowman and Littlefield Publishers, 1997.

Vitti, Mario. *I "Yenia tou Trianta:" Ideologia ke Morphi.* Athens: Ermis, 1995.

Yiannakakis, Helen. *Narcissus in the Novel: A Study of Self-Referentiality in the Greek Novel 1930–1945.* University of London: Unpublished Ph.D. thesis, 1990.

Gross, Otto (1877–1920)

Austrian psychoanalyst.

See under **Psychoanalysis.**

Gruppo 63

A group or network of left-wing Italian artists which promoted experimentalism in Italian art, and particularly in poetry.

"Gruppo 63," which was an important focal point for the Italian neo-avantgarde, was so called because it came into existence during a series of seminars, lectures, readings, and theatrical performances organized by Nanni Balestrini in Palermo, Sicily, in October 1963. Among those associated with the group are the relatively unknown Edoardo Sanguineti, Alfredo Giuliani, and Sebastiano Vassalli.

The group was particularly noted for its distrust of language, for its ironic attitude to the media, and for its desire to subvert conventional modes of artistic representation. Since language determines people's perceptions of reality it is in the interests of capitalist society for it to promote discourses which conceal its own processes and its own contradictions. The Gruppo 63 artists opposed the naturalization of the capitalist ideology by flying in the face of accepted rationality and by promoting disordered forms of discourse. Some critics argued that the group was too hermetic and that it created literary works

unreadable unless one was a member of its clique. This charge was compounded by the fact that its procedures for the inclusion or exclusion of members were sufficiently vague to invite controversy.

Gruppo 63 shared a range of interests in common with other important contemporary schools of thought in Europe. Its members were particularly interested in the work of the *Tel quel* group in Paris, in the work of the French structuralists, and in the Frankfurt School. Among its publication outlets was the political journal *Quindici,* set up in 1967 and edited first by Giuliani and then by Balestrini. The artists of Gruppo 63 saw themselves as opposing the conservatism of the neorealists in favor of a return to the innovations of the modernist avant-garde. The group held together into the 1970s. Among the writers to engage with the debates of Gruppo 63 was Umberto Eco.

Andrew Harrison

Selected Bibliography

Baranski, Zygmunt G. "Sebastiano Vassalli: Literary Lives." In *The New Italian Novel.* Edited by Zygmunt G. Baranski and Lino Pertile. Edinburgh: Edinburgh UP, 1993. 239–57.

Wagstaff, Christopher. "The Neo-avantgarde." In *Writers and Society in Contemporary Italy.* Ed. Michael Caesar and Peter Hainsworth. Warwickshire: Berg Publishers, 1984. 35–61.

Gunn, Neil Miller (1891–1973)

Scottish novelist.

Though the author of some twenty novels, characterized by a sensuous lyricism, remarkable evocations of childhood and of the sea, and suspenseful storytelling, Gunn wrote only a small number of books that are clearly, and innovatively, within a modernist locus.

The most structurally sophisticated of these is *Highland River* (1937). With reorienting flashbacks, the protagonist in philosophical free-fall, prose poetry, a subtly ironic portrayal of an intellectual exiled from his community, and a unique use of the third person with past and present tenses, *Highland River* is offered in part as a "case study" of a man's development from childhood to mature self-consciousness. The novel's structure uses disrupted chronology not only to emphasize the trauma of tragic events in World War I but, unusually, to use time's "relativity" as a way of asserting an alternative and more self-empowering idea of the individual in society, one which is not in thrall to the loss of self engendered and symbolized by **the war.**

Gunn's best-known work, *The Silver Darlings* (1941), is set in Caithness immediately after the Napoleonic wars. Its heightened synthesis of folksong, **myth,** historical detail, adventure, acute psychological observation, and symphonic recurrences in plot, nevertheless suggest an author who has absorbed modernist lessons rather than turned away from them. Following the popular and critical success of this and other novels in the 1940s, Gunn returned to more formally self-conscious works. *The Silver Bough* (1948) and *The Well at the World's End* (1951) gently satirize those who wish to observe "primitive communities" at all. At once comic and serious, their playful use of Celtic motifs produces a stylization that appears to anticipate the *knowingness* of some kinds of post-modernist fiction, though tones of af-

fection and of elegy in Gunn's work are never nullified. This paradoxical and elegiac optimism is also present in his last novels *Bloodhunt* (1952) and *The Other Landscape* (1954), both taking as a starting point a violent death and then envisaging the painful social reconstruction that ensues. *The Other Landscape*'s interest in the limits of language and human knowledge again shows the investment of fable-like stories with cooler meditations and narrative complexity. *The Atom of Delight* (1956), Gunn's last book, analyzes the first two decades of his own life which he links to writers especially important to him, including **Proust** and **Lawrence.** Its obliquity has affinities with *Highland River;* it is very much an experimental autobiography.

Richard Price

Selected Bibliography

Gunn, Neil M. *Selected Letters.* Ed. J. B. Pick. Edinburgh: Polygon, 1987.

Hart, F. R. and J. B. Pick. *Neil M Gunn: a Highland Life.* London: John Murray, 1981.

McCulloch, Margery. *The Novels of Neil M Gunn.* Edinburgh: Scottish Academic Press, 1987.

Price, Richard. *The Fabulous Matter of Fact: The Poetics of Neil M. Gunn.* Edinburgh: Edinburgh UP, 1991.

Scott, Alexander and Douglas Gifford, eds. *Neil M. Gunn: the Man and the Writer.* Edinburgh: Blackwood, 1973.

Stokoe, C. J. L. *A Bibliography of the Works of Neil M Gunn.* Aberdeen: Aberdeen UP, 1987

H

The Harlem Renaissance and Black Modernism

The Harlem Renaissance stands as a neat label for a period, running roughly from 1919 to 1932, that has come to be seen as a remarkable efflorescence of African American cultural production. Like all periodizing terms it hides as much as it describes: its dates have been contested and revised; the geography of the movement questioned; and its participants and influence considered and reconsidered with each passing generation of critics. The Harlem Renaissance remains, however, a defining period for urban African American communities and those writers and artists who chose to represent them. As Harlem, but also Chicago, Washington, Detroit, and Philadelphia, drew migrants from the South, we gain the first insights into the conditions of urban African American modernity. This means engagement with the changing technological conditions of urban life; with the speed, noise, and clutter of the new urban centers; and with consumerism, leisure, entertainment, and crime—all the characteristic features of the city in modernity. A sense of dynamic change is reflected in a wide variety of Harlem Renaissance writers and cultural commentators, from Alain Locke's celebration of the new spirit in Negro life in *The New Negro* (1926) to James Weldon Johnson's *Black Manhattan* (1930) and the controversial avant-gardism of *Fire!!* magazine (1926).

Discussion of the Harlem Renaissance and its relationship to black modernism immediately raises complex issues of racial agency and appropriation. As seminal studies such as Nathan Huggins' *The Harlem Renaissance* or David Levering Lewis's *When Harlem Was In Vogue* argue, Harlem was at least as much a construction of the white imagination as it was the site of black cultural expression or freedom. While the 1920s represent a definitive explosion in African American cultural production, it was a flowering briefly over and one that rarely embraced **the masses** of African Americans. Debates over the existence or extent of black modernism have very often stalled at these very accusations of white co-option and elitism (Huggins; Levering Lewis) but it is perhaps more useful to see the variety and richness of cultural production during the Harlem Renaissance as questioning conventional definitions of modernism *and* African American literature (Hutchinson 1–28; Balshaw 19–40). Any survey of the literature, drama, and art produced by black artists in the 1920s reveals, as Richard Powell has argued, serious engagement with the terms of American modernism as well as searching exploration of what it means to be black in white America (Bailey 16–33). Harlem Renaissance works run along a spectrum: from the romantic traditionalism of Countee Cullen's poetry and the genteel novels of Jessie Fauset; through the new women fictions of Nella Larsen, the blues poetry of Langston Hughes, the cultural nationalism of *The New Negro,* and Rudolph Fisher's urban reportage; to the avant-garde experimentation of *Fire!!* magazine, the **primitivism** of Claude McKay's novels, the vicious satire of George Schuyler and Wallace Thurman, and the sociological pessimism of Marita Bonner's *Frye Street* stories. Add to this the cubist influenced murals of Aaron Douglas, Lois Mailou Jones's Africanist inspired painting and sculpture, or the modernist/naturalist style of Archibald Motley Jr. and one is presented with a picture which amply justifies Amiri Baraka's neat assessment: "Harlem is vicious modernism: Bang/Crash" (101).

A useful register of the diversity of Harlem Renaissance modernisms can be seen in Alain Locke's *The New Negro.* Evolving out of a special issue of *Survey Graphic* magazine edited by Locke, the collection featured poetry, prose, essays, artwork, and sociological and historical analyses by virtually every African American of literary note. It has come to stand, for commentators of all theoretical and political persuasions, as *the* New Negro document, representing (variously) the most definitive statement of black modernism, a trickster mastery of form, the highpoint of the Negro vogue, a pragmatist expression of desires for social change through artistic excellence, as well as the first seeds of the eventual compromise of New Negro hopes (Baker; Gates; Levering Lewis; Hutchinson; Huggins). To paraphrase George Hutchinson, it is likely that all these views are mostly right but partly wrong. The collection has an abiding concern with the construction of urbanity as a racial attitude and as artistic impetus. This makes explicit the influence of progressive sociological narratives of urban space, drawn from the work of Robert E. Park and filtered through Charles S. Johnson (editor

of *Opportunity*—the influential Harlem based magazine—and a former pupil of Park) as an important background to Harlem Renaissance urban optimism.

In Hutchinson's view the new spirit, or cultural racialism, in *The New Negro* was in line with a more general cultural nationalism, which drew out racial and ethnic distinctiveness at the same time as articulating American values, as they were being shaped in the work of philosophers like William James and ethnographers like Franz Boas, developing what Hutchinson calls a "rhetoric of Americanism" (400). The modernist aspirations of the collection are also clearly evident. In his preface to the fiction in the collection Locke says, "It has been their achievement also to bring the artistic advance of the Negro sharply into stepping alignment with contemporary artistic thought, mood and style. They are thoroughly modern, some of them ultra-modern, and Negro thoughts now wear the uniform of the age" (50). Whether one agrees with Locke's assessment of the fiction (and not all of it fits this "ultra-modern" description), or whether one sees Locke's integrationist modernism as a useful strategy for African American artists in their period, one can see Locke draws on a notion of urban civic culture as a means to articulate a national and racial identity and literature. Locke also looks to a series of international precedents which allow him to formulate the spirit of the New Negro as well as to place the African American artistic renaissance in line with other national cultures (Irish, Mexican, Russian) the *Survey Graphic* had taken as subjects in the preceding years. Claiming Harlem as a race capital he goes on to say, "Harlem has the same role to play for the New Negro as Dublin has had for the New Ireland or Prague for the New Czechoslovakia" (7). Caught up with this is Locke's understanding of African American modernism as a projection of New Negro aspirations toward cultural renewal as well as a reflection of the changing conditions of black urban life.

Viewing *The New Negro* in this light places it in line with another 1926 text, *Fire!!* magazine. *Fire!!* was edited by one of Harlem's more controversial figures, Wallace Thurman, and the magazine represents the most deliberate attempt during the Harlem Renaissance to foster an African American modernism. The contributors to the magazine included most of the notable younger Negro writers: Rudolph Fisher, **Zora Neale Hurston,** Countee Cullen, Arna Bontemps, Gwendolyn Bennett, Langston Hughes, Aaron Douglas, Bruce Nugent, and Thurman himself. The subject matter was resolutely urban in focus, and dealt with elements of working-class life that are largely absent from *The New Negro.* The front page of the magazine, designed by Aaron Douglas, featured a stark geometric representation of a Sphinx in blocks of red and black. Viewed across its vertical axis the design revealed a stylized man's face adorned with an Africanist earpiece. The magazine's challenge to accepted models of African American writing was conceived as a stylistic break as much as a change in subject matter. The foreword stated: "FIRE . . . flaming, burning, searing, and penetrating far beneath the superficial items of the flesh to boil the sluggish blood." It echoes key modernist motifs of primitivism and exoticism, reconceptualized from an African American perspective, combining a distinctly pagan African style with an African American blues inflected spiritualism.

It was, however, the magazine's inclusion of Bruce Nugent's "Smoke, Lilies and Jade" that caused the greatest furor. The story, a stream of consciousness vignette detailing the interracial, bisexual relations of the decadent Alex, violated the boundaries of New Negro experimentation in terms of style and content. It also seemed to offer singular evidence of the pernicious influence of white exoticism on black Harlem. Looked at today the story seems interesting if relatively tame, however it does bring to the fore the significance of sexuality to the Harlem Renaissance, important given the number of major figures who were gay, despite remaining silent on the issue. It reminds us how important it is to weigh things carefully when one considers the kinds of sexual freedoms offered in Harlem's largely unlicensed and unregulated entertainment economy, as Lillian Faderman and Eric Garber have argued. Likewise, the position of women within the burgeoning race capital is as interesting as it is problematic. Carrying the double burden of structures of racial and gender oppression women writers have rarely been considered central to the Harlem phenomenon; yet the role of women artists as organizers and proselytizers for the New Negro Renaissance is crucial (Wall 1–32). The 1920s see African American women artists in the major cities working at their art for a living and finding their artistic and social contexts within the social and economic fabric of the city. Of importance are Georgia Douglas Brown's literary salon in Washington and Marita Bonner's presence in Chicago, as well as those better-known writers, such as Nella Larsen, Jessie Fauset, or Zora Neale Hurston, who found their artistic home in Harlem.

The "new woman" makes an appearance in the passing heroines of Larsen's novels—crystalizing cultural anxieties about racial identity more pointed in an urban context that offers the promise of racial and sexual anonymity. Written by and for the burgeoning black bourgeoisie, the racial conservatism of these and other passing fictions has allowed them to be too easily dismissed as peripheral to the Harlem Renaissance, with the result that the complex interdependence of racial, gender, and sexual identity they evidence has been overlooked. The passing woman can be seen as a quintessentially modern figure—characterized by her anonymity, her restless pursuit of pleasure, disavowal of family and racial belonging, as well as her enthusiastic embrace of the material experience of modern life. Her racial and class conservatism goes hand in hand with sexual radicalism. At the other extreme, Marita Bonner's despairing urban narratives present a feminized social critique of the fate of women in the rapidly expanding slum spaces of African American cities. She constructs a geography of racial disaffection and confinement in her little-known *Frye Street* stories, which construct a fictional urban neighborhood (based on an area of Chicago) revealing the transition from the optimism of 1920s Harlem toward the harshness of 1940s examinations of urban life. Across a wide variety of women's writing we see the awkward conjunction between discourses of New Negro aesthetics, burgeoning **feminism,** racial uplift, and eugenics; a difficulty which often manifests itself in anxiety around motherhood and the black woman's relationship to (and responsibilities toward) her race.

These writers offer an alternative tradition of female social protest by African American writers: a model of protest more tentative and equivocal than those rather more strident voices (like Wright or Ellison) which have played such a significant role in defining the African American literary tradition in the years following the Harlem Renaissance. This equivocal protest stands as testament to the complicating role of gender and sexuality on the experience of race in American culture (Carby, *Race Men* 1–9). It speaks to the imbrication of debates about black modernism with contemporary debates about race, gender, class, and sexuality and testifies to the enduring legacy of Harlem Renaissance cultural production.

Maria Balshaw

Selected Bibliography

Bailey, David A., ed. *Rhapsodies in Black: Art of the Harlem Renaissance.* London: Hayward Gallery, 1997.

Baker, Houston A. *Modernism and the Harlem Renaissance.* Chicago: U of Chicago P, 1987.

Balshaw, Maria. *Looking For Harlem: Urban Aesthetics in African American Literature.* London: Pluto Press, 2000.

Baraka, Amiri/Jones, LeRoi. *The Selected Poetry of Amiri Baraka/LeRoi Jones.* New York: Morrow, 1979.

Carby, Hazel. *Reconstructing Womanhood: The Emergence of the Afro-American Woman Novelist.* New York: Oxford UP, 1987.

———. *Race Men.* Cambridge, Mass., and London: Harvard UP, 1998.

Flynn, Joyce and Joyce Occomy Stricklin, eds. *Frye Street and Environs: The Collected Works of Marita Bonner.* Boston: Beacon Press, 1986.

DuCille, Ann. *The Coupling Convention: Sex, Text and Tradition in Black Women's Fiction.* New York: Oxford UP, 1993.

Garber, Eric. "'A Spectacle in Color': The Lesbian and Gay Subculture of Jazz Age Harlem." In *Hidden From History.* Ed. Martin Baum Duberman, Martha Vicinus, George Chauncey. New York: New American Library, 1989. 318–331.

Gates, Henry Louis, Jr. "The Trope of the New Negro and the Reconstruction of the Image of the Black." In *The New American Studies.* Ed. Phillip Fisher. Berkeley: U of California P, 1991. 319–345.

Honey, Maureen, ed. *Shadowed Dreams: Women's Poetry of the Harlem Renaissance.* New Brunswick, N.J.: Rutgers UP, 1989.

Huggins, Nathan. *The Harlem Renaissance.* New York: Oxford UP, 1971.

Hughes, Langston. *The Big Sea: An Autobiography.* New York: Knopf, 1940.

Hutchinson, George. *The Harlem Renaissance in Black and White.* Cambridge, Mass., London: Harvard UP, 1995.

Levering Lewis, David. *When Harlem Was In Vogue.* New York: Oxford UP, 1982.

Locke, Alain, ed. *The New Negro: An Interpretation.* New York: Albert & Charles Boni, 1925. (Rpt. New York: Atheneum, 1968.)

McCluskey, John, Jr., ed. *City of Refuge: The Collected Stories of Rudolph Fisher.* Columbia: U of Missouri P, 1987.

McDowell, Deborah E. *The Changing Same: Black Women's Literature, Criticism and Theory.* Bloomington: Indiana UP, 1995.

Scruggs, Charles. *Sweet Home: Invisible Cities in the Afro-American Novel.* Baltimore: Johns Hopkins UP, 1993.

Wall, Cheryl. *Women of the Harlem Renaissance.* Bloomington: Indiana UP, 1995.

Hauptmann, Gerhart (1862–1946)

Hauptmann's greatest works belong to the naturalist theater of the 1890s. He was first inspired as a dramatist by Ibsen, and strongly influenced by Zola's theory of *le roman expérimental* which attempted to reconcile art with nature. He used their naturalist frameworks to test how the eruption of modern ideas in the previous decades, of Marx, Nietzsche, D. F. Strauss and Ernst Haeckel, could function in German society. He experimented in symbolist, historical, neo-romantic, and neoclassical styles, and composed novels and poetry as well as plays, although few of these later works have retained a lasting significance.

His reputation was established with the premiere of *Vor Sonnenaufgang (Before Sunrise)* in October 1889 at the Freie Buhne, Berlin. The play made a huge impact on its audience with its Darwinist hero, Alfred Loth, who rejects the innocent daughter of a family of alcoholics because he believes that alcoholism is an inherited trait. This play contains ideological confusions which are present in Hauptmann's other works, since evolutionism was central to his naturalist ethos, yet here is apparently rejected. A similar effect occurs in *Einsame Menschen* (1891, *Lonely Lives*). Johannes Vockerat, a disciple of Haeckel's evolutionism, emulates the early Nietzsche's belief in the possible union between man and woman through intellect, by attempting to establish a platonic relationship with a student, Anna Mahr. The play is ambiguous about whether their aspirations fail under the conventions of his family, or from their lingering sexual desires, which leaves the audience confused over whether to accept their failure as natural, or to perceive in it a denunciation of contemporary morality.

In the play *Die Versunkene Glocke* (1897, *The Sunken Bell*) Hauptmann explored modern ideas in a neo-Romantic style. Heinrich is a Faustian character who becomes disillusioned in his social function as the bell-founder; he is inspired by the nymph Rautendlein to become a Nietzschean superman who creates bells for the sun. But he begins to resemble Alberich in Wagner's *Ring,* a tyrant over the dwarves in his foundry; he dies, conflating the affirmative Nietzschean midday with the resignatory "Nacht" of Wagner's *Tristan und Isolde.*

Hauptmann's plays were criticized by **Wedekind,** and by the later generation of modernist playwrights, for their defeatist conclusions; radical impulses are suppressed under Wilhelmine social conventions, even in *Die Versunkene Glocke* which is located in a mythological setting. Yet in *Die Weber* (1892, *The Weavers*), based on the uprising of Silesian weavers in 1844, Hauptmann pushes his chosen style of **realism** to such an extreme position that it anticipates modernist left-wing drama. The characters retain an authentic voice with their native dialect; together, they form the collective hero of the play, all carried by the tide of historical events while responding to it as individuals.

Hauptmann's works are available in Propyläen Verlag, Frankfurt am Main, and Martin Secker, London.

Carl Krockel

Selected Bibliography

Knight, K. G., and F. Norman, eds. *Hauptmann Centenary Lectures.* University of London: 1964.

Maurer, Warren R. Maurer. *Understanding Gerhart Hauptmann.* Columbia: University of South Carolina Press, 1992.

Sinden, Margaret. *Gerhart Hauptmann: The Prose Plays.* New York: Russell & Russell, 1975.

Hemingway, Ernest (1899–1961)

Despite the wild fluctuations in the literary reputation and personal fame of Ernest Hemingway, both during his lifetime and after his suicide in 1961, he may legitimately be regarded as one of the most significant writers of the twentieth century. His deceptively simple, terse prose style, in its own way as radical as the contemporaneous innovations of **Joyce** and **Eliot** (both of whom admired his writing), has spawned countless admirers and imitators. But nobody worked as hard or as long at achieving that essential tight economy of expression as Hemingway, a process in which the control of careful editing (requiring, he maintained, a built-in "shit-detector"), was every bit as important as the state of abandonment in inspired writing.

Hemingway's life can be understood as the uncompromising search for that "one true sentence" that will accurately convey the nature of experience, and was in that sense a paradigmatic manifestation of the personality of the modernist artist in exile. Throughout his extensive oeuvre there is an implicit equation between the courage and skill required to hurt or kill, (in war, bullfighting, boxing, and big-game hunting), and to face the risks of creation through writing.

Born in 1899 in Oak Park, Illinois, Hemingway grew up close to the wilderness of the Great Lakes region. His first occupation was as a reporter for the Kansas City Star: observation and clarity were to be vital to his fiction. His experience as a volunteer ambulance man on the Italian front in World War I, and his subsequent wounding, contributed the material at the core of *A Farewell to Arms* (1929), transposed to the first-person narrative of Frederic Henry. The novel recounts Henry's love for the English nurse Catherine Barkley who restores him to health in Milan,

his return to the front and the chaotic retreat after the disastrous defeat at Caporetto: "There were many words that you could not stand to hear and finally only the names of places had dignity." Henry makes his "separate peace" that is a farewell to arms, deserts and flees to Switzerland with Catherine, who is pregnant. With the death of Catherine and their baby in childbirth, (paralleling the death of his comrades in **the war**), Henry is left alone: "After a while I went out and left the hospital and walked back to the hotel in the rain."

Hemingway's first recognition came earlier in Paris, with the support of **Pound, Stein, Ford,** and **Fitzgerald:** the fifteen stories of *In Our Time* (1925) relate the youth of Nick Adams in that Great Lakes region, with vignettes of the war and bullfighting interspersed between the chapters in a kind of modernist collage. "Big Two-Hearted River," like later stories such as "A Clean, Well-Lighted Place," "The Short Happy Life of Francis Macomber," and "The Snows of Kilimanjaro" shows Hemingway at his best. His extensive output of short stories included the collections *Men Without Women* (1927), *Winner Take Nothing* (1933) and *The First Forty-Nine Stories* published with the play *The Fifth Column* (1938).

While his early Parisian days with his first wife Hadley, recounted in the posthumously published memoir *A Moveable Feast* (1964), were lived in relative poverty, later on Hemingway was able, like Fitzgerald, to command huge sums of money for anything he wrote. The magazine *Life* paid $40,000 for the serial rights alone to *The Old Man and the Sea* (1952), Hemingway's novella about a Cuban fisherman's blighted struggle to bring home a great marlin. The universality of its appeal lies in its theme of the courage needed to overcome adversity: "He was an old man who fished alone in a skiff in the Gulf Stream and he had gone eighty-four days now without taking a fish." Over five million copies of that issue sold out in days, highlighting a commercial value which was only bolstered by the award of the Nobel Prize for Literature in 1954.

Although essentially at his best as an anti-intellectual miniaturist, it is paradoxically as a writer of novels that Hemingway will be remembered and revered. Alongside *A Farewell to Arms,* the finest of these is *The Sun Also Rises* (1926), published as *Fiesta* (1927) in Britain: the first-person narrative of Jake Barnes, who has been emasculated during the war, is a vital document of the lost generation. Expatriate partying in Paris gives way to the tragic ritual of the fiesta at Pamplona, as a cast of characters, including the beautiful aristocrat Lady Brett Ashley, her lover the handsome young bullfighter Pedro Romero, and the Jewish writer Robert Cohn, battles through life and love: "At noon on Sunday, the 6th of July, the fiesta exploded. . . . It kept up day and night for seven days. The dancing kept up, the drinking kept up, the noise went on." Hemingway also wrote about the fiesta and bullfighting in non-fiction, with *Death in the Afternoon* (1932) and *The Dangerous Summer* (1985).

When Hemingway went with Martha Gellhorn, soon to become his third wife, to **Spain** to report on the civil war, (as he would later report on the Normandy landings and France in World War II), it precipitated *For Whom the Bell Tolls* (1940), well-received at the time. The long novel tells of the American, Robert Jordan, another tough Hemingway hero in another book about war and love, fighting for the loyalist cause.

Hemingway's talent, though, had long entered a decline that became terminal, no matter whether he resided in Florida, Cuba, Spain or (his final home with his fourth wife Mary), Ketchum, Idaho. The seeds of this decline were variously detectable alongside fine passages of writing in the account of his safari in *The Green Hills of Africa* (1935), and in the novel *To Have and Have Not* (1937), about the smuggler Harry Morgan. The rot had set in, the critics thought, by the time of *Across the River and Into the Trees* (1950), a much-maligned novel, itself about decline, concerning the aging Colonel Cantwell's death in Venice, mitigated only by his passion for the young Italian countess Renata.

Hemingway's frightening physical and mental decline, accelerated by injury, disease and preposterously heavy drinking ("Everybody was drunk" begins *In Our Time*) took its toll. His personality, pugilistic at the best of times and with an unpleasant tendency to turn on those who had helped him, atrophied alarmingly into irate paranoia before, like his father, he took a gun to himself. The mass of work he left behind him incomplete and perhaps incompletable, including *Islands in the Stream* (1970), *The Garden of Eden* (1987), and *True at First Light* (1999), has reputedly now all been published: while swelling his oeuvre it will do little to affect a reputation that needs no rehabilitation.

Sebastian Skeaping

Selected Bibliography

The major works of Hemingway are widely available. For the slightly complicated issue of the stories, the best solution is *The Collected Stories* edited by James Fenton (London: Everyman, 1995). The critical and biographical literature on Hemingway is vast, but the following introductory list will provide useful connections to further bibliographical resources.

Baker, Carlos. *Hemingway: The Writer as Artist.* Princeton, N.J.: Princeton U.P., 1952.

———, ed. *Ernest Hemingway: Critiques of Four Major Novels.* New York: Scribner's, 1961.

———. *Ernest Hemingway: A Life Story.* New York: Scribner's, 1969.

———, ed. *Ernest Hemingway: Selected Letters, 1917–1961.* New York: Scribner's, 1981.

Burgess, Anthony. *Ernest Hemingway.* London: Thames and Hudson, 1978.

Lynn, Kenneth S. *Hemingway.* Cambridge, Mass.: Harvard U.P., 1987.

Meyers, Jeffrey, ed. *Hemingway: The Critical Heritage*. London: Routledge & Kegan Paul, 1982.
———. *Hemingway: A Biography*. London: Macmillan, 1985.

Hesse, Hermann (1877–1962)

Although born in **Germany,** Hesse spent most of his life in Switzerland. His first novel *Peter Camezind* (1904), romantically glorified nature and love with its protagonist withdrawing from a bourgeois, urban lifestyle to his mountain birthplace. A pacifist, Hesse suffered a nervous breakdown during the First World War. In *Wanderung* (1920, *Wandering*), which incorporates poetry and sketches of the Alps, he reflects on his alternating joy before nature and his depressions. He concludes that, instead of longing for a "lukewarm, bearable center," he should "Let it storm! Let it drive you!" to experience moments of beauty. He extended his self-analyses in his novel *Demian* (1919). Emil Sinclair is dissatisfied with his lifestyle between a quiet home and aggressive outside world; his mentor Demian introduces him to the religion of "Abraxus" which combines the divine and diabolical for the fulfillment of the individual's whole self. Hesse leaves open the value of this solution, since Demian is killed in **the war** which he volunteers for, while Emil survives it, and ends the novel reflecting on the significance of Demian's death.

After visiting a sanitarium and undergoing Jungian analysis in the early twenties, Hesse continued to envisage ways of self-integration in his novels. *Steppenwolf* (1927), memorably portrays the individual's split between his humanity, and his wolf-like aggression and homelessness. In suggesting their reconciliation, Hesse now argues that the modern personality is not divided in two, but consists of many parts in play with each other; he represents them as chessmen at the "magic theater" which the Steppenwolf enters in his hope of affirming life. Steppenwolf fails the theater's tests; he holds onto the notion of his split self, and consequently murders his lover. Again the novel's ending is left open, since the murder was only playacting, and Steppenwolf is given the future opportunity to play the theater's games again until he does achieve reconciliation.

Hesse's exposure to Eastern thought, in combination with Jungian philosophy, helped him to suggest further answers to the questions set in his earlier novels, as revealed in *Siddhartha* (1922), and *Morgenlandfahrtland* (1932, *Journey to the East*). His last important novel, *Das Glasperlenspiel* (1943, *The Glass Bead Game*), borrows from their ideas. It is set in a futuristic society whose rulers devote themselves to an elaborate game as the symbol of their elevated being. One of their order, Joseph Knecht, rejects the game's refinement, and wanders with his chosen successor Tito to the physically hostile conditions of the Alps. They both jump into a freezing lake, and as in *Demian,* only the pupil Tito survives, ending the novel with vague speculations about his own possible future in the light of his experiences with Knecht.

Hesse's works are available in Suhrkamp Verlag, Frankfurt am Main, and Picador, London.

Carl Krockel

Selected Bibliography
Liebmann, Judith, ed. *Hermann Hesse*. New York: McGraw Hill, 1977.
Mileck, Joseph. *Hermann Hesse: Biography and Bibliography*. Berkeley: University of California Press, 1977.
Ziolkowski, Theodore, ed. *Hesse*. Englewood Cliffs: Prentice-Hall, 1973.

Heym, Georg (1887–1912)

Heym's poetry was posthumously illustrated by the prominent expressionist painter Ernst Ludwig Kirchner, which reflects his own central position in **expressionism.** He managed to produce a powerful body of poems and short stories during the last two years of his very short life.

Heym began writing inauspicious, sentimental nature poetry during his early teens. His mature style only emerged in 1910 when he joined the Neue Club in Berlin, where he would declaim his poetry every evening. He focused on objects in their physical construction and atmosphere, not on his own moods as he had previously done. In his series of season poems he foregrounds the color of objects, while animating and unifying the landscapes through suggesting their features acting upon each other, in a vision where "everything exists simultaneously." His explosive imagery struggles against his restrictive iambic pentameter quatrains, usually in a sonnet form. His urban poetry is most aggressively expressionistic, transposing his tactile style onto imaginary scenes; in "Der Gott der Stadt" (1910, "The God of the City") Baal expresses the malignant spirit of Berlin over its helpless inhabitants, and "War" describes how "A great city sank into yellow smoke, / Hurled itself silently into the underworld's belly."

Heym's last elegies, which include "Deine Wimpern, die langen" ("Your Eyelashes, which touch") are at least as important as his more obviously expressionist poetry; he developed a more flexible form of free verse which makes possible a more subtle and sensitive treatment of his themes of love and death.

Heym's works are available in May Niemeyer, Tübingen.

Carl Krockel

Selected Bibliography

Bridgwater, Patrick. *Poet of Expressionist Berlin: the Life and Work of Georg Heym.* London: Libris, 1991.

Krispyn, Egbert. *Georg Heym: A Reluctant Rebel.* Florida: University of Florida Press: 1968.

Hispanic American *Modernismo*

The term *modernismo,* in the Hispanic literary world, has a specific and original meaning different from Anglo-American modernism, which rather corresponds to the Spanish American *vanguardia* or avant-garde. *Modernismo* was a term used for the first time in 1888 by Rubén Darío, one of the leading *modernistas,* in order to praise the prose of a contemporary writer. In 1890, Darío himself defined *modernismo* as the "new spirit that animates a small but triumphant and superb group of Spanish American writers." Today, the term indicates, rather than a particular movement or a single school, the spirit of a whole literary epoch that covers the last two decades of the nineteenth century and the first two decades of the twentieth. This has been considered a regenerative epoch and as a bridge between **realism** and the avant-garde, and between the two centuries. Furthermore, it has often been claimed that these years marked a coming of age of Spanish American literature.

Modernista discourse was basically a syncretic blend. It was nourished, on the one hand, by French aestheticism, parnassianism, and symbolism, and on the other, by the will to revalue the indigenous past and national identity, and was driven by the desire to become cosmopolitan, on equal terms with Europe. *Modernismo* implied an aesthetic reaction against the excesses of realism and **naturalism;** it has also been understood as a spiritual struggle against the predominant modern trends of the second part of the nineteenth century in the Spanish American world: materialistic and technological progress as promoted by positivism and social Darwinism and their bourgeois trademark of "order and progress"; against the negative moral and social effects of modern capitalist industrialism and the overwhelming expansionism of the United States. Paradoxically, *modernismo* has been considered a protest against the modern way of life. It also addressed **Spain**'s parochialism and mediocrity in the sunset of its imperial days. It has been suggested that *modernismo*'s historic function was similar to that of romanticism at the beginning of the nineteen century; if romanticism was a reaction against the Enlightenment, *modernismo* was a reaction against positivism.

The pluralistic spirit of *modernismo* is projected through poetry and prose. Prose became more flexible and fluid, elegant and refined, often referred to as artistic prose. Poets tried new metrical rhythms, and also revived forgotten old ones; they provided words with new meanings and functions and enriched imagery with unusual and surprising combinations of words, sounds and meanings; *modernismo* also suggested evocative correspondences between different senses, feelings and artistic expressions. The *modernista* spirit was pluralistic mainly because of the marked personalities of each of its literary figures. Many of them emphasized the importance of form while others privileged substance. Romantic writers had sometimes tended to neglect formal perfection for the sake of spontaneity and freedom; realism had allowed poetry to become excessively referential and prosaic. French parnassianism was a source of inspiration, as the value of writing for many *modernistas* was often measured by its degree of formal refinement: *art for art's sake.* However, the sonority and lyricism foregrounded by Romantic poets were seldom rejected by *modernistas;* on the contrary, their canon extended to include the parnassian Leconte de Lisle, together with the romantic Victor Hugo and the greatest Spanish romantic poet: Gustavo Adolfo Bécquer.

Symbolism was another irresistible French influence. A new sensibility called for a renovation of traditionally referential poetics by a new system of metaphorical, symbolical, and analogical correspondences. Correspondences between different human senses and between different artistic expressions, as suggested by Baudelaire and Rimbaud, colored both poetry and prose with the use of synesthetic imagery. Certain symbolic figures quickly became trademarks of *modernismo:* the swan and the owl, the nymph and the satyr, the peacock and the centaur, the fleur-de-lys and the water lily, Leda and Medusa, Versailles and Palenque, and blue above all; this color became emblematic of *modernismo.* The new French fashion of symbolism fitted perfectly into existing Spanish American literary traditions, which were themselves rooted in symbolism (as in the Spanish mysticism of St. John of the Cross and St. Teresa of Avila in the sixteenth century, for example).

Music has always played a key role in Spanish poetry, from the sixteenth century religious texts by fray Luis de León, where music represents the harmony of man with the universe, to the romantic lyric pieces by Bécquer. However, its presence was also to be strengthened by the **impressionism** of Verlaine. *Modernismo* further stressed the aesthetic value of music to be found not merely through sound, meter and rhythm, but also *within* ideas. Darío observed: "Since each word has a soul, there is in each verse, in addition to verbal harmony, an ideal melody. Very often music comes only from the idea." Indeed, the musicality of literary language, the quest for formal perfection and also the stress on symbolism as a referential system were generally regarded by *modernistas* more as an efficient means to represent reality than as mere ornamental resources. It has been argued that swans, Versailles, and princesses made sense as weapons against the vulgarity of the industrial and commercial bourgeoisie.

Nevertheless, due to its French influences and its emphasis on formal perfection, *modernismo* was often regarded as decadent, frivolous and escapist. However, it may also be said that the aim of achieving formal perfection argues skill and maturity, and that the strong French orientation reveals, rather than escapism and simple imitation, a threefold desire: (1) to reject a materialistic daily world—a modern way of life—that lacked beauty and heroism; (2) to stand on equal terms with Europe (as represented by Paris, the cultural metropolis of the age); and (3) to accomplish a true liberation through cosmopolitanism. Indeed, this claim means that the French influence worked toward the assimilation not only of French culture but of other foreign cultural trends. **France** was used as a bridge towards the rest of the world and, therefore, as the instrument of cosmopolitanism by the young Spanish American *modernistas*. (At the same time, actual cosmopolitanism was now a real possibility, too, thanks to technological advances in travel and communications.) Moreover, exoticism and antiquity—Egypt, **Greece,** and Rome, Byzantium and the Middle Ages, the Middle and Far East—were frequently sources of inspiration for the *modernistas,* though, again, such syncretic influences were often modulated through modern French versions. In this way, *modernistas* began to use strange words, foreign terms, cultisms, and archaisms.

It has often been simplistically assumed that *modernismo* lacked political engagement, as if the aesthetic motto *art for art's sake* had ruled the entire literary production of those years. It is true that some texts may reflect this principle, but it is also true that a number of authors were radically engaged. Very often their engagement grew during their lifetime or their political orientation shifted with age; but the majority of *modernistas* looked upon themselves as a refined elite, and understood the ivory tower exile. Since there is general consensus that *modernismo* was

more the spirit of an epoch rather than a movement or a school, it is reasonable not to find a single dominant political trend among the *modernistas*. Today's criticism reads the heterogenous texts of *modernistas* as the creation of a new literary language that contributed to the representation of national cultural identities. In this sense, *modernismo* may be understood as the moment when literature in Spanish America assumed its maturity and independence from the traditional mother culture—Spain—to the degree that for the first time Spanish literature was to be strongly influenced by Spanish American writers; indeed, the most relevant young Spanish poets of the time like Manuel and Antonio Machado and Juan Ramón Jiménez, became Rubén Darío's disciples. It was the time when *modernistas* were to reveal the national identity of the language; they would also strengthen Spanish American cultural nationalism against the dangers of the interventionism of the United States in Latin America during the late nineteenth and early twentieth centuries.

Modernistas have traditionally been divided into two groups, early and late. Among the former, the most relevant are: José Martí (Cuba, 1854–95), Manuel Gutiérrez Nájera (Mexico, 1859–95), Julián del Casal (Cuba, 1863–93), José Asunción Silva (Colombia, 1865–96), and Rubén Darío (Nicaragua, 1867–1916). Among the second group are: Ricardo Jaimes Freyre (Bolivia, 1868–1933), José Enrique Rodó (Uruguay, 1871–1917), Enrique González Martínez (Mexico, 1871–1952), Leopoldo Lugones (Argentina, 1874–1938), and Julio Herrera y Reissig (Uruguay, 1875–1910).

It is within the realm of prose that one finds, between 1875 and 1882, the first signs of *modernismo,* in early texts by José Martí and Manuel Gutiérrez Nájera. Martí wrote mainly essays and poetry, but also narrative and drama. His style is elaborate and polished, and his poetry is usually straight forward, fluid, and clear. His prose, however, is more complex and often baroque. He went to Paris in 1874 and his acquaintance with impressionism made him think that one should write as if painting. A few years later, in 1881, he claimed that there was a direct relation between colors and sounds; he listed the correspondences and inaugurated the use of these kinds of synesthesia that were to be very popular among the *modernistas* later on. *Ismaelillo* (1882, *Little Ismael*), his first collection of poems, is inspired by tender memories of his absent son while Martí was in exile. *Versos sencillos* (1891, *Simple Verses*) is a collection of forty six short poems that reveal a whole world of deep feelings and emotions with a seductive musical sense and moving sincerity. Two books of poetry were published posthumously: *Versos libres* (*Free Verses*) and *Flores del destierro* (*Flowers of Exile*) which include some of his earliest poems influenced by romanticism. In spite of many romantic features, his novel *Amistad funesta* (1885, *Unfortunate Friendship*) is regarded as the first *modernista* novel. Martí also published short stories and articles addressed to "the children of America" in the four issues of his journal *La edad de oro* (1889, *The Golden Age*). His essays on politics, history, society, literature, and art, along with articles and speeches, fill 20 of the 23 volumes of his complete works. But what is probably the greatest achievement of Martí's texts is the felicitous union of poetics, morals, and politics; his texts always reveal the highest degree of sincerity and moral integrity; he strongly believed that literature had to have a social purpose, that it had to be able to improve the world. In fact all his writings, in different ways and degrees, reveal a patriotic commitment to freedom and contribute to shaping the quest for the liberation of Cuba. He spent most of his adult life in exile, fought for independence, and finally died heroically on the battlefield in Cuba, soon after the beginning of the war of independence in 1895.

Gutiérrez Nájera developed a great interest and taste for French culture, particularly for the parnassian and symbolist movements. He wrote poetry, essays, short stories, and hundreds of journalistic chronicles. He founded *Revista Azul* (1894–96, *Blue Journal*). The titles of some of his works also reveal his *modernista* use of color—*Cuentos color de humo* (*Smoke-Colored Short Stories*), *Crónicas color de rosa* (*Rose-Colored Chronicles*); *Crónicas color de lluvia* (*Rain-Colored Chronicles*), for example. He never went to France, indeed never travelled abroad at all, yet his texts, mainly his short stories and journalistic chronicles and articles, reveal playful cosmopolitan tastes; they are frequently inspired by French themes and contain numerous French allusions and terms. His style was light and graceful and usually touched with musical tones. Gutiérrez Nájera and Martí were close friends and admired each other's works; however, contrary to Martí's spirit, a great deal of Gutiérrez Nájera's texts depict a typical *modernista* commitment to *art for art's sake*. It is indeed significant that the substance of the texts of the two fathers of *modernismo* differed so radically in themes and concern; this difference would mark the two main faces of the development of *modernismo.*

Julián del Casal showed a great talent for poetry from an early age. He published two collections of poems: *Hojas al viento* (1890, *Wind Leaves*) and *Nieve* (1892, *Snow*). *Bustos y rimas* (1893, *Busts and Rhymes*), a collection of poems and prose, was published posthumously. The first volume is still very much influenced by romanticism although there is already a touch of French symbolism. *Nieve* is generally considered one of the most outstanding examples of parnassicism among the *modernistas,* and it employs a highly refined, even affected language—*aristocratic* language as it is often called—to express its predominantly pessimistic vision. Indeed, in addition to its taste for Greek antiquity and Japanese exoticism, the poetry of del Casal is characterized by its melancholic nature and its obsession with death.

José Asunción Silva lost most of his works in a shipwreck, but what remains is enough to stand as some of the most original expressions of *modernismo,* particularly his renowned poem "Nocturno" and his only novel *De sobremesa* (1925, *After-dinner*). The "Nocturno" fits form to content in a masterly way, with its poetic **expressionism** powerfully evoking the mystery of an enigmatic love encounter; while *De sobremesa* is important for reflecting the cosmopolitan and decadent atmosphere of the time, nourished by imported styles, luxury objects, literary salons, and frivolity. Silva is also remembered for his sharp criticism of the imitators and followers of Rubén Darío—the *Rubén Dariacos* or *colibríes decadentes* (decadent hummingbirds)—both in his letters and in one of his poems, "Sinfonía color de fresa con leche" ("Symphony the Color of Strawberry with Milk"), where he caricatures the excesses of exquisite *modernista* affectations.

Rubén Darío, born Félix Rubén García Sarmiento in Nicaragua, has traditionally been considered the central figure of *modernismo* partly due to the fact that the other great figures of his generation died quite young. By 1896, Darío was the only survivor, with a privilege that Martí, Gutiérrez Nájera, and Silva never enjoyed—time to mature and age: Darío still had twenty years of writing ahead of him at this point. When he was 14 he was already working as a journalist. He moved to El Salvador in 1882 where he wrote under the supervision of the poet Francisco Gavidia, who introduced him to French literature. In 1886, he moved to Chile where he wrote for newspapers and published his first books of poetry: *Abrojos* (Thistles, 1887), *Otoñales [Rimas]* (1887, *Autumnal Poems [Rhymes]*), and *Azul . . .* (1888/1890, *Blue . . .*). The two first collections are still very much influenced by the Spanish poets Campoamor and Bécquer. *Azul . . . ,* a collection of poems and short stories, is, as Darío himself declared, "thought in French and written in Spanish." Nevertheless, the book may be read as a powerful spiritual reaction against modern materialism. His extensive traveling contributed to his cosmopolitanism and put him in touch with the authors he most admired. As secretary of Nicaragua's delegation to Spain's celebration of the fourth centennial of the discovery of America, he met the leading Spanish literary figures. On his way home he met Casal in Havana and soon afterwards he was appointed Consul of Colombia in Buenos Aires. On his way to Buenos Aires, Darío stopped in New York where he met Martí, and also in Paris, where he met Verlaine. In Buenos Aires he wrote for the prestigious newspaper *La Nación,* founded the cultural journal *Revista de América,* and became the leader of a group of young writers who already called themselves *modernistas.* In 1896 he published *Los raros* (*The Odd Ones*), a collection of essays about American and European writers, and *Prosas profanas* (*Profane Prose*). This collection of poems became the most representative expression of Darío's French orientation, formal perfection, musicality, exoticism, affectation, and use of symbolic language. Here, Darío uses a wide variety of forms and meters, some of them new and others that had been forgotten. It is introduced by a prologue—"Palabras liminares"—in which he tries to define his poetry, pointing out his Spanish roots and his French tastes; it has often been read also as a general commentary on *modernismo.* In 1898, right after the Spanish-American War, *La Nación* sent him to Spain as correspondent. He established his *modernista* leadership among the Spanish writers, particularly the younger ones. His collection of poems *Cantos de vida y esperanza* (1905, *Songs of Life and Hope*) marks a turning point in his poetry. He introduces socio-political concerns for the present and future of Latin America vis-à-vis the increasing expansionism of the United States, while he traces Latin American roots to Pre-Hispanic America as well as to Spain; he also contrasts the modern materialism and pragmatism of the United States with the traditional idealism and spirituality of Latin America. (In the prologue to this collection, Darío declared himself the founder of *modernismo,* and he has been strongly criticized for this because, although he did invent the name and became the leading figure of the epoch, Martí and Gutiérrez Nájera had already produced *modernista* texts before him.) During his last years, Darío lived in Paris but went back to Latin America and also visited Spain. He published *El canto errante* (1907, *The Wandering Song*), *El viaje a Nicaragua* (1909, *The Trip to Nicaragua*), *Poema del otoño* (1910, *Autumn Poem*), and *Canto a la Argentina* (1914, *Song to Argentina*). He returned to die in León, Nicaragua. Darío assimilated the entire Hispanic heritage, from medieval Spain through the Spanish renaissance and Golden Age (sixteenth and seventeenth centuries) to romanticism; he also assimilated French parnassianism and symbolism. His creative genius and charismatic personality captivated his generation and those that followed in the twentieth century. Today, Hispanic literary history is customarily divided into "before" and "after" Darío.

Two remarkable writers associated with *modernismo* should also be mentioned here: Manuel González Prada (Peru, 1844–1918) and Salvador Díaz Mirón (Mexico, 1853–1928). González Prada introduced new metric combinations and rhythms into his poetry and was influenced by French parnassians and symbolists. His most important contributions to the spirit of the time, however, were his elegant and ironic political essays denouncing positivism, social Darwinism and the reactionary role of the catholic church. Díaz Mirón, on the other hand, began writing poetry influenced by romanticism but his technical virtuosity and formal perfection, greatly admired by Darío, soon associated him with *modernismo.*

Ricardo Jaimes Freyre's poetry is best known for his experiments with different rhythms and meters as well as by the use of exotic themes taken mainly from Scandinavian mythology and Wagnerian opera, as witnessed in his first book *Castalia bárbara* (1897, *Barbarian Castalia*). He also wrote drama inspired by biblical episodes and by the conquest of the New World, while his short stories were often inspired by China, Byzantium, and the Andean Indians. This kind of chronic exoticism, particularly the Wagnerian appeal, has often been read as another rebellion against the "vulgar" reality enhanced by the pervasive materialism of modern life. Together with Darío and Lugones, he founded the *Revista de America* in Buenos Aires.

José Enrique Rodó was the leading *modernista* essayist. His rhetoric was usually didactic and always elegant. Although his lack of philosophical rigor was not compensated for by the formal beauty of his style, his essays are noteworthy for their articulation of the *modernista* world view. He considers cosmopolitanism a necessity, as part of the syncretic formation of the American nations, and as intimately related to traditional Latin American *mestizaje.* He strongly believed in assimilation, not simple imitation. In *Ariel* (1900), his first and best known work, inspired by **Shakespeare**'s *The Tempest,* he tries to persuade Latin American youth to reject the world of Caliban—utilitarianism, pragmatism, materialism, raw sensualism—and to choose Ariel's path of spirituality, intelligence, beauty, and poetry. He identifies Latin America with Ariel and the influence of the United States with Caliban. Rodó accepted material progress, the development of science and technology, but only if guided by moral ideals and values to do with the common good, truth, justice, and, above all, beauty. According to him, beauty is the light that reveals all other moral values. *Motivos de Proteo* (1909, *The Motives of Proteus*), and *El mirador de Próspero* (1913, *Prospero's Balcony*) are his other two important books.

Illustrating again the plurality of *modernismo,* Rodó's moral aesthetic stance stands in stark contrast to the decadent aesthetic of his fellow countryman, Julio Herrera y Reissig, a poet and essayist usually associated with aristocratic sophistication and a brilliant use of synesthetic imagery and metaphor, often inspired by the use of drugs and a morbid fascination with physical and psychological diseases.

The decadence depicted in the texts of Darío's followers and imitators provoked a critical reaction. This was mainly headed by the poets Enrique González Martínez and Leopoldo Lugones. The former, a master of traditional forms, and also attracted to symbolism, immortalized his "revisionist" role when he proposed, in his best known sonnet, to "wring the swan's neck" and to replace this icon of external beauty with the figure of the owl, representing (like González Martínez's own poetry) the deeper values of intelligence, reflection, and serenity.

Leopoldo Lugones' reaction against affectation, luxury and decadence represented another step forward in the development of poetic language. With a good deal of irony and brilliant craftmanship, the Argentinian poet consistently sought to *defamiliarize* everyday language and to transform it into his own highly original kind of poetic imagery. Also a prose writer, and one of the intellectual leaders of his country, Lugones mastered several genres, encompassing historical and political writing, short fiction, and journalism. Continuing in the spirit of *modernista* musicality and grandiloquence, his first book of poems, *Las montañas de oro* (1897, *The Golden Mountains*), experiments with new poetic forms and even with orthography, while *Los crepúsculos del jardín* (1905, *Garden Sunsets*) is rich in symbolic correspondences, presenting a collection of impressionistic landscapes and still lifes, as well as expressionistic erotic encounters. The increasing importance of irony can be seen in *Lunario sentimental* (1909, *Sentimental Lunar Calendar*) where the surprising poetic transformations of prosaic language and insignificant aspects of everyday life reveal an accomplished craftmanship as Lugones achieves exquisite formal perfection with "vulgar" materials. This has also been regarded as his *modernista* will to reveal the national identity of language. *Odas seculares* (1910, *Secular Odes*), a collection dedicated to celebrate the centennial of Argentina's independence, includes "La oda a los ganados y las mieses" ("Ode to the Cattle and the Grain"), a *modernista* georgic of considerable length (around 1500 verses) that has been regarded as his single most important poem. *El libro fiel* (1912, *The Faithful Book*) mainly deals with conjugal love while *El libro de los paisajes* (1917, *The Book of Landscapes*) is a delightful tonal masterpiece whose poems often evoke programmatic musical pieces. It also includes 34 miniature poems, each one portraying a different bird. His last books of poetry are *Las horas doradas* (1922, *The Golden Hours*), *Romancero* (1924, *Collection of Romances*), *Poemas solariegos* (1928, *Ancestral Poems*), and *Romances de Río Seco* (1938). Among his prose works, *La guerra gaucha* (1905, *The Gaucho War*) includes 22 historical short stories about the war of independence, while *Las fuerzas extrañas* (1906, *Strange Forces*) and *Cuentos fatales* (1924, *Fatal Stories*) are collections of short stories, many of them containing elements of the fantastic. He also published a novel, *El angel de la sombra* (1926, *The Angel of Shadows*). A socialist and anarchist in his youth, anti-democratic and military minded later on, he shares with Martí and Darío the leadership of *modernismo*. His texts, like theirs, have successfully endured the passing of time and have become classics.

The reputations of some other *modernistas* who enjoyed fame during their lifetime have fared less well, however. This is the case of Amado Nervo (Mexico, 1870–1919) and José Santos Chocano (Perú, 1875–1934). Their styles mark another significant contrast within the realm of *modernismo*. Nervo's romantic and intimate style, his sentimentalism, and his wide thematic range made him very popular for a time, and his poetry, fiction, drama, chronicles, and criticism fill over 30 volumes; but many critics now claim that not more than 20 poems have any enduring quality. Something similar can be said of Santos Chocano's poetic impact. Inspired by Latin America's landscapes and by its history and myths, his poetry was once widely praised for its sonority, grandiloquence, and musicality; and his histrionic performances in recitals throughout the Hispanic world made him a fashionable figure for a time (he was even acclaimed as "the poet of America")—but he is now generally considered only a minor poet.

There are many other significant *modernista* writers who deserve mention. José Juan Tablada (Mexico, 1871–1945) is remembered for his cosmopolitan spirit and by his unusual imagery; his best known poems were inspired by the Japanese haiku. Guillermo Valencia (Colombia,

1873–1943) is usually identified as a classic parnassian whose poetry became a model of clarity, elegance, and sobriety. Enrique Gómez Carrillo (Guatemala, 1873–1927) is best known for the French affectation of his artistic chronicles. Enrique Larreta (Argentina, 1873–1961) was an accomplished novelist. José María Eguren (Perú, 1874–1942) developed as a poet under the impact of symbolism and often depicted themes associated with childhood, mystery, and horror. Mention should also be made of those who are frequently classified as *posmodernistas:* Horacio Quiroga (Uruguay, 1878–1937), a novelist and outstanding short-story writer; Eugenia Vaz Ferreira (Uruguay, 1880–1925), a poet of melancholy and tormented loneliness, but also of great musicality; Delmira Agustini (Uruguay, 1886–1914), whose erotic language and poetic imagery are seen to have contributed significantly to Spanish American women's poetics; Ramón López Velarde (Mexico, 1888–1921), known for his lucid, surprising and suggestive imagery and for his intense eroticism and religiosity.

The spirit and world view of *modernismo* has played a key role in revealing the national identity of language in the Spanish American countries. *Modernismo* was indeed a symptom of cultural maturity vis-à-vis decadent Spanish **colonialism** and United States expansionism. The new poetic language that emerged with *modernismo* paved the way toward the *vanguardia* or avant-garde and also toward later literary developments in Spanish America throughout the twentieth century. It contributed to the liberation of the poetic signifier and the creation of new systems of referentiality that range from avant-garde *creacionismo* to *realismo mágico*.

Juan Pellicer

Selected Bibliography

Castillo, Homero, ed. *Estudios críticos sobre el modernismo*. Madrid: Editorial Gredos, 1968.

Gullón, Ricardo. *Direcciones del modernismo*. Madrid: Alianza Editorial, 1990.

Henríquez Ureña, Max. *Breve historia del modernismo*. México: Fondo de Cultura Económica, 1962.

Jrade, Cathy L. *Modernismo, Modernity and the Development of Spanish American Literature*. Austin: University of Texas Press, 1998.

Paz, Octavio. *Los hijos del limo*. Barcelona: Editorial Seix Barral, 1974.

Schulman, Iván A. *Génesis del modernismo*. México: El Colegio de México/Washington University Press, 1968.

Schulman, Iván A. & González, Manuel P. *Martí, Darío y el modernismo*. Madrid: Editorial Gredos, 1969.

Hofmannsthal, Hugo von (1874–1929)

Hofmannsthal was born in Vienna of Austrian Jewish and Italian parentage. Usually writing under the pseudonym of Loris, his output of poetry and verse dramas throughout the 1890s was prolific. His poetry often emulates a symbolist musical effect, for example, "Vorfrühling" (1892, "Before Spring"), whose alliteration and assonance become a constitutive part of the poem's meaning. He eloquently described the anxiety of creating a world through poetry in his epigram on "Dichtkunst" (1898, "The Art of Poetry"): "Perilous, terrible art! This thread I spin out of my body / And at the same time the thread serves as my path through the air."

In his verse dramas he employs a similar language, which is in tension with a naturalistic skepticism of its relation to reality. In *Der Tor und der Tod* (1893, *Death and the Fool*) he indulges poetically in the monologue of the aesthete Claudio as he contemplates the mountains in the evening light; yet the drama is also aggressively didactic, with Claudio confessing that he always tried to "kill the urge by giving it a name"; Death parades before him the figures of those whom he failed to love, forc-ing him to be silent before his "living senses."

In "Chandos Brief" (1902, "The Letter of Lord Chandos") Hofmannsthal argued for the integrity of thought in its relation to physical reality, against the possible confusions of language in its exclusively aesthetic form. He renounced the pure lyric, and then moved to a career as a librettist and playwright. He collaborated with the composer Richard Strauss on operas such as *Elektra* (1903), *Die Rosenkavalier* (1911), *Die Frau ohne Schatten* (1919, *The Woman without a Shadow*) and *Arabella* (1933). In *Elektra* he anticipated **expressionism** with his use of **Freud**'s models of paranoia and hysteria, and by emulating Nietzsche's celebration of Dionysian tragedy. After the First World War Hofmannsthal also founded the Salzburg Festival with Max Reinhardt, for which he composed prose plays such as *Die Schwierige* (1921, *The Difficult Man*), and *Der Turm* (1925, 1927, *The Tower*). *Der Turm* is a complex symbolic work, which partly reflects Hofmannsthal's ambivalence to his society, and to his possible role as an artist in it. Prince Sigismund attempts to rule Poland according to his sensitive nature, but he is killed by the violent rebel Olivier; the first version of the play ends with the entry of a "Child king" who promises future renewal, but in the second version he is omitted, implying Hofmannsthal's more nihilistic vision of his time.

Hofmannsthal's works are available in S. Fischer Verlag, Frankfurt am Main, and Pantheon Books, London.

Carl Krockel

Selected Bibliography

Bennett, Benjamin. *Hugo von Hofmannsthal: The Theatres of Consciousness*. Cambridge University Press: 1988.

Broch, Hermann. *Hugo von Hofmannsthal and his Time*. Chicago: University of Chicago Press, 1984.

Hamburger, Michael. *Hofmannsthal*. Princeton University Press: 1972.

Huch, Ricarda (1864–1947)

Huch was described by **Thomas Mann** as "Germany's first lady" of letters. Rejecting **naturalism,** her fiction of the 1890s was highly romantic and poetic. In her most famous novel *Erinnerungen von Ludolf Ursleu dem Jüngeren* (1893, *Eros Invincible*), the narrator, who has taken refuge in a monastery, relates how his Hanseatic, patrician relatives all died for love and beauty, against morality and reason. Huch displays a powerful psychological understanding of the characters' irrational behavior, for instance portraying their glorification of love during the cholera epidemic in Hamburg as a necessary delusion in a despairing reality.

From the turn of the century to the outbreak of War, Huch wrote historical novels of heroism, such as *Die Geschichten von Garibaldi* (1906–1907, *Garibaldi and the New Italy*), in which she attempted to break the distinction between history and fiction to affirm contemporary life. As a member of the Academy of Art, she resolutely opposed the Nazis. In her last period she concentrated on studies of German history, including the Thirty Years War and the German resistance fighters in the Second World War; she also wrote autobiographical works, and critical and philosophical essays.

Huch's works are available in Kiepenheuer & Witsch, Cologne, and Gerald Howe Ltd., London.

Carl Krockel

Selected Bibliography
Bithell, Jethro. *Modern German Literature: 1850–1950.* London: Methuen, 1959.

Hulme, T. E. (1883–1917)

Thomas Ernest Hulme was born in Staffordshire, England, and educated at Newcastle-under-Lyme and St. John's College, Cambridge, from which he was expelled.

He spent some time laboring in **Canada** and then, having worked his passage home, spent a brief period in literary London before turning toward the visual arts and philosophy. He joined the army on the outbreak of **World War I** and was killed in action in September 1917. Only six of his poems were published during his lifetime; five of them as *The Complete Poetical Works of T. E. Hulme* in *The New Age* in February 1912 and later in the same year as an appendix to **Ezra Pound**'s *Ripostes* (April, 1912) and *Canzoni* (May, 1912). His essays were published posthumously as *Speculations* (1924) and *Language and Style* (1929), edited by Herbert Read. Hulme translated Henri Bergson's *Introduction to Metaphysics* and Georges Sorel's *Reflections on Violence* in 1913.

Hulme's contribution to modernism is twofold. In the first place he wrote some of the earliest of the kind of poems that were later called imagist; only Edward Storer was earlier in this line. In the second place he developed an attitude to religion that precedes and closely resembles **T. S. Eliot**'s. In an important essay ("Humanism and the Religious Attitude," in *Speculations*) he insisted, "The *divine* is not *life* at its intensest. It contains in a way an almost *anti-vital* element." In the same essay he wrote of a discontinuity between "the organic world, dealt with by biology, psychology and history and . . . the world of ethical and religious ideas" and said that this meant that "after a hundred years of romanticism, we are in for a classical revival." This puts him in the camp opposite to **D. H. Lawrence** and F. R. Leavis.

Hulme's direct influence in Britain seems to have been limited, though C. H. Sisson claims "Hardy, Shaw and Kipling were incurably pre-Hulme, whereas Pound and Eliot were post-." George Sampson, writing nearer the time, in *The Concise Cambridge History of English Literature* (1941), says that "Hulme's *Speculations* (1924) were as much an influence upon the religious thought of Eliot as his few poems upon the imagist movement associated with him, Pound and the Aldingtons from 1909 to 1917." Neither of these statements can be accepted in their entirety though certainly Eliot's thoughts about pacifism and about society resemble Hulme's in some respects and Eliot commented favorably on Hulme's poetry in his essay, "The Function of Criticism." Erik Svarny claims that Eliot came to the work of Charles Maurras and *Action Française* through Hulme (17–24). Alun R. Jones points out that Hulme's poems were written mostly before **imagism** had been thought of (33–5). Kathleen Nott believed that Eliot followed Hulme in "regarding the tradition . . . of liberal humanism as mainly responsible, not only for heresy and unorthodoxy of sensibility, but for the 'split' which took place in the seventeenth century" (9), though similar views had been held, in general terms at least, by the roman catholic communion for some longer time. Chesterton and Belloc are not usually cited as influences upon Eliot but both might be if these criteria are to be invoked. In fact it is probably more accurate to say that the tradition that influenced Chesterton and Belloc influenced the younger men as well.

Among British literary modernists only **Wyndham Lewis** really developed in the same direction, though he and Hulme quarreled bitterly and were never reconciled. Evelyn Waugh's catholicism shows some similarities with Hulme's religious thought while Grahame Greene's does not; Greene's looking more like Lawrence's more humanistic tendencies. Hulme's most obvious affinities are with the work of his friend the sculptor Henri Gaudier-Brzeska and with the futurists in **Italy** and with some aspects of constructivism in **Russia.**

Hulme avoided being rounded up by Amy Lowell into her version of the *imagistes* and does not seem to have been entirely convinced of Pound's genius but his reputation has survived these difficulties. (Other poems are published in Jones.)

Nicholas Potter

Selected Bibliography
Jones, Alun R. *The Life and Opinions of T. E. Hulme.* London: Victor Gollancz, 1960.
Nott, Kathleen. *The Emperor's New Clothes.* London, 1953.
Roberts, Michael. *T. E. Hulme.* London, 1938.
Schuchard, R. "Eliot and Hulme in 1916: Towards a Revaluation of Eliot's Critical and Spiritual Development." *PMLA* (October, 1973): 1083–94.
Svarny, Erik. *"The Men of 1914": T. S. Eliot and Early Modernism.* Milton Keynes and Philadelphia: Open UP, 1988.

Hurston, Zora Neale (1903–1960)

Zora Neale Hurston was one of the leading writers of the **Harlem Renaissance,** the literary movement in New York of the 1920s when there was an interest in black cultural forms. Here Hurston courted notoriety and controversy. Consequently, in spite of her active engagement with the movement and the essays she wrote for *Opportunity: A Journal of Negro Life,* she became noted for her appearances at parties rather than her literary contributions. Subsequently an emphasis on her personality and life-style have tended to complicate objective critical judgment. That said, however, two aspects of her biography are relevant to an analysis of her work: her childhood and education. She was born (probably) in Eatonville in Florida, where her father was mayor and her mother advised her to "jump de sun." This fed directly into her most acclaimed novel *Their Eyes Were Watching God* (1937). After a series of part-time jobs she moved to New York and studied **anthropology** under Franz Boas and her interest in black folk culture led to two collections of folklore *Mules And Men* (1935) based on material collected in Florida and Louisiana and *Tell My Horse* (1938) a study of hoodoo practices in Haiti and Jamaica.

Hurston can thus be viewed as both "insider" and "outsider": as a writer about a folk culture that she had herself experienced and as an anthropologist adopting a more scientific and objective stance. In *Mules And Men* (1935) she introduces her readership to tall-tale sessions, lying contests, jook joints and riddles expressed in a distinctive folk idiom. Previous collections had tended to disconnected anecdotes and sentimental distortion but Hurston avoids this by inventing a participatory narrator who is either a character in the tales or privy to them. However this book was criticized. A review by the critic and educator Sterling Brown attacked its failure to expose the exploitation of life in the South. Here it is possible to position Hurston as "insider," articulating her belief in "racial health" by refusing to view folklore as a symptom of a psychologically destroyed people and asserting that black culture is a distinct aesthetic system. In her essay "How It Feels To Be Colored Me" (1928) she states, "But I am not tragically colored. There is no great sorrow dammed up in my soul, nor lurking behind my eyes. I do not mind at all. I do not belong to the sobbing school of Negrohood who hold that nature somehow has given them a lowdown dirty deal."

Clearly, then, Hurston did not view African Americans as the inevitable victims of white oppression, and this led to accusations that her work serves to perpetuate minstrel stereotypes and to fuel the racism that did exist and that writers like Richard Wright sought to expose. It is hardly surprising that Wright condemned *Their Eyes Were Watching God* (1937), Hurston's second novel which develops the questions concerning sexual politics and spirituality she had addressed more tentatively in *Jonah's Gourd Vine*

(1934). This work has come to be seen as her greatest achievement and a text which, because of its concern with identity, narrative voice, and the nature of language can be validly placed within the modernist canon.

The protagonist, Janie Crawford, develops a sense of self which cuts through and exposes the inadequacy and injustice of inherited constructs of race and gender. Her grandmother, an ex-slave, alerted to Janie's imminent sexual maturity, arranges a marriage of protection to Logan Killicks, who owns property and will provide her with material comforts. However the physical demands of this marriage place Janie in the role of "de mule uh de world" that the old woman was trying to avoid so Janie leaves Killicks for Jody Starks, a younger more attractive man who spoke for "far horizon," and shaped and spurred on by white bourgeois values, does become town mayor. This marriage fails too because Starks, viewing Janie as a piece of his property, curbs her spirit and denies her a voice. Here she is constrained by constructed notions of class and femininity but, in an epiphanic moment after Starks' death, she takes off the headrag that had symbolized her entrapment.

This freedom leads her into a more equal relationship with Tea Cake Woods, a young laborer who offers Janie "de keys to de kingdom" in a partnership based on shared pleasurable play rather than ownership. That Hurston is careful not to idealize this relationship undermines criticisms concerning gender and race which have been leveled against the novel; the suggestion that Janie's personal fulfillment depends solely on her relationships with men and that Tea Cake perpetuates the one-dimensional stereo type of the happy-go-lucky nigger. His behavior after he has been bitten by a mad dog reveals a more sinister side of his personality and Janie's search for self does not end at his death. Alone and on trial for murder, she withstands sexism and racism and returns home to tell her story to a female friend. In this, significantly, Janie is helped by "Pheoby's hungry listening" in a complicated woman-to-woman narrative which frames the text.

Like other modernist writers, Hurston achieves a subtle polyphony in a variety of discourse where the voices of third person narrator and character merge with direct idiomatic dialogue. At the opening of the text an omniscient narrator comments philosophically that "Ships at a distance have every man's wish on board" and this demonstrates an understanding that neither Janie nor the other characters are able to articulate. But this privileging changes as Janie gains a sense of self and her voice becomes more apparent in the narrative. Also the third person narrative is increasingly interwoven with dialect, not only in the direct dialogue of the lying sessions on the porch, but also in the free indirect discourse of the passage where Joe, trying to impress Janie, says, "Let colored folks build things too if dey wants to crow over something." In the climactic hurricane scene Janie's insight that "Ah wuz fumblin' round and God opened the door," juxtaposed with the direct discourse of "They seemed to be staring in the dark but their eyes were watching God," indicates that the voices of character and narrator exist alongside each other. Similarly at the end of the text the cohesion between Janie's realization that "Love is lak de sea. It's a movin' thing, but still and all, and it takes its shape from de shore it meets, and it's different with every shore" and the narrator's final comment on Janie that "She pulled in her Horizon like a great fish net" signifies in narratological terms that she has achieved self-fulfillment, not only through her experiences but textually, through telling her story. She has demonstrated her ability to communicate abstractions idiomatically and has achieved the understanding of an omniscient narrator.

A further characteristic which aligns Hurston's writing to modernism is her concern with the nature of language. *Their Eyes Were Watching God* is both speakerly in its emphasis on Janie's oral telling, and writerly in its inclusion of the densely poetic image patterns that Hurston sets up to evoke Janie's emotional and spiritual development. She uses the organic metaphor of the pear tree to suggest Janie's sexual awareness and potential, hence she sees "a dust-bearing bee sink into the sanctum of a bloom; the thousand sister-calyxes arch to meet the love embrace." And this image pattern is sustained throughout the text. So after Logan Killicks' "desecrating" of the pear tree, "Janie waited a bloom time, and a green time and an orange time." She becomes disappointed and not "petal open" with Jody Starks, who had never anyway represented "sun-up and pollen and blooming trees." By contrast Tea Cake comes to be "a bee to a blossom—a pear tree blossom in the spring." This modernist preoccupation with language is also evident in Hurston's next novel *Moses, Man of the Mountain* (1939) which is a re-working of the biblical story of Moses' struggle to lead the Hebrews out of Egypt. Here she employs "a veritable thicket of similes, proverbs and metaphors" (Walker).

The 1930s marked the peak of Hurston's achievement and the controversy which emerged over the racial implications of her fiction and anthropological work persisted to the end of her life, fueled by her increasing political conservatism on racial issues. Although her autobiography *Dust Tracks on the Road* (1942) was a commercial success, even as loyal a critic as African American novelist Alice Walker calls it "oddly false-sounding," and Hurston's career took a downturn in the 1940s. She lost her enthusiasm for writing about folk culture and in her last novel *Seraph On The Suwanee* (1948) all the main characters are white. Through the 1950s she struggled to support herself and she died in 1960 in virtual obscurity and penury. However more recent criticism, most famously by Walker, has led to a rediscovery and an acknowledgment of her status and influence as a foremother of subsequent women writers.

Ann Hurford

Selected Bibliography

Walker, Alice (ed.). *I Love Myself When I Am Laughing.* New York: The Feminist Press, 1979.

I

Imagism

The literary movement, boosted by **Ezra Pound** in the autumn of 1912, which launched the careers of **Richard Aldington** and **Hilda Doolittle (H. D.).** Often characterized by scholars as rooted both in French philosophy (particularly the work of Bergson) and in the thought and poetry of **T. E. Hulme** and his circle, whom Pound came to know in London in 1908, imagism, according to Aldington in his memoir *Life for Life's Sake* (1941), was at least at first merely a label Pound used to advertise the poems Aldington and H. D. had written in Paris during the previous summer. Aldington writes that Pound was "so much worked up" by H. D.'s poems that, over tea in a bun shop in Kensington, he "informed us that we were imagists." Neither H. D. nor Aldington had ever heard of the word much less of the principles later used to define the movement. In fact, they had developed their ideas of modern poetry in part through Pound's influence and in part through their own rejection of Victorian sentimentality in favour of verse derived from their passion for Greek literature. Specifically, Aldington and H. D. had been reading the French symbolists, Villon, Verlaine, and Neo-Latin poetry, but had been translating together short epigrams from *The Greek Anthology* and writing relatively short poems in free verse which captured the subjects, spirit, rhythms, and form of the Hellenic material.

The now famous bun-shop meeting was significant on several counts. Pound slashed away with his red pencil at H. D.'s poems and signed them "H. D. Imagiste," thereby giving Hilda Doolittle the initials which would serve as her pen name through her career. Pound's "naming" of H. D. was to be for her both a burden and a limitation with which she would struggle for years (was she a developing poet in her own right or merely Pound's protegée, merely an imagist?). Imagism soon became an important movement which gathered about it a circle of early modernist writers, both British and American, and formally heralded modernism in English poetry; it also forged trans-Atlantic links and made many writers (and readers) conscious of literature and its possibilities in an entirely new way.

Pound sent Aldington's and H. D.'s poems to Harriet Monroe at *Poetry: A Magazine of Verse* in Chicago. Acting as the journal's "foreign correspondent," Pound praised the work of his friends and advertised it over the months that followed by delineating its "rules." Aldington's work ("Choricos," "To a Greek Marble," and "Au Vieux Jardin") appeared in the November issue, in which Monroe described the "imagistes" as "a group of ardent Hellenists who are pursuing interesting experiments in *vers libres*." H. D.'s work ("Hermes of the Ways," "Epigram" and

"Priapus") appeared in *Poetry* in January 1913. These poems as well as others by Pound himself and by their friends (Skipwith Cannell, John Cournos, John Gould Fletcher, F. S. Flint, **Ford Madox Ford, D. H. Lawrence,** Allen Upward, and **William Carlos Williams,** among others) soon appeared not only in *Poetry* but in *The New Freewoman* (soon to become *The Egoist*) in London. Galvanized by the freshness of this new work, Amy Lowell also became part of the group.

Informally, these young poets had developed standards for the poetry they admired and wanted to write themselves. Aldington wrote in *Life for Life's Sake*, "We wanted clear outlines, directness, concision, unhackneyed verse." Pound rather cryptically formalized imagism's "four principles" in a manifesto published in *Poetry* in March 1913:

1. Direct treatment of the "thing," whether subjective or objective.
2. To use absolutely no word that did not contribute to the presentation.
3. As regarding rhythm: to compose in sequence of the musical phrase, not in sequence of a metronome.
4. The "doctrine of the Image"—not for publication.

In order to advertise his new movement, Pound initiated a collection of work he entitled *Des Imagistes,* but by the time it appeared early in 1914, Pound was disillusioned with imagism and interested in developing a new movement he denominated **vorticism.**

Aldington, H. D., and Amy Lowell pursued the idea of an annual volume of imagist verse and produced *Some Imagist Poets* in 1915, 1916, and 1917. Working together, they published their own work as well as poems by their friends, having decided that each writer would make his or her own selection and that all poets would be equally represented and appear in al-phabetical order. Pound refused on this basis to be included. In his introduction to *Some Imagist Poets 1915,* Aldington amplified Pound's rules, stressing the use of "the language of common speech" and "the exact word" as well as "absolute freedom in the choice of subject." He explained the importance of presenting "an image," striving for poetry that was not necessarily visual but that "should render particulars exactly and not deal in vague generalities." The anthologies of this avant-garde movement managed to survive the conflict of personalities that led to Pound's defection, but they could not survive **the war.** With Aldington at the front, the project was abandoned in 1918, although Aldington would continue to draw explicitly on the continuing appeal of imagism in his two volumes of verse published just after his demobilisation in 1919: *Images of War* and *Images of Desire.*

A decade later, when all of the original imagists had gone their separate ways, Aldington edited a final "imagist" collection, designed to demonstrate the divergent artistic development since the war of all those writers who had once appeared under the movement's banner. With H. D.'s help, Aldington solicited an introduction from Ford Madox Ford and collected work that appeared in *Imagist Anthology 1930.* Lowell and Lawrence were both dead, and Pound once more refused to participate, but most of the others contributed at least one poem, if only as tribute to the movement which had encouraged their early work and given voice to an exciting experiment in early literary modernism.

Caroline Zilboorg

Selected Bibliography

Coffman, Stanley. *Imagism: A Chapter for the History of Modern Poetry.* Norman: University of Oklahoma Press, 1951.

Gage, John. *In the Arresting Eye: The Rhetoric of Imagism.* Baton Rouge: Louisiana State UP, 1981.

Gregory, Eileen. *H. D. and Hellenism: Classic Lines.* Cambridge: Cambridge UP, 1977.

Hughes, Glenn. *Imagism and the Imagists.* Stanford: Stanford UP, 1931.

Harmer, J. B. *Victory in Limbo: Imagism 1908–1917.* London: Secker and Warburg, 1975.

Jones, Peter, ed. *Imagist Poetry.* Harmondsworth: Penguin, 1972.

Laity, Cassandra. *H. D. and the Victorian Fin de Siècle: Gender, Modernism, Decadence.* Cambridge: Cambridge UP, 1996.

Pondrom, Cyrena. "H. D. and the Origins of Imagism." In *Signets: Reading H. D.* Ed. Susan Stanford Friedman and Rachel Blau DuPlessis. Madison: University of Wisconsin Press, 1990. 85–109.

Pratt, William, and Robert Richardson, eds. *Homage to Imagism.* New York: AMS Press, 1992.

Zilboorg, Caroline, ed. *Richard Aldington and H. D.: The Early Years in Letters.* Bloomington: Indiana UP, 1992.

Zilboorg, Caroline, ed. *Richard Aldington and H. D.: The Later Years in Letters.* Manchester: Manchester UP, 1995.

Impressionism

French impressionist painting, as a movement, spans the years 1868–86, the dates of first and final group exhibitions. Forerunners include Johann Barthold Jongkind (1819–91), Eugène Boudin (1824–98), and James McNeill Whistler (1834–1903); key painters are Édouard Manet (1832–83), Edgar Degas (1834–1917), Camille Pissarro (1830–1903), Claude Monet (1840–1926), Auguste Renoir (1841–1919), Alfred Sisley (1839–99), Berthe Morisot (1841–95), and Mary Cassatt (1845–1926). Impressionist painters, like naturalist writers, deal with "the raw material of experience" (Hauser 874); their world may be sunlit, as in landscapes with figures by Pissarro, Monet, and Renoir, or nocturnal, as in Whistler's nuanced *Nocturnes*. Pissarro favors rural and pastoral scenes: villages, sunlit roads and bridges, fields, orchards, gardens, roofs, parks, and rivers; Manet, Degas, Pissarro, and Monet rediscover the city: boulevards, theaters, cafés, cabarets, race-tracks, railway-stations, and cathedrals; there are glimpses of industrial suburbs and small towns on the Seine, with riverbanks, houses, and gardens. Urban impressionism is intoxicated with the rhythms of modern life, the flow of traffic, the flap of flags.

"Probably the most joyous moment in the whole history of painting," wrote **D. H. Lawrence** in his 1929 essay "Introduction to These Paintings," was "when the incipient impressionists discovered light, and with it, colour". The impact of light dissolves outlines, highlights atmosphere, and stimulates perception. Early paintings by Monet and Renoir brim with *joie de vivre*. In Renoir's *Le Moulin de la Galette* (1876), one senses the surge of life on a spring evening in Paris. The painter creates the impression of a moment, with dancing rhythms of light and shade and melodic interplay of pink and blue, green and gold, black and orange. Couples, trees, tables, chairs are dappled with light and suffused with wavelike rhythms. The breeze ruffles hair and leaves; sunlight dapples dresses; a hubbub of voices mingles with the pulse of the band; there are smells of smoke, beer, perfume, flutters of delight and laughter. The impression is one of enjoyment, freshness, vitality—a holiday atmosphere. This carefree hedonism asks only for receptivity and contemplation. The painter's perception fuses subject and object in a momentary vision.

In impressionist painting, perception is relative to the angle and moment of vision. The impressionists discovered a visual paradox. In Monet's *Impression: Sun Rising* (1872), fleeting glimpses of shapes blurred in fog cohere to form an impression more vivid than any realistic portrayal of the harbor. While illusionistic **realism** is mediated through a cognitive lens, Monet's painting dramatizes the act of seeing, at a particular moment, intensifying the impression of reality. Painters aim at a harmony of light and color: luminous air creates refractions, irradiations, a flow of colors not bound to forms. Objects are steeped in color, bodies splashed with sunlight. Complementaries oscillate and vibrate, as in the blue/gold ripples of Monet's and Renoir's *La Grenouillère* (1869), depicting a floating restaurant on the Seine, or in the blues, whites, yellows, and reds of Monet's regattas.

Fleeting atmospheres are the grail of impressionist painting. Émile Zola noted that "Colors dissolve into light in the brilliant clarity of full sunshine" (qtd. Kronegger 125, n. 16). In a series of views of Rouen Cathedral (1892–94), Monet painted the transformation of the facade by changing light: to record the changes he moved from easel to easel. In his late paintings at Giverny, Monet's vision dissolves objects into color. The viewer of the *Water-Lilies* series (1899–1926) is, at first, disoriented by the lack of landmarks, except for the blurred arch of a Japanese bridge. The huge scale makes these canvases operate like color fields that engulf the viewer, with lilies floating like tachiste blobs on the green-blue-violet water. The viewer has to step back 20 feet or so before his eye adjusts to this liquefied world. Kandinsky derived the idea of non-objective painting from one of Monet's *Haystacks* (1891), an amorphous form over which light is draped in coruscating colors.

Early impressionist brushwork is disordered, syncopated, intuitive, aiming at an overall "impression," with fragmentary touches to be reassembled by the eye. Atomization dissolves solid forms in a dance of sun motes; fragmentation causes oscillation, animating the act of seeing. Arnold Hauser comments on impressionism's reduction of life to optical surfaces, but the appeal is multi-sensory. The impressionist painter is less concerned with objects and details than movement and rhythm. To convey a sense of energy in a still medium, he emphasizes the play of light that dissolves contours. In Renoir's *Nude in the Sunlight* (1876), the female body is dappled with sunlight and reflections of foliage. Light shifts over surfaces, air is in motion; animation and nuance are more vital than statement. Sisley, Monet, and Pissarro strive for a sense of the transitory in scenes of mist, flood, melting snow, smoke, or sunshine. Life, to the impressionist, consists of a series of momentary perceptions or changing moods, from which one could abstract a metaphysic of chance and impulse. Impressionist painting represents what the eye *sees,* not what the mind "knows." Monet's atmospheric and spatial effects (Cézanne said he was "only an eye—but what an eye!") can be contrasted with Degas' structuring of space through flat areas of color, cropped forms, diagonals, and steep peripheral angles showing Japanese or photographic influence.

Literary impressionism is a pervasive tendency, rather than a movement: like Zola's **naturalism,** it deals with the raw material and sensory data of life; like Verlaine's symbolism, it is an art of nuances and suggestion. Impressionism and symbolism interact in **Conrad**'s *Heart of Darkness* (1900) and **Joyce**'s *Dubliners* (1914), where objects and characters dissolve in a flow of memories and impressions. In literary naturalism and pictorial impressionism, the flow of time is represented by a slice of life (Zola's "une tranche de vie") that implies a certain momentum. Scenes are not precognitively structured or marked off from their surroundings. Henri Bergson's emphasis on *duration,* the subjective impression of time passing, and *élan vital* (vital impulse), accords with "moments of being" in impressionist painting and in the novels of **Marcel Proust** and **Virginia Woolf.**

According to Kronegger, "Light is the soul of impressionist paintings, and the soul of impressionist literature" (42). A "painterly" style in writing foregrounds visual imagery and the play of consciousness. But while visual impressions of light, air, and color are intrinsic to painting, it takes innovative techniques to translate them into literary texts. Impressionist painting and writing validate the moment—"Life, London, this moment of June" (Woolf, *Mrs. Dalloway,* 1925); "the quick of all change and haste and opposition: the moment, the immediate present, the Now" (Lawrence, "Poetry of the Present," 1919). The ontological vision of Lawrence and Woolf reflects the "energizing of vision, which is the essence of impressionism" (Hauser 878). Vitalist motifs of spontaneous energy and instantaneous perception pervade impressionist images of "action unfolding in space" and "the breath of life" (Courthion 28). However, impressionist fascination with surfaces can produce a loss of self or decentering, a fluctuating response to rapidly changing stimuli.

Subject and object, self and other merge in the impressionist worldview. While impressionist painters convey the dance of light, writers pursue the innermost flickerings of perception. Character is no longer conceived as a solid object to be grasped and presented; it is irradiated by the stream of consciousness, destructured, pulverized into scintilla to be reassembled by the reader. Linear, chronological narrative is replaced, in "spatial form," by a network of moments that cohere in the reader's mind. The goal is simultaneous apprehension of the whole through a synthetic interrelation of parts. Impressionist narration subverts and opens up the reading experience: by refusing to tell a story sequentially, it activates perception. Fragmentary images elicit instant responses, while overall significance gradually comes into focus. The reader must fill in gaps, pick up clues, make connections. Effacing him-/herself and withholding comment, the narrator unleashes a complex play of signs, in which fictional characters dissolve into streams of consciousness, rather than being clearly anchored to identities. The reader has the role of co-creator, forming impressions that seem more like real experience, with all its ambiguity, than conceptual information. Many authors evoke perceptions through a network of motifs operating at a subliminal level and coalescing by "aesthetic vibration" (Jules Laforgue) to form an overall mood or theme. The piecing together of separate impressions parallels the "musical" harmonizing of tones or colors in painting or poetry.

Impressionist fiction, presenting apparently unstructured perceptions, validates the act of seeing over that of knowing. Moving in shifting patterns, "reality" here seems indistinguishable from illusion; all is the play of consciousness. The impressionist text foregrounds sense data, while questioning their epistemological status. Whereas cognition attempts to pin down "reality," impressionism is continual flux. As in Zeno's paradox, one cannot chart points along the flight of an arrow: consciousness, while it recalls the past and anticipates the future, flows continuously through the present. In her manifesto, "Modern Fiction" (1919), Woolf insists that "Life is not a series of giglamps symmetrically arranged; life is a luminous halo, a semi-transparent envelope surrounding us from the beginning of consciousness to the end" (106). The impressionist writer inhabits a "space/time continuum," in which there is no beginning and no end, other than the arbitary limits of the frame. He/she disrupts sequence and disperses events in nonchronological associative patterns, as in **Faulkner**'s *The Sound and the Fury* (1929). Like the painters, impressionist writers wish to keep the quality of a sketch in the finished work. Woolf's narrator in *Jacob's Room* (1922), for instance, structures the text metonymically, giving clues from which the implied reader constructs an impression of a missing self, that can only be bracketed, not presented. Everything interconnects in the modernist novel and this principle can be seen at the microlevel of the sentence, with its peripheral vision, ramifying clauses, and parallel structures.

In the narrative impressionism of Conrad and **Ford,** the text follows the order of a mind, retrospecting, anticipating, coiling back, or springing forward. Memory and association replace external reality; time is immersed in consciousness, past connects with present. Dramatized narrators and multiple viewpoints refract the action from relativized angles, distorting but intensifying impressions. Disjunct moments flow together, displaying a mind in the process of choosing or evaluating its acts. Impressionist techniques break up outlines of story and character, with juxtaposed fragments creating a more suggestive *impression* than fully constructed units would. The text presents an episodic rather than *logical* sequence. In Woolf's *To the Lighthouse* (1927), consciousness is dispersed into multiple wavelengths that supplement, contradict, or subsume each other, like the interaction of colors in painting. If naive realism looks through a textual window at a unified landscape, fictional impressionism explores a labyrinth of signs.

Whereas light-drenched impressionist painting appeals directly to the senses, the shading of impressionist fiction is more elusive. Objects and events are filtered through a focalizing subject and "reality" is identified with the shifting play of consciousness. Self is dispersed into constellations of perceptions that may be compared with the atomization of objects in impressionist painting. The canvas or text offers an array of signs from which the viewer or reader constructs a pattern. Conrad's and Ford's visual techniques include defamiliarization or "delayed decoding" (Watt), as with the heads on stakes in *Heart of Darkness,* first seen from a distance and then in startling close-up. One impression succeeds or blends into another, as in Stephen Dedalus's train journey to Cork in Joyce's *A Portrait of the Artist* (1916). Impressionist narration programs consciousness: even Christopher Isherwood's supposedly neutral "Camera Eye" in *Goodbye to Berlin* (1939) must select a focus on the passing scene.

Impressionism, as the first modernist art movement, revolutionized ways of seeing. The spectator/reader is now immersed in a subjective world of experience, with relativized viewpoints. While impressionism denies cognitive certainty, it intensifies the viewer's capacity to see and feel.

Jack Stewart

Selected Bibliography

Blunden, Maria and Godfrey. *Impressionists and Impressionism.* New York: Skira-Rizzoli, 1980.

Courthion, Pierre. *Impressionism.* Trans. John Shepley. The Library of Great Art Movements. New York: Abrams, n.d.

Hauser, Arnold. "Impressionism." *The Social History of Art.* London: Routledge, 1951. Vol. 2. 869–926.

Kronegger, Maria Elisabeth. *Literary Impressionism.* New Haven, Conn.: College & University, 1973.

Nochlin, Linda. *Impressionism and Post-Impressionism, 1874–1904: Sources and Documents.* Englewood Cliffs, NJ: Prentice-Hall, 1966.

Rewald, John. *The History of Impressionism.* 4th rev. ed. New York: Museum of Modern Art, 1973.

Stewart, Jack F. "Impressionism in the Early Novels of Virginia Woolf." *Journal of Modern Literature* 9 (1982): 237–66.

Watt, Ian. "Impressionism and Symbolism in *Heart of Darkness.*" *Joseph Conrad: A Commemoration.* Ed. Norman Sherry. London: Macmillan, 1976. 37–53.

Woolf, Virginia. "Modern Fiction." 1919. *Collected Essays.* Vol. 2. London: Hogarth, 1966. 103–10.

India

India is a continental federation of many nations in different stages of material and cultural development, with great intraregional variation and a plurality of mature literary languages each with its own particular trajectory of development. It would not be possible, therefore, for any one person to draw a complete map of literary modernism in India. A team of contributors might attempt it, if they understood the assignment in sufficiently similar terms, but in the short space available here, only a partial introductory sketch of the terrain is possible.

Either by the end of the nineteenth century or by the opening decades of the twentieth, the major Indian literary traditions register a response to the profound upheavals brought about at all levels of life by the British colonial presence. A theater of cultural encounters throughout its history, India became, in the colonial period, the ground of an East-West meeting which generated intellectual ferment and a process of modernization for the West as well as for India. An initial phase of modernization being the prerequisite for the emergence of the kind of modernism discussed in this Encyclopedia, modernist movements surface unevenly and at different times in the different regions. Thus, when modernism in the strict sense is establishing itself in Bengali poetry, Hindi poetry is going through the Chhayavad movement, which corresponds to the modernization that had happened in Bengali poetry at an earlier stage.

Though Western stimuli are important in each phase, even more important is the fact that the writers negotiate with *foreign* influences on their own terms and for their own purposes. Indigenous issues are examined in a new light because of knowledge of the *other.* In spite of variations, certain common concerns emerge and similar questions are asked. Which areas of lived reality had been underrepresented before? What kind of diction and style would give them adequate representation? How can women and the underprivileged of society acquire a voice? There is plenty of rebellion and turmoil. And new technology is as important as new ideas are, the printing-press generating the culture of magazines and printed polemics.

The two phases, first, of an initial modernization, and then, of *modernism* proper, can be seen very clearly in the case of Bengali writing. The discovery of English literature and, to a lesser extent, of some other European literatures; the influence of **Shakespeare,** the English Romantics, the nineteenth-century European novel; a rediscovery of India's past through the efforts of western orientalist scholarship; the first bursts of feminist thinking; the forging of a more supple language to accommodate the new themes; the creation of new prose genres such as the novel and the short story; the adoption of poetic forms and devices such as blank verse, the sonnet, enjambment: these belong to the first phase. The towering figure of Rabindranath Tagore (1861–1941) dominates the end of the nineteenth century and the beginning of the twentieth, his spectacular powers of self-renewal paradoxically ensuring that the first new voice after Tagore would be Tagore himself. This new voice was audible in the prose poems of *Lipika* (1922) and in several poetry collections of the thirties, in the gradual adoption of the demotic idiom (*chalit bhasha*) in preference to the literary (*sadhu bhasha*), or in a novel like *Ghare-Baire* (1916), which generated as much fierce controversy as anything written by the next generation.

The twenties, however, saw a younger generation of writers getting distinctly restless, fretting at always being in the shadow of a polymathic genius and keen to express the fractured consciousness, the spiritual uncertainties of their times. Nazrul Islam (1899–1976), with his fiery verses and songs championing liberty, equality, and secularism, was a popular new voice during this period, though he did not develop into a full-blown modernist. Modernist efforts surfaced in twenties magazines such as *Kallol, Kali-Kalam,* and *Pragati.* A degree of rebellion against Tagore was part of the show. His greatness was never challenged, but certain features of his worldview were.

Against his intuitive apprehension of cosmic and personal harmony the accent now was increasingly on the inevitability, even the desirability, of conflict and disorder; to his joy of existence were opposed passionate feelings of frustration, anguish and anger; his aesthetic gracefulness was challenged by underlining the social reality of violence, exploitation and squalor; and the mystic-religious dimension which related his love lyrics, especially of the middle period of his career, to the tradition of the Vaishnavas, Bauls and Sufis, was rejected in favour of a more overtly sex-oriented, secular and tormented eroticism. (Ray 15)

This is the core of the modernist project. There had been plenty of "tormented eroticism" in the young Tagore, but of the *Romantic Agony* brand. The new sexuality was more **Freud**-inspired. In language the steady thrust was towards the complete emancipation of the colloquial. Modernism consolidated itself in the thirties in the work of poets such as Jibanananda Das (1899–1954), Amiya Chakravarty (1901–1986), Sudhindranath Datta (1901–1960), Buddhadeva Bose (1908–1974), and Bishnu Dey (1909–1982). Each had a distinctive voice and a finely honed style of his own, but they shared an international outlook and an interest in the intellectual movements sweeping across the world in the inter-war years. In no sense imitators, their language derived in a line of direct descent from that shaped by Tagore himself in the thirties, they nevertheless mediated Western-style modernistic image-making to Bengali readers. The magazine *Kabita*, founded by Bose in 1935 and edited by him for 25 years, became the modernist poetry platform par excellence. Datta, Bose, and Dey were also major poetry translators.

There were analogous developments in fiction; from the forties onwards Marxism became an important influence;

Joyce's stream of consciousness cast its spell too. Modernism has affected virtually every field of the arts in Bengal: the visual arts (with Tagore himself as a pioneer, deeply influenced by **primitivism** and **German expressionism**), drama (Buddhadeva Bose, Badal Sircar), **film** (Satyajit Ray, Ritwik Ghatak, Mrinal Sen), and even contemporary singer-songmakers like Suman Chatterjee and Mousumi Bhowmik are artists in a modernist framework.

An intense preoccupation with the creative process marks much of the modernist consciousness. Buddhadeva Bose, who was both a great practitioner and an eloquent theoretician of modernism, provides an example of this consciousness in his poem "Magic Desk." While Zbavitel (288–89) and following him, Chatterjee and Ferdous (in Natarajan, ed., 56), cut off Bose's best poetry at *Damayanti* (1943), Bose continued to develop himself in every collection till his death, *Je-Andhar Alor Adhik* (1958) in particular being universally recognized as a landmark in modernism. The following poem, translated by myself, is from his collection *Draupadir Sari* (1948).

Magic Desk
Then brighten the lamp, and at the
    magic desk
drown yourself in the narrow pool of
    that light
whose seed engenders woman's beauty,
    whose song makes the ocean's blue
tremulous, whose chemise of
    shimmering dreams beneath the
    moon
guides the world-conquering ship to
    dash it on ancient rock.
Then brighten the lamp, the lamp that
    casts the shade
which on a wondrous endless cloth of
    grass, trees, sun
gives the earth form, the form which
    the wind shakes
for ever with a lakh of hands,—yet the
    cry of that leaf-fall

is vanquished, stilled, given a rhythmic
    pace by its art.
Then brighten the lamp, pledge
    yourself to that light
which says goodbye to youth, wipes off
    life,
pierces with color's undulations the
    core of the hot, dense mine,
and in veins of metals, in flames of
    lotuses of stone,
kindles unending, unerring, cruel
    diamonds of eyes.

Ketaki Kushari Dyson

Selected Bibliography

Das, Sisir Kumar. *A History of Indian Literature.*
Vols. VIII/1 (1800–1910) and VIII/2 (1911–
56). New Delhi: Sahitya Akademi, 1991, 1995.

Datta, Sudhindranath. *The World of Twilight: Essays
and Poems.* Calcutta: Oxford UP, 1970.

Dyson, Ketaki Kushari. "Calcutta Gemütlichkeit:
Bengali poetry after Tagore." *Poetry Review*
83:1 (Spring 1993): 26–28.

Natarajan, Nalini, ed. *Handbook of Twentieth-
Century Literatures of India.* Westport, CT:
Greenwood Press, 1996.

Nirala. *A Season on the Earth: Selected Poems.*
Trans. David Rubin. New York: Columbia UP,
1976.

Ray, Sibnarayan, and Marian Maddern, ed. *I have
seen Bengal's Face: a selection of modern Bengali poetry in English translation.* Calcutta:
Editions Indian, 1974.

Schomer, Karine. *Mahadevi Varma and the Chhayavad Age of Modern Hindi Poetry.* Berkeley
and Los Angeles: University of California
Press. 1983.

Seely, Clinton B. *A Poet Apart: A Literary Biography of the Bengali Poet Jibanananda Das
(1899–1954).* Newark: University of Delaware
Press, 1990.

Tagore, Rabindranath. *Selected Poems.* Trans. William Radice. Harmondsworth: Penguin, 1985.

Tagore, Rabindranath. *I Won't Let You Go: Selected
Poems.* Trans. Ketaki Kushari Dyson. Newcas-
tle upon Tyne: Bloodaxe Books, 1991.

Zbavitel, Dušan. *Bengali Literature.* Wiesbaden:
Otto Harrassowitz, 1976.

Interior Monologue

Joyce is probably the most well-known
user of stream of consciousness—notably
in Molly Bloom's soliloquy at the end of
Ulysses, but **Virginia Woolf** more often
employed "interior monologue" to render
the thoughts of her characters. Her practice
differs from Joyce in at least three key
ways. First, she uses many more tags, such
as "he thought" or "she wondered." Second, the style of the interior monologue is
similar from character to character—sentences, syntax, and vocabulary do not alter
as much as they do in Joyce, and this helps
to connect characters. Third, Woolf always
uses the past tense for interior monologues, to stress the importance of personal history. Overall, Woolf uses
numerous metaphors and similes for the
way the mind functions—in some of her
fiction images of thought are as common
as the thoughts themselves. The effect of
this is important in a book such as *Mrs.
Dalloway* because it allows the narrative
to skip from character to narrator to character without seeming to make abrupt
shifts. In this way, Woolf conveys what she
calls "life"—that is, the narrative can slide
between different consciousnesses for purposes of comparison and connection.

Peter Childs

Ireland

Ireland was of catalytic, yet paradoxical,
importance to the development of modernism. This quality was heightened by the
fact that the country was partitioned almost exactly half-way through the 1890–
1940 period, in 1922. Before **World War
I,** Ireland had been precocious in pioneering modernist forms and themes, partly as
a result of the tensions deriving from its
unique situation as the only metropolitan
colony in Western Europe, at once an integral part of the United Kingdom and its
most underdeveloped periphery, with a
majority of its population resentful at incorporation. The questioning of inherited
traditions stemming from such tensions
meant, as Terry Eagleton has put it, that

"[w]hat 'British' modernism there was in the late nineteenth and early twentieth centuries was largely of Irish origin" (297). Nevertheless, many of Irish modernism's major achievements took place outside Ireland itself, and modernism in the Free State suffered a dismal fate. Northern Ireland was particularly inhospitable to experiment, although it should be noted, against conventional critical wisdom, that George Russell ("AE") (1867–1935), Francis Stuart (1902–2000) and Brian O'Nolan ("Flann O'Brien") (1911–1966) were of northern provenance, and that the 1930s poetry of Louis MacNeice (1907–63) challenges realist notions of univocalism and identity. Almost uniquely, political revolution in Ireland preceded, rather than succeeding, high modernism; as a result the radical promise of a revolution of the word was effectively preempted and checked by the conservative backlash following its political equivalent. A catholic-protestant sectarian standoff between north and south, and (in different ways) within each state, made for paralysis and philistinism; this, coupled with fierce **censorship** in the south, a tiny market for *highbrow* literature and a weak publishing sector (there was no commercial poetry publisher in Ireland from 1928 to 1951), made Irish modernism from the 1920s a largely exile phenomenon.

The promising start for modernism took shape in the Celtic Revival (or Twilight) movement from the 1880s. The Revival involved a discovery (or more properly, the invention) of an indigenous Irish tradition and ethnic identity in **myth** and folklore which had its parallels in the paleomodernist interest in **primitivism** elsewhere in Europe. From the beginning, an emphasis on the poetic, otherworldly nature of the Celt displayed opposition to an England perceived as empirical and materialist, thus appropriating and giving Arnoldian categories of the Celt and Saxon a subversive twist. The chief figures included Lady Augusta Gregory (1852–1932), Standish James O'Grady (1846–1928) and—the driving force of the movement—**W. B. Yeats** (1865–1939), who fused Celticism with occult beliefs and an advanced *fin de siècle* aesthetic saturated in the *symbolisme* of de L'Isle-Adam, Maeterlinck, Huysmans, and Pater. It was an aesthetic he shared with **Oscar Wilde** (1854–1900) (who, although not a Revival activist, can be viewed fruitfully as a deconstructor of imperial metropolitan mores), with George Moore (1852–1933) and, later, with **John Millington Synge** (1871–1909). All were members of a professional or landowning ruling class who, though largely protestant, sought to reshape the increasingly resented ascendancy hegemony along nationalist but non-sectarian lines. The ever-present political dimension of cultural nationalism asserted itself more strongly with the death of Parnell in 1891, however, as the chance of a Home Rule-style, unpartitioned settlement of the Irish Question receded. Catholic nationalist middle-class energies switched to the cultural field, taking the Revival beyond clique appeal but raising the probability of a challenge to leadership of the revivalist project.

If the apotheosis of Yeats's symbolistenationalist style was *The Wind among the Reeds* (1899), his advice to J. M. Synge in 1896—to abandon being an interpreter of French literature in England for the expression of a life that is "perhaps the most primitive that is left in Europe" on the Aran Islands—showed his own awareness of a changing cultural climate and foreshadows a move from a populist to an elitist position. Nevertheless the Abbey Theatre, founded in 1899 (acquiring a permanent location in 1904), succeeded in broadening literary-cultural debate through new drama. Synge turned to writing plays in an apparently realistic Hiberno-English idiom at once stylized and earthily realistic. Courting controversy from the first, *In the Shadow of the Glen* (1903), *Riders to the Sea* (1904) and *The Well of the Saints* (1905) are lyrical dramas which rehearse the Syngean themes of solitude and community, stoicism and energy. Synge's masterpiece is *The Playboy of the Western World* (1907), whose hero is both an inspiring and liberating master of verbal pyrotechnics, and simultaneously cowardly and vicious. Synge exploits the gap between the romanticization of heroism and the facts of blood and murder in the drama of a would-be parricide whose Oedipal subtext has direct bearing on the facts of colonial infantilization and religious repression. It was the occasion of the famous riots at the Abbey Theatre at its first performance, deemed "a slander on the fair name of Ireland" because of a female character's use of the word "shift." The event marked a definitive parting of the ways between the different wings of the Revival, and the accession of middle-class catholic nationalism to cultural hegemony.

The ultimate incompatibility of the ideologies of either trend in the Revival with a freely expressive imaginative literature had long been apparent to **James Joyce** (1882–1940), whose self-exile in 1904 marked a rejection of the "periplegia" of Dublin for the purpose of attending all the more attentively to analysis of its inhabitants and their verbal transfiguration. Joyce's influence on subsequent Irish literature, modernist and non-modernist, can scarcely be exaggerated. His trajectory from **naturalism** and symbolism in *Dubliners,* ironically-framed and incipiently modernist in *A Portrait of the Artist as a Young Man,* to the high modernism of *Ulysses* (if not the proto-**postmodernism** of *Finnegans Wake*) made him a hero-figure for almost all subsequent Irish writers. Joyce's protean legacy was however a profoundly ambiguous one; if many writers heeded his call to "silence, exile and cunning," few took much more from it

than the romantic posture, or (crucially) followed his example of formal experiment (although appreciation of Joyce's Irish contexts is vital to non-Irish critics; thus, Moore's *The Untilled Field* (1903) and *The Lake* (1905) are important precursors of *Dubliners* and *A Portrait*). Similarly, Yeats's heirs—Austin Clarke, Padraig Fallon, Padraic Colum and F. R. Higgins—valorized his earlier Celticist and mythic themes in the 1920s and 1930s, pushing them, in many cases, towards a wholly anti-modernist, saccharine shamrock Georgianism, rejecting his increasingly harsh and complex later work, such as *The Tower* (1928), as "un-Irish."

The dramatist who most powerfully developed Synge's inheritance was **Sean O'Casey,** a working-class chronicler of the revolutionary moment of 1916 and its aftermath of betrayed ideals and fratricide. O'Casey's conflicting allegiances—as a Dublin protestant, socialist, one-time member of both Sinn Fein and of the Orange Order—are typical of the rich ideological contradictions of Ireland on the eve of the Easter Rising, and are articulated in the trilogy of Dublin plays, *The Shadow of a Gunman* (1923), *Juno and the Paycock* (1924), and *The Plough and the Stars* (1926). These—unlike Synge's—are in a markedly anti-heroic mode, revolutionary but pacifist; set in proletarian, inner city Dublin, they draw on its humor, song, and dialect, in the face of a growing tendency to judge plays by their "PQ," or "Peasant Quality." Resemblances to the expressionist theatre of **Toller** and **Brecht** suggest themselves, and are even stronger in later, more experimental plays such as *The Silver Tassie* (1928). By this time, however, O'Casey had moved to England in the wake of a riot and the hostile reception of *The Plough and the Stars.* The play caused deep offense by challenging the idealization of 1916 and the martyr-cult built around its leaders; in it prostitution and drunkenness are juxtaposed with patriotism, self-sacrifice is questioned, the disparity between violence and heroics exposed. Hardening orthodoxies meant that, after O'Casey, only the poetic dramas of the older Yeats continued a tradition of Irish dramatic innovation into the 1930s.

Joyce's most important follower, **Samuel Beckett** (1906–1989) became, in the 1940s, a francophone minimalist in order to evade his mentor's overpowering influence. Yet the work of the 1930s—as in *Murphy*'s (1938) satirizing of Austin Clarke and the "Cultic Toilette"—show a concern for Irish writing most cogently formulated in the review "Recent Irish Poetry" (1934). In it Beckett divided, in Manichaean fashion, the modernist sheep from revivalist goats intent only on delivering "the Ossianic goods." For Beckett the key artistic move was recognition of "the new thing that has happened . . . namely the breakdown of the object, whether current, historical, mythical or spook" (70). Accordingly, **Brian Coffey** (1905–1995) and **Denis Devlin** (1909–1959) were the only young Irish poets of promise; but Beckett placed the older **Thomas MacGreevy** (1893–1967) between these and the revivalists. This, however inadvertently, minimizes MacGreevy's achievement as the only Irish poet to have mastered Eliotic poetics; yet, if he is (almost) Ireland's **Eliot,** MacGreevy is an Eliot put through the wringer of the Western Front, prevented by its trauma from endorsing either an aestheticist or realist poetic. His poems of **the war,** "Nocturne" and "De Civitate Hominum" (like "Crón Tráth na nDéithe" ("Twilight of the Gods"), which uses *The Waste Land* as its intertext), are representative of a small but lyrical and painterly oeuvre of impasse, one ultimately seeking rapprochement with European catholic modernism which, for MacGreevy, included Joyce as well as Claudel and Jiménez. The failure of this project in an increasingly isolated Éire (to which MacGreevy had felt compelled to return after some years in Paris), combined with wartime experiences to produce a silence for nearly three decades after his *Poems* (1934).

As this suggests, MacGreevy—like Coffey and Devlin—did not, for all his formalism, share the spirit of Joycean (or Beckettian) anti-religious or anti-nationalist *non serviam.* As for modernists elsewhere—**David Jones** is an example—experimentalism accorded with ritual and orthodox faith in all three. Nor—like Beckett in this—can they be allied to the avant-garde as it is usually understood, each resisting more radical assaults on the institution of art per se (indeed it has been argued that while political conditions facilitated modernism in Ireland, the country's relative paucity of technology prevented a cultural basis for an avant-garde proper). Devlin's career was the most orthodox, as his uninterrupted publications record, and adoption by United States New Critics in the 1940s indicates. *Intercessions* (1937), his first collection, shows similarities with the verbal pyrotechnics of Hart Crane and a knowledge of the political concerns of the **Auden** generation in England, as well as the influence—almost unheard-of in Irish poetry—of French **surrealism.** But it also already reveals the closed forms, dense metaphysical argumentation and aestheticism which would recommend him to Allen Tate. Diplomatic *intercession,* indeed, often in the form of a quasi-divine female mediatrix, is frequently at the heart of Devlin's poetry, although this is more fully developed in his work of the 1950s. Devlin's relative success, during his lifetime at least, contrasts with Coffey's career, which was one of neglect and hardship registered in a long mid-life silence and later flowerings in the 1950s and 1970s. Like Beckett's, Coffey's poetry is a poetry of indeterminacy, process, rhythmic hesitancy, accumulation through repetition and an open-endedness very different from MacGreevy's or Devlin's striving for symbolic closure. Coffey studied under the French philosopher Jacques Maritain after 1933, and drew upon his neo-Thomist suspicion of the emphasis of one variety of modernism on the autonomy of the work of art and the demiurgic role of the artist, seeing them as an arrogant challenge to divine creativity. Rather, like Maritain, Coffey stressed artistic humility, the craft(ed) nature of the art object, summed up in the Scots word *makar* (or *maker*), meaning poet.

A postcolonial reading of Ireland would find no difficulty in relating the mixed fortunes of its relationship to modernism to the forging before 1916 of a national identity necessarily based on a mirror-image of the imperial power which thereafter became a straitjacket on national development. Thus, a perceived English materialism and cosmopolitan corruption were opposed by the presumed innate spirituality and chastity of the Irish "race," a cult of the peasant, and a program for Gaelicisation. From the 1920s a policy of economic self-sufficiency supportive of country against urban areas found literary equivalents in a limitedly rural literature which expressed a now-official ideology of "Irishness." This meant that the opposition to a now-moribund revivalism took the form chiefly of **realism,** not modernism (with the leading poetic realist Patrick Kavanagh (1904–67), for example, reading *Ulysses* as "almost entirely a transcription from life"). Experimentalism was seen as a self-indulgence which embattled anti-philistines could not afford. Yet, as usual in Irish culture(s), reality was more complex than first appears. Realism was certainly not wholly dominant, as Flann O'Brien's fantastically self-reflexive *At Swim-Two-Birds* of 1939 demonstrates (and as the belated impact of modernism on Irish language writing in the 1950s would show). Nor can the pre-World War II fiction of **Elizabeth Bowen** (1899–1973) or Francis Stuart be counted "realist" in any normal sense (both, like MacNeice and Beckett, possessing a dissentient, Anglo-Irish historical awareness of tradition as a form of betrayal, and of its implications in complicating realist subject-object relations in writing). Also, among Yeats's epigones, Clarke and Fallon moved, in the late 1930s, to kinds of writing containing modernist elements (the older Clarke recalling the modernist localism of **Hugh MacDiarmid,** for example). Conversely, MacGreevy and Coffey both display profoundly archaic traits; and much of what is called Irish modernism confounds simple, monolithic ideas of nationalism or internationalism, conservatism or modernism, emanating as it does from a culture (or cultures) which do not conform to standard Anglo-U.S. or European models. In this sense it is appropriate that the critical jury should still be out on whether Yeats can be categorized as a modernist; that *Ulysses* may equally well be described as an anti-novel as a novel; and that Moore's masterpiece, *Hail and Farewell* (1911–1914), should be a mélange of fiction, autobiography and cultural history. In the long run, arguably, it is precisely this kind of hybrid evasion of critical definition which will be seen as the most distinctive aspect of the exceptional Irish contribution to modernism.

John Goodby

Selected Bibliography

Beckett, Samuel, "Recent Irish Poetry." *Disjecta: Miscellaneous Writings and a Dramatic Fragment.* Ed. Ruby Cohn. London: John Calder, 1983. 70–76.

Brown, Terence. *Ireland: A Social and Cultural History 1922–85.* London: Fontana Press/HarperCollins, 1985.

Cairns, David, and Shaun Richards. *Writing Ireland: Colonialism, nationalism and culture.* Manchester: Manchester UP, 1988. (See especially 58–138.)

Coughlan, Patricia, and Alex Davis, eds. *Modernism and Ireland: The Poetry of the 1930s.* Cork: Cork UP, 1995.

Davis, Alex. *Denis Devlin.* Dublin: Irish Academic Press, 2000.

———. "'No Narrative Easy in the Mind': Modernism, the Avant-Garde and Irish Poetry." In *For the Birds: Proceedings of the First Cork Conference on New and Experimental Irish Poetry.* Ed. Harry Gilonis. Sutton: Mainstream Poetry Press; Dublin: hardPressed Poetry, 1998. 37–50.

———. "Irish Poetic Modernisms: A Reappraisal." *Critical Survey* 8:2 (1996): 186–197.

Eagleton, Terry. "The Archaic Avant Garde." In his *Heathcliff and the Great Hunger: Studies in Irish Culture.* London, Verso, 1995. 273–319.

Foster, John Wilson. *Colonial Consequences: Essays in Irish Literature and Culture.* Dublin: Lilliput Press, 1991. (See especially 44–59.)

Goodby, John, and Maurice Scully, eds. *Colonies of Belief: Ireland's Modernists.* Special Issue, *Angel Exhaust* 17 (Spring 1999).

Kiberd, Declan. *Inventing Ireland: The Literature of the Modern Nation.* London: Jonathan Cape, 1995. (See especially 33–50, 137–238.)

McCormack, W. J. *From Burke to Beckett: Ascendancy, Tradition and Betrayal in Literary History.* Cork: Cork UP, 1994. (See especially 307–23.)

Italy

Modern Italian literature emerges from, and responds to, two overwhelmingly significant historical events: the unification of the country in 1861, and the rise and fall of the fascist party.

In the novel, Italian **realism,** epitomized in its early days by the work of Alessandro Manzoni (1785–1873), examined the miseries of the poor in the new Italy. Luigi Capuana's (1839–1915) "verismo" movement was a native version of Zola's French naturalist movement: **Giovanni Verga,** who is associated with the "Veristi," writes of the experiences of Sicilian peasants in a realist style that, in its attention to regional variations of language, gestures towards the psychological emphases of the major modernists. Other novelists, like Grazia Deledda (1871–1936), combined an interest in "verismo" with a style drawn from decadent writings. With **Italo Svevo,** who was born and lived in the cosmopolitan port of Trieste, the Italian novel takes on a more recognizably international modernist flavor. Svevo, whose work was promoted by **James Joyce,** was heavily influenced by **Freud,** and he helped to develop the range of the narrated **interior monologue** and stream-of-consciousness techniques. Italian reviewers were slow to recognize the innovative qualities of his work. Alberto Moravia (1907) has been said to show the influence of Svevo. His novels explore sexual experience in undermining the bourgeois way of life. He was married to **Elsa Morante,** a fellow anti-fascist, whose work is influenced by **Katherine Mansfield.** Together with **Natalia Ginzburg,** Morante is considered the most important modern Italian female writer. Cesare Pavese (1908–1950) and **Elio Vittorini** both translated, and were influenced by, English and American writers, including **Stein** and **Faulkner** (Pavese) and **D. H. Lawrence,** Faulkner, and **Hemingway** (Vittorini). Vittorini's strong anti-fascism informs his work both thematically and stylistically. In the period after the Second World War, "neorealism" sought to restore a political directness to literature, stressing the importance of content rather than form. Italo Calvino's published fiction starts out in the neorealist vein but soon transforms itself into his complex and meditative mature style, with its blending of folktale and literary parody. Calvino's engagement with the international literary scene, and his association with the structuralists in Paris, registers an opening-up of post-war Italian writing that also finds expression in the formation of **Gruppo 63,** a network of Italian writers who promoted a form of experimental writing reflecting their interest in theoretical developments in **France** and **Germany.**

In poetry, three names dominate the late nineteenth-century Italian scene: Giosuè Carducci (1835–1907), Giovanni Pascoli (1855–1912), and Gabriele D'Annunzio. The latter of this trio was the dominant figure of the Italian Decadence, and the fame won by his sensational works and excessive lifestyle casts a shadow over the first decades of the new century. As a response to D'Annunzio's sensational excesses, the Crepuscolari ("Twilight") poets cultivated an unpretentious, conversational poetry that dwells on simple, everyday life and objects. It mourns the passing of one age, but cannot embrace the arrival of a new one. Among the major exponents of this crepuscular poetry are Marino Moretti (1885–1979) and Guido Gozzano (1883–1916). In direct contrast to these poets, the futurists, under the leadership of **Filippo Tommaso Marinetti,** embraced the future and its trappings (machinery, the impersonal climate of the cities, mass warfare) with a sensational violence reminiscent of D'Annunzio, whom they constructed as a symbolist lover of antiquity. In poetry, the futurists promoted a freeing of the word from the constraints of grammar and punctuation. Their dictum, "Parole in libertà" (words in freedom), called for poems whose words—italicized, enlarged, made bold—were spread across a page in imitation of newspapers and billboards, and of the chaos created by the phenomenon of speed. These innovations produced a poetry best suited to violent declamation: a form, together with that of the manifesto, which Marinetti perfected in his tireless efforts to gain a wider audience for **futurism.** The movement contributed significantly to experimentalism in painting, sculpture, drama, and architecture. It was finally co-opted into the fascist party. **Giuseppe Ungaretti** was, like Marinetti, born in Egypt and educated in French, but, though he mixed early in his life with a number of the futurists in Paris, his academic disposition is in direct opposition to futurist irrationalism, and his style and metaphysical themes are his own. He has, however, been dubbed an "Hermetic" poet because of the difficulty of much of his verse. Eugenio Montale (1896–1982) has also been classed as an "Hermetic" poet. Among other notable modern Italian poets are Umberto Saba (1883–1957), and Salvatore Quasimodo (1901–1968), who won the Nobel Prize for Literature in 1959.

In the theater, despite the innovations of the futurists in developing a participatory form of "Variety Theater," **Luigi Pirandello** is the single major figure. His self-reflexive plays, in their questioning of the forms of mimetic theater, retain a central place in the history of modern drama. His *teatro nuovo* (new theater) also makes strides towards the establishment of a *teatro del grottesco* (theater of the grotesque), an Italian version of the "Theater of the Absurd."

Andrew Harrison

Selected Bibliography

Bondanella, Peter, and Bondanella, Julia Conaway, eds. *Dictionary of Italian Literature.* Westport, Connecticut: Greenwood Press, 1979.

Brand, Peter, and Pertile, Lino, eds. *The Cambridge History of Italian Literature.* Cambridge: Cambridge University Press, 1996.

J

James, Henry (1843–1916)

There are several good reasons *not* to include Henry James in any consideration of modernism. The most obvious are anecdotal. The James who visits the 1910 London exhibition of **post-impressionism**—a *locus classicus* in the history of English modernism—in the company of Roger Fry is assigned, in **Viriginia Woolf**'s recording of the scene, the part of the great old man somewhat bewildered by the pictorial innovations of Matisse and Picasso he is being invited to take in (Torgovnick 45).

Other reasons are more central to the general issue, having to do with the established usage and usefulness of the term, its rather coercive circularity. Modernism would appear to prove its heuristic usefulness as the name referring to an artistic project of which certain works by **Eliot, Pound,** and **Joyce** are the exemplary, performative instances: modernism is thus the label conveniently attached to the works of the writers just mentioned, and to any other works from the same period exhibiting a family-resemblance to this limited number of *strong* canonical examples. In which case, the term would appear to function like any other nodal point around which literary history organizes its narrative. For however insistent the modernist invocation—by its canonical practitioners or its academic analysts—of *fragmentation* as the modality constitutive of its aesthetic, however insistent the implication of

a break with prior, established literary modes, and the reference to either an intentional modernist *disordering* of form or a resigned submission to the disorder of its material, it is nonetheless evident that, when considered as a term which articulates a particular moment of literature, modernism both subscribes to and consolidates the orthodox idea that a canon does indeed exist, composed of the defining instances represented by a small number of literary works, upon which, like any other movement or moment, modernism lays its claim to epochal status, its capacity to situate other works and other periods, as either *premodernist* or *postmodernist.*

The term would thus appear to function, whether in the ordinary practice of critical judgement or in the grander narrative of literary history, with the normative thrust proper to any classical *art poétique. Modernism* has its defining instances—the writers just mentioned; its crowning moment—between 1910 and 1930; and, presumably, its secondary, outer constellation: **Lawrence,** Woolf, **Hemingway** for example, writers ultimately less heroic, being more congenial, more reader-friendly. Modernism has its precursors and its cases of epigonic belatedness. Any attempt to situate the Jamesian "house of fiction" in relation to the modernist project might thus constitute even less than an embarrassing *mésalliance,* being more in the nature of a blind date bringing face-to-face two parties who, their respective defining qualities having been examined, decide there is nothing to warrant any further engagement. For there can be little point in regarding James as either a "precursor" or a peripheral instance of modernism. The dates are wrong. James is a writer who, in his autobiography, *A Small Boy and Others* (1913), evokes the Paris of the early years of the Third Empire—well before the debacle of 1870, and a world away from the "grand Niagara" of the outbreak of war in 1914 (James, *Letters,* 713). His artistic career begins in the 1860s, around the moment when early **impressionism** was beginning its celebration of the ambient world, long before the Woolfian change in the human character, round about December 1910. Our aim is thus to determine whether or not James the author, and modernism, as the name given to a problematic common to a number of major literary projects of the early twentieth century, can, or should, be best regarded as separate entities, best evaluated in isolation. We shall therefore try to outline the Jamesian project—its conditions, ends, and instruments—in order to see whether it can be adequately described on its own (Jamesian) terms, independently of any reference to the modernist project. In which case, James stands alone, or at least, elsewhere, his enterprise having been elevated on grounds other than those of modernism. If however there *does* exist a perspective enabling us to align James and the general problematic of modernism, the implication we should then face is that modernism is more than the inventory of its manifest rhetorical traits or mannerisms: Joycean epiphanies, Conradian narrative "open-endedness," citational collage, a rhetoric of dissonance, and ironic shifts (Jameson 16).

The Jamesian "Art of Fiction"

James began his career as a writer of fiction in 1865 with "The Story of a Year,"

published in the *Atlantic Review.* The complete Jamesian harvest, fifty years later, amounts to an immense, but clearly-outlined oeuvre. For despite reference to the "textual chaos" of James's work (Freedman 247)—a simple matter of magnitude—the ordinary reader, on taking up a Jamesian text, constantly has the sense of being on (generically) familiar ground. There are novels and there are short-stories, or "tales," to use the rather unmodernist-sounding title of the twelve-volume edition; there is also a *Complete Plays of Henry James* (1949). There is certainly no Jamesian poetry, no poetic drama, there are no prose-poems. The history of the publication of James's fiction is that of the author's largely successful endeavor to find an audience on both sides of the Atlantic; of his exploitation of the possibilities of serial publication (*The Portrait of a Lady* (1880–81) was serialized both in England and in the States); of his ability to place stories in commercially-viable magazines aimed at a distinguished, cosmopolitan readership—and not in the "little" magazines, kept going through a combination of avant-gardist militancy and a neo-aristocratic patronage. With one exception, James's art demonstrates the successful adjustment of an authorial offer to the demands of a distinguished bourgeois public, on the terms, accepted by both parties, of the free market of publication. The one exception is James's failed courtship of success in the commercial London theater, an ambition fuelled by his admiring observation of the art of the stage on the mid-nineteenth century Parisian boulevards. James's celebration of Parisian and London commercial success testifies to his espousal of a protocol which all subsequent revolutions within the theater would vehemently refuse. The aesthetics and politics of Wagner, **Synge**'s pursuit in an imaginary Irish west of a mode of speech not yet contaminated by the metropolitan vulgate, **Yeats**'s attempt to erase the indignity of personality, establishing in its place the mask of impersonality: these are just a few of the numerous enterprises of theatrical renewal which turned their backs on those codes within which James sought his triumph.

The Jamesian achievement is thus equidistant from an aristocratic system of patronage and fealty and from the male-diction—and its transvaluating election—of an opus that is anti-bourgeois, precisely to the extent that it is commercially prob-lematic, destructive of, or indifferent to, the conventional terms of readability and reception, terms which mirror those of a liberal, non-preferential protocol of bour-geois exchange. Whatever the complexi-ties of the Jamesian "late" style, the writing, when read according to the James-ian paradigm, does remain on the "read-able" side of the Barthesian division of writing between a *lisible* mode—represen-tational, transitive, communicational—and a *scriptible* mode of instransitive reflexivity and textual involution (Barthes 10). Insofar as the division proposed and valorized by Barthes is a recapitulation of the terms in which canonical modernism proposes its own self-definition, on which it stakes its claim to epochal significance, James's pursuit of an audience through the established procedures of the literary market-place would seem closer to Zola's celebration of commercial publication as the concomitant of the novelist's unre-stricted exploration of the society which he must address and represent, in which he finds himself living and writing (Zola 57). The Jamesian posture, its confident antic-ipation of a public reception, can be further qualified, and more clearly distin-guished from subsequent ones. For the posture would appear to imply an optimis-tic, liberal confidence in the enhancing possibilities of all modes of exchange—commercial, linguistic, intersubjective, moral, cultural. The question is of course a vexed one: to the extent that James dra-matizes or reflects the contradictions of a later, corporate capitalism, and the migra-tions far more massive than the individual transatlantic relation which it sets in mo-tion—consider the immense distance separating the 1878 *Daisy Miller* from the 1907 *The American Scene*—the Jamesian aesthetic can be said to move to a more distraught, anxiously "modernist" mode. But let us not collapse the distinctions too soon. A certain Jamesian belief in the *ne-cessity* and *adequacy* of art means that the enterprise can be opposed both to the (modernist) exposure of the logic of rep-resentation to its unaccommodated, unap-peased other (whether figured as a transcendent or as an abysmal, infernal force), and to the (postmodernist) vacuity of a self-perpetuating exchange—of signs, images, words—whose logic is that of an all-pervading immanence, without any vertical reference to a substance or burden of meaning with which the exchange might, however obliquely, be engaged with.

A consideration of the substantial Jamesian corpus of non-fiction enhances our sense that its overall architecture is as clear as it is compliant with the conven-tions of *belles lettres*. There is the vast cor-respondence charting the preoccupations of a man of letters; there are the essays in the appreciation of Italian art; the travel essays; and, most importantly, two com-plementary, flanking bodies of writing, vi-tal to any assessment of the designs and accomplishments of the Jamesian edifice: the *Notebooks,* in which the writer con-signs the initial motif or *"donnée,"* of whose possibilities or "reverberations" the novel is the consummate elaboration; the critical essays, James's reflection on his own practice and on that of his peers, which leave little doubt that it is his own art which is the exemplary, defining in-stance. The tone of the 1882 essay, "The Art of Fiction," is as patient as it is as-sured. Nothing could be farther from the nervous energies of the futurist or vorticist tracts of the 1910s, or from the note of cultural exhaustion and dereliction—the sense of language's necessity and of its poverty—audible in the Eliot of the early twenties or in the tones of Heidegger's *Sein und Zeit* (1927, *Being and Time*), published a few years later.

The overall effect of the Jamesian opus thus suggests the folly of regarding James as, in any sense, a precursor or occasional member of the modernist movement. One is left, on the contrary, with the conviction that the Jamesian art of fiction is a definitive consummation: both the expression and—by way of its restorative powers—the confirmation of a series of enabling conditions, within the restricted economy of literature and within the general economy of a culture. When considered together, as a certain organization of the social world, as a socially-endorsed trust in the intentional and transitive properties of language, these conditions, restricted and general, amount to *the conditions of representation,* of which James is the exemplary case and final achievement—and of which modernism is the disruption or termination, for reasons having to do both with the internal aesthetic economy and, more fundamentally, with the general logic of an economy (that of capitalism), a politics (that of mass democracy, the modernist reaction to which is fraught), and a cultural condition marked by the acute sense both of the accumulated sedimentation of symbolic forms and generic codes, and their disqualification as a foundational support authorizing either the secure lyricism of full voice, devoid of ironic inflection, or the critical examination of things as they are in the present (modern) predicament. In other words, the modernist moment has to do with the disestablishment of the codes of romantic poetry and those of an art of the representational novel, of which James is a master.

James and Modernism

The first, somewhat naive option—to regard James as an early or minor modernist—is therefore to be discarded. The alternative option—to consider James solely on his own terms, making no attempt to situate him within the confines of an aesthetic or a cultural problematic that is not his—is equally naive. The heroic, high modernism of 1922 retroacts upon prior achievements, in compliance with the general axiom stated by Eliot in his essay "Tradition and the Individual Talent" (Eliot 15). Modernism creates and recreates what precedes it, causing us to appraise and requalify what comes before it and after it, just as a non-tonal, serialist **music** requalifies and foregrounds the "tonality" of other types of music (Jameson 17–25). It is thus important, in any consideration of James, that we do try to measure James against modernism, that we define how the Jamesian protocol of representation harnesses language for tasks quite different from those which, for example, Joyce set himself as an artist. A consideration of the relation between James and modernism will thus foreground the nature of the representational protocol, just prior to its disestablishment by modernism. In return, we may gain a stronger sense that the defining—enabling and disabling—trait of the modernist predicament or project is the exhaustion of this same representational protocol, for reasons that the culture we inhabit is still trying to come to terms with. The retroactive effect of the modernist problematic upon our reading of James can also alert us to the hovering instability of the Jamesian enterprise, poised between the phenomenological disclosure of the world and the experimentation of linguistic enclosure.

Let us go back therefore to our remark that the banal contingencies of generational divides inclined us not to regard James as a modernist. The same can also be said of Monet (1840–1926), not usually included in the art history of modernist painting, whose beginning one generally locates in the years 1905–06. Just as Monet, in his painting, through the endeavor to reproduce the illuminating, impressive force of the world, becomes, should the spectator look too closely, or from too oblique a perspective, a modernist *malgré lui,* inasmuch as he forces the viewer to face up to the constitutive materiality of paint on the canvas, the Jamesian style of the late novels (most notably in *The Golden Bowl*), in its attempt to remain true to the inner drama of consciousness, may write its way to a point where it overcharges the syntactic frame, thereby precipitating a discursive blur which, far from revealing a state of consciousness, confronts the reader with the unrelieved enclosure of language. In adopting such a perspective on the Jamesian opus, it is the modernist problematic which, as the mode still, and of necessity, conditioning (only modernism can make us "post-modernists": the later vantage-point supposes the earlier one) our access to the world of social experience, to the successive sedimentations of cultural forms, establishes the terms, not to be easily shuffled off, within which we can now read James, comprehend his enterprise.

It does in fact prove rather easy to read James not as a precursor, but as a fully-fledged modernist, as one who writes into a certain number of his fictional enterprises the conditions rendering impossible the emergence of any final resolution, any final establishment not predicated on the (limited, conditional) credit to be granted to a partial subjective voice or point of view. Vargish and Mook (1999) can thus argue the case for the inclusion of James among the major, canonical modernists, in the company of novelists such as Conrad, **Kafka,** Joyce, and **Faulkner,** painters such as Picasso and Braque, and physicists such as Einstein and Mach. Our intention is not

to suggest that all cases and points of view are equally valid, when examining the Jamesian achievement in relation to the question of modernism. Vargish and Mook, in their focus upon the emergence of an aesthetic which explores the way in which any disclosure or construction of meaning—any significant formation of the world—is conditional on the constructive power of a precisely-angled discursive or pictorial agency, highlight what is perhaps one particular strand of modernism, and one specific dimension of the Jamesian enterprise. Like the "linguistic turn," the "subjective turn" is a crucial aspect of modernism, as it also is of the Jamesian project: *The Sacred Fount* (1901), a first-person narrative, is probably the strongest exploration by James of the condition of narratively-framed subjective "undecidability," where, in the absence of any external touchstone of truth, madness and revelation are inextricably fused, there being no point beyond the fictional field from which to tell the difference. A "linguistic turn" and a "subjective turn" are however both of them aspects of a more general modification.

Vargish and Mook envisage modernism as an experimentation of the preemptive and involutive inclusiveness of "field models" (104). Such a paradigm ensures that it is not only possible, but, perhaps, even inevitable that the Jamesian opus be comprehended from within modernism's own defining conditions: on modernism's own terms. However, in all logic, the inclusive potency of a "field model" can equally operate from the other side of the relation. That is, we can legitimately redefine the problematic or project of modernism from within the general "field model" of the Jamesian "house of fiction," the latter understood as a vantage-point open upon the social world and upon the major drama of consciousness, upon the drama of doing and of making, of shoring and storing up. Both *The Portrait of a Lady*

(1881) and *The Golden Bowl* (1904) present us types of the modern collector, Gilbert Osmond and Adam Verver, in retreat from the Yeatsian "filthy tide" of the vulgar modern, in search of forms, edifices, locations, through which to satisfy a rage for order and to amass the "fragments" of a (fantasized) unity of culture or being which one might shore against one's ruin. James presents and motivates the modernist meditation upon the monumental accumulation of the past, its newly-visible and thoroughly modern availability as a precious, no longer operative, museum-world of artifacts, here and now, in the fleeting fluidity of the present. Osmond and Adam Verver strive willfully to alter the "terrible denudation" (James 133) of their original American ego, through an enterprise involving the appropriation of whatever has been best thought and best spoken, or most artistically, exquisitely, figured. The aim is of course Arnoldian. Between the (English) Victorian mid-century and the (American) new century there is however an enhanced sense of the need for cultural accumulation, so that a thoroughly modern denudation be given its preserving figure or envelope, coupled with a sense of the impropriety of these foregrounded, fetishized forms, their ironic inaptitude as vessels within which to accommodate the charge of current, modern experience in waiting for its symbolic treatment. The Jamesian idiom continually reverberates with the drama of consignment and containment: "precious vessels," "golden bowls," boats that do, or do not, "leak." James goes beyond the compact which, through the securities of genre, regulates the free, collaborative exchange between the nineteenth-century novelist and his readers. James shares the hyperbolic modernist faith in the necessity of art, as an enterprise of consignment and conservation. Rarely however is he visited by any modernist agnosticism as to the efficacy of his adopted artistic form, its virtues as an instrument of conservation and enhancement, through its active elaboration of the meaning implicit and germinal in any given mundane experience. He can analyze and distance himself from Gilbert Osmond's religion of fetishizing accumulation, a petrifying cult to be distinguished from the "religion of doing" to which James subscribes. He shares with the modernist generation the conviction that the artistic enterprise concentrates the essential "ado" of the drama coextensive with the more general, social enterprise of culture. His own artistic project, James regards as a perfective reworking of, or supplement to, what remains undone or unfinished in the general culture. In this he is unlike the French symbolists, and unlike the exemplary art of Mallarmé; unlike the modernists, who owe so much to these precedents. Yeats, **Beckett**, Eliot—Joyce also, at least until the emergence of Leopold Bloom—are antithetical artists. They strive to define or forge the heroic archetype of gesture and literary form, and the type of a renewed—perhaps to the point of its ultimate negation—speech, to be set against the fallen ordinariness of action and idiom.

James, by contrast, would have wished to remain to the end an artist of conservation and of tutoring, faithful to the art of drawing from a *donnée* its endless potential for reverberation, in accordance with the rules of a moral and aesthetic creed which confronts a predicament of dissociation and rupture, by way of an art of interminable relation, confident in its capacity to restore: to remake the golden bowl as it was to have been, "without the cracks." A story such as "The Bench of Desolation" (1910), an essay such as "The American Scene" (1907), carry the suggestion that the late James is made to face up to an unnamable tenor located at the abysmal extremity of familiar experience, for which his art of representation finds no adequate vessel or vehicle, as a modernist beast in a jungle grows up around and beneath and inside the house of fiction.

Cornelius Crowley

Selected Bibliography
Barthes, Roland. *S/Z.* Paris: Seuil, 1970.
Eliot, T. S. *Selected Essays.* London: Faber, 1932.
Freedman, Jonathan, ed. *The Cambridge Companion to Henry James.* Cambridge: Cambridge UP, 1998.
James, Henry. *Hawthorne.* In *The Critical Muse: Selected Literary Criticism.* Ed. Roger Gard. Harmondsworth: Penguin, 1987.
———. *Letters.* Vol. 4. Cambridge: Harvard UP, 1984.
Jameson, Fredric. *Postmodernism, or The Cultural Logic of Late Capitalism.* London: Verso, 1991.
Torgovnick, Marianna. *The Visual Arts, Pictorialism, and the Novel. James, Lawrence, and Woolf.* Princeton, New Jersey: Princeton UP, 1985.
Vargish, Thomas and Delo E. Mook. *Inside Modernism. Relativity Theory, Cubism, Narrative.* New Haven: Yale UP, 1999.
Zola, Emile. "L'Argent dans la Littérature." In *L'encre et le sang.* Brussels (Belgium): Editions Complexe, 1989.

Japan

Japanese modernism emerged in the early 1920s in reaction, first, to the dominant Japanese form of **naturalism,** which had been characteristic of *Watakushi Shousetsu* or "I" novels since the 1900s (after Émile Zola's naturalism was first introduced in 1889 by Mori Ohgai—later to become one of Japan's greatest novelists); and, second, to the contemporaneous development of radical proletarian literature. Roughly speaking, the main period of modernism in Japan extends for two decades from the early 1920s to the outbreak of World War II, though there was also some revival in the post-war period.

It is usually said that Japanese modernism started with the birth of Yokomitsu Riichi's "Shinkankakuha" or "School of New Sensibilities" in 1924. However, by this time, the major avant-garde theories and movements from Europe had already begun to exert an influence on Japanese literary circles; and, in particular, **futurism, dada, surrealism,** constructionism, **expressionism,** and **cubism** all contributed significantly to the growth of modernism in Japan. The earliest introduction was futurism, the manifesto of which was translated in 1909, again by Mori Ohgai, just three months after **Marinetti**'s "Manifeste du Futurisme" was first published in Paris (in February 1909).

Dada and surrealism, however, were perhaps the most immediately and productively influential of the European movements in terms of actually generating new works by Japanese writers. In particular, they inspired the work of three poets: Murayama Kaita's pioneering dadaist poems, *Kaita no Utaeru* (1920, *Thus Sings Kaita*), Takahashi Shinkichi's *Dadaist Shinkichi's Poems* (1923), and Nishiwaki Junzaburo's surrealist *Spectrum* (1925) and *Ambarvalia* (1933). Dadaism was introduced in 1920 and 1922 respectively by the literary critic Wakatsuki Yasuharu and by the poet and translator Horiguchi Daigaku, and the works by Murayama and Takahashi represented a radical challenge not only to conventional Japanese society but also to the dominant circle of traditional Japanese poets. However, though a promising genius, Murayama died at the age of 25; and Takahashi soon abandoned the Western theory and turned to Buddhism as his basic philosophy. As for surrealism, it was Nishiwaki himself who introduced it to Japan both as a critic and through his own surrealist poems. He was highly unusual for his time in that he was a writer who had recently lived in England and who had direct contact with the contemporary literary scene in Europe (among other things, he enjoyed a friendship with **T. S. Eliot,** as well as with other English authors). While studying in Oxford, he had his book of poems, *Spectrum,* published by an English press, and he contributed a poem called "A

Kensington Idyll" to *The Chapbook* (no. 39) in 1924. When he came back to Japan in 1925, he wrote many surrealist poems as well as books and essays on surrealism; *Ambarvalia* is considered to be an epoch-making surrealist work in the history of Japanese poetry.

And then comes Yokomitsu's "School of New Sensibilities" with the publication of a short story, "Atama Narabini Hara" ("Head and Belly") in 1924, which is often said to have proclaimed the birth of new sensibilities accompanied by new forms of expression (see Yokomitsu's 1928 essay, "Shinkankakuha Bungaku no Kenkyu"—"A Study of Literature of the School of New Sensibilities"). The emergence of this school was, as Yokomitsu's contemporary, Chiba Kameo, said in 1935, "the birth of [Japanese] modernist literature" (Ito 144). It was, as it were, a herald of a new age, especially coming just one year after the Great Kantou Earthquake of 1923 which left nothing but a heap of shattered ruins where the old Tokyo had once stood. The chief exponents of the new school, beside Yokomitsu, were Kawabata Yasunari and Nakagawa Yoichi. In 1925, Yokomitsu said of the new school that it was a literary syncretism of futurism, cubism, expressionism, dadaism, symbolism, constructivism, and *Neue Sachlichkeit* ("new objectivity").

Yokomitsu made his debut as a novelist with *Nichirin* (*The Sun*) in 1923, a novel set in ancient Japan and partly influenced by Gustave Flaubert's *Salammbô* (translated into Japanese by Ikuta Choukou in 1913) (Odagiri Hiroko 40–74). But Yokomitsu's new style was more effectively demonstrated by two stories with modern settings: the above mentioned "Atama Narabini Hara," which appeared in the first issue of *Bungei Jidai* (*The Literary Age*), the main journal established for his school in 1924; and "Haru wa Basha ni Notte"(1926, "Spring in a Surrey"), which deals with the themes of love and death within the style of new sensi-

bilities (though it also owes something to the Norwegian novelist Alexander Kielland's "Hopes Clad in April Green" and "Withered Leaves"). While he last applied the style of new sensibilities to a novel called *Shanghai* in 1932, Yokomitsu had by then started to cultivate a more Proustian style, developed in *Shin-en* (1930, *The Imperial Mausoleum*) and *Kikai* (1931, *Machine*), novels in which he anticipated Ito Sei's use of a Joycean style of stream of consciousness (as mentioned below).

Kawabata's *Kanjou Soushoku* (*The Decoration of Feelings*) and Nakagawa's *Kooru Butojou* (*The Frozen Dance Stage*) (both 1926) are also representative works of the school of new sensibilities, being characterized by their expression and depiction of delicate feelings. (Like Yokomitsu with *Kikai,* Kawabata went on to experiment with the stream of consciousness style in *Suisho Gensou* (*Crystal Fantasy*) in 1931.) Beside these novelists, Fujisawa Takeo, too, is regarded as a writer of the school of new sensibilities: his story of 1925, "Kubi" ("Head") was highly praised as a work of the new school by Yokomitsu, although Fujisawa later joined the Marxist camp of writers.

Six years before Yokomitsu's "Atama Narabini Hara," another type of new sensibility had already been demonstrated by the poet and novelist, Satou Haruo, who, inspired by various contemporary Europeans, wrote a novel called *Den-en no Yuutsu* (1918, *Melancholy in the Countryside*), whose subjective style, full of poetic metaphors, was entirely different from traditional Japanese naturalism. Though he did not subsequently pursue the style in his later novels, Satou will be remembered as a modernist for this one novel.

Yokomitsu's *Bungei Jidai* finally lost its power in 1927, challenged by the ever-growing power of Marxism and proletarian literature (whose representative writers were, among others, Kobayashi Takiji, Aono Suekichi, Nakano Shigeharu, Hayama Yoshiki, Murayama Tomoyoshi). *Bungei Jidai* was succeeded in 1928 by a new journal called *Shi to Shiron* (*Poetry and Essays on Poetry*), edited by Haruyama Yukio. During its existence, this became probably the most powerful vehicle for introducing European modernism into Japan, and representative contributors were the poet, Nishiwaki, and novelists Yokomitsu, Ito Sei and Abe Tomoji (an exponent of intellectualism). The journal, however, ended its life in 1933.

Modernism as a literary term (which, incidentally, Yokomitsu and Kawabata did not like) had established itself in Japanese literary circles, and had become a catch word, by the end of 1930. Although Marxism became increasingly influential and popular among Japanese writers and intellectuals, modernism was supported by a new movement promoting "art for art's sake" called *Shinkou Geijutsuha* formed expressly in order to challenge the rise of materialistic philosophy and proletarian literature. The new movement developed into a fashionable form of Japanese modernism and was championed by Ryutanji Yuu, who, in 1930, wrote a collaborative novel called *The Year 1930* with Asahara Rokurou and Hisano Toyohiko. (None of these three novelists produced any significant work subsequently, however.)

Another new literary movement was introduced in the 1930s from the West. James Joyce's *Ulysses* was translated between 1931 and 1934 by Ito Sei (who also translated **D. H. Lawrence**'s *Lady Chatterley's Lover* in an abridged version in 1935, and in an unabridged version in 1950). Ito was not only a translator but also a novelist, and, in 1937, he wrote his own novel, *Yuuki no Machi* (*A Ghost Town*), in which he successfully employed Joyce's technique of stream of consciousness. Ito's style came to be known as *Shin Shinri Shugi* ("the School of New Psychology") and *Yuuki no Machi* is generally regarded as the most representative work

of "new psychology" in Japan. While Ito did not further develop the Joycean style in his later novels, Hori Tatsuo explored a similar style under the influence of Marcel Proust's **interior monologue,** and his Proustian masterpieces are *Kaifukuki* (1931, *The Recuperation Period*), *Utsukushii Mura* (1933, *A Beautiful Village*), and *Kaze Tachinu* (1936, *Le vent se lève*), in which Hori uses Paul Valéry's phrase "Le vent se lève, il faut tenter de vivre" as epigraph (borrowed from Jacques Rivière's "Florance").

A final feature of Japanese modernism is its debt to *Neue Sachlichkeit* or "the New Objectivity," which was first introduced from **Germany** by a literary critic, Chino Shoushou, in 1929. Two years later a poetry journal called *Neue Sachlichkeit Literature* (no. 1, 1931) was established and its first issue contained poems by Murano Shirou, "Nenrei" ("Age") and "Nichibei Taikou" ("A Contest between Japan and the US"), and Sasazawa Yoshiaki, "Yuubin" ("Mail"). Although there were no subsequent issues of the journal, this first and last one is considered to have contributed to the creation of new poetry in the 1930s. In 1939, Murano wrote further Neue Sachlichkeit poems in *Taiso Shishu* (*Poems of Physical Exercises*), but these were followed by no other creative Neue Sachlichkeit poets.

Since, as has been made clear here, Japanese modernism in its main period could not claim its own identity apart from the constant influence from European modernist movements, it was perhaps inevitable that there should have been complaints from critics like Ikuta Choukou in 1925 and Koboyashi Hideo in 1929, that Japanese modernist writers, especially those of the school of new sensibilities, were too dependent on, and derivative from, their European counterparts. But, throughout this period, it is also fairly clear that Japanese writers were able to absorb the European influences very quickly and to adapt them for their own ends in trying to create original modernist works and a new Japanese literature generally.

Although Japanese modernism declined during World War II, it found its voice again after the war in the works of some important novelists. For example, Nakamura Shin-ichirou makes use of Proustian psychological technique in *Shi no Kage no Motoni* (1947, *Under the Shadow of Death*); Ito Sei this time applies aspects of Lawrence's sexual vitalism to his novels, *Hi no Tori* (1953, *Phoenix*) and *Henyou* (1968, *Transformation*); Abe Koubou creates a Kafkaesque picture of isolation in *Suna no Onna* (1962, *A Woman in Sand*); and in his last novel, *Genka* (1965, *Phantasm*), Umezaki Haruo employs a Woolfian style in exploring a hypochondriac's unconsciousness.

(This article owes much to the comments of Professor Odagiri Hiroko, as well as to the works on Japanese literary history listed in the selected bibliography below.)

Iida Takeo

Selected Bibliography

Campbell, Alan. "Shinkankaku School." *Kodansha Encyclopedia of Japan*. Vol. 7. Tokyo: Kodansha, 1983.

Chiba, Sen-ichi. *Modernism no Hikaku Bungakuteki Kenkyu* (*A Comparative Literary Study of Modernism*). Tokyo: Oufu, 1998.

Ichiko, Teiji, ed. *Nihonbungaku Zenshi* (*The Comprehensive History of Japanese Literature*). Vol. 6. Tokyo: Gakutousha, 1978.

Ito, Sei, Kamei Katsuichirou, Nakamura Mitsuo, Hirano Ken, and Yamamoto Kenkichi, eds. *Nihon Gendai Bungaku Zenshu* (*The Collected Works of Modern Japanese Literature*). Supplementary Vol. 2: *Nihon Gendai Bungakushi* (*The History of Modern Japanese Literature*) Part 2. Tokyo: Kodansha, 1980.

Iwanami Kouza: Nihonbugakushi (*Iwanami Lecture Series: The History of Japanese Literature*). Vol. 13. Tokyo: Iwanami-shoten, 1996.

Keene, Donald. *Dawn to the West: Japanese Literature in the Modern Era*. 2 Vols. New York: Holt Rinehart and Winston, 1984.

Nakamura, Mitsuo. *Nihon no Gendai Shousetsu* (*Modern Novels of Japan*). Tokyo: Iwanami-shoten 1968.

Nakamura, Shin-ichirou. *Kono Hyakunen no Shousetsu* (*Novels of the Past One Hundred Years*). Tokyo: Shinchousha, 1974.

Odagiri, Hideo, "Modernism." In *Nihon Daihyakka Zensho* (*Encyclopedia Nipponika 2001*). Vol. 22. Tokyo: Shogakkan, 1988.

Odagiri, Hiroko. *Yokomitsu Riichi: Hikaku Bungakuteki Kenkyu* (*Yokomitsu Riichi: A Comparative Study*). Tokyo: Nansou-sha, 1980.

Sasaki, Kiichi, "Modernism Bungaku" ("Modernist Literature"). In *Nihon Kindai Bungaku Daijiten* (*The Grand Dictionary of Modern Japanese Literature*). Ed. Nihon Kindai Bungakukan. Vol. 4. Tokyo: Kodansha, 1977.

Yoshida, Seiichi, and Inagaki Tatsuo, eds. *Nihon Bungaku no Rekishi* (*The History of Japanese Literature*). Vol. 12. Tokyo: Kadokawa-shoten, 1968.

Jones, David (1895–1974)

Anglo-Welsh poet, artist, and essayist. Though a monoglot Englishman born in Brockley, Kent, Jones identified himself from an early age with his Welsh patrimony: his father had come from a Welsh-speaking family in Holywell, Clwyd, but, entirely typically for the time, he had been discouraged from speaking his native language by parents who wanted their son to "get on." His mother was an Englishwoman from a family of London boatbuilders: already it is possible to see in Jones's own family that fruitful admixture of the Cockney and the Welsh which energizes so many passages of Jones's first published poem, *In Parenthesis* (1937). He showed early talent in drawing and attended the Camberwell School of Art from 1909 until the outbreak of the First World War, in which he served as a private soldier with the Royal Welsh Fusiliers from late 1915 until March 1918; his experience on the Western Front influenced all his subsequent life and writing. It finds its most astonishing and powerful expression in *In Parenthesis,* which many consider to be both his finest poetic work and a key text of modernism.

Years before *In Parenthesis* came to be written, however, Jones underwent another formative experience in his life and art: his conversion to roman catholicism, which occurred in 1921, the same year in which he met and formed a close association with the artist Eric Gill. During the 1920s Jones spent long periods living in the artistic communities established by Gill in Ditchling, Sussex and later in Capel-y-ffin in the Black Mountains of South-East **Wales.** The period at Capel-y-ffin was particularly significant in shaping Jones's artistic vision of the Welsh landscape and in bolstering his perception of his own Welsh identity and allegiance. Just as R. S. Thomas in the later twentieth century makes his stand against the Machine, so David Jones in his day opposed what he saw as a manipulative technocracy which attempted to eliminate cultural difference and to make the role of the artist irrelevant. In his clear ideological championing of man-the-maker and his use of the sign, the idea of Wales functioned for Jones as an important alternative to a contemporary urban, English society which he felt to be hostile and philistine. He argued for the need to resurrect and recall the whole matter of Wales, a Wales which arose from within a disintegration. Jones's Wales is not a monolithic concept but consists of what he terms "a great confluity and dapple" and, in a self-conscious echo of Hopkins, of "things counter, pied, fragmented, twisted, lost" ("Wales and the Crown" (1953) in *Epoch and Artist,* 46). Jones's distinctive watercolor landscapes are an expression of this fragmented yet fluid vision; reminiscent of the works of Cézanne and, occasionally, of Matisse, these paintings are nevertheless idiosyncratic expressions of recognizably Welsh scenes. As an engraver, Jones easily surpassed the work of his mentor, Eric Gill, particularly in his illustrations for Coleridge's *Rime of the Ancient Mariner,* which Jones interprets in a characteristically sacramental way.

Although Jones was an adherent of tradition, and indeed a believer in certain universals (at least after his conversion to roman catholicism) he was also a modernist artist who worked only with fragments and shards of **myth** and memory, shaping them into works of epic scope and ambition. *In Parenthesis* is the best example of this. More approachable than his later epic, *The Anathémata, In Parenthesis* focuses on **the war** experiences of a common soldier, John Ball, and his companions, following them as they approach the front line. The chaos of war experience, its surreality and unexpected humor, as well as its brutality, are poignantly expressed in the prose-poem's modernist style and structure. Allusions to a wide range of other literary texts, including the ancient Welsh epic, the *Gododdin,* succeed in placing this war in the broad historical sweep of all wars, drawing not a despairing moral but an optimistic one, emphasising brotherhood and the unquenchability of the human spirit.

Jones remained true to his own idiosyncratic modernist aesthetic in his later writings, notably in *The Anathémata* (1952) which **Auden** regarded as the best long poem written in English in this century. Subtitled "Fragments of an Attempted Writing," the poem ransacks again the mythological material of Celtic and other European origin which he had used as an underlying patterning for *In Parenthesis,* focusing in the later poem on the central image of the ship and telling of the sea voyages which brought successive cultures and beliefs to these islands. Underneath the densely allusive texture reminiscent of **Eliot**'s mode and method in *The Waste Land* is a devotional poem which celebrates the Christian sacraments.

Jonathan Miles accurately describes Jones's work as a "bricolage of intellectually assimilated elements invigorated by the unique music of his diction." Like his close friend, the Welsh poet and playwright **Saunders Lewis** (to whom Jones dedicated his 1959 book, *Epoch and Art-*

ist) Jones's work as poet and artist can be said to have embraced an unlikely alliance between absolute religious orthodoxy and extreme artistic innovation.

Katie Gramich

Selected Bibliography

Agenda 11: 4 (Autumn/Winter, 1973–4). Special David Jones issue.

Blamires, David. *David Jones: Artist and Writer.* Manchester: Manchester UP, 1971.

Hague, René. *David Jones.* Cardiff: University of Wales Press, 1975.

———, ed. *Dai Greatcoat: A Self-Portrait of David Jones in his Letters.* London: Faber, 1980.

Mathias, Roland. "David Jones: Towards the 'Holy Diversities.'" *A Ride Through the Wood: Essays on Anglo-Welsh Literature.* Bridgend: Poetry Wales Press, 1985.

Matthias, John, ed. *David Jones: Man and Poet.* University of Maine Press, 1989.

Miles, Jonathan. "David Jones and the Right Wing." *The New Welsh Review* 5 (Summer 1989): 57–61.

———. *Backgrounds to David Jones: A Study in Sources and Drafts.* Cardiff: University of Wales Press, 1990.

———. *Eric Gill and David Jones at Capel-y-Ffin.* Bridgend: Seren, 1992.

Poetry Wales 8: 3 (Winter 1972). Special David Jones issue.

Ward, Elizabeth. *David Jones—Mythmaker.* Manchester: Manchester UP,1983.

Joyce, James (1882–1941)

James (Augustine Aloysius) Joyce, novelist, was born in Dublin, **Ireland,** in 1882 and died in Zurich, Switzerland, in 1941. He was educated at Clongowes Wood College, Sallins, Co. Kildare (1888–1891); Belvedere College, Dublin (1893–1898); and University College Dublin (then the Royal University) (1898–1902). He was the eldest son of John Stanislaus Joyce and Mary Jane Joyce (née Murray). Mary Jane Joyce was a devout catholic who went through fifteen pregnancies before she died of cancer in 1903. Her suffering and death haunt Stephen Dedalus throughout *Ulysses.* John Joyce was a talented but reckless man whose wit, love of **music** and drink, as well as his anticlericalism, inspired numerous characters in his son's writings. He appears most prominently in *A Portrait of the Artist as a Young Man* and *Ulysses* as Simon Dedalus, a middle-class catholic from Cork who squanders his income and his inheritance. When his father died in 1931, James Joyce told a friend that "[t]he humor of *Ulysses* is his; its people are his friends. The book is his spittin' image."

While at Belvedere College James Joyce was elected prefect of the Sodality of the Blessed Virgin Mary, but his religious faith waned and his literary interests grew. At college he studied modern languages and befriended Vincent Cosgrave, John Francis Byrne, and George Clancy, who as Lynch, Cranly, and Davin respectively were to provide foils for Stephen Dedalus in *A Portrait.* He was also friendly with Richard Sheehy whose sister Mary most likely inspired Emma Clery in *Stephen Hero* (1944) and E. C. in *A Portrait of the Artist as a Young Man* (1916). In 1900 he began to write prose sketches which he called epiphanies and which in *Stephen Hero, A Portrait,* and *Ulysses* signal moments of heightened perception. Among the early important influences were **Hauptmann,** Ibsen, Dante, and **Yeats.**

In 1903 he spent several months in Paris reading Aristotle and the works of St. Thomas Aquinas. He also discovered Dujardin's novel *Les lauriers sont coupés* (1888) which he later credited as the source of his own use of **interior monologue.** He returned briefly to Dublin as his mother was dying, but in 1904 left again for good with Nora Barnacle. They spent the rest of their lives together, but married only in 1931, to protect the inheritance rights of their two children. They lived in Trieste and Zurich before settling in Paris after **World War I.**

Joyce is among the most influential artists of the twentieth century, his eclectic work encompassing characteristics of various key literary movements, including symbolism, **realism, naturalism,** modernism, and **postmodernism.** His first published work was *Chamber Music* (1907), a volume of verse. This was followed by ***Dubliners*** (1914), a collection of short stories published after serious difficulties and delays. **Ezra Pound** reacted enthusiastically to *Dubliners,* and his support was to be crucial to Joyce's career. *A Portrait of the Artist as a Young Man* appeared serially in *The Egoist* in 1914–15 before being published in 1916. Part of a first draft appeared in 1944 as *Stephen Hero.* Joyce's only extant play, *Exiles,* was written in Trieste in 1914 and first published in London in 1918 by Grant Richards. Yeats turned down the play for the Abbey Theatre. *Exiles* has been criticized for lacking in dynamism, and opinion remains divided on how successful a drama it is. The play, influenced by Ibsen and Gerhart Hauptmann, presents the relationship between an exiled author, Richard Rowan, and his non-literary wife Bertha after their return to Dublin, and their relations with a long-time friend of Richard's, Robert Hand, and Robert's cousin Beatrice. *Exiles* is an important transitional piece between *A Portrait of the Artist as a Young Man* and *Ulysses,* and it focuses on several themes found throughout Joyce's works, including exile, love, doubt, seduction, and betrayal.

His famous novel *Ulysses* was published in Paris in 1922 and hailed as a work of genius by **T. S. Eliot, Hemingway** and others, but it was banned in the United States until 1933 and in England until 1936. *Ulysses* revolutionized the novel formally and structurally and decisively influenced the development of the stream of consciousness technique. ***Finnegans Wake,*** published in 1939, is Joyce's last and most innovative work. Both it and *Ulysses* gave new dimensions to the idea of polyphonic and dialogical texts, and *Finnegans Wake* in particular pushes language and linguistic experiment to their extremes.

From *Dubliners* onwards Joyce's major works are marked by an aesthetic discontinuity which challenges readers by leaving them to their own devices. His works are typically modernist in their awareness of cultural relativism and of the workings of the unconscious mind, in their persistently experimental display of linguistic self-consciousness, and in their use of **myth** as a structural principle. Joyce is not typically modernist, however, in his obsession with the ordinary and the commonplace, nor was he a right-winger. His works are truly democratic yet ruthlessly avant-garde. Joyce is a profoundly comic writer whose work shows up the gratuitousness of all meaning and, like the world itself, he is amenable to any number of readings.

Joyce's major works are dealt with in separate entries; the following is a brief description of his minor works.

Joyce's essay "The Day of the Rabblement" (1901) was inspired by his reaction against what he considered the insularity of the Irish Literary Theatre (later the Abbey Theatre). The broadside attacks **W. B. Yeats** and the other leaders of the dramatic movement for "surrender[ing] to the popular will" of an increasingly nationalistic and pietistic Ireland: "The Irish Literary Theatre must now be considered the property of the rabblement of the most belated race in Europe." When the essay was turned down by *St Stephen's,* a newly founded undergraduate magazine at University College, Dublin, Joyce printed it privately along with a tract on women's rights by his classmate Francis Skeffington.

"The Holy Office" (August 1904; printed Trieste, June 1905) is a satirical broadside in which Joyce again attacks the Irish Literary Revival for what he saw as its hypocrisy and self-deception. As an antidote to the spirituality of the Revival's leading writers, Joyce's rhyming poem angrily declares his intention to use candor as a means of "Katharsis" for "their timid arses."

Chamber Music (1907), Joyce's first published work, consists of thirty-six lyric poems about love and its failure. With a recommendation from Arthur Symons, it was published in London in 1907 by Elkin Mathews. The poems contain many of the themes of his later works, such as jealousy, betrayal, rejection, loneliness, the allure and frustrations of love. They resemble Elizabethan lyrics, but are clearly influenced by the lyrics of Yeats. Although occasionally striking they are imitative and often trivial. Joyce intended that *Chamber Music* be set to music. In a letter of July 19, 1909 to G. Molyneux Palmer he wrote that the "book is in fact a suite of songs and if I were a musician I suppose I should have set them to music myself." The work has been set to music by many composers including Palmer, W. B. Reynolds, Samuel Barber and Anthony Burgess.

When Roberts of Maunsel & Co. reneged on his contract to publish *Dubliners* and the printer John Falconer destroyed the sheets already printed in 1912, Joyce in bitter response wrote a satire entitled "Gas from a Burner" (1912). The rhyming invective, written mostly in Roberts' own voice, treats with much sarcasm his role as publisher to the Irish Literary Revival. "Gas from a Burner" was originally issued as a broadside, and is reprinted in *The Critical Writings of James Joyce.*

Infatuation in Trieste, sometime between 1911 and 1914, with some of his younger students prompted Joyce to compose some ironic observations and erotic feelings which were posthumously published as *Giacomo Joyce* in 1968, edited with an introduction and notes by Richard Ellmann. Joyce transposed parts of these sketches into *A Portrait of the Artist as a Young Man, Exiles* and *Ulysses.*

Pomes Penyeach (1927) collects a dozen poems with "Tilly" thrown in for good measure. Most were written in Trieste between 1913 and 1915; and some added later in Zurich and Paris. They are the reflections of a mature man, disparate but generally personal. The poems are less lyrical than *Chamber Music,* but still heavily metered. The collection was first published by Shakespeare and Company in Paris in 1927, and in 1932 a limited edition was published in London by Desmond Harmsworth with illuminated letters designed by Joyce's daughter, Lucia.

Critical Writings gathers 57 critical pieces written by Joyce between 1896 to 1937. The collection, edited by Ellsworth Mason and Richard Ellmann, was published in 1959 and contains essays, lectures, newspaper articles, broadsides in verse, book reviews, letters to editors, and program notes.

In a letter to his grandson Stephen Joyce on August 10, 1936, Joyce incorporated a children's story called *The Cat and the Devil.* The fable is set in Beaugency, a small French town on the River Loire, and tells the story of how the Devil builds a bridge across the wide river in exchange for the soul of its first traveler. Beaugency's Lord Mayor, Monsieur Alfred Byrne, outwits the Devil by making a cat cross the bridge first. *The Cat and the Devil* was published posthumously in 1964, with illustrations by Richard Erdoes.

Christine O'Neill

Selected Bibliography

Attridge, Derek and Daniel Ferrer, eds. *Post-Structuralist Joyce.* Cambridge: Cambridge UP, 1984.

———, ed. *The Cambridge Companion to James Joyce.* Cambridge: Cambridge UP, 1990.

———. *Peculiar Language: Literature as Difference from the Renaissance to James Joyce.* London: Methuen, 1988.

Brown, Richard. *James Joyce and Sexuality.* Cambridge: Cambridge UP, 1985.

Budgen, Frank. *James Joyce and the Making of Ulysses and Other Writings.* Oxford: Oxford UP, 1989.

Cheng, Vincent J. *Joyce, Race, and Empire.* Cambridge: Cambridge UP, 1995.

Ellmann, Richard. *James Joyce.* Oxford: Oxford UP, 1959; rev. 1982.

Fargnoli, A. Nicholas and Michael Patrick Gillespie. *James Joyce A to Z: The Essential Reference to the Life and Work.* New York: Facts on File, 1995.

Herr, Cheryl. *Joyce's Anatomy of Culture.* Urbana and Chicago: U of Illinois P, 1986.

Kenner, Hugh. *Joyce's Voices.* Berkeley: University of California Press, 1978.

MacCabe, Colin. *James Joyce and the Revolution of the Word.* London: Macmillan, 1978.

MacNicholas, John. *James Joyce's 'Exiles': A Textual Companion.* New York: Garland, 1979.

Mahaffey, Vicki. *Reauthorizing Joyce.* Cambridge: Cambridge UP, 1988.

Nolan, Emer. *James Joyce and Nationalism.* London and New York: Routledge, 1995.

Peake, Charles H. *James Joyce: The Citizen and the Artist.* Stanford, Ca.: Stanford University, 1977.

Scott, Bonnie Kime. *Joyce and Feminism.* Bloomington: Indiana UP, 1984.

Jung, Carl Gustav (1875–1961)

Swiss psychiatrist and originator of Analytical Psychology.

See under **Psychoanalysis.**

K

Kafka, Franz (1883–1924)

Kafka's visionary prose is almost exclusively drawn from his experiences in his native city, Prague, as the eldest son of a strict, lower-middle-class family. His doctorate in law and his career at the Workers' Accident Insurance Office which he retained throughout most of his writing life both provided sources for his dissections of bureaucracy. His psychological insights are partly drawn from his difficult relationships with women such as Felice Bauer and Milena Jesenka, and with his father, all of which are partly recorded in his letters to them. Finally, his Jewish identity encouraged his interests in Yiddish theater and Zionism. His subtle and elusive style simultaneously incorporates these elements into his writing, which include the themes of father-son conflict, artistic solitude, bureaucratic totalitarianism, and spiritual redemption. Kafka also dealt with these issues in his diaries, which help to shed light on his fiction.

Early in 1912 Kafka began his first novel *Der Verschollene* (1927, *Amerika*); he first intended it to be an imitation of a Dickens *bildungsroman,* but it also embodied the qualities of his later writing. It includes Kafka's concern with the arbitrariness of the law, as its hero Karl Rossmann unsuccessfully defends a ship's stoker for trying to wrest him from his uncle, and, later, Karl is accused by the head waiter of the Hotel Occidental for leaving its elevator unattended for a couple of minutes. Also, there is the Oedipal scenario of Karl desiring Brunelda, but being ousted by the vagabond Delamarche who leaves him on the balcony; this scene reenacts Kafka's childhood trauma of being left outside on the balcony during the night by his father. Finally, the novel is uncompleted, but promises Karl's reconciliation with American society through joining the Nature Theater of Oklahoma, which is perhaps based on Kafka's impressions of Yiddish theater.

Kafka regarded his composition of the short story "Das Urteil" (1916, "The Judgment") in one night during 1912 as the birth of his mature style. It begins apparently naturalistically in the dialogue between Georg Bendemann and his elderly father, until his father cries "No!," declaims a completely different interpretation of their relationship, and orders George to drown himself. In the same year Kafka wrote "Die Verwandlung" (1915, "The Transformation"), perhaps his most perfect work, about Gregor Samsa, who turns into an insect overnight. Kafka holds in balance the themes of Oedipal conflict in Gregor's relationship with his father, and spiritual messianism at his death, in an apparently realistic, yet symbolic style.

In the novel *Der Prozess* (1925, *The Trial*), written in 1915, Joseph K. is accused of an unspecified crime, and wanders through scenes evoking the workings of an impenetrable and unanswerable social system which has pronounced judgment on him. The novel also explores how the individual psychologically internalizes the oppression that originates from society; in the cathedral the priest tells Joseph the parable, which Kafka separately published as "Vor dem Gesetz" (1919, "Before the Law"), of the man who fails to pass the guard to the doorway of the law, because of his lack of inner will, not because he is prevented by any outside authority. In the same year Kafka also wrote a related short story, "In der Strafkolonie" (1919, "In the Penal Colony"), about a machine which executes its victims by inscribing its judgment on their bodies.

In 1917 Kafka experienced the first symptoms of tuberculosis, which was to prove fatal. In 1922 he wrote his last (unfinished) novel, *Das Schloß* (1926, *The Castle*), about a land surveyor, K., who attempts to integrate with the inhabitants of a village and gain access to their castle. The symbolism of the castle is multivalent, including social alienation, father-son conflict, authority and power, and spiritual redemption. Although Kafka intended a "happy" ending for K., as he had done for Karl Rossmann, the fragment which he completed suggests that the castle is as inaccessible to him as freedom from guilt was to Joseph K., as every action that K. undertakes for his goal achieves nothing.

Kafka's most important other pieces at the end of his life include "Der Hungerkunstler" (1922, "The Hunger Artist"), and "Josefine die Sängerin" (1922, "Josephine the Singer"), which share the theme of the poet's inability to be a prophet and leader of his people in the modern world. The Hungerkunstler's once elevated art of starving himself is ignored by the people, who become fascinated by the vitality of a caged panther; the significance of Josephine's performing art, like that of the Yiddish theater and of Kafka's own writing, is undermined since it has lost its prophetic role for her race of mice.

Kafka's works are available in S. Fischer Verlag, Frankfurt am Main, and Penguin and Minerva, London.

Carl Krockel

Selected Bibliography

Anderson, Mark M. *Kafka's Clothes.* Oxford: Clarendon Press, 1992.

Kuna, Franz. *On Kafka: Semi-Centenary Perspectives.* London: Paul Elek, 1976.

Robertson, Ritchie. *Kafka: Judaism, Politics, and Literature.* Oxford: Clarendon Press, 1985.

Speirs, Donald, and Beatrice Sandberg. *Franz Kafka.* London: Macmillan, 1997.

Klein, Melanie (1882–1960)

Austrian psychoanalyst, based in London from 1926.

See under **Psychoanalysis.**

L

Lacan, Jacques (1901–1981)

French psychoanalyst.
See under **Psychoanalysis.**

Lasker-Schüler, Else (1869–1945)

After the failure of her first marriage, Lasker-Schüler embarked on a bohemian lifestyle and literary career, publishing *Styx* in 1902. In this first volume of poetry she transposes her moods onto a universal scale, for example in "Mein Tanzlied" ("My Dancing Song"), where the poetic persona describes herself dancing exuberantly for "thousands of years, / since my first eternities." As in all of her later poetry, she uses language to free herself from the material world, and to locate her identity in distant realms as a woman, Jew, and artist.

From 1901 to 1911 she was married to Herwarth Walden who edited expressionist poetry in his periodical *Der Sturm*. She became a central personality among the circle of expressionists in Berlin, addressing poems to **Gottfried Benn, Franz Werfel,** Georg Grosz, **Georg Trakl,** and Franz Marc. With or without their influence, her images in *Meine Wunder* (1912, *My Wonder*) became bolder in their detachment from material reality. She tried to identify herself with Biblical mythology in "Die Stimme Edens" ("The Voices of Eden"), and with nature in her love poetry, as in "Behind Trees I take Shelter" where her "eyes rain," and her arms grow into her lover like ivy.

In *Hebräische Balladen* (1913, *Hebrew Ballads*), Lasker-Schüler acted as the poetic voice of her race by writing on Biblical themes; she attempts to overcome her temporal remoteness in "Mein Volk" ("My People"), by listening to the "echo" within herself of her fellow Jews crying out to God. Emigrating from **Germany** during the rise of Nazism, she settled in Palestine in 1940, where she lived in poverty. In her last collection, *Mein blaues Klavier* (1943, *My Blue Piano*), she transcends her dispossessed state in her own homeland through poetry, maintaining in "An meine Freunde" ("To my Friends"), that she was "Still cradling the moon / Between my lips."

Lasker-Schüler's works are available in Kösel Verlag, Munich, Jewish Publications Society, New York.

Carl Krockel

Selected Bibliography
Cohn, Hans W. *Else Lasker-Schüler: The Broken World*. Cambridge: Cambridge UP, 1974.
Grunfeld, Frederic V. *Prophets Without Honour*. New York: Holt, Rinehart and Winston, 1979.

Lawrence, D. H. (David Herbert) (1885–1930)

D. H. Lawrence, novelist, short-story writer, poet, travel writer, translator, essayist, dramatist and letter-writer, was born in the small mining town of Eastwood, near Nottingham, the fourth child of Arthur John (1846–1924) and Lydia Lawrence (1851–1910). Arthur Lawrence was a coal-miner who in the course of fifty years working underground experienced the changes in working-practices brought about by the mechanization of the industry: any independence he had had as an individual worker (and butty) was effectively destroyed. Lawrence's mother's family, originally lower middle-class, had suffered financial disaster in the Nottingham lace-industry's crash back in the 1840s; and to make matters worse, her father had been badly injured at work as an engineer. Lydia—in spite of attempts to work as a pupil-teacher—had been forced into employment as a sweated home-worker in the lace industry. The experiences of their parents not only left the Lawrence children permanently divided in loyalty, but would play a large part in Lawrence's writing about independence and the modern world.

Always a voracious reader, during his teacher-training course at Nottingham University College (1906–08), Lawrence began reading significantly modern authors such as William James (1842–1910); moving to London as a schoolteacher in 1908, he discovered (for example) the work of Friedrich Nietzsche (1844–1900). He wrote fiction and poetry in his spare time, but within three years had with extraordinary luck been taken up by several of the important literary communities of his time. His first breakthrough came in the autumn of 1909: some poems attracted the attention of Ford Madox Hueffer (later **Ford Madox Ford**) (1873–1939) at the *English Review.* Hueffer not only printed them, but read the manuscript of *The White Peacock* (1911) and wrote to the publisher William Heinemann recommending it. He also got Lawrence to write more about his mining background: Law-

rence almost immediately wrote the story "Odour of Chrysanthemums" (1911) and his first play, *A Collier's Friday Night* (1934); in 1910 he would write a second play, *The Widowing of Mrs. Holroyd* (1914). Through Ford, Lawrence got to know the American poet **Ezra Pound** (1885–1972), who did what he could to publicize Lawrence; while by the end of 1911 Lawrence had become an intimate friend of the publisher's reader Edward Garnett (1868–1937), who regarded **Joseph Conrad** (1857–1924) as the greatest modern master, and who badly wanted to attract Lawrence's work to his own publisher Gerald Duckworth. It indicates Lawrence's refusal to conform to literary expectations that none of these contacts would much influence his subsequent writing.

Again, within five years of first meeting Hueffer, Lawrence would be acquainted with all the significant modernist movements of the pre-war period; but he would break with Garnett over his refusal to revise his novel *The Sisters* as Garnett demanded in 1914; and he started to resent the way in which Hueffer and Pound treated him as a spokesman for the working class. By 1914, via **Katherine Mansfield** (1888–1923) and John Middleton Murry (1889–1957), Lawrence had become acquainted with the work of artists such as Henri Gaudier-Brzeska (1891–1915), Pablo Picasso (1881–1973), and Jacob Epstein (1880–1959); he had also got to know the Russian nineteenth century writers like Fyodor Dostoyevsky (1821–81) who influenced modernism so profoundly. He also knew the milder English Georgian poets in the circle around Edward Marsh (1872–1953); while in Italy in the spring of 1914 he had become aware of the Italian futurists, and was especially interested by the writing of **Filippo Tommaso Marinetti** (1876–1944) and the sculpture of Umberto Boccioni (1882–1916). A review he had written for the last issue of Murry's *The Blue Review* in July 1913, describing the German writer **Thomas Mann** (1875–1955) as belonging to another generation—"Thomas Mann is old—and we are young" (*Phoenix* 313)— might have been a prelude to a declaration of loyalty to modernist art and writing: he even thought of his own novel *The Sisters* as "a bit futuristic," though "quite unconsciously so" (*Letters* ii 182).

Lawrence did not, however, ally himself with any of the English or Continental literary or artistic circles where the various forms of modernism grew or flourished. He believed that Conrad belonged to a superseded generation; he had no sympathy with Pound, or with the English vorticists such as F. S. Flint (1890–1935) and **Wyndham Lewis** (1884–1957), whom he met and argued with in 1915; his own knowledge of industry as his parents and grandparents had experienced it would probably have prevented him from linking up with movements which hymned mechanism and progress. And although Amy Lowell claimed him as an imagist, he had no real sympathy with the group: he was not at the "Imagist Dinner" of July 17, 1914, for example, which the poets **Richard Aldington** (1892–1962), **H. D.** (1886–1961), Pound, Flint, and Hueffer all attended. His reaction to the formal experiments of the painter Duncan Grant (1885–1978), whose work he saw in January 1915, was uncompromisingly dismissive: "Tell him not to make silly experiments in the futuristic line, with bits of color on a moving paper" (*Letters* ii 263). Gerald Crich, in *Women in Love* (written 1916–18, pub. 1920), getting to know the artistic and intellectual café crowd in London and sensing sexual license, asks Birkin: "All loose?" Birkin replies: "In one way. Most bound, in another. For all their shockingness, all on one note" (617–20). The remark sums up Lawrence's attitude towards wartime modernist experiment: he saw it not only as fashionable but predictable. He

was sufficiently detached (by class and background) from London and other metropolitan literary circles deliberately to exile himself from them; during **the war** he lived mostly in Cornwall and Derbyshire, a long way from the metropolis. Although he did know individuals—such as H. D. between 1915 and 1918, and Aldington from 1914 to 1930—they were not partners in movements, any more than were the younger advanced contemporaries he got to know late in 1915, Aldous Huxley (1894–1963), the musician Philip Heseltine (1894–1930), and the writer Dikran Kouyoumdjian (1895–1956), later the famous popular novelist Michael Arlen. As soon as Lawrence could leave England at the end of the war, he did, and thereafter lived through a series of exiles; he belonged to no group, and maintained relations with only a few of his contemporaries, such as **E. M. Forster** (1879–1970).

Characteristically, however, Lawrence also wanted to know what was supposed to be the most significant serious contemporary fiction. In July 1922 he remarked to a friend "I shall be able to read this famous *Ulysses* when I get to America," and soon after arriving he asked his New York publisher "Can you also send me a copy of James Joyce's **Ulysses**. I read it is the last thing in novels. I'd best look at it" (*Letters* iv 275, 306). He was not impressed: "*Ulysses* wearied me: so like a schoolmaster with dirt and stuff in his head: sometimes good, though: but too mental" (*Letters* iv 345).

It is probably not a coincidence, either, that Lawrence's own formal literary experiments nearly all belong to the 1920s; his adoption between 1920 and 1921 in *Mr. Noon, Aaron's Rod* and *Fantasia of the Unconscious* of a button-holing and sarcastic narrator ("dear reader"); his assertions of the fictional nature of what he was writing, in *Aaron's Rod* and *Kangaroo;* his use of a narrative technique akin to **film** in

Sea and Sardinia, where sections are constantly broken up by lines across the page (at one time he thought of calling the book *Sardinian Films*); his use of quotations from newspapers in one chapter of *Kangaroo;* his creation, in his final revision of his book *Studies in Classic American Literature* in America 1922–23, of an outrageously hard-hitting technique of short paragraphs and extreme assertions. He appears to have been demonstrating that anything the modernists could do, he could do too. As late as 1929, he would develop a new kind of poetic technique in his book *Pansies,* characterized by doggerel, slangy, crude, "unpoetic" verse, very different from his own Whitmanesque free-verse. Late in 1929, he was (among the last things he ever wrote) experimenting with the prose-poem (e.g. "Fire").

He was also able to identify and to welcome modernist techniques in, for example, the work of **John Dos Passos.** Reviewing *Manhattan Transfer* in 1927 as "the best modern book about New York that I have read," he memorably described its technique as that of the "movie picture with an intricacy of different stories and no close-ups and no writing in between. Mr. Dos Passos leaves out the writing in between." What made Dos Passos's work special to him was that "the confusion is genuine, not affected; it is life, not a pose" (*Phoenix* 364). His friendship with (and liking for the work of) the Danish painters Knud Merrild (1894–1954) and Kai Götzsche (b. 1886), both influenced by Picasso and Braque, suggests how open he could be to the modern (and the modernist) in some contexts.

He would, however, attempt to be crushing about modernism in 1923, when in his essay "The Future of the Novel" he mocked "the pale-faced, high-browed, earnest novel" as written by Joyce, **Marcel Proust** (1872–1922), and the English writer **Dorothy Richardson** (1882–1957). He claimed that such writing was "dying

in a very long-drawn-out fourteen volume death-agony" because it analyzed too much: "if I liked to watch myself closely enough, if I liked to analyse my feelings, minutely, as I unbutton my pants, instead of saying crudely I unbuttoned them, then I could go on to a million pages instead of a thousand . . . After all, the absorbing adventure of it! Which button did I begin with?" (*Study of Thomas Hardy* 151–2). And in 1928, after reading parts of Joyce's "Work in Progress" in *transition,* he commented: "What a clumsy *olla podrida* James Joyce is! Nothing but old fags and cabbage-stumps of quotations from the Bible and the rest, stewed in the juice of deliberate, journalistic dirty-mindedness—what old and hard-worked staleness, masquerading as the all new" (*Letters* vi 508). Lawrence was always more an enemy of what he took to be affectation than of experiment as such; what angered him was the pretentious, not the modern. His own experiments in the years 1926–28 revealed how seriously he challenged the conventions. His painting "Dandelions" showed a man pissing, his pictures were prosecuted in London in 1929 because of their depiction of the human body, his novel *Lady Chatterley's Lover* (1928) took a vast amount of courage to write and publish, and his version of Christ in *The Escaped Cock* (1929) outraged many of his contemporaries. In 1922 he had groaned about his audience, "They want things modern and thrilling; ah, they weary me" (*Letters* iv 309). His own challenges to the modern, and his own happiest encounters with modernism, demonstrated his loyalty to **realism** about emotional and bodily experience: the "thrilling," like the experiments of modernism, too often suggested emotional detachment.

John Worthen

Selected Bibliography

With the exception of the Lawrence item listed below, all citations from Lawrence's works and letters are from the standard scholarly edition published by Cambridge University Press. Lawrence's works are also widely available in Penguin. The primary bibliography is Warren Roberts and Paul Poplawski. *A Bibliography of D. H. Lawrence.* 3d ed. Cambridge: Cambridge UP, 2001.

Ellis, David. *D. H. Lawrence. Dying Game 1922–1930.* Cambridge: Cambridge UP, 1997.

Kinkead-Weekes, Mark. *D. H. Lawrence. Triumph to Exile 1912–1922.* Cambridge: Cambridge UP, 1996.

Lawrence, D. H. *Phoenix.* Ed. Edward D. McDonald. New York: Viking Books, 1936.

Nehls, Edward. *D. H. Lawrence. A Composite Biography.* Madison: Wisconsin UP, 1957–59.

Worthen, John. *D. H. Lawrence. The Early Years 1885–1912.* Cambridge: Cambridge UP, 1991.

Lawrence, D. H. (Fiction)

Locating Lawrence's fictional work within modernism has always posed a challenge. Lists of key modernist novels rarely omit *Women in Love* (1920), and might include *The Rainbow* (1915) or even *The Plumed Serpent* (1926), but the presence of two or three novels in such lists does not necessarily qualify their author for inclusion among the writers who created literary modernism in the years before and after **World War I.** Emphatically excluded from **Wyndham Lewis**'s "men of 1914," Lawrence is similarly absent from some more recent genealogies of modernism. Yet he clearly belongs among those who made the early twentieth century revolution in literature, and the continuing debate about his relationship to the work of his contemporaries suggests a need to "place" him somewhere.

The difficulties involved in that placing originate in the nature of Lawrence's work and the terms in which modernism has been defined. For some critics, Lawrence's strength lies in his challenge to the assumptions of modernism, as he develops existing fictional modes without subjecting them to such extreme subversions as his contemporaries. For others, the self-evident "newness" of his work suggests that the difficulties lie less in Lawrence's individual practice than in the limitations and exclusions of academic typology. If the distinguishing features of modernism are assumed to be aesthetic innovation and the search for impersonality in narration, then the low priority Lawrence gave to style for its own sake and the persistence in his work of a clearly heard narrative voice would exclude him from the modernist canon. A more broadly configured concept of modernism, however, which takes into account the contrasting and competing literary modes of the years 1900–1930, and embraces the use of **myth,** the representation of consciousness, and the concern with otherness, can easily accommodate Lawrence's achievement.

A further problem lies in Lawrence's hostility to what would now be seen as modernist practices. In November 1909, he defined the difference between himself and **Ezra Pound**—"his god is beauty, mine, life" (*Letters* i 145); Pound may have demanded that artists should "make it new," but Lawrence continued to place the claims of truth to experience over those of art for its own sake. In 1913, reviewing **Thomas Mann**'s *Death in Venice,* he saw the German author as a member of the school of Flaubert in his "craving for form in fiction" and as having "never given himself to anything but his art." Further, Mann is "the last sick sufferer from the complaint of Flaubert . . . [who] . . . stood away from life as from a leprosy," and who, like Flaubert, regards physical life as "a disordered corruption, against which he can fight with only one weapon, his fine aesthetic sense, his feeling for beauty, for perfection" (*Phoenix,* 308, 309, 312). Lawrence regarded such work as nihilistic, exhibiting a self-loathing which can only be resolved in a perfectionist aesthetic, and in fictional acts of suicide.

When he wrote this review, Lawrence had already struggled with the relationship between form and experience as he completed the final version of *Sons and Lovers*. In a letter of June 1912 he remarked that the novel was "not so strongly concentric as the fashionable folk under French influence . . . want it" (*Letters* i 417). "I tell you it has got form—*form*," he insisted to his editor Edward Garnett in November of the same year, and challenged Garnett to "tell me if I haven't worked out my theme, like life, but always my theme. Read my novel . . . If *you* can't see the development—which is slow like growth—I can" (*Letters* i 476–7). Again, Lawrence's insistence on the organic nature of artistic creation is in direct opposition to the school of Flaubert: the painstaking search for the apt word, the perfect form, the theoretical justification of artistic practice and the resulting loss of spontaneity.

The White Peacock. Lawrence's early novels find him negotiating with inherited nineteenth century models. Jessie Chambers's recollections suggest that Lawrence, as early as 1906, the year in which he began work on the novel that became *The White Peacock* (1910), was beginning to reflect on the conventions of **realism.** George Eliot, the main precursor of his first novel, offered a number of starting-points: structurally "to take two couples and develop their relationships" (*Personal Record* 103) and texturally to seek a balance between external and internal action. The resulting novel is a version of the Hardy-Eliot realistic/pastoral, an idyll undermined and challenged by the complexities of individual destiny, intellectual doubt and the relationship of human life to the natural world; Lawrence himself described it as "a decorated idyll running to seed in realism" (*Letters* i 185). This mixture of modes may account for the uneasiness of the novel's structure: quite early on, Lawrence abandons any attempt to maintain the conventions of the first person narrator, allowing Cyril Beardsall to recount events and thoughts to which he cannot have access. Cyril's role develops

into that of a chorus or commentator on the action, the type of the detached intellectual artist, with an aesthetic outlook which serves as a plausible starting-point for fine writing. The novel reflects Lawrence's own reading in the skeptical and pessimistic literature of the late nineteenth and early twentieth century, such as Darwin, Schopenhauer, and Haeckel. He uses these ideas to subvert the idyllic genre and allows circumstances to destroy the two characters most at ease in their surroundings: George Saxton, the farmer, whose strength lies in his ability to work with nature, but who is fatally weakened by his love for the high-spirited Lettie; and Annable, the gamekeeper, an ex-vicar who has abandoned the life of the mind to be "a good animal" (*White Peacock* 151), but whose understanding and acceptance of nature cannot protect him from the fragility of the individual life. The overt announcement of such themes is a weakness in the novel, as is the self-consciously literary quality of some of the writing, as if Lawrence is over-anxious to assert his status as a novelist. Yet in its concern with marriage, self-fulfilment, and the integrated self and in its adumbrations of later characters, it begins to explore the material which would dominate the next phase of Lawrence's fiction.

Sons and Lovers (1913; 1992) was Lawrence's first major novel, and although in many respects its structure and texture conform to the conventions of realism, it shows how Lawrence was beginning to explore both the thematic material and the representations of consciousness that would become the distinctive features of his most mature work. The text published in 1913, pruned by Edward Garnett of about one-tenth of Lawrence's manuscript material, invalidated some of Lawrence's claims for the shape of the novel; the reconstructed text of 1992 restores the author's careful balancing of elements. Nonetheless, in terms of plot and patterning, even the 1913 text displays the emergence of Lawrence's interest in pairs of contrasted siblings and in individuals caught between lovers who represent different aspects of their needs, with whom they struggle for individual identity. William Morel is destroyed by the demands of his pursuit, encouraged by his mother, of social advancement, and his passion for a woman who can never meet his (or his mother's) exacting demands. Paul is torn between three women, for even after Mrs. Morel's death his complex attachment to his mother continues to interfere with his relationships with Miriam and Clara. Paul is also trapped in his parents' marital conflict, between his mother's reserve, intellectualism, and social aspiration, and his father's more instinctual and physical approach to life. The presence of the latter in his personality is less apparent to Paul than it is to the reader, and it is notable that the balance of sympathies in the dramatization of scenes involving the father is at odds with the evident preferences of the narrative voice. That voice is least audible in scenes where competition for Paul's affection is least at stake (though Mr. Morel has no more than a dim awareness of such competition) and in some passages his view is allowed to prevail without interference from the narrative voice.

If the presence of such a voice, functioning in the text as a totalizing narrative against which the novel's other discourses may be checked, is a central distinguishing feature of realism, and its absence the mark of a text that aspires to modernism, then *Sons and Lovers* stands between the two. Side by side with narrative interventionism exists a supple employment of free indirect speech, which at its most successful allows a complex interplay between the workings of different consciousnesses in the novel, creating a sense of drama and conflict at a level beneath or beyond that which is spoken or enacted. This developing sense of intense and deep-seated internal conflict is strengthened by Lawrence's use of the natural world as a source of images and external representations of the characters' states of mind, so that the novel has, for instance, a rich and complex pattern of flowers and bird calls, used both literally and symbolically. Paul detests Miriam's possessive attitude to flowers, preferring to maintain a cool, appreciative distance. At the same time, in a number of key scenes, particular flowers acquire intense personal significance. This aspect of the novel is successful because it is related to nature in a larger sense, in its concern with the relationship of the individual to the cosmos, and the theme is more fully integrated into the drama of *Sons and Lovers* than in Lawrence's previous novels (*The Trespasser* was published in 1912), where his method of introducing such issues is often to have either the characters or the narrator discuss them. The final pages of *Sons and Lovers,* which find Paul on the brink of extinction, still caught in an emotional tangle between his mother and Miriam, and conscious of his own inconspicuousness in the face of an indifferent universe, are a triumphant integration of the novel's narrative and thematic elements.

The Rainbow. Before *Sons and Lovers* had achieved its first published form, Lawrence announced a decisive break with the kind of novel it represented. He was by now at work on the earliest versions of the material that would become *The Rainbow* and *Women in Love,* and in letters to Garnett he described his new novel as "really a stratum deeper than I think anybody has ever gone, in a novel . . . It is all analytical—quite unlike *Sons and Lovers,* not a bit visualised" (*Letters* i 526), and as "written in another language almost . . . I shan't write in the same manner as *Sons and Lovers* again . . . in that hard violent style full of sensation and presentation" (*Letters* ii 132). Lawrence's engagement with **Italian futurism,** although short-lived and highly qualified, came at this time and enabled him to focus some of his ideas. Lawrence approved of **Marinetti**'s refusal to separate human beings from the rest of the physical universe and of his search for a language to express the presence of non-human forces in nature and the individual. In June 1914 he told Garnett that he found the "certain moral scheme" within which fictional characters were conventionally presented to be restrictive and deadening, an artistic straitjacket from which he sought release. Marinetti's insistence on "that which is physic—non-human, in humanity . . . the inhuman will . . . physiology of matter" seemed to offer such a release. Characteristically, however, Lawrence disagreed with what he saw as a reductive element in futurist thought, which described humanity solely in scientific language: "instead of looking for the new human phenomenon, they will only look for the phenomena of the science of physics to be found in human being" (*Letters* ii 182–3). Lawrence rejected "the old stable ego of the character" in order to reveal another ego, which "passes through allotropic states which . . . are states of the same single radically-unchanged element"— carbon rather than coal or diamond. Garnett should not expect "the development of the novel to follow the lines of certain characters: the characters fall into the form of some other rhythmic form, like when one draws a fiddle-bow across a fine tray delicately sanded, the sand takes lines unknown" (*Letters* ii 184). In both cases Lawrence's analogies were drawn from the physical sciences, but he sought a relationship between science and art and an expressive language different from that proposed by the futurists, which would enable him to reveal that in his characters which is both human and individual as well as nonhuman and universal.

The first outcomes of Lawrence's new approach can be found in the final versions of the stories, such as "The Prussian Officer" and "Odour of Chrysanthemums," revised in the summer and early autumn of 1914 and published in *The Prussian Officer* in November of that year. It was also in late 1914 that he wrote "Study of Thomas Hardy," with its attack on the defeatism of modern literature and the artist who places his "thumb in the scale," and its assertion of the need for "the perfect union" (*Study* 126–7) of Man and Woman, Love and the Law. This remarkable text, a combination of literary criticism, philosophy and passionate personal statement, is rightly regarded as central to Lawrence's development in a crucial phase of his career. It is less an outline of the "philosophy" that will be illustrated in novels and short stories than another way of engaging with a similar body of material, a labile primary text rather than an authoritative statement of a stable position.

That "stratum deeper" of which Lawrence wrote is certainly present in *The Rainbow,* which is notable for the ways in which it seeks to represent individual consciousness and to embody those aspects of the self hidden from or only partly knowable by the self. The novel's repetitions, which for some readers are a mark of Lawrence's stylistic failure, are his attempts at that embodiment, less repetitious than rhythmic, and mimetic of the wave-like or spiralling movements of consciousness. The point is not to reach a fixed conclusion by following a logical, ratiocinative line, but to dramatize the self in flux. At the same time, however, the novel is full of the kind of visualization which Lawrence claimed to have abandoned. The internalized element of *The Rainbow* is rooted in and issues from a securely realized everyday life, encompassing the farming world of the Brangwens, Will's work and his pastimes of gardening and woodcarving and Ursula's career at college and as teacher. If the characters can conceive of themselves in mythical or spiritual terms, as do the

Brangwen men in their relationship with the earth, they cannot ignore their participation in a changing society and its history: both dimensions are announced in the novel's opening pages. The life of three generations of Brangwens is touched at every point by history: the coming of canal and railway, the encroachments of ugly industrialization, expanding educational opportunities. Similarly, many of its most memorable scenes are triumphs of realism: Tom and Anna feeding the cows, Tom's speech at Will and Anna's wedding, Ursula's fierce struggles with her pupils. Yet these and many other scenes also confront the characters with other forces, figured by a subtle deployment of the imagery of moon, mirror, arch, doorway, and rainbow. Tom's experience with Anna, reminiscent of his own childhood and set against Lydia's birth-cries, places the characters in contact with cycles of fertility and renewal, as does the pregnant Anna's naked dance in the moonlight. When Will and Anna stack corn stooks together in the moonlight, the dance-like pattern of their movements emphasizes their participation in a cosmic, universal process, just as their reactions to Lincoln Cathedral establish the terms of their later conflicts. Ursula's experiences in Wiggiston, which appear to offer a straightforwardly transcribed naturalistic description of industrial ugliness, are conceived on a level of nightmare which is only resolved in the novel's final vision. Although Lawrence claimed to have gone through a decisive watershed in his work, the rich satisfactions of *The Rainbow* derive from its combination of mimesis and poesis, of history and myth, of the visualized and the visionary.

Women in Love. For many readers, *Women in Love* is Lawrence's most unequivocally modernist novel, and is seen as one of a group of works from the years 1920–25 which represent the era of high modernism. It shares with Ezra Pound's *Hugh Selwyn Mauberley* (1920), **T. S. El-**iot's *The Waste Land* (1922), **James Joyce**'s *Ulysses* (1922), and **Virginia Woolf**'s *Mrs. Dalloway* (1925) a sense of crisis and fracture, of a civilization collapsing in the years during and after **the war.** The novel's exact historical setting is unclear, however, a deliberate move by Lawrence, for whom the general effect of the age on his characters was more important than their exact location in time, as he made clear in the novel's "Foreword": "I should wish the time to remain unfixed, so that the bitterness of the war may be taken for granted in the characters" (*Women in Love* 485). This is in marked contrast to *The Rainbow* which has a firm chronology, readily established from the few dates mentioned in the text. *Women in Love* also differs from its predecessor in its structure: it has none of the organic, cyclical pattern of *The Rainbow,* a pattern which is maintained even at moments of deep crisis— indeed, its crises may be related to or palliated by recourse to that rhythm. The later novel has continuity of plot, but its frequent changes of scene and breaks in the action (for a novel of similar length it has 32 chapters to *The Rainbow*'s 16) give it a disjointed, dislocated atmosphere.

The characters also appear in various degrees disaffected and ill at ease. Birkin's intermittent misanthropy, Gudrun's restlessness, Gerald's dissatisfaction with his role as industrial magnate and his father's despair at the loss of a paternal relationship with his employees, are all marks of the novel's concern with people who are in some sense wanderers, lacking fixed homes or any sense of rootedness. Such links as they have to the social world are weak and easily broken, as when Ursula and Birkin resign from their jobs by telegram. Ursula, although in many ways a very different character from the Brangwen daughter of *The Rainbow,* has moved decisively from the sheltering arch of home, which in the earlier novel was always ready to receive her, however much she sought to rebel against its constraints. The Brangwen family home in which the sisters are living at the beginning of the novel seems less of a protective haven, and is threatened by invasions from a new and more troubling world.

Equally notable are the novel's frequent eruptions of violence and anger, usually involving the attempted domination of the will: Gerald forcing the horse to confront the train, Hermione's attack on Birkin, Birkin and Ursula's arguments, Birkin throwing stones at the moon's reflection in a pond. The sources of this violence differ, however: the conflicts between Birkin and Ursula are the sparks thrown off by a live relationship that is constantly in flux, the outcome of the struggle for "star equilibrium," whereby characters can achieve fusion without sacrifice of separateness. Gudrun and Gerald, on the other hand, are fascinated by what repels them. Gudrun hates the ugliness of the mining town of Beldover, yet is drawn back to it and to Gerald, the mineowner: when they kiss under the same bridge where miners take their lovers, their identification with the life of the town seems complete. This sense of *nostalgie de la boue* is intensified when Gerald brings to Gudrun's bed the mud from his father's grave, an incident which in turn is part of the steady accretion of death in and around the Crich family: the drowning of the young couple, Mr. Crich's death and Gerald's act of self-extinction.

Art occupies a central place in the novel, and this has been taken as another mark of its modernism. Certainly it is a mark of its *modernity,* for *Women in Love* is full of references to contemporary artists and artistic movements, and there is an argument, between Gudrun and the corrupt artist Loerke on one side and Ursula on the other, in which the novel appears to discuss the terms of its own making. Ursula wishes to return art to its origins in the artist's experience and its effects in the real world, but Loerke tells her that she " ' . . . *must not* confuse the relative world of action with the absolute world of art' " (431), while Gudrun asserts that " ' . . . life doesn't *really* matter—it is one's art which is central' " (448). These statements of modernist aesthetic doctrines run counter to Lawrence's own advocacy of a revolution in favor of life. Yet, in *Women in Love,* it is dangerous to assume that any character acts as a mouthpiece for Lawrence's own ideas: other characters constantly challenge, deride and subvert Birkin's opinions, just as the narrative refuses to underwrite wholeheartedly the positions they may adopt. In many respects the novel, in keeping with its atomistic structure, remains a series of contending language zones, from which no reconciling total vision can possibly emerge— even one as willful as that which ends *The Rainbow.* The artistic argument between Ursula and Loerke remains unresolved; so, famously, does that between Ursula and Birkin which ends the book, a refusal of resolution that has seemed to many readers the novel's most characteristically modernist gesture.

The early 1920s. The Lost Girl (written and published 1920), *Mr. Noon* (unfinished; written 1920–1, part 1 published 1934, full text 1984), *Aaron's Rod* (written 1917–21, published 1922) and *Kangaroo* (written 1922, published 1923) share some structural, thematic and textual features. The first three of these novels begin in a small Midlands town, a satirical recreation of Lawrence's Eastwood. A sudden crisis, usually the culmination of a long-standing sense of dissatisfaction with the constrictions of English provincial life, propels the protagonists to leave and travel to another country: in all three cases, Italy. As they begin to travel through continental Europe, Alvina Houghton, Gilbert Noon, and Aaron Sisson become more aware of the insularity and deadness of England and experience reality on a larger scale, geographically, morally, and historically. In *Kangaroo,* where Richard Somers' wartime experiences are recounted in retrospect, the break is more radical, because post-war Europe as a whole is seen as compromised, and the characters need to search for an even newer world—first in Australia and then in America.

The characters' sense of emotional liberation and expanded opportunities is related to their search for fulfilling emotional relationships, the outcomes of which are different in each novel. The tense, uncertain ending of *The Lost Girl* leaves Alvina alone in a remote Italian village, hoping that her husband will survive the war and return to her. Aaron Sisson, having escaped a worn-out marriage, finds no greater fulfilment in any later sexual relationship and at the end of the novel is equally uncertain about the future. The second part of *Mr. Noon* asserts the importance of a reciprocal relationship between man and woman in terms reminiscent of *The Rainbow* and even *Women in Love* and its atmosphere of impassioned discovery is still present when the manuscript breaks off. *The Lost Girl* and *Aaron's Rod,* however, together with *Kangaroo* and *The Plumed Serpent* (written 1923–25, published 1926), present sexual relations in terms of a different power dynamic, which asks questions about the submission of women to men, and of men to a charismatic leader.

In the early 1920s, Lawrence's fiction also began to change in other ways. *Aaron's Rod* and *Kangaroo,* like *Women in Love,* are fragmented, less organic narratives than *The Rainbow,* a development related to Lawrence's sense of the war's effect on the sustaining discourses of European society. In Lawrence's earlier fiction there had been a predominating narrative voice, often absorbed into or merged with a character's voice but never quite without the tones of an authoritative omniscient narrator. This voice begins to falter in *Women in Love* and playfully draws attention to itself in *The Lost Girl;* in *Aaron's Rod,* however, it is foregrounded in defense of its own role, and confronts "the gentle reader" as an antagonist: "Don't grumble at me then, gentle reader, and swear at me that this damned fellow wasn't half clever enough to think all these smart things and realise all these fine-drawn-out subtleties. You are quite right, he wasn't, yet it all resolved in him as I say, and it is for you to prove that it didn't" (*Aaron's Rod* 164). In *Mr. Noon* Lawrence further centralizes the technique of the narrator as protagonist, in debate with readers who are teased and berated by an author who claims to be embattled by hostile and uncomprehending critics, and who needs to re-establish the right to be in command of his novel: "Am *I* writing this book, or are you? Let me tell you, even if, gentle reader, you happen to be a wonderful, chirping, gentle, soft-billed gosling of a critic, gentilissimo, *I* am writing this book, and it is *not* being chirped out by you" (*Mr. Noon* 137). Nor can readers assume that the narrative will take any form that their reading of other novels may have led them to expect; they are constantly reminded of the text's fictionality, and must accept a narrative that flouts accepted modes of character development. Similarly in *Kangaroo* the narrative voice challenges the reader about the nature of the text: "Chapter follows chapter, and nothing doing . . . If you don't like the novel, don't read it" (*Kangaroo* 284). After the difficulties of 1915–1920, Lawrence felt he could no longer rely on his audience and the society it represented to accept and understand his work. He is seeking an audience, a voice in which to address it and a means of asserting his ownership of his novels.

When he was writing *Kangaroo* Lawrence described it as "such a novel! Even the Ulysseans will spit at it" (*Letters* iv 275). He was conscious that to render

Richard Somers' sense of dislocation he must find a form which avoided both the stereotypes of popular fiction and the exaggerated self-conscious of the modern serious novel, among which he counted *Ulysses,* which he read at this time. He found Joyce's novel wearisome, cerebral and full of childish self-absorption, offering the reader little more than a chaotic potpourri. Out of this brief and hostile engagement with Joyce came the first of a number of important critical essays. The first of these "The Future of the Novel," written and published (as "Surgery for the Novel—Or a Bomb" in 1923) was a specific response to Joyce, **Proust,** and **Dorothy Richardson.** There then followed, in the summer and autumn of 1925, five essays which bore a similar relationship to Lawrence's work as did "Study of Thomas Hardy" a decade earlier. "Morality and the Novel," "The Novel," "Art and Morality," "Why the Novel Matters," and "The Novel and the Feelings" are much-quoted, but often simply to explain Lawrence's "intention" in a particular text or as expositions of his "theory" of novel-writing. Yet the form, technique, and critical procedures of these essays sometimes throw more light on Lawrence's fiction than do the ideas they put forward. The informal, challenging style of Lawrence's recent novels is here used for critical purposes, so that ideas are presented less through argument, logic, or textual analysis than through anecdote, parable, image, and symbol. The tone is in turns impassioned, angry, witty, ironical, farcical; the argument has no apparent linear progression; it swirls and swoops, twists and creeps, before bursting on the unsuspecting reader like a revelation. In a sense, the form of these essays is an anticipation of the concerns of Lawrence's subsequent career, as he became interested in the potential of myth and in healing what he saw as an artificial division between the novel and philosophy, or the novel and the gospels.

America and "The Plumed Serpent." Lawrence went to America in 1922, the year in which the anticipatory *Studies in Classic American Literature* was published. At first he found it "a land of tight, iron-clanking little *wills*" (*Letters* iv 311) and was disappointed that it did not reanimate his creative energies, but he was impressed by the size and beauty of the landscape and its potential for connection with a lost pagan vision. *The Plumed Serpent,* first written as "Quetzalcoatl" in 1923 (published 1995), is set in Mexico, which Lawrence visited in 1923 and 1924–5, and is an account of a search for that lost vision. It draws on material from Mexican history and mythology as background to a story of modern politics and spiritual revival. Kate Leslie flees from an exhausted post-War Europe in search of renewal, and is drawn to "the great, opened-out cosmos" of the Mexican landscape with its sense of a lost "subtle dark, consciousness" (*Plumed Serpent* 421, 415). She becomes involved with a cult-like political movement, which seeks to revive the Aztec worship of the god Quetzalcoatl, whose incarnation Don Ramón declares himself to be. His chief follower is General Cipriano, with whom Kate has a relationship in which she is required to be submissive and deny her own sexuality.

The novel thus brings together the developing concerns of Lawrence's work in the early 1920s: despair with Europe, political leadership, spiritual renewal, and sexual submissiveness in women. Further explorations of these themes can be found in other American stories such as "The Princess" and "The Woman Who Rode Away" (both written and published 1924–5). These stories, like *The Plumed Serpent,* have proved distasteful to many readers, and have been dismissed as misogynistic, phallocentric fantasies with fascistic tendencies, similar to those in works by **Yeats,** Eliot, and Pound. "The Woman

Who Rode Away," particularly, has been deplored for its dehumanization and sacrifice of a woman, apparently for the sake of a pagan vision to which Lawrence is assumed to give his approval. Subsequent readings have been more lenient, and concentrate on Lawrence's use of mythical material and emphasize his shifts in narrative tone and his interrogation, through the spirited Kate Leslie, for instance, of the validity of modern political attempts at spiritual renewal. "The Princess" is an inverted version of the rape-fantasy, in which the Sleeping Beauty refuses to be woken by the man's sexual power and thus destroys him. *St. Mawr,* the other major short novel of this period, ends with a similar inversion of values, as Lou Witt is left with a vision of the American landscape as " 'something big, bigger than men, bigger than people, bigger than religion' " (*St Mawr* 155).

The final phase. Lawrence returned to Europe for the last time in 1925, and in 1926 he made his final journey to England, a visit which enabled him to recover the Midlands as subject and setting for his fiction. *Lady Chatterley's Lover* (written and published, 1928), notorious for its sexual content, is equally concerned with political issues, and Lawrence's balancing of these elements can be traced through the novel's early versions, written in 1926 (published as *The First Lady Chatterley,* 1944) and 1927 (published as *John Thomas and Lady Jane,* 1972). The novel has the mythical dimensions of the preceding phase, while the sylvan setting in which the lovers meet offers a redeemed version of the compromised idyll of *The White Peacock.* Wragby Hall, with its maimed and impotent owner, is a symbol of a paralyzed country, undermined by industrial conflicts and mechanized money-based relationships, where men and women are cut off from the vital sources that would give them energy and self-respect. Mellors, a combination of vitalism

and intellect, articulates the novel's critique of materialism, expressing the desire to "live beyond money" (*Lady Chatterley* 300). It is in the tender, reciprocal relationship between Constance Chatterley and Oliver Mellors that some kind of redemption can be achieved. But the novel offers no total vision of social renewal, like that at the end of *The Rainbow:* the lovers, with their expected child, hope to withdraw together to a small farm where they can foster "the little pentecost flame" (*Lady Chatterley* 301) that exists between them.

"Autobiographical Fragment," written in the autumn of 1927, begins as another of the brief "autobiographies" that Lawrence wrote in the last few years of his life, in which he nostalgically celebrates the Midlands of his childhood. But this narrator falls asleep and wakes one thousand years later in a utopian society; the piece thus demonstrates how Lawrence, even while writing *Lady Chatterley's Lover,* was seeking new modes of expression. *The Escaped Cock* (written in 1928–9, published with this title in 1929, also known as *The Man Who Died*) is a tender, rapt, and yearning myth of renewal which moves decisively beyond realism. The risen Christ, weary of his mission, no longer wishes "to lay the compulsion of love on all men"; he finds joy in "the stirring of the phenomenal world" (*Escaped Cock* 34, 30), but is fearful of returning to a world, where he has been hurt and betrayed. His relationship with a priestess of Osiris who overcomes his fear of touch and connection, and who at the end of the story is carrying his child, brings him to rebirth into full humanity.

The mythic, non-realistic turn of Lawrence's late works might seem to place him firmly among the modernists, but his use of myth is quite different from that of Joyce or Eliot, who largely seek in myth a set of correspondences. The elaborate structure of *Ulysses,* which mimicks and modifies that of Homer's epic, is used by

Joyce to illustrate the universality of human experience through time. For Eliot, in spite of his claims for the underlying motifs of *The Waste Land,* myth can only have a fragile and fragmentary status as a sustaining vision. Although Lawrence was conscious of the universalizing and transcendent potential of myths, when he came to use them in works as various as *The Plumed Serpent, Lady Chatterley's Lover,* and *The Escaped Cock* he was less interested in their *content* than in the worldview from which they arose. Lawrence's use of myth is related to his central metaphor of the journey or quest, and through it he seeks a true and vital relation to the phenomenal world and the renewed sense of connection that he always desired.

Peter Preston

Selected Bibliography

With the exception of the two Lawrence items listed below, all citations from Lawrence's works and letters are from the standard scholarly edition published by Cambridge University Press.

Bell, Michael. *D. H. Lawrence. Language and Being.* Cambridge: Cambridge UP, 1992.

———. *Literature, Modernism and Myth. Belief and Responsibility in the Twentieth Century.* Cambridge: Cambridge UP, 1997.

Ellis, David and Howard Mills. *D. H. Lawrence's Non-Fiction. Art, Thought and Genre.* Cambridge: Cambridge UP, 1988.

"ET" [Jessie Chambers]. *D. H. Lawrence. A Personal Record.* London: Jonathan Cape, 1935.

Fernihough, Anne. *D. H. Lawrence: Aesthetics and Ideology.* Oxford: Clarendon Press, 1993.

Hyde, G. M. *D. H. Lawrence.* London and Basingstoke: Macmillan, 1990.

Lawrence, D. H. *The Escaped Cock.* Edited by Gerald M. Lacy. Santa Barbara, California: Black Sparrow Press, 1976.

———. *Phoenix. The Posthumous Papers of D. H. Lawrence.* Edited by Edward D. McDonald. London: Heinemann, 1936.

Martin, Graham. "Lawrence and Modernism." In *D. H. Lawrence in England and Italy.* Edited by George Donaldson and Mara Kalnins. London and Basingstoke: Macmillan Press, 1999, 135–153.

Pinkney, Tony. *D. H. Lawrence.* London: Harvester Wheatsheaf, 1990.

Pykett, Lyn. *Engendering Fictions. The English Novel in the Early Twentieth Century.* London: Edward Arnold, 1995.

Worthen, John. *D. H. Lawrence and the Idea of the Novel.* London and Basingstoke: Macmillan, 1979.

Lawrence, D. H. (Poetry)

D. H. Lawrence's poetry constitutes a significant body of writing not only in terms of Lawrence's own life and art, but also in terms of early twentieth-century modernist verse more generally. His poetry collections include *Love Poems and Others* (1913); *Amores* (1916); *Look! We Have Come Through!* (1917); *New Poems* (1918); *Bay* (1919); *Birds, Beasts and Flowers* (1923); *Collected Poems* (1928); *Pansies* (1928); *Nettles* (1930); "More Pansies;" and "Last Poems" (1932). These poems chart an experimental progression through different styles in the attempt to establish a satisfactory method through which to articulate an idiosyncratic view of society and humanity.

The earliest poems are characterized by an attempt to emulate conventional rhyming forms and a growing awareness of the limitations of such forms. There are a few successful rhyming poems, including four poems written in Lawrence's native Eastwood dialect, which compelled **Ezra Pound** to nominate him for the Polignac prize. Yet Lawrence generally associated regulated, rhyming verse with vacuous sentiment, and the most interesting early poems, such as "The Wild Common," reveal an attempt to stretch an ostensibly conventional rhyming form to its limits. For instance, the line "Rabbits, handfuls of brown earth, lie" is followed by one containing twice the number of syllables. The word "lie" is rhymed with "I" at the end of the next line, but the "I" affords no sense of closure, as it forms part of an enjambment ("when I / Move. . . . "). The use of irregular line lengths and the conscious overriding of end-rhymes through linguistic continuity, foreshadow the free-verse later adopted by Lawrence (and never relinquished). This was a method he consciously derived from **Walt Whitman,** the poet he once placed beside Dante and **Shakespeare** as among his greatest literary precursors.

Free-verse is the dominant and successful medium in *Look! We Have Come Through!,* an autobiographical collection charting the development of the relationship between Lawrence and his wife Frieda after their elopement in 1912. The poems oscillate between hope and despair, struggling with the unfamiliar emotion of utter dependence, and the psychological instability thereby occasioned. Free-verse is at times employed effectively, contracting and expanding, oscillating between balance and dislocation, in order to convey these shifting instabilities. Yet it is often considered to be in the later volume, *Birds, Beasts and Flowers,* that Lawrence creates his unified masterpiece in free-verse.

The unity of this collection is evident both in style and subject-matter, as the poems describe aspects of the natural world, emphasizing both the affinity and "otherness" which are characteristic of man's relation to nature. The line "But must I confess how I liked him" from "Snake" might be contrasted with the poem "Fish" which emphasizes the futility of any attempt to adopt the perspective of an intrinsically "other" creature, provoking the helpless and rather chilling insight, "I didn't know his God." These poems are among the most frequently anthologized of Lawrence's poetry: lines from "Snake," for example, are often cited in order to indicate the mimetic quality of Lawrence's writing. This poem in particular reveals the ability of free-verse to expand and contract in a manner appropriate to the image.

The *Birds, Beasts and Flowers* poems are not only significant in their successful realization of an appropriate poetic medium. These poems also echo the "modernist" preoccupation with mythic archetypes: they are richly allusive, creating links between past and present through reference to landscape and location. "Cypresses," for example, identifies in the trees described layers of symbolism relating to the language and culture of the previous inhabitants of that area: namely the lost Etruscan race that became the focus of Lawrence's travel book *Sketches of Etruscan Places* (1932). Vivid description of the trees as "supple, brooding, softly-swaying pillars of dark flame" is therefore combined with a constant awareness of the "Etruscan-dusky, wavering men of old Etruria" who (according to Lawrence) understood the "meaning" of life. In this poem, Lawrence imaginatively reinvigorates the present through reverting to a symbolically conceived mythic past, advocating a "deliberate return in order to get back to the roots again, for a new start" (Lawrence, *Apocalypse* 137). His many imaginative depictions of such a "return" engage with three crucial intertexts within the corpus of Lawrence's reading: namely James Frazer's *The Golden Bough;* E. B. Tylor's *Primitive Culture,* and Gilbert Murray's *Five Stages of Greek Religion.* These intertexts tend to advocate an interpretation of society that emphasizes its progression beyond **primitivism** and savagery to civilization. Lawrence, in *Birds, Beasts and Flowers* as in numerous other poems and prose works, demands a redefinition of such terms as savagery, and an awareness that in many ways so-called "primitive" cultures were superior to our own. Lawrence was not alone in this respect: the redefining of the present in terms of the past was a feature of "modernist" writing, as is indicated by the extensive use of anthropological and mythological reference within **T. S. Eliot**'s *The Waste Land.*

Lawrence's startlingly prolific late poetry, composed in 1928–1930, reveals that having established free-verse as a satisfyingly enabling medium, he was concerned with new kinds of formal experiment. The poetry of this period includes aphoristic, epigrammatic verse stylistically emulating the 17th century French writing of Pascal, La Bruyère, and La Rochefoucauld (in *Pansies*), as well as biting social satire or "doggerel" (in *Nettles*). The final unfinished manuscript collections ("More Pansies" and "Last Poems") are diverse in subject-matter, engaging with aspects of philosophy, religion, astronomy, psychology, and **anthropology** in order to provide suitable contexts for exploring contemporary modes of living. The scope of mythological reference evident in *Birds, Beasts and Flowers* is again reflected here—most conspicuously in the allusions to Persephone, Hades, Odysseus, and Dionysus in "Bavarian Gentians," "The Greeks Are Coming," "The Argonauts," and "Middle of the World"—while free-verse is again highly effective as the chosen medium.

In his essay "Poetry of the Present," Lawrence gives his own definition of the free-verse poetry he considered to be innovatory, distinguishing it from the "unfree," fettered verse of his precursors: "We can get rid of the stereotyped movements and the old hackneyed associations of sound or sense . . . We can be in ourselves spontaneous and flexible as flame, we can see that utterance rushes out without artificial foam or artificial smoothness" (*Complete Poems* 184). In moving away from the rigidity of fixed nineteenth-century forms, adopting an alternative aesthetic and extending this in order to conform to his own definitions of modernity, Lawrence's poetry is clearly significant among early twentieth-century modernist writings.

Bethan Jones

Selected Bibliography

A variorum edition of Lawrence's poems, edited by Christopher Pollnitz, will soon be published by Cambridge UP. The most authoritative Complete and Selected editions currently available are cited below.

Aldington, Richard. "Introduction to 'Last Poems' and 'More Pansies.' " *The Complete Poems of D. H. Lawrence*. Vol II. Ed. Vivian de Sola Pinto and Warren Roberts. London: Heinemann, 1964.

Ellis, David. "Verse or worse: the place of 'Pansies' in Lawrence's Poetry." In David Ellis and Howard Mills. *D. H. Lawrence's Non-Fiction: Art, Thought and Genre.* Cambridge: Cambridge UP, 1988.

Gilbert, Sandra. *Acts of Attention: The Poetry of D. H. Lawrence.* Ithaca and New York: Cornell UP, 1972.

Laird, Holly. *Self and Sequence: the Poetry of D. H. Lawrence.* Charlottesville: UP of Virginia, 1988.

Lawrence, D. H. *Apocalypse and the Writings on Revelation.* Ed. Mara Kalnins. Cambridge: Cambridge UP, 1980.

———. *Birds, Beasts and Flowers.* London: Cresset Press, 1930.

———. *The Complete Poems.* Ed. Vivian de Sola Pinto and Warren Roberts. London: Penguin, 1993.

———. *Selected Poems.* Ed. Mara Kalnins. London: Dent, 1992.

Pollnitz, Christopher. "Raptus Virginis: The Dark God in the Poetry of D. H. Lawrence." *D. H. Lawrence: Centenary Essays.* Ed. Mara Kalnins. Bristol: Bristol Classical Press, 1986.

———. "Cough-Prints and Other Intimacies: Considerations in Editing Lawrence's Later Verse." *Editing D. H. Lawrence.* Ed. Charles L. Ross and Dennis Jackson. Ann Arbor: University of Michigan Press, 1995.

Sagar, Keith. "The Genesis of 'Bavarian Gentians.'" *The D. H. Lawrence Review* 8 (Spring 1975): 47–53.

Smailes, T. A. "D. H. Lawrence: Seven Hitherto Unpublished Poems." *The D. H. Lawrence Review* 3 (Spring 1970): 42–46.

Lewis, Saunders (1893–1985)

Playwright, poet, novelist, and literary critic. He was born in Wallasey to a prominent Welsh Calvinistic Methodist family. He studied English and French at the University of Liverpool but his studies were interrupted by the outbreak of the First World War. He served as an officer with the South Wales Borderers in **France, Italy,** and **Greece.** On returning to England, he took a first in English at Liverpool, writing a dissertation on English influences on eighteenth-century Welsh verse, which became his first publication: *A School of Welsh Augustans* (1924). Thereafter he worked as a librarian for a short period and then as a lecturer in Welsh at the University College of **Wales** in Swansea. Politically active, he was one of the founders of Plaid Cymru, the Welsh Nationalist Party, in 1925, and was its President from 1926. In 1932 he became a convert to roman catholicism. In 1936 he and two fellow Welsh nationalists, D. J. Williams, and Lewis Valentine, committed an arson attack on Royal Air Force buildings destined to become a bombing school on the Lleyn peninsula in North Wales. They were tried, convicted and imprisoned for this largely symbolic action. Significantly, a Welsh jury refused to come to a verdict in the case and the three had to be tried in the Old Bailey in London. Saunders Lewis's impassioned political speech from the dock in defence of his actions has become legendary. On release from prison, Lewis was dismissed from his post at the University of Wales, Swansea and thereafter sustained himself through journalism, teaching, and farming. Later, he was appointed lecturer in Welsh at the University of Wales, Cardiff. He was a skillful political journalist and made a key intervention in Welsh political and social life in 1962, when he broadcast a radio lecture entitled "Tynged yr Iaith" ("The Fate of the Language") the rhetorical power of which was sufficient to lead directly to the founding of "Cymdeithas yr Iaith Gymraeg" ("The Welsh Language Society") which was, and is, committed to securing the future of the Welsh language through direct, non-violent political action.

In addition to the public, political role outlined above, Saunders Lewis was also one of the most prominent—some would say undoubtedly the greatest—Welsh playwright and poet of the twentieth century. His first play, *The Eve of St. John,* was in English but soon after its completion in 1921 Saunders Lewis decided to write no more in that language but to dedicate himself to the Welsh language and to enriching its literature. His plays often have historical or mythological themes and tend to explore moral conflicts and dilemmas, including clashes between the personal and the political. Others are set in contemporary Wales and address issues of Welsh identity and allegiance. Lewis's poetic language is grand and powerful, indeed visionary. It has been suggested that the French classical dramatist, Corneille, is the dominant influence on the plays. At the same time, there is no doubt of the modernist nature of these works which create visions of grandeur in the midst of what Lewis regarded as a decadent and crumbling world. His historical characters often speak in a slightly archaic language betokening their elite status and high honor. Lewis invented for himself an idealized vision of aristocratic, Catholic, medieval Wales, which he passionately espoused in opposition to the dominant Welsh ideology of nonconformity, liberalism, and the cult of the *werin* (common folk). His acknowledged masterpieces include *Gwaed yr Uchelwyr* (1922, "The Blood of the Nobility"), *Blodeuwedd* (1948), *Siwan* (1956), *Brad* (1958, "Treason"), and *Esther* (1960). As the titles suggest, Lewis excelled at the creation of powerful female protagonists. Many regard *Siwan* as his greatest work. Based on real events and characters in early thirteenth-century Wales, the play focuses on the moral choices and passions of Siwan (Joan) the daughter of the English King John, who had been married to the Welsh prince, Llywelyn Fawr, and who committed adultery with a young nobleman called William de Braose (Gwilym Brewys in the play) who was executed when Llywelyn discovered their affair. The execution, which takes place offstage and is described to the manacled Siwan by her maid, is at the center of the play, but the play's power lies in its deep psychological insight into the characters of Siwan and Llywelyn and in the sheer beauty of the language.

Lewis wrote only two novels, namely *Monica* (1930) and *Merch Gwern Hywel* (1964, "The Daughter of Gwern Hywel"). The former, which has been translated into English by Meic Stephens, is certainly a modernist text, notably out of character with the Welsh novelistic tradition. It focuses on a repulsive anti-heroine and explores in a cold and merciless way the lives of contemporary characters who are deracinated, immoral, and faithless.

It is possible to discern strong parallels between Saunders Lewis and **T. S. Eliot.** Both seemed to embody the aesthetic of high modernism and to combine the most rigorous traditionalism (such as a strong allegiance to a ritualistic Church) with a fearless artistic iconoclasm. Both were men born outside the ancestral homeland to which they returned and dedicated themselves to "purifying the language of the tribe." Both were also incisive and influential literary critics who, arguably, "created the taste by which their work was enjoyed." Neither was a particularly prolific poet, but both produced poems which seem to encapsulate and express the spirit of the age, Eliot in *The Wasteland* (1922) and Lewis in *Y Dilyw 1939* ("The Flood 1939"). There are also parallels with the work and aesthetic of the Anglo-Welsh poet and artist **David Jones,** who became a close friend of Lewis's.

Saunders Lewis's achievement is truly remarkable. There are many within Wales who violently disagree with his elitism, his conservatism, and his questionable rapprochement with extreme right-wing politics, but no one can deny the enormous influence of his work nor the enduring value of his literary oeuvre.

Katie Gramich

Selected Bibliography

Clancy, Joseph P. (trans. & ed.) *The Plays of Saunders Lewis.* Four volumes. Llandybie: Christopher Davies, 1985–6.

———. (trans. & ed.) *Saunders Lewis: Selected Poems 1893–1985.* Cardiff: University of Wales Press, 1993.

Griffiths, Bruce. *Saunders Lewis.* Writers of Wales Series. Cardiff: University of Wales Press, 1989.

Jones, Alun R. & Gwyn Thomas, eds. *Presenting Saunders Lewis.* Cardiff: University of Wales Press, 1983.

Jones, Harri Prichard, Mair Saunders Jones & Ned Thomas, eds. *Saunders Lewis: Letters to Margaret Gilcriest.* Cardiff: University of Wales Press, 1993.

Rowlands, John. *Saunders y Beirniad.* Caernarfon: Pantycelyn, 1990.

Williams, Ioan. *A Straitened Stage: A Study of the Theatre of J. Saunders Lewis.* Bridgend: Seren, 1991.

———, ed. *Dramau Saunders Lewis: Y Casgliad Cyflawn.* Caerdydd: Gwasg Prifysgol Cymru, 1996.

Lewis, Wyndham (1882–1957)

Writer, essayist and polemicist, Wyndham Lewis was one of the most versatile personalities of English modernism. **T. S. Eliot** dubbed him the greatest prose writer of his generation, but, unlike Eliot and the other "men of 1914" (**Pound** and **Joyce**), he was not only a writer but also one of the most significant painters of the twentieth century.

He was born to an American father and a British mother on board his father's yacht off the coast of Amherst, Nova Scotia, Canada. After passing his infancy in New England, he was educated in England, first at Rugby and then in London, where he studied at the Slade School of

Art (1898–1901). The most decisive period of his formation was spent in Paris (1902–08), from where he made important visits to Madrid and Munich. This experience rendered him the most cosmopolitan of the English modernists, exposing him directly to the extraordinary cultural ferment of the *ville lumière* (he always considered Paris to be his "university"). Here he had the opportunity to observe closely (and probably enter into contact with) the literary and artistic avant-garde (Apollinaire, Modigliani, Derain, Picasso, **Gertrude Stein**). He also attended Bergson's lectures at the Collège de France. During his stay in Paris, Lewis read the Russian classics (Gogol, Dostoevsky) in the French translation. Another important encounter ("a paramount influence") was with the works of Nietzsche.

Upon his return to London, these cultural stimuli allowed him to operate with an independent and radical attitude amid a backward and notoriously conservative local culture. His first novel, *Mrs. Dukes' Million* (published posthumously in 1977, but probably written between 1907 and 1908) is characterized by an incredible multiplication of narrative incidents and an ever accelerating **rhythm** of plot. In spite of the work's adherence to the conventions of the late Victorian novel, this extraordinary merry-go-round of *coup de théatre,* doublings, and masquerades reveals the experimental tendencies that Lewis would display in the following years. The short stories written between 1909 and 1911 are awkward and stylistically immature (thoroughly revised in 1927, they were collected under the title *Wild Bodies*). However these sketches are important both thematically and ideologically. Set in Brittany ("a barbaric environment"), they deal with marginalized characters (tramps, eternal pensioners, acrobats, etc.). In these stories, as in the works that follow, Lewis was not searching for a nature uncorrupted by industrial civilization. At no point did he long for a pastoral retreat; rather he was fascinated by the primordial energy and anarchy that animated these outcasts, by the body in all its unpredictability and wildness.

As a painter, Lewis is best known as the founder and leader of **vorticism,** an independent British artistic movement, begun in 1914 with the aim of reconciling the stasis of **cubism** and the dynamism of **futurism.** The vorticist experiment resulted in implosive and semi-abstract forms, characterized by rigid and clear-cut outlines. Notwithstanding his harsh criticism of **Filippo Tommaso Marinetti,** Lewis adopted many of the techniques of self-promotion and provocation advocated by the futurists. This is evident in the bold and aggressive typography of the magazine BLAST (The Review of the Great English Vortex), in which he fervidly publicized the vorticism movement (the magazine survived only for two issues, 1914 and 1915). Apart from manifestos and other notes that appeared in BLAST, Lewis published a *pièce* that can be considered the earliest and most radical work of the English avant-garde, *Enemy of the Stars.* In this prose poem, ostensibly a theatrical *pièce,* Lewis attempts for the first time to apply the techniques of abstract painting to a written text. This experiment continues in *Tarr,* which many critics consider to be his most successful novel (written before **the war,** it was first published in 1918, then revised in 1928 for a second edition that softened many of the more daring avant-garde features of the original). Set in Paris during the early years of the twentieth century, *Tarr* describes with great verve the relations that develop within a group of "bourgeois-bohemians" who inhabit the artistic society of Montmartre. The narrative scheme does not allow Lewis to conduct abstract experiments with language (although there remain some eloquent traces of this in the first edition). Nonetheless, he introduces another innovation—a vigorous technique of "external" or plastic characterization, which has great visual impact even in those parts that (following the influence of Dostoevsky) analyze the lacerations of the soul. As a writer, Lewis conducted a harsh polemic against the interior narrative style of Joyce and **Virginia Woolf,** preferring instead a hard, violent, and dynamic speech-action that refuses all psychologism. In *Tarr,* the ludic dimension of *Mrs. Dukes's Million* reemerges in a more spectacular manner, so much so that it becomes a kind of "laughter-in-action."

In his copious post-war narrative production, Lewis abandoned his most daring **formal experimentation** (in parallel with the return of figuration in his painting), but without eliminating all the characteristics of the innovative style he developed during his avant-garde period. The *rappel à l'ordre* also influenced Lewis on the ideological level. Throughout the 1930s, the writer and painter (whom **Auden** describes as "that lonely volcano of the Right") displayed strong affinities with reactionary French thought. The "external style" was stretched to the point where it became a poetics of the "Great Without," manifesting itself eventually in what most readers consider to be the dull and long-winded descriptions of *The Apes of God* (1930). In this satirical *roman à clef,* Lewis employed grotesque caricatures to parody the life and culture of the **Bloomsbury** set, a prominent group of London artists and intellectuals that he had already (in a famous prewar polemic with Roger Fry) accused of aesthetic dilettantism. Of the ambitious epic-visionary narrative project that was to constitute a tetralogy named *The Human Age,* Lewis would publish only three volumes: *The Childermass* (1928), *Monstre*

Gay, and *Malign Fiesta* (both of 1955). A less polemical and more creative Lewis can be discerned in *The Revenge for Love* (1937), a novel set in **Spain** during the period of the Civil War and in *Self-Condemned* (1954), a semi-autobiographical narrative that recalls his self-imposed exile in Canada.

Though often erratic and repetitive, Lewis's essays are occasionally lucid and thought-provoking—for example, *The Art of Being Ruled* (1926), which expresses sympathy for fascism, and *Time and Western Man* (1927), which contains a well-known attack upon Joyce's *Ulysses.* His warming to Nazism in *Hitler* (1931) brought him ostracism, giving rise to an isolation that his militant self-declaration as "enemy" of the establishment did little to allay (*The Enemy,* 1927–29, was the title of an art magazine that consisted almost entirely of Lewis's own contributions). The critiques of T. S. Eliot, Virginia Woolf, Gertrude Stein, and **Hemingway** in *Men Without Art* (1934) are interesting because they are polemics conducted within the militant avant-garde. Notable also are the autobiographical reconstructions in *Blasting and Bombardiering* (1937) and *Rude Assignment* (1950).

Giovanni Cianci

Selected Bibliography

(Note: Most of Lewis's books are available in editions published by Black Sparrow Press, California.)

Cianci, Giovanni, ed. *Wyndham Lewis: Letteratura/ Pittura.* Palermo: Sellerio, 1982.

Cork, R. *Vorticism and Abstract Art in the First Machine Age.* 2 vols. London: Fraser, 1976

Dasenbrock, R.W. *The Literary Vorticism of Ezra Pound and Wyndham Lewis.* Baltimore: Johns Hopkins UP, 1985.

Jameson, Frederic. *Fables of Aggression: Wyndham Lewis as Fascist.* Berkeley, California: U of California P, 1979.

Kenner, Hugh. *Wyndham Lewis.* Norfolk, Va, 1954.

Meyers, Jeffrey. *The Enemy: A Biography of Wyndham Lewis.* London and Henley: Routledge, 1980.

Meyers, Jeffrey, ed. *Wyndham Lewis: A Revaluation.* London: The Athlone Press 1979.

Michel, W. *Wyndham Lewis: Paintings and Drawings.* London: Thames and Hudson, 1971

Lindegren, Erik (1910–1968)

Swedish poet and critic who made his debut with *Posthum ungdom* (1935, *Posthumous Youth*), in which a formally conventional poetry gives expression to feelings of spleen. His modernist breakthrough is *mannen utan väg* (1942, Eng. trans. *The Man Without a Way,* 1969) a collection of forty "exploded sonnets" capturing a sense of despair and anguish characteristic of the literary climate of the forties. It gains its poetic effect from the tension between a strictly controlled form and a disharmonious imagery. Lindegren here combines a surrealistic imagery and a mythical method reminiscent of **T. S. Eliot.** *Sviter* (1947, *Suites*) marks a new stage in Lindegren's poetic development: a movement away from the bold modernism of the previous collection towards a more easily accessible, musically structured, and romantically oriented expression. In 1947 Lindegren also published a group of ecphrastic poems, lyrical interpretations of Swedish modernist paintings, some of which are included in *Sviter.* Lindegren's fourth and final lyrical phase is represented by *Vinteroffer* (1954, *Winter Sacrifice*) where themes of frozenness and petrifaction combine with a strong metapoetical drive. A selection of Lindegren's literary criticism appears in the collection *Tangenter* (1974, *Keys*).

Mats Jansson

Selected Bibliography
Cullhed, Anders. "Tiden söker sin röst." *Studier kring Erik Lindegrens mannen utan väg.* Stockholm: Bonniers, 1982.

Lysell, Roland. *Erik Lindegrens imaginära universum.* Stockholm: Doxa, 1983.

Lowry, (Clarence) Malcolm (1909–1957)

Lowry is chiefly famous for his phantasmagoric Mexican novel *Under the Volcano* (1947), a highly complex late modernist *tour de force* which follows the day-in-the-life approach of **Joyce's** *Ulysses* and **Woolf's** *Mrs. Dalloway,* but which draws on Lowry's personal interests in romanticism, **expressionism,** symbolism, and the cabala.

Lowry was born in Liscard, Cheshire and attended the Leys School, Cambridge, before entering St. Catharine's College, Cambridge in 1929. The years 1927 to 1930 were eventful ones in which Lowry worked aboard the SS *Pyrrhus* (which provided the source material for his first novel *Ultramarine* (1933)), studied in **Germany** (where he discovered a lifelong love of German films, particularly those of the Ufa school), made himself apprentice in Boston to one hero, Conrad Aiken, and traveled to Norway to meet and pay homage to another of his literary inspirations, Nordahl Grieg.

In 1934 he married the actress Jan Gabrial, who became the model for Yvonne in *Under the Volcano.* Their marriage was tempestuous from the first, hindered by Lowry's prodigious drinking, which landed him in Bellevue Hospital's Psychiatric Wing in 1935 (providing the source material for his novella *Lunar Caustic*). The following year, the peripatetic Lowrys settled in Cuernavaca, where Lowry soon began writing his masterpiece (initially as a short story). *Under the Volcano* would take ten years to revise as he added layer upon layer of mythological reference, mystical symbolism, and literary allusion. Set on the Day of the Dead, November 2, 1938, the novel charts the final twelve hours in the life of a British ex-consul in the Mexican town of Quauhnahuac (a fictionalized Cuernavaca). Though most frequently localized through the mind of the Consul, the book uses other characters as narrators and its first chapter is set exactly one year in the future, after the Second World War has started. In conventional terms little happens, as the Consul embarks on a drinking spree, while his wife, who has temporarily returned to him, and his brother, who has been fighting in **Spain,** try to keep him from harm, whether self-inflicted or at the hands of the corrupt Mexican police. The book's fascination lies in its exemplary use of modernist devices: symbolism, expressionist imagery, **interior monologue,** mythological allusion, defamiliarization, time-shifting, fast-cutting, and intensely resonant, rhythmical, poetic prose. Like Joyce's *Ulysses* it is a book about everything: politics, history, Western literature, religion, psychology, and human relationships. The single best way to approach the novel is undoubtedly through Lowry's long letter (reprinted in the 1985 Penguin edition) to his British publisher, Jonathan Cape, detailing and defending the book's dense construction and intricate organization.

In 1937, Lowry's first wife finally left him as he completed the first of four drafts of *Under the Volcano.* In 1940 he married Margerie Bonner and the two of them lived most of the next 15 years in a shack in Dollarton, British Columbia. These were the most productive years of Lowry's life, when he finished *Under the Volcano* (in December 1944) and worked on his novels *Dark as the Grave Wherein My Friend Is Laid* and *October Ferry to Gabriola,* together with the short-story cycle *Hear Us O Lord from Heaven Thy Dwelling Place* and many other projects, including an exegesis and filmscript of *Tender is the Night.*

None of these works was published in Lowry's lifetime. *Lunar Caustic* appeared in 1958, while Lowry's other major work, the volume of short stories *Hear Us O Lord* was released in 1961 (his *Selected Poems* were published the following year). This collection contains some of his best writing in its experimental, arguably postmodernist, fictions such as "Through the Panama" and idyllic meditations like "The Forest Path to the Spring." Unusually for Lowry, the stories focus on couples genuinely in love, acts of kindness or charity, and intimations of a benign divinity.

Two unfinished novels followed: *Dark as the Grave Wherein My Friend Is Laid* (1968) and *October Ferry to Gabriola* (1970). These later books continue the themes of Lowry's earlier work: eviction, failure in social responsibility, debilitating introspection, supernatural forces, guilt over plagiarism, paranoia relating to authority, and a progressive loss of self-control. The earlier book is largely based on his own experience, as is nearly all of Lowry's work to some degree, and concerns a novelist's nightmarish return trip to Mexico (which the Lowrys made in January 1947). The central character is a novelist, Lowry's primary alter-ego Sigbjörn Wilderness, who has had a book about Mexico rejected and sets off in search of a good friend who appeared in his novel and was his guardian angel but who is now discovered to be dead. Lowry once called it an "under *Under the Volcano*" and the narrative's chief interest lies in its tangential relation to the earlier novel. *October Ferry to Gabriola* was never meant to follow the pattern of familiar novels, but it is very unclear how it might have appeared had Lowry ever finished it. The key incidents and preoccupations are clearly lifted from Lowry's life: the guilt over the suicide of a school friend; the burning down of the house belonging to the central couple, Ethan and Jacqueline Llewelyn; the occult figure or white wizard, McCandless; the fixation with eviction, guilt, and drunkenness. The published novel, edited by Lowry's wife, with only flashes of prose which indicate that it is by the same writer as *Under the Volcano,* is still underdeveloped.

Lowry, who never felt his work was finished even when published, considered all his writing to be connected and to be organic. In both these senses he referred to his writings as "The Voyage That Never Ends," a series of seven projected parts, including all the major fiction he had worked on. This was as an extension to his first plan to fashion a modern Divine Comedy from *Under the Volcano* (hell), *Lunar Caustic* (purgatory) and an unpublished novel called "In Ballast to the White Sea" (paradise). *Under the Volcano* remains Lowry's only exceptional novel, though several of the short stories are also excellent, and when he died in Sussex, a probable suicide, he was once more struggling against depression, alcohol dependency, and crippling self-doubt.

Peter Childs

Selected Bibliography
Bareham, Tony. *Malcolm Lowry.* London: Macmillan, 1989.
Day, Douglas. *Malcolm Lowry.* Oxford: Oxford UP, 1973.

M

MacDiarmid, Hugh (Christopher Murray Grieve) (1892–1978)

Some of the defining aspects of Hugh MacDiarmid's career and achievement seem recognizably, even typically modernist. His struggle towards maturity in a cultural backwater, his drive to find forms and idioms adequate to a Freudian sense of the material basis of consciousness, his insistence alike on the primacy and opacity of language, his contempt for the comfortable certainties of the bourgeois, his commitment to "difficulty," his High Cultural distaste for the middle ground of human experience and his attraction to totalitarian ideologies (albeit of the Left rather than the Right) partake of a familiar pattern. Yet in other respects MacDiarmid's case is unusual, even idiosyncratic. He conducted his career not from London or Paris but from the little seaside town of Montrose, Angus, where he worked as a journalist, and subsequently from the remote Shetland island of Whalsay. He committed his most energetic work to the old Teutonic language of the Scottish Lowlands rather than the emerging imperial *lingua franca* of **Conrad, Joyce,** and **Pound.** He had almost no access to an international readership—much of his poetry was published by small Scottish publishers, frequently with print runs of hundreds rather than thousands—and he was denied the kind of informed critical reception which sustained the careers of his English, Irish, and American contemporaries.

The central ambiguities of MacDiarmid's art are bound up with questions of language. The mere fact of his employment of Scots in the poetry of the earlier part of his maturity foregrounds linguistic issues, while the more memorable and sustained stretches of the Anglophone verse of the increasingly problematic later career pursue what he called "A Vision of World Language." MacDiarmid's Scots usage is undeniably conservative in its harking back to the work of the late medieval *makars,* its subservience to romantic ideas of national reawakening and racial *ur-motives,* and in the resolutely rural and even peasant origins of many of its most vivid idioms. It is emphatically modern, however, in its valorization of the local and the particular, its distrust of abstraction (a distrust which links it to the widely disparate literary practices of Hopkins, **Yeats** and Joyce, for example) and above all in its repeated demonstration of the *a priori* nature of language and, where the act of poetic creation is concerned, the secondariness of thought, imagination and inspiration to verbal impulse. The question which provides the title of a poem by W. S. Graham, a leading Scottish poet of a later generation, underlies many of the characteristic procedures of MacDiarmid's verse: *What is the Language Using Us For?*

The rebarbative character of MacDiarmid's Scots has been exaggerated; indeed, the energetic beginner is less likely to be baffled by the Lowland idioms themselves than by the poetry they facilitate. Vehement, self-dramatizing, obsessed with the need for a mutation in consciousness, and yet constantly undercutting its swank with tenderness and its apocalyptic hankerings with a comic earthiness, the bulk of this writing does not begin to accord with the ironizing imperatives of twentieth-century English and American verse. It looks less odd, however, in the company of German expressionist and Russian futurist poetry. MacDiarmid had a wide if not always deep knowledge of contemporary European writing and he was keen to confound British (or as he would have termed it, "English") insularity by replicating in the "technique and ideation" of his own writing some of the most far-reaching and self-consciously progressive developments in European literature.

MacDiarmid's "ideation" links him to English language modernism, too, however, especially in its late romantic manifestations. He shares with **Wallace Stevens,** the contemporary he most admired, a concern with epistemological processes and with poetry's capacity to create meaning in the wake of the collapse of traditional values and interpretations. His dedication to "the extension of human consciousness" (a pseudo-Marxist phrase to which he defaulted from the 1920s to the last year of his life) involved commitment not only to revolutionary politics but to what Stevens and the romantics called Imagination. In the earlier part of his career, in particular, he sought to revalidate a faith in the cultural centrality of poetry which may be thought of as pre- rather than post-Victorian. As in the case of Yeats, he could be a romantic in the modern age partly because he looked on his own small, historically beleaguered country as a field of unexplored possibility, a reservoir of immeasureable potential. Yet he is unique among the English language

modernists in the intensity (and perhaps the crudeness) of his belief in the possibility of an imminent transformation in general consciousness; at various stages of his career and with varying degrees of contradiction he looked to nationalism, communism, Social Credit, and technological advance to facilitate the "upwelling of the incalculable" for which he longed.

The ingenious lyrics of *Sangschaw* (1925) and *Penny Wheep* (1926) were to some degree a by-product of the furious program of cultural agitation the poet launched on his return to **Scotland** after serving with the Royal Army Medical Corps in the Great War (see **The War**), in a Herculean or perhaps Quixotic effort to transform the cultural condition of Scotland. "His anonymous and pseudonymous habits of authorship and journalism render any attempt to estimate [his] literary size . . . quite out of the question yet," observed Grieve of A. R. Orage in the *Dunfermline Press* in 1922, and he might well have been commenting on himself. In the 1920s, along with the copy he turned out for his day job as a reporter for *The Montrose Review,* he published millions of words unsigned, under his Grieve patronymic, and under such aliases as A. K. Laidlaw, James Maclaren, Gilliechriosd Mac a'Ghreidhir, J. G. Outterstone Buglass, Isobel Guthrie (mistress of a notably masculine style), and, eventually, Hugh MacDiarmid. Articles, essays, causeries, reviews, announcements and fugitive pieces of all sorts appeared in school magazines, national and provincial papers, educational and literary journals and also in the short-lived but influential periodicals he edited from his council house in Montrose (*The Scottish Chapbook,* 1922–23; *The Scottish Nation,* 1923; *The Northern Review,* 1924). The polyphonic command with which this teeming prose discharges the tasks of reportage, fulmination, reminiscence, cultural theorizing, literary appreciation and disappreciation, protest, and showing off offers a counter-part for the baffling heterogeneity of the poetry as a whole. Despite the committed and even vituperative nature of much of the material, the overall impression is of a kind of neutrality, the diversity of attitude and flexibility of register suggesting a sensibility as excited by the nature as by the content of utterance. MacDiarmid was fond of citing Yeats's proposition that "words alone are certain good," and his prose no less than his verse can be said to spring out of its own self-delight.

It was perhaps this faith in the intrinsic interest of words, along with a perverse fascination with the possibility of creating a fully contemporary poetry in Scots—a possibility he had derided at length in his cultural propaganda—which sent the poet to the Scots lexicon in 1922. In August of that year, in the Montrose Public Library, there occurred the first and most dramatic of the conversions which characterize the development of Grieve/MacDiarmid's career. It is appropriate to the romantic dimension of his poetry that key moments in its creation should have involved surrender to an impulse destructive of an established literary "self," and the hasty invention of a new persona capable of encompassing the energies which had overwhelmed the old one. Playfully at first but soon in total and astonished earnest, the poet began tessellating words and phrases from Scots dictionaries. The result was the stream of "cosmic" lyrics collected in *Sangschaw* and *Penny Wheep,* and the supersession of C. M. Grieve, scourge of the Scots revivalists, by the *makar* Hugh MacDiarmid.

The lyrics are notable for the extreme economy with which they evoke the grandeur and desolation of interstellar space, and for their tough-minded faith in the human as the sole source of meaning. With an iconography drawn variously from contemporary physics, folk superstition, and traditional Christian theology, they mea-sure the earthly against the celestial to intimate a sort of skeptical, unsentimental preference for the local, the domestic, the demotic over the universal, the affected, the aristocratic. MacDiarmid's early verse is "actualist" as opposed to idealist; its radically anti-Platonic bias places it at the furthest possible remove from the poetry of W. B. Yeats. The lyrics are close to the poems of Wallace Stevens, however, at least in their sense of the withdrawal of the deity from the cosmos and their anxiety to find significance in the earthly (though a handful of more or less conventionally Christian poems in *Sangschaw* and *Penny Wheep* illustrate how difficult it is to generalize about MacDiarmid's metaphysics). Technically they range from the experimental to the traditional. The metrical structures as well as the perspectives of some of them (notably "The Watergaw," "The Sauchs in the Reuch Heuch Hauch," and "The Eemis Stane") are determined in large degree by the inherent energies of the particular words, phrases, and proverbs MacDiarmid sets about accommodating in poetic form. Linguistic predetermination contributes to the workings even of poems which can at first sight appear deeply conventional. "Crowdieknowe," for example, owes its existence to the poet's creatively mistaken reading of the name of Middlebie Kirkyard as "Crowded Knoll" (the churchyard is adjacent to Crowdie-knowe—i.e., "Porridge Knoll"—Farm). The phrase "croodit clay" in line seven offers the key to the genesis of the text. It is worth noting also that the speaker's rejection of the "trashy, bleezin' " angels of the Resurrection in favor of the glowering denizens of Crowdieknowe is at once continuous with an ancient Scottish tradition of the comic macabre and consistent with MacDiarmid's distinctively materialist cast of mind.

Perhaps the most brilliant expressions of that materialism are to be found in "Ex Vermibus" and "Scunner." Rejoicing in the rhotic phonology of Scots, the first of these pieces inverts the medieval Chain of Being to identify the wriggling worms eaten by the fledgling as the the source of the birdsong which lights up the heavens. "Scunner" investigates and ultimately celebrates sexual disgust in a dramatized recognition of the bodily origins of consciousness. The swift density of the poem's argument may owe something to MacDiarmid's association with Herbert Grierson, who pioneered the revival of interest in John Donne, and who was Professor of Rhetoric in Edinburgh University when his anthology *Metaphysical Lyrics and Poems* came out in 1921, occasioning **T. S. Eliot**'s celebrated review in the *Times Literary Supplement.*

There is no doubting the modernist character of the lyrics' linguistic eclecticism and experimentalism. Yet a crucial factor in the poet's response to the lexicon in 1922 was his return to the language he had heard at the knee of his barely literate mother in Langholm in the 1890s. For MacDiarmid did not so much "discover a voice" as unlock a whole affective idiom, a mode of being as well as a means of expression, when he laid himself open to the dictionary. This is borne out by the emotional range and subtlety of the lyrics and by the successful approach of the first of them, "The Watergaw," to a complex of unresolved feelings regarding the death of his father in 1911. MacDiarmid did not write in Langholm Scots—like other surviving dialects too far gone in decay to support serious composition—but it was his intimate language in a way that English, identified by his class all over the borders with privilege, hypocrisy, and an over-refinement of feeling, could never be; it equipped him to respond with an almost neurological urgency to the locutions he found in the dictionary, and to bring them semantically and rhythmically alive by coaxing them into relationships with words and speech patterns familiar from childhood.

The private and the public come together in *Sangschaw's* release of linguistic energies associated with suppressed tendencies in MacDiarmid's own personality and with political possibilities foregone by his nation. But if the lyrics are nationalist in stance, their nationalism is wholly implicit. The germ of much else that would be noisily assertive in MacDiarmid's subsequent career can be found in these delicate, compressed, supremely tactful little poems. The interstellar vistas of "Au Clair de la Lune" and "The Eemis Stane," for instance, prefigure the Anglophone Shetland poetry's awe before the silence of inanimate nature, but the lyrics counter their intimations of estrangement with a near feminine sympathy rooted in the homeliness of Scots.

The second of MacDiarmid's "conversions" involved surrender to a figurative, rather than a linguistic dynamic. *Penny Wheep's* "To One Who Urges More Ambitious Flights" had trumpeted his preference for "wee bit sangs" over long poems. In the spring and summer of 1926, however, what had begun as a middle-length demonstration of the flexibility of "Synthetic Scots" was transformed into the 2,684 line *A Drunk Man Looks at the Thistle* by the poet's "letting himself go" (his own phrase) in pursuit of the furthest implications of his whisky-thistle-moon symbolism. Suggestive of little more than a droll concern with the emblems of Scottish nationality, the title promises nothing of the agonized, vituperative and intermittently ecstatic reverie on the dualities of experience MacDiarmid's sequence actually delivers. Yet the title has its prosaic accuracy, for it is his sometimes befuddled but never less than ardent contemplation of the disfigured, ridiculous, sod-rooted but doggedly aspirant weed towering between himself and the moon which elicits the protagonist's fantastically resourceful eloquence. While the self-possessed artistry of the "early lyrics" contrasts sharply with the reach and sprawl of the prose of the same period, already by 1926 the slap of the journalist was beginning to combine with the dash of the poet: *A Drunk Man* may have serious claims to be considered the most linguistically and philosophically resourceful text of British poetic modernism, but it is often dismayingly ragged in style. In his subsequent career stylistic continence ceased to be a priority for MacDiarmid in any of his media, though he could still occasionally achieve it in all of them.

Contraries are the key to both the philosophical and aesthetic progression of *A Drunk Man*. The effort to sustain them, however, proved exhausting. In the first two "Hymns to Lenin," "Water of Life," "Tarras," "Depth and the Chthonian Image," "Whuchulls," and other poems written in England between May 1931 and August 1932, the tension between demotic instinctualism and hermetic alienation slackens, as the ground is prepared for a rejection of the former—and of the Scots which epitomizes it—in the *Stony Limits* volume of 1934. The named poems were intended, along with a few dozen other extant pieces, for an ambitious work of intellectual self-portraiture to be called *The Muckle Toon,* which in turn was to constitute the first volume of a five-volume epic, *Clann Albann.* Even in its scattered, incomplete form, the *Muckle Toon* material elaborates an impressive **myth** of personal and political evolution, creating a figurative *nexus* linking Langholm's rivers to the water of life, Noah's flood to the Bolshevik tide, the Scottish borders to the frontiers of consciousness, and the poet's boyhood to the infancy of mankind. Criticism has scarcely begun to acknowledge the symbolic richness of the poetry of this phase of MacDiarmid's development.

Clann Albann was knocked off course by a third "conversion" in May 1933, when the poet, nearly broken after a series of personal calamities, moved to the treeless (and publess) island of Whalsay in the Shetlands and, over a period of about six weeks, wrote most of the contents of *Stony Limits* along with a mass of other material. These early Shetland poems are unique in MacDiarmid's development alike in their quantity and variety. Elaborate propaganda odes on Social Credit jostle with satirical squibs, exercises in scientific speculation, alternately cheerful and despondent lyrics about the state of Scotland, and various more or less unclassifiable bits and pieces. Easily the most ambitious and innovative writing from this unprecedented, terminal burst of creativity is to be found among two constellations of poems, one in Scots, the other in English, in which MacDiarmid explores some of the contrasting implications of what is registered as an overwhelmingly urgent new theme—isolation. A letter to William Soutar (July 5, 1933, National Library of Scotland) reveals that he was quite consciously striving for variety in his Shetland output. The multifariousness of creation is one of the obsessions of the Scots cluster and it seems reasonable to assume that the diversity of *Stony Limits* and of the other material produced at this time—in mood, technique, and perhaps even in quality—was intended to reflect something of that multifariousness.

Luridly sexual, mesmerized by the randomness of the physical processes underlying consciousness, threatened by the swarming fecundity of biological life, and aghast before a God whose manifestations can neither be ignored nor endured, the Scots poems dramatize a surrender to unreason. The English ones, conversely, celebrate the determination of the intellect— or of *an* intellect—to preserve its authority by curbing the instincts and affections: asexual, "austerely intoxicated" ("On a Raised Beach") by the geological realm's indifference to consciousness and exhilarated by its sub-biological bareness, they insist with a paradoxically Calvinistic vehemence that the God in whom the Western mind has traditionally tried to ground its being has withdrawn forever beyond reach. "Ex-Parte Statement on the Project of Cancer," "Shetland Lyrics," "Ode to All Rebels," "Harry Semen," and "Tam o' the Wilds and the Many-Faced Mystery" are the major writings of the Scots cluster; "In Memoriam: Liam Mac 'Ille Iosa," "Vestigia Nulla Retrosum" (an extraordinary, linguistically synthetic elegy on **Rainer Maria Rilke**), "Stony Limits," and "On a Raised Beach" of the English.

The fact that MacDiarmid's career both as a Scots and as a lyric poet effectively comes to an end in these poems contributes to the impression that the Shetland work plays out an inner conflict of great and destructive intensity, a conflict which so implicated the sources of his creativity that it was to be resolved only at the expense of his gift. The split in *Stony Limits* between Scots and English, feeling and reason, release and control may indeed reflect something of the psychological dynamic which issued in the author's collapse and hospitalization in 1935. The extent to which these are *experimental* poems must not be lost sight of, however. "Tam o' the Wilds and the Many-Faced Mystery," for instance, is, at three hundred and fifty lines, an extended exercise in demotic Scots—arguably MacDiarmid's only genuinely vernacular Scots poem— and also an essay in taxonomical precision. Its low-key idiom offers one solution to the problem of reconciling the demands of lyrical and scientific utterance, the fleering rhetoric of "Ex-Parte Statement on the Project of Cancer" another. Similarly the almost deranged personalism of many of the poems in the Scots group and the puritanical impersonality of the English ones can be seen—partly at least—in exploratory terms, as projections to their natural extremes of the necessary propensities of those languages in the hands of a writer brought up in a Scots-speaking environ-

ment. Just as Grieve's speculative deployment of the resources of the Scots lexicon in 1922 had released him into an affective mode from which he had been cut off by his education, so his adventuring among the contents of *Chambers Twentieth Century English Dictionary* in 1933 admitted him to a world beyond emotion. The linguistic psychology of the *borderer,* that is to say, rather than the personal psychology of C. M. Grieve *in extremis,* can be invoked to account for the schism between the two major clusters of writing of the *Stony Limits* phase of the career.

"On a Raised Beach" reflects Shetland's bleak simplicities of light, stone, and water, objectifying in terms of the islands' rugged foreshores MacDiarmid's sense of having arrived at the bedrock of existence, and essaying a "scientific" style, bare of ornament but packed with arcane geological and archeological terminology, in which the utter neutrality of the material universe can be acknowledged and grimly celebrated. The implacable topography of Shetland is accommodated in an implacable English rhetoric; the elemental pose forecloses on the wayward and the irrational, disabling the fluidity of mood and insight for which the Scots lyricism had been remarkable. "On a Raised Beach" can be seen as a late variation on the romantic crisis poem, a text which rewrites Wordworth's great "Ode" in terms of the certainty of extinction rather than the hope of immortality, and which goes much further than Stevens's almost immediately contemporary "The Idea of Order at Key West" in adapting Arnold's "Dover Beach" to the relentlessly materialistic perspectives of twentieth-century thought.

Most of the work on the composition of the enormous open-ended poem from which *In Memoriam James Joyce* (1955) and *The Kind of Poetry I Want* (1943; 1961) were quarried appears to have taken place in Shetland from 1936 to 1939. (The poet returned to the Scottish mainland in

1941.) This writing has been the subject of sympathetic attention in recent years as criticism has come to question the status of the division between poetry and prose and to cherish reminders (in which late MacDiarmid is, to say the very least, unusually rich) of the dependence of new texts on old. *A Drunk Man* had mourned the lost opportunities inherent in every act of choice; that problem disappears in the late work, where particulars are admitted in such equivalent and polyglot profusion that the organizing, registering, evaluating "I" is obliterated. *Song of Myself,* the *Cantos* and the *Maximus Poems* are sometimes invoked as parallels for MacDiarmid's "poetry of fact," but where **Whitman,** Pound, and Olson were concerned to develop a new poetic acoustic, the Scottish poet seems for pages at a time eager to dispense with aural considerations altogether. And yet this *"divertissement philologique,"* this "schlabone, bordatini, and prolonged scordatura," has its moments of surprise and discovery, typically achieved by a juxtaposition of phrases or whole passages in disparate specialized or technical vocabularies. With its destabilization of subjectivity, its insistent intertextuality, its general if not total eschewal of the metrical and stylistic charms traditionally seen as essential to the art, this "poetry of fact" may be said to mark the end of MacDiarmid's career as a modernist and to represent the first stirrings of British literary **postmodernism.**

Patrick Crotty

Selected Bibliography

A multi-volume authoritative edition of the poems is in preparation under the general editorship of Alan Riach. *Complete Poems* (3d ed. 2 vols. Ed. Michael Grieve and W. R. Aitken. Manchester: Carcanet, 1993) presents most of the texts, if in a chronologically problematic manner. The main prose texts have appeared in ten volumes in Carcanet's *MacDiarmid 2000* series (ongoing from 1992). Kenneth Buthlay's *Hugh MacDiarmid* (Edinburgh: Oliver and Boyd, 1964; rev. Edinburgh: Scottish Academic Press, 1982) and **Edwin Morgan**'s *Hugh MacDiarmid* (Harlow, Essex: Longman, for the British Council, 1976) are the most dependable general studies. Alan Riach's *Hugh MacDiarmid's Epic Poetry* offers a clear-sighted, sympathetic account of the later work. Riach's book includes an extensive bibliography of primary and secondary sources.

MacGreevy, Thomas (1893–1967)

Thomas MacGreevy's attenuated poetic achievement—he published only a single volume of poetry, *Poems,* in 1934—may be seen as indicative of the wider predicament of experimental poetics in the **Ireland** of his time. MacGreevy's cultural contribution is eclectic—as Director of the National Gallery of Ireland, and as author of the first monographs on **T. S. Eliot** and Jack B. Yeats—and yet the eccentric trajectory of the publication of MacGreevy's poems, from the leading avant-garde little magazines of Europe and America like *transition* and *The Dial,* to homegrown Irish and Church-sponsored journals such as *The Capuchin Annual* and *The Father Mathew Record* begs the question, what kind of modernism is MacGreevy's? Described by **Wallace Stevens** as a man "at the heart of his time," MacGreevy's poetry yet inhabits a liminal space between the poles of abstraction and representation, between the plural experiments of European and Euro-American modernisms and a monolithic Irish nationalism.

Samuel Beckett's assessment of MacGreevy, in his essay "Recent Irish Poetry" (1934), casts the world of Irish poetics as a Manichean universe, where the "antiquarians" or followers of **W. B. Yeats** who pursue revivalist themes, are characterized by their "flight from self-awareness" and are countered by the self-aware countertradition represented by emergent poets such as **Denis Devlin** and **Brian Coffey,** whose work forms "the nucleus of a living poetic in Ireland." Like Coffey and Devlin, MacGreevy is aware of a "rupture in the lines of communication." Yet MacGreevy occupies an "independent" position between Beckett's opposing camps of poets, and as an independent he has not proved easily assimilable to that literary criticism which has adopted Beckett's bipartite construction of Irish poetry in the period.

MacGreevy can indeed be seen as an independent and even paradoxical figure: he had served in the British Army in **World War I** but vehemently opposed British imperialism in Ireland; he was a catholic nationalist but at the same time was a cosmopolite; as a modernist antithetical but drawn to the European imagination of **Joyce,** MacGreevy was regarded with suspicion in De Valera's Ireland, where cultural as well as economic protectionism proved hostile to continental modernist innovation.

MacGreevy's poetics are foregrounded in his monograph *Richard Aldington. An Englishman* (1931), this despite the different, and in MacGreevy's eyes opposed, nationalities of the two writers (the book would more accurately be titled "Richard Aldington. An Englishman, by Thomas MacGreevy. An Irishman"). Here, MacGreevy gives a twist to the critical given about modernism and the First World War—the barrage of war fragmenting old forms—and gives a crucial context for his own modernism. For MacGreevy, being part of the collective experience of the war also serves to differentiate him, not only from the slightly younger Coffey (b. 1905) and Devlin (b. 1908), but also from other modernist poets of his own generation—Eliot, Joyce, **Pound**—who did not fight in the war, and who could thus steal a march on the traumatized combatants.

In his "war" poems, "Nocturne," and "De Civitate Hominum," MacGreevy draws attention to the gap, the no man's land, between metaphor and reality. "De Civitate Hominum" can be read as a meditation on the insufficiency of both representational and experimental language, as a self-reflexive meditation on the poet's art in time of war—MacGreevy questions the adequacy of his own returning painterly metaphor, counterpointing it with direct speech and with grim referents in the warscape to which he is witness. At the end of the poem, the world is left in limbo, waiting for God's "reply."

Much of MacGreevy's poetry is written on the interface of art and religion. If Joyce can be seen as the artificer of catholicism, for MacGreevy **epiphany** is finally religious epiphany, even if assisted by or described in analogs derived from the arts, as in his poem "Gloria de Carlos V." Although MacGreevy signed his name to the manifesto "Poetry is Vertical," which declares "the autonomy of the poetic vision," art for him is not autonomous or self-sufficient. Where Beckett tries to secularize MacGreevy—describing his poetry in terms of "prayer that is a spasm of *awareness*"—MacGreevy himself often desecularizes other writers, especially Joyce. MacGreevy was one of the twelve contributors to the defense of Joyce's *Work in Progress,* but as his essay for *Our Examination Round His Factification For Incamination of Work in Progress,* titled "The catholic element in *Work in Progress*" shows, if MacGreevy was disciple to Joyce's master, he was a disciple with a firm agenda of his own. MacGreevy is a poet who has frequently been *written over* by or absorbed into the wider ambits of the better-known writers with whom he associated, but he could also write others over in his own image, and according to his own lights.

The differences between the catholic and the protestant mind—this is a principal way in which MacGreevy theorized his contemporaries. MacGreevy's poem "For an Irish Book, 1929" again acts to "catholicize" Joyce, as the pun in the poem's typescript title, "Re Joyce," makes apparent. Here, Joyce's *Work in Progress* is described in the metaphor of a rich fig tree manured by "a dung of English literature" and a "slag of catholic theology."

In his unpublished memoir of Joyce, MacGreevy argues that "*Work in Progress* was to be a restatement of the *Purgatorio* in terms of the modern world" and in his 1950 essay states that Joyce's text is "an evocation in transitional language of an appropriately purgatorial state of being." So, Joyce becomes the writer of limbo for MacGreevy, himself a writer *in* limbo, a writer who occupies Beckett's "position intermediate" between the opposing camps of modern Irish poetics.

MacGreevy moves from an aesthetic derived from that rupture in the lines of communication caused by World War I and the resultant crisis in representation—as he says in *Aldington,* "The war bust it all up"—to the posited integration of a pan-European catholic vision, a kind of European Union, its common currency a common catholic heritage. MacGreevy's essay on Joyce in *Our Exagmination,* which is itself part of a collaborative defense of Joyce, also posits a wider collaboration, relating as it does Joyce's *Work in Progress* to the catholic vision of Dante and Vico.

Yet his European-catholic vision did not guarantee creativity for MacGreevy himself, who published very little poetry between 1934 and a brief late recovery of voice in the early 1960s. The Breton context of his last poems, "Breton Oracles" and "Moments Musicaux," suggest that MacGreevy's earlier and ambitious project of a Euro-catholic modernism has been replaced by a more localized vision of Celtic union. MacGreevy's flawed but fascinating achievement is as a modernist who could at times become thoroughly entangled in the nets of nationality, language, and religion.

Lee Jenkins

Selected Bibliography

Coughlan, Patricia and Alex Davis, eds. *Modernism and Ireland: The Poetry of the 1930s.* Cork: Cork UP, 1995.

Davis, Alex. *A Broken Line: Denis Devlin and Irish Poetic Modernism.* Dublin: University College Dublin Press, 2000.

Goodby, John and Maurice Scully, eds. "Colonies of Belief." Special issue of *Angel Exhaust* 17 (Spring 1999).

Jenkins, Lee. *Wallace Stevens: Rage for Order.* Brighton: Sussex Academic Press, 1999.

Schreibman, Susan, ed. *The Collected Poems of Thomas MacGreevy. An Annotated Edition.* Dublin and Washington D.C.: Anna Livia Press and The Catholic University of America Press, 1991.

Mahler, Gustav (1860–1911)

After attending the premiere of Mahler's Eighth Symphony in September 1910, **Thomas Mann** wrote to the composer describing him as the man who "represents the art of our time in its profoundest and most sacred form." The occasion had been an unexpectedly unalloyed triumph for a musician whose conducting career had aroused controversy because of his exacting perfectionism and whose compositions had generally been greeted with reserve, bafflement, and even downright hostility. The triumph was short-lived, however. Within a year, at the age of only fifty, Mahler was dead.

The developing appreciation of Mahler's genius has been one of the phenomena of twentieth-century music. For the first half of the century, his symphonies were castigated as the overblown last-gasp outpouring of the late romantic tradition, only performed by his former pupil conductors like Bruno Walter and Otto Klemperer out of misguided loyalty. "We just don't want Mahler here," the English musicologist Donald Mitchell was told, as if Mahler were some undesirable immigrant. Since the 1960s, however, the Mahler symphonies have blazed their way into the central repertoire of every world-class orchestra, seeming to catch, in a musical language that moves with compelling drama between beauty and brutality, nostalgia and irony, something close to the spirit of the troubled twentieth century. "How blessed to be a tailor!" Mahler once cried in despair after the public rejection of his Fifth Symphony. "Oh that I might give the Symphony's first performance fifty years from now!" The prophecy was uncannily accurate: his time did come and it took half a century. Such landmarks as Jascha Horenstein's unforgettable Royal Albert Hall performance of the Eighth Symphony in 1959 and Leonard Bernstein's impassioned cycle of the complete symphonies in the 1960s marked the beginning of a Mahler resurgence that, forty years on, shows no sign of abating.

"A symphony is like the world," Mahler told Sibelius, "it must embrace everything." He stretched the boundaries of the symphonic structure to its limit and beyond, recognizing that what he had to say would require a new form. The scope is vast: his symphonies can sometimes have five or even six movements rather than the conventional four and, in contrast to the thirty minute duration of the classical symphonies of Haydn and Mozart, can last well over an hour. The orchestral and vocal forces required are formidable: like Beethoven, Mahler uses choral forces to augment his symphonic argument—not just in one symphony but in three. For works that are a kind of spiritual autobiography, this could seem monstrously egotistical, but the feelings the music evokes—exultation, childlike wonder, love of Nature, crises of faith, and doubt—are at the heart of the twentieth-century experience and the reason that, in Aaron Copland's words, his music is so "extraordinarily touching."

In one way, Mahler is a nineteenth-century throwback, steeped in the romantic tradition, a musical Dostoyevsky who took musical romanticism to new extremes of nobility and neurosis. In another sense,

though, he is a modern, the tensions of whose musical personality express the restless instability of the new age and anticipate the sardonic irony and tortured **expressionism** of Schoenberg and Berg, and later of Shostakovich and Britten. Like many modernists (it goes with the territory), Mahler felt himself an outsider—"thrice homeless," as he put it, "as a native of Bohemia in Austria, as an Austrian among Germans, and as a Jew throughout the world." (On this latter point, he controversially converted to catholicism to ease his way into the conductorship of the Viennese State Opera, but this has always been taken as more to do with career than conviction: it did not prevent his music from being banned by the Nazis.) Also like other modernists, he was ahead of his time, expressing ideas and feelings in a personal language that was not immediately understood. What was the clue to a musical style that seemed a strange, self-conscious mixture of high and low forms, that juxtaposed the simple with the sublime, the deliberately vulgar with the transcendentally beautiful? He was famously psychoanalyzed by **Freud,** who diagnosed a mother fixation that not only affected the way Mahler walked (a curious jerking movement that seemed subconsciously to empathize with his mother's lameness) but affected his compositional technique: these extreme stylistic contrasts were traceable, Freud surmised, to a childhood memory when the distressed young Mahler rushed out into the street during one of the many terrifying parental rows and, in his mood of emotional turmoil, suddenly heard the jolly strains of an organ-grinder. The moods in his music are mercurial. Like another Bohemian Jew and great artist, **Franz Kafka,** Mahler's work is full of spooky satire and the sense not of certainty and control but of inquiry and quest.

Many writers were to be inspired by Mahler. **Arthur Schnitzler** said that "of all the creative musicians of our time, none has given me more than Gustav Mahler." There have, for example, been poems written in his honor, notably Stefan Zweig's "The Conductor"; and a book by David Holbrook that draws elaborate parallels and contrasts between the artistic personalities of Mahler and Sylvia Plath. But if there is one major masterpiece of literary modernism that is inconceivable without the inspiration and example of Mahler, it is Thomas Mann's novella, *Death in Venice* (1913), his story of an artist's infatuation with an adolescent boy in a Venice that is being slowly contaminated by plague. The story came to Mann, he said, when he heard the news of Mahler's death. Although the specific incident which forms the basis of *Death in Venice* has no authenticated equivalent in Mahler's own life and although the hero Aschenbach in the novella is a writer not a composer, Mann uses some biographical details of Mahler (his age and appearance, the tragic death of one of his children, even some of his artistic ideals) to clinch the connection with Aschenbach.

In Mann's conception, the chief thing shared by Aschenbach and Mahler, as well as their incomparable artistry, is that both are the last of their line. Both stand, Janus-faced, between two worlds. Aschenbach stands between the world of the conscious and the subconscious, order and chaos, classical control and Dionysian excess, even life and death: at any moment, the former could slip into the latter. Mahler too stands between two worlds (the "dual one" as Leonard Bernstein called him), his music oscillating between the highest expression of late nineteenth-century romanticism and early twentieth-century modernism. Although it is always difficult to attach a precise meaning to a musical composition, authorities such as Alban Berg and Bruno Walter are agreed that Mahler's last completed work, the Ninth Symphony, is essentially a sonic presentation of death—and, like *Death in Venice*, not simply about the death of one particular artist but about the death of a whole culture and society. Mann's story has begun on "a spring afternoon in that year of grace 19—, when Europe sat upon the anxious seat beneath a menace that hung over its head for months." Similarly, the "volcanic eruptions" (Walter's phrase) that puncture Mahler's Ninth and occasionally threaten to tear it apart from within, seem to justify Leonard Bernstein's description of its prophetic significance: "ours is the century of death and Mahler its musical prophet." Much of the power of these great works comes from the sense of the artists having, as it were, caught something in the air—a sense of a Europe about to tear itself apart in a genocidal global war, and possibly of a century that will dice tantalizingly with total annihilation. Certainly modernism's fascination with the abyss and the apocalypse achieves two of its finest, most disturbing expressions in these works of Mann and Mahler.

Neil Sinyard

Selected Bibliography

Bernstein, Leonard. *The Unanswered Question.* Cambridge, Massachusetts and London: Harvard UP, 1976.

Cooke, Deryck. *Gustav Mahler: an introduction to his music.* London: Faber, 1980.

Floros, Constantin. *Gustav Mahler: the symphonies.* Aldershot: Scolar Press, 1993.

Mitchell, Donald, ed. *Gustav Mahler: Memories and Letters: Alma Mahler,* London: John Murray, 1968.

Walter, Bruno. *Gustav Mahler.* London: Severn House Publishers, 1975.

Mann, Heinrich (1871–1950)

The elder brother of **Thomas Mann,** Heinrich Mann was born in Lübeck. His early novels vary in style, from the satirical *Im Schlaraffenland* (1900, *In the Land of Cockaigne*) to the decadence of *Die Göttinen* (1903, *The Goddesses*). *Die Kleine Stadt* (1909, *The Little Town*) anticipates his transition to the role of social and political chronicler of his time in its dissection of the social relationships among the inhabitants of an Italian town.

His *Kaiserreich* trilogy forms a powerful analysis of authoritarian structures in **Germany,** including *Der Untertan* (1918, *The Man of Straw*). It introduces modern psychological insights, such as Diederich Hessling's sado-masochism in decorating the headmaster's cane and satisfaction when being punished, up to the climax of facing the Kaiser's "power which transcends us and whose hoofs we kiss." Yet the novel as a whole is a realist *bildungsroman* of Hessling's unscrupulous rise to power as an industrialist.

In the 1920s Mann found his realist style inadequate for depicting the upheaval of modern Europe; he observed that "It seems difficult to me to write a social novel and a real novel today. Too many facts obscure one's vision." Apart from his political astuteness as a spokesman for democracy, his most significant achievement in this period was the *Henri Quatre-Romane* (1935, 1938), a historical study which obliquely incorporates commentary on German politics.

Carl Krockel

Selected Bibliography

Mann's works are available in Aufbau Verlag, Berlin, and Penguin, London.

Hamilton, Nigel. *The Brothers Mann: The Lives of Heinrich and Thomas Mann, 1871–1950 and 1875–1955.* London: Secker & Warburg, 1978.

Linn, Rolf N. *Heinrich Mann.* New York: Twayne Publishers, 1967.

Roberts, David. *Artistic Consciousness and Political Consciousness: The Novels of Heinrich Mann, 1900–1938.* Bern: Lang, 1971.

Mann, Thomas (1875–1955)

Regarded as the most important novelist in **Germany** in the twentieth century, Thomas Mann confronts its crucial historical and cultural issues. His literary career began after his father's death in 1891, which freed him from an impending professional career. He moved to Munich, where he remained until his self-exile to the United States in 1933. His novels chronicle the ideological crises of Germany throughout the first half of the twentieth century.

In his first novel, *Buddenbrooks* (1901), Mann charts the "decline," as he puts it in his subtitle, of a mercantile family in the nineteenth century, from the robust Johannes Buddenbrook, to his great-grandson, little Hanno. As a naturalist novel, it explores Germany's transition from a burgher patrician society to a modern bourgeois one, but it is also indebted to the late romantic tradition of Schopenhauer, Wagner, and Nietzsche. Thomas, Hanno's father, appears to fail in business because of his overly conservative approach to trade, but Mann also implies that he is spiritually renouncing his will. In Hanno's character Mann has also borrowed from Nietzsche's ideas on the artist's cultural strength flourishing in a declining civilization. Mann orders the novel's episodes of decadence through the Wagnerian leitmotif, which develops a symbolic meaning independently of references to history.

Between *Buddenbrooks* and his next major novel Mann wrote *Tonio Kröger* (1903), *Tristan* (1903), and *Der Tod in Venedig* (1912, *Death in Venice*), all of which explore the bourgeois artist's alienation from the activities of his class, and from the beauty which he can only objectify and celebrate, not possess. In *Der Tod in Venedig* an aging author, Gustav von Aschenbach, muses on the significance of his obsession with a beautiful young boy called Tadzio. His attempt to glorify his obsession as an artistically ideal, platonic love is strained by the Venetian atmosphere of disease and decay, and by his own failing health. Ultimately, however, his aspiration to immortalize the object of his desire in the face of death takes on a heroic and tragic power.

From 1912 Mann worked on *Der Zauberberg* (1924, *The Magic Mountain*), which incorporates the arguments between himself and his brother Heinrich, and within Germany at large during the First World War. The character Hans Castorp weighs up the dialogue between the Italian liberal Settembrini and the anti-humanist Naphta, who argues for political authoritarianism and cultural irrationalism. Their arguments gradually lose significance after Hans' **epiphany** in the chapter "Schnee" ("Snow"), during which a vision of Greek youths is countered by a baby being thrown into a cauldron by witches. Hans concludes that, regardless of the truth of Settembrini's and Naphta's positions, death must be acknowledged and life pursued. In the novel Mann was attempting to master his late romantic heritage, in the wake of the First World War, whose militarism he had associated with it; he wished to establish a perspective which could contribute to the stability of the Weimar Republic, whose foundations were as uncertain as his own conclusions to the novel.

During the thirties Mann composed his four-part novel *Joseph und seine Brüder* (1933–1942, *Joseph and His Brothers*), a reinterpretation of part of Genesis, which narrates the transition from tribal society to an individualistic society, and the religious development from **myth** to God. Jacob lives exclusively in a mythological world view; his son Joseph is exiled from his clan to the "modern" society of Egypt where he learns to control his fate through rationally responding to the historical events into which he has been thrown. Mann's perception of the biblical family reflects his own dualistic notion of Germany, of its primeval mythological culture and modern rational civilization which he had depicted in *Der Zauberberg*.

After his self-exile from Germany, Mann publicly dissociated himself from Nazism in 1936. He moved to the United States in 1938 and became a citizen in 1944. He returned to Switzerland after the war. During this period Mann wrote essays and delivered speeches on German cultural figures such as Schopenhauer, Nietzsche, Wagner, and Goethe, the latter to whom he devoted his novel *Lotte in Weimar*. Mann's last great novel *Doktor Faustus* (1947), the modernist answer to Goethe's *Faust,* was a culmination of Mann's inquiries in his essays and novels. The composer Adrian Leverkühn represents the anti-humanism of German culture; his life is depicted by the thorough, if unimaginative, schoolmaster Serenus Zeitblom. Leverkühn is fascinated by Wagner's **music,** and like Nietzsche, suffers from syphilis which eventually causes madness. He devotes his last work to reversing the affirmation "it must be" of Beethoven's String Quartet in C-sharp Minor, with his own nihilistic "it must not be." Leverkühn represents the trend of German culture which Mann believes fed into Nazism, and partly represents his younger self, which in turn is depicted by the conservative Zeitblom, who echoes Mann's older self.

Carl Krockel

Selected Bibliography

Mann's works are available in S. Fischer Verlag, Frankfurt am Main, and Penguin and Minerva, London.

Bloom, Harold, ed. *Modern Critical Views: Thomas Mann.* New York: Chelsea House, 1986.

Hayman, Ronald. *Thomas Mann.* London: Bloomsbury, 1995.

Heller, Erich. *Thomas Mann: The Ironic German.* New York: Paul P. Appel, 1973.

Reed, T. J. *Thomas Mann: The Uses of Tradition.* Oxford: Clarendon Press, 1996.

Mansfield, Katherine (1888–1923)

Short-story writer, born Kathleen Mansfield Beauchamp in Wellington, New Zealand.

Her father was a prominent banker; the family of five children was brought up in comfortable wealth and inculcated with respectability by their socially punctilious mother. Mansfield attended schools in Wellington and in London, England, where she eventually stayed, seeing no future for her own ambitions as a writer in a New Zealand which she regarded as stuffy and backward. Escape from the confines of her family was also a priority. While pregnant by another, she married George Bowden in 1909 but left him immediately, fleeing to Bavaria where she suffered a miscarriage. Her family deeply disapproved of Mansfield's sexual indiscretions and recklessness.

She began publishing stories in the avant-garde magazine, *The New Age,* in 1910 and brought out her first volume of stories, *In A German Pension,* in the following year. At about the same time she met the critic and writer John Middleton Murry with whom she began a long and complex liaison, culminating in marriage in 1918. She also developed important relationships with other innovative writers of the period, including **Virginia Woolf** and **D. H. Lawrence.** Her health was always precarious and for the last few years of her short life she spent long periods abroad, mainly in the south of **France,** in an attempt to ameliorate her worsening tuberculosis. *In a German Pension* was followed by the publication of *Bliss and Other Stories* in 1920 and *The Garden Party and Other Stories* in 1922. Despite her illness, the last three years of her life produced some of her most technically assured and sensitively executed work. She died in 1923 at the age of only thirty-four. A number of other collections of stories, her letters, and her journal, edited by Murry, appeared posthumously.

In 1915 Mansfield began work on a strongly autobiographical novel, entitled *The Aloe,* which was later revised and published (by Virginia and Leonard Woolf) as *Prelude* in 1918. In October, 1915, Mansfield's only brother, Leslie, was killed in the First World War and the enormous sense of loss and despair felt by the writer finds its way into the elegiac quality of *Prelude,* which is, among other things, an evocation of their childhood in New Zealand. The work signals a return to Mansfield's creative sources, focusing on a New Zealand family much like the Beauchamps and the complex interrelationships among its members.

Works such as *Prelude, At the Bay, The Daughters of the Late Colonel* and *The Garden Party* (1922) display Mansfield's skills as a modernist writer experimenting with different stylistic methods of depicting consciousness. Many of the stories deal with the complexities and tensions of family relationships; most focus on central female characters and explore the contradictions and frustrations of women's lives in a new, apparently more liberated age. Mansfield's earlier stories are more overtly feminist, while the later work retreats from open political statement in favor of a more stylistically subtle approach to similar material. While patriarchal figures are routinely and scathingly satirized, matriarchal figures are by no means idealized. Indeed, maternity is viewed in highly ambivalent terms. At the same time, the tensions and pleasures of female sexuality are foregrounded and explored in the work of Mansfield in a way which is unparalleled in that of any of her contemporaries, except perhaps **Lawrence** and **Jean Rhys.**

Mansfield is a key figure in the development of modernist prose. She was experimenting with **interior monologue** and with new ways of exploring characters' consciousness at a time when neither **Joyce** nor **Woolf** had yet published their major works. Her lyrical style is also marked by economy and an extreme sensitivity to the nuances of relationships between parents and children, wives and husbands, siblings and, perhaps most remarkably, among children. In her mature work, the narrative moves effortlessly and fluidly among the psyches of the various characters, presenting not only their differing points of view but also a kaleidoscopic narrative "world." The extreme precision and control of Mansfield's technique is remarkable. Her non-linear handling of time in the stories also deserves mention as a significant modernist innovation, for the narrative moves backwards and forwards temporally in harmony with the thoughts and memories of the central characters. Mansfield's work is also marked by a democratic spirit, in that the delicate instrument of her prose is as likely to explore the psyches of uneducated maids and very young children as it is those of pompous businessmen and domineering matriarchs.

Mansfield's reputation suffered after her death partly because of the way in which her widowed husband attempted to create a hagiographic account of her life and work. In more recent times, however, and particularly with the new feminist reappraisal of modernism, Mansfield has been accorded a central place in the movement. Her influence on the genre that she radically redefined, namely the short story, is in itself sufficient to ensure that she is recognized as one of the major literary innovators of the first half of the twentieth century.

Katie Gramich

Selected Bibliography

Alpers, Anthony. *The Life of Katherine Mansfield.* London: Jonathan Cape, 1980.

Kaplan, Sydney Janet. *Katherine Mansfield and the Origins of Modernist Fiction.* Cornell UP, 1991.

Michel, Paulette and Michel Dupuis, eds. *Fine Instrument: Essays on Katherine Mansfield.* Sydney: Dangaroo, 1989.

Middleton Murry, John, ed. *The Journal of Katherine Mansfield.* Definitive edition. London: Constable, 1954.

O'Sullivan, Vincent and Margaret Scott, eds. *The Collected Letters of Katherine Mansfield* vols. 1–4. Oxford: Oxford UP: 1984–1996.

Parkin-Gounelas, Ruth. *Fictions of the Female Self: Charlotte Bronte, Olive Schreiner, Katherine Mansfield.* London: Macmillan, 1991.

Pilditch, Jan. *The Critical Response to Katherine Mansfield.* London: Greenwood, 1996.

Robinson, Roger, ed. *Katherine Mansfield: In From The Margin.* Louisiana State UP, 1994.

Tomalin, Claire. *Katherine Mansfield: A Secret Life.* Harmondsworth: Penguin, 1988.

Marinetti, Filippo Tommaso (1876–1944)

Poet, novelist, dramatist, and writer of manifestos, Marinetti is best known as the founder and leader of the Italian futurist movement. He was born in Alexandria, Egypt, of wealthy Italian parents, and educated at a French Jesuit school. He studied at the Sorbonne in Paris, and at Pavia and the University of Genoa. He graduated in law from the latter university with a thesis on parliamentary government in 1899, but would never practice, choosing instead to take up his literary interests.

Marinetti began by writing free-verse poetry in French under the influence of the symbolists, with some success. On moving to Milan in 1905 he dedicated himself to a literary career, founding the international journal *Poesia,* which promoted experimental European writing. His pre-futurist works include the poetry collection *La Conquête des Étoiles* (1902, *The Conquest of the Stars*) and the satirical tragic play *Le Roi Bombance* (1905, *King Carousing*). He also wrote a novel, *Mafarka le Futuriste* (1910, *Mafarka the Futurist*), for which he was tried and convicted on grounds of publishing pornographic material. Marinetti issued the founding manifesto of **futurism** in the Parisian newspaper *Le Figaro* on February 20, 1909. He traveled widely—and most notably to **Russia** and England—promoting the central tenets of the movement. His great skills as a writer of manifestos and as a declaimer of futurist ideas earned him the title of "the caffeine of Europe." The innovations he proposed in theater and poetry, and his promotion of the new art of **film,** were arguably a greater legacy than any of his individual works.

After the First World War Marinetti forged links with Mussolini, but, though he hoped that it would represent a political enactment of futurist aesthetic ideals, Marinetti swiftly became disillusioned with fascism. He left the fascist party in 1920, but became reconciled to Mussolini at a later date, becoming a member of the Italian Academy in 1929. His connections with fascism have meant that his work, and that of the futurists more widely, received little critical attention until recent years. His importance as the founder and promoter of Italian futurism (the first international avant-garde movement) is now universally recognized.

Marinetti's writings have been published in **Italy** by Mondadori in a volume entitled *Teoria e invenzione Futurista,* edited by Luciano De Maria (1968). This volume also contains dates and places of publication for the various writings.

Andrew Harrison

Selected Bibliography

Blum, Cinzia Sartini. *The Other Modernism: F. T. Marinetti's Futurist Fiction of Power.* London: University of California Press, 1996.

Marinetti, F. T. *Selected Writings.* Trans. R. W. Flint and A. A. Coppotelli. London: Secker and Warburg, 1972.

The Masses

During the nineteenth century the world's population increased dramatically. In Europe, despite large-scale migrations in periods of economic depression, the population still increased by about 75 percent between 1830 and 1914. In industrialized countries this growth was most apparent in urban areas, and it was largely from these areas that pressure for democratization made itself felt during the later part of the nineteenth century. Extensions to voting rights were achieved fairly rapidly, and even though by the time of the First World War universal adult suffrage was still a long way off in most countries, the Western world "was plainly moving towards systems of politics based on an increasingly wide electorate dominated by the common people" (Hobsbawm, 87). Democratization and the spread of literacy went hand in hand, and again it was in the towns of protestant Europe that educational developments were most marked. Britain's Education Acts of 1870 and 1891 helped to bring literacy rates in England and **Wales** into line with many other parts of northern Europe, to the point that when lists of soldiers dead and missing in the First World War were posted, almost everyone was able to read them.

The newly-expanded reading public found plentiful and affordable reading matter in the popular newspapers and magazines that emerged in the later nineteenth century. In Britain the Victorian periodical market had already expanded rapidly by the 1890s, with numerous monthly and weekly titles, some of them illustrated, and most of them offering a miscellany of informative articles, serialized fiction and perhaps some poetry. Much cheaper weekly magazines began appearing from the 1880s, their composition aptly represented in the title of the popular *Tit-Bits* (1881–1984), made up of snippets of news, entertaining information, letters, quizzes, and fiction, including, in the early years, stories by **Conrad** and Bennett. A similar mixture appeared in other penny weeklies such as *Answers,* and magazines aimed at specific readerships such as *Home Chat* for housewives. The latter titles were owned by Alfred Harmsworth (later Lord Northcliffe) whose media empire soon included two mass-circulation newspapers, the *Daily Mail* and *Daily Mir-*

ror. The *Daily Mail,* founded in 1896, was the first newspaper in the world to reach sales of over a million, its circulation figures and advertising revenue spiralling upwards together. The *Mail's* mixture of news, features, and competitions owed something to the sensationalist "yellow journalism" of the American press, and the formula was so effective in Britain that when the Canadian-born Lord Beaverbrook applied it to the *Daily Express* at the end of the First World War the circulation of the *Express,* too, rapidly climbed towards the million mark.

The pressures of the new journalism are often seen as one of the key factors leading to the stratification of literature during the late nineteenth and early twentieth centuries. H. G. Wells, who popularized the American terms "high-brow" and "low-brow" to describe major divisions in British culture at this period, went so far as to claim that the historical gulf between "readers" and "the non-reading mass" was dissolved into mere "differences in educational level" by the early twentieth century (Carey, 6). The fact that new novels were often sold at several different price levels, according to the binding, suggests that there was certainly some concurrence of taste across widely differing income levels. But high culture's scorn for the indisputably popular range of literature characterized as low-brow was a pale thing compared with its fear of mass culture in the shape of tabloid newspapers and, later, Hollywood-dominated **cinema.**

This fear of commercialized and Americanized mass culture has sometimes expressed itself as regret for the erosion of some more genuine working-class culture that is supposed to have existed in the past. However, such views now appear to be part of a general tradition of cultural pessimism that existed in Britain from the time of Matthew Arnold (at least), and rose to a crescendo in the writings of **T. S. Eliot** and F. R. Leavis, with echoes still heard in the

work of Raymond Williams. Since then, **postmodernism** has effectively renegotiated the relationship between high art and mass culture.

Lynda Prescott

Selected Bibliography

Carey, John. *The Intellectuals and the Masses.* London: Faber & Faber, 1992.
Hobsbawm, Eric. *The Age of Empire, 1875–1914.* London: Abacus, 1994 [1987].
Huyssen, Andreas. *After the Great Divide: Modernism, Mass Culture and Postmodernism.* Bloomington: Indiana UP, 1986.

Metaphor and Metonymy

In his article "Modernism, Anti-Modernism and Postmodernism," and at length in his book *The Modes of Modern Writing: Metaphor, Metonymy, and the Typology of Modern Literature,* David Lodge advances his theory that modern literature swings between two dominant poles of imagery. He takes his lead from the Russian formalist Roman Jakobson's belief, through his study of aphasiacs, that metaphor and metonymy correspond to the selection—or substitution—and combination axes of language (Lodge also argues that some modern writers, such as **Beckett** and **Stein,** aspire "to the condition of aphasia"). Metaphor works by substituting one word or image for another in terms of resemblance. By contrast, metonymy works by contiguity and association, and replaces an object with its attribute ("the deep" instead of "the sea"). Metonymy is often considered also to include *synecdoche,* which replaces the part for the whole ("sails" for "ships") or the whole for the part ("England played football last night").

For Jakobson, the distinction between metaphor and metonymy can explain numerous cultural differences: films are metonymic, drama metaphoric; prose and the epic are metonymic, poetry and the lyric are metaphoric; **Freud**'s interpretation of dreams refers to metonymic aspects to dreamwork (condensation and displacement) and metaphoric aspects (identification and symbolism). For Lodge, the value in the theory lies in its explanatory power when considering literary shifts over time. Romanticism was characterized by metaphor in its representation of the individual and his or her imaginative life in reaction to classicism's metonymic imagery used to describe the social. **Realism** was again metonymic, while modernism swung the pendulum in the opposite direction once more. In the twentieth century the process appears accelerated. The socially aware political writers of the thirties favored metonymy while the late modernists (Durrell, Beckett, **Lowry**) staged a recovery for metaphor before the down-to-earth postwar authors (Larkin, Amis, Wain, and so on) again championed a realist style. Finally, postmodernism witnesses a resurgence of metaphoric writing, in its use of the fantasy mode, in its radical dismantling of character and plot, and particularly in its experiments with language.

The most important distinction to arrest our attention here is that between the primarily metonymic genre of realism and the metaphoric modes of modernism. This distinction can be demonstrated at the level of titles: *David Copperfield, Middlemarch, Mary Barton,* and *Northanger Abbey* are indicative of realist writers' metonymic penchant for the representative and the social, using a part to represent the whole (the individual or town representing the populace or the country); by contrast, *Heart of Darkness, To the Lighthouse, The Waste Land,* and *The Rainbow* are metaphoric titles not to be taken at face value in terms of reference or resonance. It is easy to find exceptions, but the general point is defensible. It is also noticeable in modernism that when an apparently metonymic title is used, its symbolic significance is particularly high, as with *A Passage to India, The Good Soldier,* or *The Golden Bowl.* Similarly, the distinction can

be argued at the level of character description: Dickens's writing is predominantly metonymic (Micawber's cane or Mrs. Sparsit's Roman nose) while **Virginia Woolf**'s rendition of character is typically metaphoric (Clarissa Dalloway is associated with a bird, with the color green, and so on—nothing she owns is ever solidly connected with her).

Lodge would be the first to urge limitations to and reservations over the theory, but the first qualifying comment must be that the terms are relative. It is often not easy to decide whether a description or a title is metaphoric or metonymic (e.g. *Bleak House* on the one hand or "The Garden Party" on the other). Post-structuralist theory additionally reminds us that all language is symbolic in that it is not the thing to which it refers; and also many metaphors evolved from metonyms. However, while prose generally veers towards metonymic representation more than poetry does, the greater a literary style, such as that of the modernists, tends towards dense, poetical imagery, the more it is likely to gravitate towards the metaphoric.

Peter Childs

Selected Bibliography

Lodge, David. *The Modes of Modern Writing: Metaphor, Metonymy, and the Typology of Modern Literature.* London: Arnold, 1977.
———. "Modernism, Anti-modernism, and Postmodernism." In his *Working with Structuralism.* London: Routledge, 1981. 1–16.

Moore, Marianne (1887–1972)

"Miss Moore's poems form part of the small body of durable poetry written in our time," wrote **T. S. Eliot** in 1935 (Tomlinson 65). Though Moore has yet to secure her properly central position in the modernist canon, her contemporaries frequently cited her work to exemplify the procedures and styles that may serve to define what modernism was: according to **Pound,** Moore wrote "logopoeia": "a dance of the intelligence among words" (Tomlinson 46); for **William Carlos Williams,** Moore's scrupulous powers of observation made for a poetic that valued "edge-to-edge contact" (Tomlinson 57); for **Wallace Stevens,** her "skilful expression of the genuine" made her exemplary for his new conception of the romantic (Stevens 778). One of the exotic creatures that appears in Moore's menagerie is the chameleon, and it is perhaps because her poetry was so well adapted to its literary environment that its own contours have tended, until recently, to fade from view. Since the centenary of her birth there has been a marked resurgence of interest in Moore's poetry, and she now figures not only, in Williams's phrase, as "a rafter holding up the superstructure of our uncompleted building" (*Autobiography* 146), but as an extraordinarily innovative and accomplished poet in her own right.

Marianne Craig Moore was born in 1887 in Kirkwood, Missouri. Her father had suffered a nervous breakdown, and Moore was raised by her mother and maternal grandfather. She graduated from Bryn Mawr College in 1909, and having moved to Greenwich Village in 1918, lived in New York for the rest of her life. Perhaps the most striking aspect of her biography was Moore's close relationship with her mother: the two women lived together until Mary Warner Moore's death in 1947. In the late 1910s Moore's poems began to appear in the transatlantic little magazines (*The Egoist, Poetry, Others*) alongside those of **H. D.** and the imagists, Pound, Eliot, Stevens, and Williams. As editor of *The Dial* from 1925 to 1929 she was increasingly influential in shaping the modernist canon, and as an established poet was a significant forebear to younger writers, of whom Elizabeth Bishop is the most prominent.

Moore's second book *Observations* (1924) won the *Dial* award and perhaps

best exemplifies her characteristic topics, idioms, and forms. The poems, famously imagined as "imaginary gardens with real toads in them" ("Poetry") situate zoological and verbal specimens, curios and artifacts in carefully cultivated formal environments. Moore's syntax and vocabularies juxtapose the "plain American which cats and dogs can read" ("England") with a fastidious idiom and tone capable of Jamesian archness: "one has one's preferences in the matter of bad furniture" ("People's Surroundings"). This crossbreeding of styles is also manifested in Moore's "hybrid method of composition." The quotation marks that season her poetry and the Notes that accompany them signal an intertextual method notable for its eclecticism: "Marriage," for example, conjoins a line from *The Tempest* with an article from a woman's magazine; Edmund Burke consorts with a fashion advertisement. Though, as in "Marriage," Moore often wrote in free verse, she also experimented with and perfected an unusual syllabic form in which carefully counted syllables make a visual grid-pattern that cuts across units of grammar and sense (in, for example, "The Fish" and "The Steeple-Jack"). America's entry into World War II signaled a marked turn in Moore's poetry: in the 1940s her reticence, indirections, and polyphonic methods gave way to the more direct lyric voice of "In Distrust of Merits" and "What Are Years." The death of Moore's mother in 1947 may account in part for her turning to the lengthy and absorbing project of translating La Fontaine's *Fables*.

Moore's 1952 *Collected Poems* earned her the Bollingen and National Book Awards, and a Pulitzer Prize. In her later years she became something of a national mascot, a figure all too easily caricatured: the eccentric maidenly lady in the tricorn hat, a frequenter of zoos with a predilection for amphibians and elephants as well as the minor prophets and baseball. Most recently, Moore made a guest appearance in Ted Hughes's *Birthday Letters* (London: Faber, 1989): he remembers her as "daintiest curio relic of Americana" (75). Clearly a more robust and substantial figure than these caricatures allow, Marianne Moore finds a genuine place in the canon of American modernist poetry.

"Omissions are not accidents" warns the epigraph to the *Complete Poems,* the only readily available volume of Moore's poetry. This collection includes only 125 of the 192 poems Moore published in her career, many of them significantly revised (Margaret Holley's appended bibliography gives a chronological account of Moore's *oeuvre*). The *Selected Letters* are the best means of accessing Moore's life and contacts, while the *Collected Prose* evidences her voracious reading habits. Numerous unpublished notebooks, conversation diaries, and poetry drafts are housed in the Moore Collection at the Rosenbach Museum and Library, Philadelphia.

Fiona M. Green

Selected Bibliography

Costello, Bonnie. *Marianne Moore: Imaginary Possessions.* Cambridge, Mass.: Harvard UP, 1981.

Holley, Margaret. *The Poetry of Marianne Moore: A Study in Voice and Value.* Cambridge: Cambridge UP, 1987.

Leavell, Linda. *Marianne Moore and the Visual Arts: Prismatic Color.* Baton Rouge: Louisiana State UP, 1995.

Molesworth, Charles. *Marianne Moore: A Literary Life.* New York: Atheneum, 1990.

Moore, Marianne. *The Complete Poems.* 1967. Rev. ed. New York: Viking, 1981; London: Faber, 1984.

———. *The Complete Prose of Marianne Moore.* Ed. Patricia C. Willis. New York: Viking, 1986. London: Faber, 1987.

———. *The Selected Letters of Marianne Moore.* Ed. Bonnie Costello, Celeste Goodridge and Cristanne Miller. London: Faber, 1998.

Schulze, Robin G. *The Web of Friendship: Marianne Moore and Wallace Stevens.* Ann Arbor: University of Michigan Press, 1998.

Slatin, John M. *The Savage's Romance: The Poetry of Marianne Moore.* Philadelphia: Pennsylvania State UP, 1986.

Stevens, Wallace. "A Poet That Matters." 1935. *Wallace Stevens: Collected Poetry and Prose.* New York: Library of America, 1997.

Tomlinson, Charles, ed. *Marianne Moore: A Collection of Critical Essays.* Englewood Cliffs, NJ: Prentice Hall, 1969.

Williams, William Carlos. *The Autobiography of William Carlos Williams.* New York: Random House, 1948 (rptd. New York: New Directions, 1967).

Willis, Patricia C., ed. *Marianne Moore: Woman and Poet.* Orono: National Poetry Foundation, University of Maine, 1990.

Morante, Elsa (1918–1985)

Novelist, short story writer, poet, translator and essayist, Morante, who was married to Alberto Moravia, is, together with **Natalia Ginzburg,** considered the most important modern Italian female writer.

Morante's constant theme is the conflict between illusion and reality. The illusions of youth and the personal values of the individual conflict with the disillusionment of adolescence and the pressures exerted by corrupt and indifferent social institutions. Morante's work may be said to move from a more detached "literary" position to a position of political engagement. Her first novel, *Menzogna e sortilegio* (1948, *House of Liars*), the family saga of a southern Italian bourgeois family and the destructive consequences of its flight from historical reality into fantasy, is said to be influenced in its lyricism by **Katherine Mansfield,** whose work Morante translated. Her later novels were *L'Isola di Arturo* (1957, *Arthur's Island*), *La Storia* (1974, *History: A Novel*), and *Aracoeli* (1982, *Aracoeli*). *L'Isola di Arturo* concerns an adolescent boy's rude awakening from dreams of his dead mother and his over-idealized father. *La Storia* is set in the time of the Second World War and traces the tragically short life of Useppe, a child who is born to a woman after her rape by a German soldier. The novel achieved great popularity in **Italy** but commentators often criticize its overtly ideological focus and the resultant simplicity of its style. *Aracoeli,* her bleakest novel, reveals the mental and social alienation of its narrator, a middle-aged homosexual man.

Morante also produced a children's adventure book, *Le bellissime avventure di Cateri dalla trecciolina* (1942, *The Marvellous Adventures of Kathy Pigtail,* later revised and expanded), two collections of short stories, entitled *Il gioco segreto* (1941, *The Secret Game*) and *Lo scialle andaluso* (1963, *The Andalusian Shawl*), and two anthologies of poetry which reflect the Marxist-Christian tone of her later works: *Alibi* (1958, *Alibi*) and *Il mondo salvato dai ragazzini* (1968, *The World Saved by Children*).

Morante's works are published in Italy by Einaudi. English translations are available through various publishing houses in England and America. A bibliography of her works is contained in Caesar (1984).

Andrew Harrison

Selected Bibliography

Caesar, Michael. "Elsa Morante." In *Writers and Society in Contemporary Italy.* Edited by Michael Caesar and Peter Hainsworth. Warwickshire: Berg Publishers, 1984, 211–233.

Kalay, Grace Zlobnicki. *The Theme of Childhood in Elsa Morante.* University of Miss.: Romance Monographs, 1996.

Wood, Sharon. "The Bewitched Mirror: Imagination and Narration in Elsa Morante." *Modern Language Review* 86.2 (1991): 310–21.

Morgan, Edwin (b. 1920)

Morgan's push, as poet, teacher, translator, playwright, librettist, man of letters and *honnête homme,* is energized and sustained by a deep understanding of the liberating forces unleashed by the shock of the new. He has always kept moving in the revitalized spirit of bringing the contemporary and near together with ancient or far-distant cultures: a major characteristic of modernism. Yet, if his work sometimes finds expression in linguistic pyrotechnics, it also embraces the post-nuclear sense of radical egalitarianism. Born in 1920, his first flourishing came with *The Second Life* (1968), with its influences evident: Black Mountain and "Beat" poets, South American "concrete" poets, European and especially Eastern European poets. Morgan had already translated Montale (1959) and various Russian poets (1961). However, this distinctively "postmodern" debut had strong roots in the modern movement itself.

Combining humanitarian sympathy with exceptional virtuosity nourishes and excites Morgan's prodigious variety, in translations of Mayakovsky (into Scots— the impact is stronger in the rebarbative, "defamiliarized" tongue), in "Glasgow Sonnets" (urban renewal is welcomed as the human cost is counted), in *Instamatic Poems* (newspaper clippings transformed to verse emblems, news that stays news indeed), in poems that give voices to the voiceless (the songs of the apple, sensual and sexy; the hyena, hideously sinister; the Loch Ness Monster, hilariously glum), in science fiction poems (astronauts cut their umbilical line to earth and float out "in an impeccable trajectory," keeping "a voyaging generation voyaging" in "space that needs time and time that needs life").

In *Sonnets from Scotland* (1984) interstellar travellers see the nation in new ways, imagining its neglected aspects, dream or reality, terrible or wonderful. For Morgan, technology is the cure for its own corruption. With courage born of the deepest faith in the radical hopes engendered in the modern movement, Morgan affirms, in "The World" (*The New Divan,* 1977) his belief that "what's been made" does not clutter the spirit. But this healthy appetite also thrives on hostility to convention and opposition to establishment. "The Fifth Gospel" begins with a call to overthrow the law and the prophets and calls, not the sinners, "but the virtuous and law-abiding, to repentance." Blakean energy is released with comic zest in the improprieties of "Some Rules for Dwarf-Throwing" and is emphatic in "The World of Things Undone" (*Virtual and Other Realities,* 1997).

Morgan's solidarity with creativity and his quick humor counter modernism's lingering tones of confession, alienation, and victimization. He acknowledges both the saturnine (*Demon,* 1999, begins, "My job is to rattle the bars") and the transcendent (a 2000/2001 project controversially dramatizes the life of Christ). In *Hold Hands Among the Atoms* (1991), he warns the iconoclasts of post-Soviet Europe how carefully the past must be preserved, how witless mass destruction is, but he insists, repeating the line three times emphatically, "The futurists, united, shall never be defeated."

His lifelong commitment to Glasgow has always complemented his eagerness to travel, curiosity unabated, wisdom lightly carried. In 1985 he blew the award money for a poetry translation prize on a day-trip to the North Pole to meet Santa Claus. After years of cloaked homosexuality, his public declaration of being gay coincided with the year when Glasgow was proclaimed "European City of Culture" (1990) and, internationally, eyes were turned upon it. This courageously asserted the continuity between personal and civic identities, enacting much more an optimism reminiscent of Leopold Bloom than the inner-city anxieties of **Eliot**'s wastelanders or **Kafka**'s accused or incarcerated. Morgan was made the city's first poet laureate in October 1999.

When asked to choose an object that might exemplify the twentieth century for an exhibition at the new Museum of Scotland in 1998, he opted for a Soviet-made 45 r.p.m. record of Yuri Gagarin's voice from lunar orbit: a symbol of old "new technology" but a potent reminder of how the human voice speaks across languages, motives, desires, aspirations, and distances, from the far reaches of space.

Alan Riach

Selected Bibliography

Carrell, Christopher, ed. *Seven Poets.* Glasgow: Third Eye Centre, 1981.

Crawford, Robert and Hamish Whyte, eds. *About Edwin Morgan.* Edinburgh: Edinburgh UP, 1990.

Morgan, Edwin, ed. *Collins Albatross Book of Longer Poems.* London & Glasgow: Collins, 1963. (Includes texts of Yeats, Stevens, Williams, Pound, Eliot, and others, from Chaucer to Ginsberg, all annotated by Morgan.)

———. *Essays.* Cheadle Hulme: Carcanet New Press, 1974.

———. *Provenance and Problematics of "Sublime and Alarming Images" in Poetry.* London: The British Academy, 1977.

———. *The South Sea Brotherhood: A poem from the Fort Baskerville Golf Club.* Glasgow: At the celebrated Partick Press, 1989.

———. *Collected Poems.* Manchester: Carcanet, 1990.

———. *Collected Translations.* Manchester: Carcanet, 1996.

Whyte, Hamish, ed. *Nothing Not Giving Messages: reflections on work and life.* Edinburgh: Polygon, 1990.

Music

The early years of the twentieth century were characterized by radical developments in the field of music that both reflected and influenced parallel movements across the arts. Modernism in music broke with traditional modes of writing dependent on a diatonic system (rooted in the use of major and minor keys), and challenged the narrative-like structural coherence which had reached a dramatic culmination in the large-scale post-romantic works of Richard Wagner, Richard Strauss, and **Gustav Mahler.** Claude Debussy referred to Wagner's music as a "beautiful sunset which was mistaken for a dawn," and composers of this period recognized the need for innovation and experiment rather than mere imitation of revered precursors. As in literature, this innovation took many different forms and cannot be discussed exhaustively. It is possible, however, to give some indication of the principal developments through identifying key figures and discussing seminal works.

Paul Griffiths locates the earliest clear manifestations of modernism in the flute melody from the opening of Debussy's *Prélude à L'après-midi d'un faune,* written in 1892–94. This melody breaks free from tonality and conventional harmonic structures and has the feeling of a free improvisation rather than a logical development: it sounds hesitant and exploratory. Rhythmically, too, the melody is striking: the tempo fluctuates, employing irregular rhythms, adding to the spontaneous, improvised effect. It feels wayward and unconstrained rather than regulated through strict measurement of time. The orchestration is characterized by delicate color and shading, and lines are created that are suited only to a particular instrument. The work in general seems impressionistic and dream-like rather than adhering to a clearly defined narrative development.

Debussy's subsequent works continued radically to undermine pre-existing models; yet they remained accessible to audiences and did not provoke the kind of hostility generated by the works of his two contemporaries, Arnold Schoenberg and **Igor Stravinsky.** Debussy's *Jeux*—characterized by an unpredictable shifting in different directions—was performed in the same month (May 1913) as Igor Stravinsky's *The Rite of Spring* in Paris. Stravinsky's music had previously been experimental, as is indicated by his use of polytonality (different keys heard simultaneously) in *Petrushka.* Yet audiences were unprepared for the new dynamic force achieved in *The Rite of Spring.* Inspired by a dream in which solemn elders sit in a circle, watching a girl dance herself to death in ritual sacrifice, the work echoes

the preoccupation with **anthropology** and **primitivism** in the writings of numerous literary modernists. Rhythm, rather than harmony, is the binding force and driving impetus underlying the work. In the "Sacrificial Dance" in particular, Stravinsky uses unequal "cells" rather than conventional phrases, manipulated through repetition and variation within frequently changing time-signatures. Stravinsky's ballet score caused an outcry: it was immediately perceived as a barbaric and violent subversion of an entire musical tradition.

The works of Arnold Schoenberg (1874–1951) and his disciples (referred to as the Second Viennese School) were analogously subversive, and provoked extreme antagonism. Schoenberg's shift into atonality was perhaps the most startling and radical of the modernist period, as it entailed a denial of the tonal foundation of all music since the seventeenth century, on which had rested all faculty for response and comprehension. Significant composers before Schoenberg had pushed to the brink of atonality then sharply retreated, the most notable being Strauss in *Salome* and *Elektra;* Sibelius in his fourth symphony; Mahler in the "Adagio" (the only completed movement of his tenth symphony); and many works by Alexander Skryabin (1872–1915). Schoenberg, however, was the one to take the plunge.

Schoenberg first abandoned tonality in 1908 while working on settings of poems by **Stefan George**: two for the final movements of his second string quartet (1907–8) and the rest for a cycle of fifteen songs from "Das Buch der Hängenden Gärten" (1908–9). Schoenberg later wrote that he was "intoxicated by the first words in the text, without in the least caring for the further development of the poem, without even noticing it in the ecstasy of composing. . . ." Yet rather than simply being a result of somnambulistic writing, Schoenberg's use of atonality here seems to have been a response to key images of waiting and apartness in George's poem. Another contributory factor may well have been biographical: he was at that time experiencing disillusionment and depression as a result of his wife leaving him in order to live with the painter Richard Gerstl. Schoenberg was utterly committed to the idea of the artist as someone who should penetrate beneath models and stereotypes in order to portray the deepest, darkest depths of the psyche and personality. A restless, searching style would have been appropriate for voicing the disturbance inherent in his own life at that time.

The most significant underlying motive, however, was the fact that Schoenberg believed strongly in the necessity of music moving beyond the tonal barrier. He felt this was an inevitable consequence of what had gone before—even though he experienced an overwhelming sense of loss, resulting from his denial of the Austro-German tradition that he so loved and revered. He felt himself driven onward by a subconscious force: an experience he described as like having "fallen into an ocean of boiling water."

Schoenberg was followed into atonality by his first and most talented pupils—Alban Berg (1885–1935) and Anton Webern (1883–1945)—though he emphasized the importance of individual style and placed no compulsion on them to adopt his methods. Webern followed directly, also using the poetry of George in the fourteen songs of 1904–09 to lead him into atonality; while Berg's set of songs based on poems by Hebbel and Mombert followed in 1909–10. Yet the work of these two composers was utterly distinctive, rather than weakly imitative. Schoenberg's style was a profound, intense and self-searching kind of **expressionism,** while Webern was concise and lyrical, and Berg wistfully retrospective.

It is interesting that Schoenberg went through relatively barren periods after

adopting atonality; and that he, Webern and Berg found it increasingly difficult to write atonal instrumental music. A literary text seemed necessary to compensate for the loss of coherence previously provided by tonality. However, in 1921 Schoenberg announced that he had found a method for providing atonality with a kind of order: namely serialism. In serialism, the twelve notes of the chromatic scale are arranged in a fixed order, thus functioning as a framework from which melodies and harmonies can be constructed. This method provides a degree of harmonic coherence, as it ensures consistency of interval patterns. This system, which has since been criticized as both mathematical and mechanical, gave Schoenberg a compositional freedom previously lacking. Significantly, in the period 1920–23 he composed instrumental rather than vocal works, namely "Five Piano Pieces," "Serenade for Septet," and "Piano Suite." Serialism, for Schoenberg, resulted in a reversion to more traditional forms, and a shift away from tortured self-expression. In later years, he reverted to tonal as well as serialist compositions, allowing the musical idea to dictate his choice of form.

Webern experienced an analogous liberation through serialism, composing the "String Trio" in 1927 which was his first significant instrumental piece for thirteen years. Unlike Schoenberg, however, Webern never turned back to tonal methods once he had adopted serialism: if anything, he increased the rigidity of his methods. Berg found such methods laborious, and created a half-tonal serialism evident for instance in his opera *Lulu.* He attempted to amalgamate serialism and tonality, while Schoenberg used both methods but kept them stringently apart.

It is important to recognize that not all composers moved into atonality as a response to the Second Viennese School. In **Russia,** for instance, the composer Nikoloy Roslavets (1880–1944), who came close to anticipating aspects of Schoenberg's later serialism, approached atonality through the late works of Skryabin. In America, composers such as Charles Ives, Carl Ruggles, and Henry Cowell came to atonality from an entirely different point of view from that of Schoenberg—ignoring tradition rather than developing from it. Modernist music in America moved towards a futurist preoccupation with embodying aspects of the modern world through a cultivation of the "art of noise." Luigi Russolo (1885–1947) was perhaps the most persistent of the futurist composers, going to great lengths to create new machines such as his "intonarumori," in order to produce crackling sound effects. Edgard Varèse (1883–1965) profited from such techniques, although he did not feel the need to create his own instruments to achieve the desired effects. Instead he generated startling sounds through his original and highly inventive use of percussion, employing such means to reflect the uproar of the modern world through other methods than direct imitation. He followed with interest the early development of electrical instruments, and predicted the immense impact of such resources when they became sufficiently advanced.

It was largely through the work of Henry Cowell (1897–1965) that much experimental work was published in America in the early twentieth century. His New Music Edition was distinguished by its lack of dogmatic exclusivity, and encouraged an open-mindedness among his American contemporaries, such as Harry Partch (1901–74) and John Cage (1912–1992). Cowell's late discoveries arising from his own experiences as a composer were published in the book *New Musical Resources,* in 1930.

While American composers between the wars were exploring new musical resources, more tentative ideas were being developed in Europe. Conscious of tradition, yet feeling the need to rebel against post-Wagnerian late romanticism, European composers turned to popular music—particularly jazz—in order to serve modern social and political purposes. Many early jazz styles had originated in African music, which was alien to Western concepts of harmony and thus provided an alternative to the diatonic system. They were characterized by exciting new beat combinations, derived, for example, from West African "polyrhythm," in which "contrasting rhythmic patterns are superimposed to create textures of considerable complexity" (Cooke, 11). "Swung rhythm" was a trademark of jazz, as was the syncopation employed in "ragtime" (from "ragged time"): a style that particularly influenced many notable modernist classical composers. The new rhythmic impetus derived from jazz could infuse classical music with energy and vitality. In addition, elements such as the "blue note," the "dirty sound" of jazz and the use of portamento (sliding between notes) were adopted and employed successfully within modern classical music.

In Europe, from the early 1900s, many significant and highly influential figures assimilated jazz in their compositions. Debussy heard ragtime music performed by a marching band created by John Philip Sousa (1854–1932), probably in Paris in 1900, leading to his attempt to synthesize ragtime and concert music in several works. In the "Golliwog's Cakewalk" from *Children's Corner Suite* (1908), Debussy emulated the music of Scott Joplin: perhaps the most famous ragtime composer and performer. In this piece, Debussy also included a quotation from Wagner's *Tristan und Isolde,* thus employing an ironic juxtaposition for the purpose of satire. He subsequently used rag elements in *Le petit nègre* (1909), and also in the preludes "Minstrels" (1910) and "General Lavine: excentric [sic]" (1913). In 1917 Erik Satie (1866–1925) incorporated references to ragtime songs by Irving Berlin in his ballet

Parado. Stravinsky created a series of works in which he manipulated rag elements through ingenious distortion. *The Soldier's Tale* (1918) was the first work of this type, followed by the solo piano piece *Piano-Rag-Music* (in 1919) and *Ragtime for Eleven Instruments* (1919).

The jazz vogue intensified and reached its height in the twenties, with the treatment of jazz elements still varying from serious to satirical. Francis Poulenc satirized convention through adopting a vulgar form, while Darius Milhaud exploited Afro-American primitive force in *La création du monde* (1923)—referred to by Paul Griffiths as a "sleazy jazz-ballet." Maurice Ravel incorporated a blues movement in his Violin Sonata (1923–27), and adopted "swing" elements for his Piano Concerto in G (1931). Ernst Krenek showed that he could include jazz among his multiplicity of early romantic and classical styles, as shown in the opera *Jonny spielt auf* (1922–26), which achieved considerable popularity worldwide.

It is interesting that American composers were not at the forefront of those who integrated aspects of jazz into their works before 1920. One notable exception was Charles Ives in his *Piano Sonata* (written around 1909), which subjects ragtime elements to an idiosyncratic process of distortion. It was in fact in the 1920s that Americans began seriously to respond to the European jazz vogue. Aaron Copland's *Piano Concerto* of 1926 may be taken as a paradigm of American art-jazz composition, in its energy and ebullience. George Gershwin (an accomplished "stride" pianist in the 1920s) famously used jazz to great effect in his *Rhapsody in Blue* of 1924.

The appropriation of jazz by classical composers was echoed in the process by which jazz musicians and composers similarly used classical models. Joseph Lamb (1887–1962), for instance, adopted an unusual minor key for his "Ragtime Nightingale" (1915), emulating aspects of the piano music of Chopin and Liszt. Classics were also made subject to the "jazzing up" process that was later frequently dismissed as tasteless and inappropriate.

The cross-fertilization across musical traditions described above was symptomatic of the process of radical change throughout the crucial early years of the twentieth century. As in literature, the results of such experimentation were often startling and subversive, provoking antagonism rather than admiration. Yet we can now identify the most influential figures of this period as pioneers, who expanded the possibilities of pre-twentieth century music beyond all imaginable bounds through their creativity, vision, and perseverance.

Bethan Jones

Selected Bibliography
Cooke, Mervyn. *Jazz.* London: Thames and Hudson, 1998.
Griffiths, Paul. *Modern Music: A Concise History from Debussy to Boulez.* London: Thames and Hudson, 1986.
Schuller, Gunther. *Early Jazz.* New York: Oxford University Press, 1968.

Musil, Robert (1880–1942)

Musil's greatest work, *Der Mann ohne Eigenshaften* (1952, *The Man without Qualities*), to which he devoted most of his literary career, without completing, is considered to be one of the most important novels of the twentieth century. He studied mathematics, philosophy, and psychology at Berlin University, and then worked as a civil servant before concentrating on literature. He regarded his writing as a synthesis between literature and philosophy; his early works, the novel *Die Verwirrung des Zöglings Törless* (1906, *Young Törless*) and the play *Die Schwärmer* (1920, *The Enthusiasts*), concentrate on the interplay of characters' experiences and the development of their philosophical attitudes.

Der Mann ohne Eigenschaften is a vast, multivalent novel, into which Musil incorporated various streams of modern culture. It is driven by the opposing strains which are associated with the naturalist and expressionist aspects of modern German culture. The novel is arranged around Ulrich, whose personality does not develop like that of the protagonist of a *bildungsroman,* because he lacks "qualities" as a character, which makes him the ideal observer of his environment. Musil attempts to analyze contemporary history in Ulrich's extended philosophical dialogues and monologues. Also, the discussions among Vienna's upper classes in the "Parallel Campaign" on how to celebrate Emperor Franz-Joseph's seventieth jubilee in 1917, turns into a quest for the single unifying idea of the Austro-Hungarian Empire, then of modern Europe. Yet Ulrich's lack of qualities begins to signify his tragic flaw as a modernist hero, and, for Musil, his own weakness as a modernist artist, as the upheaval of historical events disrupted his attempts to complete the novel. The series of analytical dissections are gradually revealed as a facade for the characters' interests, such as the industrialist Arnheim's desire to control a group of oil fields. Against the apparent objectivity of the dialogues, Ulrich desires to let go of himself, to envisage an alternative to modern life; this vitality is also manifested in the characters' sexual desires for each other and in the psychopath Moosbrugger. In the uncompleted third part of the novel, Musil attempts to reconcile objective analysis with subjective desire in Ulrich's platonic relationship with his sister Agathe, through which he gradually develops qualities with which to respond to the world at large. Yet their relationship often threatens to spill over into incest, and to become a mode of existence which excludes the outside world.

Carl Krockel

Selected Bibliography

Musil's works are available in Rowohlt, Hamburg, and Picador, London.

Hickman, Hannah. *Robert Musil and the Culture of Vienna.* London: Croom Helm, 1984.

Luft, David S. *Robert Musil and the Crisis of European Culture 1880–1942.* Berkeley: University of California Press, 1980.

Payne, Philip. *Robert Musil's "The Man Without Qualities": A Critical Study.* Cambridge: Cambridge UP, 1988.

Myth

The last years of the nineteenth century were characterized in literature by the demise of **realism,** and a developing preoccupation with aesthetic form. The artist was increasingly envisaged as a manipulator of reality—a myth-maker—rather than as someone concerned with faithfully representing the actual. The artist frequently turned to mythic archetypes in order to articulate the present, thus transforming a work into a dual system, in which the narrative is enriched through functioning on two or more levels. The preoccupation with myth in the modernist period was widespread across all literary genres: it was prevalent (for example) in the fiction of **Joseph Conrad, James Joyce,** and **D. H. Lawrence;** and the poetry and plays of **W. B. Yeats** and **T. S. Eliot.**

The myth of psychological journeying underlies Conrad's *Heart of Darkness,* in which Marlow travels not only down the Congo to the heart of **Africa**—or the dark continent—but to the heart of all that is malign, evil, and nihilistic in the heart of man. In Joyce's *Ulysses,* the psychological journey experienced by Leopold Bloom is grafted onto a specific myth, through the appropriation of a precursive literary text: namely Homer's *Odyssey.* Literary artifice is emphasized by the correlation between Joyce's chapters and each episode of the Homeric tale: Joyce adopts the intertext as a structural framework for his novel. The mythological location, Hades, reflects the psychological hell that Joyce creates for Bloom (for example in the Circe chapter)—revealing one way in which an underlying myth can inform aspects of characterization as well as style. **Pound** referred to Joyce's novel as "a new Inferno in full sail," indicating the way in which models from the past can be reinvigorated through mythic transformation in a modern setting.

Yeats's poetry and plays reveal the way in which myths, tales, and legends associated with a country or place can lie at the heart of texts that simultaneously possess contemporary relevance. He felt that it was possible to establish a national identity through poems and plays infused with reference to ancient ritual and pagan beliefs, at a time when political **Ireland** had lost much of its significance. Early poetry collections such as *Poems* (1895) and *Wind Among the Reeds* (1899) possess a dreamlike quality resulting from their preoccupation with myth and folklore. His early plays depict characters who often appear superficial, yet acquire depth through their symbolic resonance: for instance, in *Cathleen ni Houlihan* the old woman represents the spirit of Ireland. In his later plays, Yeats turned to pure images and stylization, divorcing figures from their social contexts, but maintaining mythic elements. In his *Four Plays for Dancers* (1921) he adopted the mode of dance to explore the underlying theme: namely art itself. Here, Yeats identifies with the mythological character Cuchulain, recreating myths in order to reflect the mythmaking process itself.

Yeats derived his model for these plays and many others from Japanese Noh drama, which he encountered through his work with Ezra Pound. In 1917 Yeats stayed at Stone Cottage, Sussex, where Ezra Pound worked as his secretary. Pound was editing translations of the Japanese Noh plays: a kind of symbolic, stylized drama for small groups of initiates. Rather than appearing archaic, the Japanese style, when performed on a European stage, created an effect of strangeness and radical subversion of tradition. The borrowing of Oriental models became a staple of the modernist period in literary and other modes, as is evident, for example, in **Stravinsky**'s *Les Noces.*

In his poetry, Eliot cultivated a strangeness achieved through intertextuality and the appropriation of numerous myths. He advocated poetry that was impersonal and historical, arising from a familiarity with the entire tradition of European literature. Hence the scope of reference in *The Waste Land,* which engages with a multiplicity of sources. Literary texts mentioned specifically in Eliot's "Notes" include the Bible, St. Augustine's *Confessions,* Ovid's *Metamorphoses,* Webster's *White Devil,* Kyd's *Spanish Tragedy,* Milton's *Paradise Lost,* Baudelaire's *Fleurs du Mal* and many others. Eliot's inclusion of notes with the poem suggests self-referentiality; yet the notes themselves indicate that a broader reading experience is necessary. Eliot suggests, for instance, that a reader of the poem might wish to refer to Jessie L. Weston's book on the Grail legend—*From Ritual to Romance*—in order to gain insight into his text.

In "Ulysses, Order and Myth," Eliot claims that he wrote *The Waste Land* according to a "mythic method," through which he could give "a shape to the immense panorama of futility and anarchy which is contemporary history" (*Selected Prose* 177). In addition to Weston's book, introducing the Grail legend as one mythic framework for *The Waste Land,* Eliot refers to Frazer's *The Golden Bough,* and specifically to the two books entitled *Adonis, Attis, Osiris.* The vegetation ceremonies to which Eliot frequently alludes indicate the anthropological origin of key parts of the poem. Eliot explains in the notes that "The Hanged Man" of the poem—a member of a traditional tarot pack of cards—was associated in his mind with the "Hanged God" of Frazer, as well as with the hooded figure portrayed in part V of the poem.

In addition to Eliot and many other writers of the modernist period, D. H. Lawrence was profoundly influenced by anthropological texts: notably *The Golden Bough* (again with particular reference to the material discussing dying and reviving gods) and E. B. Tylor's *Primitive Culture*. Lawrence's fascination with myths is reflected in works written throughout his life, but seem most prevalent in the later period. *The Plumed Serpent* engages with myths surrounding the ancient serpent-god, Quetzalcoatl; "The Woman Who Rode Away" dramatizes a situation in which a Western woman infiltrates a Red Indian community, finally dying in ritual sacrifice; *Sketches of Etruscan Places* portrays Lawrence's version of the long-extinct inhabitants and deities of Tuscany; while *Apocalypse* embodies a radical re-interpretation of St. John's *Revelation*. The story "The Escaped Cock," constituting another rewriting of Christian myth, is perhaps the text in which Lawrence is most clearly indebted to Frazer. The story of Christ (in Part 1) is subsequently juxtaposed (in Part 2) with the dying and reviving gods (in this case Isis and Osiris) of *The Golden Bough*. The disillusioned Christ-figure, cut down too soon from the cross, rejects his mission and receives a new kind of resurrection and fulfillment through sexual awakening.

It is interesting that in *The Escaped Cock* Lawrence describes a Christ-figure who progresses in wisdom and knowledge in order to assume his subsequent symbolic role as Osiris. Paganism is dislocated from its historical context and envisaged as an enlightened step beyond Christianity. Lawrence's use of myth in this way is symptomatic of the modernists' imaginative treatment of the past, which was (as Eliot believed) projected into early twentieth-century literature to give shape artistically to a fragmenting world.

Bethan Jones

Selected Bibliography

Butler, Christopher. *Early Modernism*. Oxford: Oxford UP, 1994.

Cowan, J. C. *D. H. Lawrence's American Journey: A Study in Literature and Myth*. Cleveland, Ohio and London: Press of the Case Western Reserve University, 1970.

Eliot, T. S. *Selected Prose*. Ed. Frank Kermode. London: Faber and Faber, 1975.

———. "Ulysses, Order and Myth." *Dial* (November 1923).

Frazer, James. *The Golden Bough*. Vol. 4. London: Macmillan, 1927.

Levenson, Michael, ed. *The Cambridge Companion to Modernism*. Cambridge: Cambridge UP, 1999.

Tylor, Edward B. *Primitive Culture*. London: John Murray, 1903.

N

Naturalism

An extreme form of **realism** in novels, short stories and plays: naturalist works rejected idealizations of human life and focused instead on the forces of heredity and environment that shape and drive human nature. Naturalist writings are informed by Darwin's theories of evolution, Comte's application of biological models to the study of society, and Taine's application of theories of determinism to literature.

Critics often trace the origins of literary naturalism back to the publication of *Germinie Lacerteux* by Jules and Edmond Goncourt in 1865. It was another Frenchman, Émile Zola, who formulated a manifesto-piece for naturalism: he wrote "Le roman expérimental" ("The Experimental Novel") in 1880. Drawing continual parallels between his own literary aims and the aim of experimental medicine, Zola casts the novelist as pathologist and suggests that he study the effects of heredity and environment on character with scientific objectivity. The essay accompanies Zola's hugely ambitious series of twenty "Rougon-Macquart" novels, in which a family line is traced through several generations.

Naturalist writers frequently set their works in slum areas, depicting modern urban environments and the effects they have on their inhabitants. Important writers associated with naturalism include Guy de Maupassant in **France;** George Moore and George Gissing in Britain; Theodore Dreiser, **Frank Norris,** and Stephen Crane in America; Anton Chekhov and Maxim Gorky in **Russia.** In the theater, dramatic naturalism is linked to the names of Henrik Ibsen, August Strindberg, and **Gerhart Hauptmann.** Naturalism developed along slightly different lines in **Italy,** in the "verismo" movement associated with **Giovanni Verga** in the 1880s. Naturalist writings exercised an important influence on the modernists: **Marinetti** names Zola among his main influences in the formation of **Italian futurism.**

Andrew Harrison

Selected Bibliography

Baguley, David. *Naturalist Fiction: The Entropic Vision.* Cambridge: Cambridge UP, 1990.

Furst, Lilian R., and Skrine, Peter N. *Naturalism.* London: Methuen, 1971.

Nelson, Brian, ed. *Naturalism in the European Novel: New Critical Perspectives.* New York and Oxford: Berg Publishers, 1992.

Pizer, Donald. *The Cambridge Companion to American Realism and Naturalism: Howells to London.* Cambridge: Cambridge UP, 1995.

Neo-Impressionism

The neo-impressionist movement (1883–91) treated form and color scientifically. In Georges Seurat's *divisionism* (or "pointillism"), natural colors were divided into primary components; when rhythmically juxtaposed on canvas, the complementary patches recombined optically to intensify luminosity. While Seurat (1859–91) coined the term "chromo-luminarism" for his method, which analyzes refraction of sunlight and redistributes forms in calculated designs, the influential critic, Felix Fénéon, gave currency to the term "neo-impressionism." Reacting against the hazy atmospheres of **impressionism,** Seurat aimed to enhance clarity and design by division of color, intensification of optical effects, and modelling of space. His method was based on the color theories of Eugene Chevreul, Charles Blanc, and Ogden Rood and the "Scientific Esthetic" of Charles Henry, which related line to emotion. By the laws of contrast, a color gains intensity when juxtaposed with its complementary and the effect is increased when separate patches of color are applied to the canvas and mixed optically, rather than on the palette. The pointillist method of stippling with dots of blue and yellow gives an impression of green, while blue and red make purple. By "simultaneous contrast," a bright color gives rise to a fleeting after-image of its complementary.

Seurat imposes pattern on the random phenomena of light and atmosphere. He gained control from his method, building up hieratic designs in his large-scale tableaux, *Une Baignade, Asnières* (1883–84) and *A Sunday Afternoon on the Island of La Grande Jatte* (1884–86). The stillness and poise of the figures in *Une Baignade* creates a timeless moment; the intricate, logical pattern of *La Grande Jatte* composes a social tableau like that of an Egyptian frieze or Byzantine mural. In *La Grande Jatte,* "[the] geometrical rigidity" of the figures, "the elaborate planning of detail," and "the use of multiple perspective" produce a strange feeling of stasis (Shone 38). A hieratic design is imposed on the bustle of modern life: individuals, arrested in characteristic poses, are subsumed in social rhythms; moving or resting figures are arranged in a harmonious design by the divisionist technique.

Charles Henry's laws of line contributed to Seurat's modeling of space. Henry "set out to discover which spatial *directions* are expressive of pleasure or dynamogeny, and which of pain or inhibition"; he also related *warm* and *cold* colors to emotional states (Rewald 126). Exploiting this knowledge, the painter could make lines and colors more directly expressive. In Seurat's *Une Baignade,* for instance, one notes "the perfection of the overall harmony, the continual transaction between line and line, colour and colour, the disposition of light and dark accents" (Shone 23). Roger Fry analyzes Seurat's "art of hollowing out a canvas" and asks: "Who before Seurat ever perceived exactly the possibilities of empty space?"—all areas of the pictorial surface "become the elements of a plastic design" (Fry 189).

If Seurat's method is scientific, his vision is poetic; despite the flatness and rigidity of forms, the neo-impressionist painter (like the impressionist) aims to capture an image of life, but in a depersonalized, stylized synthesis. Even Camille Pissarro (1830–1903), founding father of impressionism, temporarily adopted the style. But while Seurat's painstaking method of applying innumerable dots of paint gave him a sense of control, Pissarro ultimately found it too restricting. The method did not suit all temperaments: less original artists were absorbed by it and reduced to imitation; many (like Van Gogh) tried some version of it and then moved on. Paul Signac (1863–1935), who championed the movement, achieved radiant form in coastal landscapes and city scenes that outdo Seurat's in sheer luminosity. Fénéon, whose portrait he painted against an abstract background of spiralling colors, admired his "highly decorative art, which sacrifices the anecdote to the arabesque, nomenclature to synthesis, the fugitive to the permanent" (see Rewald 124). Signac's book, *D'Eugène Delacroix au Néo-Impressionisme* (1899; Paris: Hermann,

1964) is a major contribution to the study of color in painting. Henri-Edmond Cross (1856–1910), Maximilien Luce (1858–1941), and Albert Dubois-Pillet (1846–90) also created harmonies in a range of tones using the pointillist method.

Neo-impressionism coincided with the rise of literary symbolism, which spread doctrines of aesthetic modernism. Gustave Moreau's dream visions, based on literature, inspired symbolist writers like J.-K. Huysmans, while Odilon Redon's strange visions intrigued Paul Gauguin and Stéphane Mallarmé. "For the exact translation of its synthesis," declares Jean Moréas in his symbolist manifesto, "symbolism requires an archetypal and complex style," while for Gustave Kahn "[it] objectif[ies] the subjective (the externalization of the Idea) instead of subjectifying the objective (nature seen through the eyes of a temperament)" (see Rewald 134). Moving away from **naturalism** towards supernaturalism, the symbolists called for "a return of the imagination to the epic and the marvelous" (Rewald 134). Key figures, such as Mallarmé, Paul Verlaine, and Jules Laforgue turned away from sunlit surfaces to an inner world of dreams, supporting the shift from naturalism and impressionism to mysticism and the occult. While opposed to scientism, their poetry was in accord with the neo-impressionist emphasis on formal beauty and the logic of design.

Seurat's concepts can be set beside **Virginia Woolf**'s manifesto, "Modern Fiction" (1919), where the image of a "luminous halo of consciousness" recalls impressionist vision, while the formal ordering of "a myriad impressions" relates to post- or neo-impressionist "crystallization." Seurat's goal, like Cézanne's, was uniformity of design, or what Édouard Dujardin called a "total impression." Urged by Fry to seek verbal equivalents for plastic form, Woolf fused impressionist textures (in imagery) with post-impressionist

structures (or "spatial form") and neo-impressionist modeling of time. As Seurat "hollow[ed] out a canvas" (Fry), Woolf "[dug] out beautiful caves" (*A Writer's Diary* 60), that connect characters across space and time, and link the present moment with the past through a flow of memory and perception.

Jack Stewart

Selected Bibliography

Courthion, Pierre. *Georges Seurat.* Trans. Norbert Guterman. New York: Abrams, n.d.

Fry, Roger. *Transformations.* London: Chatto, 1926.

Herbert, Robert L. *Neo-Impressionism.* New York: Guggenheim Foundation, 1968.

Rewald, John. *Post-Impressionism: From van Gogh to Gauguin.* 3rd ed. rev. New York: Museum of Modern Art, 1978.

Shone, Richard. *The Post-Impressionists.* London: Octopus, 1979.

Sutter, Jean, ed. *The Neo-Impressionists.* Greenwich, Conn.: New York Graphic Soc., 1970.

Woolf, Virginia. "Modern Fiction." 1919. *Collected Essays.* Vol. 2. London: Hogarth, 1966. 103–10.

———. *A Writer's Diary.* London: Hogarth, 1953.

The New Woman

A figure of social rebellion and cultural mythology, the New Woman stands on the cusp between the nineteenth-century "woman question" and its transformation into a distinctly modern, twentieth-century concern with the sexual meaning of femininity, epitomized in the **psychoanalysis** of **Sigmund Freud** and the so-called "sex science" (or sexology) of Havelock Ellis. The New Woman was a genuinely political figure, who emerged from feminist movements of the 1870s and whose very existence was linked to fundamental reforms of ninetenth-century society, most notably in women's access to higher education and in the relative financial independence this started to bring middle-class young women.

Sarah Grand, a novelist, journalist and feminist activist, is commonly credited with the naming of this figure as a "New Woman" in an 1894 article in the *North American Review.* Together with *Nineteenth Century* and the liberal feminist journal *Shafts,* this was one of the main debating grounds for proponents and critics of the New Woman. The phenomenon of the New Woman was felt on many fronts—from the literary press and women's magazines to the London stage and the pages of the New Women's fiction. But what exactly did the New Woman represent? By her critics she was portrayed as a headstrong, excessively intellectual and abominable imitation of masculinity. Dressed in short hair and sturdy clothes, smoking cigarettes and riding bicycles, the usually bespectacled New Woman represented a physical challenge to the codes of respectable feminine behavior. Brandishing a latchkey (a symbol of independence), reading her books and walking unchaperoned, the New Woman was condemned for her willful desire for emancipation and for her supposed betrayal of woman's true maternal role.

Such attacks emerge strongly in the essays of older female commentators such as Eliza Lynn Linton whose anti-feminist polemic against "Wild Women" (a term in use before "New Woman" and without any of the positive connotations) begins an article of 1891 thus: "All women are not always lovely, and the wild women never are. As political firebrands and moral insurgents they are especially distasteful, warring as they do against the best traditions, the holiest functions, and the sweetest qualities of their sex. Like certain 'sports' which develop hybrid characteristics, these insurgent wild women are in a sense unnatural" (Linton 79). In her desire to control her own fertility and her refusal to be valued for her maternity alone, the New Woman seemed indicative of a wider degeneracy which threatened western civilization. For this reason, feminist critics such as Anne Mclintock have reassessed

the work of New Woman writers such as Olive Schreiner, pointing to the intersection of colonial and sexual discourse in their work. In the 1890s, non-procreative sex was not a matter of personal choice, but was considered a dereliction of duty to Empire and a threat to "the stability of society and the well-being of the race" (Linton 79).

The tone of crisis detectable in Linton's rhetoric emerges from wider *fin de siècle* concerns with subjectivity and sexuality. As Lyn Pickett argues, the New Woman and the Decadent (epitomized in the figure of **Oscar Wilde**) are key elements in the wider avant-garde challenge to nineteenth-century society which later modernist novelists all sought to develop. **E. M. Forster**'s Schlegel sisters in *Howard's End,* **D. H. Lawrence**'s Ursula and Gudrun in ***The Rainbow,*** and Miriam Henderson in **Dorothy Richardson**'s *Pilgrimage* are, to different degrees, New Women. In the theater, the New Woman first appears on stage in Henrik Ibsen's *A Doll's House* (first performed in Britain in 1889) and is more explicitly the subject of Sydney Grundy's *The New Woman* (1894) and **George Bernard Shaw**'s *Mrs. Warren's Profession* (1893).

An undoubted influence on modernist fiction, the cultural phenomenon of the New Woman deserves to be understood as a self-standing literary movement which reached its high point in the work of novelists—both male and female—of the 1890s. Sarah Grand's best-seller *The Heavenly Twins* (1893) is one of the most significant novels and displays a common narrative structure (found also in Olive Schreiner's *The Story of an African Farm*) of taking two sisterly women as contrasting test cases for the fate of the New Woman and her more conservative counterpart. This contrast is thrown into starkest relief when discussing the matter of sexuality. Hence Grand's New Woman, Evadne, refuses sexual relations with her husband on the basis of his pre-marital sexual adventures, whereas her traditional, feminine twin, Edith, consents to and suffers the consequences of intercourse with a syphilitic husband.

The subject of sexual disease within marriage is also central to Emma Brooke's novel *A Superfluous Woman* (1894) and Ellis Ethelmer's poem, "Woman Free" (1893). Elsewhere, the subject of childbirth within marriage and its effects on women's physical and mental health dominates, as in the case in much of Mona Caird's journalism and novels, including her *Daughters of Danaus* (1894), and in Grand's second novel, *The Beth Book* (1897), where on the very first page we read: "She was weak and ill and anxious, the mother of six children already, and about to produce a seventh . . . It was a reckless thing for a delicate woman to do, but she never thought of that. She lived in the days when no one thought of the waste of women in this respect, and they had not begun to think for themselves." Not all New Women novelists were opposed to marriage or maternity, as both Menie Muriel Dowie's *Gallia* (1895) and Iota's (K. M. Caffyn) *A Yellow Aster* (1894) testify. Even Caird, a veteran campaigner of the feminist protests against the 1870s Contagious Diseases Acts, viewed marriage as reformable, providing it evolved on the basis of mutual, spiritual friendship.

In their artistic practice as well as their politics, New Women novelists sought to make new the methods of narrative fiction as they challenged the conventions of nineteenth-century **realism.** In her foreword to *The Story of an African Farm* (1883), for example, Schreiner sets her stall by a new method of literary representation which sacrifices the securities of realist plots in order more accurately to reflect the dissonances and incoherences of human life: "Here nothing can be prophesied. There is a strange coming and going of feet. Men appear, act and re-act

upon each other, and pass away. When the crisis comes the man who would fit it does not return. When the curtain falls no one is ready." An early manifesto of modernist method, Schreiner's work shares with other New Women novelists a formal as well as social concern with the role of fantasy and imagination in the human psyche. This innovative method is put to best use when evoking the suffocations of duty endured by powerless subjects (usually women and children) trapped by their place in the world (an excellent example is the impressive opening chapter of *The Story of an African Farm*). The attempt to render the internal anxieties of the mind as they are experienced, marks Schreiner's work as "modernist" and her technique as a precursor to the more fully developed stream of consciousness of **James Joyce, Dorothy Richardson,** and **Virginia Woolf.** Equally important to the narrative structure of New Woman writing is the dramatic use of an overtly political discussion on the rights and wrongs of women staged between the New Woman and a central male figure. It is worth bearing in mind here that politics for these writers did not mean textual politics alone; in her time, Schreiner was known as much for her socialist sympathies as for her literary achievements (see, for example, her *Women and Labour* 1911). It is the structural balance between a didactic feminist fiction and a modern mode of writing which makes the New Woman's literature central to our understanding of the late nineteenth and early twentieth centuries.

Ruth McElroy

Selected Bibliography

Further primary texts which are usually included under the category of New Woman literature are:

Cunningham, Gail. *The New Woman and the Victorian Novel.* London: Macmillan, 1978.

Grant Allen, *The Woman Who Did* (1895); Mary Cholmondeley, *Red Pottage* (orig. 1899; Virago, 1985); Ella Hepworth Dixon, *The Story of a Modern Woman* (1894); George Egerton

(Mary Chavelita Dunne), *Keynotes* and *Discords* ((1893, 1894, reprinted together by Virago, 1983), and *The Wheel of God* (1898); George Gissing, *The Odd Women* (1893); and Thomas Hardy, *Jude the Obscure* (1895).

Gardner, Viv and Susan Rutherford, eds. *The New Woman and her Sisters: Feminism and Theatre 1850–1914.* London: Harvester, 1992.

Ledger, Sally and Allison Ledger. *The New Woman Fiction and Feminism at the Fin de Siècle.* Manchester: Manchester UP, 1997.

Linton, Eliza Lynn. "The Wild Women as Social Insurgents." *Nineteenth Century* 30 (1891): 79–88. See also Mona Caird's response in the following volume, 596–605.

Marks, Patricia. *Bicycles, Bangs and Bloomers: the New Woman in the Popular Press.* Lexington, KY: Kentucky UP, 1990.

McClintock, Anne. *Imperial Leather.* London: Routledge, 1995.

Pickett, Lyn. *The Improper Feminine: The Women's Sensation Novel and the New Woman Writing.* London: Routledge, 1992.

———, ed. *Reading Fin de Siècle Fictions.* London: Longman, 1996.

Showalter, Elaine. *A Literature of Their Own.* Princeton: Princeton UP, 1977.

Norris, Frank (Benjamin Franklin Norris) (1870–1902)

U.S. novelist, journalist, essayist, and short story writer.

Norris's most important works are *McTeague* (1899), concerned with the rise and fall of a physically powerful but stupid San Francisco dentist, and the first two volumes of an unfinished "trilogy of wheat": *The Octopus* (1901), portraying a violent and political struggle between Californian growers and a monopolistic railroad that fixes transportation rates to gain possession of the land; and *The Pit* (1903), which follows the progress of the grain through the Chicago stockmarket and shows the effect of price fluctuations on lives.

With critics generally divided over whether Norris is a romantic or a realist, rather than a naturalist in the manner of Zola, as he regarded himself, it may seem perverse to include him in the modernist project. Nevertheless, after reading the manuscript of *Lord Jim* (1900) while working for publishers Doubleday, Norris declared himself a passionate follower of **Conrad.** As Jennifer Boyd argues, Norris similarly tries "to make you see" (Conrad, Preface to *The Nigger of the Narcissus*). Trained as a painter in London and Paris, he uses spatial images, repetitions, parallels and other structural patternings in tension with the linearity of his chronological narration. The penultimate chapter of *The Octopus,* for example, employs crosscutting to juxtapose starkly contrasting but connected simultaneous scenes some fifteen years before the technique became common in **cinema.** In an essay, "The Responsibilities of the Novelist," Norris writes of the impossibility of objective **realism,** "for you are not only close to the canvas, but are yourself part of the picture." Where spatiality supplants linearity, and the artist's presence comes before things as they are, is arguably where modernism begins.

Norris's **naturalism** also prepares the way for modernism in its conception of the alienated, divided character. Although he propounded a somewhat mechanical social Darwinist view of human interaction determined by hereditary, environmental, and economic pressures, Norris's concern with experiences shaped by powerful impersonal forces is recognizably modernist. Uncontrollable impulses Norris understood as atavism are broadly comparable to what **psychoanalysis** would come to term the unconscious; external influences—capitalism, mechanization, urban anonymity, anomie, rapid communications—are foregrounded over the moral concerns, humanism, or attempts at comprehensive description found in much nineteenth-century realism.

Norris's prose lacks the linguistic experimentation associated with modernism, and its commitment to scientism necessitates a detached, often superior, point of view. Even so, certain images transcend the melodramatic, clunking obviousness of the bulk of the writing. The final scene of *McTeague,* where the protagonist ends up handcuffed to his dead nemesis in the middle of Death Valley, while providing a moral ending, implies a bleakness and absurdity, reinforced in the dialogue, worthy of **Beckett.** Descriptions in *The Octopus* of the locomotive, "that terror of steel and steam," anticipate the contradictory fascination and horror of technology found in **futurism**.

Nigel Morris

Selected Bibliography

Boyd, Jennifer. *Frank Norris: Spatial Form & Narrative Time.* New York: Peter Lang, 1993.

Graham, Don (ed.). *Critical Essays on Frank Norris.* Boston, Mass.: G.K. Hall & Co., 1980.

O

O'Brien, Kate (1897–1974)

The Irish-born writer Kate O'Brien produced nine novels in a writing career lasting from the 1930s until the late 1950s.
Although her working life was spent
mainly in Britain, her fiction deals mainly
with Irish protagonists or Irish settings.
Her novels chart the emergence of a catholic bourgeoisie in **Ireland** in the late
nineteenth century and she focuses on the
aspirations of her young female protagonists for independence within this emergent and conformist class. As a result her
fictions are produced from the conflict between her need to idealize her own class
and a modernist interest in interiority and
in the solitary imaginations of her characters. In a lecture on **Joyce,** she once defined her sense of the novelist's task in the
following way: "You take your material
from outside. Once you settle with it, once
you know what it says to you, it is yours
and it is for you to re-create it in your
terms, to give it back to life, illuminated
and translated by you. That is the business
of being an artist." Ireland, illuminated and
translated into idealized fiction, this was
Kate O'Brien's theme.

To a degree, she was a novelist of transition, relying on the **realism** of the
nineteenth-century novel and her fictions
adhere to the formal structures of the bourgeois novel. At the same time, within these
civilized, reflective narratives, she formulated an aesthetic which challenged assumptions about the consoling nature of
bourgeois art. In her novel *Mary Lavelle*
(1936), she celebrated the disruptive potential of primitive ritual in the representation of the bullfight as witnessed by the
eponymous heroine, Mary Lavelle: "Here
was madness, here was blunt brutality,
here was money-making swagger—and all
made into an eternal shape, a merciless
beauty, by so brief an attitude . . . Here was
art in its least decent form, its least ex-
plainable or bearable. But Art, unconcerned and lawless."

In her early novels, *Without My Cloak*
(1931) and *The Ante-Room* (1934), she remade her native Limerick as the Irish town
Mellick and dramatized the conflict between communal belief and individual
imagination in the context of the bourgeois
family unit. Kate O'Brien's project as novelist was clearly feminist and these first
novels portray female protagonists inhibited by the demands of catholic conscience
in their quest for selfhood. Her fictions are
strictly realist in form but, with her third
novel *Mary Lavelle* (1936), Kate O'Brien
began to move her fictive perspectives
away from the limitations of the Irish
bourgeois family novel and towards an
imagined, bohemian Europe. In these novels, O'Brien extended her representation
of dissident sexualities and thus subverts
the catholic ethos of her native Ireland. As
a consequence, *Mary Lavelle* was banned
in Ireland for O'Brien's considered portrayal of lesbian desire and adulterous pas-

sion. Her next novel *Pray for the Wanderer* (1938) was a direct attack on **censorship** and on the patriarchal control of creativity in Ireland and elsewhere. With the outbreak of the Spanish Civil War, Kate O'Brien aligned herself on the side of the Republicans and against the fascist nationalist side and her travel book *Farewell Spain,* a liberal humanist plea for "man's courageous heart," was the cause of an embargo on her entering Spain for the next twenty years. Her 1941 novel *The Land of Spices* was also banned, this time for a one-sentence reference to homosexuality: "She saw her father and Etienne in the embrace of love." This banning led to a parliamentary debate in Ireland and a relaxing of the censorship laws. Her most successful novel, *The Lady* (1946) was a complex response to the experience of the Second World War and an attack on the curtailment of individual liberty under fascism in Europe. In the novel, O'Brien took an historical episode, the imprisonment of Ana De Mendoza, the Princess of Eboli, by King Philip II of Spain and refashioned it into a parable of resistance and a defense of individual conscience. As the protagonist, Ana tells her authoritarian king: "My private life is truly private . . . I own it, Philip. If I do wrong in it, that wrong is between me and heaven." In her final novel, *As Music and Splendour* (1958), O'Brien realizes her utopian vision of an autonomous selfhood for her young Irish women. The novel charts the careers of two Irish opera singers in **Italy** and the material and artistic success of the world of opera brings them release from their Irish "selves" and a consequent freedom in terms of a European bohemianism. Kate O'Brien died in 1974 and many of her novels went out of print but much of her work has been reissued by Virago and other feminist publishing houses and her fiction is now the focus for scholarly research and interest.

Eibhear Walshe

Selected Bibliography

Dalsimer, Adele. *Kate O'Brien: A Critical Study.* Dublin: Gill and Macmillan, 1990.

Reynolds, Lorna. *Kate O'Brien: A Literary Portrait.* Gerrards Cross: Colin Smythe, 1987.

Walshe, Eibhear, ed. *Ordinary People Dancing: Essays on Kate O'Brien.* Cork: Cork University Press, 1993.

———. *Kate O'Brien: The Life of an Imagination.* Cork: Cork University Press, 2000.

O'Casey, Sean (1880–1964)

Sean O'Casey was born a protestant in Dublin in 1880. The fortunes of the family began to slide after the death of his father in 1886 and O'Casey, the youngest child, grew up in respectable poverty, though surrounded by tenements where the poorest of the mostly catholic working classes lived in scandalously overcrowded and unhygienic squalor. O'Casey was never reduced to such circumstances, but his reputation is inextricably linked with those people for whose welfare he agitated and whose language he immortalized.

Because of congenital eye trouble, O'Casey may have had difficulty learning to read. It is certain that he quickly acquired a passion for books and for sonorous speech, such as he found in **Shakespeare** and the Authorized Version of the Bible. He gave early evidence of this while leading the prayers in St. Barnabas's Church. Coincidentally, political oppression and poverty had hindered the spread of formal education among the lower orders of Irish society. As a consequence, at the turn of the century the literacy rate was so low as to allow a predominantly oral society to survive. Like **Joyce** before him and Behan after him, O'Casey exploited the color and energy of oral speech, especially in his Abbey plays, *The Shadow of a Gunman* (1923), *Juno and the Paycock* (1925), and *The Plough and the Stars* (1926).

Although he abandoned religious practice around 1910, O'Casey was instinctually protestant. From a staunchly unionist background and with two brothers in the British army, he became an enthusiastic nationalist until he decided that Irish nationalism was essentially bourgeois and conservative and uninterested in bettering the conditions of the working class. His decision was prompted by the arrival in Dublin of the labor leader Jim Larkin, the subsequent lock out, and the founding of the Irish Citizen Army in 1913. Crucial to O'Casey's drama is his belief that 1913 was the missed opportunity of Irish political life. Instead of seizing the opportunity to achieve a genuine revolution, the Irish working class was deluded by nationalists into joining a revolution that offered it nothing but suffering and death. After his resignation from the Irish Citizen Army in 1914 O'Casey took no further part in Irish politics; he concentrated on writing and in 1923 *The Shadow of a Gunman* was produced by the Abbey to popular acclaim. In this and in the two other Abbey plays he lacerates all political formations, Right and Left, celebrating individual kindness as heroic and exposing political idealism as self-deceptive posturing.

Hailed by **Yeats** as a genius, O'Casey proceeded with his dramatization of the suffering of the Irish working class by dealing with **World War I.** Meanwhile he went to London for productions of *Juno and the Paycock* and *The Plough and the Stars.* Internationally famous, he was befriended by **Bernard Shaw,** Augustus John, and members of the British upper class. His success seemed complete when, at the age of forty-seven, he married Eileen Carey, a young Irish actress, but marriage was not to be the only major change in his life. In 1928 he was (and with good reason) shocked when *The Silver Tassie* was rejected by the Abbey, a theater he could claim to have saved financially. In turn he rejected the Abbey and spent almost all the rest of his life in England.

Though it was thematically logical for a dramatist of the Dublin working class to move on to the trauma of the Great War, O'Casey had also moved on from the **realism** that characterizes the Abbey plays to the extra-realism that characterizes their successors. He had taken some liberties in the Abbey plays while generally remaining within the parameters of working class speech. In the later works he transcended realism and used a wide range of extra-realist devices—symbolist settings, allegorical characterization, choric chants, **music,** song, **dance**—and occasionally wrote scenes, such as Act Two of *The Silver Tassie* and Act Three of *Red Roses for Me,* that are expressionistic. The most contentious element of the later plays is the dialogue, which throws off the restraints of vernacular speech and seeks poetic richness, as **Synge**'s did, through intensification of imagery, **rhythm** and, especially, alliteration. Many would argue that O'Casey did not achieve Synge's success and that the dialogue of the later plays tends towards overindulgence and self-parody.

The warm reception in London encouraged O'Casey to use a canvass broader than that provided by the inner city of Dublin and it also released an innate disposition to preach the socialist gospel of perfectability. *Within the Gates* (1934), set in Hyde Park, is a highly stylized morality with a Young Woman as its focus. *The Star Turns Red* (1940) is a theatrical hymn to communism; O'Casey, whose political career had been a long series of resignations, remained a strangely loyal Stalinist until the end. *Red Roses for Me* (1943) is a lyrical version of a theme—a saintly labor leader is killed during a Dublin strike—that O'Casey had used in one of his earliest efforts, *The Harvest Festival,* written in 1919 but rejected by the Abbey.

When World War Two was won, O'Casey's fanaticism softened and, if the texts of his dramatic sermons remained starkly clear, the tone was less strident and more humorous: the *good* are sub-angelic and the *evil* are objects of ridicule rather than fiends to be exorcized. In *Purple Dust* (1945) he presents the **Ireland** which will dominate the late plays: a stylized rural setting where a younger generation, imbued by the spirit of ancient paganism, struggle against the tyranny of their puritanically narrow-minded and economically voracious elders. The most successful of the late plays is *Cock-a-Doodle-Dandy* (1949) in which exuberant sexuality is incarnated as an enormous cock which drives the gerontocracy of Nyadnanave into superstitious panic. The other plays—*The Bishop's Bonfire* (1955), *The Drums of Father Ned* (1959), *Behind the Green Curtains* (1962)—suggest that, on the whole, O'Casey had come to believe that Ireland's best chance of salvation was through exuberant sociality rather than dogmatic socialism.

Throughout his life he embroiled himself in feuds and controversies and between 1939 and 1954 he published six large volumes of imaginative autobiography in which he generally comes off better than his enemies. His reputation will depend on his plays. Though there are occasional efforts to argue otherwise, it is almost certain that the Abbey plays will be seen as his masterworks. Though not an innovator, he was the first to represent convincingly on stage the extravagant language and manners of the Dublin tenements, the first to deal directly with recent political events. For a few years he worked in a comi-tragic vein which invited the audience to laugh at politics and then suddenly subverted the laughter by showing the consequences of politics. For almost a hundred years the Abbey plays have continued to win new audiences.

Colbert Kearney

Selected Bibliography

Fallon, Gabriel. *Sean O'Casey: The Man I Knew.* London: Routledge and Kegan Paul, 1965.

Hogan, Robert. *'Since O'Casey' and Other Essays on Irish Drama.* Gerrards Cross: Colin Smythe, 1983.

Hogan, Robert and Richard Burnham. *The Years of O'Casey, 1921–1926: A Documentary History.* Gerrards Cross: Colin Smythe, 1992.

Holloway, Joseph. *Joseph Holloway's Abbey Theatre.* Ed. Robert Hogan and Michael J. O'Neill. Carbondale: Southern Illinois UP, 1967.

Hunt, Hugh. *Sean O'Casey.* Dublin: Gill and Macmillan, 1980.

Kosok, Heinz. *O'Casey the Dramatist.* Gerrards Cross: Colin Smythe, 1985.

Krause, David. *Sean O'Casey: The Man and His Work.* London: MacGibbon and Kee, 1960.

Krause, David and Robert G. Lowery, eds. *Sean O'Casey: Centenary Essays.* Gerrards Cross: Colin Smythe, 1980.

Lowery, Robert, ed. *Essays on Sean O'Casey's Autobiographies.* London: Macmillan, 1981.

———. *O'Casey Annual Nos 1, 2, 3.* London: Macmillan, 1982/1983/1984.

Margulies, Martin B. *The Early Life of Sean O'Casey.* Dublin: Dolmen Press, 1970.

Mikhail, E. H. and John O'Riordan, eds. *The Sting and the Twinkle.* London: Macmillan, 1974.

Murray, Christopher. *Twentieth-Century Irish Drama: Mirror up to Nation.* Manchester: Manchester UP, 1997.

O'Casey, Sean. *Autobiographies.* 2 vols. London: Pan Books, 1980.

———. *Feathers from the Green Crow: Sean O'Casey 1905–1925.* Ed. Robert Hogan. London: Macmillan, 1963.

———. *The Green Crow: Selected Writings of Sean O'Casey.* London: Virgin, 1994.

———. *The Harvest Festival.* Foreword by Eileen O'Casey and introduction by John O'Riordan. Gerrards Cross: Colin Smythe, 1980.

———. *The Letters of Sean O'Casey.* 4 vols. Ed. David Krause. London: Cassell, 1975; New York: Macmillan, 1980; Washington, DC: Catholic U of America P, 1989, 1992.

O'Connor, Garry. *Sean O'Casey.* London: Hodder and Stoughton, 1988.

Schrank, Bernice. *Sean O'Casey: a research and production sourcebook.* Westport, CT: Greenwood Press, 1996.

Schrank, Bernice and William W. Demastes. *Irish Playwrights, 1880–1995: A Research and Production Sourcebook.* Westport, CT: Greenwood Press, 1997.

Williams, Raymond. *Drama from Ibsen to Brecht.* Harmondsworth: Pelican Books, 1973.

O'Neill, Eugene (1888–1953)

No American dramatist better captures the currents and contradictions of literary modernism than Eugene O'Neill. His plays mark a distinct break with the romantic optimism and melodramatic claptrap that were dominating the commercial American theater in the early twentieth century. In rebellion against the Irish catholic morality and bourgeois values of his deeply dysfunctional upbringing, O'Neill transformed serious American drama through his self-conscious, Nietzschean desire to write big plays on big ideas. It would be no exaggeration to state that modern American drama begins with O'Neill.

The range and inventiveness of O'Neill's work are astonishing. He created terse, poetic dramas based on his experience at sea. He created realistic and expressionistic works that examined the lives of characters who existed at the periphery of society. He wrote historical dramas and extravaganzas that examined America's fascination with materialism. He created lengthy plays, steeped in Freudian and Jungian thought, that examined the loss of faith and decay of values in modern society. These works aspired to capture the narrative form of the novel and to become modern versions of Greek tragedies. Ultimately, however, O'Neill's greatest subject was himself. Few playwrights have been as autobiographical, both consciously and unconsciously, as Eugene O'Neill.

In an era of increasing moral relativism, O'Neill was interested primarily in writing tragedy. In 1923 he explained, "I see life as a gorgeously-ironical, beautifully-indifferent, splendidly-suffering bit of chaos, the tragedy of which gives Man a tremendous significance, while without losing his fight with fate he would be a tepid, silly animal. I say 'losing fight' only symbolically, for the brave individual always wins. Fate can never conquer his—or her—spirit." The impact of fate in the affairs of humankind would be a thematic obsession with O'Neill through all of his plays, from his very first, *A Wife for a Life* (1913) to his very last, A *Moon for the Misbegotten* (1943).

O'Neill boldly experimented with a variety of dramatic and literary devices. Using devices from masks to soliloquies, he challenged conventional expectations and found a theatrical language and form that best suited the stories he was telling. His formalistic experiments invigorated and bemused the Broadway stage, and they aligned American drama, for the first time, with avant-garde European developments. This created an unprecedented international interest in his work which resulted in his being awarded the Nobel Prize for Literature in 1936. It is ironic that O'Neill's posthumous reputation is largely based on the realistic, autobiographical dramas he created after 1936 and not his earlier, more self-conscious, modern works.

Eugene Gladstone O'Neill was born October 16, 1888 at a theatrical hotel, the Barrett House, in New York City. His father was the handsome and talented Irish-born actor James O'Neill. The father enjoyed early acclaim in classical roles where he appeared opposite some of America's greatest stage stars, but he was still haunted by the deprivations and hardships of his immigrant childhood. Because of this, he sacrificed the promise of his early career for easy fame and fortune and spent years barnstorming the country as Edmond Dantes in an adaptation of Dumas fils' *The Count of Monte Cristo*. He performed the play over 4,000 times between 1883 and 1912, but would come to regret his capitulation to popular taste. His career brought him material success, but little artistic satisfaction, and in time the father's example would forever steel the son's determination that he would "never sell out."

O'Neill's mother, Ella Quinlan O'Neill, was shy, refined, devoutly catholic and convent-educated, but she was temperamentally unsuited to cope with the peripatetic lifestyle of a professional actor. Her disdain for a life spent on trains, backstage in theaters, and in lonely hotel rooms would be shared by her youngest son Eugene, who spent the first seven years of his life traveling with his parents on his father's theatrical tours.

The O'Neills had three sons: James Jr., Edmund (who died in infancy while his parents were on tour), and Eugene. Eugene's birth was difficult and his mother's recovery slow. In order to ease her pain and relieve her anxiety, Ella O'Neill's doctor gave her morphine, which at the time was widely used as medicine. This was the beginning of an addiction that would last over twenty-five years. The dark family secret would only be revealed to Eugene—by his father and brother—when he was 15. The revelation came after a harrowing episode in which Ella O'Neill tried to commit suicide. The episode would forever haunt O'Neill. As Edmund, his alter ego, bitterly confesses in *Long Day's Journey into Night* (1940), "God, it made everything in life seem rotten!" The experience precipitated O'Neill's loss of faith in catholicism and the God who had deserted his mother. It was at this time, with the encouragement and example of his wastrel brother Jamie, that he began to drink and whore.

During the summer months, when not touring, the O'Neills resided in New London, Connecticut, a city where James O'Neill had investment and real estate holdings. Their summer home was called the Monte Cristo cottage, and it served as the inspiration for the settings in several of O'Neill's plays such as *Ah, Wilderness!* (1933) and *Long Day's Journey into Night* (1940). As a boy in New London, O'Neill developed a fascination with the sea where he would spend hours reading, sketching, and swimming. The reading, especially, seemed to offer him a refuge from the insecurities of his troubled family life.

O'Neill's formal education began in 1895 when he was sent away to a catholic boarding school. Then in 1902, he was enrolled at Betts Academy, a non-sectarian private school where he stayed until 1906. In that same year, he entered Princeton University. At Princeton, he was rebellious, drifting, and unengaged by his studies, but O'Neill read intensely and dreamed of being a poet. He immersed himself in the works of the pre-Raphaelite and symbolist writers, and, most importantly, he read Nietzsche's *Thus Spake Zarathustra*. This book, he said, influenced him "more than any book I've ever read." O'Neill was taken with its imaginative and mystical mixture of allegories, parables, and oracular statements, including the statement Edmund quotes in *Long Day's Journey into Night:* "God is dead: of His pity for man hath God died."

During this same period, O'Neill saw his first performance of one of Henrik Ibsen's works. The play was *Hedda Gabler* and starred the charismatic Russian-born actress, Alla Nazimova. O'Neill used his father's free passes to see the production ten times and said that "The performance discovered an entire new world of drama to me. It gave me my first conception of a modern theater where truth might live." This was a truth that O'Neill had found sorely lacking in his father's theater.

In 1907, O'Neill was dismissed from Princeton for "poor scholastic standing." His father secured him a job as a secretary for a mail-order firm, but he proved incapable of holding down any regular job for long. During the next six years he lived "on the edge." He fell in love and married Kathleen Jenkins, but his parents objected to the relationship and soon, with their assistance, he deserted his pregnant bride and left to prospect for gold in Honduras. He returned to the States six months later with a tropical fever and tried to work briefly with his father in the theater. Soon, however, he was on his way to Buenos Aires. Now O'Neill, destitute and drinking, was living the life of a bum on the docks, working odd jobs and occasionally shipping out on ocean voyages. When he returned to New York, he lived at Jimmy the Priest's, a waterfront dive for derelicts that he would later immortalize in *The Iceman Cometh* (1939) as Harry Hope's saloon and rooming house. There, in January of 1912, O'Neill attempted suicide by taking a drug overdose, but was saved by friends who found him in a coma. At last, he began to struggle back from the brink of oblivion. He rejoined his family, briefly acting with his father and brother in a truncated, vaudeville version of *Monte Cristo.* In the summer, he returned to New London and worked for a short time as a newspaper reporter, but his health had deteriorated, and he was now diagnosed with tuberculosis.

On Christmas Eve of 1912 he was admitted to Gaylord Farm, a private sanatorium for the treatment of his disease. Commenting on this period, O'Neill said, "It was at Gaylord that my mind got a chance to establish itself, to digest and valuate the impressions of the many past years in which one experience was crowded on another with never a second's reflection. At Gaylord I really *thought about* my life for the first time, about past and future." It was at this time that O'Neill decided to become a playwright, and he spent his confinement devouring modern European drama. He read **Synge, Yeats,** Gregory, Brieux, **Hauptmann,** Ibsen, and most importantly, August Strindberg. O'Neill found much to admire in Strindberg's bleak and brutal depiction of family and marital relations. He also admired Strindberg's frank exploration of his own tortured biography. In Strindberg, he found a writer who moved away from a raw, melodramatic **naturalism** to a "supernaturalism" that captured the **rhythm** and the bizarre imagery of dreams. In 1936, when O'Neill accepted his Nobel Prize, he called Strindberg "the greatest genius of all modern dramatists" and credited him with inspiring him to write for the theater.

At age 24, after five months in the sanatorium, O'Neill was released. Now declared "cured," he returned to New London determined to write for the stage. In a short time, he wrote his first one-act plays. For all their deficiencies, these plays contain, in embryonic form, situations, themes, characters, and ideas that he would reiterate and develop as he matured as a playwright. With the financial support of his father, five of the plays were privately published under the title *Thirst* in 1914. The most important of these early works was *Bound East for Cardiff,* the first of his memorable sea plays.

Aware of the weaknesses in his work, that same year he applied to study playwriting in a unique post-graduate program at Harvard University. Under the tutelage of Professor George Pierce Baker, O'Neill was determined "to be an artist or nothing." The year he spent at Harvard provided him with a structured approach to dramatic composition, but Baker's most vital lesson may have come through urging his students "to believe in our work and to keep on believing."

The beginning of O'Neill's playwriting career coincided with the emergence in America of the noncommercial, experimental "little theater" movement. Modeled on earlier European "independent theaters" such as the Théâtre Libre in Paris and the Abbey Theatre in Dublin, the "little theaters" were dedicated to presenting modern work and fostering the development of new American playwrights. Organizations such as the Washington Square Players, founded in New York in 1914, were America's first true off-Broadway theaters.

In 1916, O'Neill became involved with one of the most important of these early amateur groups. On July 28, 1916, the Provincetown Players in Provincetown,

Massachusetts presented *Bound East for Cardiff* at their small Wharf Theater. Emboldened by the play's success, they transferred the production in November to the MacDougal Street Theater in Greenwich Village. These, the first performances of a play by Eugene O'Neill, introduced his work to the New York theater scene. The partnership between O'Neill and the Provincetown Players was inspired. The company provided sympathetic collaborators and support for a series of productions that would capture the attention of audiences, critics, publishers, and commercial producers. It was also through his work with the Provincetown Players that O'Neill met the writer Agnes Boulton, the woman who would become his second wife in 1918.

During the period from 1916 to 1920, O'Neill wrote a number of one-act and full-length plays. *The Long Voyage Home, The Moon of the Caribbees,* and *Ile* established his reputation as a realist whose plays were reminiscent of the writings of **Joseph Conrad.** Works such as *Before Breakfast* were Strindbergian in their conception and their exploration of domestic relationships. *In the Zone, The Sniper,* and *Shell Shock* dealt with the Great War and its aftermath. Other plays of the period focused on contemporary social and political issues, such as race in *The Dreamy Kid.*

The 1920s were a remarkable decade for O'Neill. He abandoned the one-act form and, in short order, wrote *Beyond the Horizon, The Emperor Jones, Anna Christie,* and *The Hairy Ape.* These four plays would secure his national and international reputation. *Beyond the Horizon* (1920) and *Anna Christie* (1921) were realistic works that won Pulitzer Prizes for Drama in 1920 and 1922. *Beyond the Horizon* examined the tragic and ironic consequences that befall two brothers who forsake their dreams. In the *New York Times,* Alexander Woollcott called the play an "absorbing, significant, and memorable tragedy."

Anna Christie told the poignant story of three inarticulate people: Chris, the old captain of a sea-going barge; Anna, his daughter and a former prostitute; and Mat, an Irish stoker in love with Anna. In this drama of abandonment, reunion, and reconciliation, Anna summarizes the play's main point when she says, "Don't bawl about it. There ain't nothing to forgive, anyway. It ain't your fault, and it ain't his neither. We're all poor nuts and things happen, and we just got mixed in wrong, that's all." *Beyond the Horizon* and *Anna Christie* quickly established O'Neill on Broadway as America's most important serious playwright.

In 1920, the Provincetown Players produced *The Emperor Jones,* and in 1922, *The Hairy Ape.* O'Neill had deemed the plays too experimental for commercial Broadway productions. Both plays used expressionistic devices to examine the demise of classic outsiders: Brutus Jones, the black, outlaw dictator of a tropical island, and Yank, the powerful yet sensitive brute from the stoke hole. Both characters are alienated from society and doomed by historical and cultural forces beyond their control. Yet, the two emerge as heroic in their struggles with fate, and O'Neill's studies of race and class retain a real power on the stage.

More ambitious works followed. *All God's Chillun Got Wings* (1924) examined racial intolerance. *Desire Under the Elms* (1924), a stark drama, modeled on Euripides' *Hippolytus,* explored the struggle between a father and his son for possession of the family farm and for the love of the father's new, young wife. *Marco Millions* (1925) pitted Marco Polo, the quintessential materialist, against the poetry and spirituality of the mysterious East. *The Great God Brown* (1925) experimented with the use of masks and investigated the differences between the public and private personae of the characters. In *Strange Interlude* (1927), the stream-of-consciousness technique of the modern novel was merged with Freudian psychology to create a complex portrait of a self-absorbed woman, Nina Leeds, and the men in her life. The nine-act play, which was presented with a dinner break, made extensive use of asides that allowed the characters to give voice to their inner thoughts. It won O'Neill his third Pulitzer Prize and was his most popular and profitable work.

The public triumphs of the 1920s were marked by personal tragedy. Between 1920 and 1923, O'Neill's father, his mother, and his brother died. James O'Neill lived long enough to witness the success of *Beyond the Horizon*. Ella O'Neill died in 1922 while in San Francisco with her son Jamie. A year later Jamie was dead from the chronic effects of alcoholism. By 1926 O'Neill himself was seeking psychiatric counseling to help him stop his own drinking. The treatment was successful, but his problems continued. In 1927 he deserted his wife and two young children to be with Carlotta Monterey, an actress he would elope with in 1930. Carlotta devoted herself to "the Master." She provided O'Neill with the attention, care, and security he had always wanted from his mother. She successfully played the roles of mother, lover, and wife, and after O'Neill's death, she became the fierce and eccentric guardian of his literary reputation.

O'Neill was at the pinnacle of his popular and critical acclaim when he completed *Mourning Becomes Electra* in 1931. His epic, eleven-act resetting of Aeschylus' *Orestia* in post-Civil War New England was a conscious effort to mythologize American history and a textbook application of Freudian theory. The grandeur of O'Neill's conception impressed many critics who declared it his greatest play. *Ah, Wilderness!* in 1933 was a complete anomaly, a celebration of family and small-town life in turn-of-the-century New England. O'Neill described the play as "the way I would have *liked* my boyhood to have been." It was his only comedy and,

ironically, it proved to be one of his most popular works.

In 1934 O'Neill was diagnosed with a nervous disorder thought to be Parkinson's disease. Over the next ten years, the disorder would debilitate him to the point that he would stop writing, but in the meantime he devoted himself to a massive, eleven-play cycle dealing with American history from 1775 to 1932. The cycle was entitled *A Tale of Possessors, Self-Dispossessed,* but only two plays, *A Touch of the Poet* (1942) and *More Stately Mansions* (left unfinished in 1939) survive from it. Shortly before his death, O'Neill, with Carlotta's assistance, burned the unfinished drafts of the cycle to prevent them from being completed by someone else.

O'Neill interrupted work on the cycle to write what were to be his last completed works: *The Iceman Cometh* (1939), *Long Day's Journey into Night* (1940), *Hughie* (1942), and *A Moon for the Misbegotten* (1943). In these plays, O'Neill exorcized the ghosts that had haunted him all his life. These intensely personal and private works focused on his family and his own life. They were written at a time when his reputation was in eclipse and he had nothing to lose.

The Iceman Cometh examined the consequences of living without illusions. In the play, the charismatic Hickey extols to the wreckage that inhabits Harry Hope's saloon the virtues of living without pipe dreams. The monumental drama in four long acts looks back to Gorki's *Lower Depths* and, at the same time, forward to **Beckett**'s *Waiting for Godot*. It was the last play by O'Neill to be presented on Broadway during his lifetime.

Long Day's Journey into Night is a "play of old sorrow, written in tears and blood." O'Neill stipulated that it should not be produced until twenty-five years after his death, for here, the fictionalized O'Neills torment each other with the past. In this, their unending cycle of verbal assaults and apologies anticipates Sartre's *No Exit*. O'Neill concentrated the traumatic events of his youth into one harrowing evening and created an unflinching family portrait. Considered by many critics to be the greatest American play of the twentieth century, it received the Pulitzer Prize when it was presented in New York in 1956, three years after O'Neill's death.

Finally, *Hughie*, a one-act coda to *The Iceman Cometh*, and the elegiac *A Moon for the Misbegotten* allowed O'Neill to make peace with the memory of his older brother Jamie. The relationship between James Tyrone Jr. and Josie Hogan, whom O'Neill describes as "so oversized for a woman that she is almost a freak," is particularly poignant in *A Moon for the Misbegotten*. O'Neill invests Josie, his archetypal mother/lover figure, with a sensitivity and humanity that sets her above the rest of his female characters. It is Josie who provided James with the redemption and peace he so desperately seeks, a redemption and peace that sadly seems to have eluded O'Neill.

O'Neill's final years were consumed by failing health, an inability to write, and bitter domestic quarrels with Carlotta. Tragedy struck one last time in 1950, when his first son and namesake, Eugene O'Neill Jr., a once promising classics scholar, committed suicide. Isolated from his old friends and estranged from his children, he died on November 27, 1953 at the Hotel Shelton in Boston. His final words resonate the irony of a curtain line for one of his tragedies: "I knew it, I knew it! Born in a goddamn hotel room and dying in a hotel room!"

Note on Productions. O'Neill's reputation was rescued from obscurity after his death by a new generation of theater artists who rediscovered the power of his plays in performance. International interest was first focused on O'Neill's late plays during the world premier of *A Long Day's Journey Into Night*, directed by Karl Ragnar

Gierow, at the Stockholm Royal Dramatic Theatre in February 1956. The Royal Dramatic Theatre, with a long history of producing O'Neill's dramas going back to 1923, also premiered *A Touch of the Poet* in 1957, *Hughie* in 1958, and *More Stately Mansions* in 1962.

In May 1956, José Quintero directed an acclaimed production of The *Iceman Cometh* at the Circle-in-the-Square Theatre in New York with Jason Robards as Hickey. The production was a revelation. It inspired Carlotta to offer Quintero the American rights to *A Long Day's Journey into Night* (with Robards as James Tyrone Jr.) which was presented on Broadway in 1956. Both Quintero's directing and Robards' acting careers were distinguished by their many associations with O'Neill's plays. In 1964 they collaborated on the New York premier of *Hughie*, and in 1973 on an important revival of *A Moon for the Misbegotten* with Colleen Dewhurst as Josie Hogan.

Each decade has brought forth notable productions that have introduced O'Neill's plays to new audiences. Laurence Olivier played James Tyrone in Michael Blakemore's production of *A Long Day's Journey into Night* at the National Theatre in 1971. In 1986, the English director Jonathan Miller staged a controversial production of the play with the popular film actor Jack Lemmon as James Tyrone, and an unknown Kevin Spacey as Edmund. In 1999, Spacey played Hickey in Howard Davies' highly praised National Theatre production of *The Iceman Cometh* in London and New York. O'Neill's plays have also served as the catalyst for experimental productions by directors interested in challenging the realistic aesthetic. **Germany**'s Peter Stein produced a striking production of *The Hairy Ape* in Berlin in 1986 that wed O'Neill's text to the visual world of *The Cabinet of Dr. Caligari*. Even more radical and controversial was Elizabeth LeCompte's 1998 Wooster Group production of *The Emperor Jones* where the role of Brutus Jones was played by a white woman in black face. These productions persuasively demonstrate the continuing fascination with O'Neill's plays.

Robert C. Hansen

Selected Bibliography

Bogard, Travis. *Contour in Time: The Plays of Eugene O'Neill.* Fair Lawn, N.J.: Oxford UP, 1972.

Floyd, Virginia. *The Plays of Eugene O'Neill: A New Assessment.* New York: Frederick Ungar Publishing, 1985.

Gelb, Arthur, and Barbara Gelb. 1962. *O'Neill.* New York: Harper and Row, 1987.

Houchin, John, ed. *The Critical Response to Eugene O'Neill.* Westport, Conn.: Greenwood Press, 1993.

Sheaffer, Louis. *O'Neill: Son and Playwright.* Boston: Little, Brown and Company, 1968.

———. *O'Neill: Son and Artist.* Boston: Little, Brown and Company, 1973.

Smith, Madeline, and Robert Eaton. *Eugene O'Neill: An Annotated Bibliography.* Hamden, Conn.: Garland, 1988.

Objective Correlative

For **T. S. Eliot**, the purpose of art, and therefore language in poetry, was to codify an emotion, to represent an "internal reality." Eliot famously wrote in his 1919 essay on Hamlet that: "The only way of expressing emotion in the form of art is by finding an 'objective correlative'; in other words, a set of objects, a situation, a chain of events which shall be the formula of that *particular* emotion." In *Hamlet,* **Shakespeare** attempted to express the "inexpressibly horrible," and failed because Hamlet's feeling (his disgust for his mother) is greater than the situation Shakespeare represents. The expression of emotion through a chain of events is arguably what we have in Eliot's *The Waste Land:* a sequence of objects and situations which attempts to express the sense of sterility in the postwar Western world. The association of thought and feeling provides an intellectual mapping of the individual's emotional experience.

Peter Childs

Selected Bibliography

Eliot, T. S. "Hamlet and His Problems." In his *Selected Essays.* New York: Harcourt, Brace, 1950.

P

Pessoa, Fernando (1888–1935)

One of the most interesting and complex figures of Western literature in the twentieth century, Fernando Pessoa is best known for his heteronyms. The story of the genesis of the heteronyms was told by Pessoa, in the year of his death, in a letter addressed to Adolfo Casais Monteiro, a young poet and critic of *presença* (see **Portugal**). Pessoa's heteronyms are, literally, "other names" which Pessoa himself (or "orthonymous" Pessoa) gave to "other poets" he discovered in himself and under whose different personalities he wrote. Dozens of "other names" have been found among the vast number of manuscripts left by Pessoa (in the famous "arca" [trunk]), but the most important of the heteronyms, those responsible for some of the most original poetry written in the West in this century, are, besides Pessoa himself, Alberto Caeiro, Ricardo Reis, and Álvaro de Campos. The name of Bernardo Soares, a semi-heteronym according to the poet, and the author of an extraordinary fragmentary piece of poetic prose, posthumously published in 1982 as *Livro do desassossego* (*The Book of Disquietude*), must also be added to Pessoa's "drama em gente" ("drama in people," Pessoa's own phrase for the poetic phenomenon of himself). At the very beginning of the nineteenth century, Friedrich Schlegel spoke of "Unverständlichkeit" (Incomprehensibility) to identify the complexities and paradoxes of lyric poetry. Pessoa's "desassossego" (disquietude) is perhaps the best term of all to characterize Western modernity's deeper loss of grounds for meaning in its utmost consciousness of the opacity of language.

Pessoa was born in Lisbon in 1888, and died in the same city in 1935. He lived in Lisbon most of his life, except for a brief but very important period of his childhood and adolescence, during which he was in South Africa. After Pessoa lost his father at age five, his mother remarried, and in 1896 sailed for Durban to join her husband who had been recently appointed the Portuguese consul there. Seven-year old Fernando Pessoa traveled with her. He stayed for ten years and all his elementary and secondary schooling took place in English schools in South Africa. This experience was to leave a strong mark upon him. A contemporary of all the major Anglo-American modernist poets (he was born exactly the same year as **T. S. Eliot**), Pessoa received an elementary and secondary education in Durban that was similar to theirs. The Portuguese poet was also widely and deeply read in English Literature, wrote some very interesting and accomplished poems in English (including a handful of very early ones signed by Alexander Search, one of his first heteronyms), and the roots of his poetic theory and practice reach equally into Portuguese Literature and the Anglo-American literary tradition.

There is no indication that Pessoa was acquainted with the innovative poetics of Eliot or **Pound** during the first decades of the century, though he, too, was an attentive reader of *Nouvelle Révue Française* and well acquainted with the French symbolists. But the literary and artistic issues he was concerned with were similar to theirs, namely Eliot's aesthetics of objectivity. Like Eliot, Pessoa took an interest in Edgar Allan Poe's poetics of form and ratiocination. Even if, again like Eliot, he did not admire Poe's poems very much, Pessoa produced brilliant translations of some of them (e.g., "The Raven" ["O corvo"]). The relevance of Rimbaud's "je est un autre" for the theorization of a modernist poetics of impersonality cannot be ignored in Pessoa's case either, but his encounter, early on in his career, with **Walt Whitman,** the poet whose "I" is often "not the me myself," has been also duly acknowledged as a major influence in the appearance of the heteronyms (Pessoa/ Campos's celebrated "Saudação a Walt Whitman" ["Salutation to Walt Whitman"] dates from 1915). **Shakespeare**'s soliloquies, Keats's characterless poet, and Browning's dramatic monologues were also important for their development, as is clear in a very interesting fragment of about 1930, titled "Os graus da poesia lírica" ("The Degrees of Lyric Poetry").

Pessoa could actually be claimed by the Anglo-American poetic tradition as one of its most exquisite poets. This is not to say that the Portuguese modernist poet is to be judged primarily for his poetry written in English, quite the opposite. Pessoa's heavily convoluted English poems sound somewhat old-fashioned and stilted, and convey little of the striking freshness and revolutionary innovation in which his best Portuguese poetry excels. But they do teach us a great deal about Pessoa's conception of himself as a poet. In a letter addressed in the early thirties to João Gaspar Simões, a young literary critic also related to the *presença* group and Pessoa's

future biographer, Pessoa explains (as if to exonerate himself from possible charges of impropriety concerning two of the poems, the homoerotic "Antinous" and the ambiguously heteroerotic "Epithalamium") that his objective in writing those poems was to get "obscenity" out of his system and thus prepare to engage in "superior mental processes."

Whether, after the English poems were written and published (*Antinous,* 1918; *35 Sonnets,* 1918; *English Poems I and II,* 1921; and *English Poems III,* 1921), the poet succeeded in earning the integrity of mind he believed was being disrupted by the "obscene element," most critics of Pessoa would seriously doubt. The English poems and the way Pessoa was to view them years later may well be one more instance of Pessoa's most remarkable feature as a poet, his self-interruptive imagination, which the heteronyms best express. By writing the English poems ostensibly in order to heal himself from fracture, Pessoa is but repeating in another fashion the paradoxical self-inventing gesture of interrupting himself in order to "other" into many different selves his nonetheless one poetic (or fictional) self. The famous heteronyms of Pessoa, whose name of course means "person" and derives from the Latin *persona* (mask), are thus the poet's most complex fictional gesture of self-objectification, that is to say, of othering himself ("outrar-se" is Pessoa's coinage for this gesture of becoming other persons, "pessoas," not Pessoa), while keeping intact the fiction of the integral subject, or selfsame person (Pessoa), as precisely what it is also: a fiction. The first half of the twentieth century in the West was indeed witness to the development of an *impersonal* poetics of "objectivity," notably in Pound and Eliot, which might best be described, albeit by a term that is etymologically a paradox, as *Pessoan.* Pessoa's heteronyms are therefore best understood as a theatrical device by which the modern lyric subject deals with the problem of its own theoretical status by disappearing into its own objectification as various *personae,* or poetic masks. A fuller understanding of this problematic would have to take into account Pessoa's lyricization of drama in the unfinished "subjective tragedy" of "Fausto" ("Faust," the earliest fragments date from 1908) and "O marinheiro, drama estático" ("The Mariner, Static Drama," 1915).

For a while after his return to Portugal from South Africa in 1905, the young Pessoa attended the school that would later become the Faculty of Letters of the University of Lisbon, with the intention of obtaining a higher degree in Arts and Letters. He dropped out of school a few months after enrollment and never graduated, but he was by then already reading extensively in Portuguese literature. It was around 1908, he said once, after he read *Flores sem fruto* and *Folhas caídas,* by Almeida Garrett (1799–1854), that Pessoa decided to write all his major poetry in the Portuguese language. But he went on writing in English all his life, though mainly prose. He was also interested in Greek and German philosophy (Nietzsche was to make a strong impression on him), was aware of turn-of-the-century discussions of identity, sexuality, deviance, and normalcy (Max Nordau; Cesare Lombroso; Havelock Ellis; Edward Carpenter), and was both attracted by and critical of the aestheticism of Walter Pater and **Oscar Wilde.**

Pessoa also toyed for a while with the idea of going into the publishing business but the project soon fell through. All his life, Pessoa earned his living by working for import/export companies and taking care of commercial translations and correspondence, somewhat like Bernardo Soares, the author/protagonist of *Livro do desassossego.* Almost like self-effacing Bernardo Soares, who wrote the amazing "fragments" of his *journal intime* unbeknownst to all the others at the office, Pessoa published relatively little during his lifetime (the present controversy surrounding the publication of the "definitive edition" of his works is a fascinating issue in literary history) and led a very quiet, inconspicuous personal and social life. The only relationship of a romantic or sexual kind that is known of in his life is his Platonic attachment to Ophelia Queiroz, a colleague at one of the offices he worked in, to whom he wrote a series of love letters over a short period of time in the twenties. But Pessoa was not destined for the "common" bliss of bourgeois life, as at one point he explained to her. His "fate" had rather to do with "another Law" and with "Masters who neither consent nor pardon."

Pessoa's life was the "terrible mission" of poetry, as he himself insists in a letter written to his friend, Armando Côrtes-Rodrigues, as early as 1915. Pessoa's commitment to poetry, indeed, to *Portuguese* poetry, had already been evident in a series of articles he published in *A Águia* in 1912. Writing then about "the new Portuguese poetry," Pessoa elaborated at some length the current sociological and psychological conditions which, according to the poet, would inevitably force the emergence of a "supra-Camões" and an exceptionally fertile and brilliant era of poetic production in Portugal. *Mensagem* (1934, *Message*), the only major book of poems published by Pessoa during his lifetime and under his own name, a quintessentially modernist long poem made up of short lyrics skillfully combining the epic, lyric and dramatic modes (it can be best compared to Hart Crane's *The Bridge* [1930] in form, content, and intent), is a kind of elegiac counter-celebration of the Portuguese nation and sea-borne empire as sung by Luís de Camões (1525?–1580) in the great national epic *Os Lusíadas* (1572, *The Lusiads*). Pessoa's prophecy of a modern poet whose excellence was to supersede that of Camões may be seen as fulfilling itself in the heteronymic poet's multifaceted poetry.

Côrtes-Rodrigues was also a poet, as were all Pessoa's closest friends, Mário de

Sá-Carneiro foremost amongst them. In 1915 they were all engaged in putting together the first "little magazine" of Portuguese modernism, *Orpheu,* of which only two issues were to come out that same year. A third issue never got beyond the galley proofs for lack of funds. By then, Pessoa and his major heteronyms were already producing some of the most revolutionary poetry of the century. According to Pessoa, the first heteronym to appear, in the "ecstactic" writing of the sequence of poems titled *O guardador de rebanhos* (*The Keeper of Sheep*) in 1914, was Alberto Caeiro, the "master" of them all. "Disciples" of this seemingly artless pastoral yet wholly contrived poet of naturalness are, besides orthonymous Pessoa, Ricardo Reis, physician, latinist, and author of epicurean Horatian odes, and Álvaro de Campos, futurist, "sensationist," and Whitmanian singer of the ambiguities of nation, poetry, identity, and sexuality.

A very selective introductory sample of Pessoa's poetic work would have to include, besides the lyrical counter-epopee of *Mensagem* and a number of the highly self-conscious poetic fragments of *Livro do desassossego,* a choice of poems by Pessoa himself, Campos, Reis, and Caeiro. The theory of the heteronymic fiction makes "Autopsicografia" by orthonymous Pessoa mandatory. "Autopsychography" is the poem that defines the self-interruptive poet as a faker, feigner, or pretender: "O poeta é um fingidor./Finge tão completamente/Que chega fingir que é dor/A dor que deveras sente." ("The poet is a faker. He/Fakes it so completely,/He even fakes he's suffering/The pain he's really feeling.") Then, Álvaro de Campos and his "faked" trajectory from decadent "Opiário" ("Opium Eater") to the great futurist/decadent odes, "Ode triunfal" ("Triumphal Ode") and "Ode Marítima" ("Maritime Ode") (all dated 1915, though, actually, "Opiário" was written *after* the odes); the Nietzschean "Ultimatum" included in *Portugal Futur-*

ista (1917) (see Portugal); and the non-metaphysical musings of "Tabacaria" (1933; "Tobacco Shop"): "Não sou nada./Nunca serei nada./Não posso querer ser nada./À parte isso, tenho em mim todos os sonhos do mundo" ("I'm nothing./I'll always be nothing./I can't even wish to be something./Aside from that, I've got all the world's dreams inside me.") A complex alcaic ode by Ricardo Reis would also have to be included, perhaps, "De novo traz as aparentes novas" ("Again the new spring brings," 1923), in which Pessoa, born in Lisbon, arrogantly compares himself favorably to Homer, the greatest of all poets: " . . . e tu, que Ulisses erigira,/Tu em teus sete montes,/Orgulha-te, materna,/Igual desde ele às sete que contendem/cidades por Homero . . ." ("and you, who Ulysses had founded,/you, on your seven hills,/be maternally proud./For you are equal, because of him,/to the seven cities that claim Homer . . ."). Finally, from Alberto Caeiro, he of the "clear gaze," a poem about being not a poet. "E há poetas que são artistas" ("And there are poets who are artists," 1923) is the poem in which the fiction of the poet's artlessness is deconstructed by the obvious inevitability of the constructed poem itself: "E há poetas que são artistas/E trabalham nos seus versos/Como um carpinteiro nas tábuas! . . .//Que triste não saber florir!" ("And there are poets who are artists/And work on their poems/Like a carpenter on his planks! . . .//How sad, not knowing how to bloom! . . .").

With very few exceptions, all Pessoa's works were published posthumously. It all started in the 1940s with the Ática series, launched by some of Pessoa's *presença* friends and admirers, including Casais Monteiro, Gaspar Simões, and Jorge de Sena. In the 1960s, two distinguished Pessoan scholars, the Portuguese Jacinto do Prado Coelho and the German Georg Rudolf Lind, brought out two volumes of prose essays, some of them written originally in English. Prado Coelho was also responsible for the first edition of *Livro do desassossego* (1982). In the late 1980s a team of specialists known as "Equipa Pessoa" was officially appointed to work anew on the manuscripts in the infamous "arca" towards "the definitive edition." Imprensa Nacional-Casa da Moeda has already published several volumes. However, given the controversy launched by another distinguished Pessoan scholar, Teresa Rita Lopes, after the publication of the "Álvaro de Campos" volume, what was meant to be the definitive text of an author rapidly became a battlefield of problematic authorships and contested identities. Fortunately, the convenient two-volume pocket edition of *Obra poética* (*Poetry*) and *Obras em Prosa* (*Prose*) by Aguilar of Rio de Janeiro (1960), frequently updated in the course of its many reprints, is still available. The publishing house, Assírio & Alvim (Lisbon), is currently bringing out several volumes of what claims to be the complete Pessoa.

Pessoa has been translated into many languages. His best known and most successful translators into English are Jean R. Longland, Edwin Honig and Susan Brown, Peter Rickard, Jonathan Griffin, F. E. G. Quintanilha, Suzette Macedo, George Monteiro, Richard Zenith, Margaret Jull Costa. A convenient anthology by some of the same and several other translators is *A Centenary Pessoa,* edited by Eugénio Lisboa and L. C. Taylor (Manchester: Carcanet, 1995).

Maria Irene Ramalho de Sousa Santos

Selected Bibliography

Bréchon, Robert. *Étrange Étranger: Une Biographie de Fernando Pessoa.* Paris: Christian Bourgois, 1996.

Coelho, Jacinto do Prado. *Unidade e Diversidade em Fernando Pessoa.* 1950. Lisboa: Verbo, 1982.

Crespo, Angel. *La Vida Plural de Fernando Pessoa.* Barcelona: Seix Barral, 1988.

Güntert, Georges. *Das Fremde Ich: Fernando Pessoa.* Berlin: Walter de Gruyter & Co., 1971.

Hamburger, Michael. *The Truth of Poetry: Tensions in Modernist Poetry since Baudelaire.* London: Weidenfeld and Nicolson, 1969.

Josipovici, Gabriel. *The Lessons of Modernism and Other Essays.* London: Macmillan, 1977.

Lourenço, Eduardo. *Fernando Pessoa Revisitado: Leitura Estruturante do Drama em Gente.* Porto: Inova, 1973.

Perrone-Moisés, Leyla. *Fernando Pessoa: Aquém do eu, Além do Outro.* S. Paulo: Martins Fontes, 1982.

Sacramento, Mário. *Fernando Pessoa: Poeta da Hora Absurda.* 1958. Porto: Inova, 1970.

Sadlier, Arlene. *An Introduction to Fernando Pessoa: Modernism and the Paradoxes of Authorship.* Gainsville: U P of Florida, 1998.

Seabra, José Augusto. *Fernando Pessoa ou o Poetodrama.* S. Paulo: Perspectiva, 1974.

de Sena, Jorge. *Fernando Pessoa & Ca. Heteronímica.* 2 vols. Lisboa: Edições 70, 1982.

Tabucchi, Antonio. *Il Poeta e la Finzione: Scritti su Fernando Pessoa.* Genova: Tilgher-Genova, 1983.

Pirandello, Luigi (1867–1936)

Though perhaps best known for his innovative and influential work as a playwright, Pirandello was also a prolific poet, short story writer, novelist, and essayist. He was born in Southern Sicily, where his father was a wealthy sulphur merchant. He studied at the universities of Palermo, Rome, and Bonn (**Germany**), graduating from the latter with a doctorate in romance philology. Afterwards, he married and settled down in Rome with his three children. His personal life was to be marked by tragedy. In 1903 the flooding of his father's sulphur mines left him bankrupt: a blow which precipitated his wife's breakdown and descent into paranoia and insanity. His response to her condition is often said to inform his pessimistic but compassionate outlook.

Pirandello began by writing lyrical poetry and short stories. His first major critical success came with the publication of the novel *Il fu Mattia Pascal* (1904, *The Late Mattia Pascal*). His early prose writings show the influence of **Verga**'s "verismo" movement, but his interests were always strongly philosophical. His relativism and anti-rationalism are fully expressed in his work for the theater, which occupied his attention during **the war.** Pirandello sought to make his audience aware of the theatricality of existence: his plays are highly self-conscious, forcing their audiences to relate to the action on stage by eschewing the comforts of illusion and the willing suspension of disbelief. His most famous trilogy of plays is *Sei personaggi in cerca d'autore* (1921, *Six Characters in Search of an Author*), *Ciascuno a suo modo* (1924, *Each in His Own Way*), and *Questa sera si recita a soggetto* (1930, *Tonight We Improvise*). Some critics consider *Enrico IV* (1922, *Henry IV*) his masterpiece.

Pirandello's political leanings are unendearing. He joined the fascist party in 1924, and Mussolini funded his own theater company, Teatro d'Arte di Roma, from 1925 to 1928, when it disbanded. He was awarded the Nobel Prize for Literature in 1934. His influence is widely felt, especially in the work of Camus, Sartre, Ionesco, and **Beckett,** and in the formation of a Theater of the Absurd.

Andrew Harrison

Selected Bibliography

The standard edition of Pirandello's works is published in **Italy** by Mondadori. English translations are widely available through various publishing houses. A bibliography of his works is contained in Giudice (1975).

Bassanese, Fiora A. *Understanding Luigi Pirandello.* Columbia: University of South Carolina Press, 1997.

Caputi, Anthony. *Pirandello and the Crisis of Modern Consciousness.* Urbana: University of Illinois Press, 1988.

Giudice, Gaspare. *Pirandello: A Biography.* London: Oxford UP, 1975.

The Politics of Modernism

The politics of modernism are as disparate and various as the diversity of aims, movements, forms, and techniques from which it is composed. If it is possible to identify a single political perspective characteristic of modernism it is a shared rejection of the values and cultural practices of a rather broadly defined bourgeoisie. In visual art, for example, critics sympathetic to the post-impressionist exhibition, which came to Britain from Paris in 1910, saw nineteenth-century British painting as symptomatic of a bourgeois culture that reduced human experience to an unthreatening and comfortable sterility. According to Richard Muther this was an art in which, "everything must be kept within the bounds of what is charming, temperate and prosperous without in any degree suggesting the struggle for existence" (Holbrook Jackson 274).

Marinetti's Futurist Manifesto, which appeared in *Le Figaro* in 1909, reflects a similar rejection of the values of an earlier literature that is seen as willfully soporific and hostile to action. "Up to now literature has exalted a pensive immobility, ecstasy, and sleep. We intend to exalt aggressive action, a feverish insomnia, the racer's stride, the mortal leap, the punch and the slap" (Kolocotroni 251). The futurist "punch and the slap" reflects a hostility, and an implied violence, towards bourgeois cultural institutions which overlaps with both the surrealist and dadaist aspiration to destroy the existing social order: " . . . every means must be worth trying, in order to lay waste to the ideas of *family, country, religion*" (Breton 128).

As Raymond Williams has pointed out, however, this shared preoccupation did not produce a unified politics: " . . . within what may at first hearing sound like closely comparable denunciations of the bourgeois, there are already radically different positions, which would lead eventually . . . not only to different but to directly opposed kinds of politics: to fascism or to communism; to social democracy or to conservatism and the cult of excellence" (Williams 1989: 55). Williams points out that modernism has been as easily associated with an aristocratic distaste for spiritually narrow bourgeois values as with a proletarian resistance to the commodification of the results of artistic labor. In different historical contexts and by different movements the modernist artist was conceived, analogously at least, as both alienated laborer and "true aristocrat." By 1920, for example, in *En avant Dada* Richard Huelsenbeck makes an explicit connection between dadaism and the German left and deplores the bourgeois economic interest in art. "Dada is German bolshevism. The bourgeois must be deprived of the opportunity to 'buy up art for his justification' " (Harrison 259). A year earlier he demands centralized state support for artists and intellectuals. In "What is Dadaism and What does it want in Germany" he calls for, "Daily meals at public expense for all creative and intellectual men and women" (Harrison 256).

In Marinetti's Futurist Manifesto, on the other hand, modern civilization is seen as degenerate and in need of purging of its weak elements. The "young and strong *Futurists!*" must be protected from the constraining influence of the past which provides "a solace for the ills of the moribund, the sickly" (Kolocotroni 253). **Futurism**'s famous glorification of war, "the world's only hygiene" (Kolocotroni 251), celebrates irrational creativity as the necessary alternative to bourgeois preoccupations with domestic stability. From a condemnation of the bourgeois failure to recognize the value of artistic creativity it is an easy step to a wholesale condemnation of a proletarian mass seen as incapable of comprehending authentic art. **Italian futurism**'s valorization of what it perceived as the strong individual artist's struggle against the debilitating effects of social constraint, including "moralism, feminism, every opportunistic or utilitarian cowardice" (Kolocotroni 251), resulted in an open support for Italian fascism under Mussolini.

Marinetti's fear of cultural degeneration was shared by the so called "men of 1914" whose hostility to the cultural values of Victorian humanism and sentimentality led not only to a radically impersonal poetics but to more or less extreme right wing sympathies. These ranged from **T. S. Eliot**'s anglo-catholic Christian conservatism to **Wyndham Lewis**'s relatively short lived support for Hitler in the early nineteen thirties and **Ezra Pound**'s public endorsement of both Hitler and Mussolini during the second world war.

The rejection of liberal bourgeois sensibilities from both the right and the left, although overwhelming, was not the only modernist response to the new century however. While the various members of the **Bloomsbury** group were also, in Leonard Woolf's words, in " . . . conscious revolt against the social, political, religious, moral, intellectual and artistic institutions, beliefs and standards of our fathers and grandfathers" (Williams 1980: 153), it was a liberal and reformist revolt. In 1924 **Virginia Woolf,** for example, expresses her excitement at the possibilities for social and cultural change at the end of the Edwardian era by comparing the Victorian cook, who dwells "like a leviathan in the lower depths silent, obscure, inscrutable;" with the Georgian cook who she describes as " . . . a creature of sunshine and fresh air; in and out of the drawing-room, now to borrow the *Daily Herald,* now to ask advice about a hat" (Woolf 92). Where the poetic and political values of the men of 1914 advocate an escape from what they perceived as the disorder of recent and contemporary history, particularly the growing emphasis on individualism, personality and consumerism, Woolf's modernism is firmly embedded in the elaboration of the social effects of all of these. Her Georgian cook's free passage from the "lower depths" of the kitchen to the drawing-room suggests a social mobility and an engagement with mass and consumer culture, represented by the *Daily Herald* and the hat, that would have been anathema to Eliot or Pound. Her critique of Eliot's intolerance of "the old usages and politenesses of society—respect for the weak, consideration for the dull!" (Woolf 109) is also at complete odds with Marinetti's preoccupation with both breaking with the past and protecting the strong from the weak and is characteristic of a liberal and inclusive version of modernism.

The relatively recent inclusion of Virginia Woolf in the modernist canon reflects another aspect of the politics of modernism. Her reintroduction is an early example of the retrospective interpretation and reconstruction of modernism by literary criticism subsequent to the modernist period. The American New Criticism of the 1940s which included the criticism of T. S. Eliot, did much to consolidate a specifically Anglo-American right leaning version of modernism. The modernist canon established in the forties and fifties has since that time been reconsidered from a range of theoretical and historical perspectives. This revaluation has often sought to replace Eliot's call for modern poetry to "escape from personality" with an attention to examples of modernist writing that have addressed the modern experience from a range of geographically, historically, and culturally specific perspectives. Critics such as Houston Baker, Nathan Huggins, and George Hutchinson, for example, have considered the relationship of African American writers of the **Harlem Renaissance** to modernism. Shari Benstock and Bonnie Kime Scott discuss the work of neglected women modernists and James Arnold and Gregson Davis, amongst others, demonstrate the relationship between Caribbean poets of the *Négritude* movement with European modernism. This ongoing revaluation has changed the political landscape of modernism significantly.

The politics of modernism also includes debate regarding the relationship between politics and art as different but related forms of social practice. Hand in hand with the modernist rejection of established cultural norms is its rejection of traditional modes of representation, particularly **realism,** in which earlier forms of cultural expression are often seen as inadequate to the task of reflecting the new modern world and the new modernist sensibility. This *avant-garde* aspect of modernism has been viewed with suspicion by a broad range of political orthodoxies leading to significant debate concerning the relationship between aesthetics and politics.

The polemical exchange that took place between **Bertolt Brecht** and Georg Lukács during the 1930s reflects two polarized perspectives of this debate. Writing from the political left Lukács saw the experimental writing of the modernist *avant-garde* as failing to address the objective processes of history. He argues that **naturalism,** and later modernism, emphasizes subjective experience at the expense of objective reality subordinating reality to the processes of writing. In "a reversed order of significance" he argues "the object is made a symbol" (Lukács 131) rather than having significance independent of language. Lukács rejects what he calls the formalism of *avant-garde* writing and argues that it is incapable of dealing accurately with political processes. Brecht's response to this political critique argues that Lukács' continued valorization of the critical realism of the previous century is itself formalist as it emphasizes a literary form that was developed in response to an earlier economic paradigm. For Brecht new historical and political circumstances require new modes of expression.

Variations on the basic principles of this debate have appeared in a variety of different contexts both at the time and since. It has found echoes, for example, in modern feminist and post-colonial studies. In this sense questions regarding the politics of language initiated during the modernist period remain relevant to the present day.

Simon J. Ross

Selected Bibliography

Arnold, A. James. *Modernism and Negritude: The Poetry and Poetics of Aimé Césaire.* Cambridge, Mass.: Harvard UP, 1981.

Baker, Houston. *Modernism and the Harlem Renaissance.* Chicago: Chicago UP, 1987.

Blair, Sarah. "Modernism and the Politics of culture." *The Cambridge Companion to Modernism.* Ed. Michael Levenson. Cambridge: Cambridge UP, 1999. 157–173.

Bloch, Ernst, et al. *Aesthetics and Politics.* London: New Left Books, 1977.

Breton, André. *Manifestoes of Surrealism.* Trans. Richard Seaver and Helen R. Lane. Michigan: University of Michigan Press, 1969.

Davis, G. *Aimé Césaire.* Cambridge: Cambridge UP., 1997.

Eliot, T. S. *Selected Essays.* London: Faber and Faber, 1951.

Harrison, Charles, and Paul Wood, eds. *Art in Theory 1900–1990.* Oxford: Blackwell, 1992.

Jackson, Holbrook. *The Eighteen Nineties. 1913.* London: Pelican, 1939.

Kime-Scott, Bonnie. *The Gender of Modernism.* Indiana: Indiana UP, 1990.

Kolocotroni, Vassiliki, et al., eds. *Modernism: An Anthology of Sources and Documents.* Edinburgh: Edinburgh UP, 1998.

Lovell, Terry. *Pictures of Reality.* London: BFI Publishing, 1980.

Lukács, Georg. "Narrate or Describe." 1936. In *Lukács, Writer and Critic and other Essays.* Ed. Arthur Kahn. London: Merlin Press, 1970, 110–148.

Tzara, Tristan. *Seven Dada Manifestos and Lampisteries.* Trans. Barbara Wright. London: Calder Publications, 1977.

Williams, Raymond. "The Bloomsbury Fraction." *Problems in Materialism and Culture.* Verso: London, 1980. 148–169.

———. "The Politics of Modernism." *Against the New Conformists,* Ed. Tony Pinkney. London: Verso, 1989.

Woolf, Virginia. "Mr. Bennett and Mrs. Brown." *The Captain's Deathbed and Other Essays.* Ed. Leonard Woolf. Hogarth: London, 1950. 90–111.

A Portrait of the Artist as a Young Man (1916) and *Stephen Hero*

A partly autobiographical novel by **James Joyce** which describes Stephen Dedalus's growing disillusionment with the constraints of Irish society and his gradual sense of his own destiny as poet. It traces his physical and spiritual liberation from the ties of family, nationality, and religion. Having appeared in serial form in *The Egoist* during 1914–15, *A Portrait of the Artist as a Young Man* was his first published novel in 1916.

The novel is written in carefully crafted prose and skillfully arranged in five chapters spanning events from Stephen's infancy to his student days around the turn of the century. As the title suggests, the novel focuses on the young man and budding artist in a series of tableaux. The successive chapters, subdivided into sections, show Stephen overcoming the internal and external forces that prevent his soul from taking flight. Chapter One deals with Stephen's earliest days at home and with his life at boarding school where he is bullied by older boys but stands up to one of his teachers, who punishes him unjustly, by appealing to the Rector. Chapter Two speaks of Stephen's growing love of literature and his family's diminishing fortunes. At college he stands out intellectually and wins a prize, but predictably fails to stop his family sliding into poverty; the chapter closes with Stephen's first sexual encounter with a prostitute. The third chapter consists largely of a hell-fire sermon delivered during a college retreat and Stephen's reaction to it. Terrified by the preacher's powerful rhetoric, Stephen resolves to confess his mortal sins and repent. Chapter Four describes Stephen's zealous if short-lived mortifications; how he decides against a religious vocation when the director of studies suggests it; and how he opts for an artistic vocation instead. In Chapter Five Stephen refuses to become involved in the Irish nationalist movement, and he rejects Irish catholicism as well as his family. He outlines to a friend his aesthetic theory which, for him, has come to replace catholic dogma. The novel closes with Stephen Dedalus, who is set to leave claustrophobic **Ireland** behind, famously declaring: "I go to encounter for the millionth time the reality of experience and to forge in the smithy of my soul the uncreated conscience of my race."

The choice of the name Dedalus recalls the legendary craftsman and inventor who made the Cretan labyrinth and fashioned wings for himself and his son Icarus. *A Portrait of the Artist as a Young Man* is prefaced by an epigraph from Ovid's *Metamorphoses* (VIII, 188) evoking Daedalus and ends with an appeal to him as "Old father, old artificer."

The novel radically departs from conventional modes of representation right from the start. It opens in the third person with an unmediated fairy tale which the father tells young Stephen; develops abruptly through a rendering of the linguistic abilities and concerns of early childhood; and ends in the first person with the diary entries of the young artist—an open form which resists closure in typical Joycean fashion. Questions of narrative viewpoint are raised throughout the text as it partly suggests Stephen's development and partly comments on it. Ultimately it is impossible to assess the novel's attitude to its main protagonist as it fluctuates between sympathetic understanding and ironic detachment.

The novel evolved through a series of radical changes. Joyce had written an essay entitled "A Portrait of the Artist" which the Irish literary magazine *Dana* declined to publish in 1904. Almost immediately he began revising and expanding the essay into a book-length work of largely conventional writing provisionally entitled *Stephen Hero* which traced the evolution of an artist from infancy to his university days. While living in Paris, Joyce gave the manuscript of *Stephen Hero* to Sylvia Beach who sold it to the Harvard College Library in 1938. Theodore Spencer first published a manuscript fragment under the title *Stephen Hero* in 1944, despite a letter of April 22, 1939 written by Paul Léon on Joyce's behalf expressing unease at the prospect of the fragment's publication.

Setting out from a radically altered conception in 1907 Joyce reworked *Stephen Hero* into *A Portrait of the Artist as a Young Man* retaining many of the characters and incidents, but abandoning the realistic form in favor of a much more flexible style. He greatly condensed the material, removed all authorial discourse, and boldly juxtaposed a variety of styles including the elaborate prose of the 1890s and naturalistic description. The narrative, rather than being strictly linear, was made to consist of a series of episodes, with thematically related vignettes. The episodes and vignettes were then linked by motif-like phrases which alter ever so subtly to indicate Stephen's growing emotional and mental vocabulary. Such internal echoes and correspondences make *A Portrait of the Artist as a Young Man* extraordinarily dense and allusive. The absence of narrative comment forces the reader to engage actively with the text.

Christine O'Neill

Selected Bibliography

Beja, Morris, ed. *James Joyce:* Dubliners *and* A Portrait of the Artist as a Young Man: *A Selection of Critical Essays.* London: Macmillan, 1985.

Deane, Seamus, ed. *A Portrait of the Artist as a Young Man.* Harmondsworth: Penguin, 1992.

Ellmann, Maud. "Disremembering Dedalus: A Portrait of the Artist as a Young Man." In *Untying the Text: A Poststructuralist Reader.* Ed. Robert Young. Boston: Routledge & Kegan Paul, 1981.

Gabler, Hans Walter. "Towards a Critical Text of James Joyce's *A Portrait of the Artist as a Young Man.*" *Studies in Bibliography* 17 (1974).

Gifford, Don. *Joyce Annotated: Notes for* Dubliners *and* A Portrait of the Artist as a Young Man. 2nd ed. Berkeley, Los Angeles and London: U of California P, 1982.

Kershner, R. B. Jr., ed. *James Joyce: A Portrait of the Artist as a Young Man.* Boston and New York: Bedford Books of St. Martin's Press, 1993.

Schutte, William M, ed. *Twentieth Century Interpretations of* A Portrait of the Artist as a Young Man. Englewood Cliffs, N.J.: Prentice Hall, 1968.

Staley, Thomas F. and Bernard Benstock, eds. *Approaches to Joyce's Portrait. Ten Essays.* Pittsburg and London: University of Pittsburg, 1976.

Portugal

When the long poem, *Tabacaria,* signed by Álvaro de Campos and beginning with the lines "Não sou nada / Nunca serei nada" ("I am nothing / I shall never be anything") was published in the review *Presença* in 1933, it is arguable that the "nada" in the poem refers to its author, **Fernando Pessoa** (1888–1935), given the isolation to which contemporary Lisbon had condemned him. But such a declaration of non-existence can be applied to Portuguese modernism itself, for although the movement had manifested itself in several forms as early as 1914—in the review *A Renascença,* in poetry and fiction by Mário de Sá-Carneiro (1890–1916) (*Dispersão, A Confissão de Lúcio*), and in the poems of *Distância* by Alfredo Guisado (1891–1975)—it was not until much later that it met with any public or critical recognition.

It was briefly a *succès de scandale* in 1915 with Mário de Sá-Carneiro's *Céu em Fogo,* and, most notoriously, with the two numbers of *Orpheu* published by Fernando Pessoa and Mário de Sá-Carneiro; but manifestations of modernism in 1916—the two reviews *Exílio* and *Centauro,* and an exhibition by the painter Amadeo de Souza-Cardoso (1887–1918)—were once more generally ignored. Modernism be-

came a police matter when the review *Portugal Futurista* was seized in 1917; and in the same year the painter, writer and playwright Almada Negreiros (1893–1970) published two futurist books, *A Engomadeira* and *K4 Quadrado Azul.* But after four years of modernist activity, the reading public (if it took any notice of them at all) was merely contemptuous or abusive toward the group of artists it designated indiscriminately as "futurists." In a precise historical sense, therefore, Portuguese modernism did not even begin to exist. Or rather, it began to exist—perhaps as elsewhere in Europe—only in retrospect, as we shall see.

Symbolism had found itself in a similar situation of invisibility. At least two of its great names, the poets Camilo Pessanha (1867–1926) and Ângelo de Lima (1872–1921), had written a large part of their work back in the nineteenth century, but they remained obscure until the emergence of the modernist aesthetic being discussed here. Ângelo de Lima was "discovered" by *Orpheu 2* and Camilo Pessanha was given prominence in *Centauro* in 1916. Such acts of revaluation demonstrate the aesthetic affinity between symbolism and modernism, but they also show how little avant-garde art coincided with public expectations. (And if modernism openly admitted its debt to its symbolist masters, it nevertheless carried a good deal further their attempts to reinvent and revitalize language.)

The very cosmopolitan nature of Portuguese modernism meant that artists quickly responded to contemporary developments elsewhere in Europe and this encouraged the emergence of an avant-garde group in Lisbon which followed the precepts of the cubist or futurist vanguard by publishing provocative texts in the press or promoting public meetings for the reading of manifestos, asserting through the slightest gesture and in each and every line of their verses their passion for challenging and rupturing the accepted forms of the past. Key moments in the development of this movement were Pessoa's newspaper contributions in 1915; the "vertiginista" manifesto of Raul Leal (1886–1964), *O Bando Sinistro,* from the same year; Almada Negreiros' manifesto *Anti-Dantas* and his support for Amadeo de Souza-Cardoso's exhibition, both in 1916; and the Futurist Conference which took place in Lisbon in 1917, at which the same Almada Negreiros presented another key manifesto, the *Ultimatum.*

During these years, the hostility or the silence of the public had their counterpart in the intense inner vitality of the modernist group. Their "eccentric" life, recorded for posterity in notes left by Pessoa and in the correspondence of Sá-Carneiro, had a theoretical core which grew out of the influence of symbolist and vanguardist traditions. This resulted, at first, in the poetics of *paulismo* characterized by the theme of the division of the self and by extensive rhetoric, bordering on the subversive. The beginnings of paulismo, which had *A Renascença* as its unofficial vehicle, are to be found in the 1913 texts of Sá-Carneiro and Pessoa, who circulated manuscripts that gave rise in 1914 to the above-mentioned books of Sá-Carneiro and Guisado. Paulismo quickly grew into *interseccionismo,* which had its starting point in **cubism.** Pessoa considered publishing a manifesto that would launch it as a vanguard movement, but this did not come to fruition. Some of its best examples are the poetry of Sá-Carneiro in the collection *Indícios de Oiro* (published posthumously in 1937) and *Chuva Oblíqua,* a long poem by Pessoa published in *Orpheu 2.* The same issue of *Orpheu* included reproductions of the interseccionista paintings of Santa Rita Pintor. Later on, the last stage of this movement was called *sensacionismo. Orpheu* 3, which was to act as its official organ, never saw the light of day, owing to lack of funds. Drafts for a manifesto, penned by Pessoa, who planned the international launching of this "ism," still survive, but the key texts of "sensacionismo" are the great odes of Álvaro de Campos, published in *Orpheu 1* and *2,* as well as Almada Negreiros' *Cena do Ódio* (which had been projected for number 3).

Sensacionismo had obvious points of contact with **futurism,** despite the fact that it did not follow **Marinetti**'s teachings. Its stance was one of rupture with traditional forms. As such, it did not need to follow the programs received from Europe. Its synchronization with the avant-garde was deeper and more immediate. The greatest Portuguese painter of modernism, Amadeo de Souza-Cardoso, declared in an interview that he did not follow any "ism" and yet followed them all simultaneously. What mattered to him was variation itself, the experiment with several aesthetic possibilities opened up by avant-garde art. Something similar could be said about Fernando Pessoa: what emerges from the radical crisis of the self as a guarantor of meaning, underscored by his heteronymic proliferation, is a coherent body of work shaped by variability or essential poetic multiplicity.

This heroic period of Portuguese modernism was followed by a gradual adaptation for greater public consumption. Gone were the days of revolution. Thus the review *Contemporânea,* which had a period of regular publication in 1922 and 1923, and in which the modernists were largely published, looked like a glossy magazine. As for *Athena,* edited by Pessoa and with five issues in 1924–1925, it separated the realm of literature from that of painting, in an effort of organization and appeal. In the 1920s, a new provocation of the public, this time based on homoerotic themes, was enacted by the second modernist generation, particularly in the persons and works of António Botto (1897–1959) and Judith Teixeira (1880–1959), but arguably without the explosive quality of the previous decade. António Ferro (1895–1956), who had been part of the *Orpheu* group while still very young, remained active as an author of manifestos, a man of the theater and a journalist and went on to become responsible for a politics of culture and propaganda during Salazar's dictatorship.

Finally, any assessment of Portuguese modernism would remain incomplete without reference to the decisive role played by the review *Presença* from 1927 to 1940, and more particularly to the significant body of criticism published therein by José Régio (1901–1969), João Gaspar Simões (1903–1987), and Adolfo Casais Monteiro (1908–1972). It was undoubtedly thanks to their efforts that the label of modernism as we perceive it today came into being, as well as the recognition of the undisputed genius of those whom they called masters, Fernando Pessoa, Mário de Sá-Carneiro, and Almada Negreiros. In short, it was *Presença* that built the bridge that took the generation of *Orpheu* to the future.

Fernando Cabral Martins

Selected Bibliography

Guimarães, Fernando. *Simbolismo, Modernismo e Vanguardas.* 2nd ed. Porto: Lello, 1992.

Júdice, Nuno. *A Era de "Orpheu."* Lisboa: Teorema, 1986.

Lourenço, Eduardo. *Tempo e Poesia.* Porto: Inova, n.d.

Pessoa, Fernando. *A Centenary Pessoa.* Ed. Eugénio Lisboa and L.C. Taylor. Manchester: Carcanet, 1995

Quadros, António. *O Primeiro Modernismo Português.* Lisboa: Europa-América, 1989.

Sá-Carneiro, Mário de. *Lúcio's Confession.* Transl. Margaret Jull Costa. Sawtry: Dedalus, 1993.

Seabra, José Augusto. *Poligrafias Poéticas.* Porto: Lello, 1994.

Post-Impressionism

The post-impressionist period extends from the last impressionist exhibition in 1886 to the rise of **cubism** in 1906. The term was coined for Roger Fry's London exhibition "Manet and the Post-Impressionists" in 1910, which included Cézanne, Gauguin, van Gogh, Matisse, and Picasso; the Second Post-Impressionist Exhibition (1912) included the Fauves, Vlaminck, Derain, and Braque. Post-impressionism aims at harmonies of pure color and form, asserting decorative and structural principles. According to Fry, who claimed that aesthetic responses to art are based solely on formal interrelations, the post-impressionists were concerned with "plastic equivalents" for spiritual reality, rather than atmospheric impressions. They were responding to new aesthetic forces: (1) Japanese art, especially the woodblock prints of Hokusai and Hiroshige; (2) photography, with its angles of vision that cropped figures; (3) pure or unmixed colors, often applied straight from the tube; (4) scientific *divisionism* (see **Neo-Impressionism**); (5) symbolism. The major figures are Paul Cézanne (1839–1906), Vincent van Gogh (1853–90), and Paul Gauguin (1848–1903). Reacting against the amorphous textures of **impressionism,** post-impressionists aimed at clear modeling of space, using color and line arbitrarily to heighten design. Maurice Denis stated that "a painting, before becoming a war horse, a nude woman or some anecdote, is essentially a flat surface covered with colors arranged in a certain order" (see Kelder 192–93).

Post-impressionists searched for form in substance. As Schapiro says, "[p]ure painting meant the dedication to the visual as a complete world grasped directly as a structure of tones, without intervention of ideas or feelings . . ." (*Cézanne* 24). This emphasis on the concrete reality of the medium has affinities with the "poésie pure" of Mallarmé, which created an autoreferential world of verbal textures and nuances. But Cézanne, in his groundbreaking art, was mainly concerned to grasp and express underlying structures of nature. He wanted "to redo Poussin after nature" and advised Émile Bernard to "deal with nature as cylinders, spheres, cones, all placed in perspective so that each aspect of an object or a plane goes toward a central point" (*Letters* 296). He attempted to develop an original intuition (or "petite sensation"), by translating material into plastic forms, and maintained that "[the] writer expresses himself through abstractions whereas the painter is concrete through line and color, his feelings, his perceptions" (*Letters* 297).

Cézanne could look at his own head as objectively as at an apple. **D. H. Lawrence** celebrated this "appleyness" of his painting, its rendering of sensuous solidity; and, although Lawrence's phenomenalism is the opposite of Fry's formalism, both critics praised Cézanne for struggling to grasp the object as it is in itself and for smashing clichés. Cézanne felt the need to overcome habit and recover a pristine vision. Lily Briscoe, **Woolf**'s artist in *To the Lighthouse,* seeks similarly to capture "that very jar on the nerves, the thing itself before it has been made anything" (193); she "[wants] to be on a level with ordinary experience, to feel simply that's a chair, that's a table, and yet at the same time, It's a miracle, it's an ecstasy" (193, 202). So the natural, in its density and complexity, appears miraculous in Cézanne's still-lifes.

According to Fry, Cézanne's painting reduces "actual objects" to "*pure elements of space and volume*" (58); the forms then assume an equivalent reality of their own. As he struggles to articulate a natural vision, Cézanne achieves "a dynamic and not a static equilibrium" (Fry 62). In order to build a harmonious architecture of planes and shapes, he deforms the contours of objects. Cézanne reconstructs the image of space through mutual readjustment of geometric forms—just as Lily reminds herself "to put the tree further in the middle" (*To the Lighthouse* 84). His landscapes rest on a harmony of straight

and arabesque lines, cubes and rectangles, in which spatial modelling presents an animate image of stillness. He constructs his paintings on "a geometrical scaffolding," yet builds up "a smouldering glow of colour" from "innumerable touches" (Fry 70). In still lifes and landscapes, he strives to combine recessive depth with the flat surface of the picture plane.

In Cézanne's painting, an ordered sequence of planes is "modified everywhere by an infinity of minute movements" (Fry 62). Objects are assembled, as design dictates, without regard for exact proportion or position. Dark edges, adjacent tones, and color contrasts emphasize shapes and volumes. A deep contemplation of nature lies behind Cézanne's "plastic construction" (Fry), in which forms converge and diverge. In the still lifes, firmly cohering shapes and planes combine "solidity, weight, opacity, and transparency" (Schapiro, *Cézanne* 96). In the *Portrait of Gustave Geffroy* (1895), one can see "a rare union of the realistic vision of a piece of space . . . [with an] effort to adjust all that is seen in a coherent balanced structure" (Schapiro 94). In his late landscapes of *Mont Sainte-Victoire* (1904–06), Cézanne, finding an outlet for pent-up baroque impulses, loosens form in a rhapsodic harmony of blues and greens.

The post-impressionist artwork fuses surface and depth, color and mass, texture and structure. Cézanne sought "harmony" and "synthesis" (Fry 64) in a "geometric" use of color; Woolf's surrogate artist conceives her work in comparable terms: "Beautiful and bright it should be on the surface, feathery and evanescent, one colour melting into another like the colours on a butterfly's wing; but beneath the fabric must be clamped together with bolts of iron" (*To the Lighthouse* 171). Her image of art is a paradigm of the post-impressionist synthesis of surface and structure. Just as Cézanne "[transposes] all the data of nature into values of 'plastic colour'" (Fry 69), Woolf transposes psychological data of perception and memory into structurally linked streams of images.

Van Gogh, who painted the sombre *Potato Eaters* (1885) in earth-tones, lightened his palette after he came to Paris in 1886 and encountered neo-impressionism. Although he never adopted Seurat's method systematically, he learned to surround objects with auras of complementary color. After he moved to Arles in 1888, his paintings drew intensity from the clash of complementary colors. In 1890 Albert Aurier described van Gogh as a symbolist: his studies of irises, sunflowers, an old bridge, are so charged with feeling as to symbolize inner states (see Pickvance, Appendix III, 310–15). But van Gogh's symbolism did not refer to a world of dreams or ideals, as did Bernard's: he simply strove to maximize the force of "complementary colors, their mingling and their opposition, the mysterious vibrations of kindred tones" (*Complete Letters* 3: 26). In his portraits, he used resonant color to intensify spiritual expression: "I want to paint men and women with that something of the eternal which the halo used to symbolize, and which we seek to convey by the actual radiance and vibration of our coloring" (*Complete Letters* 3: 25). Such expressive use of the medium became a hallmark of aesthetic modernism.

Van Gogh sought the strongest possible expression of *life* through "intense colour"; in Provence, "[he saw] things with an eye more Japanese" (*Complete Letters* 2: 513; 590) and Japanese vision encouraged him "[to] use color more arbitrarily, in order to express [him]self forcibly" (*Complete Letters* 3: 6). His attempt to express repose through simplified colors and lines in *The Artist's Bedroom at Arles* (1888) combines Japanese design with Seurat's theories. His handling of the reed-pen in drawings also shows Japanese influence, as he constructs compact designs from a dense calligraphy of strokes. Casting off the somber tones of the North, van Gogh in Arles reveled in a range of bright tones, painting "[the] town violet, the orb [of the sun] yellow, the sky blue-green. The wheat . . . old gold, copper, gold-green or gold-red, gold-yellow, bronze-yellow, green-red" (3: 493). Aurier marvelled at his dazzling color: "He is . . . the only painter who perceives the chromatism of things with this intensity, with this metallic, jewellike quality" (Pickvance 314). While risking his sanity in "the blazing sun" for that "high note of yellow," van Gogh studied the effects of contrast, discovering that "*[t]here is no blue without yellow and without orange*" (*Complete Letters* 3: 491). In *The Starry Night* (1889), he was "driven by an irresistible urge to express his visual experiences" (Rewald 18), just as D. H. Lawrence felt compelled to express a "visionary awareness" in *The Rainbow*. As his tumultuous brushwork unleashed unconscious forces, van Gogh's creative struggle fused subject and object in an expressionist vision of space.

While Cézanne and van Gogh painted directly from nature, Gauguin was stimulated by dreams and imagination. He saw the motif as a mere pretext for decorative or symbolic creation and wrote: "Art is an abstraction; derive this abstraction from nature while dreaming before it . . ." (see Rewald 178). Gauguin cultivated primitive life in Brittany, Martinique, Tahiti, and the Marquesas, seeking power of expression through radical reduction and distortion. Like the literary symbolists, he wanted his painting to penetrate to the "mysterious centre of thought" (see Shone 66). While Cézanne valued logical analysis and construction, Gauguin aspired to visionary symbolism. In *Vision after the Sermon: Jacob Wrestling with the Angel* (1888), he dramatizes the peasant mind by combining real and imaginary worlds in a single tight-knit design. Adopting Japanese form-language, he bisects the picture space with a strongly marked diagonal, distorting size and shape, and marking off zones by arbitrary color contrasts. In this artful synthesis, the motif of primitive religion is shaped by the painter's sensibility, which selects, excludes, abstracts, and heightens. After emigrating to the South Seas, Gauguin fused "contemporary and archaic motifs, Christian and Maori beliefs, Polynesian, Javanese, Egyptian and even Greek-inspired design" (Shone 94) in sensual and dreamlike visions, culminating in the panoramic triptych, *Where Do We Come From? What Are We? Where Are We Going?* (1897).

Édouard Dujardin, the inventor of stream-of-consciousness, gave the name *cloisonnisme* to a style invented by Louis Anquetin and Émile Bernard that marks off forms with heavy outlines—the "violent and decisive color," enclosed within borders, "emphasizing the design" (Dujardin; see Rewald 176). *Cloisonnism* merged with *synthesism,* in which, as Gauguin says, "the *synthesis* of form and color [is] derived from the observation of the dominant element only" (see Rewald 178). The simplified pattern emphasizes the artist's vision, relating synthesist painting to symbolist poetry. Paul Sérusier and the Nabis group were attracted to Gauguin's art by "the presentiment of a higher reality, a predilection for the mysterious and unusual, a tendency towards reverie, a mental luxury" (Dom Verkade; see Rewald 262). Instructed by Gauguin, Sérusier painted his near-abstract *Talisman,* signifying "that every work was a transposition, a caricature, the passionate equivalent of a sensation experienced" (Maurice Denis; see Shone 66–67).

Post-impressionist painting presents an imaginative synthesis of forms in a decorative or striking pattern. Cézanne, the pioneer of modernism, was fully engaged in a study of the visual world and an exploration of his own sensations and per-

ceptions. While van Gogh merged his being with the motif, Cézanne detached himself from it in order to contemplate it more profoundly. Gauguin, "dreaming before [nature]," expressed the power of the primitive and of reverie, anticipating the more abstract harmonies of Henri Matisse (1869–1954). The "aesthetic attitude" to their medium of Cézanne, Gauguin, and Matisse is in accord with the literary modernism of **T. S. Eliot, James Joyce,** and Virginia Woolf, while van Gogh's expressionist vision has marked affinities with Lawrence's.

Jack Stewart

Selected Bibliography

Cachin, Francoise. *Gauguin.* Trans. Bambi Ballard. Paris: Flammarion, 1988.

Cézanne, Paul. *Letters.* Ed. John Rewald. Trans. Seymour Hacker. Rev. ed. New York: Hacker, 1984.

Fry, Roger. *Cézanne: A Study of His Development.* 1927. New York: Noonday-Farrar, 1968.

Hammacher, A. M. *Genius and Disaster: The Ten Creative Years of Vincent van Gogh.* New York: Abrams, n.d.

Kelder, Diane. *The Great Book of Post-Impressionism.* New York: Abbeville, n.d.

Nochlin, Linda. *Impressionism and Post-Impressionism 1874–1904: Sources and Documents.* Englewood Cliffs, N.J.: Prentice-Hall, 1966.

Pickvance, Ronald. *Van Gogh in Saint-Rémy and Auvers.* New York: Metropolitan Museum of Art, 1986.

Rewald, John. *Post-Impressionism: From van Gogh to Gauguin.* 3rd ed. rev. New York: Museum of Modern Art, 1978.

Schapiro, Meyer. *Paul Cézanne.* New York: Abrams, n.d.

Shone, Richard. *The Post-Impressionists.* London: Octopus, 1979.

Stewart, Jack F. "Color in *To the Lighthouse.*" *Twentieth Century Literature* 31 (1985): 438–58.

———. "Spatial Form and Color in *The Waves.*" *Twentieth Century Literature* 28 (1982): 86–107.

van Gogh, Vincent. *The Complete Letters of Vincent van Gogh.* 2nd ed. Boston: New York Graphic Soc., 1978. 3 vols.

Woolf, Virginia. "The Post-Impressionists." In her *Roger Fry: A Biography.* 1940. London: Peregrine-Penguin, 1979. 129–57.

———. *To the Lighthouse.* 1927. London: Hogarth, 1967.

The Post-Impressionism Exhibition, 1910

"In or about December 1910, human character changed." So wrote **Virginia Woolf** in her famous essay of 1924, "Mr. Bennett and Mrs. Brown." Woolf was often deliberately playful and provocative in her artistic pronouncements: she was never, however, frivolous. The date she cited was carefully chosen: a conscious allusion to the first post-impressionist exhibition at the Grafton Gallery in London, which was the first extensive viewing that people in England had been given of the work of painters such as Cézanne, van Gogh, Gauguin, and Picasso. The change in human character Woolf was suggesting was not so much a change of personality *per se,* but a way of *perceiving* personality (1910 was also the year when Freud gave his lecture on the origins and development of **psychoanalysis**) and also on the way of *presenting* character, in paint and in print. In the early twentieth century, artists in different fields were seeking a new language or mode of expression to render what the art critic Roger Fry called "the sensibilities of the modern outlook."

It was Fry who had organized the Exhibition, which had actually been opened to the press on November 5th (Virginia Woolf had quite properly allowed some time for its impact to be felt). The date is memorable because one critic, Robert Ross (perhaps best remembered as a friend of **Oscar Wilde**) immediately suggested that what these painters were up to was roughly analogous to what Guy Fawkes had planned for the Houses of Parliament: "revealing the existence of a widespread plot to destroy the whole fabric of European painting." The Exhibition achieved huge publicity and notoriety: it was widely denounced as pornographic, degenerate

and evil, and became, in the critic Ian Dunlop's words, "the high-water-mark of public concern for art in Britain."

Whether Fry had anticipated such a response is difficult to say. The Exhibition had been organized in something of a rush. Desmond MacCarthy, who wrote the introduction to the catalogue, was fearful that because of the frequent last-minute changes, the numbers of his entries would get mixed up, and he would wind up describing a portrait, say, of a nude girl as "station master at Arles." Even the title of the Exhibition—"Manet and the post-impressionists"—was more opportunistic than a carefully considered artistic statement. "Let's just call them post-impressionists," declared Fry when they were stuck for a title. "At any rate they came after the impressionists." The label remained because it had a certain appropriateness, stressing both a continuity with **impressionism** but also a distinction from it. It was strange that the showing should have been greeted as the latest outrage of the new century. Most of it was taken up with works by painters already dead and with paintings that had been done in the 1880s and 1890s.

The outcry is even more intriguing when one considers the identity of the paintings put on show that caused such offense. These included: Cézanne's *Madame Cézanne in Armchair;* Matisse's *The Girl With Green Eyes;* van Gogh's *Sunflowers* and *Crows in the Wheatfields;* Gauguin's *Christ in the Garden of Olives, Eve During The Fall* and his Tahitian pictures; and Picasso's *Nude Girl With a Basket of Flowers.* In other words, the Exhibition comprised some of the paintings that were to become the most popular, and priceless, of the twentieth century. Tastes change, of course, but it is still worth asking why the critic of *The Times,* C. J. Weld-Blundell could say that, on the evidence of this Exhibition, **post-impressionism** was "like anarchism in politics . . . the rejection of all that civilisation had done." The critic Wake Cook went further: "the whole show," he said, "was intentionally made to look like the outpouring of a lunatic asylum." Van Gogh's *Crows in the Wheatfields,* according to the correspondent in *The Tatler,* baffled spectators, who could not decide whether it most resembled a prairie fire or a smoking ham omelette.

Undoubtedly part of the hostility was conservative in origin: these painters were attempting to tear up tradition. If writers were being exhorted by **Ezra Pound** to "make it new," the clarion call for the post-impressionists was: "Dare all." "Nobody is astonished any more," grumbled Gauguin and set about changing that. But it was not change for change's sake. There was a conviction that the impressionists had pushed representation to such a point of perfection that it seemed futile to continue along the same road: a new path must be found. (Contemporary writers were having the same feelings about **realism** after George Eliot and Tolstoy, and composers having the same feeling about romanticism after Wagner and **Mahler.**) Moreover, with the perfection of the photograph and the coming of the **film** camera, representation no longer seemed valid or appropriate as a painter's primary goal. In his catalogue introduction, MacCarthy would talk of a shift away from the external world to a "synthesis of design." Roger Fry referred to the artist's relinquishment of an attempted resemblance to the natural world in his work in favor of the creation of "a purely abstract language—a visual music." If the artist was shifting away from **naturalism** and the environment, what was he shifting towards?

The move was towards self-expression. "Before the easel, the artist is slave neither to the past, the present, nature nor even his neighbour. Himself, always himself," said Gauguin, adding: "I am content to search my own self and not nature." This in turn involved a different way of looking at painting. As the critic Clive Bell argued, the question one should ask of a painting now was not "What does this picture represent?" but "What does it make us feel?" In these terms, a picture like van Gogh's wheatfield is more a depiction of a mood than a colored photograph. Reviewing the second post-impressionist exhibition in 1912 (which followed hard on the heels of the spectacular and scandalous success of the first), that perhaps surprising champion of most things modern, Rupert Brooke proposed that the chief object of a good modern painting was not to give an impression of what the painter saw but to give an expression of what the painter felt.

The impact of this artistic movement on writers was considerable. That traditional Edwardian and tepid modernist, **E. M. Forster** was unsurprisingly shocked by the Exhibition. Similarly, in that throwback to the Victorian triple-decker, John Galsworthy's *The Forsyte Saga* (1906–28), the author notes that his hero, Soames Forsyte buys a Gauguin not because he likes it but because it is fashionable. "He had bought the ugly great thing before the war," wrote Galsworthy, "because there was such a fuss about these post-impressionist chaps." By contrast, **Katherine Mansfield** would claim that looking at the paintings of van Gogh taught her something about writing, which she identified as "a kind of freedom, a shaking free." Similarly, Arnold Bennett, who had been shocked by the London response which he saw as a humiliating demonstration of English insularity and complacency, thought post-impressionism had momentous implications for the writer. If some novelist were to do in words what those men had done in paint, he would say, then we might be disgusted with the whole of modern fiction, feel that we had been concerning ourselves with inessentials, and might have to start again.

Ironically, it was to be on precisely those grounds that Bennett was to be attacked by Virginia Woolf in "Mr Bennett and Mrs Brown" and in her later essay, "Modern Fiction": namely, that writers like him, Galsworthy, and H. G. Wells had indeed been concerning themselves with inessentials and with an arid observation of everyday trivialities. "Life was not at all like this," she wrote. What was needed was a new form that reflected the uniqueness of the individual mind and found a way of articulating the previously unexpressed and inexpressible. In short, what was required was an art less sociological and more psychological, and not externally but internally directed. The post-impressionists seemed to have effectively portrayed not so much how the world looks but how the artist feels: a diagram of his mind. Writers like Woolf, **D. H. Lawrence, Marcel Proust, James Joyce,** and **Dorothy Richardson** were similarly to experiment with fresh ways of uncovering the modern consciousness and the subconscious. In the process, and in its manner of representation, human character changed.

Neil Sinyard

Selected Bibliography

Bullen, J. B., ed. *Post-Impressionists in England: the Critical Reception.* London: Routledge, 1988.

Dunlop, Ian. *The Shock of the New.* London: Weidenfeld & Nicholson, 1972.

Fry, Roger. *Vision and Design.* London: Chatto & Windus, 1929.

Tillyard, S. K. *The Impact of Modernism.* London: Routledge, 1988.

Woolf, Virginia. *Roger Fry.* London: Chatto & Windus, 1940.

Postmodernism

What might be acceptable as a "definition" of postmodernism in an encyclopedia clashes in many ways with the ideas most associated with postmodernism. Systematic, totalizing, or encyclopedic knowledge, accurate definition, precise determination, and conceptual clarity do not sit well with the common valorization within postmodernism of randomness, plurality, discontinuity, disruption, and contingency.

What Is Postmodernism?

In the view of its detractors, postmodernism is thoroughly "postmodern" in its plurality, or, less respectfully, in its conceptual incoherence. By the early 1990s, it could be argued that "there is no unified postmodern theory, or even a coherent set of positions" to be identified (Best and Kellner 2). According to Alex Callinicos' critique, "Matters weren't helped by the fact that lead producers of the discourse such as Jean-François Lyotard and Charles Jencks offered definitions which were mutually inconsistent, internally contradictory and/or hopelessly vague" (Callinicos 2). The scholarly disagreement concerning the meaning of postmodernism is examined by Ihab Hassan:

> postmodernism suffers from a certain *semantic* instability: that is, no clear consensus about its meaning exists among scholars. The general difficulty is compounded in this case by two factors: (a) the relative youth, indeed brash adolescence, of the term postmodernism and (b) its semantic kinship to more current terms, themselves equally unstable. Thus some critics mean by postmodernism what others call avant-gardism or even neo-avant-gardism, while still others would call the same phenomenon simply modernism. This can make for inspired debates. (Hassan 149)

What postmodernism is *not,* is a clearly defined historical period. Laurence Sterne's *Tristram Shandy* (1759–1767), with its self-reflexive and self-defeating narrative structures, incorporates recognizably postmodernist features. What can be said, however, is that twentieth-century postmodernism is a reaction to and considers itself a break from the alleged failings of modernism.

Elitism/Commercialism

Postmodernists, in the words of Lance Olsen, are liable to speak of a strain of "cryptofascistic elitism" in modernism (Olsen 144). Leaving its own politics aside for the moment, and making allowances for a desire to "throw into high relief the novelty and difference of postmodernism," it can still be argued that "where the modernists repudiated and sought to camouflage their reliance on popular-art models, . . . postmodernists have tended openly to advertize theirs" (McHale, *Constructing Postmodernism,* 226). To Callinicos' disdain, postmodernism is as pleased to theorize about "any old soap opera" (Callinicos 170) as about more respectable literary or artistic work. The need to posit a genuinely "postmodern break," however, rests upon often tendentious constructions of its supposed opposite, modernism. In their analysis, Best and Kellner maintain that any "desire for radically new art forms" is replaced in postmodernism "by pastiche, quotation and play with past forms, irony, cynicism, commercialism, and in some cases downright nihilism" (Best and Kellner 11). Not all these features are unknown in high modernist works.

Cyberpunk

This brand of popular science fiction, the latest manifestation of postmodernist fiction, has, at least, never been threatened with co-option into the high modernist canon. *Cyberpunk* works have been called "the apotheosis of postmodernism" (Csicsery-Ronay, Jr. 182). Cyberpunk narratives accept that "the real and the true are superseded by simulacra and the hyperreal" (Csicsery-Ronay, Jr. 193); paradoxically, this is the "postmodern reality," the truth, that cyberpunk works seek to portray. The "apotheosis of postmodernism" thus comes full-circle back to pre-modernist **realism:**

> postmodern SF should be seen as the breakthrough "realism" of our time. It is

an art form that vividly represents the most salient features of our lives, as these lives are being transformed and redefined by technology. It also seeks to empower us by providing a cognitive mapping that can help situate us in a brave new postmodern world that systematically distorts our sense of who or where we are, of what is "real" at all, of what is most valuable about human life. (McCaffery 16)

What cyberpunk and postmodernist fiction represent and imitate, as Brian McHale confirms, "is the pluralistic and anarchistic ontological landscape of advanced industrial cultures" (McHale, *Postmodernist Fiction,* 38), or, in Larry McCaffery's terms, "the world space of multinational capitalism" (McCaffery 12). For its materialist and Marxist critics, postmodernism is the cultural dominant associated with post-industrial capitalism.

"The Logic of Late Capitalism"

Fredric Jameson, in a influential formulation, sought to identify the social and historical basis of the emergence of postmodernism as a cultural product:

> theories of the postmodern . . . bring us the news of the arrival and inauguration of a whole new type of society, most famously baptized "postindustrial society" (Daniel Bell) but often also designated consumer society, media society, information society, electronic society or "high tech," and the like. Such theories have the obvious ideological mission of demonstrating, to their own relief, that the new social formation in question no longer obeys the laws of classical capitalism, namely, the primacy of industrial production and the omnipresence of class struggle. The Marxist tradition has therefore resisted them with vehemence . . . (Jameson 3)

Postmodernism and commodity capitalism are perceived as eminently compatible allies in the Culture Industry, with its rapid turnover of mass-produced *aesthetic* commodities. By their own ability to account for postmodernism as a cultural phenomenon arising from a particular historical socioeconomic base, Marxism and materialism seek to reinstate the superiority of their own theoretical analyses. As merely another cultural product, postmodernism falls within Marxism's area of socioeconomic expertise. Postmodernism, however, considers itself able to encompass and account for Marxism instead.

Metanarratives

"I define *postmodernism* as incredulity toward metanarratives," says Jean-François Lyotard (Lyotard xxiv). One such metanarrative is Marxism. As Thomas Docherty confirms:

> Lyotard has argued that it is becoming increasingly difficult to subscribe to the great—and therapeutically optimistic—metanarratives which once organised our lives. What he has in his sights are totalising metanarratives, great codes which in their abstraction necessarily deny the specificity of the local and traduce it in the interests of a global homogeneity, a universal history. Such master narratives would include the great narrative of emancipation proposed by Marx; the narrative of the possibility of psychoanalytic therapy and redemption proposed by Freud; or the story of constant development and adaptation proposed under the rubric of evolution by Darwin. (Docherty 11)

Metanarratives are precisely those global explanatory theories which are not eclectic, random or discontinuous; postmodernism might exist to disrupt their orderly and systematic operation. Postmodernist discourse would identify the base/superstructure model within Marxism as a metaphor or an organizing principle rather than simply descriptive of the actuality of economic and cultural interdependence. Such

models may be pragmatically useful; postmodernism would deny that they could be *true*.

Enlightenment Reason

Postmodernism also reassesses the emancipatory credentials of Enlightenment reason. The "enlightenment project" of eighteenth-century philosophical rationalism was crucial, Best and Kellner argue, to "the American, French, and other democratic revolutions which attempted to overturn the feudal world and to produce a just and egalitarian social order that would embody reason and social progress" (Best and Kellner 2). Thomas Docherty, from a Derridean and postmodernist perspective, describes science, instrumental knowledge and reason itself very differently:

> Reason is racist and imperialist, taking a specific inflection of consciousness for a universal and necessary form of consciousness. Here Derrida exposes the West's tendency to legitimise itself: the West is reasonable because it says so, and, since it is the definer and bearer of reason, it must be universally reasonable to accede to this proposition. This, as Derrida argues, is clearly a false and troubling logic. (Docherty 13)

Yet as Callinicos notes, theorists and philosophers important to the emergence of postmodernism, Friedrich Nietzsche and Martin Heidegger, Jacques Derrida and Michel Foucault, seem to face a contradiction "in using the tools of rationality—philosophical argument and historical analysis—in order to carry out the critique of reason as such" (Callinicos 26). Postmodernism also attracts many other self-reflexive, and apparently self-defeating, paradoxes to itself.

Self-Reflexive Paradoxes

When postmodernist discourse tries to undermine the very concept of *truth,* it cannot help but imply that it is true that there is no truth. This is a self-reflexive paradox. There are other "deep contradictions spinning at the core of the anti-ideological ideology" of postmodernism (Olsen 142). As Best and Kellner argue, " 'postmodern theory' may seem problematical, since postmodern critiques are directed against the notion of 'theory' itself" (Best and Kellner x). If postmodernism seeks to be genuinely new and confrontational, then, Olsen asks, "How long can the experimental actually remain experimental, the subversive actually subversive, before we simply become accustomed to a certain level of shock, a certain system of 'anticonventions' which are themselves conventions?" (Olsen 145). Postmodernism's co-option into the operations of commodity capitalism prompts a further query: "The big question for 1980s art is whether any authentic countercultural art can exist for long without being transformed into self-annihilating simulations of themselves for mass consumption, furthering central cultural aims" (Csicsery-Ronay, Jr. 183). Is Lyotard's critique of metanarratives, of Marxist or Enlightenment provenance, itself a metanarrative? Analogous problems are associated with the attempt to treat postmodernism as one more academic concept or genre. To securely define postmodernism is simultaneously to negate its meaning. Olsen describes the process: "To bring postmodernism into academic discourse is to begin to traditionalize postmodernism, to stabilize a way of thinking whose essence is destabilization. As soon as we have agreed upon a menu for postmodernism, petrifaction has begun" (Olsen 146). What might save postmodernism from petrifaction is the inability of academic discourse finally to agree what its *essence* (*destabilization* or otherwise) actually is.

Brian McHale opens up another way of approaching postmodernism: "Whatever we may think of the term, however much or little we may be satisfied with it, one thing is certain: the referent of 'postmodernism,' the *thing* to which the term claims to refer, *does not exist*" (McHale, *Postmodernist Fiction,* 4). Instead, "postmodernism exists discursively, in the discourses we produce *about* it and *using* it" (McHale, *Constructing Postmodernism,* 1). Postmodernism is merely a "discursive construct" (McHale, *Postmodernist Fiction,* 4). If postmodernism is what we make it, then there is no adequate definition or final truth to be set down about the meaning of the term. McHale, perhaps, can provide a postmodern definition of postmodernism; he deals in pluralistic "narratives" rather than "truths:"

> Several versions of this story have already been told, so it is important to distinguish among better and less good stories—"better" not in the sense of objectively *truer* (a criterion discredited by the constructivist approach), but in terms of such criteria as rightness of fit, validity of inference, internal consistency, appropriateness of scope, and above all *productivity.* (McHale, *Constructing Postmodernism,* 9)

McHale can only offer a further narrative about postmodernism; the constructivist argument contradicts itself if it claims that its own account is *true*. It is the *productivity* of a narrative about postmodernism, its ability to provoke further argument, discussion and criticism, which is the key to its use-value; as under the terms of Lyotard's "postmodern condition," "it is now dissension that must be emphasized" (Lyotard 61). But can either McHale, valuing pluralism, or Lyotard, recommending dissension, really want us simply to agree with them?

Sue Wilson

Selected Bibliography

Best, Steven and Douglas Kellner. *Postmodern Theory: Critical Interrogations.* London: Macmillan, 1991.

Callinicos, Alex. *Against Postmodernism: A Marxist Critique.* Cambridge: Polity Press, 1989.

Csicsery-Ronay, Jr., Istvan. "Cyberpunk and Neuromanticism." *Storming the Reality Studio: A Casebook of Cyberpunk and Postmodern Science Fiction.* Ed. Larry McCaffery. Durham: Duke UP, 1991. 182–193.

Docherty, Thomas. "Postmodernism: An Introduction." *Postmodernism: A Reader.* Ed. Thomas Docherty. New York: Harvester Wheatsheaf, 1993. 1–31.

Hassan, Ihab. "Toward a Concept of Postmodernism." *Postmodernism: A Reader.* Ed. Thomas Docherty. New York: Harvester Wheatsheaf, 1993. 146–156.

Jameson, Fredric. *Postmodernism, or, The Cultural Logic of Late Capitalism.* London: Verso, 1991.

Lyotard, Jean-François. *The Postmodern Condition: A Report on Knowledge.* Trans. Geoff Bennington and Brian Massumi. Manchester: Manchester UP, 1984.

McCaffery, Larry. "Introduction: The Desert of the Real." *Storming the Reality Studio: A Casebook of Cyberpunk and Postmodern Science Fiction.* Ed. Larry McCaffery. Durham: Duke UP, 1991. 1–16.

McHale, Brian. *Postmodernist Fiction.* London: Routledge, 1987.

———. *Constructing Postmodernism.* London: Routledge, 1992.

Olsen, Lance. "Cyberpunk and the Crisis of Postmodernity." *Fiction 2000: Cyberpunk and the Future of Narrative.* Ed. George Slusser and Tom Shippey. London: University of Georgia Press, 1992. 142–152.

Pound, Ezra Loomis (1885–1972)

American poet, translator, critic and economic and political polemicist.

Ezra Pound was born in Hailey, Idaho, on October 30, 1885. The family moved back east before he was one year old, settling in Wyncote near Philadelphia, where his father worked in the United States Mint, in 1892. Pound claimed that he always felt "foreign" in suburban Philadelphia but his upbringing was not particularly eventful or traumatic. Perhaps the event of his boyhood was his tour of Europe with "Aunt Frank" (Frances Amelia Weston) in 1898. Pound soon visited Europe again, in 1902 and 1906, but it was that first trip he particularly recalled in the *Pisan Cantos* (84:553).

In 1901 Pound enrolled at the University of Pennsylvania. He transferred to Hamilton College, New York, in 1903 and returned to Pennsylvania as a graduate student in 1905. He was awarded an M. A. in 1906 and began to work for a Ph.D., but within a year he had accepted a teaching post in Romance Languages at Wabash Presbyterian College, Crawfordsville, Indiana. Crawfordsville and the flamboyant young Pound were a mismatch from the outset, and his academic career ended after one semester. He left Wabash in February 1908 and the next month sailed for Europe, going first to **Spain** and **Italy** and then, in August, to London. In Venice he had a manuscript collection of poems printed as *A Lume Spento* (1908, "With Tapers Quenched").

The little that Pound had published before leaving the United States—a verse translation in Hamilton College's literary magazine (1905) and a handful of articles including a review of Péladan's *Le Secret des Troubadours* (1906)—is of scant interest. It should, however, be noted that many of the traits and concerns that would later be seen as characteristically "Poundian" were, to a greater or lesser extent, present in 1908. He saw himself as a poet and a cosmopolitan (his "Latin Quarter" ways were unfavorably remarked upon) and had begun to develop an iconoclastic social style. His literary formation was incomplete but its outline was visible: the Classics, the troubadours and medieval litterature generally, Browning and the already admired **W. B. Yeats** (who read at Pennsylvania in 1903).

London 1908–1920. Pound arrived in London in 1908 with only *A Lume Spento* to establish his *bona fides* as a poet, but by the end of 1909 he had published *Personae* and *Exultations,* and was a rising star in literary circles. The next year saw the publication of *The Spirit of Romance* and, in America, of *Provença,* a selection from his two earlier books plus a section of new poems, published in London as *Canzoni* (1911). *The Spirit of Romance* is Pound's first attempt at an extended treatment of Provençal literature; Pound believed that, for the initiated, troubadour poetry celebrated a "love cult" (deriving ultimately from the mysteries of Eleusis) that held that coitus led to mystical illumination—a theory elaborated in the later essay "Psychology and Troubadours" (1912). In 1912 Pound published *The Sonnets and Ballate of Guido Cavalcanti* and *Ripostes.*

The contemporary reader is likely to find Pound's early poetry affectedly antiquarian, with its archaic themes, diction, and syntax, but it is often technically accomplished and there are several striking poems such as "Sestina: Altaforte" and "The Seafarer." In *Ripostes,* under the influence of **Ford Madox Ford,** who insisted that "poetry should be written at least as well as prose," Pound begins to experiment with a more modern idiom and with *vers libre.* Ford's influence was more apparent in *Cathay* (1915) and *Lustra* (1916). The translations of Chinese poetry in *Cathay* were the first results of Pound's work on the papers of the American orientalist Ernest Fenellosa (which he had received in 1913). In *Lustra* Pound emerges as a self-consciously, even aggressively, *modern* poet dealing directly with the contemporary world in a language stripped of archaism and the *poetic.* The outstanding poem of the volume, "Near Perigord," deals with the matter of Provence in a modern idiom and is a complex and subtle exploration of the relationship between poetry and history.

The key to Pound's early poetry and its relation to his work as a whole is provided by the title of his 1909 volume *Personae,* a title which later became a generic term for all Pound's poetry outside the *Cantos.* Looking back on his development as a poet as a "search for oneself" and for "sincere self-expression," Pound wrote in 1914: "I began to search for the real in a book called *Personae,* casting off, as it were, complete masks of the self in each poem" (*Gaudier-Brzeska* 85). A persona is neither the *I* which equates to or is congruent with the poet in romantic and other expressive schools of poetics, nor the autonomous fictional *I* of the dramatic monologue. Rather, the persona articulates a series of shifts and displacements between the two; it may even be described as deconstructing the distinction, which goes back through Aristotle to Plato, between speaking in one's own voice and assuming the voice of another. Thus Pound's concern with "masks," although the term looks back to **Wilde,** links his poetic practice, almost from the beginning, with modernist poetics of impersonality and with a wider modern questioning of received models of the self and of individual identity. This "search for the real" through personae is central to Pound's two major pre-*Cantos* works, "Homage to Sextus Propertius" (1919) and "Hugh Selwyn Mauberley" (1920).

Pound detected in the Latin poet Sextus Propertius a quality he termed "logopoeia" that classical scholars had missed or misread. Defined by Pound as "the dance of the intellect among words" (*Literary Essays* 25), in practice it is close to the wider sense in which irony is used by literary critics. Speaking through the mask of Propertius, in a series of very free translations, Pound makes this quality apparent and reveals behind the "logopoeia" Propertius' ambiguity about Roman imperialism. The relation between the poet and the mask is complex and reciprocal, and Propertius articulates Pound's ambiguous position as an émigré American living in the capital of the British Empire in 1919. The privileged position of Classics in the education of the British ruling class of the period makes the poem's questioning of the received truths of Victorian classicism, and subversion of its discourse, a telling, if somewhat oblique, critique of imperialism.

Pound described "Mauberley" as a "popularisation" of "Propertius." This may be true if it is read as a criticism of contemporary London; in "Mauberley" (and particularly in Section IV which deals with **the war** and its immediate aftermath) Pound's criticisms are more direct and explicit and so of more immediate impact. On another level "Mauberley" may be read as a culmination, and critique, of Pound's search for himself and for "sincere self-expression." If a persona may be said to comprise of a voice, a self or an individuality, plus a style, then "Mauberley" anatomizes the disjunction of the two; the poem traces a process of "diastasis" (separation) by which the persona dissipates into voiceless style and style-less voice.

Although the best of his criticism ("The Serious Artist" or "How To Read") is of interest in its own right, Pound believed that the primary function of criticism was "to forerun composition, to serve as gun-sight" (*Literary Essays* 75). This does not make criticism a secondary or ancillary activity. Indeed, his practice, in poems such as "Near Perigord" and "Propertius," of "criticism in new composition" calls into question the distinction between poetry and criticism. Pound's critical acumen was most apparent in his recognition and fostering of new talent. Many benefited from this (including Robert Frost, **William Carlos Williams,** and **Ernest Hemingway**) but his efforts on behalf of **James Joyce** and **T. S. Eliot** stand out. He met Eliot and began corresponding with Joyce in 1914, when both were virtually unknown, and he immediately set to work on their behalf: helping their work into publication, writing laudatory reviews and generally promoting their reputations. For this alone Pound must be considered a

decisive influence on the development of modernism. Pound also helped Eliot, as he had earlier helped Yeats, by providing detailed criticism of his work; most famously, he helped Eliot revise the first draft of *The Waste Land* (1922), which Eliot then dedicated to Pound.

Imagism and **vorticism** illustrate Pound's abilities as a literary entrepreneur. Pound began to speak of "*Les Imagistes*" and to hint at an elusive "doctrine of the image" in 1912. No such school existed but he created it by signing a set of **Hilda Doolittle**'s poems "H. D. Imagiste" and having them published in *Poetry*. In "A Few Don'ts by an Imagiste" (1913) Pound expounded the tenets of "imagisme"—"direct treatment of the object," concision and precision; they are not new or distinctive and no coherent poetics can be obtained from them (or from his 1914 anthology *Des Imagistes*). As a publicity stunt or marketing ploy "imagisme" was a success, but by 1914 it had served its turn and Pound moved on to vorticism. When Amy Lowell wanted to continue putting out imagist anthologies (three more appeared), Pound tried, unsuccessfully, to sell her the "brand name." Kayman gives a good account of all of this. Pound did not create vorticism but he made the same strategic use of it as he made of imagism; Pound's vorticism was essentially a more ferocious imagism.

London, Paris, Italy, 1920–1944: The Cantos (1). By 1920 Pound was tired of London, and London tired of him, and at the end of the year he announced that he was leaving for Paris. Pound may have hoped to repeat in Paris the successes of his early years in London; if so he was disappointed, and by early 1924 he had moved on to Rapallo.

Pound began work on the *Cantos* in late 1915 (claims for an earlier genesis cannot be sustained by bibliographical or biographical evidence). In 1917 he published "Three Cantos" (the "Ur-Cantos") and he continued working, fitfully and uncertainly, on his "long poem" until 1922 when he began composing the "Malatesta Cantos." When these were published in July 1923 the enterprise coalesced around them and within six months he had completed the first installment of the *Cantos,* published as *A Draft of XVI Cantos of Ezra Pound for the Beginning of a Poem of some Length* (1925).

The "Malatesta Cantos" (8–11)—Pound's multifaceted portrait of the Renaissance ruler of Rimini, Sigismondo Malatesta—are the poem's first sustained attempt to "include history" and so constitute its beginning as a modern epic. The references to laurels and to Calliope in the opening lines of Canto VIII clearly signal Pound's epic ambition, and it is in the "Malatesta Cantos" that the characteristic features of Pound's historical narrative are first encountered: the insertion into the texts of historical documents and fragments; and the ellipsis, elision and startling juxtapositions that mark Pound's practice of quotation.

Two of Pound's maxims, "an epic is a poem containing history" and "poetry asserts positive" (*Literary Essays* 86, 324) convey the essence of his modern epic: its concern with history as "a light for the future" (*Selected Prose* 366) and its didacticism ("'History is a school book for princes,'" *Cantos* 54:280). Michael Bernstein argues that the *Cantos* should be read as a public poem whose function it is to celebrate and transmit the record of the "tribe's" achievements; it is public in that it deals with "public events" and is "addressed to the citizen, not to the private individual" (71). This model of the epic is not an eccentric or idiosyncratic one. **Gertrude Stein** called Pound a "village explainer," and he was, by all accounts, a remorseless pedagogue but the didactic element of the *Cantos* stems as much from the generic imperatives of the epic as from Pound's compulsion to instruct.

While working on the "Malatesta Cantos" Pound made two visits to Italy; between those visits, in October 1922, Mussolini's fascist party came to power. This conjunction of events is significant. Lawrence Rainey has established that Pound was an admirer of Mussolini by 1923 and that the "Malatesta Cantos" and fascism are inextricably linked (Rainey, 1997). Does this mean that the *Cantos* is a fascist poem? This question cannot be satisfactorily answered on the level of opinion or by counting the flattering references to Mussolini in the poem. "An epic," Pound asserted, "cannot be written against the grain of its time . . . the writer of epos must voice the general heart" (*Spirit of Romance* 216); an idea also expressed in the poem itself (9:722). In other words, an epic narrative imitates or corresponds to a larger master narrative and ultimately its coherence derives from it. Pound misread fascism as the "grain of his time," and wrote his epic accordingly. The *Cantos* grew steadily in the 1920s and 1930s—*A Draft of XXX Cantos* (1930), *Eleven New Cantos XXXI–XLI* (1934), *The Fifth Decad of Cantos [XLII–LI]* (1937) and *Cantos LII–LXXI* (1940)—castigating economic error and multiplying instances of sound governance (with lyrical and mystical interludes). Their tendency was clear enough but any overarching design or form remained elusive.

Converted to the Social Credit economics of Major C. H. Douglas, whom he met in 1917, and further radicalized by World War I, Pound's political and economic concerns were well to the fore by the early 1920s. Initially, Pound may have hoped that fascism would actually implement the economic and cultural policies he favored, but even though these hopes failed to materialize, he became increasingly committed to Mussolini's regime and by the 1930s was an ardent and wholehearted advocate of fascism. Pound remained in Italy during the Second World

War and began writing and broadcasting for Rome Radio in 1940. He continued to do so after the United States entered the war and he was indicted for treason in July 1943. In his broadcasts, Pound denied any treasonable intent but the published transcripts show that they were, and were patently intended to be, pro-Axis propaganda (see Doob). In places, they are marked by virulent anti-Semitism.

Pisa, Washington D.C., Italy, 1945–72: The Cantos (2). In May 1945 Pound was taken into custody by the United States Army and held at the Army Disciplinary Training Center (D.T.C.) near Pisa until he was repatriated in November to answer the charge of treason. Early in 1946, a jury declared Pound to be of "unsound mind" and unfit to stand trial; he was then committed to St. Elizabeth's Hospital for the Criminally Insane in Washington, D.C. (where he was to remain until 1958). The case was a controversial one and has remained so. Precarious as Pound's situation was, more was at stake than the fate of a single individual. Pound was not alone among writers and intellectuals in being attracted to fascism, and his case raised questions about the responsibility and accountability of artists and the relation between literature and politics. In 1949 these issues were brought to the fore when Pound was awarded the Bollingen Prize for the *Pisan Cantos* (published in 1948 but written at Pisa). The Bollingen committee (which included T. S. Eliot and **W. H. Auden**) took the position (one not shared by Pound) that poetry and politics were separate matters.

The defeat of the Axis powers was catastrophic for Pound and for the *Cantos;* he had intended his epic to celebrate the advent of a new order and predicated its success upon the success of that order. The *Pisan Cantos* are the response to this and they chart the process of Pound putting back together the pieces of himself and his poem; they return to the task of "shoring fragments against ruin" with which he began. Pound's desperate situation (cf. 74:444; 76:472) gives the sequence urgency and directness while the D.T.C. and its day to day life provides unity and a dramatic counterpoint to its other elements (elegiac evocations of his London years, Confucian philosophy and invocations of the harmonious world of **myth**). In the context of the poem as a whole, the *Pisan Cantos* should not be seen as a change of direction, much less as a change of heart, but as a tactical *démarche;* Pound remains adamant (even defiant) in his views and positions, surrendering nothing of his "city of Dioce" (74:448). This is one of the poem's types of the "Ideal City"; in the *Pisan Cantos* it is described, in a recurring phrase, as being "now in the mind indestructible." This move from the realm of the imminent to the immanent does not, I believe, mean that Pound had given up the idea that the "city of Dioce" could, and would, be built in this world. His new order survived in memory (76:471) not as an unrealizable ideal but as a practical proposition awaiting its historical moment and the *Cantos* would now serve as the vehicle of its occult survival and, for the initiated, its blueprint. His belief that the mysteries of Eleusis had survived into the Christian era to emerge in Provence furnished a model of such occult survival.

The *Pisan Cantos* are a stunning display of authorial power: in them Pound puts his derailed epic back on track and drives it forward. But Pound had known from the beginning that the poem could not be sustained, or brought to a conclusion, by a single individual working "against the grain." Installments of the *Cantos* continued to appear—*Section: Rock Drill 85–95 de los cantares* (1955), *Thrones, 96–109 de los cantares* (1959) and *Drafts & Fragments of Cantos CX–CXVII* (1970)—but, while these are of interest in themselves and do add to the poem, with each successive volume it became increasingly clear that there would be no ending. By the time of *Drafts & Fragments,* Pound can still assert that "it coheres all right" but he is compelled to add, "even if my notes do not cohere" (116:811).

After his release from Saint Elizabeth's, Pound returned to Italy. He is said to have continued working on the *Cantos* until he died (in Venice on 1 November 1972) but it is unlikely that any currently unpublished material will add significantly to the poem as it now stands.

Pound's description of Sigismondo Malatesta as "a failure worth all the successes of his age" (*Guide to Kulchur,* frontispiece) has been applied to Pound himself, and as a verdict on the *Cantos* it is undeniably seductive. However, the concept of "failure" requires some qualification. Pound's inability to bring the *Cantos* to a conclusion, as sketched out above, cannot be seen as a failure in the terms in which the poem was originally conceived; indeed, Pound's inability to finish the Cantos could be seen as a measure of his success in writing a "poem including history." The *Cantos* radically disconcert the suppositions of formalism in all its guises, but this does not make them incoherent, formless, or a failure. To approach the *Cantos* with the *a priori* assumption that a poem is an autonomous verbal icon, or that literary works spend themselves in their textuality and linguisticality and that outside these there is nothing (or nothing of which it is possible to speak), is effectively to pre-empt any discussion of them as "a poem including history," driven by a strong referential imperative, and this cannot be an adequate critical response. It cannot be denied, nor should it be regretted, that Pound did not succeed in producing a modern epic celebrating, and sustained by, the triumph of fascism; but as a record of Pound's engagement with fascism, which although extreme was not aberrant or idiosyncratic, the *Cantos* are,

if not the great "modernist epic" Pound intended, an epic of modernism.

Stephen Wilson

Selected Bibliography

Bernstein, Michael Andre. *The Tale of the Tribe: Ezra Pound and the Modern Verse Epic.* Princeton N.J.: Princeton UP, 1980.

Doob, Leonard W., ed. *Ezra Pound Speaking: Radio Speeches of World War II.* Westport and London: Greenwood Press, 1978.

Kayman, Martin A. *The Modernism of Ezra Pound: The Science of Poetry.* London: Macmillan, 1986.

Pound, Ezra. *The Cantos of Ezra Pound.* 4th collected ed. London: Faber and Faber, 1987. (Citations in the text give canto and page numbers.)

————. *The Collected Shorter Poems.* London: Faber and Faber, 1952. Rptd 1973.

————. *Gaudier-Brzeska: A Memoir.* 1916. New York: New Directions, 1970.

————. *Guide to Kulchur.* 1938. London: Peter Owen, 1966 (4th. impression).

————. *The Literary Essays of Ezra Pound.* Ed. T. S. Eliot. London: Faber and Faber, 1954.

————. *Selected Prose 1909–1965.* New York: New Directions, 1973.

————. *The Spirit of Romance.* 1910. New York: New Directions, 1968.

Rainey, Lawrence. *Institutions of Modernism: Literary Elites and Public Culture.* New Haven and London: Yale UP, 1998.

Tryphonopoulos, Demetres P. " 'That Great Epic Year': Ezra Pound, Katherine Ruth Heyman and H. D." In *Ezra Pound and America.* Ed. Jacqueline Kaye. London: Macmillan, 1992.

Primitivism

Primitivism takes divergent forms, as suggested by Lovejoy and Boas's "chronological" and "cultural," "soft" and "hard" modes. If "cultural primitivism" is the desire of "civilized" people for a simpler, more authentic lifestyle, aesthetic primitivism is the fascination with tribal artifacts—religious icons, fetishes, reliquaries, or ceremonial objects. Michael Bell distinguishes between "primitive animism" and "conscious primitivism" in **D. H. Lawrence**'s novels and a similar distinction may be made between instinctual and formal primitivism in the arts. The longing for a Golden Age or lost paradise is a recurrent symptom of advanced civilization: it springs from rebellion against restraints and a longing for self-renewal. "Primitivism" ambiguously indicates regressive or progressive tendencies; it can be seen either "as a symptom of cultural disaffection [or] as a sign of life" (Varnedoe, "Contemporary" 682). A shift from perception to conception and from empathy to abstraction accompanied the turn from **impressionism** to symbolism, in the late 1880s, and this reorientation prepared the ground for primitivism. In 1984, the Museum of Modern Art staged an exhibition, " 'Primitivism' in 20th Century Art," where the key term, supposedly devoid of Darwinian overtones, still stirred up controversy. Despite inevitable ethnocentric associations (see Torgovnick, ch. 1), William Rubin's art-historical use of the term seems clear enough: switching the focus off ethnology, he shows how modern artworks were inspired by tribal art ("Introduction").

Modern primitivism begins with Gauguin, whose *Vision after the Sermon: Jacob Wrestling with the Angel* (1888) juxtaposes the everyday world of Breton peasants with a symbolic dreamworld, dissolving barriers between objective and subjective, physical and spiritual. Varnedoe sees *Vision* as a stylistic "manifesto of primitivism" ("Gauguin" 184). From 1891 to 1903, Gauguin lived in Tahiti and the Marquesas, drawing eclectically on Egyptian, Greek, Medieval, and Javanese court styles, which he tranposed into Polynesian settings, as in *Ia Orana Maria* (1891) and *Ta Matete* (1892). Gauguin constructed a legendary identity as a "savage;" his lapsing back into a simpler, more sensuous way of life combined nostalgia for a lost paradise with a deep interest in symbolism and **myth** (see *The Moon and the Earth,* 1893). From the French patriarchal/colonial viewpoint, Gauguin's primitivizing

was regression or subversion; from that of the artist, it was cultivation of soul and senses.

In 1906–07, Maurice Vlaminck, André Derain, and Henri Matisse discovered African and Oceanic masks and carvings in Paris. Vlaminck acquired three West African sculptures and a white Fang mask, which he sold to Derain; Matisse showed a small African carving to Picasso at **Gertrude Stein**'s. While the Fauves did not make much structural use of African art, except for Matisse's *Blue Nude* (1907) with its dramatic torsion, avant-garde artists quickly felt the impact of such objects. The qualities of tribal art that appealed to them were "rawness, *non finito,* geometricity, and the emphasis on extremes of invention" (Rubin, "Introduction" 17). After stumbling upon some masks in the ethnographical wing of the Trocadéro Museum in June 1907, Picasso developed a strong affinity for tribal art. He repainted the two right-hand faces of *Les Demoiselles d'Avignon* as savagely distorted masks—an act of exorcism as much as innovation. Picasso intuitively responded to the *mana,* or psychic force, in African artifacts: "For me the [tribal] masks were not just sculptures," he told André Malraux. "They were magical objects . . . intercessors . . . against unknown threatening spirits. . . . They were weapons—to keep people from being ruled by spirits, to help free themselves" (see Rubin, "Picasso" 255).

But Picasso also linked tribal art with the solution of formal problems, deriving his experimental shorthand from the starkly reductive forms of African sculpture. As D. H. Lawrence wrote in his 1925 essay "Art and Morality," "[the] African fetish-statues have no movement, visually represented. Yet one little motionless wooden figure stirs more than all the Parthenon frieze." The cubists incorporated African form-language into a search for underlying structures that had begun with the geometrizing of Cézanne. Carl Einstein, in *L'Art negre et l'art oceanien* (1919), took a formalist view of African masks, dismissing the notion of crude distortion: "Their expression flows from their construction, from the accentuation of planes by large masses. It is from the play of lines that they derive their effects" (see Paudrat 159). Picasso, in his primitivizing phase (1907–08), moved from Iberian to African art, abstracting geometric forms, yet empathizing deeply with the expressive powers that mobilized his own creativity. African fetishes "seemed animated by the irrational forces of sorcery" (Paudrat 142), which could be used to access the repressed potential of the unconscious. Thus Lawrence's Birkin, in the "Fetish" chapter of *Women in Love* (1920), is initiated into cultural otherness by encountering the *mana* of an African sculpture that embodies extreme sensation.

African sculpture, cutting into the grain of the wood, emphasizes deep structure, "plasticity," and the "tactile"; Oceanic sculpture highlights "pictorial structure," "surface decoration," and the "visual" (Rubin, "Introduction" 41, 47). African art had a major impact on cubists and expressionists, Oceanic on the surrealists. Parisian circles associated Oceanic art with sensuality, magic, and myth, African with "something more fetishistic, magical, and, above all, potentially malefic—far closer in mood to **Conrad**'s *Heart of Darkness* than to Gauguin's *Noa-Noa*" (Rubin, "Picasso" 259). Tribal objects were catalysts for the European unconscious and primitivism could take idyllic or demonic forms. Rubin compares "[the] archetypal 'night journey' of the soul" in *Heart of Darkness* (1900) with Picasso's *Demoiselles,* which "express[es] something alien, menacing, and virtually unutterable" ("Picasso" 259). The primitive awakens an echo in the modern soul of libidinal forces it thought it had overcome. While Europeans were

colonizing **Africa,** primitive artifacts were colonizing the European imagination. In Conrad's novella, "the wilderness" echoes within Kurtz, because he is "hollow at the core;" in **Yeats**'s "Second Coming," evil reverberates with passionate intensity, because the ideals of civilization are exhausted.

Expressionists sought revitalization in the dynamic forms of tribal art, which Kirchner discovered in the Dresden Ethnographical Museum around 1904. The barbaric stripping-off of appearances appealed to them, but their "conscious primitivism" was more ambivalent, "confront[ing] the raw with the sophisticated, the natural with the cultured" (Gordon 372). The sheer physicality of the creative act, reflected in the vigorous anatomical distortion of tribal carving from Cameroon or Congo, appealed to *Die Brücke.* As Nolde put it: "What we enjoy, probably, is the intense and often grotesque expression of energy, of life" (Nolde; see Gordon 383). Expressionists linked this creative urge—Alois Riegl's "religious sensuality of art"—with nineteenth-century blood-and-soil philosophies of Ludwig Klages and Alfred Schuler, as well as with Nietzsche and **Whitman.** While German expressionists "revived Romantic ideals of tapping into the lifeblood of nature" (Masheck 94), Lawrence developed a cult of "blood consciousness," based on the primitive anthropology of Edward Tylor and Sir James G. Frazer.

Expressionists aspired to recapture authentic powers of vision from primitive art: the challenge was to find outward forms to match their inner feelings. Nolde, who affirmed that "[i]nstinct is ten times what knowledge is" (see Haftmann 24), visited New Guinea in 1913–14 and became an advocate of "primordial being." Primitivists wanted to slough off the effects of modern industrial civilization and re-root themselves in nature. The postwar twenties brought "[an] aspiration of passionate naturalness, of being grounded like some supposed peasant in the true, raw earth" (Masheck 115). Expressionists and surrealists embraced tribal art as the clue to long-forgotten mysteries: although tribal forms are rigidly codified by tradition, as can be seen in the distinctive style languages of Kifwebe and Fang masks, European artists often took them to be the expression of individual talent and emotion.

Primitivism in the arts was supported by investigations of the "primordial mind" in anthropology. European thinkers such as Frazer, Lévy-Bruhl, **Freud,** and **Jung** were studying "primitive mentality" and the surrealists followed their lead. Desiring to contact "the Spirit world and the realm of the dream," they felt an affinity for "the art of the Primitive, the child, and the insane" (Maurer 546, 538). André Breton attended voodoo ceremonies in Haiti and attempted to recapture "the primitive vision"; Max Ernst adopted a bird-totem and practiced shamanism. Joan Miró's paintings, composed of biomorphic and geometric shapes, show an affinity with prehistoric pictographs like those of the Altamira caves. The strong attraction of the tribal for the civilized was based on a sense of exotic Otherness, yet archetypal unity underlies cultural diversity. Rubin compares the Moon/Sun face in Picasso's *Girl before a Mirror* (1932) with a painted Kwakiutl mask from British Columbia: these two-faced images of psychic and cosmic duality manifest an extraordinary affinity ("Picasso" 330). Primitivism broke down cultural barriers, so that human experience could be recognized or articulated in a vast variety of forms.

Primitivism involved reduction, selection, displacement, distortion, and heightening, as painters translated a form-language derived from three-dimensional masks and carvings to a flat surface. The Fauves and Picasso felt a strong affinity for African masks. Even Braque, who did not use their form-language, said: "The African masks . . . opened a new horizon to me. They made it possible for me to make contact with instinctual things . . ." (see Rubin, "Picasso" 307). Masks were worn in tribal dances to impersonate spirits and so came to symbolize altered states of consciousness or metamorphosis. Masks and costumes, which appealed strongly to the surrealists, are related to ritual, play, and caricature, which "involves both artistic aggression (against the object) and psychic regression (to childlike play)" (Gordon 381). Paul Klee felt that "[c]hildren, the insane, and primitive peoples all still have . . . the power to see" (see Laude, "Klee" 487)—that is, in a directly visionary way. Ideographic systems, like that of Zaire, attracted Klee, who built up a matching lexicon of signs; his pictorial language in *Picture Album* (1937) mediates dreams and the unconscious, giving the painted signs a pre-verbal universality.

European sculptors responded directly to the sheer force of African art. "The demonic power, the often overt sexuality, the extraordinary formal variety, and the inner logic," writes Wilkinson, "were the characteristics of tribal art that had such a liberating and far-reaching influence on the work of Picasso, Brancusi, Epstein, and Moore" (423). Lawrence's Birkin recognizes the cutting edge of expression in the "fetish," where the face of a woman in labor is "abstracted almost into meaninglessness by the weight of sensation beneath." Birkin, who sees "hundreds of centuries of development in a straight line, behind that carving" (*Women in Love,* Cambridge UP, 1987: 79), is one of Rubin's "vanguard modernists [who] told us decades ago that the tribal peoples produced an art that often distilled great complexity into seemingly simple solutions" ("Introduction" 71).

Primitivism is ambiguously oriented to remote cultures and to civilized man's own inner being. On the strength of the fetish, Birkin imagines that "that which was imminent in himself must have taken place in these Africans" (253). Attracted to, yet dreading, a sensual knowledge that would submerge the mind, he uses tribal icons as a means of psychic and cultural divination.

The negative side of primitivism, as a symptom of civilized consciousness, involves regressive fantasy or sadomasochistic atavism—as with Lawrence's artist Gudrun, whose "nostalgia" stems from a dual desire to obliterate hypertrophied mental consciousness in "dark" sensuality and to exploit a "lower" order of being for libidinal gratification. According to Varnedoe, "[Jean] Dubuffet's literal *nostalgie de la boue* sought to fuse the untempered physical and emotive aggressivity he sensed in tribal objects with the unpoliced force found in the graffiti . . . of the modern city" (637). Contemporary primitivism, involving multimedia and environmental art, draws on prehistoric earthworks and artifacts as well as textual sources by Antonin Artaud, Georges Bataille, Michel Leiris, Claude Lévi-Strauss, and Gilles Deleuze. In its search for roots, authenticity, and expressive power, modernism was deeply fertilized by tribal art. Contemporary artists now have access, through reproductions and exhibitions, to a worldwide pool of artistic resources and many have shown an elective affinity for the "primordial."

Jack Stewart

Selected Bibliography

Abrams, M. H. "Primitivism and Progress." *A Glossary of Literary Terms.* 6th ed. New York: Harcourt, 1993. 169–71.

Bell, Michael. *Primitivism.* London: Methuen, 1972.

Gauguin, Paul. *Noa Noa: The Tahiti Journal of Paul Gauguin.* Trans. O. F. Theis. San Francisco: Chronicle, 1994.

———. *The Writings of a Savage.* Ed. Daniel Guerin. Trans. Eleanor Levieux. New York: Viking, 1978.

Gordon, Donald E. "German Expressionism." Rubin, ed. Vol. I. 369–403.

Haftmann, Werner. *Emil Nolde.* New York: Abrams, n.d.

Laude, Jean. *The Arts of Black Africa.* Trans. Jean Decock. Berkeley: U of California P, 1971.

———. "Paul Klee." Rubin, ed. Vol. II. 487–501.

Lévi-Strauss, Claude. *Tristes Tropiques.* Trans. John and Doreen Weightman. New York: Atheneum, 1974.

Lovejoy, Arthur O. and George Boas. *Primitivism and Related Ideas in Antiquity.* New York: Octagon, 1965.

Masheck, Joseph. "Raw Art: 'Primitive' Authenticity and German Expressionism." *Res* 4 (1982): 92–117.

Maurer, Evan. "Dada and Surrealism." Rubin, ed. Vol. II: 535–93.

Paudrat, Jean-Louis. "From Africa." Trans. John Shepley. Rubin, ed. Vol. I. 125–75.

Rubin, William, ed. *"Primitivism" in 20th Century Art: Affinity of the Tribal and the Modern.* 2 vols. New York: Museum of Modern Art, 1984.

———. "Introduction." Rubin, ed. Vol. I. 1–81.

———. "Picasso." Rubin, ed. Vol. I. 241–343.

Stewart, Jack. " 'Primitivism' in *Women in Love.*" In his *The Vital Art of D. H. Lawrence: Vision and Expression.* Carbondale: Southern Illinois UP, 1999. 94–116.

Torgovnick, Marianna. *Gone Primitive: Savage Intellects, Modern Lives.* Chicago: U of Chicago P, 1990.

Varnedoe, Kirk. "Contemporary Explorations." Rubin, ed. Vol. II. 661–85.

———. "Gauguin." Rubin, ed. Vol. I. 179–209.

Wilkinson, Alan G. "Paris and London: Modigliani, Lipchitz, Epstein, and Gaudier-Brzeska." Rubin, ed. Vol. II. 417–51.

Proust, Marcel (1871–1922)

French novelist, author of *A la recherche du temps perdu.*

Proust was born and educated in Paris; his father was an eminent neurologist, his mother from a wealthy and cultured Jewish family. His first compositions appeared in symbolist reviews in the early 1890s; in 1896 he published a collection of short stories and poems (in prose and verse), *Les Plaisirs et les jours* (Pleasures and Days).

Between 1895 and 1899 he worked on a largely autobiographical novel; the drafts of this unfinished project were eventually published as *Jean Santeuil* in 1952. He subsequently translated two works by Ruskin (*La Bible d'Amiens* in 1904, *Sésame et les lys* in 1906); a series of pastiches of famous French writers appeared in *Le Figaro* in 1908–09, and were later published in *Pastiches et mélanges* (1919). From 1909 onwards Proust was working on what would eventually become *A la recherche*. At this early stage, Proust was uncertain as to whether it would be a work of fiction or criticism; much of the critical writing was published in 1954 as *Contre Sainte-Beuve*. Proust's fame, however, rests securely on *A la recherche,* a seven-volume *roman-fleuve* published between 1913 and 1927. The second volume, *A l'ombre des jeunes filles en fleurs,* was awarded (controversially) the Prix Goncourt in 1919. Proust was still revising the fifth and sixth volumes at the time of his death, from pneumonia, in 1922; the last three volumes were published posthumously.

A la recherche is generally considered the most significant work of fiction published in **France** in the twentieth century. It narrates the life of a young man who in many ways resembles the author, recounting his childhood in Combray and Paris, his various emotional attachments, his forays into the aristocratic society of the Faubourg Saint-Germain, and his eventual discovery of his vocation as a writer. On one level, *A la recherche* can be read as a fictionalized autobiography, tracing the evolution of a figure similar to, but not to be identified with, the author Marcel Proust. Traditional readings have stressed the convergence between character, narrator, and author in the last volume of the book—this in spite of Proust's disclaimers (most notably in an interview dating from 1913, in which he states that "le personnage qui raconte, qui dit: 'Je' [. . .] n'est pas moi" ("the character who narrates,

who says 'I' . . . is not me") (*CSB* 558). The "nouveaux critiques" of the 1960s and 1970s followed Proust on this, stressing the divergences between author and narrator, and indeed the irrelevance of the question to the properly literary examination of theme, form, and technique. Recently, the generic ambiguity, or hybridity, of *A la recherche* has again begun to attract critical attention: Leo Bersani talks of a "non-attributable autobiographical novel" (Bersani 404), which Margaret Gray glosses as "the fictive life of a fictive narrator, belonging to no-one" (Gray 44).

Bracketing for a moment the autobiography question, one might be tempted to see *A la recherche* as a variation on the *roman d'apprentissage* model—what German critics would call a *Künstlerroman,* the narrative of an artistic vocation (indeed, Proust himself described his novel as "l'histoire d'une vocation"). This thematization of art and writing is something *A la recherche* shares with many major modernist fictions—André Gide's *Les Faux-monnayeurs,* **James Joyce**'s *Portrait of the Artist,* **Thomas Mann**'s *Doktor Faustus.* Traditional readings, following the narrator's own "aesthetic theory" as expounded in *Le Temps retrouvé* (the final volume of *A la recherche*), have tended to present art, the narrator's belated discovery of his literary vocation, as the (largely unproblematic) resolution of the novel: the narrator will discover and/or create—this is a central tension within the work—his authentic self in the act of writing his projected novel.

This discovery/creation of the "vrai moi" and the "vraie vie" is achieved through writing; but a crucially necessary precondition for this is the recovery of the writer's past through (involuntary) memory. The distinction between voluntary and involuntary memory is a thematic lynchpin of *A la recherche,* even if (as Gérard Genette has remarked) Proust's textual practice is rather more complex than the narrator's commentary thereon (Genette 270). Involuntary memory provides both material and model for the projected novel. It brings back past moments ("le temps perdu") with a completeness and vividness which the snapshots of voluntary memory cannot match. It also, in its dyadic structure, resembles metaphor, since both involve a linking between two similar but discrete elements. Metaphor condenses objects or images which share certain features or qualities; involuntary memory brings together moments from past and present which are linked by the occurrence of similar sensations.

In fact, the distinction between voluntary and involuntary memory—important though it is in the narrator's aesthetic theory and practice—does not entirely do justice to the complex and subtle shifts of remembering and association which we can trace in the text of *A la recherche*. Often the text suggests or enacts patterns of association between images, sensations, ideas, moments, which are based neither on a near-identity of perceptions (as with involuntary memory) nor on the willed and contingent connections of voluntary memory. Indeed, the network of associations extending through the narrator's mind and Proust's text can at times call to mind the complex mental structures **Freud** describes in his case histories.

Proust's concern with the workings of memory underlines the importance of time in the novel (as indeed do the novel's title, and its first and last words). A stated intention of narrator (and author) was to write a work of fiction which does not neglect the fourth dimension, to depict "une psychologie dans le temps" (*CSB* 557). This led early critics to link Proust and Bergson (his near-contemporary and relative by marriage). However, as Proust himself was the first to point out, his conception of time and memory is in fact very different from Bergsonian "durée" ("duration"), laying much greater stress on

intermittence and discontinuity. And Bergson's system has no equivalent of Proustian involuntary memory.

Proust's preoccupation with time, as one might expect, has formal ramifications, especially in the first volume of *A la recherche,* where we find the famous description of involuntary memory in the "madeleine" episode, and the interpolated retrospective narrative of "Un amour de Swann." Thereafter, though, the narrative line of *A la recherche* is surprisingly chronological. There are certainly great variations in the pace of the narrative (Genette's category of "duration"), but the order of the narration corresponds in general to the temporal sequence of the events narrated. We should perhaps look elsewhere for major innovations in narrative structure—especially, perhaps, to the combination (or interweaving) of narrative-descriptive and what we might call discursive modes in the narrative voice. Various critics have commented on the importance of "la démonstration"—of argumentation—in *A la recherche:* the extraction of "lois générales" of human behavior, motivation and consciousness is a conspicuous, and acknowledged, element in the work.

Another major structural innovation in *A la recherche*—one which we find, in slightly different forms, in other major modernists (Joyce, Mann, **Woolf, Broch**)—is the use of what has sometimes been called musical form: principles of textual organization based on, or showing affinities with, the forms of sonata or symphony or (in the case of Proust) of Wagner's "Musikdrama," with its pervasive structuring device of the leitmotiv. The opening passage of *A la recherche* has frequently (and controversially) been described as the "overture;" certainly the recurrence of images and motifs in the novel does show some parallels with Wagner's use of the leitmotiv (for example, Saint-Loup's monocle as a parodic variation on Siegfried's spear). The role of more traditional forms like the sonata should not be underestimated: the compositions of the fictional composer Vinteuil which play such a major role as "mises en abyme" in the novel are a sonata and a septet. In fact, Proust's narrator draws on a variety of metaphors to describe the structure of his work: some of these (the quartet, the cathedral) are derived from the major arts, but others (some of the more memorable ones, perhaps) are drawn from humbler fields of creative activity, like dressmaking (Fortuny's robes) and cooking (Françoise's famous "boeuf en daube").

The role of metaphor and analogy in Proust's writing is hard to overstate. We have already indicated the structural parallels which link metaphor (on a textual level) and involuntary memory (on a psychological or phenomenological one). The search for analogy is also, of course, a fundamental principle of mental functioning in general: in a crucial passage discussing the most profound and persistent of those partial selves which coexist in the (total) self, we find mention of "un certain philosophe, qui n'est heureux que quand il a découvert, entre deux oeuvres, entre deux sensations, une partie commune" (a certain philosopher who is only happy when he has discovered a common element linking two works or two sensations, *RTP*, III, 522). The human mind, in Proust's vision, ceaselessly and restlessly establishes links and associations between objects, sensations, ideas. This is not always a conscious process: indeed, more fertile connections are often forged below the threshold of awareness. Proust himself described *A la recherche* as "une suite de 'Romans de l'Inconscient' " (a series of 'novels of the unconscious,' *CSB* 558), and the oneiric element in Proust's vision was noted early on by Edmund Wilson, who described it as "a true dream-novel" which has "the harmony, development and logic of the unconscious" (Wilson 145).

The writing of the self, in its conscious and unconscious aspects, is a (perhaps the?) central concern of much modernist fiction; *A la recherche* represents one of the summits of this mode of "subjective realism." As mentioned earlier, *A la recherche* (at least according to traditional readings) culminates in the (projected) discovery of the narrator's true self ("le vrai moi") in the act of writing. Becoming a writer, or any form of artist, means finding a style, which—the narrator affirms—is a matter not of technique but of vision. So we find an expressivist theory of style in tandem with (on a thematic level) a profound exploration of the self: the *subject* (in both senses) of *A la recherche* is the narrator—the texture, structure, evolution of his consciousness. The narrator's life provides the raw material for his art; conversely, artistic form and expression are presented as the (potential) consummation of the life.

Writing, then, functions as an ordering and indeed interpretation of (remembered) experience: the composition of the projected novel involves not only the recollection of past experience through involuntary memory, but also—a concomitant process—the deciphering of the images which memory and perception throw up. The task of writing is essentially that of reading the signs of the "livre intérieur," the inner book made up of sensations and impressions buried deep in the mind. There are, however, other important elements in the writing of the self in *A la recherche,* chief among them the pivotal notion of the "intermittences du coeur," intermittences of the heart. This is exemplified when Marcel, bending down to tie his shoe-laces, is suddenly overwhelmed with grief at the death of his grandmother, which had occurred much earlier in the narrative. The narrator sees this as evidence that our emotional self is discontinuous, that (as with memory) the full range of our emotional resources is not always accessible to us. The link with involuntary memory, its sporadic and unpredictable irruption into consciousness, is clear; likewise its importance for that central Proustian principle, the multiplicity of the self. (As early as the 1920s, Proust's friend and editor, Jacques Rivière, presented this as the foundation of Proust's psychology, and the decisive contrast with the dualist Freudian paradigm of mental conflict between conscious and unconscious.)

Intermittence and the death of the (partial, provisional) self is at the center of Proust's very original exploration of love and desire. In *A la recherche,* falling out of love involves such a profound emotional shift that the narrator describes it as the death of the self: a striking example occurs early in *A l'ombre des jeunes filles en fleurs,* when Marcel has become indifferent to Gilberte. On a traditional reading of *A la recherche,* the multiplicity and discontinuity of the self is overcome at the end of the novel, when the narrator discovers how to express/create the true (permanent, underlying) self through involuntary memory and writing (or writing based on the resources of involuntary memory). More recent critics, however, have often tended (to a greater or lesser extent) to read "against the grain," to interpret the final revelations of *Le Temps retrouvé* as just one (albeit the most intense) in the series of epiphanies, of "moments bienheureux," which Marcel has experienced in the course of the novel. This would imply that the aesthetic theory expounded by the narrator is not necessarily definitive, that it should not automatically be read as a complete resolution of the tensions and conflicts which have up till then informed Marcel's existence.

A la recherche explores the narrator's subjectivity with unparalleled subtlety; but how does that affect the presentation of the other in the novel? Various critics (most prominently Deleuze) have argued that the primacy accorded to subjective vision means that other figures in the novel come across as (to a great extent) projections of the narrator's self. This seems especially compelling in the case of the major love objects—Gilberte, Oriane, and above all Albertine, the "être de fuite" par excellence, whose "self" Marcel never manages to fix, capture, or define. This dramatizes one of the narrator's more compelling "lois générales": desire for the other on the one hand whets the urge to know; but it also disperses and fragments the object, thus making it unknowable. Desire sharpens attention and awareness; this makes the object more complex, more difficult to fix and immobilize within the bounds of a specific "character" or "self." Moreover, not only is the object of desire in perpetual movement; the universal law of change also affects the desiring subject, whose shifts are obviously reflected in, or on to, the object. This lability of both subject and object (of perception, knowledge) is of course at the root of Proust's "psychologie dans le temps."

Style (verbal, artistic), as mentioned above, is presented as the most complete and satisfactory expression of subjectivity, of personal vision: "[le style] est la révélation . . . de la différence qualitative qu'il y a dans la façon dont nous apparaît le monde" (Style is the revelation of the qualitative difference in the way the world appears to [each of] us, *RTP,* IV, 474). How is this reflected in the text of *A la recherche?* The distinctive features of Proust's writing, by common consent, are to be found in syntax and imagery. The most striking syntactic feature is the famously (or notoriously) lengthy Proustian sentence. J. P. Houston comments perceptively on the function of these sentences, how they encapsulate an impression, a complex and self-contained "moment" of the kind which forms the basis and raw material of *A la recherche:* "Proust's sentence structure is intended to bind together the most varied materials into new wholes, new total impressions, where the accessory is as essential as the main object of contemplation" (Houston 248). Metaphor we have already mentioned; suffice it to say that it exemplifies the condensing and conjoining activity of the mind, in perception, thought and memory. Proust (or his narrator) is quite explicit about the importance of metaphor, presenting it as the foundation of authentic art: "la vérité ne commencera qu'au moment où l'écrivain prendra deux objets, posera leur rapport . . . et les enfermera dans les anneaux nécessaires d'un beau style" (Truth will only begin [to appear] when the writer takes two objects, posits the connection between them, . . . and encloses them within the necessary links of a beautiful style, *RTP,* IV, 468). However, Genette, in an influential article entitled "Métonymie chez Proust" (Genette 41–63), subjects the narrator's theory to scrutiny, comparing it with Proust's textual practice in *A la recherche,* where metaphors often arise from previous metonymic links, images juxtaposed on the diegetic level of the text. An example might clarify this: the steeples of a church in Combray are compared to ears of corn; a little earlier, we find the description of the church surrounded by cornfields. Hence the proximity of elements in the fictional universe of the novel seems to generate the comparison or metaphor in the narrator's discourse.

In many respects Proust's writing seems to exemplify perfectly the "poetic prose" so prevalent in modernist fiction—Woolf, Joyce, **Faulkner**, Broch. But the interplay of **metaphor and metonymy** complicates the picture: *A la recherche* shows a subtle interweaving of poetic prose based on metaphor and a more realist mode based on metonymy—though the latter bears little relation to the "littérature de notations" which Proust's narrator criticises and parodies in the pastiche of the Goncourts' style in *Le Temps retrouvé.*

As we have said, Proust is surely one of the summits of modernist subjectivism; but as his fascination with Balzac, and in-deed Saint-Simon, would indicate, there is a salient, and sometimes neglected, strand of what one might call social realism in *A la recherche.* This is not perhaps of a sort to satisfy a Lukács: Proust describes the *moeurs* of a certain (aristocratic) stratum of French society around the turn of the century, but he lacks the totalizing ambitions so central in (for example) Balzac's "social zoology." But *A la recherche* does trace the evolution and decline of a certain class through *fin de siècle* and *belle époque* society, exhibiting great attentiveness to subtle signs of social interaction; this complements and counterbalances his mappings of inner experience.

Proust's preeminent position in early twentieth-century French literature seems assured; indeed, some would make even greater claims for him. Walter Benjamin asserted in 1929 that "this great special case of literature . . . constitutes its greatest achievement of recent decades" (Benjamin 203). Much later, in his study of Tolstoy and Dostoyevsky, George Steiner suggests that *A la recherche* is, in certain respects, more central even than the work of the two great Russians. Certainly the influence of *A la recherche* on subsequent writers has been enormous and undisputed: from Sartre, who parodies the "petite phrase" of the Vinteuil sonata in *La Nausée,* to the major exponents of the *nouveau roman* (Sarraute, Butor, Simon, Robbe-Grillet), all of whom acknowledge a debt to *A la recherche.*

Situating Proust more precisely in literary history, however, has proved more problematic. As indicated earlier, Proust could in no sense be considered a follower of **realism:** the Goncourt pastiche alone demonstrates that. And yet he is an avid reader of Balzac and of Flaubert (the latter admittedly for his "génie grammatical" rather than for his themes and subjects). Edmund Wilson stresses the symbolist vein, making much of Proust's use of musical form: "Marcel Proust is the first important novelist to apply the principle of symbolism in fiction" (Wilson 111). It is hard to dispute the influence of Wagner on *A la recherche,* but we should remember Proust's reservations about symbolist excesses, expressed notably in an early article entitled "Contre l'obscurité" (*CSB* 390–95). Among his nineteenth-century precursors, Proust seems to have felt the closest affinity with those great writers of poetic prose, Chateaubriand and Nerval, and with Baudelaire.

Perhaps the most satisfactory attempt to situate Proust in literary and intellectual context has been made by Antoine Compagnon. Compagnon meticulously traces the richness and complexity of Proust's affiliations (with Baudelaire, Huysmans, Fauré . . .), concluding that Proust is "the last writer of the nineteenth century and the first of the twentieth, who both was intimately attached to the *fin-de-siècle* and miraculously escaped from it" (Compagnon 7). It is undeniable that the most varied strands of nineteenth-century thought and art are interwoven in his work; but it would still be hard to see *A la recherche* as a (belated) nineteenth-century novel. The meticulous mapping of subjectivity, the reflexive preoccupation with the activity of writing and the figure of the writer— the writing of self, with the accent on both elements—predominate in Proust's great novel. Despite clear divergences in form and sensibility, these central concerns align Proust more closely with his major contemporaries—Gide, Joyce, Mann, **Musil,** even Woolf—than with those great (and greatly admired) nineteenth-century French precursors, Balzac, Stendhal, and Flaubert.

Robin MacKenzie

Selected Bibliography

Benjamin, Walter. *Illuminations.* Ed. H. Arendt. London: Fontana, 1973.

Bersani, Leo. " 'The Culture of Redemption': Marcel Proust and Melanie Klein." *Critical Inquiry* 12.2 (Winter 1986): 399–421.

Bowie, Malcolm. *Proust among the Stars.* London: Harper Collins, 1998.

Compagnon, Antoine. *Proust between Two Centuries.* Transl. R. Goodkin. New York: Columbia University Press, 1992.

Deleuze, Gilles. *Proust et les signes.* 4th edition. Paris: Presses universitaires de France, 1976.

Genette, Gérard. *Figures III.* Paris: Seuil, 1972.

Gray, Margaret. *Postmodern Proust.* Philadelphia: University of Pennsylvania Press, 1992.

Houston, John Porter. *The Traditions of French Prose Style.* Baton Rouge and London: Louisiana State University Press, 1981.

Proust, Marcel. *A la recherche du temps perdu.* General ed. J.-Y. Tadié. 4 vols. Paris: Gallimard, 1987–89.

———. *Contre Sainte-Beuve.* Ed. P. Clarac and Y. Sandre. Paris: Gallimard, 1971.

———. *Remembrance of Things Past.* Transl. C.K. Scott-Moncrieff and Terence Kilmartin. 3 vols. Harmondsworth: Penguin, 1983.

Rivière, Jacques. *Quelques progrès dans l'étude du coeur humain.* Re-edition, in *Cahiers Marcel Proust,* 13. Paris: Gallimard, 1985.

Steiner, George. *Tolstoy or Dostoevsky: an Essay in Contrast.* 2nd ed. London: Faber, 1980.

Wilson, Edmund. *Axel's Castle.* Re-edition. London: Fontana, 1974.

Psychoanalysis

The term *psychoanalysis* is used to denote both the theories about the nature and development of the human mind, and also the therapeutic practices, that were first evolved by Sigmund Freud in the 1890s and that have subsequently been further developed by his followers. It thus indicates a tradition of theories and practices different from those deriving (for example) from Adler's "individual psychology," **Jung**'s "analytical psychology," or from the host of more recent psychotherapies that may or may not use psychoanalytic ideas and techniques.

The origins of psychoanalysis in the 1890s were contemporary with those of modernism, although its roots lay in the materialism of late nineteenth-century science, and in Freud's belief that mental events have causes in the same way that physical events do. Freud's hope was to establish a universal science of mind—an ambition which brought psychoanalysis into conflict with the cultural relativism that followed in the wake of widening historical and anthropological knowledge during the modernist period. Freud's psychic determinism also aroused opposition on religious grounds from people believing in the spirituality of mind, and on artistic grounds from people championing its creativity. Much of this opposition crystallized around the status of art.

There was thus a measure of ideological non-conformity between psychoanalysis and modernist culture, and much of its history, and the criticism that it faced, may be read in terms of this non-conformity. To its enemies, psychoanalysis seemed a symptom of the very disease it was trying to cure; to its adherents, it offered the only way to understand, and perhaps to cure, the mental illnesses endemic in contemporary society.

Beginnings: The Study of Hysteria

Psychoanalysis originated in Freud's work with hysterical patients, and in his meditations over the fact that they suffered from functional disorders with no organic cause. A patient might be unable to move an arm, for instance, and yet the nerve pathways that permit such movement be quite undamaged. The cause of such disorders was found to lie in mental trauma, of which the symptom was either a direct or symbolic expression. Patients vomiting regularly at the sight of food might do so either because the original trauma occurred during a meal-time, or because they were being asked to "swallow" something "disgusting" that they found "indigestible." Hysterical illnesses were thus expressions of a patient's experience, defenses against intolerable feelings of fright, anxiety, shame or pain. As Freud and Breuer wrote in their "Preliminary Communication" (1893), "*hysterics suffer mainly from reminiscences*"; and it was the great achievement of their *Studies on Hysteria,* which followed in 1895, that a condition that had been previously under taboo, and stigmatized as degenerate, was suddenly made accessible to understanding, even legitimated as a response to circumstance. Freud was beginning, in Foucault's words, to open up "the possibility for reason and unreason to communicate in the danger of a common language."

From a psychological point of view, what was important about hysterical illness was that the patients remained ignorant of its cause. Their reminiscences were unconscious; and it was upon this fact that Freud built the theoretical edifice of psychoanalysis. If hysterical illnesses were the product of a process of splitting, or dissociation—the mind's defense against intolerable pain, fear or desire—it followed that there must be unconscious processes within the mind ("the unconscious"), and a process for making those processes unconscious ("repression"). But since that which was repressed remained dynamic within the mind, expressing itself in the disguised form of symptoms, there must also be processes of mental transformation whereby energy is transferred from one object to another ("displacement"); and it was the job of the therapist to unravel this process, decoding the symptomatology and symbolism of illness in order to locate its cause—a process undertaken by encouraging patients to talk, at first under hypnotism and later simply in a position of relaxation, obeying the basic injunction to say whatever came into their heads ("free association"). The difficulty that patients found in carrying out this command was seen to be yet a further act of self-defense ("resistance").

Traditionally, although a few doctors had identified the male hysteric, hysteria was thought to be a woman's disease; and it is notable that all the patients whose histories were given by Breuer and Freud in their *Studies on Hysteria* were women. There is an important difference, however; these women were listened to, and the causes of their condition traced to the suffocating circumstances of their lives, and particularly their sexual lives, within patriarchal society. Flaubert's *Madame Bovary* (1857) was the first literary text to use female hysteria as a means of social criticism, but such texts multiplied under modernism. **Henry James** made elaborate play out of the possibilities and limitations of contemporary discourses of hysteria in *The Turn of the Screw* (1898), while Freud's own influence on the literature of hysteria can be seen in a novel like May Sinclair's *The Life and Death of Harriett Frean* (1922). Freud's notable openness to women's versions of their own experience, however, is less prominent in his later *Fragment of an Analysis of a Case of Hysteria* (1905), the case-history of "Dora," which has become a touchstone for feminist debate about the degree of Freud's collusion with patriarchal repressiveness.

The Oedipus Complex

Freud quickly began to apply the psychological insights gained through the study of hysteria both to the other neuroses and to the mind in health. Everywhere he found traces of unconscious mental processes banished from consciousness by repression; and increasingly he came to believe that what had been repressed was not always the trauma of fright or physical pain but the shame of sexual fantasy and desire. This privileging of sexuality might be accounted for in a number of ways. It might be explained sociologically in terms of the constraints exerted by Viennese patriarchy upon the middle-class young women who made up so much of Freud's clientele; it might be explained philosophically in terms of the late nineteenth-century desire to examine human behavior in

terms of the biological instincts that supposedly inspired it; and of course it might be explained personally in terms of the secret preoccupations of Freud himself. Freud's emphasis upon the ubiquity of sexual desire helped to lift a profound and often pathogenic social taboo; but in so far as it led to the consideration of illness largely from an intrapsychic perspective, it was also responsible for deflecting attention away from something that Freud himself often repeated—the fact that, as in Dora's case, illness is often the result of traumatic or abusive interpersonal relationships.

The most momentous of Freud's theories about human sexuality was his formulation in a letter of 1897 of what is now called the Oedipus complex. His self-analysis following the death of his father in 1896 had revealed to him that as a child he had been "in love with my mother and jealous of my father"—a pattern which patients' revelations had then confirmed as universal to childhood. This theory has since proved useful in exploring the triangular asymmetry of growing up as a self of one particular sex, while excluded from participating in a parental relationship involving both sexes; and yet in its original formulation it was asymmetrical in its neglect both of the female child and of the different family constellations encountered by succeeding brothers and sisters. In this sense the Oedipus complex in 1897 was very much the theory of an eldest son—a defect that Freud partially remedied later in *The Ego and the Id* (1923), where he explored the love and hate felt both by girls and boys for both parents. The early conception of the Oedipus complex, however, became amongst the most widely known of all Freud's theories, helping to structure such works as **Lawrence**'s *Sons and Lovers* (1913) and **Joyce**'s *Ulysses* (1922), while the latter conception perhaps helped to shape **Virginia Woolf**'s *To the Lighthouse* (1927).

The Interpretation of Dreams (1900)

Freud first published his work on Oedipal theory in *The Interpretation of Dreams* (1900), in the context of a discussion of *Hamlet* which, when expanded by Ernest Jones in his essay "A Psycho-Analytic Study of Hamlet" (1910), reverberated throughout the modernist period and accelerated the development of a specifically psychoanalytic literary criticism.

The Interpretation of Dreams was the first of Freud's two most important works. He argued that dreams were material phenomena like any other, and hence that they must have causes. Dreaming was not simply something that we do, for which *reasons* may be found, as Wittgenstein was later to argue, but a predetermined activity for which *causes* may be found. The search for those causes presented the scientist both with peculiar difficulties, since they were unconscious, and with peculiar opportunities, since *the interpretation of dreams is the royal road to a knowledge of the unconscious activities of the mind.*" Freud's approach to the problem of interpretation was typically bold. He argued that all dreams (except traumatic dreams) originated in an unconscious wish, which it was the business of the dream to gratify—but to gratify only in disguised form, since the true nature of the wish (usually infantile and sexual in origin) remained repressed even during sleep. A dream was thus a compromise formation between an inadmissible desire and a censoring agent within the mind, and its business was to preserve sleep. A nightmare was a dream whose compromise had proved ineffective, and where the anxiety caused by the repressed desire had awoken the dreamer.

We all dream; and while Freud's theory of dreams was a by-product of his work on the neuroses, he quickly saw the proximity between health and illness, with the same defenses at work in each case, although not with equal success. In this sense, he wrote later, a healthy person is "virtually" a neurotic, since his dreams perform the same function as the symptoms of the neurotic: they express in disguised form the desires against which they are also defenses. It was these desires that Freud sought to make his patients "admit" through interpretation of their dreams—an activity in which (as with the behavior and the speech of the hysteric) the non-rational was once again made subject to a rational scientific discourse.

Freud's distinction between "reason" and "unreason," however, expresses a view of mental structure and functioning that often caused difficulties for creative artists. He postulated two kinds of process in the mind: "primary processes," glimpsed in the "unreason" of dreaming, and "secondary processes," seen in the "reason" of everyday discursive thinking. Both processes, he thought, aimed at gratification, the former by hallucination (as when babies suck to recreate the absent breast) and the latter by adaptive behaviour (as when babies learn to wait). Freud thought of the primary processes as non-adaptive, recognizing neither time nor space, and condemned to work symbolically through hallucinated images that were substitutes for the real repressed objects of desire. He had no place in his scheme for what creative writers since the romantics had called "imagination," and did not guess that the baby hallucinating the breast might in fact be engaged in a highly adaptive behavior lying at the root of imagination. Instead, he privileged secondary over primary processes, in a way typical of late nineteenth-century positivism. He undervalued the non-discursive thinking that goes into art, and although he knew that artistic creativity was more than merely a neurotic symptom, he had no adequate way of saying why this might be so. The imaginative activities of the various art-forms constituted the necessary absence out of which the narratives of a scientific psychoanalysis emerged. In the words of Ernest Jones, art evinced "the conscious working out of unconscious wishes of childhood origin," and early psychoanalysts felt themselves free to treat artists, like dreamers, as "virtual" neurotics. It is ironic that *The Interpretation of Dreams,* which did so much to assimilate neurotic to normal behavior, should have no other course but to refer the normal creative impulse to neurotic motivation.

The result of Freud's work on dreams, on "Freudian slips" in *The Psychopathology of Everyday Life* (1901) and on jokes in *Wit and Its Relation to the Unconscious* (1905) was to heighten awareness amongst modernist authors of the importance of unconscious over conscious mental processes. Schopenhauer, Nietzsche, and French symbolism had already prepared the ground, and **Conrad**'s *Heart of Darkness* (1898) makes clear the conformability of pre-Freudian modernism to the weltanschauung of psychoanalysis. Many of the new techniques evolved by later modernist writers were attempts to articulate the power, both creative and disruptive, of the unconscious. Lawrence's development as a major writer is inseparably bound up with his attempt to integrate what he had gathered of psychoanalysis with wider traditions of romantic creativity. The new prose of *The Rainbow* (1915) and *Women in Love* (1920), like the stream-of-consciousness techniques of Joyce and Woolf, and the symbolist methods of **Eliot** and **Pound,** were attempts to utter an unconscious which had been defined in part by Freud. Pound in 1913, describing the image of **imagism** as "that which presents an intellectual and emotional complex," followed "the newer psychologists" in his definition of "complex," while the disrupted surface of *The Waste Land* (1922) parallels the discontinuous experience of the ego beset by

the unconscious in an alien world. Ironically, however, such alienation was enhanced by the instinct-theory upon which psychoanalysis was based, as Freud himself made clear in describing the three great wounds dealt by history to "the general narcissism of man." First, he said, Copernicus had displaced the earth from its position as the center of the universe; then Darwin had displaced man from the center of the animal creation; and now psychoanalysis had displaced the ego from the center of the human self.

Three Essays on the Theory of Sexuality (1905)

Freud always held a dual instinct theory which saw the self as riven by internal conflict; and in 1905 the conflict lay between the ego-instincts (those belonging to self-preservation) and the sexual instincts (those belonging to the reproduction of the species). Libido was the mental energy that belonged to the sexual instincts, and it involved the self in further conflicts still, at first because of the biological incapacity of the small child in the Oedipal situation, and later on because of the restraints imposed upon desire by social convention. Freud's sense that frustration was inherent in the human situation was no doubt partly responsible for the stoical, even tragic tone of much of his writing. It did not, however, prevent him from attacking the "unnatural" sexual conventions of contemporary society, where the anxiety caused by frustration led far too often to repression and neurosis. The alternative redeployment for instinctual energy was sublimation by unconscious symbolization into activity of a non-instinctual and socially acceptable kind.

Freud's *Three Essays on the Theory of Sexuality* (1905) constitute the second of his two most important books, opening up for discussion another area that, like dreams, had hitherto lain beyond rational explanation and, despite the recent growth of sexology, usually under taboo—the sexual perversions and deviations. The *Essays* draw up a comprehensive theory of human sexual development, tracing the usual emergence of adult heterosexuality out of infancy, and attributing alternative sexualities to fixation at early stages of development. At the heart of Freud's theory is his conception of infantile sexuality. Sexuality, he argued, does not suddenly originate at puberty; individuals reach puberty only with a history of bodily pleasures already behind them, and also with a history of mental projections and identifications arising out of the Oedipal situation. These were the most decisive forces in determining the adult's future sexual character. The infant's bodily pleasures, as it negotiated the oral, anal, and then genital stages of its development, helped to determine its future sexual aim, while its Oedipal projections and identifications established a psychic bisexuality whose particular composition helped to determine its future sexual object. In widening the scope of sexuality in this way, Freud was able to do justice to the observable facts of infant behavior, to stress an essential continuity throughout the different stages of human development, and also to identify the source of all the perversions in the normal behavior of the infant (whom he called "polymorphously perverse"). It is notable that Freud does not refer to homosexuality as a perversion, but only as a deviance from the biological norm in the nature of object choice. His tone throughout is liberal and ironically tolerant of the diverse expressions of human sexuality.

It was typical of Freud's boldness that, as he had ascribed so many dreams to desire, he should ascribe so many human actions to libido; yet his boldness was in line with much biological and philosophical thinking of the time. Schopenhauer's will-to-live, popularized on the stage by Wagner's operas and plays like **Shaw**'s *Man and Superman,* was later invoked by Freud

himself as one antecedent. By 1900 the erotic had become so widely privileged in **Germany** as the *primum mobile* of life and the *sine qua non* of spiritual health that Martin Green has spoken of an "erotic movement" and identified the maverick psychoanalyst **Otto Gross** as one of its leading figures. From 1907 until his death in 1920 Gross attempted to put the insights of Freud and Nietzsche to the services of sexual and political revolution by acting out the desires that German patriarchy tried to repress. "The philosophy of the unconscious," he declared, "is the philosophy of revolution." In puritan England meanwhile, Edward Carpenter was celebrating the "unconscious, even though human, instincts and forces" which Nature had implanted in human beings. His intention, like that of the sexologist Havelock Ellis, was to establish a more informed and tolerant view of human sexualities, and to promote a newly feminized kind of masculinity over the "beefy self-satisfaction" typical of the men of his day. These English and German traditions met powerfully in the work of D. H. Lawrence, who almost certainly knew Carpenter's work and whose wife Frieda had been greatly influenced by an affair with Otto Gross in 1907.

The Psychoanalytic Movement: Expansion and Dissent

At the start of 1906 the knowledge and practice of psychoanalysis was still largely confined to Jewish circles in Vienna, and to the small discussion group which since 1902 had met on Wednesday nights in Freud's waiting room. But all that was about to change, not least because of the interest that Freud's ideas had aroused in the Burghölzli hospital in Zurich, where in 1904—the same year as Puttnam in America—Jung had already attempted an analysis. From 1906 the spread of psychoanalytic ideas began to accelerate. A string of interested foreigners came to visit Freud, many of them inspired by what they had learned at the Burghölzli, before returning to practice psychoanalysis at home: Jung, Eitingon, Binswanger, and Abraham in 1907, Ferenczi, Jones, and Brill in 1908. There was an International Congress in April 1908 for the "friends of psychoanalysis," at which the *Jahrbuch,* the first psychoanalytic periodical, was launched. Then, in 1909, Freud and Jung were invited to America by Stanley Hall to lecture at Clark University; and in 1910 there was a second conference at Nuremberg, where the International Psychoanalytic Association was set up with Jung as its President. Its aims were to safeguard the purity of psychoanalytic doctrine, to monitor the quality of psychoanalytic publications and to establish a constitution for the local psychoanalytic groups that were springing up. At this conference too, a second psychoanalytic periodical, the *Zentralblatt,* was launched.

Since 1908 this organizational expansiveness had been matched by an expansiveness in the range of psychoanalytic enquiry. Freud had begun it in 1907 with the publication of his first full-length discussion of a literary text, *Delusions and Dreams in Jensen's "Gradiva."* In 1908 Riklin published a work on fairy-tales, Otto Gross celebrated the cultural perspectives offered by psychoanalysis, and the flood-gates of applied psychoanalysis opened up. Literature, art, mythology, **anthropology,** religion, and fairy-tales were all investigated, with Freud himself taking a leading role with *Leonardo da Vinci* (1910) and *Totem and Taboo* (1912–13). Clearly by 1910, with the Oedipus complex now firmly established at its core, psychoanalysis was offering itself as what George Eliot's Casaubon had called a Key to all Mythologies. What had begun as a therapeutic practice with pretensions to medical science was fast developing its own weltanschauung, with principles of

enquiry that, unusually for a science, were policed against unorthodoxy; and with that policing, of course, came dissent.

It was in 1911–12 that the two major splits came. First of all, in 1911 Alfred Adler was pressurized into resignation from the Viennese Psychoanalytic Society on the grounds that his views were incompatible with those of psychoanalysis. He did not believe in the sexual origin of the neuroses, but saw them instead as the result of over-compensation for "organ inferiorities;" and in 1912 he developed this biological theory by declaring that a sense of inferiority might also be socially instilled (the so-called "inferiority complex"). Neurosis was thus a factitious compensation for weakness, epitomized by the small boy and his "masculine protest" against his father. Whereas self-confidence betokened a person at ease with the world, Adler defined the will-to-power in neurotics as that which led them away from the challenges of the real world and the human community into a fictional world of make-believe. These ideas lay at the root of the movement that Adler was later to establish under the name of Individual Psychology.

The quarrel with Jung that followed in 1912 was more momentous, both in its nature and its implications. If Freud's theories were the expression of his personal and professional experience, so too were Jung's; but their experiences were crucially different. While Freud had been primarily concerned with neurosis, Jung had been working with schizophrenics—with people who had difficulties in finding a self within which to be ill—and the main preoccupation of Jung's thinking, as it came to define itself against Freud's, was with the ways in which human beings might discover their selfhood. He was interested less in causation, more in the teleological purposes which direct people to find their fulfillment in some particular way of life; less in desire, more in aspiration; less in positivism, more in phenomenology. With Jung, a younger man than Freud, something of the modernist sense of the provisionality of the self entered psychoanalysis.

The theoretical differences between the two men emerged in 1912 with the publication of the second part of Jung's book *Transformations and Symbols of the Libido* and with the Fordham lectures which he delivered later that same year in America; and they center upon the two related issues of Jung's desexualized view of libido and his existential view of the causes of neurosis. Libido, Jung argued, is best conceived in terms of the Schopenhauerian will-to-live, of that unknowable mental energy which human beings experience as will and desire—an energy first expressed as hunger, and later as sexuality, but that increasingly throughout evolutionary history has freed itself from an exclusively sexual orientation in order to pursue other desires, predicated upon ever more complicated adaptations to reality. As birds build elaborate nests, human beings build cantatas and cathedrals. Art, myth, and religion are thus not primarily for Jung the expression of unconscious neurotic conflict; they belong amongst the natural activities of the human animal, providing hermeneutical tools that image the various destinies awaiting us in life. It is amongst these destinies that individuals find their life-tasks; and it is here that the neurotic quails and the schizophrenic fails.

Jung, like Adler, saw the causes of neurosis as lying in the cowardice, inertia, or plain insensibility with which the individual ducked the challenges implicit in the maturational processes. Unlike Freud, who looked to the past to discover the causes of mental illness, Jung approached the problem from the other side: the infantilism present in neurosis was not the result of past fixation but of regressive libido in the present—libido which, balked in its aspirations and desires, could only discharge itself by flowing back into earlier com-

plexes and reactivating them. The Oedipus complex was not for Jung the universal scenario of infantile desire but the neurotic result of a cowardly regression away from the challenges of adulthood. In Jung's view the task of therapy was to dissipate the lures of regression, to identify amongst them the genuine prospective desires of the unconscious, and thus to release libido to fulfil its chosen tasks. Although depoliticized and desexualized, it was the therapy that Otto Gross had dreamed of—a therapy in pursuit of an endless process of Nietzschean self-overcoming.

By 1914 Jung was suggesting that the methodology of psychoanalysis was closer to that of literature and art than to science, and that its business lay not with interpretations of the past but with constructions for the future, bringing the patient's frustrated aspirations into a richer relationship with life through the use of such unconscious typologies as emerge in myth. A man facing his mid-life crisis might, for example, take strength from his own unconscious image of a wise old man. In *Psychological Types* (1920), where he developed an earlier distinction between introvert and extrovert, he began to call the man's unconscious image of the female the "anima," and the woman's unconscious image of the male the "animus." All these images he called "archetypes," and located them in the "collective unconscious" of mankind as the product not of human culture but of man's biological nature. Freud attributed Jung's popularity to his disavowing the doctrines of infantile sexuality and the sexual origin of the neuroses; but it is clear from the periodical writings of 1916 onwards, when Constance Long published Jung's *Collected Papers in Analytical Psychology,* that it was Jung's constructivism, his "spirituality," his friendliness towards myth, religion, and to a lesser extent towards art that helped the spread of his ideas.

The Great War and the Popularization of Psychoanalysis

The spread of psychoanalytic ideas in the United States has been documented by Nathan Hale in his two-volume *Freud and the Americans;* but there is as yet no comparable work about Britain. It was, however, around 1912 that knowledge of psychoanalysis began to extend beyond the small groups of doctors and sexologists to whom it had hitherto been confined. It was in 1912 that *The New Age* consciously pioneered an interest in psychoanalysis by stirring up a controversy about Ernest Jones's interpretation of *Hamlet.* It was in 1912 too that D. H. Lawrence, engaged in rewriting *Sons and Lovers,* met Frieda Weekley; and in 1913 May Sinclair funded the establishment of the Medico-Psychological Clinic in London, offering psychoanalytic and other treatments predominantly for women.

What speeded up this slow process of percolation, however, was the outbreak of war, when the Freudian model of hysteria proved to be of great practical use in treating the bewildering variety of traumatic symptoms popularly known as "shell-shock." The anthropologist and psychologist W. H. R. Rivers was influential in making Freud's ideas respectable, while the psychoanalysts themselves were not slow to seize the propaganda opportunities offered them in the new military hospitals. Despite the utility of Freudian ideas about repression, dissociation, unconscious processes and conversion, however, a consensus of opinion rapidly emerged amongst British doctors that war-shock invalidated Freud's theory of the sexual origin of the neuroses. The underlying conflict here, they argued, was not between sexual desire and social convention, but between the instinct for self-preservation and the military ideals of manliness and courage. The psychoanalysts retaliated by pointing out that

only a small number of soldiers actually succumbed to illness, and that in these cases there must have been a predisposing cause in the individual's early sexual history.

It was through war-shock too that Freudian ideas first significantly entered British fiction. **Rebecca West**'s *The Return of the Soldier* (1918) was the first English novel about war-shock and its treatment by psychoanalysis; D. H. Lawrence explored the spurious ideals of masculinity that underlay war-shock in *Aaron's Rod* (1922) and *Lady Chatterley's Lover* (1928), while Virginia Woolf did the same from a feminist standpoint in *Mrs. Dalloway* (1925). Siegfried Sassoon's *Sherston's Progress* (1936) described his war-time experiences under Rivers at Craiglockhart Hospital, Edinburgh, where Wilfred Owen had also been hospitalized. This episode has recently been fictionalized by Pat Barker in her *Regeneration* trilogy (1991–5).

Last Years: Freud's Second Model of the Mind

After the war, Ernest Jones set about securing the future of psychoanalysis in Britain. In 1919 he dissolved the London Psycho-Analytical Society, many of whose members had defected to Jung, and reconstituted it in a purged form as the British Psycho-Analytical Society. In 1920 he founded the *International Journal of Psycho-Analysis,* and in 1924 established the Institute of Psycho-Analysis in London, followed in 1926 by the London Clinic of Psycho-Analysis. Also in 1924 he arranged for the Hogarth Press, run by Leonard and Virginia Woolf, to publish psychoanalytic literature on behalf of the Institute—a sign of the connection between **Bloomsbury** and psychoanalysis that was to be so important for the future of psychoanalysis in Britain. It was the Hogarth Press that was later to publish the Standard Edition of Freud's works (1953–74) under the editorship of James Strachey.

These post-war years were the years of maximum public interest in psychoanalysis, and also of its acceptance in cultural circles as a discourse shaping modern perspectives of subjectivity. As Lawrence wrote in *Psychoanalysis and the Unconscious* (1921), "The Oedipus complex was a household word, the incest motive a commonplace of tea-table chat. Amateur analysis became the vogue." Aldous Huxley satirized one such analysis in "The Farcical History of Richard Greenow" (1920). Even writers as skeptical of psychoanalysis as Virginia Woolf engaged its characteristic concerns, while at the start of the 1930s the poet and novelist **H. D.** underwent a series of analyses that culminated in two analyses with Freud in 1933 and 1934, described later in her book *Tribute to Freud.*

Freud's most interesting theoretical work in these years is found in *Beyond the Pleasure Principle* (1920), where he postulated a death instinct (Thanatos) to counterbalance the sexual and self-preservation components of the life instinct (Eros), and more importantly in *The Ego and the Id* (1923), where he replaced his earlier bipartite picture of the mind with a new tripartite one. The unconscious is now reformulated as the id, an unstructured mental area where instinctual drives pursue gratification by means of the primary processes. The conscious mind is reformulated as the ego, a part of the id which may be modified and subsequently structured in response to its experiences of the outside world. The new concept introduced by Freud is that of the superego. This was the part of mind to which self-consciousness belongs, and which is structured at an early age by internalization of the parents; hence it too has an important unconscious element, responsible for the ferocity with which people often judge both themselves and others. *The Ego and the Id* also reformulates the Oedipal stage, describing for the first time the positive and negative reactions of the child towards each parent, and studying the asymmetry of the developmental processes undergone by boys and girls. This work lays the ground for Freud's later work on the psychological structuring of male and female, that has since attracted the critical attention of many feminist writers amongst others. The writing of this period marks the culmination of Freud's movement away from his early preoccupation with the disjunctions between conscious and unconscious; it shows instead an interest in the structuration of the ego and its necessary renunciations which underlies his last two big works, *The Future of an Illusion* (1927) and *Civilization and Its Discontents* (1930).

Later Developments: France and England

Despite Freud's earlier attempts to police the border-lines of psychoanalytic doctrine, many significant developments occurred during the last years of his life, most notably in England with Melanie Klein, and in **France** with Jacques Lacan. Klein arrived in London from Berlin in 1926, and her work helped to establish the school of "object-relations" psychoanalysis that was to culminate in the work of Donald Winnicott. These are perhaps the three theorists who have made the greatest contributions to psychoanalysis since Freud.

Klein's originality stemmed from her work with children, whom she analysed through their play. This enabled her to conceptualize pre-Oedipal stages of development in which the child's relationship with its mother assumed primary importance—an emphasis noted by recent feminist critics, who have aligned Virginia Woolf's later work with Klein's at this point. Klein postulated a primary ambivalence in the infant towards its mother, so that each child must first negotiate what she called the "paranoid-schizoid position," in which the mother's breast is perceived alternately as a good and as a bad "part-object," first ideal and then persecutory. Secondly the child must then negotiate the "depressive position," in which the mother is gradually perceived as a whole person and the child must wrestle with the consequences of its own aggressivity towards her. This aggression Klein saw as a defensive projection of the death-instinct—a Freudian concept that she alone amongst major theorists found useful. Failure to negotiate the paranoid-schizoid position led to psychotic illness, she believed, while failure to negotiate the depressive position led to neurosis. On the other hand, a successful outcome to the depressive position involved the child in reparative activity towards its mother which Klein thought lay at the roots of its future artistic creativity. A marked feature of Kleinian theory, however, is its emphasis upon the inner drama of the child's fantasy-life at the expense of its actual experiences with its real mother.

Lacan developed his psychoanalytic thinking partly in hostility to the English tradition inaugurated by Klein; he disliked its preference for the later over the earlier Freud, and its concern for the processes of ego-integration in early infancy. Instead, he returned to Freud's early work on the unconscious, exploring its implications in a modernist spirit hostile to the traditional positivism of psychoanalysis and revelling in the instabilities that he thought characteristic of all human thought, identity, and language. Taking his cue from Saussure, Lacan evolved a psychoanalysis only minimally attached to the objective world of historical fact and etiology, and situated it instead (in one sense where it already was) in the intersubjective continuous present of the linguistic communications between patient and therapist. People, he argued, are driven not by instinct but by the insatiability of a desire that, deprived forever of its infantile satisfactions, flees in an endless series of deferrals from object to object in search of that which can never again be found. It is in language that this desire is both disguised and disclosed, and in the interconnected symbolisms of the unconscious that are only accessible through language. Yet language must be taught to know itself in all the slippages and volatility which the unconscious brings. It must be rescued from the fixities of what Lacan called the "Imaginary Order," the world of presumed certainties about our own knowlege and self-knowledge which is the illusory achievement of human culture; and here lies the peculiar task for Lacanian psychoanalysis. Each young child, he argued, is seduced into misrecognition of itself at "the mirror-stage;" it enters a world of illusory, potentially pathogenic certainties whose prescriptions and proscriptions overwrite the lability and insatiability of desire. Lacan's distrust of the mental world resembles that of Bergson or Lawrence; and it is the aim of his therapy to enable his patients to pass from the fixations of the "Imaginary Order" to what he called the "Symbolic Order" where the endless slippages of desire may be both acknowledged and enjoyed. Subjection to the split between conscious and unconscious may be relished by the individual subject, as Lacan himself exemplifies in the playfulness, difficulties and disrupted surfaces of his writings.

Winnicott's work, like Klein's but unlike Lacan's, is empirical in manner, and relies upon extensively quoted case-histories. It avoids the tragic tone of Freud and the tragic jesting of Lacan, preferring instead, in the Darwinian tradition of the later British school, to believe with tempered optimism in the essential adaptiveness of the human species to the world. It is a psychoanalysis attuned to ideas of health rather than of sickness, and its attention falls not upon the internal world of the individual child, as in Klein, but upon the relationship between child and its real mother. While Lacan had focused upon the castrating power of the Oedipal father, barring desire for the mother and bringing about an endless deferral of pleasure whose absence-presence he symbolized in the phallus, Winnicott focused instead upon the facilitating presence of the pre-Oedipal mother, and her power to create in the infant a good-enough sense of self, an "I" that is substantial and not illusive as in Lacan. For Winnicott the baby finds itself in the "mirror" of its mother's eyes; and his formulation suggests how the object-relations school in its turn evolved partly in reaction to Lacan.

The mother's first task, Winnicott says, which is also the daily achievement of the "good-enough" mother, is to meet her baby's demands in full. The baby cries, the breast appears, and the baby, secure in its "holding environment," enjoys an illusion of omnipotence that corroborates its energy, its aggressiveness and its "primary creativity." Aggression is its way of making the world feel real to itself. Gradually, sensing her baby's increasing ability to tolerate disappointment, the mother then begins to let it wait; and sometime during this process of benign disillusionment, the child discovers a "transitional object"—a teddy bear, perhaps, or blanket—whose value is that it exists in the real world while at the same time being suffused with symbolic value as a representative of the absent mother. If presence for Lacan is haunted by absence, absence for Winnicott is a form of presence; and the transitional object, where subject and object paradoxically intertwine, is the start of that spontaneous and creative activity called "playing" which will, in time, if unhampered by the need to comply, lead into the rich cultural life of adulthood. Unlike classical analysts Winnicott is interested not so much in instinct and desire as in the periods of relaxation that come between. His concern is for the nurturance of an integrated sense of self within which desires and instincts can be accommodated; for ego-relations rather than id-relations; for affection rather than erotics. His ideas only reached their fulfilment in the 1960s and 1970s; but they were perhaps the first psychoanalytic theories to embody both the strengths and weaknesses of the post-romantic Bloomsbury culture in which Winnicott had grown up, and in which British modernism had first begun to explore and test the ideas of Freud.

John Turner

Selected Bibliography

Bowie, Malcolm. *Lacan*. London: Fontana, 1991.

Gay, Peter. *Freud: A Life for Our Time*. London: Dent, 1988.

Green, Martin. *The von Richthofen Sisters*. New York: Basic Books, 1974.

———. *Otto Gross. Freudian Psychoanalyst. 1877–1920*. Lewiston, NY: Edwin Mellen Press, 1999.

Hinshelwood, R. D. "The Organizing of Psychoanalysis in Britain." *Psychoanalysis and History* 1.1 (1998): 87–102.

Hogenson, George B. *Jung's Struggle with Freud*. London: Notre Dame Press, 1983.

Kerr, John. *A Most Dangerous Method: The Story of Jung, Freud, and Sabina Spielrein*. London: Sinclair-Stevenson, 1994.

Phillips, Adam. *Winnicott*. London: Fontana, 1988.

Rycroft, Charles. *The Innocence of Dreams*. London: Hogarth Press, 1979.

Segal, Hanna. *Klein*. London: Fontana, 1979.

Showalter, Elaine. *The Female Malady: Women, Madness and English Culture, 1830–1980*. New York: Pantheon Books, 1985.

Stone, Martin. "Shellshock and the psychologists." *The Anatomy of Madness: Essays in the History of Psychiatry*. Ed. W. F. Bynum et al. Vol. 2. London: Tavistock, 1985. 242–71.

Sulloway, Frank J. *Freud, Biologist of the Mind: Beyond the Psychoanalytic Legend*. New York: Basic Books, 1979.

Wollheim, Richard. *Freud*. London: Fontana, 1971.

R

Realism

Realism has been an issue in philosophy and in aesthetic representation since Aristotle, but, in discussions of modernism, it is usually used to denote a style of fiction which came to prominence in the eighteenth century and shared much in common with historical, journalistic, or biographical writing. *Classic realism,* which flowered in the nineteenth century, has been delineated by Roland Barthes, Colin MacCabe, and Catherine Belsey. It is a term used to describe the work of such writers as Honoré de Balzac, Charles Dickens, Elizabeth Gaskell, and George Eliot: novels with reliable narrators who deal with contemporary social and political problems. The principal features of realism (opposed to the earlier Romance) are: narrative authority and reliability, a contemporary setting, recognizable characters, representative locations, ordinary speech, linear plots, and extensive use of free indirect discourse. Modernism challenged many of these conventions, particularly in terms of narrative technique, character portrayal, self-referentiality, and linearity. However, *realism* appealed as a term for many writers we would now consider modernist: for example, both **Henry James**'s "psychological realism" and Dostoyevsky's "Higher Realism" were attempts to go beyond realism but to retain its belief in the faithful representation of life.

Peter Childs

Selected Bibliography
Belsey, Catherine. *Critical Practice,* London: Methuen, 1980.

Rhys, Jean (Ellen Gwendolen Rees Williams) (1890–1979)

Novelist and short-story writer, born at Roseau on the Caribbean island of Dominica, the daughter of a Welsh father and a Creole mother.

Rhys's father was a Welsh-speaking doctor originally from Caernarfonshire in North-West **Wales,** while the maternal Lockhart family had Scottish ancestry but had been plantation owners on Dominica for several generations. Rhys experienced a lonely childhood, feeling estranged from her strict mother, and was early aware of the racial and cultural tensions of the island of her birth. As a writer, Rhys was to excel in the depiction of her heroines' alienation and estrangement; it is perhaps not unreasonable to suggest that such feelings were intimately known to the author from an early age. Growing up on an island whose population was predominantly black and poor, Rhys felt acutely her own unwanted position as a member of a privileged white elite, the remnant of a plantocracy which had lost virtually all of its former economic power. Her own family had been the owners both of a plantation and of the slaves who labored there but, at the period of emancipation in the mid-nineteenth century, the slaves had rebelled and set fire to the plantation. This episode in her family history was transmuted by her, years later, into an extraordinarily powerful scene in her best-known novel, *Wide Sargasso Sea* (1966). Despite this familial and racial allegiance with the former slave-owners, Rhys as a young girl identified strongly with the black people and culture which surrounded her. One of her heroines states "I always wanted to be black," while another makes the following categorical distinction: "Being black is warm and gay, being white is cold and sad." Nevertheless, Rhys's racial attitudes were always ambivalent; it would be a misapprehension of her work to regard it as simply championing the cause of black people.

Rhys was also influenced by the linguistic diversity of her background: the French patois which was the language of the majority on the island of her birth finds its way into some of her work, as does English Caribbean dialect, though most of her narrative is in standard English. Nevertheless, linguistic codes and rules are a recurring preoccupation in her novels: often, her heroines do not, or cannot, "speak the same language" as those who oppress or exploit them, or even those who would have them join their exclusive group. Although Rhys left Dominica at the age of sixteen, the experiences she had during those early years were crucially formative: she remained emphatically a Caribbean writer, even when she lived and wrote of characters adrift at the edges of European cities. Rhys attended school in Cambridge, England and spent a brief, unhappy period in the Royal Academy of Dramatic Art. On

her father's death, she became estranged from her family and began a series of poorly paid jobs, including chorus girl and artist's model, which placed her at the margins of respectability in an English society which was riven by class divisions and blinkered by insularity. She met a much older, wealthy man, who became her lover and benefactor. These experiences are rendered in fictionalized form in her later novel, *Voyage in the Dark* (1934).

In 1919 Rhys married Jean Lenglet, a Dutch writer, and with him travelled to continental Europe. They lived a precarious life, which became all the more dangerous when Rhys's husband was extradited as a criminal, so that she had to fend for herself. **Ford Madox Ford,** then an influential novelist and editor, became her mentor and lover; her experiences with him and his partner, Stella Bowen, are given vindictive fictional form in the novel *Quartet* (1928; originally entitled *Postures*). However, before the relationship with Ford soured, he had facilitated the publication of her first book, a collection of stories entitled *The Left Bank and Other Stories* (1927). Although, as the title of this collection suggests, Rhys was living in Paris at a time of extraordinary artistic vitality, she never truly became a part of the expatriate modernist set of the left bank. She remained a lonely and vulnerable individual, who nevertheless in retrospect can be seen as forging for herself a new, and distinctively modern novelistic idiom. In the aforementioned novels and stories, as well as in *After Leaving Mr. Mackenzie* (1930) and *Good Morning Midnight* (1939) Rhys created archetypal representations of the alienated and deracinated woman, living in liminal spaces of angst and anomie. The Jean Rhys heroine, who differs slightly in the separate texts but has strong basic similarities, is on the one hand a passive victim of patriarchal economic, sexual, and psychological exploitation, and on the other a powerfully dissident figure who refuses to acknowledge the validity of moral categories and class distinctions.

In her experiments with narrative style Rhys shows herself to be a true modernist, in that she mixes modes with a deliberate and disorienting carelessness for the reader's welfare. Symbolically dense **interior monologue** is often cut across by realistic dialogue and naturalistic description of urban and island landscapes. Rhys also frequently has recourse to free indirect style, which takes the reader uncomfortably close to her suffering heroines.

There is a hiatus in Jean Rhys's career as a writer between 1939 and 1966, which biographer Carole Angier terms "the lost years." In 1934 she had married her second husband, Leslie Tilden Smith, and in the same year the relative success of *Voyage in the Dark* seemed to bode well for Rhys's future career as a writer. However, the next two novels were not critically successful and Rhys herself was at the same time succumbing to alcoholism; again, her experiences were translated into fiction for Sasha, the protagonist of *Good Morning, Midnight* has "the bright idea of drinking [her]self to death." As early as 1939 Rhys had written a version of her most acclaimed novel, *Wide Sargasso Sea,* but she had burnt it in despair; then, after the death of her second husband in 1945, came a long period of silence, in which Rhys wrote very little. In 1966 her third husband, Max Hamer, died and her first novel for twenty-seven years appeared, to instant critical success. *Wide Sargasso Sea* is, from one point of view, a bold rewriting of *Jane Eyre,* taking Brontë's mad creole woman out of her attic and placing her at the center of her text, giving her a voice and a life. From another point of view, it is the culmination of all of Rhys's brilliant and lacerating forays into autobiography. It is a post-colonial text, boldly reinscribing literary and imperial history from the point of view of the marginalized female. It is also a text which makes telling parallels between patriarchal power structures and those of empire, while revealing clearly that men can be victims of oppressive structures, just as women can. The novel gives triumphant expression to Rhys's visionary, poetic style and, for the first time, she gives a direct and haunting evocation of the landscape and atmosphere of her native island, Dominica. Although Rhys wrote a number of excellent stories and an unfinished autobiography in the next thirteen years before her death in 1979, she never surpassed the great achievement of *Wide Sargasso Sea.*

Katie Gramich

Selected Bibliography

Angier, Carole. *Jean Rhys: Life and Work.* Harmondsworth: Penguin, 1992.

Emery, Mary Lou. *Jean Rhys at "World's End": Novels of Colonial and Sexual Exile.* Austin: University of Texas, 1990.

Frickey, Pierrette, ed. *Critical Perspectives on Jean Rhys.* Washington D.C.: Three Continents Press, 1990.

Harrison, Nancy R. *Jean Rhys and the Novel as Women's Text.* Chapel Hill: University of North Carolina Press, 1988.

Howells, Coral Ann. *Jean Rhys.* Brighton: Harvester Wheatsheaf, 1991.

Maurel, Sylvie. *Jean Rhys.* Basingstoke: Macmillan, 1998.

Nebeker, Helen. *Jean Rhys, Woman in Passage.* Montreal: Eden Press, 1981.

O'Connor, Teresa F. *Jean Rhys: The West Indian Novels.* New York UP, 1986.

Staley, Thomas F. *Jean Rhys: A Critical Study.* London: Macmillan, 1979.

Thomas, Sue. *The Worlding of Jean Rhys.* London: Greenwood, 1999.

Wyndham, Francis and Diana Melly, eds. *Jean Rhys: Letters 1931–66.* London: Andre Deutsch, 1984.

Rhythm

E. M. Forster, and his critics, have used the term *rhythm* to denote the structural use of leitmotifs or "repetitions with variation" in fiction which depends upon expanding symbols. Rhythm then refers to the repeated use of phrases, words, incidents, or characters to create a rhythmic effect in the evolution of a text's themes. The technique is apparent in **Forster**'s *A Passage to India,* and in particular in the use made of the echo which haunts Adela and Mrs. Moore after their visit to the Marabar Caves.

Peter Childs

Selected Bibliography
Brown, E. K. *Rhythm in the Novel.* Toronto: University of Toronto Press, 1950.

Richardson, Dorothy (1873–1957)

A prolific writer of fiction and essays, Dorothy Richardson's best known work is *Pilgrimage,* a thirteen-volume novel made up of the following: *Pointed Roofs* (1915); *Backwater* (1916); *Honeycomb* (1917); *The Tunnel* (1919); *Interim* (1919); *Deadlock* (1921); *Revolving Lights* (1923); *The Trap* (1925); *Oberland* (1927); *Dawn's Left Hand* (1931); *Clear Horizon* (1935); *Dimple Hill* (1938) and *March Moonlight* (1967). A selection of her shorter works appears in her *Journey to Paradise,* selected and published in 1989.

That Dorothy Richardson's fiction has not found its way into the standard syllabuses of English literary studies is not entirely surprising; that it has never gained the honorable recognition of either **Marcel Proust**'s *A la recherche du temps perdu* or **James Joyce's** *Finnegans Wake* certainly is. Why, in the common library of literary modernism, is Richardson squeezed out by the great, often unread yet canonical work of Proust on the one hand, and by the more widely read Joyce and **Virginia Woolf** on the other? Although the case of Woolf herself militates against any simple answer along the lines of gender, Woolf's insights into the sexual politics of writing are nevertheless pertinent here, for the sheer vastness and for-

mal innovation of Richardson's narrative might be more assimilable were it not to center on the unremarkable life of an ordinary young middle-class English woman—Miriam Henderson—who provides the sole consciousness of *Pilgrimage.* The question of whether this singularity is the novel's great strength or its major weakness is one of the most hotly contested issues amongst Richardson's readers. Derek Stanford, for instance, argues that "All we can say is that the unrelieved impact of the ego, in life as in art produces monotony. We tire ourselves and we tire others also; and Miriam is, in her effect, truly life-like" (qtd. Bronfen 223). Certainly, Miriam is often far from likeable, trapped as she is the mindset of middle-class English femininity even as she seeks to demolish its petty refinements and privileges. Miriam is a complex, often understated character whose impressionistic narrative often glides over us. On other occasions, however, she calls us up sharply in order to question the patriarchal status quo. The doubting, uncertain, and questioning nature of *Pilgrimage*'s feminine consciousness is the source of its philosophical and political interest, but it is also in many ways mundane, porous, and mildly melancholic as it seeks to re-invent the representation of everyday life at the turn of the century (the novel stretches from 1891–1912). Richardson's claim to be recognized as a key modernist figure lies principally in her avant-garde stylistic innovations, most notably her pioneering use of what May Sinclair first termed "stream-of-consciousness," pre-dating the more renowned achievements of Joyce and Woolf. If Woolf, in *A Room of One's Own,* is right in arguing that a woman's life is not deemed "serious" because it is lived principally within the domestic world of women, then a two thousand page novel which does just that is hardly likely to meet the criteria of standard literary judgement.

Richardson's own life began in Abingdon, Berkshire in 1873. She was born the daughter of Charles Richardson, a businessman who made his short-lived wealth from the grocery trade, and Mary Taylor, the daughter of a long-established gentry family from East Coker, Somerset. This conjunction of trade and county reveals itself in Richardson's fiction as an acute sensitivity to the structures of feeling of middle-class life. In particular, Miriam Henderson's oblique angle of vision (she often sits in corners of rooms or looks askew at the society around her) uncovers the rifts and tensions within the English middle classes at a time when what it meant to be middle class—the economic and social practices which made one respectable and secure—were changing rapidly. Like **T. S. Eliot,** Richardson looks at office workers, clerks and tradesmen as the new inhabitants of the quintessentially modern city, but where Eliot sees a hellish unleashing of faceless men and women, Richardson writes from the interstices of the middle-class—she is at once a participant and a critical observer. Miriam Henderson's exploratory consciousness is Richardson's fictional vehicle for animating these class politics, although they receive a far clearer, and more consistently socialist airing in her articles for the political journal, *Ye Crank*. Her on-going dialogue with "The Odd Man" in *Ye Crank* Winter/Spring editions of 1907 is an especially lively example of her rigorous and passionate concern with the technicalities of socialist politics. This is one example of where the author and her autobiographical character differ, for Miriam is haunted by quite contradictory impulses. On the one hand, she displays the characteristic anxiety of the lower middle-classes, who both desire to emulate and yet disdain those above them whose wealth and social status are far more assured. On the other hand, Miriam's (like Richardson's) own semi-bohemian existence places her in direct conflict with the petty worldview of a philistine class. This disdain and cultural distance is emblematic of much literary modernism and it makes Miriam a close fictional relative of **E. M. Forster**'s Schlegel sisters: "I am unsociable, I suppose—she mused. She could not think of any one who did not offend her. I don't like men and I loathe women . . . She thought of the fathers of girls she knew—the Poole girls, for instance, they were to be independent, trained and certificated—she envied that—but her envy vanished when she remembered how heartily she had agreed when Sarah called them sharp and knowing . . . Mr. Poole was a business man . . . common . . . trade . . . If pater had kept to grandpa's business they would be trade, too—well-off, now—all married. Perhaps as it was he had thought they would marry" (*Pointed Roofs* 31–2).

In the late nineteenth century, it was middle-class girls' widening access to education and to paid, semi-professional work, which was one of the most profound and lasting changes to social class formation and gender relations. At the age of 17, Dorothy Richardson took up a post as governess in Hanover, **Germany,** much as Miriam Henderson does in the first volume of *Pilgrimage, Pointed Roofs*. In the novel, Miriam enjoys the challenges and freedoms of financial independence and in this respect she is representative of the *fin de siècle* **New Woman**'s challenge to the traditional place of women within the home. However, for Richardson and her fictional alter ego, paid work was a necessity rather than a choice given her father's constant financial difficulties. In 1893, while Richardson was governessing in London and the Home Counties, Charles Richardson was declared bankrupt and the stress and shame endured by this middle-class family was instrumental in Mary Richardson's suicide while vacationing with Dorothy in Hastings in 1895. Thereafter, Richardson moved to London where she worked as a secretary, journalist, and translator. She became an active figure in the intellectual society of London, encountering a range of religious and political groups, from the Quakers to Russian anarchists; more scandalously, she had a short-lived affair with H. G. Wells. In 1909, she suffered a nervous breakdown in Switzerland, but three years later began writing *Pointed Roofs* which was published in 1915. In 1917, she married the artist Alan Odle. Between 1916–1938, Richardson published the further 11 volumes of *Pilgrimage* with the final volume, *March Moonlight,* being published posthumously in 1967.

The canonical neglect which Richardson's work has suffered does not reflect a lack of interest by her contemporaries. Jean Radford, for example, points to how, in 1928, Dorothy Sayers' fictional detective, Lord Peter Wimsey, lists Richardson alongside Woolf, May Sinclair, and **Katherine Mansfield,** as women writers who are emblematic of a specifically modern woman reader. Despite this, and despite collaborating with key literary figures such as Winifred Bryher, **Ford Madox Ford,** and **H. D. (Hilda Doolittle),** Richardson never enjoyed popular or widespread critical success.

Not surprisingly, it is feminist literary critics who have led the revaluation of Richardson's work, beginning in 1977 with Gloria Gilkin Fromm's biography and followed in 1979 by Virago's re-publication in four volumes of *Pilgrimage.* Gillian Hanscombe's 1982 study is a response to Fromm and is the first extensive critical work to position Richardson as a feminist writer. The monographs that have emerged in the 1990s principally read Richardson through the contemporary critical lenses of French feminist and post-structuralist approaches to subjectivity, narrative, and gender.

The Foreword commissioned by her publishers, Dent, for the 1938 publication of 12 of the 13 volumes which make up

Pilgrimage reads as both a defense and an ironic rejoinder to those unwilling to forge the new interpretative practice demanded by this modernist fiction of consciousness: "the author of 'Pilgrimage' must confess to an early habit of ignoring, while writing, the lesser of the stereotyped system of signs, and, further, when finally sprinkling in what appeared to be necessary, to a small, unconscious departure from current usage" (p. 12). Richardson's own extensive graphological signs include ellipses, dashes, and broken paragraphs. Littering the text, they are the material signs of a writer refusing the restrictive patterns of **realism.** Instead, the prose spills out into the gaps between words, the spaces of meaning which the Victorian novel never seeks to chart but which, in reading *Pilgrimage,* we are required to attend to as the sites of a consciousness in development. Such a profusion of punctuation draws attention to itself, breaks the illusions of a seamless realism and self-consciously highlights the progress of the narrator's thought as it is being narrated. The circularity of Miriam's conscious mind, her meditative quarrel with herself, reads like an example of what the French feminist, Julia Kristeva, describes as a "subject in process": "The drive had been too short. . . . Bennett's friends had given the Corries wrong ideas about her. They wanted a governess. She was not a governess. There were governesses . . . the kind of person they wanted. It was a mistake; another mistake . . . the brougham made a beautiful dull humming, going along a tree-lined tunnel . . . What did the Corries want of her, arriving in their brougham? What did they expect her to do? . . ." (*Honeycomb* 352). It is not that arrival is unimportant to Richardson, but that the process of journeying is far more significant and more of an aesthetic challenge to represent in the modern novel. Characteristically, it is the intensity and simultaneity of experience, the disorderly structure of the mind's journey, which Miriam's consciousness places center stage and which so fundamentally opposes the strictures of the traditional novel, as Miriam herself comments:

> But in *all* the books about these people [the English], even in *novelettes,* the chief thing they all left out, was there. They even described it, sometimes so gloriously that it became *more* than the people; making humanity look like ants, crowding and perishing on a vast scene. Generally the surroundings were described separately, the background on which presently the characters began to fuss. But they were never sufficiently shown as they were to the people when there was no fussing; what the floods of sunshine and beauty indoors and out meant to these people as single individuals, whether they were aware of it or not. (*Deadlock* 243)

It is just this writerly critique and syntactical, graphological innovation which led Virginia Woolf in a review of *Revolving Lights, Pilgrimage's* seventh volume, to credit Richardson with "inventing a sentence which we might call the psychological sentence of the feminine gender. It is of a more elastic fibre than the old, capable of stretching to the extreme of suspending the frailest particles, of enveloping the vaguest shapes" (*Times Literary Supplement,* May 1923). Innovative Richardson certainly is, but it must be noted that her modernism finds its roots in **the New Woman** writings of a novelist such as Olive Schreiner whose foreword to *The Story of an African Farm* bears remarkable similarity to Miriam's own readerly manifesto for fiction.

Neither Dorothy Richardson's concern with the visual nor her modernism are confined to her fiction; they structure both her journalism and her critical essays on **film** published as a column entitled "Continuous Performance" in the journal *Close-Up*

which remained in print from 1927 until 1933. It is not surprising that these essays have, until very recently, demanded even less attention than Richardson's fiction; after all, cross-disciplinary research and an attention to film as the art form of the twentieth century are relatively recent arrivals. However, as Susan Gervitz's excellent study of Richardson's narrative theory shows, it is through reading Richardson intertextually that we see her modernism most clearly. When critics follow Richardson into the cinema—out of the **Bloomsbury** attic room of her own which she cherished as a space for her writing—we find a woman enthralled and challenged by the new representational techniques and narrative methods of film.

Going to the movies is an intellectual, philosophical, as well as aesthetic revelation for Richardson in her own quest for "a contemporary pattern" of narrative fiction able to engender the simultaneity of disparate objects and feelings which she saw as the hallmark of human consciousness. In her foreword to *Pilgrimage,* Richardson describes the stream of consciousness technique as "slow motion photography." What some of Richardson's critics perceive as Miriam's depthless, superficial consciousness is in fact testimony to the role of the screen in Richardson's prose. In its marked disposition towards metonymy (see **Metaphor and Metonymy**), her prose displays a filmic quality, as if the novelist's pen were establishing a panoramic shot which enacts rather than tells the narrative by panning around a scene and pursuing a chain of associations. Film's great strength as a quintessentially modern art form is that it allows us to see a scene whole and from numerous perspectives, as the great Russian filmmaker, **Sergei Eisenstein** argued, "In a single cinematographic act, the film fuses people and a single individual town and country. It fuses them with dizzying change and transfer. . . . [w]ith its ability to follow watchfully not only the clouds gathering in the hills, but also the swelling of a tear from beneath an eyelash" (qtd. Gervitz 67). It is film's capacity for synthesis which appeals to Richardson as an artist but it is a thoroughly gendered appeal: "The film . . . in the day of its innocence, in its quality of being nowhere and everywhere, nowhere in the sense of having more intention than direction and more purpose than plan, everywhere, by reason of its power to evoke, suggest, reflect, express from within its moving parts and in their totality of movement, something of the changeless being at the heart of all becoming, was essentially feminine" (Richardson, "The Film Gone Male," 1932, 37). The tremendous value Richardson places on synthesis is even more apparent in an article written 15 years earlier and whose tone we hear later in the twentieth century in the work of Simone de Beauvoir, Luce Irigaray and Julia Kristeva: ". . . the fact of woman remains, the fact that she is relatively to man, *synthetic*. . . . Men tend to fix life, to fix aspects. . . . Let anyone who questions the synthetic quality of women ask himself why it is that she can move, as it were, in all directions at once, why, with a man-astonishing ease, she can 'take-up' everything by turns, while she 'originates' nothing. . . . And let him further ask himself why the great male synthetics, the artists and mystics, are three-parts woman" ("The Reality of Feminism," 1917, 244–5).

The insistence on an understanding of femininity as a synthetic consciousness open to both male and female writers suggests that Richardson was at one with Woolf's theory of **androgyny** and open to charges of an essentialist, bourgeois **feminism.** However, Richardson was a vigorous critic of the liberal feminism underpinning the suffrage movement of the turn of the century, describing it as "a class feminism—feminism for ladies" (ibid. 242). One way of resolving or at least un-

derstanding this contradiction is by appreciating that for Richardson socialism was not simply an economic or political philiosophy, but a profoundly spiritual way of living in the world. Her article on feminism cited above, for instance, comes from the journal *The Ploughshare: A Quaker Organ of Social Reconstruction.* Elsewhere, Richardson argues that "the ideals that are developing in relation to modern socialistic [sic] thought seem to me a testimony to the indomitable spirituality of humanity" (*Ye Crank,* January 1907, 33). At the heart of this dual concern with socialism and spirituality lies Quakerism. Richardson had first-hand experience of a Quaker community when she returned from Switzerland following her nervous breakdown and it appears in the guise of the Roscorlas's retreat of *Dimple Hill.* She also wrote two scholarly works on the subject, *The Quakers Past and Present* and *Gleanings From the Work of George Fox* (both 1914).

Contemplative, socially engaged, and aesthetically innovative, Dorothy Richardson's contribution to literary modernism promises to be more fully recognized in our postmodern and multi-media times. One can also hope that a time will come when feminist theories of national identity will enable Richardson to be read as the specifically English writer which *Pilgrimage* so clearly shows her to be.

Ruth McElroy

Selected Bibliography

Abel, Elizabeth, Hirsch, Marianne and Langland, Elizabeth, eds. *The Voyage In: Fictions of female development.* Hanover: University of New England Press, 1983.

Barrett, Michele and Radford, Jean. "Modernism in the 1930s: Dorothy Richardson and Virginia Woolf." In *1936: The Sociology of Literature. Volume 1: The Politics of Modernism.* Ed. Francis Barker et al. Colchester: University of Essex, 1979.

Bronfen, Elisabeth. *Dorothy Richardson's Art of Memory.* Manchester: Manchester University Press, 1998.

Felber, Lynette. "A Manifesto for Feminine Modernism: Dorothy Richardson's Pilgrimage." In *Rereading Modernism: New Directions in Feminist Criticism.* Ed. Lisa Rado. New York, 1994.

Fromm, Gloria Gilkin. *Dorothy Richardson: A Biography.* London: Univeristy of Illinois Press, 1977.

Gervitz, Susan. *Narratives Journey: The Fiction and Film Writing of Dorothy Richardson.* New York: Peter Lang, 1996.

Hanscombe, Gillian. *The Art of Life: Dorothy Richardson and the Development of Feminist Consciousness.* London: Peter Owen, 1982.

Radford, Jean. *Dorothy Richardson.* London: Harvester Wheatsheaf, 1991.

Sinclair, May. "The novels of Dorothy Richardson." (1918). In *The Gender of Modernism.* Ed. Bonnie Kime Scott. Bloomington: University of Indiana Press, 1990.

Thomson, George. *A Reader's Guide to Dorothy Richardson's Pilgrimage.* Greensboro, 1996.

Rilke, Rainer Maria (1875–1926)

Rilke was born in Prague, and spent most of his life traveling throughout Europe. Although he maintained a distance from other writers, his poetry is indebted to modernist art; it shares the modernist concern of *schauen,* the active construction of reality as it is known and experienced, and the artist's relationship with God in this process of creation.

Rilke's first poetry, such as the collections *Dir zu Feier* and *Mir zu Feier* (1897–1899, *In your Honour* and *In my Honour*) emulates the ornamental effects of *Jugendstil,* with an occasionally awkward syntax at the expense of rhyme. In his next cycle, *Das Stunden-Buch* (1905, *The Book of Hours*), he developed a sparser style, and introduced themes of the artist's relation to God, as well as his own loneliness and death, themes which would preoccupy him for the rest of his career. The poetic persona, Apostol, is fascinated by the individuality of Renaissance art which is opposed to his artistic tradition of icon painting; he loses his ability to depict God, whom he wishes to rebel against as his Father, but then suggests reconciliation with Him as his son.

In *Das Buch der Bilder* (1906, *The Book of Images*) Rilke began to focus on the act of perception, from the influence of Auguste Rodin, and the Worpswede artists' community. It included the expressionist painter Paula Modersohn-Becker, to whom Rilke addressed his "Requiem für eine Freundin" (1908, "Requiem for a Friend"), praising how she had painted people "from the inside / driven in the forms of their being." Rilke envisaged a relationship between depicting spiritual and objective worlds, declaring in "Forschritt" ("Progress") that "I feel myself more familiar with the Nameless / with my senses."

In *Neuer Gedichte* (1907–1908, *New Poems*) he established his style of "thing-poetry" which portrays its subjects objectively through isolated details and subtle shade, while implying their symbolic value by linking them to other objects and to the poet's thoughts. Through the rhythmical descriptions of pacing and gazing through bars in "Der Panther," he suggests the animal's entrapment in a cage and its smothered vitality. Rilke's semi-autobiographical novel, *Die Aufzeichnungen des Malte Laurids Brigge* (1910, *The Notebooks of Malte Laurids Brigge*), is a *bildungsroman* of a young poet who learns to reject his preconceptions to perceive the world as it is constructed from its details, while acknowledging his limitations in attempting to emulate God's act of creation.

Rilke's culminating achievements are the *Duineser Elegien* (1923, *Duino Elegies*) and *Die Sonnette an Orpheus* (1923, *Sonnets to Orpheus*) in which he returns to the problematic relationship of the poet to material and spiritual reality, to his physical impulses and the angels who represent God's will. In the first "Elegie" he is terrified of the angels, feeling inadequate before them. In the seventh "Elegie" he withstands the despair over his mortal limitations and confronts them. Finally, reconciliation with the angels and death is achieved, symbolized by the dead youth who continues to experience the cycles of life in another world. In the *Sonnette* Rilke continues his theme, stating that "Song is being" and for a God this is easy, but posing the question "when will we *be?*" Orpheus, as the archetypal poet whom Rilke aspires to, maneuvers between physical and spiritual reality, life and death.

Carl Krockel

Selected Bibliography

Rilke's main works are available in Insel-Verlag, Frankfurt am Main, and Random House, New York.

Baron, Frank, Ernst S. Dick, and Warren R. Maurer, eds. *Rilke: The Alchemy of Alienation.* Lawrence: Regents Press of Kansas, 1980.

Casey, Timothy J. *Rainer Maria Rilke: A Centenary Essay.* London: Macmillan, 1976.

Paulin, Roger, and Peter Hutchinson. *Rilke's Duino Elegies.* Riverside: Ariadne Press, 1996.

Wood, Frank. *Rainer Maria Rilke: The Ring of Forms.* New York: Octagon Books, 1970.

Roth, Henry (1906–1995)

U.S. novelist, metalworker, psychiatric attendant, waterfowl farmer, and mathematics and Latin tutor.

Born in Tysmenitz, Galicia, an Austro-Hungarian village, Roth immigrated to New York, aged two. He started his novel *Call It Sleep* (1934), based on his childhood in the Lower East Side and Harlem, as a twenty-one-year-old student when he moved in with anthropology professor and poet Eda Lou Walton. She encouraged his writing and introduced him to the work of **Joyce, Eliot,** and Frazer, all recognizable influences on Roth's nevertheless unique novel.

Acclaimed on publication as a modernist masterpiece, *Call It Sleep* came too late to be unproblematically received as such. Its multiple allusions, symbolic structures, and multilingual puns—comparable in places to *Finnegans Wake*—were not universally recognized. Ironically it suffered from selective attention to one discursive strand, becoming celebrated as a proletarian novel for its detailed, naturalistic evocation of slums and streetlife. Some critics rejected the experimental form, narration, and language as affected and obscure. Politically committed during the Depression, Roth took seriously complaints such as an anonymous review in *New Masses* berating "young writers" squandering "their working class experience . . . as material for introspective, febrile novels." Proletarianism, like modernism, declined as war loomed; *Call It Sleep* went out of print, largely forgotten.

Certainly some phrases and snatches of dialogue remain impenetrable, but in the context of a deceptively direct, clear narrative voice, these can be seen as conveying the protagonist's lack of understanding as he encounters various languages and mysterious cultural signs during his odysseys along teeming sidewalks, on rooftops, and across wasteland. A Jew among gentiles, one of the last generation of Yiddish speakers, a child among adults, and a European country boy who knows corn and wildflowers only from his mother's cheap picture print, David represents the outsider. His alienation, displacement and sensitivity are expressed in a supple and curiously uncentered style that weaves stream-of-consciousness, **interior monologue,** free indirect discourse and limited objective narration. His thoughts are primarily in Yiddish, as is the speech of his family and immediate community which are interspersed with snatches from Hebrew and Aramaic; these appear as though translated into more or less Standard English, although occasional words and phrases remain in the original, explained or not, depending on David's understanding, while Polish, his mother and aunt's secular language, remains mysterious. Difference is unmarked except when they and other immigrants use English, presented almost phonetically as David hears it and thereby rendered "foreign." The idioms and cultural resources of these languages enable dialogic productivity, in the Bakhtinian sense, as David proceeds on his journey, never completed, toward American identity: the Promised Land reverts to Babel, vibrant cacophony, with speech embedded among bewildering urban sounds and sensations.

David's quest culminates in repeating a prank, executed initially as a dare to appease some *goy* children and deny his Jewishness, that involves thrusting his father's metal milk dipper between streetcar tracks to create a blinding arc. Replete with sexual and religious connotations, his near-fatal electrocution epitomizes the novel's strategies. His Oedipal parental relationships, symbolized by his ankle becoming burnt, are resolved when his Goliath- (and Thor-) like father finally accepts his paternity. David's Excalibur, likened to the Statue of Liberty's torch and the Christian cross that fascinates him, releases Isaiah's holy light (remembered from Hebrew lessons), counterpart of peace-bringing thunder from *The Waste Land* and oriental myths, allaying his associated fears of darkness and sexuality. Language and imagery drawn almost directly from **Ulysses** describes orgasmic purification by that most potent symbol of modernity, electricity; the city grid short-circuits through him, bringing transport to a halt, suggesting momentary connectedness with his surroundings in a chapter that expands beyond his focalization into an impressionistic montage of disembodied Manhattan voices.

Following the mixed reception of *Call It Sleep,* Roth contracted a second novel with Scribners editor Maxwell Perkins, part of which was published as work in progress. The protagonist, a communist proletarian experiencing ideological confusion, mirrored Roth, increasingly frustrated by his life of privilege and patronage in bohemian Greenwich Village. Having broken his difficult relationship with Walton, after which he married pianist and composer Muriel Parker, Roth suffered possibly the longest writer's block in history.

Jewish critics persistently championed *Call It Sleep* as the most important Jewish-American novel of the first half of the century. It was eventually republished in 1960, the later paperback becoming a million-copy bestseller. Roth was now claimed as a major American modernist and as a displaced European modernist. The heteroglossic form of the novel, contradicting the myth of America as melting pot, ensured continuing interest as multiculturalism evolved in the seventies and eighties, conferring new recognition as an ethnic document.

A 1968 University of New Mexico **D. H. Lawrence** Fellowship, acknowledging the novel's renewed status, took the Roths to Albuquerque, where they settled. Although a collection of stories and interviews, *Shifting Landscape,* had appeared in 1987, Roth astounded the literary world with a second novel in 1994. *A Star Shines Over Mt. Morris Park* is the first volume of *Mercy of a Rude Stream,* a projected six-part work. An account of New York during **World War I,** it is a third-person, fragmented chronology of childhood interrupted by the storyteller's meditations in the present and dialogues with his alter-ego over questions of veracity and the problems of writing. Of the 1457 manuscript pages Roth left for posthumous publication, Volumes 2, 3, and 4, *A Diving Rock on the Hudson* (1995), *From Bondage* (1996) and *Requiem for Harlem* (1998) have so far appeared. While these carry Roth's disclaimer that they are not autobiography, they contain a fictional author with the same name as his protagonist

(Ira): both characters experience events known to have involved Roth, concordant with *Call It Sleep.* Volume 2 recounts Ira's struggle with reading *Ulysses,* and his disillusion with Joyce's novel over sixty years. It also expresses ambivalence towards Eliot, ranging from initial enthusiasm and identification with the poet's anti-Semitism, to horror after the Holocaust.

Nigel Morris

Selected Bibliography

Wirth-Nesher, Hana (ed.). *New Essays on Call It Sleep.* Cambridge and New York: Cambridge University Press, 1996.

Russia

The Russian contribution to modernism in all the arts was so large and so radical that one might be forgiven for believing the kinds of exaggerated claims contained in comments by (for example) John Middleton Murry (on Dostoyevsky), James Stephens (on Rozanov) and **Virginia Woolf** ("if the Russians are mentioned one runs the risk of feeling that to write of any fiction save theirs is a waste of time"), telling us in no uncertain terms that literary modernism was anticipated, if not invented, by the work of earlier writers in Russia, especially Fyodor Mikhailovich Dostoyevsky. The "modernist" Dostoyevsky was in turn anticipated by Gogol, lauded by Nabokov (1944), and by Lermontov, whose *A Hero of Our Time* was "discovered" by **James Joyce** as a sort of *Portrait of the Artist* before the event (see Kenner 215). Both these Russian writers can be seen as forerunners of Dostoyevsky's fascination with a kind of depth-psychology qualitatively different from the psychological cause-and-effect narratives of the great realists in other cultures; and by virtue of which he attracted much comment in his own time and later. The influential *Kratkaya Literaturnaya Entsyklopedia,* for instance, promotes Dostoyevsky to unequivocal pride of place in the evolution of "Modernizm," which it defines in existentialist terms by reference to displacement, alienation, and the struggle with form and language (Surkov; my translation). This is, it says, a living tradition passing through the work of Andrei Bely (6) to Sartre and Camus into present-day writing (the latter-day Dostoyevskians Shestov and Rozanov, both of whom also influenced **Lawrence,** should be, and indeed often are, mentioned in this context). Dostoyevsky still had a world of ethical imperatives to control his vision of "the man in man" and the formal relativism of what Mikhail Bakhtin later called his "polyphonic" method; but with Andrei Bely, his natural heir and successor, "Already the boundaries between human consciousness and the surrounding world melt down and become effaced in the phraseological whirlwind" (Surkov, vol. 4: 908; my translation).

Andrei Bely is the pseudonym of Boris Nikolayevich Bugaev (1880–1934), whose contribution to Russian literature in the modernist era was unparalleled. Poet, theorist, essayist, Bely broke new ground in every genre, mainly as a consequence of introducing into Russian the symbolist (mostly French) preoccupation with the metaphysics of representation which had begun with Baudelaire and continued with Mallarmé and Rimbaud (of all the French symbolists, Rimbaud may take most credit for inventing the "alchemy of the word" that so strongly influenced the Russians). Bely's mystical but often grotesque intelligence also had a native Russian pedigree, and the nineteenth-century Russian preoccupation with the city of St. Petersburg fuses with the special paranoia of Baudelaire's alienating Paris to bear a new and strange fruit in Bely's masterpiece *Petersburg* (1918).

Like Joyce's and **Proust**'s "stream of consciousness," the "method" of Bely and others cannot be understood simply as an extension of, or deviation from, the methods of the great realist novelists. A new spirit is at work overturning formal and ethical values. In Russia, inevitably, this became linked with the Revolutions of 1905 and 1917, both in fact and in fancy, in the eyes of Russians as well as abroad (which is not to say that most Russian writers, by any means, "accepted" the October Revolution's values). This revolutionary modernism involved all the arts in one way or another, and in its turn it produced a powerful aesthetic theory, known as the "Formal Method" (cf. Ehrlich), which soon began to evolve into rich and diverse genres and types, linking up especially with the revolutionary new art of **film,** as well as the already modernist art of theater from Chekhov through Stanislavsky to Meyerhold (which in turn involved large numbers of talented painters and designers). Konstantin Stanislavsky (1863–1938) founded the Moscow Art Theater in 1898. His tour of Europe and the United States gave currency to the "method" which became the basis of the New York Actors' Studio style. Vsevelod (actually Karl Teodor) Meyerhold (1874–1940) was with the Art Theater from its foundation, but from 1918, when he was made People's Commissar for Theater, his style diverged sharply from Stanislavsky's, and his "biomechanics" used abstract "constructivist" sets, circus routines, gymnastics, and above all the idea of the actor as a puppet. Many postwar directors, especially in Eastern Europe, drew extensively on his radical ideas.

The Dostoyevskian prose revolution, therefore, was not an isolated phenomenon. In poetry, a more extreme kind of experimentalism was born out of the symbolist explorations of sound and sense, **rhythm** and form, in the work of Alexander Blok (1880–1921), a **Yeats**-like poet whose *The Twelve* (1918) notoriously—but very persuasively—celebrated the Revolution in terms of Christ's rule on earth, in a vivid image of Bolshevik soldiers marching with Christ at their head. (*The Twelve* welcomes the Revolution as a great cleansing flood of antihumanism, but Blok never became an apologist of the new social order and his enthusiasm was short-lived.) Blok's fascination with murky and macabre urban landscapes permeated by a melancholy eroticism is close to **T. S. Eliot**'s. The much-quoted poem *Nieznakomka, The Stranger* (1906) is representative: "On the lake the rowlocks creak and a woman shrieks, while in the sky the moon's/disk, inured to everything, leers senselessly" (Obolensky 262). The tone strongly resembles that of many poems by Eliot, who found in Joyce's *Ulysses* a new "mythic method" adequate to explore contemporary reality ("anarchy and futility"). Blok embodies in his poetry the metaphysical critique of history which the Silver Age philosophers also expounded in very persuasive and influential terms. Nicolas Berdyaev, for example, asserted in *The Meaning of History* (1923) that

> Each man represents by virtue of his inner nature a sort of microcosm in which the whole world of reality and all the great historical epochs combine and coexist. He is not merely a minute fragment of the universe, but rather a world in his own right, a world revealed or hidden according as consciousness is more or less penetrating and extensive. In this development of self-consciousness the whole history of the world is apprehended, together with all the great epochs which historical science investigates. (Cited in Ellman and Feidelson.)

It would be no exaggeration to say that what Berdyaev has written here (which is echoed by Soloviev, as well as by the highly original, very personal writings of Rozanov, or Shestov's anguished skepticism) represents a modernist crux. Coming as *we* moderns do at the end of a vast era of history, which *we* increasingly have the means to study objectively and understand fully, *we* are forced to recognize that certain elements of the human condition, notably aging and death, elude our comprehension.

One might, however, have supposed (as Eliot said) that we no longer needed *the past* as a living reality, when we understand the world (through science) so much better than our ancestors did. But this understanding, our shared knowledge, leaves the big questions unanswered. The value of an individual life resides in the creative access that any individual has to the ground of his or her own being, and our civilization, as Nietzsche told us in *The Birth of Tragedy* (1872), is ringed around by the gods we have driven out of the city, waiting to repossess their territory. This new genre of Dostoyevskyan urban poetry in Blok, with its irrationalism and its quest for the "unknown woman" who embodies the yearning psyche of the poet, is continued in the work of Vladimir Mayakovsky (1893–1930) (who declared in his autobiographical fragment "I myself" that nature was "not up to date enough") and Nikolai Gumilyov (1886–1921) among others, where it also serves as the occasion for radical psychological and verbal innovations coming from other quarters (the fusion of poetry with painting and the fine arts, theater in all its ramifications, the new linguistics, and the findings of a massively accelerating tradition of anthropological research, and in Mayakovsky's case with Marxist politics as well). Gumilyov was an exoticist rather than an urbanist, but between 1918 and 1921 he wrote one masterly urban poem, *The Runaway Tramcar,* which uses a cityscape to express the creative possibilities of a new sort of disorientation, urban and psychological at once: "A sign-board . . . The letters, suffused with blood, spell 'green-grocer'; here, I know,/instead of cabbages and swedes they sell dead heads" (Obolensky 300–303).

The kinds of structural analysis of narrative inaugurated by **anthropology** later developed into a powerful anthropological critique of culture in the hands of Vladimir Propp (1895–1970) (see, for example, his *Morphology of the Folk Tale* of 1928) and his heirs, who in turn drew extensively upon the methods of the formalist movement. Although Russian literary historians, taking their cue from Nikolai Gumilyov, who coined the term, still like to call the modernist era the "Silver Age" in Russian letters (see Georgiyeva) to distinguish it from the "Golden Age" inaugurated by Pushkin (1799–1837), the creative explosion that occurred at this time had repercussions which impacted on world culture and art via linguistics and (appropriately) cinema, drama, and the fusion of theory and practice in the plastic arts.

Although the term "Silver Age," enshrined in Russian literary history, seems oddly apologetic to non-Russians, one should not lose sight of the fact that (influenced by the late Tolstoy, as well as Dostoyevsky) the term is designed to characterize a period of spiritual revival, with Vladimir Soloviev (in one influential version of the phenomenon) at its head. This new spirituality issued in heterodox forms, so that Christian values were accompanied by the strange millenarian, messianic, and revolutionary impulses which went right to the heart of Russsian modernism. Certainly, the combination of autocratic rule with new forms of spirituality, and the beginnings of a modern historical and sociological critique of culture, pushed the Russian intelligentsia into the foreground of their society to a degree probably unparalleled in any other European culture. For many decades to come it was the writers and artists of Russia who constituted the real political opposition. Seminal texts in this regard were Berdyaev's *The Spiritual Crisis of the Intelligentsia* (1910) and *The Crisis of Art* (1918), and Fedotov's *Tragedy of the Intelligentsia* (1926). Especially acute was the question of *roots:* whether the Russian intelligentsia had any (i.e., in *the people*), or whether they ought to have some, or whether roots were a good thing or a bad thing, or whether talk of roots was meaningless.

All of this is manifest in the visionary work of Velimir Khlebnikov (1885–1922), one of the strangest and most puzzling talents in the history of literature ("Much of his verse resembles fragments of some vast unfinished epic poem, pagan and pantheistic" says Dimitri Obolensky). Not for nothing did Henryk Baran set Khlebnikov firmly at the head of his admirable study of Russian poetic modernism. In purely literary-historical terms, his work belongs with, indeed inaugurates, that of the futurists. Russian **futurism** was more "transcendental" than the Italian version (see **Italian Futurism**): Mayakovsky was the leader of the so-called "cubo-futurist" wing, which went in for machines and cities, but in the name of liberating the human spirit; the "Ego-Futurism" of Igor-Severyanin and Shershenevich has been neatly characterized by Renato Poggioli as more "up-to-date" than "modern," basically a sort of "salesmanship." However, Khlebnikov's strange art of controlled psychosis is a blend of nostalgia, nationalism, infantilist regression, and startling creative inventiveness, especially in its language. He is not "modern" in the tough, urban way that Mayakovsky is modern. Sometimes he reads like a verbal fusion of Henri (le Douanier) Rousseau with Salvador Dalí; sometimes more like a set of illustrations from Ferdinand de Saussure's *Cours de Linguistique General* (1916) (which was disseminated in Russia via the teaching of Baudouin de Courtenay in St. Petersburg). His early death in the famine of 1922 snuffed out his work, but not his influence. In a poem like "dyr bul shchyl"—these words have no referential meaning, but could be imagined to be component syllables of meaningful words within the Russian phonological system— Khlebnikov inaugurated concrete poetry in a special Russian idiom, a return to the roots of the Russian language and the combinatorial possibilities of Russian philology, with sound generating meaning. The gestural possibilities of the new "sound poetry" were developed and extended, especially by his most often quoted poem "Zaklyatie smekhom"("Incantation by Laughter"), which runs a series of brilliant variations on the morphological, phonological, lexical, and phonetic possibilities of the word "smekh" (laughter), while at the same time extending the expressive possibilities of the Russian verse line towards a sort of grammatical infinity. The effect is jovial, sinister, comic, and liberating. The poem raises the question of the (un)translatability of poetry yet again: I quote some early lines in two different English versions which could be two quite different texts, they are so utterly unlike each other:

> O you laughniks, laugh it forth!
> You, who laugh it up and down, laugh
>   along so laughily;
>   *(Markov and Sparks)*

> Hlahla! Uthlofan, laughlings!
> Who lawghen with lafe, who hlachen
>   lewchly.
>   *(Schmidt)*

Maybe it is the more nonsensical poem/ translation that means more, because of the more radical choices that have been made by the translator in relation to the semantic/structural possibilities inherent in the source text. The special brilliant syntactical and sonic combination here should not allow us to lose sight of the other aspect of Khlebnikov I have mentioned, however: his profound nostalgia for a proto-Slavonic landscape populated by shamans like himself and wild, beautiful, mythological, or mythologized, animals out of a savage fairy tale. In the end the real key to his work may reside in what the great formalist analyst Yuri Tynyanov called a verse where "the child and the savage were the new poetic protagonists, suddenly scrambling the fixed norms of metre and of verse" (quoted in Surkov, vol. 4: 910; my translation).

Essentially, it was the Dionysiac energies liberated by Khlebnikov that Mayakovsky harnessed to his massive critique of industrialism and modernity called cubo-futurism. Mayakovsky had a combination of critical acumen and creative originality that made him the foremost poet of socialism, accepted as such (enthusiastically) by Stalin and (regretfully) by Pasternak. Mayakovsky was privileged (by virtue of this) to exercise a certain condescension toward other important poets of his time who could not share his revolutionary enthusiasm, most notably Sergey Esenin (the "Russian **Dylan Thomas**," though he is both more lyrical and more lucid), particularly in the notable tract *How are Verses Made* of 1926 (the year of Esenin's suicide, and four years before his own). In early works like his short autobiography, "I myself," and the masterly urban narrative poem "A Cloud in Trousers" (*Obloko v Shtanakh,* 1914/15; in *How Are Verses Made?*), Mayakovsky combines elements of **Whitman,** Dostoyevsky, and some cubist painterly devices transposed into words, and shapes a psychoanalytical narrative with an authentic tragic resonance tricked out in melodramatic gestures and prophetic, Nietzschean intonations.

His self-imposed enlistment to the Soviet cause (as with **Eisenstein**) did nothing to damage his gifts as one of the greatest love poets in Russian literature (see especially *Pro Eto* of 1923) but gave him in addition a wide range of satirical materials which he used to excellent effect (39). The jargons of sovietism, used to marvelous effect by Mayakovsly, who relished them, are particularly well conveyed by **Edwin**

Morgan's Lallans Scots versions, *Wi the haill voice.* The work of Viktor Pertsov and others kept alive the modernist Mayakovsky in the midst of the relentless sovietization of his work. In our time, no book or exhibition devoted to the Russian avant-garde could omit the graphic work which linked him with Rodchenko, El Lissitsky, and others. (The recent two-volume collection of pieces by Nikolai Khardziev contains a number of contributions relevant to Mayakovsky, most notably "Poeziya i Zhivopis' Ranny Mayakovsky," 18–98).

Of course, like some other Russian writers and artists of the Revolutionary period, Mayakovsky tended to identify with an over-personalized version of the prevailing political impetus, without recognizing perhaps that the revolutionary literary-historical road led almost inevitably from Lunacharsky and Trotsky to Zhdanov and worse. This does not alter the fact that he accomplished an aesthetic transformation of poetry of a Brechtian power and authority.

In this, one might compare his work with Eisenstein's. From the elemental wave breaking over the sea wall at the beginning of *The Battleship Potemkin* (1925), Eisenstein's unique film sense subsumes his own radical Oedipal energies to his empathic feeling for the limitless power of the camera eye to transpose and transform a kind of dream-work textured from a "cut-up" reality, a sort of pansexualism, as well as the eye of the caricaturist trained on classic Russian fiction, Japanese wood-block prints, poster art, and theater (including several non-European traditions). For him, and for other Russian artists (Tatlin, Goncharova, Malevich) the Revolution meant not so much a body of dogma as a conceptual framework that could contain, and *theorize,* all these diverse elements and more. A new created universe was coming into being (see Yakimovich). The montage effect which was crucial to Eisenstein's development as an artist (see his *The Film Sense,* 1963), had been practiced by Mayakovsky as well, and by prose writers like Boris Pilnyak, best known for his novel *The Naked Year* (1921). (Surkov damns Pilnyak with faint praise as too "literary," but his mannerist prose, with its sardonic wordplay and strange bursts of lurid imagery, communicates in a most original way the desperate sense of the disappearance of all cultural landmarks and boundaries in Russia at the time). Eisenstein it was, however, who refined montage into a powerful instrument of analytical and synthetic vision. The much-quoted Odessa steps sequence of *The Battleship Potemkin* is a masterly dream-fusion of displacement and condensation whereby stone lions rearing up, and boots marching down, are superimposed in an instant of time—like the image and the vortex of Anglo-American **imagism** and **vorticism** in poetry—to expose "reality" to a play of energies which overwhelm it, or subvert it, in order to tease out another, hidden narrative which enters into a radical dialogue with the "given" images of the real.

A larger, more contentious or polemical conceptual order is the outcome, but the process matters more than the product because it is by tracing its developing contours that a critical raising of consciousness occurs. Mayakovsky's longer poems, from *Pro Eto* to *Vladimir Ilyich Lenin,* enact their radical meanings with a similar gestural authority. The cinema, the supreme aesthetic product of the age of mechanical reproduction, subverts the reproductive process at its very outset, "laying bare" its powerful machinery (like the theater of Meyerhold and Brecht). Later in his career come the anti-German propaganda film *Alexander Nevsky* (1938) and the unfinished Stalinist epic *Ivan the Terrible* (1944–46), both masterpieces of an increasingly theatrical vision of history as a bloody charade justified only by the tragic sense of form. *Ivan* offers a psychotic vision of a period of history which is as much the postwar Soviet Union as it is sixteenth-century Russia, riddled with intrigue, suspicion, and gratuitous violence. But with Eisenstein there is everywhere the recognition that meaning in art, like victory in war, or the succession to a throne, hangs upon a handful of contingent images perfectly placed:

> The first task is the creative breaking-up of the theme into determining representations, and then combining these representations with the purpose of bringing life to *the initiating image of the theme.* And the process whereby this image is perceived is identical with the original experiencing of the theme of the image's content. . . . We shall find that a similar crowd of pictures, carefully selected and reduced to the extreme laconicism of two or three details, is to be found in the finest examples of literature. (Eisenstein 44)

This is, of course, pretty much what Russian formalism tried to tell us. Evolving hand-in-hand with the poetics of Khlebnikov, Mayakovsky, and Eisenstein, the work of Viktor Shklovsky, Yuri Tynyanov, Boris Eikhenbaum, Roman Jakobson, and many others (see Lemon and Reis), formalism—or as they liked to call it "the formal method"—is the modernist aesthetic *par excellence.* The much-cited essay by Viktor Shklovsky known in English as *Art as Technique* (in Lemon and Reis, 3–24) sets the tone for the whole movement by presenting a theory of art which cocks a snook at Aristotle's doctrine of mimesis in order to build a new theory of how art "works" on the basis of models drawn from the new linguistics and anthropology (Nietzsche's radically un-Aristotelean theory of tragic art *The Birth of Tragedy* (1872) influenced all aspects of Russian modernism, not least the work of the so-called formalists). If Aristotle (and the **realism** which justified itself by reference to his work) thought that art was concerned above all with making an image of reality, representing it, "*ut pictura poesis*," Shklovsky thought that art was concerned above all with a series of *interventions* into the world of the real and the codes by which it was constructed: the codes themselves were built into our perception of things. If traditional literary history had given the writer a privileged place as the final arbiter of the moral values and the verisimilitude of his creation, the God of the fictional universe, Shklovsky gave pride of place to the *medium* of art and its *language* (in the fullest sense).

The "making new" of art (in **Ezra Pound**'s phrase—see his *ABC of Reading* (1934) and *Make it New* (1934), which are close to formalism in spirit and manner) is based upon the principle of what Shklovsky called "defamiliarization" (*ostranenie*), and the main examples he gives are (paradoxically) from Tolstoy, though he subjects Tolstoy rather perversely to a "strong reading" *against* the doctrine of realism. What counts in Tolstoy, according to Shklovsky, is the prolongation of the process of perception whereby an event becomes an experience (Lemon and Reis 12). Habit devours our lives: "works, clothes, furniture, one's wife, and the fear of war." By disrupting the codes (sometimes by extreme forms of parody, which becomes, for the formalists, central to the "making new" process), writing "makes the stone stony," restores the sensation of life. One of Shklovsky's more basic examples (but still in keeping with the spirit of his venture) is that of Tolstoy's short story "Kholstomer" where a horse speaks, providing an estranged Swiftian perspective on a world of cruel and foolish human transgressions of the laws of nature and of God. What Shklovsky began in this essay he continued in his classic study of Sterne's novel *Tristram Shandy* (1759–67), where the convolutions of the mannerist

narrative—interrupting itself, going back and forth in time and space—are so thoroughgoing that they allow Shklovsky to speak of "the device laid bare" (as opposed to Tolstoy's art, which in the end naturalizes its contradictions).

> Sterne even lays bare the technique of combining separate story lines to make up the novel. In general, he accentuates the very structure of the novel. By violating the form, he forces us to attend to it; and, for him, this awareness of the form through its violation constitutes the content of the novel. (*Sterne's Tristram Shandy* in Lemon and Reis, 30)

Already in *Art as Technique* Shklovsky had moved from the "motivated" device (e.g., narrating from the viewpoint of a horse for satirical purposes) to the "unmotivated" device in the full conviction of the gratuitousness of art-language:

> I personally feel that defamiliarisation is found almost everywhere form is found . . . an image is not a permanent referent for those mutable complexities of life which are revealed through it, its purpose is not to make us perceive meanings, but to create a special perception of the object. . . . In my article on plot construction I write about defamiliarisation in psychological parallelism . . . to transfer the usual perception of an object into the sphere of new perception. (In Lemon and Reis, 18)

Mayakovsky's *How Are Verses Made* (1926) is especially interesting for the way it yokes together futurist experiment, communist politics, and formalist theory in the short-lived moment of cultural history that also contains the major innovations of Eisenstein and Meyerhold. To show the reader how texts are "made" was central to the formalist demythologizing of the creative process (Eikhenbaum's title *How Gogol's Overcoat Was Made* is symptomatic). Similarly, Eisenstein's montage principle foregrounds the complex devices a film uses to create visual equivalents for conceptual processes: far from being disguised by the flow of events or the development of characters, the devices are laid bare. In Meyerhold's theater, similarly, there is a method quite unlike the Stanislavskyan **naturalism** that underpinned the marvelous art of Chekhov (who used it to puncture the illusions and aspirations of the Russian bourgeoisie and intelligentsia). Meyerhold, by contrast, develops a narrative of gesture for its own sake, so that a kind of gestural logic of mime is counterpointed with the logic of the text, outpacing it, anticipating it, interrupting it. These kinds of stylizations undermine verisimilitude but (strangely enough) by doing so they allow the reader to participate more completely in the creative process, as if we were always on the stage ourselves, or in the writer's study participating in the process of writing. In Mayakovsky's expanded metaphor of the city the materialist critique of cultural production is accompanied by a wildly romantic self-dramatization that transposes the action on to the cosmic plane of a "magical universe:"

> I walk along, waving my arms and mumbling almost wordlessly, now shortening my steps so as not to interrupt my mumbling, now mumbling more rapidly in time with my steps. So the rhythm is established and takes shape—and rhythm is the basis of any poetic work, resounding through the whole thing. Gradually you ease individual words free of this dull roar. . . . Where this dull roar of a rhythm comes from is a mystery. In my case it's all kinds of repetitions in my mind of sounds, noises, rocking motions, or in fact of any perceptible repetition which comes to me as a sound shape. (*How Are Verses Made?* 68)

Evidently, the mysticism behind Khlebnikov's poetics remained, even when cubo-futurism and constructivism had adapted them to a more material end.

Outside of futurism and its associated cultural processes, acmeism may have been the most powerful Russian modernist poetic movement. It consciously opposed (as Renato Poggioli has said) the Dionysiac impulse which lent itself to a revolutionary art, and instead cultivated an Apollonian calm which was intended to check the obscurantist tendencies in the symbolist movement and its successors. It is close to Anglo-American imagism in form, content, and doctrine (and takes its origins from the 1910 manifesto by Mikhail Kuzmin in the pages of the journal *Apollo* entitled "On Beautiful Clarity") (Poggioli 213). It is also worth mentioning here that *Apollo* first published Mandelshtam, also in 1910. Acmeism proper, however, stems from Gorodetsky and Gumilev, whose ideas Poggioli compares to **T. E. Hulme**'s in the context of Anglo-American imagism. Gumilev calls for "a more precise notion of the tie between subject and object" than the symbolists had evinced. A sort of acceptance of the created world on its own terms had a special significance in a culture which, looked at historically, was riven by metaphysical and political turmoil (by no means at an end, however). A personal voice of a quieter, more reflective kind than Russian literature had been used to entered the scene. Mandelshtam, for instance, creates a poetic world "saturated with objective details" and like the other poets in this category he has a strong preference for strictly regulated forms which seem classical but in fact contain subtle shifts of meter or semantic associations which (like Eliot's early lyrics) introduce a very idiosyncratic note underlining an uncompromisingly personal vision which works on traditional, mythic, and historical topics (again like Eliot) to redefine "tradition" and the writer's relationship with it. He brought his curious classicism and fascination with etymology (which have been referred back to Lomonosov) to a Revolution which (as he said himself) had no need for his gifts. It is ironic that he died a victim of what used to be referred to euphemistically as the "cult of personality." Poggioli compares him to de Chirico and the classical period of Picasso (fascinated by "the heavy rigidity of inorganic matter," 312), but it is the coolness that counts.

Two women poets (at least) also play a crucial role in Russian modernism, Anna Akhmatova and Marina Tsvetayeva, the one limpid, translucent, with a strong sense of tradition, and the other (as Dmitri Obolensky says) full of "whirling and staccato rhythms" (xxvi), the one living her long life in Russia and writing powerful threnodies for the sufferings, and the victims, of Russian history, the other living in emigration then returning, disastrously, to the Soviet Union. Akhmatova, as well as being a major poet, is unusual in the Russian poetic tradition because she combines her creativity with a marvelous critical sense (like Eliot, or Lawrence) so that she does what Eliot did and weaves into her own output as a poet a modernist revaluation of past Russian writing. By doing so she also constructs (as Eliot did in *Four Quartets* and Lawrence in *Lady Chatterley*) a powerful myth of historical identity and national consciousness. The early acmeist poetry, however, is most representative of her modernism. Tsevtayeva, married to a White Guard officer, turned her back on the Revolution and emigrated to Paris; by doing so, perhaps she gave to her collections of the late twenties that formalist series of "shifts" (in register, vocabulary, rhythm, and syntax) which became her distinguishing feature, linking her with the (otherwise quite different) futurists. Like Akhmatova, Tsvetayeva too developed a flexible, alert critical prose.

The question of what might constitute the "norms" of literary Russian, hanging over from the nineteenth century, was sharpened by revolution and war and the radical disruption of academic canons which accompanied them. In the famous Sterne essay, Shklovsky notes the foregrounding of the narrator in what Russian literary tradition calls "skaz:" a gestural miming of the articulatory process. The classic study of this is Eikhenbaum's essay on Gogol's short story *The Overcoat*. This essay is central to Russian modernism in its rejection of the historical/emotive readings of Gogol's drama of the "little man" in favor of a more abstract, conceptual reading of the "voicing" of the tale, or what Eikhenbaum calls "sonic gesturing" (which also means locating Gogol's story in a world analagous to that of Khlebnikov's strange mythologies). The displaced protagonist who acquired so much intellectual weight in Dostoyevsky's work is here a marionette-like figure (in some ways like **Stravinsky**'s *Petrouchka*) made up of repeated narrative stammerings "orchestrated" with great brilliance and interspersed with atmospheric set pieces. A similar "quarrel with realism" informs Roman Jakobson's *On Realism in Art*, which renegotiates the conventions of literary realism on the basis of some very original categories of reader/writer relations based on what a reader expects from the "category" of realism, and what a writer adopts from the realist tradition and "makes new." Jakobson's fascination with the differentiation of the processes of representation and interpretation integrates the critical and the creative act in typical formalist style:

> While in painting and in the other visual arts the illusion of an objective and absolute faithfulness to reality is conceivable, "natural" (in Plato's terminology), verisimilitude in a verbal expression or in a literary description obviously makes no sense whatever. Can the question be raised about a higher degree of verisimilitude of this or that trope? Can one say that one metaphor or metonymy is conventional or, so to say, figurative. . . . As tradition accumulates, the painted im-

age becomes an ideogram. . . . We no longer see a picture. The ideogram needs to be deformed. (*On Realism in Art,* in Matejka and Pomorska, 39)

In this way, *realism* becomes the most relativistic of concepts. In order to perceive a represented object as real we participate in a complex relation of codes in which artist and viewer (or reader) measure a perceived reality in relation to their expectations, radical or conservative, of what constitutes the real. Elsewhere, and in subsequent work as one of the century's foremost linguisticians, Jakobson extended his "modernist" preoccupation with the relation of syntagma to syntax.

The formalist critique developed and grew, nourishing (for example) the **music** of Prokofiev and the theatre of Meyerhold, whose art, unfairly disparaged by Poggioli (69), developed as the antithesis of Stanislavsky's. The two opposed styles both fed, later, into the American "method" (thanks to Lee Strasberg and others), which left its mark permanently on Hollywood movies, maybe even created a distinctively "filmic" style of acting. Russian prose and poetry continued to explore new forms of writing and sensibility despite (or because of) terrible political pressures. The whole formalist venture was regarded with suspicion by the communist authorities, so that when Mikhail Bakhtin wrote his classic study of Dostoyevsky, despite the fact that his theory of polyphony was clearly indebted to formalism, he was careful to cover up the affinity by means of some swift diversionary tactics. Nevertheless, modernism continued to grow and flourish. Citing just seven out of scores of instances of highly original modernist prose writing taking the modern tradition forward into the postwar era, one might note in particular Bely's Joycean *Petersburg* (1918); the imagistic *Konarmiya* (1926, *Red Cavalry*) by Isaac Babel (1894–1941); the polyphonic *The Master and Margarita* (written 1938, published

1973) by Mikhail Bulgakov (1891–1940)—probably the best-loved Soviet novel, as popular in the satellite countries as it was in the USSR when at last it found a publisher (an abridged version appeared in a journal in 1966–7); *Zavist'* (1927, *Envy*) by Yuri Olesha (1899–1960); Boris Pilnyak's *The Naked Year* (1921); the dystopian *My* (1921, *We*) (which profoundly influenced George Orwell, who read it in French) by Evgeny Zamyatin (1884–1939); and the late symbolist *Dr. Zhivago* (1957) by Boris Pasternak (1890–1960).

The poetry of Mandelshtam, Akhmatova, Tsvetayava, and Pasternak may be said to show the modernist aesthetic evolving naturally out of the futurist/formalist radical critique of language, towards a new sense of an unbroken tradition which for historical reasons always remained to be defined, as the writers in question bore witness to the inhumanity and philistinism of the Soviet regime, and created for themselves that rich inner space which is still so vibrant in Russian writing (though post-Soviet capitalism seems set to destroy it). Other major writers had emigrated never to return, foremost among them perhaps Vladimir Nabokov (1899–1977), who achieved the seemingly impossible feat of becoming more famous as a writer in his adopted language than he was in his native land (where a revaluation of his work is currently taking place).

Pasternak is of course a major writer both in poetry and in prose, and his case may be taken as symptomatic of both the power of Russian modernism and the pressures which beset it. His autobiographical writings constitute one of the most important prose testimonies of the era (especially the splendid *Okhrannaya Gramota* (1931), translated into English as *Safe Conduct*). Somehow indulged by Stalin, maybe as a reward for his translations from Georgian, Pasternak survived only to be condemned by the new Soviet leaders in the early years of the technocratic revolution which had no use for his intense individualism (when his extraordinary modernist novel *Dr. Zhivago* was vilified). The recent publication of Nikolai Khardzhiev's collected essays has thrown an interesting sidelight on Pasternak's tribulations in the thirties. In a piece called "The History of an Article" ("Istoriya odnoy stat'i (o Borise Pasternake)" 330–344), Khardzhiev writes about the problems he experienced getting his essay *On Boris Pasternak* published. In the course of his correspondence he was even told by the editor of *Literaturnaya Gazeta* that Pasternak had rejected the piece and chosen one by another author. The article was dropped, despite protests from Viktor Shklovsky, who was a member of the editorial committee, and only saw the light of day forty years later (though Khardzhiev enjoyed respect in the USSR as a major authority on Russian modernism). This kind of tale, as significant in its way as the horror stories of imprisonment and execution, and multiplied thousand of times over throughout the USSR, forms an intrinsic part of the story of Russian modernism.

But the content of the article is at least as interesting as its fate, and bears witness to what, for the righteous, had evidently proved offensive in modernism by 1932. It is a twenty-year survey and shows very vividly what is distinctive in Pasternak's work from the outset: his "spacious lyricism," his "incantatory" repetitions, the typical clash of lyrical pathos and facticity. In order to communicate succinctly a vivid sense of development in a small compass, Khardzhiev makes use in his essay of analytical-synthetic strategies drawn directly from formalism. Terms such as "the poetic system," "intonation," "medium of formal renewal," "functions," "transformation of the genre," "lexical dissonance," "shifts," "associative series" (of a generic convention), "associative leaps," and very detailed analysis of imagery above all,

brand Khardzhiev (it seems) one of the damned and despised brigade of formalists. But of course, like the formalists proper, he uses his analytical strategies to provide a method which will reveal the growth and transformation of creative processes in such a way as to repudiate those critics (he quotes in particular V. Shershenevich) who had dismissed Pasternak's "neologisms" and "odd vocabulary."

It is precisely by virtue of his precise, spare, formalist commentary on Pasternak's imagery that Khardzhiev can show how this "metaphysical" poet, who was deeply influenced by **Rilke** and other Western modernists (especially French symbolists), and whose poetry is an intimate record of a sustained growth and development of sensibility, could work as deeply and creatively inside the Russian language as the more doctrinaire Khlebnikov with his experimental "slavisms." This was the basis of the earliest work of Pasternak in the so-called "Centrifuge" (founded in 1914), and the characteristic syntactical energy (rivaling the futurists) persisted even when Pasternak's poetry seems to be working exclusively through richly associative chains. As with Blok, a narrative component is generally visible, or half-visible, at the heart of the lyrical process: this is nowhere more apparent, of course, than in the poems which compose the subtext of *Dr. Zhivago,* the novel which brought Pasternak fame in the West and which is written in a style which tells us on every page that the deep subjectivity of literary modernism remained a burning concern for Russian writers (as it did for the whole of the communist world, as a sort of opposition to the Party line).

Nabokov (1899–1977) is a case of a much more cosmopolitan but equally personal, egocentric creative genius who reaches back into the traditions of Russian literature in order to move forward into the world of **postmodernism** (which is, at any rate, where many of his commentators place him, though he never seemed much inclined to identify himself with this position). Taking off from Gogol, and reading Gogol through the eyes of Bely and the formalists, Nabokov combined parody, translation, satire, and the grotesque with his innate lyrical gift in order to turn Russian fiction inside out, ending up with the consummate art of his sensational masterpiece *Lolita*. The novel is not self-evidently Russian, and its landscape is of course American; but in its embattled advocacy of the literary culture as the bearer of meaning, the validation of subjective experience, however strange, and the one bright undefiled source of language, it is thoroughly Russian. Like Meyerhold, Nabokov was fascinated with the automaton-figure that enters Russian literature from German romanticism and thrives there (maybe because, as Poggioli suggests, autocracy of one kind or the other denied individual freedom). Like Lawrence, whom he disliked, he finds erotic motifs and sexual fantasies permeating human behavior and creativity at every level (in V. V. Rozanov he shared a source with Lawrence). He hated the Soviet system as passionately as Orwell, but his satires on totalitarianism, *Bend Sinister* and *Invitation to a Beheading* build their monstrous visions on formal paradoxes rather than on moral propositions or political satire (Surkov says of the latter novel that it is influenced by **Kafka** and Proust, but both novels are fantasies of dystopian police states which (among other things) parody Kafka and Proust). This refusal to moralize is also perhaps why *Lolita* has been (of late) disparaged somewhat, as if it were a plea for the rights of the child abuser, rather than a study of the perverse creative flights of the imagination. When, or maybe even before, he became the doyen of the interpretation industry, Nabokov first wove the whole analytical business into a fictional narrative, *Pale Fire* (1962), in which he satirizes critics and himself as well—the

great Pushkin scholar—in the figure of the man writing the impossible biography, and the futile footnoter. Then he built himself into his own critical biography, and wrote a succession of late, short works, often very moving, where the artist, Prospero-like, says a long farewell to his books. Something of great moment is coming to an end in Nabokov's late work. One way of saying what this something was, is to go back to a writer Nabokov greatly admired, Andrei Bely.

Bely's novel *Petersburg* is, from one angle, a massive updating of what has been called "the Petersburg theme" in Russian literature, which is itself a focal point of the Russian sense of modernity. From Pushkin's *The Bronze Horseman* (1833) through the short stories of Gogol and the novels of Dostoyevsky to Bely and beyond, St. Petersburg has challenged Russian writers to make sense of this monument to classical perfection and the power of human inventiveness which at the same time bears witness to one man's tyranny and the wanton disregard for human suffering which sprang from it. Strongly reminiscent of Joyce's *Ulysses* (another novel where a phantasmagoric city is the real "hero") especially those sections (like *The Sirens*) where Joyce, whose ear was as acute as Bely's, takes music as his narrative paradigm, Bely's novel unfolds in a sequence of loosely juxtaposed tableaux, propelled by the dynamics of its own linguistic inventiveness as much as by any action. Its translators say of it:

> Bely even claimed that *Petersburg* had been built on a system of sound. . . . "I have the impression that 'll' is the smoothness of form: Apo-*lll*-on; 'pp' is the pressure created by covering surfaces (walls, the bomb); 'kk' is the height of insincerity; Ni-*kkk*-olai . . . *kkk*-lanyalsya na, *kk*-a-*kk* la-*kk*, par-*kk*-eta-khkh ('Nikloai . . . bowed on the varnish-like parquet floor'); 'sss' are reflections; 'rr' is the energy of the explosion (beneath the

covering surfaces); *prr-0-rr* yvv v *brr*-ed ('a breakthrough into delirium') . . ." Bely went on to say that in the composition of the novel sound was preexistent, and "content" formed around it: "Later I myself stumbled on the connection—which surprised me—between the verbal instrumentation and the story line (which came into being involuntarily)." . . . From the very first page we are conditioned to listen as well as look. (*Petersburg* xvii)

What we are listening to is not just an organized pattern of sounds. It is also one of the numerous instances of a modernizing of the device of *skaz* in Russian writing, the self-dramatizing, quasi-improvised narrative which the formalists were so enthralled by. In a sense, nothing has changed since Gogol: the automated figures of the bureaucrats go about their mechanical business filling out the author's rambling lines with gratuitous gesturings and posturings and strings of arbitrary signifiers. Dostoyevsky's "suddenly" (the monstrous power of contingency) is pressed into service on all sides.

The symbolic object at the heart of Bely's narrative is Nikolai's bomb: to blow up his father, Petersburg, the world, the universe of the imagination, and of narrative. The urban landscape of St. Petersburg is evoked less naturalistically than the Dublin of Joyce's *Ulysses* (published five years later) yet unmistakably for anyone who has read *Crime and Punishment* or Pushkin's poem *The Bronze Horseman.* Pushkin and the monument to Peter the Great which his great poem anathematizes both play roles in Bely's novel, evoking autocracy, the power of art, and the menace of retribution hanging over this grotesque Gogolian world of balls, civil servants, marital infidelities, and desperate revolutionary fervor. With great skill Bely orchestrates a kind of symphonic poem of the metropolis in which something like Edgar Allan Poe's "Masque of the Red

Death" acts itself out anew, with its focal point in the red domino (is it Nikolai's?) that marks out the subversive figure who symbolically inaugurates the apocalyptic violence and chaos of the years that were to follow. The latter half of the narrative is organized around the suspense created by the "sardine tin" (the bomb which takes a hundred and fifty pages to blow up in Apollon Apollonovich's study). Madness and childish/childhood memories mingle in Nikolai's mind:

> He awoke from his dream. He understood: his head was lying on the sardine tin.
> A dreadful dream. But what was it? He could not recollect. His childhood nightmares had returned: Pepp Peppovich Pepp, swelling from the little blob, was in the sardine tin—Pepp Peppovich Pepp is a Party bomb, chirring inaudibly; Pepp Peppovich Pepp will expand and expand. And Pepp Peppovich Pepp will burst! (*Petersburg* 168)

The texture and structure of Bulgakov's extraordinary *The Master and Margarita* (1938) are very unlike those of Bely's novel. For one thing, it was published much later than the heyday of modernism, and contains elements of political satire that place it firmly in the period following modernism. It is more like Huxley than like Joyce. Nevertheless, it adopts a Dostoyevskyan multiple narrative, splicing together in an open-ended way a religious story based on Scripture, and attributed to its hero "The Master," with powerful components of fantasy and surreal improvisations, and its radical experimentalism is modernist. Bulgakov is the heir to such writers as Bely and Pilnyak (whose *The Naked Year* is a sort of cubist deconstruction of the immediately postrevolutionary period), and his remarkable power of survival in an increasingly forbidding political culture testifies to his deep understanding of the historical moment to which his novel *really* belongs, the 1920s rather than the 1930s.

The events of *The Master and Margarita* weave together parallel stories involving Christ, the Devil, the Master, and the poet Ivan Bezdomny, all inhabiting worlds which are marginally compatible and interrelated, but radically dissimilar. Into the comfortable but corrupt world of Moscow men of letters comes a demonic presence masquerading as con man and conjurer, accompanied by his familiars. His intervention precipitates a string of bizarre events which land Bezdomny in a mental hospital where the boundaries of fantasy and reality are tested (foreshadowing ominously the abuse of psychiatric medicine in the USSR). His public performances probe the validity of the economic reforms of the 1920s (the so-called New Economic Policy) and highlight the black-marketeering and speculation which turned this era of "liberalization" into something peculiarly false and unreal (as Pasternak noted) in the history of the Soviet state. In a sense, this topic (the illusory "freedom" based upon an equally illusory flow of capital, foregrounded in Woland's conjuring tricks) serves as a controlling metaphor for the whole fantasy narrative in which the unhappy wife Margarita acquires a new identity as the naked demonic accomplice of "the Master," who is the author of the Christ-narrative embedded in a tale of belief and disbelief encompassing a series of time-loops (under the Devil's control) in which characters with the unlikely (musical) names of Berlioz, Rimsky, and Stravinsky are tossed about in a Witches' Sabbath (or carnival) of madness, degradation, and death. Ivan is left at the end sadder and wiser as a consequence of his "lunacy;" maybe it was all a dream, but there is no way of resolving the question of how reality and fantasy accommodate each other, at least not in Russia. Bulgakov's career, under the strange protection of Stalin (like Pasternak's), may

serve to conclude this overview of Russian modernism. All his work continues to engross readers, but for many, *The Master and Margarita* has a special status as a wayward yet terribly focused masterpiece which somehow managed to combine modernity with some very traditional Russian preoccupations, and gave voice to an era which might easily have crushed it (and its author) mercilessly.

The legacy of Russian modernism is huge, as I have tried to suggest. With the end of Soviet power, reputations have been overturned (though the attempts to dislodge such giants of socialist art as Eisenstein and Mayakovsky have been very inconclusive). Maxim Gorky is definitely "out" (despite his very considerable talent), because he can be shown to have been instrumental in engineering the downfall of writers he did not approve of. The institutional figure of Gorky may be said to have been replaced by the much more contentious Andrey Platonov (1899–1951), whose work takes on the question of the proletariat's historical role, and the ultimate significance of the Revolution, in quite different terms, a fusion of satire (of Soviet bureaucracy), a sort of mystical populism, with curious assimilations of the spoken idiom, and (to borrow some phrases from L. A. Shubin in Surkov's encyclopedia) "a sort of thinking aloud, when thought is only just being born, rousing itself, and accommodating itself to reality" (Surkov, vol. 5: 790). Equally interesting is the quasi-documentary element in Platonov's work, which often spoke out so freely and frankly that the writer created political difficulties for himself (to avoid which he sometimes adopted pseudonyms). But if the "socialist realist" novelists and those akin to them are now disparaged, the line of Mayakovsky (passing through Yevtushenko and others), which means a public poetic voice, has not disappeared.

The rewriting of Russian cultural history has of course made room for those great emigrés in all the arts whose contribution was enormous, but was only grudgingly recognized, if at all, in their homeland. Foremost among these are perhaps **Igor Stravinsky,** whose ballet scores, especially *The Rite of Spring,* may be said to have taken the crucial step beyond Skryabin's mysticism and established Russian modernism in music as a global presence. Vladimir Nabokov, who in some important respects resembles him, while undergoing some curious reappraisals in the West, is now an established classic in Russia. Moscow audiences are also discovering, with some surprise, how well Nabokov's novels lend themselves to the stage (vivid dramatizations of *Lolita* and *Laughter in the Dark,* for example, have recently been performed at Moscow's Sphere theater). The Soviet years, during which modernism waned as it did everywhere else, nevertheless kept alive the heritage of such writers as Pasternak and Mayakovsky in a very public way (Pasternak via the *cause celebre* of his reviled novel, and Mayakovsky as the instigator of a school of poetry which managed to persuade the world that it was typically Russian). And the peculiar isolation and constraints imposed on Russian culture in this period bore a kind of fruit in the seriousness with which the literature of the modernist period was read—in tiny editions which appeared all too rarely (sometimes available only for hard currency, and passed around avidly). The formalist heritage in literary theory engendered not only the much-admired (and much-misunderstood) Bakhtin, but also the Tartu school of semiotics. At the beginning of the twenty-first century, a vigorous revaluation of some of the so called forbidden classics of philosophy and literary interpretation (I think particularly of Shestov and Rozanov) is taking place, showing clearly how significant they were in carrying what one might call "the Dostoyevsky tradition" forward into French and German literature, and thence onward into the powerful existential tradition: the revised interest in Kierkegaard (for example) undoubtedly owes a great deal to Western readings of Bakhtin.

George Hyde

Selected Bibliography

Bakhtin, Mikhail. *Problemy Tvorchestva Dostoevskogo* (Leningrad 1929). Tr. as *Problems of Dostoevsky's Poetics.* Manchester: Manchester UP 1984.

Baran, Henryk. *Poetika Russkoi Literatury Nachala XX Veka.* Moscow: Progress Publishers 1993. (Authorized translation from English.)

Bely, Andrei. *Petersburg.* (1918). Tr. Robert A. Maguire and John E. Malmstead. Hassocks: Harvester Press, 1979.

Ehrlich, Victor. *Russian Formalism: History, Doctrine.* 'S-Gravenhage: Mouton and Co., 1955.

Eikhenbaum, Boris. "The Structure of Gogol's 'The Overcoat'"(1918). *Russian Review* 22 (1963): 377–399.

Eisenstein, Sergey. *The Film Sense.* London: Faber and Faber, 1963.

Ellmann, R., and D. Feidelson, eds. *The Modern Tradition.* Oxford, Oxford UP 1964.

Georgiyeva, Tatyana. *Russkaya Kultura: Istoriya i Sovremennost'.* (*Russian Culture: History and the Present*). Moscow: Yurait, 1999.

Hyde, G. M., *Vladimir Nabokov: America's Russian Novelist.* London: Marion Boyars 1976.

Jones, M., and R. Miller. *The Classic Russian Novel.* Cambridge: C.U.P. 1998.

Kenner, Hugh. *James Joyce.* Oxford: Oxford UP, 1965.

Khardziev, Nikolai. *Stat'i ob Avangardie.* Moscow: RA, 1997.

Lemon, L., and Reis, M. *Russian Formalist Criticism: Four Essays.* Lincoln: U of Nebraska P, 1965.

Markov, Vladimir, and Merrill Sparks, eds. *Contemporary Russian Poetry.* London: MacGibbon and Kee, 1966

Matejka, L., and K. Pomorska. *Readings in Russian Poetics.* Cambridge, Mass: MIT Press.

Mayakovsky, Vladimir. *Pro Eto.* Moscow/Petrograd, Gosudarstvennoe Izdatelstvo 1923. (A masterpiece which has never found the right English translator, though it may be read in Herbert Marshall's version: London: Dobson, 1965.)

———. *How Are Verses Made?* (1926) Tr. G. M. Hyde. Bedminster: The Bristol Classical Press, 1990.

———. *Wi the haill voice: 25 poems by Vladimir Mayakovsky translated into Scots by Edwin Morgan.* Oxford: Carcanet Press, 1972.

Murry, J. M. *Dostoevsky.* London: Cape, 1916.

Nabokov, V. V. *Gogol.* Norfolk, Conn.: New Directions, 1944.

———. *Strong Opinions* New York: McGraw-Hill 1973.

Obolensky, Dimitry, ed and tr. *The Penguin Book of Russian Verse.* Harmondsworth: Penguin, 1962.

Poggioli, Renato. *The Poets of Russia.* Cambridge, Mass: Harvard UP, 1960.

Schmidt, Paul. *Velimir Khlebnikov, the King of Time.* Cambridge, Mass: Harvard UP, 1985.

Stephens, James. *Foreword* to V. V. Rozanov, *Fallen Leaves,* tr. S. S. Koteliansky. London: The Mandrake Press, 1929.

Surkov, A. A. et al., *Kratkaya Literaturnaya Entsiklopedia.* Moscow, Izdatel'stvo Sovetskaya Entsiklopedia, 1967.

Woolf, Virginia. "Modern Fiction" (1919). *The Common Reader* series one. London: The Hogarth Press, 1925.

Yakimovich, A. *Magicheskaya Vselennaya (Magical Universe).* Moscow: Galart 1995.

S

Scandinavia

The breakthrough of modernism in the Scandinavian countries generally occurred later than in the Anglo-American world and was not without important links to Anglo-American and other modernist predecessors and movements on the international scene.

The first Swedish writer who consciously linked himself with international modernist movements was Pär Lagerkvist. In 1913 he formulated his aesthetic program in *Ordkonst och bildkonst* (*Word Art and Pictorial Art*) referring to **cubism** and **expressionism.** His most significant early work is the poetry collection *Ångest* (1916, *Anguish*), in which a new expressionist imagery breaks forth. But it was in the Swedish-speaking part of Finland that lyrical modernism had its stronghold and most prominent advocates in the twenties. **Edith Södergran**'s work had an enormous influence on poetic modernism in Swedish literature. Her poetry ranges from triumphant **expressionism,** first formulated in *Septemberlyran* (1918, *September Lyre*), to cosmic mysticism in a highly charged and intense imagery. Her five collections of verse now stand out as modernist cornerstones. Södergran's Fenno-Swedish contemporary Elmer Diktonius also voiced expressionist views of life in his poetry, often in a concrete, dense and fragmented imagery. Diktonius' aesthetics also connects with Anglo-American **imagism.** In

1924 he published eight poems by **Ezra Pound** in translation. Central figures in this pioneering Fenno-Swedish movement are also the modernist poets Gunnar Björling and Rabbe Enckell. The Swedish poet Birger Sjöberg must be considered one of the most original and important renewers of poetic language in this context. With *Kriser och kransar* (1926, *Crises and Wreaths*) he creates a new, concrete and complex metaphorical language of immense importance for the further development of lyrical modernism in Sweden. At the beginning of the 1930's several new modernistic poets break through. First and foremost was Artur Lundkvist, a central figure in the group of poets, The Young Five, that emerged around 1930. From then on Lundkvist came to be a central force in Swedish modernism for almost half a century. In his own early poetry he related to international modernism, which he also introduced in several essay collections. Of chief importance for the later development of Swedish modernism is *Ikarus' flykt* (1939, *The Flight of Icarus*) in which Lundkvist introduces, among others, **Joyce, Eliot, Faulkner,** as well as French **surrealism.** In 1932 **Gunnar Ekelöf** made his debut with the poetry collection *sent på jorden* (*Late Arrival on Earth*), for its time a sensational modernist work with its shockingly bold imagery, now clearly one of the most important achievements in the history of Swedish modernism. The year 1932 also saw the

Swedish translation by Erik Mesterton and Karin Boye of Eliot's "Det öde landet" (*The Waste Land*), which proved to be of great significance for the general breakthrough of Swedish lyrical modernism in the 1940s. Furthermore this breakthrough was made possible by a new generation of literary critics strongly supportive of the modernist innovations in poetry. The leading figures of the forties generation are the poets and critics **Erik Lindegren** and Karl Vennberg. Lindegren in *mannen utan väg* (1942, Eng. tr. *The Man Without a Way,* 1969) created a modernist milestone which, in a formally disrupted language, epitomized much of the ideological despair and pessimism of the forties period. Vennberg's skeptical and analytical poetry was characteristically expressed in the collections *Halmfackla* (1944, *Straw Torch*) and *Tideräkning* (1945, *Chronology*). A poet of international stature writing in the central modernist tradition of Eliot and Pound is **Tomas Tranströmer,** who even in his first collection *17 dikter* (1954, *17 Poems*) displayed his highly concentrated and metaphorical language. Modernistic means of expression have gradually become more diversified and specialized, exemplified during the 1950s and 60s on the one hand by an experimental *concrete* poetry and on the other by a striving towards a more directly communicative *new simplicity.* The development of modernism in prose was slower and not as radical as in the lyrical genre. During the 1920s and 30s the novel was, with few exceptions, dominated by the conventional realistic tradition. During the 1940s a bolder modernist renewal of the literary form can be noticed. Eyvind Johnson could be characterized as a moderate modernist forerunner, and in the early novel *Kommentar till ett stjärnfall* (1929, *Commentary to a Falling Star*) he introduced Joyce's technique of **interior monologue.** Tage Aurell's short stories from the 1930s and 40s make use of a very original and extremely compressed narrative technique. During the 1940s leading novelists Lars Ahlin and Stig Dagerman both indulged in modernist experiments in form and style. Ahlin's boldest was the novel *Om* (1946, *If*), expressing his highly personal aesthetics of communication, and in Dagerman's *De dömdas ö* (1946, *Island of the Doomed*) one meets with a style verging on modernist prose poetry. Gösta Oswald's novel *En privatmans vedermödor* (1949, *A Private Individual's Hardships*) is an exclusively modernistic experiment striving to break up conventional genres and pointing towards a new form of prose. The modernist generation of the 1940s paved the way for prose writers of the coming decades, who could follow in their paths, developing and refining, new modernist techniques, as in the experimental prose of the 1960s, represented, for example, by the writings of Torsten Ekbom.

In Norway, modernism did not break through until after the Second World War. In the interwar period, Norwegian literature is to a large extent characterized by traditional and conventional means of expression, and there is no radical or general renewal of literary form. International modernist movements such as expressionism, at this time well known in the neighboring Nordic countries, had little or no impact on Norwegian literature. Part of the reason for the relatively slow development of modernism in Norway may be the strong public position of an older and formally more traditional generation of poets in the 1930s. However, there are individual modernist precursors even in the 1930s, and in the writings of such poets as Claes Gill, Rolf Jacobsen, and Emil Boyson modernistic modes of expression can be traced. The year 1949 has been hailed as the symbolic starting-point for a broad and general modernist breakthrough. This year saw the publication of Gunnar Reiss-Andersen's poetry collection *Prinsen av Isola og andre dikt* (*The Prince of Isola and Other Poems*) and of Paal Brekke's *Skyggefektning* (*Shadow Fencing*), both making use of modernist techniques. In 1949 Brekke also published his translation of Eliot's seminal modernist poem *Det golde landet* (*The Waste Land*), and Norwegian poetry now started to employ radicalized modernistic techniques inspired by Eliot's aesthetics. During the first years after the war and into the 1950s Norwegian prose was dominated by a strong tradition of psychological **realism.** One notable exception is Brekke's novel *Aldrende Orfeus* (1951, *Aging Orpheus*) where one finds a style and form reminiscent of Joyce's *Ulysses*. In the 1960s members of the influential literary group *Profil,* such as the novelists and short-story writers Dag Solstad and Espen Haavardsholm, argued against the psychlogical-realistic novels pleading for modernist experiment and a renewal of literary form.

As in Norway, a general breakthrough of modernism in Denmark does not commence until the end of the 1940s. But early signs of an influence from international modernism in the writings of individual precursors are perhaps more notable in Danish letters. For example expressionistic echoes can be heard in Emil Bønnelycke's early poetry from the century's second decade. An important pre-war modernist forerunner is Gustaf Munch-Petersen, fully accepted only by the modernists of the 1940s. In his poetry of the 1930s he was strongly influenced by French surrealism, and in *19 Digte* (*19 Poems*) from 1937 one finds the earliest influence in Danish poetry of an imagist technique in the manner of Pound. Munch-Petersen also displays affinities with the Fenno-Swedish modernists, notably Elmer Diktonius and Edith Södergran. This modernist prewar renewal of literary form mainly concerns the lyrical genre, whereas the corresponding development in prose comes later and extends over a longer period of time, though Tom Kristensen's novel *Hærværk* (1930,

Havoc) must be mentioned as one early exception where the formal and stylistic similarities with Joyce's *Ulysses* are apparent. A broad and general modernist breakthrough gradually sets in during the 1950s when a new modernist generation gathered round the periodical *Heretica* (1948–53), also introducing international modernism: Sartre, **Kafka,** Eliot. In 1948 Eliot's *Ødemarken* (*The Waste Land*) came out in a Danish translation by Tom Kristensen. *Heretica's* first two editors Thorkild Bjørnvig and Ole Wivel in various ways in their own writings can be seen as representatives of the Danish modernist breakthrough.

Mats Jansson

Selected Bibliography

Aadland, Erling. "Forundring. Trofasthet." *Poetisk tenkning i Rolf Jacobsens lyrikk.* Oslo: Gyldendal, 1996.

Algulin, Ingmar. *Den orfiska reträtten. Studier i svensk 40-talslyrik och dess litterära bakgrund.* Stockholm: Almqvist & Wiksell International, 1977.

Arnald, Jan. *Genrernas tyranni. Den genreöverskridande linjen i Artur Lundkvists författarskap.* Stockholm: Aiolos, 1995.

Beyer, Edvard. " '-et dikt mot verden'. Temaer og faser i Paal Brekkes lyrik." In Beyer's *Forskning og formidling.* Oslo: Aschehough, 1990, pp. 160–181.

Bredsdorff, E., et al. *Introduction to Scandinavian Literature.* Cambridge: CUP, 1951.

Brostrøm, Torben. *Modernisme før og nu.* København: Gyldendal, 1983.

Espmark, Kjell. *Själen i bild. En huvudlinje i modern svensk poesi.* Stockholm: Norstedts, 1977.

———. Livsdyrkaren Artur Lundkvist. *Studier i hans lyrik till och med Vit man.* Stockholm: Bonniers, 1964.

———. Harry Martinson erövrar sitt språk. *En studie i hans lyriska metod 1927–1934.* Stockholm: Bonniers, 1970.

Jansson, Mats. Tradition och förnyelse. *Den svenska introduktionen av T. S. Eliot.* Stockholm/Skåne: Symposion, 1991.

———. Kritisk tidsspegel. *Studier i 1940-talets svenska litteraturkritik.* Stockholm/Stehag: Symposion, 1998.

Lundberg, Johan. Den andra enkelheten. *Studier i Harry Martinsons lyrik 1935–45.* Uppsala: Vekerum förlag, 1992.

Rossel, Sven H, ed. *A History of Scandinavian Literatures.* 3 vols. Lincoln and London: U of Nebraska P, 1992–96.

Vosmar, Jørn, ed. *Modernismen i dansk litteratur.* København: Fremad, 1967.

Schnitzler, Arthur (1862–1931)

Schnitzler was born in Vienna, a city he often used as the setting for his plays and prose works. He combines his psychological studies with a form of **realism,** placing members of different social classes in erotic encounters with each other. His early career in psychopathology, which included the study of **Freud**'s works, prepared him for his primary concerns of characters' psychology. Freud in turn admired the way Schnitzler's plays encourage the audience to analyze the characters' erotic crises as though they had been triggered by an earlier trauma; he even felt that Schnitzler had anticipated his theories in *Der Sohn* (1982, *The Son*), in which a character's hysteria has been induced by infantile trauma.

In his first successful play, *Anatol* (1893), Schnitzler portrays his hero's picaresque series of sexual adventures. Anatol is split between his attitude to women as objects of sexual pleasure, and his encounters with them as unrepeatable, transcendental experiences. He has a collection of boxes containing souvenirs of his many affairs, treasuring each of them; he is devastated on learning that a woman, who is immortalized by one of his boxes, has since married and forgotten their encounter.

In the more socially complex *Liebelei* (1896, *Love Games*), an affluent gentleman, Fritz, dies in a duel against the husband of his lover. He spends the previous evening with his other lover Christine, whose lower social status has discouraged him from committing himself to her. On learning that Fritz has died for another woman, Christine is devastated, and her love for him is upheld as the play's moral center.

Schnitzler caused riots of protest in 1920 during the premiere of *Reigen* (1903, *Merry-Go-Round*), a cycle of ten dialogues between lovers, linked by the theme of betrayal. It begins with a prostitute and a soldier, and ends with a count and the same prostitute. It is poised on the irony of its whole structure revealing the leveling effect of sexuality, while each character treats the other according to his or her social position.

Schnitzler's later achievements are represented in his novels and shorter novellas. The novel *Der Weg ins Freie* (1908, *The Road to the Open*) treats the problem of Jewish identity in Vienna, with the failed relationship between Georg von Wergenthin and his non-Jewish lover Anna Rosner. Schnitzler's later novella *Flucht in die Finsternis* (1931, *Flight into Darkness*), is a study of the destructive consequences of a character's persecution mania.

Carl Krockel

Selected Bibliography

Schnitzler's works are available in S. Fischer Verlag, Frankfurt am Main, and Methuen, London.

Allen, Richard H. *An Annotated Arthur Schnitzler Bibliography.* Chapel Hill: University of North Carolina Press, 1966.

Swales, Martin. *Arthur Schnitzler: A Critical Study.* Oxford: Oxford UP, 1971.

Thompson, Bruce. *Schnitzler's Vienna: Image of a Society.* New York: Routledge, 1990.

Schwitters, Kurt (1887–1948)

Schwitters' career centered in Hanover, where he was born, until his exile from Nazi **Germany** in 1937, later settling in Britain. His poetry mediates between the contradictory trends of **expressionism,** which was oriented to the individual subject, and **dada,** which struck outwards to the social and political realms.

His early poetry is suffused with the expressionist desire to regain contact with nature and feeling, yet also includes elements foreign to it. For example the viscerally expressive use of alliteration in "Quakes one within / Quivers one" in the poem "Nachte" (1918, "Nights"), is juxtaposed with playful lines such as "Sleekly stabs fish in the whip-air" which contribute to the poem's **rhythm,** not to its meaning. After the 1918 revolution Schwitters felt that "Everything had broken down . . . new things had to be made from fragments;" he began to construct collages and assemblages from refuse and found materials. In his poem "An Anna Blume" (1919, "Eve Blossom"), his interruptions are borrowed from newspaper cuttings and scraps of conversation, combining romantic proclamations with football chants—"E easy, V victory, E easy." Yet this poem was rejected by dadaists such as Huelsenbeck for a lack of aggression and deflating irony against its romantic sentiments. Excluded from the Berlin Dada Fair in June 1920, Schwitters was later joined by Tristan Tzara, Hans Arp, and Theo van Doesburg in the "Manifest Proletkunst" which rejected politicized art.

Schwitters attempted to combine his poetry with other arts, for the ultimate "union of art and non-art," which stresses the disruptive incongruity between its heterogeneous elements. His 1920s picture poems included "Cigarren" ("Cigars") which resembles a long stream of smoke. His recitals became a form of musical concert, in which he spoke his sound poems to the melodies of Chopin. Yet in some of these works the tension between subject and form is lost, as they are reduced to mere formalist pattern-making. In his greatest poem though, the "Ursonate" ("Primal Sonata"), he created a musical structure out of primitive sounds; the opening, explosive "Fümms bö wö tää zää Uu" and the lyrical "Jüü-Kaa" are repeated

and varied within a sophisticated, modern architectural whole.

Carl Krockel

Selected Bibliography
Schwitters' works are available in DuMont Buchverlag, Cologne, and Penguin, London.

Elderfield, John. *Kurt Schwitters.* London: Thames and Hudson, 1985.

Steinitz, Kate Trauman. *Kurt Schwitters: A Portrait from Life.* Berkeley: University of California Press, 1968.

Scotland

The impact of modernism in Scotland is principally associated with the Scottish Renaissance Movement, the term usually applied to the literary and cultural regeneration of Scotland initiated by **Hugh MacDiarmid** (C. M. Grieve) in the 1920s. More precisely, the term might be located in what happened between the first appearance of MacDiarmid's lyric poetry in Scots in 1922 and the publication of a series of highly controversial and iconoclastic essays by C. M. Grieve, "Contemporary Scottish Studies," in *The Scottish Educational Journal* from 1925–1927. C. M. Grieve/Hugh MacDiarmid, as poet, critic, and cultural revolutionary, effected an assault upon the intellectual and emotional conventions of his era.

On December 4, 1925, Grieve wrote: "A certain type of critic is apt to say that the movement so far has consisted only of propaganda—only 'of the posters'—that the actual work has still to be done. This is a mistake. The Scottish Renaissance has taken place. The fruits will appear in due course. Earlier or later—it does not alter the fact. For the Scottish Renaissance has been a propaganda of ideas and their enunciation has been all that was necessary." The "ideas" were essentially to end the reliance upon sentimental, stereotypical representations of Scotland that had become common through the late nineteenth century and to bring modern Scottish culture into alignment with the most advanced European thought and avant-garde artistic techniques. MacDiarmid attacked and destroyed as many existing preconceptions responsible for the status quo as he could, in religious, political, and social terms and on every other front.

He edited three anthologies of new **Scottish poetry,** *Northern Numbers,* in which work by the old guard was seen alongside that of new poets. For example, "Isle of My Heart" by Donald A. Mackenzie is familiar, sentimentally nostalgic for "the dear days that were," in the "sweet" Hebrides. By contrast, John Ferguson's sonnets about unemployed chorus-girls and music-hall comedians, bank accountants, and the inmates of a sanatorium, are shocking; Roderick Watson Kerr (known as "the Scottish Siegfried Sassoon"), wrote bitterly of prostitution, urban squalor, and Christian Mission halls for the poor. His proto-feminist verse is reflected in the editorial policy of the third and most radical of the anthologies. Of twenty contributors, ten are women. No editor of Scottish poetry before or since has done so much to insist that the voices of women be heard to represent the nation.

MacDiarmid/Grieve also included theater and fiction in his vision of a "modernist" Scotland. Experimental theater movements, working-class theater, the Scottish National Players (in the 1920s) and Ewan MacColl and Joan Littlewood's Theatre Workshop (in the 1940s) were encouraged, alongside radical journalism and avant-garde novels such as the early work of **Neil Gunn** and the later achievement of **Lewis Grassic Gibbon.** The whole matter of Scotland's linguistic diversity required reconsideration; cultural criticism needed to adapt to modernist aesthetics. In 1926, MacDiarmid recognized *Ulysses* and *The Waste Land* as the two works which will "survive as the representative expressions of early twentieth century life and thought in the English language." Few of his con-

temporaries were as acute in their literary perceptions.

The Scottish Renaissance went further. The artist William Johnstone (1897–1981) referred in his autobiography *Points in Time* (London: Hutchinson, 1980) to the composer F. G. Scott (1880–1958), MacDiarmid, and himself as the "Three Borderers" setting out heroically, like the three musketeers, to modernize Scottish culture. Scott, Johnstone wrote, became greatly excited by the prospect of "a Scottish Renaissance of the arts" and envisaged the three friends at the core of it, "all having a revolutionary point of view," raising the standard of the arts "right from the gutter into something that would be really important." Johnstone pointed out that Scott's song-settings of MacDiarmid's poems "broke entirely new ground . . . It was the birth of a twentieth-century Scottish Renaissance." No British composer of the time is closer to Schoenberg than Scott. The lasting impact of modernism upon composers such as Ronald Center (1913–1973) and Ronald Stevenson (b. 1928) and the painters James Cowie (1886–1956), William Crozier (1897–1930), and William McCance (1894–1970) deserves further study also. Individual artists established their own dynamic after the impact of modernism but in many cases the renewed idea of national potential charged their creativity, so they sought to establish a common ground of social identity along with the virtue of unsentimental "impersonality."

Crucial in the development of the movement was the role played by newspapers and little magazines: *The Scottish Chapbook* (1922–23), *The Scottish Nation* (1923), *The Northern Review* (1924), *The Pictish Review* (1927–28), *Scots Independent* (1927–33), *The Scots Observer* (1927–34), *The Modern Scot* (1931–34), and *The Free Man* (1932–35). Some Scottish writers also contributed to the London-based journals like *The New Age* and *New Britain* and to more widely-distributed national press in Scotland. (Full details and examples of MacDiarmid's contributions to these periodicals may be found in Hugh MacDiarmid, *The Raucle Tongue: Hitherto Uncollected Prose,* Manchester: Carcanet, 1996–98.)

In Scotland, the most important long-term effect of this effort towards revitalization has been the general overhaul of the nation's various and complex cultural identity, with new histories of Scottish literature, art, music and economic and social development offering new ways of comprehensively understanding a national culture, before, through, and after its participation in the rise and fall of the British Empire. Later scholarly excavations like William Donaldson's discovery of popular prose fiction in Victorian newspapers also coincided with new creative energies, prodigious, innovative, and internationally acclaimed.

Alan Riach

Selected Bibliography

Lindsay, Maurice. *Francis George Scott and the Scottish Renaissance.* Edinburgh: Paul Harris, 1980.

MacMillan, Duncan. *Scottish Art 1460–1990.* Edinburgh: Mainstream, 1990.

Purser, John. *Scotland's Music: A History . . .* Edinburgh: Mainstream, 1992.

Walker, Marshall. *Scottish Literature Since 1707.* Harlow: Longman, 1996.

Scottish Poetry 1922–1999

The impact of modernism's aesthetic and political aspects affected the arts in **Scotland** generally through the work of **Hugh MacDiarmid** and his associates in the "propaganda of ideas" generated in the 1920s under the banner of the Scottish Renaissance. Poetry led the movement in Scotland but it reached into all forms of cultural expression, with the composer F. G. Scott, the painter William Johnstone, the historian G. P. Insh, and various edu-cationalists, dramatists, and others. In later Scottish poetry (more, perhaps, than in prose fiction or drama) written during MacDiarmid's lifetime and sometimes with his direct encouragement, the force of modernism continued to be felt. (See entry on **Scotland.**)

Most of the Scots poets who began writing seriously during and after World War II remained cautious about both Mac-Diarmid's extremism and the endless possibilities entertained by **postmodernism**'s refusal of closure, which effectively endorsed statelessness. A small group may be named as representative. The long-term strategies of modernism evident in their work might best be understood not as belatedness but as a considered development and application of the radical possibilities modernism introduced.

The breakthrough in modern Gaelic poetry effected by Sorley Maclean (1911–1996) in his first book *Dain do Eimhir* (1943) brought a profound knowledge of the traditions of Gaelic poetry, song, and history together with a sensibility marinaded in Grierson's metaphysical poets, read alongside **Yeats** and **Eliot.** From these roots, Maclean developed a poetry dealing directly with war, love, the nuclear threat, and the disassociated sensibility of the later twentieth century, in lyrical, muscular, anxious, and passionate verse of enormous dignity and attractiveness.

Another Gaelic speaker whose work in prose fiction, radio drama, and above all, poetry, reflects an increasingly confident negotiation between the urgencies of place and dislocation, Iain Crichton Smith (1928–98) brought a kindly and quizzical humor to bear on matters of grief and despair. "The White Air of March" is a late Gaelic version of *The Waste Land* tainted with humor, uncertainly balanced between the extremes of anguish and absurdity.

The urbane humor and wit of Robert Garioch (1909–81) belies the darker and austere war poet of "The Wire" and "The Muir" while his translations from the sonnets of the Roman Giuseppe Belli, are a perfect fit for the human scale of his native Edinburgh, with its civic pretensions, poverty, and pain. The balance in the poetry of Norman MacCaig (1910–96), between Edinburgh and Highland landscapes, between celebration and mourning, between simple assertion and subtle inquiry, rejects the authority of pronouncement for a world of continual qualification. While a schoolmaster looks out a window through eyes that read Latin and Greek, a boat is rounding the point in Gaelic.

The catholic, liturgical, heavily freighted verse of George Mackay Brown (1921–96) has its own affinities with that of Eliot and **Auden,** and most evidently that of Mackay Brown's mentor, Edwin Muir (1887–1959). Muir's poetry itself is distinctive, fresh, and clearly within the modernist spirit. It appealed to T. S. Eliot directly, who published it at Faber and Faber and edited and introduced a selection of it. Eliot also published W. S. Graham (1918–86), who evolved a slow, fluent, intense, lyrically meditative poetry in English.

During World War II, Eliot seems to have come close to giving the Faber imprimatur to MacDiarmid's epic *In Memoriam James Joyce.* Eliot described it as "a very fine monument to Joyce . . . there is a great deal in it that has my sympathy as well as my admiration"—but he excused himself from taking it on with reference to wartime paper shortage. In Scots, Sydney Goodsir Smith (1915–75) effectively invented a loose, rambling, free-verse idiom for his larger-than-life Falstaffian persona, most eloquently in the love poems of *Under the Eildon Tree.* In tighter form, he also translated Alexander Blok's "The Twelve" to brilliant effect.

The linguistic versatility, imagistic precision and prosodic accomplishment of these poets and others suggest a long wave of influence reaching from the modern movement through and alongside MacDiarmid, into the 1960s. Perhaps this is most clearly seen in Goodsir Smith's neo-modernist (still largely impenetrably coded) prose masterpiece of farraginous excess, *Carotid Cornucopius* (1964) (which, MacDiarmid claimed wildly, did for Edinburgh what **Ulysses** did for Dublin).

However, the manifold legacy of modernism in Scottish poetry is most fully encountered in the work of **Edwin Morgan** (b.1920) and the poets who have grown up in the company of his multi-faceted and encouraging example, including Veronica Forrest-Thomson, Liz Lochhead, Carol Ann Duffy, Jackie Kay, Richard Price, Peter McCarey, John Burnside, and others.

Alan Riach

Selected Bibliography
O'Rourke, Daniel, ed. *Dream State: The New Scottish Poets.* Edinburgh: Polygon, 1994.

Shakespeare 1890–1940

Shakespeare criticism in the period is marked by the self-conscious spirit of innovation we associate with modernism in general. In Shakespeare studies, the conflict between moderns and the nineteenth-century tradition centers on the whole conception of dramatic character. Just as modernist fiction challenges the Victorian and Edwardian conventions of characterization, so some Shakespearean critics take issue with the psychologizing of characters that dominates nineteenth-century commentary on Shakespeare's plays.

The character-centered approach to Shakespeare begins in the eighteenth century but comes of age in the nineteenth, fuelled by the romantic interest in the human personality and assisted by the ascendancy of the realist novel and the naturalistic stage. Coleridge, for example, in his Shakespearean lectures of 1811–12, announces the new primacy of character as he praises the subtle veracity with which the dramatist represents "all the minutiae of the human heart" (Foakes 78). He also insists that the characters are true to the fundamental laws of human nature and therefore have a universality that renders Shakespeare the poet of all ages. Coleridge argues that this timeless fidelity to nature is made possible because Shakespeare reproduces or exaggerates facets of his own personality in his creations as well as entering empathetically into characters of all kinds.

Coleridge's view is echoed in a number of key nineteenth-century studies. William Hazlitt, in *Characters of Shakespear's Plays* (1817) declares that Shakespeare creates "living men and women . . . who speak and act from real feelings" (Hazlitt 74). Edward Dowden's influential study, *Shakspere: A Critical Study of His Mind and Art* (1875), though recognizing the part played by source material and convention, and seeing the plays as representing Shakespeare's struggle for self-mastery, nonetheless assumes the psychological subtlety and consistency of the characterization. Important commentaries on the female characters make the same assumptions. Anna Jameson's *Shakespeare's Heroines* (1832) engages in close scrutiny of the characters' feelings; while Helena Faucit's *On Some of Shakespeare's Female Characters* (1885) offers observations on character which stem from her performances as a Shakespearean actress in the 1830s and 1840s. Faucit tends to apply an inventive overlay to the text, elaborating the characters' feelings like an actress working her way into a role. Even more adventurous excursions are made by Mary Cowden Clarke in *The Girlhood of Shakespeare's Heroines* (1850–52). Her account of the putative childhoods of the characters, inventing data not supplied by Shakespeare himself, represents an extreme form of character-criticism cut loose from the moorings of the plays.

The character-centered approach reaches its apotheosis in A. C. Bradley's monumental *Shakespearean Tragedy* (1904). Bradley's analysis of *Hamlet, Othello, King Lear* and *Macbeth,* the four principal tragedies in his view, occupies a unique place in critical history as the single most influential work in its field, and the most controversial. He famously renders the tragedies as stories of exceptional beings with one overdeveloped trait of character that colludes with circumstances to bring about the catastrophe. He emphasizes the centrality of character in the tragic process: "The dictum that, with Shakespeare, 'character is destiny' is no doubt an exaggeration . . . but it is the exaggeration of a vital truth" (Bradley 13). He also asserts the importance of self-division within the protagonists: it is in "the maturest works," he argues, "that this inward struggle is most emphasised" (Bradley 18). In the case of Macbeth, for example, Bradley describes a hero whose internal conflict between ambition and conscience is heightened by his vivid imagination. The witches provoke his ambition but do not create it, and the play insists on "the natural psychological genesis of Macbeth's crimes" (Bradley 345).

The extent to which Bradley applies a realist frame of reference to the plays is vividly illustrated by the presence of a number of "Notes" appended to the volume. In these addenda Bradley explores matters of detail that he does not consider substantial enough to have a direct bearing on his main argument. These are, on the whole, questions that might occur in the study rather than obtruding in the theater, but they are set out with a gravity that belies their peripheral status. Thus we have "Note CC. When was the murder of Duncan first plotted?" (480) and "Note DD. Did Lady Macbeth really faint?" (484). Bradley tries to answer these questions by holding a magnifying glass up to the dramatic representation; but what he unintentionally reveals is the openness of the text at certain key points, and its unresponsiveness to the realist mode of analysis. He states his conviction that Lady Macbeth's faint after the discovery of the murder is genuine and not a pretence to distract attention from her husband's suspicious response to questioning; but he also admits: "I am not aware if an actor of the part [in Shakespeare's theater] could show the audience whether it was real or pretended" (486). The discussion hints at complex issues relating to the semiotics of drama and the limits of authorial control. If the conventions of Jacobean acting were incapable of communicating Lady Macbeth's state of mind unproblematically, the result would have been an irresolvable ambiguity that compromised the unity and verisimilitude of the mimesis. Bradley evades these difficult matters by adducing the authority of the dramatist: Shakespeare knew whether he meant the faint to be real, and he might have instructed the actor. The whole discussion, however, is unsatisfactory and leaves us with a sense of the inadequacy of some of Bradley's critical apparatus.

The early twentieth century brings a reaction against character-criticism. Tolstoy is a precursor of this reaction, as he struggles to admire Shakespeare but finds it impossible to do so. His observations differ markedly from the eulogies of nineteenth-century critics: he challenges the plausibility of the characters and denies that they are individualized through language ("Shakespeare and the Drama," translated 1907). Tolstoy still judges the characterization from a realist standpoint—he is actually attacking decadence and the formalism he sees as its most dangerous literary symptom—but the mere fact that he denigrates Shakespeare's art and punctures the rhetoric of nineteenth-century criticism is historically significant. Robert Bridges (*On the Influence of the Audience on Shakespeare's Drama,*

1906) remarks on the inconsistency in the character of Macbeth, arguing that Shakespeare seems to enjoy breaching plausibility. Bridges suggests that Shakespeare makes too many concessions to Elizabethan popular taste and implies that there is a lack of discipline in his dramatic technique, declaring that he "will risk, or even sacrifice, the logical and consistent" to create surprise (Bridges 16).

Perhaps the most powerful attack on character-criticism is mounted by L. L. Schücking (*Character-Problems in Shakespeare's Plays,* translated 1922). As part of a general thesis on romantic Shakespeare criticism, Schücking sets out to define "the limits of Shakespearean realism" (Schücking 60). He argues that the search for consistency in Shakespeare's characters represents an anachronistic projection of realist expectations onto the plays. He proposes instead that Shakespeare's art combines sophisticated and primitive elements, the latter including the uncritical adoption of plot material from the sources. There are moments of psychological realism, he concedes, but no consistent attempt to harmonize character and language. In short, Schücking agrees with Ben Jonson that Shakespeare lacks art, if by art we mean "the conscious and consistent observation of certain clearly formulated rules in the treatment of reality" (202). One cardinal principle is, however, deemed by Schücking to be evident: Shakespeare never intends to be obscure, and therefore the less ingenious our exegesis, the more likely it is to be in tune with the dramatist's technique. This calls into question the nice psychological inflections that are the stock-in-trade of the character-critic, in the area of character motivation, for instance. As Schücking puts it, "We are justified, as a rule, in adding a motive only when no sense results without it" (235).

In the 1930s, the continuing devaluation of Bradley is accompanied by the growing tendency to analyze Shakespeare's plays as modernist poems, unified by patterns of imagery and symbol. G. Wilson Knight's essay "On the Principles of Shakespeare Interpretation" (1930), in a volume introduced by **T. S. Eliot,** sets out a number of propositions that subsequently prove influential. A Shakespeare play, he argues, "is set spatially as well as temporally in the mind . . . there are throughout the play a set of correspondences which relate to each other independently of the time-sequence" (Wilson Knight 3). He goes on to define thematic and poetic patterns such as the death-theme in *Hamlet* (the Ghost functioning as its poetic symbol) and the intelligence-intuition antithesis in *Troilus and Cressida.* Wilson Knight does not deny the importance of narrative in the audience's experience of a play, and indeed his background in Shakespearean acting and directing informs all his commentary, but he rejects the nineteenth-century notion of character because "it is so constantly entwined with a false and unduly ethical criticism" (9), in which the critic forensically judges the morality of stage figures by analogy with real life. In Wilson Knight's view, such criticism fails to appreciate the play as a poetic construct, "a visionary whole, close-knit in personification, atmospheric suggestion, and direct poetic-symbolism" (11).

More acerbic and polemical is L. C. Knights's celebrated attack on Bradley in *How Many Children Had Lady Macbeth?* (1933). Knights's title, suggested by F. R. Leavis, parodies Bradley's "Notes" and indicates the impatience of 1930s Cambridge criticism with the portrait-gallery view of Shakespeare. Knights argues that by treating stage figures as living beings we not only sacrifice critical objectivity but "lose the dramatic pattern and are inhibited from the full complex response which a play of Shakespeare's can evoke" (Knights 28). Knights attacks what he sees

as Bradley's false assumptions about the nature of drama. *Macbeth,* he urges, is not a set of tiresomely incomplete data on characters; instead it is "a dramatic poem" (7), which works by "calling into play, directing and integrating certain interests" (37). Significantly, Knights asserts that the play, as a construction of images and motifs, has more in common with Eliot's *The Waste Land* than with the social and psychological realism of Ibsen's *A Doll's House* (34). The reference to Eliot's text helps to contextualize Knights's attack, linking it to the contemporary attempt to see the Shakespeare play as a poem and to the broader modernist rejection of nineteenth-century critical methods.

These strictures and the change in critical fashion of which they form a part have had a far-reaching effect on Shakespeare criticism. Schücking, Wilson Knight, and Knights have provided a valuable check on the excesses of character-criticism and have discouraged the application of inappropriate criteria to Shakespeare's art. Character has come to be seen as a product of diction, imagery, genre, and structure, and criticism has been richer as a result. But it would be wrong to suppose that Bradley has been effaced by his opponents, though some critical surveys state or imply as much. The truth is more complex, as Anne Ridler, surveying the scene in 1963, points out: while it seemed in 1935 that "the aesthetic of that great critic A. C. Bradley was discredited," by the 1960s the dust had settled on the debate and it had again "become respectable to direct attention to the psychological truth of his [Shakespeare's] creations" (Ridler vii). Patrick Murray, writing in 1969, echoes Ridler's findings when he maintains that drama provides "an image of human activity," and that, while a dramatic character is clearly not synonymous with a real person, we cannot avoid using our "experience of human character" when discussing stage figures (Murray 17).

Another look at the early twentieth century reveals why character-criticism survives the apparently terminal onslaught. Several substantial studies simply carry forward the nineteenth-century method. E. K. Chambers, in *Shakespeare: A Survey* (1925) draws on Dowden and Hazlitt, seeing the characters as psychologically credible. Harley Granville-Barker's *Prefaces to Shakespeare* (five series, 1927–47) brings the perspective of the actor and producer to bear on the plays: his empathetic response to character and precise definition of mood changes reflect his keen awareness of performance. H. B. Charlton's *Shakespearian Tragedy* (1948) is the work of a self-confessed 'devout Bradleyite' (Charlton 4). Also important is the fact that Bradley's theoretical opponents find themselves at times slipping into the supposedly discredited discourse. E. E. Stoll, for instance, is usually associated with the reaction against character-criticism, but his analysis of *Romeo and Juliet* (*Shakespeare's Young Lovers*, 1937) discusses the lovers in incongruously psychological terms at times. Romeo he describes in classic nineteenth-century fashion as "a prey to his imagination," while Juliet's temperament is "simpler . . . more naive and individual . . . pervaded with her girlish playfulness" (Stoll 25, 28). The repeated intrusion into Stoll's analysis of the critical maneuvers he purports to reject suggests how deep-seated is our tendency to respond to dramatic characters as if to living beings. Any critical formula that omits this important element is likely to prove impracticable. It is interesting to note a timely acknowledgement of this by Wilson Knight, who, in 1947, declares that his earlier comments on character analysis were "never intended to limit the living human reality of Shakespeare's people" or "to repudiate the work of A. C. Bradley" (Wilson Knight v).

The reaction against character-criticism, then, has itself been moderated by the recognition that dramatic action is inevitably interpreted with some reference to actual human behavior. The debate has been well documented by Katharine Cooke (*A. C. Bradley and His Influence in Twentieth-Century Shakespeare Criticism,* 1972). What has emerged is a partial rehabilitation of Bradley that allows critics to speak of character-psychology without self-justifying preliminaries. Clearly an approach in terms of individual psychology will not be equally applicable to every kind of drama and every stage figure. Due weight having been given to dramatic form, however, it would seem that we are now free to discuss character not merely as a convenient shorthand for structural or rhetorical effects, but as an integral part of drama.

The whole debate constitutes a model of critical movement and counter-movement, including the part played by meta-critical surveys (like this one) that tend to simplify critical history and accentuate the pendulum-swings of critical fashion. The controversy is paradigmatic in another way, too. It suggests the capacity of authoritative criticism to disarm potentially radical movements by assimilating them in an attenuated form: thus character-criticism persists with some minor modifications that take account of the objections made to it. There is a much more recent parallel. John Drakakis, writing in 1985, warned that "the continuities of Shakespeare criticism and textual and historical scholarship all exert a powerful institutional brake upon any attempt to diverge from the order of concepts and methods they have sought to establish for themselves" (Drakakis 22–23). He wrote, of course, as Marxist, feminist, and poststructuralist critics challenged the traditional intepretative procedures of Shakespeare studies. Fifteen years on, it is difficult to see what the fuss was about. The Shakespeare establishment, no monolith but an evolving organism, has adapted to the new discourses, internalizing some and marginalizing others. It is business as usual.

James Cunningham

Selected Bibliography

Bradley, A. C. *Shakespearean Tragedy.* London: Macmillan, 1904.

Bridges, Robert. *On the Influence of the Audience on Shakespeare's Drama.* 1906. New York: Haskell House, 1966.

Chambers, E. K. *Shakespeare: A Survey.* London: Sidgwick and Jackson, 1925.

Charlton, H. B. *Shakespearian Tragedy.* Cambridge: CUP, 1948.

Cooke, Katharine. *A. C. Bradley and His Influence in Twentieth-Century Shakespeare Criticism.* Oxford: Clarendon Press, 1972.

Cowden Clarke, Mary. *The Girlhood of Shakespeare's Heroines.* London: J. M. Dent, 1906.

Dowden, Edward. *Shakspere: A Critical Study of His Mind and Art.* London: Henry S. King & Co., 1875.

Drakakis, John, ed. *Alternative Shakespeares.* London and New York: Methuen, 1985.

Faucit, Helena. *On Some of Shakespeare's Female Characters.* London and Edinburgh: William Blackwood and Son, 1891.

Foakes, R. A., ed. *Coleridge on Shakespeare: The Text of the Lectures of 1811–1812.* London: Routledge and Kegan Paul, 1971.

Grady, Hugh. *The Modernist Shakespeare: Critical Texts in a Material World.* Oxford: Clarendon Press, 1991.

Granville-Barker, Harley. *Prefaces to Shakespeare.* 2 vols. Princeton: Princeton UP, 1947.

Hazlitt, William. *Characters of Shakespear's Plays.* London: Everyman, 1906.

Jameson, Anna Brownell. *Shakespeare's Heroines: Characteristics of Women, Moral, Poetical and Historical.* 1832. London: George Bell & Son, 1879.

Knight, G. Wilson. *The Wheel of Fire: Interpretations of Shakespearian Tragedy.* Revised ed. London: Methuen, 1949.

Knights, L. C. *How Many Children Had Lady Macbeth?* Cambridge: The Minority Press, 1933.

Murray, Patrick. *The Shakespearian Scene: Some Twentieth-Century Perspectives.* London: Longman, 1969.

Ridler, Anne, ed. *Shakespeare Criticism 1935–1960.* London: OUP, 1970.

Schücking, L. L. *Character-Problems in Shakespeare's Plays.* 1922. Gloucester: Peter Smith, 1959.

Stoll, E. E. *Shakespeare's Young Lovers.* London: OUP, 1937.

Tolstoy, Leo. "Shakespeare and the Drama." In his*"What is Art?" and Essays on Art.* Trans. Aylmer Maude. London: World's Classics, 1930.

Shaw, George Bernard (1856–1950)

Writing in *The Dial* in 1921, **T. S. Eliot** observed: "Hardy is Victorian, Shaw is Edwardian. Shaw is, therefore, more interesting to us, for by reflecting on his mind we may form some plausible explanation . . . about what in retrospect the 'present' generation will be found to have been." Eliot's contrast is interesting: Shaw himself often pointed out that being born in Dublin in 1856, of impoverished genteel protestant stock, he, in fact, pre-dated the impact of Darwin; and, it is a critical common-place that from the 1880s to his death in 1950, in his commitment to socialism, particularly fabianism, and to often quirky social reforms—not least his famous Jager suit, and efforts to reform the English alphabet—he represented the last gasp of a kind of Victorian confidence, what he himself called "the general march of enlightenment" (see Greene). However, as Eliot suggests, it might equally be argued that Shaw anticipates a worldview and a range of literary techniques more commonly seen as modernist.

In a life which lasted nearly a century Shaw was nothing if not prolific. He wrote five largely unsuccessful novels, thirty full length plays and many shorter dramatic pieces, nine volumes of **music** criticism in addition to theater, literary and social criticism, and, most astonishingly of all, over a quarter of a million letters. He reluctantly accepted the Nobel Prize for Literature in 1925 (interestingly the prize money was used to aid the translation of Swedish literature, not least the works of Strindberg). On his death, Shaw—or at least the persona he created for himself, "G. B. S."—was arguably one of the most famous figures in the world.

In 1891 Shaw published the critical study *The Quintessence of Ibsenism.* He found in Ibsen a fellow critic of Victorian cant; but it is true to say that, as with many of his critical studies, *The Quintessence* tells us more about "G. B. S." than about his apparent subject. He writes, opposing what he called elsewhere "the sweet-shop view of theatre," of the well-made play, and the contemporary interest in **naturalism,** that dramatists should abandon the "old stage tricks" of encouraging audience identification in favor of a "forensic technique" of "disillusion and penetration;" and he wished the playwright to make "free use . . . of all the rhetorical and lyrical acts of the orator, the preacher and the rhapsodist." In these demands more than one critic has seen Shaw as "jump-starting a thrust toward modern drama" (Innes 55; see also Davis 58ff).

However, Shaw's first play *Widower's Houses,* performed in 1892 by J. T. Grein's Independent Theatre Society, which had done so much to popularize Ibsen, was subtitled a "Realistic Play." At one level it is, indeed, a social problem play about slum landlords; and it forms part of a group collected as *Plays Unpleasant* (1898) with *Mrs. Warren's Profession,* a play about prostitution and the staple Victorian figure of the fallen woman, and *The Philanderer,* a play about sexual hypocrisy. A character in *Mrs. Warren* might be said to sum up Shaw's naturalistic strain in the phrase "Life is what it is, and I am prepared to take it as it is." However, it is also arguable that Shaw is subverting the conventions he seems to employ: thus, for example, in *Widower's Houses,* in a move repeated more famously in *Pygmalion* (1916), the attack on capitalism is most powerfully made through the unrealistic, sudden, and almost pantomime transformation of the former servant Lickcheese into (a parody of) a man of property. Many critics have found in the abandonment of **realism** in these early plays, already ar-

gued for in *The Quintessence,* anticipations of Giraudoux, Anouilh, and **Brecht** (see Davis 141ff and Holroyd, vol. 2, 136).

In *Plays Unpleasant* and its companion *Plays Pleasant* (1898), including *Arms and the Man,* Shaw also initiated an interest in the play as both a material and literary product. He began a long-standing practice of providing his plays with prefaces and explanatory matter, sometimes longer than the plays themselves. Part of his motivation was commercial—novel sized books would sell at the price of novels. However, one might also argue that he was largely responsible for the more general shift into considering contemporary drama as serious literature to be read as well as simply watched for diversion.

Both the non-naturalist Shaw and the Shaw who was concerned with drama as more than "sweet-shop" can be seen in *Man and Superman* (1903). Another reworking of the courtship comedy, this can also be seen as an attack on Victorian ideas in its characterization of Ramsden, the outdated radical. It also provides evidence of Shaw's own abiding interest in technological advances with its *coup de théâtre* introduction of an automobile onto the stage. Later, through the speeches of the arms manufacturer Undershaft in *Major Barbara* (1905), he would link mechanical obsolescence with the need for moral relativism.

Man and Superman is perhaps most interesting for its use of an extended dream sequence (modeled on the Don Juan story), which Berst sees as "second cousin to Strindberg dream plays" (128); and for Shaw's discussion in his preface to the play of what, foreshadowing Bergson's *Creative Evolution* (1907), he calls the Life Force. This idea, revisited in the mammoth *Back to Methuselah* (1921)—a multi-part play about the history of mankind from Adam and Eve to "as far as thought can reach"—can be seen as a Nietzschean one in which certain individuals are agents of human improvement. It is both an attack on a kind of mechanical Darwinism, and an acceptance of constant change. Yet there is a profound uncertainty as to the point of this change: utopia is only achieved in *Methuselah* in the very distant future; and Don Juan asks "Does this colossal mechanism have no purpose?" Indeed, after the impact of **World War I,** Shaw envisages the future apocalyptically in the conclusion of *Heartbreak House* (1919).

The most striking aspect of the Don Juan dream sequence is the extent to which it is a static discussion—an often-criticized quality of Shaw's drama as a whole; yet, here, and in the "disquisitory plays" *Getting Married* (1908) and *Misalliance* (1909), in which traditional dramatic high spots are deliberately kept off stage, Shaw's "plays of ideas" might be said to anticipate the "rational drama" of Brecht and, later, Edward Bond.

Such links can be made even more firmly between later dramatists and the techniques employed by Shaw in his history plays. At the beginning of *Caesar and Cleopatra* (1898), for example, the audience is addressed directly, and the character of Britannus is presented anachronistically as a member of the Victorian middle classes, his blue woad playfully suggesting blue-suited respectability. In *St. Joan* (1923), Warwick is able to predict Joan's historical significance, and the "Epilogue" breaks the time-frame of the drama, foreshadowing the alienation effects of much modern drama.

From *The Quintessence* to plays written well into the twentieth century, it is characteristic of Shaw, as Stephen Watt has observed, to "heighten the audience's consciousness of its own participation in a theatrical event" (Innes 213). Shaw himself spoke of the necessary "staginess" of his drama and this was part of his proposed "forensic" method to make audiences and readers question their beliefs. It is in this,

perhaps, that his relevance to Eliot and subsequent generations lies. Rather than being seen as one of the last Victorians, then, Shaw might be said to have achieved—to some extent—his own immodest aim: "to incarnate the Zeitgeist" of the early twentieth century.

Paul Wright

Selected Bibliography

Berst, Charles. *Bernard Shaw and the Art of the Drama.* Urbana: U of Illinois P, 1973.

Davis, Tracy C. *George Bernard Shaw and the Socialist Theatre.* Westport CT: Greenwood Press, 1994.

Greene, Nicholas. "The Edwardian Shaw or the Modernist That Never Was." *High and Low Modernisms.* Ed. Maria DiBattista and Lucy McDiarmid. Oxford: OUP, 1996. 135–47.

Holroyd, Michael. *George Bernard Shaw.* 5 vols. London: Chatto and Windus, 1988–93.

Innes, Christopher. *The Cambridge Companion to Shaw.* Cambridge: CUP, 1998.

Laurence, Dan H. *Bernard Shaw: Collected Letters* 4 vols. London: Max Reinhardt, 1965–88).

————. *Bernard Shaw: Collected Plays* 7 vols. London: Max Reinhardt, 1970–4.

Shaw, G. B. *The Complete Works.* 36 vols. London: Constable; New York: Dodd Mead, 1931–50.

Slavic Modernism in Central and Eastern Europe

The modern movement in the Slavic countries of Central and Eastern Europe emerged from the blending of international influences with the local literary traditions. The major influences nurturing modernism emanated from **France, Russia,** and the German-speaking countries. It is part of the enigma of the phenomenon that it swept more or less at the same time through countries of different economic and social development. Yet two different rhythms in the emergence of the tendency can be outlined pertaining to location: Polish, Czech, and Slovak modernism in Central Europe springing up in the conditions of a buoyantly expanding capitalism had a different chronology, a different generic profile, and a different set of representative figures from Bulgarian, Serbian, Croatian, Slovenian, or Macedonian modernisms taking place in the more rural Southeastern Europe. The national question also played an important part in determining trends and influences: pre-war partitioned Poland, for example, had several intellectual centers because the German, Austrian, and Russian sections were submitted to very different influences and languages; while the post-war Czech avant-gardist movement in the Masaryk Republic was fascinated with French **surrealism** and thus totally overlooked the most original literary figure of German-speaking Prague, **Franz Kafka.**

The literary past of different Slavic countries was also an important factor for the different degrees of assimilation of the modernist spirit. While the Polish and Czech Moderna had the traditions and conventions of literary **naturalism** to break away from, modernist experimentation in the Balkan countries developed within the framework of relatively new, post-liberation literatures. The modernist sensibility in Bulgarian, Serbian, or Slovenian letters is often coupled with an awareness of the need to open up the provincial national literature to European influences in order to accelerate its advance. Hence the focus of Bulgarian or Serbian symbolist poetry on forging linguistic and poetic means to express complex spiritual and contemplative states rather than playing excessively with language. This may also explain why the modernist impulse in the Balkan Slavic literatures was altogether alien to the impersonality doctrine of Anglo-American modernism.

Of course, in such a short space it is not possible to do full justice to the literatures of each individual country within the Slavic world. Thus, this entry focuses mainly on Bulgarian and Polish literatures, with the hope that they can serve as indicative examples of the development of modernism in the Slavic countries of Central and Southeastern Europe.

Polish Modernism

Modernism was a powerful trend in Poland equally affecting the major genres of poetry, drama, and the novel. It falls neatly into two periods: 1890–1918, the Young Poland, its heyday spanning the decade between 1899 and 1909; and the avant-garde movements gathered round the *Skamander Review* in Warsaw and the First and Second Vanguards in Cracow in the independent Poland of the twenties. The clear-cut periodization shows how closely literary developments in Poland were affected by the country's partitioning and subsequent restoration of independence in 1918. The name "Young Poland" is used by Polish scholars to describe the changes in sensibility and style referred to as decadence, symbolism, **impressionism.**

The early years of Young Poland were characterized by an aesthetic and philosophical revolt against the utilitarian ideals of **realism** and positivism, and the beginnings of the revolt were connected to a growing familiarity with French, English, and German poetry in translation. A literary magazine in Warsaw, *Życie* (*Life*), edited by Zenon Przesmycki (pen name: Miriam) in 1887 published translations of Edgar Allan Poe, Baudelaire, Verlaine, and Swinburne. In the early 1890s Przesmycki's translation of Arthur Rimbaud's *Le bateau ivre* and Antoni Lange's translation of Baudelaire's *Les fleurs du mal* introduced the generation's two most important influences, while the dramas of Maurice Maeterlinck and Henrik Ibsen had gained popularity too.

The crisis of the positivist weltanschauung also encouraged interest in German idealistic philosophy. The most influential initiator of Young Poland, Stanisław Przybyszewski (1868–1927) introduced Nietzsche as early as 1892. Between

1905 and 1912 Nietzsche's works were published in translation and exerted a strong influence on Berent, Wyspiański, and Leopold Staff. In the decade preceding the outbreak of **World War I,** Henri Bergson and Søren Kierkegaard were translated. The powerful influence of German intellectual life on Young Poland could be explained by the fact that a part of partitioned Poland was in **Germany.** Przybyszewski had studied in Berlin, and his first works, written in German, brought him fame in the bohemian circles of that city. "Young Germany" was closely linked with Young **Scandinavia** and Przybyszewski was very much in touch with these movements through personal contacts. He was the pioneer who focused the disparate tendencies which went into the making of Young Poland. Before it became Young Poland, the movement was known as Przybyszewski's Moderna.

The first phase of Young Poland culminated around 1900. In 1899, Przybyszewski published his important manifesto "Confiteor" stating his intense concern for aesthetic values and denouncing the utilitarian purpose of art. Art that creates *value* became the object of worship. Przybyszewski's notion of the "naked soul" to be expressed in art revealed his interest in the primordial, subconscious powers which had kinship both with **Freud**'s unconscious and with Nietzsche's Dionysian force: "I stated that 'the naked soul' exists beyond all the external acts of that little normal soul, of our poor infinitely poor consciousness" (quoted by Miłosz 332). Another example of strong German influences was the fruitful and lasting friendship between Wacław Rolicz-Lieder (1866–1912) and the German poet **Stefan George.** Lieder's poetry also exemplifies a fresh cosmopolitanism combining the influence of French Parnassians, symbolists, Oriental motifs, and old Polish poetry. A graduate of the Ecole des Langues Orientales, Lieder translated Persian poets. Another oriental influence came through the work of Antoni Lange (1863–1927) who popularized Indian philosophy and literature and translated from Sanskrit (Bhagavad-Gita).

Apart from literary and philosophical borrowings, Polish modernism was shaped by the specific political conditions and the strong native romantic tradition. The powerful revival of Polish romanticism in the early twentieth century had its roots in the external circumstances of Poland's partitioning and the new hopes for independence in the wake of Russia's defeat in the Russian–Japanese war of 1905. Nationalist sentiments and idealistic hopes for independence found an outlet in poetry. Kazimierz Tetmajer (1865–1940) was one of the first to draw heavily on his native Tatra mountains and their oral folklore to render melancholy *fin de siècle* motifs. The poetry of Jan Kasprowicz (1860–1926) also shows an infatuation with the Tatras. His best-known free-verse hymns in two volumes, *Ginącemu światu* (1902, *To a Dying World*) and *Salve Regina* (1902), translate themes of universal suffering into particular misfortunes befalling Polish peasants. Kasprowicz's most characteristic quality is the blending of his philosophical and religious meditations with the Polish landscape, peasant life and themes from folklore—for example, in *Moj Świat* (1926, *My World*). The mystical vein of Polish romanticism was continued by Tadeusz Miciński (1973–1918) who was fascinated by Hindu religious philosophy, cabala, and occultism.

The melancholy and despair of Przybyszewski's Moderna as well as the mannerism of its symbolist aesthetics were gradually superseded by new developments in Polish writing. One of the strongest theoretical attacks came in 1909 when Stanisław Brzozowski (1878–1911) wrote his 600-page long *The Legend of Young Poland* in which he criticized Moderna's romantic decadence and aestheticism.

Also critical of Moderna's extreme states of mind was one of its former members, Leopold Staff (1878–1957), whose later work developed along classical lines. Recurring images of nature in his work celebrate the joy of life and endorse simple action as against the pessimism of thought. An accomplished scholar, his range was wide, from Heraclitus, the Greek sophists, and Old Chinese poetry, to Horatio, St. Francis of Assisi, Nietzsche, and Henri Bergson.

Bolesław Leśmian (1878–1937), considered to be the most accomplished Polish poet of the twentieth century, introduced linguistic experimentation based on folk songs and ballads. He elaborated a language of his own to express a private, tragic vision which drew on his anthropological studies of primitive religions and on his fascination with nature. He faced the dilemma of agnosticism through the poet's effort to create a semantic world of make-believe, which he saw as man's only solace. In his important *Treatise on Poetry* (1937), he analyzed the duality of poetic and colloquial language proclaiming the autonomous status of the former. His **myth**-creating imagery and his agnosticism recall the poetry of **William Butler Yeats.** A new voice in Polish poetry was Tadeusz "Boy" Żeleński (1874–1941). Beginning as a witty script writer for a cabaret in Cracow, in 1913 Żeleński produced a volume of satirical verse and songs called *Słówka* (*Little Words*). His unpretentious use of colloquial language, his humor and epigrammatic terseness paved the way for a radical change in poetry away from Moderna's mannerism and spirituality. Further testimony of the dwindling respect for the profundity of Young Poland lies in the work of Adolf Nowaczyński (1876–1944), a poet and pamphleteer who worked in the satirical vein. In *Małpie zwierciadło* (1902, *Monkey's Mirror*) he made fun of the "academic prophets" and "alcoholics" of the Moderna. Mention might also be made here of Jan Lemański (1866–1933) who resurrected the traditional verse fable for his own modern purposes.

The Polish theatrical repertoire during the era of Young Poland included the most important European modernist drama in translation: the plays of Henrik Ibsen, August Strindberg, the Germans Hermann Sudermann and **Gerhart Hauptmann, Oscar Wilde, George Bernard Shaw** and William Butler Yeats. Shaw was one of the most applauded contemporary playwrights, to the extent that between the wars some of his plays had their world or continental premiere in Warsaw. Many Polish poets wrote symbolist plays (Tetmajer, Kasprowicz, Staff). However, the most important accomplishment in drama belongs to the reformer of the Polish theatre, Stanisław Wyspiański (1869–1907).

Indebted to the romantic theater of Adam Mickiewicz (1798–1855) and his Paris lecture on the Slavic drama, Wyspiański brought new ideas to the theater, helping to overcome Moderna's devotion to art as an absolute. According to Moderna, "literature has no more right than an actor while the actor is as much a component of theatrical art as the decor" (Leon Schiller, quoted by Miłosz 354). The theatrical spectacle was for Wyspiański a unity of word, color, **music,** and movement thus striving after a new syncretism. His cycle of plays *Wesele* (*The Wedding*), *Wyzwolenie* (*Liberation*), *Legion* (*The Legion*) and *Acropolis* introduced national themes. Symbolist techniques hitherto associated with individualistic art, were applied to treat national problems and the fate of a whole community. The staging of his play *The Wedding* in Cracow in 1901 produced a powerful impact and opened up a new era in the Polish theater. Between the wars Leon Schiller's continued experimentation and his theory of monumental theater helped to consolidate this trend away from naturalism.

Avant-garde experimentation in fiction is connected with the names of Stanisław Brzozowski and Karol Irzykowski (1873–1944). Brzozowski's second novel *Sam wśród ludzi* (1911, *Alone Among Men*) is the Polish modernist *bildungsroman* and the most Dostoyevskian of Polish novels. A story of the intellectual maturing of a young man during the 1830s, the novel offers an analysis of Russian, German, and Polish mentalities and has complex portraits of priests which anticipate **Thomas Mann**'s portrait of a Jesuit priest in *The Magic Mountain* ten years later. Irzykowski's self-reflexive novel *Paluba* (1903, *The Hag*), with its generic mix, limited narrator, and Freudian plunge into the subconscious, it is a true precursor of the modernist European novel of the twenties. His probings into psychology and his experimentation with the aesthetics of the novel stand out yet more starkly when set against the socially committed neoromantic novels of the most important Polish fiction writer of the first quarter of the twentieth century, Stefan Żeromski (1864–1925)—his novels include *Popioły* (1904, *Ashes*) and *Przedwiośnie* (1925, *Before the Spring*)—and against the huge epic novel of 1924 Nobel prize winner Władysław Reymont (1867–1925), *Chłopi* (1902–09, *The Peasants*).

With the establishment of Poland's independence in 1918 the post-war generation of poets including Jarosław Iwaszkiewicz, Antoni Słonimski, and Julian Tuwim felt free from commitment to national-patriotic themes and focused on formal linguistic experimentation. There were two centers—Warsaw (the Skamander poets) and Cracow (the "Switch" constructivists of the First Vanguard).

In a manifesto published in the *Skamander Review* in Warsaw in 1920 the young post-war generation called themselves "poets of the present" who worshipped life and believed that "the greatness of art does not appear in subjects, but in the forms through which it is expressed" (quoted by Miłosz 386). Compared to Russian acmeists, the Skamander poets introduced everyday speech and colloquial idioms and sought to liberate poetry from the verbosity of Young Poland. The linguistic brilliance of Julian Tuwim (1894–1953) was coupled with an interest in demonology, an ever-present theme in his early work, *Czyhanie na Boga* (1918 *Ambushing God*), *Socrates Tańczący* (1920, *Dancing Socrates*), *Słowa we krwi* (1926, *Words in Blood*). Jarosław Iwaszkiewicz (1894–1980) was compared to Oscar Wilde and to Russian symbolists. His *Octostychy* (1919, *Octostichs*) offers a daring experiment with metrics and assonance. His *Dionizje* (1922, *Dionysiacs*) presents a highly personal interpretation of the myth of Dionysus. The poetry's fantastic explosion of color and dissonant jarring rhythms have prompted Miłosz to describe this as "perhaps the only truly expressionistic volume of poems published in Poland after WWI" (Miłosz 390). Antoni Słonimski (1895–1976) wrote intellectual poetry distanced from emotions, yet managed still to convey a deep joy in life in works such as *Droga na wschod* (1924, *Road to the East*) and *Z dalekiej podrozy* (1926, *From a Long Journey*).

Cracow witnessed the birth of another avant-garde group, The First Vanguard of the 1920s, known as the constructivists. They gathered round the *Switch* review edited by Tadeusz Peiper (1891–1969) between 1922–1923 and 1926–1927. The Switch group—Peiper, Julian, Przyboś (1901–70), Jan Brzękowski (1903–83)—criticized Skamander's propensity for lyricism, for the exploitation of the subconscious, and for an excessive concern with language. They laid emphasis instead on construction and spatiality, and favored emotional detachment and rational control. Przyboś, for example, reflected this tendency in his essays where he promoted new architecture and nonfigurative painting.

The joyful, light-hearted experimentation in poetry that dominated the twenties, gradually dwindled in the thirties. It was supplanted by politically committed poetry ringing catastrophic and apocalyptic notes in anticipation of the new world cataclysm.

Bulgarian Modernism

The radical reorientation in Bulgarian letters tagged as the era of symbolism occurred roughly between 1905 and 1923. The second wave of experimentation, often referred to as "September poetry," occurred between 1923 and 1930. This entire period, particularly the time between 1905–1915, are years of notable literary productivity concentrated in the capital city of Sofia, which was the only center of modernism. The symbolist school in Bulgaria, as elsewhere in Europe, played an essential role in the preparation of subsequent modernist developments.

The age of individualism began as an impulse to open up post-liberation Bulgarian letters to Western European influences, French and German in particular. The initiators were the group that formed round the *Misl* journal edited by the literary critic Kristju Kristev between 1892 and 1907 and consisting of Pencho Slaveikov, Petko Todorov, and Pejo Javorov. A major advocate of disinterested art, Kristev (1866–1919) published a series of articles in 1903 on the tendentiousness of letters, condemning literature in the service of social causes and arguing in favor of the autonomous status of art. The dominating figure was the poet Pencho Slaveikov (1866–1912) who, having studied in Germany, translated Nietzsche, introduced German idealistic aesthetics (Wilhelm Wundt), and promoted German culture through a collection of translations, *German Poets* (1911).

His early poetic collection, *Epic Songs* (1896–98), contains poems on both folk motifs and such figures as Shelley, Michelangelo, and Beethoven, thus already revealing his life-long concern to make the best in world culture accessible to Bulgarians while also highlighting the value of the national tradition. Underlying his aesthetic credo is the neo-classical ideal of beauty and truth, fused with an admiration for Nietzschean individualistic genius. Inspired by Mickiewicz's Polish epic, *Pan Tadeusz,* his long poem about Bulgarian liberation struggles, *A Song of Bloodshed* (*Karvava Pesen,* 1893), was the first attempt at a Romantic national epic in Bulgarian letters. Slaveikov's most original work is *The Isle of the Blest* (1910), an anthology of poetry by fictional poets for whom Slaveikov supplied both biographies and samples of their work. Slaveikov's poetry is more interesting today as an illustration of his philosophical and aesthetic views rather than for its literary merits, but it played a crucial role in promoting the era of individualism.

It took the major talent of Pejo Javorov (1878–1914) to effect the first significant shift into introversion in modern Bulgarian poetry. Although beginning with socially oriented poetry fused with folk motifs in the 1890s, Javorov became the precursor of Bulgarian symbolism in his mature collections, *Insomnia* (*Bescanizi,* 1907) and *Following the Shadows of the Clouds* (*Podir Senkite and Oblatzite,* 1910). Here opposites intertwine to create a stark dramatic quality and dynamism—love and death, loneliness as a cherished and loathed state, terror and fascination with death, writing as a painful catharsis. The recurrent theme of the tortured soul's oscillations between the angelic and the demonic recalls the notion of the "naked soul" introduced by the "satanist" Przybyszewski, with whom Javorov has been compared. Critics also point to connections between Javorov and Nietzsche in their negation of absolutes, their disdain for the crowd and the glorification of the poet's personality; and between Javorov and Maurice Maeterlinck in their sense of man's hopelessness and helplessness (Moser 143).

The poetry of Dimcho Debeljanov (1887–1916) combines lyricism with a calm contemplative vein. His work is influenced by the Russian and French symbolists Brjusov, Blok, Baudelaire, and Verlaine in particular. His mature writing between 1911–1915 gives shape to standard *fin de siècle* motifs of melancholy, despondency, death. His elegies, which are unique in Bulgarian letters for their lyrical flow and sonority, introduce the important modernist theme of recollection and memory. His programmatic *Cerna Pesen* (*Black Song*) develops the romantic theme of creation-dissolution through the light-darkness imagery which underlies his entire work. As in Javorov's poetry, individual self-consciousness is asserted through suffering which stems from deeply felt private sorrows.

Although arriving late, symbolism was the most consistent school in Bulgarian literature. It grew out of French, German, Austrian, Russian, and Polish literary influences: Baudelaire, Mallarmé, Verlaine, Rimbaud, Dehmel, **George, Rilke,** Przybyszewski, Balmont, Blok and Brjusov. The debt of Bulgarian symbolists to French sources is particularly great. Most of them had resided in France (Yavorov, Liliev, Emanuil Popdimitrov, Dimiter Boiadjiev), absorbing French culture and French symbolist poetry at first hand. In 1905 the journal *Hudozhnik* (*Artist*) published the programmatic symbolist poem "Novijat den" ("The New Day") by the most consistent Bulgarian symbolist, Teodor Trajanov. Several journals nurtured symbolism thereafter, the last and most influential one, *Hyperion* appearing until as late as 1931. The movement had its theoreticians in Dimo Kiorchev, Ivan Radoslavov, and Ljudmil Stoyanov, whose foreword to his collection of poems *Vi-*

sions at the Crossroads (1914) refers to **Oscar Wilde** in presenting a view of art divorced from reality, morality, and "truth" (Wilde was the major British influence on Bulgarian poets at this time).

Teodor Trayanov—whose pantomime version of Wilde's *The Happy Prince* was staged at the Volksoper in Vienna in 1914—lived in the Austrian capital in the war years, where he met Rilke, **Hugo von Hofmannsthal, Arthur Schnitzler** and Stefan George. The poems in his most outstanding collections *Regina Mortua* (1909) and *Hymns and Ballads* (1912) are typical symbolist pieces clearly evincing the influence of Austrian modernism in their motifs of death and dissolution and their ornate and sensuous nature imagery. Drawing on Christianity, oriental beliefs, and the classical pagan heritage (*Hymns to Astarte,* for example), Trayanov's work exhibits a strong vein of eclectic mysticism. Nikolai Liliev (1885–1960) came to be known as "the poet's poet" for his self-conscious linguistic experimentation. His collections *Ptici v Noshtta* (*Birds in the Night,* 1918) and *Lunni Petna* (*Moonspots,* 1922) develop leitmotifs of loneliness and pensive melancholy through exquisitely polished short verses playing on assonance and rhyme.

Bulgarian symbolists generally had a strong sense of the literary tradition within which they worked, and this was typically expressed by incorporating quotations in French into their verse or by dedicating poems to their fellow writers. Another tendency, initiated by Yavorov and developed by all, was the use of an Old Bulgarian lexicon, along with Russian borrowings which often lead back to Old Bulgarian through Church Slavonic. The introduction of Old Bulgarian was used to give their poetry a magic otherworldly quality to stress the artificiality of the "supreme" language.

The overcoming of symbolism coincides with dramatic events for Bulgaria:

the defeat in World War I, the abortive September uprising of 1923, and the political reprisals of 1925 against writers and intellectuals. These upheavals had a sobering effect on the younger adherents of symbolism who slipped from the symbolist orbit in two ways: by abandoning symbolist themes and turning to real life for their subjects; and by attempting to liberate language from "the ivory tower" of symbolist aesthetics. The period from 1919 to 1925 witnessed a proliferation of "isms" on the literary scene, with symbolism ceasing to exist as a movement by 1925. **German expressionism** and Russian **futurism** played a central role, particularly influencing the work of Geo Milev (1895–1925).

One of the most authoritative journals between the two wars was *Zlatorog* (*The Golden Horn*) edited by the critic Vladimir Vassilev and publishing nearly all the best writers in Bulgaria. The other avant-garde journal was *Vezni* (*The Scales,* 1919–22), started by Geo Milev. Carrying symbolist poetry as well as translations from Oscar Wilde's work and modernist art, *Vezni* recorded the shift to **expressionism** in Bulgarian letters during its period of publication. Geo Milev himself had participated actively in German literary life, contributing to the German expressionist periodical *Die Aktion* and observing events in Berlin in 1918–1919 during his second stay in Germany. His interest in expressionism went together with an ideological shift leftwards which he proclaimed in his new journal *Plamak* (*Flame*), where in 1924 he printed his expressionist pieces, the poems "Ad" ("Hell"), "Septemvri" ("September") and "Grozni prozi" ("Ugly Prose Pieces"). In his masterpiece, the poem "September," Milev translates the real-life events of the September uprising into typical expressionist motifs: the impoverished masses who are bearers of the highest humanity become "ecstatically destructive" in their anarchic revolt; their liberated energies are like a flood, like a wild animal, casting down God and envisioning paradise on earth. The poem's tone and style, the experiment with typography, the stepped lines, and, above all, the catalogs of verbless nouns and adjectives working toward an emotional climax reveal the other important influence on Milev's work, the Russian futurist, Vladimir Mayakovsky. The poem's impact was so strong that Milev was brought to court to answer for it. Sentenced to a year's imprisonment, he then vanished in the wave of political reprisals in 1925.

The other trend in the post-war experimental poetry, prose, and painting which dominated the 1920s and 30s, was a renewed concern with the rich national heritage of folk songs, myths and legends as well as peasant thematics. Behind this impulse was the modernist fascination with the primitive and the unconscious, born of a disillusionment with an increasing urbanization and mechanization in the postwar period. Folk material fused with **formal experimentation** underlies the work of Nikola Furnadjiev (*Proleten Viatar/Spring Wind,* 1925) Asen Razcvetnikov (*Zertveni kladi/Sacrificial Pyres,* 1924), the prose-writer Anton Strashimirov (*Xoro/Round-Dance,* 1926), the poet Elisaveta Bagryana (*Vechnata I Svyatata/ The Eternal and the Sacred,* 1927). Angel Karalijchev (*The Stone Bridge on the Rosica,* 1925) was part of an influential group of avant-garde painters who used the Bulgarian translation of the German *Heimatskunst* to give a name to their movement which sought to paint peasant subjects in a stylized, two-dimensional, and decorative manner.

The concern with folk material has been a strong undercurrent in Bulgarian modernist writing from the very outset. It is particularly prominent in the prose and drama of the period, though this is relatively small in volume. In his first work of symbolist prose, *Bogomil Legends* (1912), Nikolai Rainov (1889–1954) created highly stylized, two-dimensional, anti-naturalist characters. In his subsequent work (*Visions from Ancient Bulgaria,* 1918, *Book of the Czars,* 1918, and *The City,* 1919) he drew on ancient Bulgarian legends, writing about the glories of medieval Bulgaria in a densely metaphorical language. A conscious stylist, Rainov himself acknowledged his debt to Petko Todorov (1879–1916) and the latter's interest in the unconscious. In his *Idylls* (1908) and his folklore dramas *The Builders* (1902), *The Woodsprite* (1903), and *Zmei's Wedding* (1910) (to mention but a few), Petko Todorov interweaves the fantastic with the realistic, utilizing folklore motifs to outline archetypal situations. The work of the major playwright of the period, Pejo Javorov, *In the Outskirts of Vitosha* (1911) and *When the Thunder Strikes* (1912), takes Bulgarian drama in exactly the opposite direction. His dramas are skillful psychological pieces centered on the conflict between sexual passion and conventional morality and manifesting the influence of Henrik Ibsen and Anton-Chekhov.

The drama and the fiction of the period could not match the achievements of poetry, particularly the lyric poem, which was the genre that attracted the best talents. Thanks to the modernist ferment and the concentration of talents in the 1910s and 1920s, the period is seen to be one of the most productive in Bulgarian literature, which from then on began to shake off its provincialism and to emerge on the international literary scene. With the advent of the thirties, modernist experimentation gradually faded away.

Stefana Roussenova
and Wassil Balewsky

Selected Bibliography

Barac, Antun. *A History of Yugoslav Literature.* Belgrade: Committee for Foreign Cultural Relations, 1955.

Encyclopedia of World Literature in the 20th Century. New York: Frederick Ungar, 1967–71.

French, Alfred. *The Poets of Prague.* London: Oxford University Press, 1969.

Kadic, Ante. *Contemporary Serbian Literature.* The Hague: Mouton. 1964.

Mihailovich, Vasa D, ed. *Modern Slavic Literatures: A Library of Literary Criticism.* New York: Frederick Ungar Publishing Co., 1976.

Miłosz, Czesław. *The History of Polish Literature.* London: The Macmillan Company, 1969.

Moser, Charles A. *A History of Bulgarian Literature: 865–1944.* The Hague. Paris: Mouton. 1972.

Novak, Arne. *Czech Literature.* Ann Arbor: Michigan

Rechcigl, Jr., Miroslav. *Czechoslovakia Past and Present.* The Hague: Mouton, 1968.

Vaupotic, Miroslav. *Contemporary Croatian Literature.* Zagreb: Croatian P.E.N. Club, 1966.

Wellek, Rene. *Essays on Czech Literature.* The Hague: Mouton, 1963.

Södergran, Edith (1892–1923)

Fenno-Swedish poet, born in St Petersburg.

Södergran is one of the most influential poetic modernists in the Swedish language. She made her debut with the poetry collection *Dikter* (1916, *Poems*) in which her free verse and catalog technique appeared modern for its time. The poetic diction ranges from intense emotional reactions expressed by a first-person speaker, to concrete and realistic images of nature and scenery. In *Septemberlyran* (1918, *September Lyre*) she gave voice to a triumphant, expressionist view of life inspired by Nietzsche. Here one finds the highly charged poetic idiom characteristic of Södergran which is further developed in *Rosenaltaret* (1919, *Rose Altar*), her most openly Nietzschean collection. This is followed by *Framtidens skugga* (1920, *Shadow of the Future*) where a cosmic and ecstatic view of life also takes form. In *Landet som icke är* (1925, *The Land That Is Not*), published posthumously, a more moderate and religious tone can be heard. Södergran also published a collection of aphorisms, *Brokiga iakttagelser* (1919, *Miscellaneous Observations*). A collection of Södergran's letters is available in *Ediths brev* (1955, *The Letters of Edith*), edited by her friend, the literary critic Hagar Olsson. A selection of Södergran's earliest poetry has been published as *Vaxdukshäftet* (1997, *The Oilcloth Booklet*). Södergran's poetry has been translated into several languages. An English translation is *The Collected Poems of Edith Södergran* (1980).

Mats Jansson

Selected Bibliography

Brunner, Ernst. Till fots genom solsystemen. *En studie i Edith Södergrans expressionism.* Stockholm: Bonniers, 1985.

Evers, Ulla. Hettan av en gud. *En studie i skapandetemat hos Edith Södergran.* Göteborg: Skrifter utgivna av Litteraturvetenskapliga insititionen vid Göteborgs universitet, 1992.

Hedberg, Johan. Eros skapar världen ny. *Apokalyps och pånyttfödelse i Edith Södergrans lyrik.* Göteborg: Daidalos, 1991.

Schoolfield, George C. Edith Södergran. *Modernist Poet in Finland.* Westport & London: Greenwood Press, 1984.

Södergran, Edith. *Collected Poems.* Trans. Martin Allwood. Mullsjö, Sweden: Anglo-American Center, 1980.

Witt-Brattström, Ebba. Ediths jag. *Edith Södergran och modernismens födelse.* Stockholm: Norstedts, 1997.

Spain

In Spain, modernism, as defined in 1934 by Federico de Onís, relates to "the universal crisis of letters and the spirit which initiates around 1885 the dissolution of the nineteenth century;" it "manifested itself gradually in art, science, religion and all other aspects of life, and possessed, therefore, all the characteristics of a profound historical change which continues today" (Onís xv). Modernism signifies the gamut of experimental literary and artistic forms emerging in the period between the 1890s and 1930s as a response to the experience of modern urban life. The turn of the century was marked by the contours of change and a concomitant awareness that society and social relations exist in a permanent state of flux. The loss of Spain's colonies (Cuba, Puerto Rico, Philippines) in 1898 had provoked a sense of discontinuity and disempowerment, and a questioning of self and other. Urban migration led to tensions in what was perceived to be the newly emergent mass culture, and industrialization and transportation made the world at once smaller and infinitely larger. In what would become known as the crisis of modernism, huge advances in technologies and science meant new ways of viewing the world, and precipitated fears surrounding the role of the human self in the universe. Above all, art reflected this sense of crisis, in "different formal articulations of the same sense of loss of wholeness and depth—whether of the things or of the self" (Graham and Labanyi 12).

Experimental cultural forms played on a disruption of the processes of representation, as if the unproblematic solidity of things and of the self which **realism and naturalism** announced could not now describe human experience. These works characteristically substituted multidimensional space for unilinearity, and were self-reflexive, pointing to an ironic self-awareness of the processes of artistic creation. Rather than a movement, modernism in Spain was more of a process, subject to individual and semi-collective challenges, motivations, and realignments.

Furthermore, the political ambiguity of modernism in Spain is notorious: "those artists who embraced communism, those who embraced fascism, and those who rejected politics altogether—to take only three of the many positions adopted—all saw themselves as radicals responding to the dislocating forces of the times" (Graham and Labanyi 13). Radically distinct initiatives and ventures, with different motivations and directions equally aspired to literary experimentation in a process which challenged what had gone before.

Artists and writers in Spain, although composed of heterogeneous factions, were nevertheless involved in a paradigmatic shift in artistic practices, consonant with the wider European and Anglo-American movements taking place at the same time elsewhere.

While Jencks apparently finds the term "modernism" in the third century, most commentators agree that it did not enter general usage as a movement and critical category in the English-speaking world until the 1950s (Williams 34). Spanish-speakers, however, used the designation, "modernismo" a generation earlier. Perry Anderson writes that, "we owe the coinage of 'modernism' as an aesthetic movement to a Nicaraguan poet, writing in a Guatemalan journal, of a literary encounter in Peru." Rubén Darío (1867–1916), the Nicaraguan poet in question, spearheaded the movement, with his *Azul* (*Blue*) from 1888 being taken as its keystone text. **Hispanic American** *Modernismo* reached its fullest development around 1910 in the pages of the Mexican poet Amado Nervo's *La Revista Moderna* (*The Modern Review*) and focused on developments in poetry. Darío's *modernismo* was a narrowly defined, self-conscious movement, inspired by French *symbolisme* and parnassianism, and arguably it declined in Spanish-America with Darío's death in 1916. *Modernismo* asserted Spanish-American emancipation in cultural and intellectual terms from Spain, and with it, "to use Darío's metaphor, it sent the galleons back to *la madre patria*" (the mother-land) (Hart 26). *Modernismo* was subsequently taken up in Spain, with leading intellectual and literary figures contributing to the debate on definitions. "I don't know exactly what this business of *modernistas* and *modernismo* is, such diverse and opposing things are given these names that there is no way to reduce them to a single category," wrote Miguel de Unamuno in 1918, and it is partly the conflicts within the modernist current in Spain, its propensity for dialogue in time and place, that has constituted its inner dynamic.

Stephen Hart has outlined some of the contradictory views of *modernismo* presented both during and since the movement. He notes that while many cite Darío as the founder of the movement, (Salinas [1941], Díaz-Plaja [1951], Henríquez-Ureña [1954] and others), there are those (Manuel Pedro González, Ivan Schulman) for whom Martí and Nájera are its true founders. Furthermore, while some critics see *modernismo* as symptomatic of a paradigm-shift taking place across modern Europe (what Davison [1966] refers to as the "epochal" view), sensitive to the larger cultural watershed of the modern age, still others see *modernismo* as a movement with Spanish and Spanish-American proponents, distinct from Brazilian *modernismo,* Catalan *modernisme,* Anglo-American and European modernism, which arose out of the crisis of values in Latin America caused by the positivist critique of religion and metaphysics (Hart 26).

In part, the contention surrounding definitions of modernism in Spain is due to the misunderstandings and slippage between Castilian *modernismo* and European and Anglo-American "modernism." John Butt has written of the "unfortunate and idiosyncratic use of the term *modernismo* for what in any other country would be called symbolism." *Modernismo,* like the Catalan *modernisme,* is possibly best seen, then, as a precursor of "modernism," a view taken by Everdell (7). Butt writes that the unity of Castilian literature in the 1890s, viewed as a complex reaction to positivism and realism, has not yet been fully understood, nor have we "grasped how in that complex unity was born modernism—in the European sense of the word, which is hardly ever used in Hispanic Studies." This absence of an all-embracing term to describe modernist endeavor in Spanish seems exemplified by the work of Pablo Picasso, who is often featured in English-language accounts of "modernism," yet in Hispanic studies is described as "avant-garde," "cubist," or "surrealist," rather than "modernist." Furthermore, as Mary Lee Bretz (2001) points out, accounts of European modernism largely overlook modernist endeavor in Spain, a phenomenon which is highlighted by the fact that Spanish philosopher José Ortega y Gasset is often cited as a paradigmatic figure in European modernism. Thus, for Bretz, Ortega "becomes the explicator of a European modernist canon that excludes Spanish writers and culture" (27). She remarks, "the persistent recourse of Ortega as an expert on modernism in studies that exclude, deny, or devalue Hispanic modernism raises the question of how a major theorist of the movement arose in a nation with no equivalent cultural development" (28). According to Butt, a full account of Castilian modernism is yet to be written, something that he deems "unlikely until a Castilian translation of the word 'modernism' is found" (Butt 5).

Thus, while commentators of European and Anglo-American "modernism" critique the homogenization of radically disunited practices into a "canonized" movement long after a period which knew little of the term itself (Williams 34), in Spain those diverse and contesting theories and practices, often assembled into movements and processes which at times overlapped, are understood as differentiated initiatives and not grouped together under the umbrella term of modernism. In 1934 Onís pointed the way for an understanding of modernism in Spain which would stretch from Darío's *modernismo* towards the radical impulses of what he termed the *ultramodernistas,* what we now often designate the opening moments of the avant-garde. Modernism in Spain, then, is best understood in terms of the geographical and historical specificity of Spain (a country composed of separate and often culturally autonomous regions), with a cognizance of its emotional and ideological ties, (its inflections from Europe, Anglo-, and Spanish-America) as a series of challenges, initiatives, and modifications by a collection of artists who saw themselves as individually and semi-collectively (whether or not they belonged to "Generations" or movements) responding to the dislocating forces of the times, and which arguably spans from the 1890s to the end of the Spanish Civil War in 1939.

In Spain, modernism's pre-history can be located in the evolution of the work of Benito Pérez Galdós, Leopoldo Alas (also known as *Clarín*), and the novelist and feminist Emilia Pardo Bazán (Miller 1105). The Spanish realist novel developed later than its European counterparts, so that novelists had a knowledge of earlier foreign realists (Balzac, Zola, Dickens, Tolstoy and Flaubert), which gave their work "a conscious self-reflexivity rarely found in the nineteenth-century novel outside Spain," a metafictional dimension which had recourse to the heritage passed down by Cervantes (Labanyi 4). Moreover, in the 1880s and 1890s the novels of Galdós, Alas, and Pardo Bazán began to deal less with the depiction of reality, and more with individuals' self-deception and inner conflicts. In an 1881 review of Galdós's *La desheredada,* Alas indicates that his focus is "the interior revelation of a mind" rather than the description of the exterior world. Alas praises the use of dialogue and free indirect style: "presented not as a monologue but as if the author were inside the characters and the novel were coming from inside their heads" (Labanyi 47). The narrator of *La desheredada* is endowed with a psyche, afflicted by fears about the city's transition to modernity, and "uses irony to establish a complicity between himself and his reader against a character's self-deluded opinion," which undermines any single view of reality with the juxtaposition of others that negate it (Sieburth 48). This trend towards interiorization and ironic distance anticipated the modernist rupture with representationalism.

In 1897 Galdós spoke of the reasons behind this change in literary emphasis. Galdós now saw the middle-classes as a self-interested bourgeoisie which he had lost interest in depicting, preferring instead to take the path of interiorization in his writing. The transition he had recently observed in society was producing the need for new literary forms. These had not yet appeared, but "human ingenuity lives in all surroundings, and it sends forth its flowers in the gay porticoes of splendid architecture as well as among sad and desolate ruins" (Labanyi 38). From this perspective then, modernism in Spain is created amidst a lack of faith in the past and present of national life, and takes the form of an individualistic search for new forms, which will rise out of the "desolate ruins" of the literary dissolution of the nineteenth century indicated by Onís.

Two literary movements were ushered in shortly before the turn of the century, whose members and concerns often converged: the so-called *Generation of 1898* and *modernismo,* the Castilian form of the Spanish-American current initiated by Darío. Darío's poem "El cisne" ("The Swan") expresses most unequivocally his aesthetic vision: "the neck of the great white swan which questions me," not only establishes the image of the aristocratic poet, but also makes a visual pun on the similarity between the form of a swan's neck and that of a question mark (Hart 33). From this blend of experimental form and idea "la nueva Poesía" (new Poetry) would be hatched. In Spain *modernismo* brought about a reinvigoration of Castilian poetic language and sensibility and by the late 1890s the poetry of Antonio Machado

(1875–1939), Juan Ramón Jiménez (1881–1958) and Ramón María del Valle-Inclán (1866–1936) rivaled that of symbolist poets elsewhere, although they would later turn away from early *modernista* concerns and form. Many *modernistas* were reacting against naturalism and the excesses of romanticism. Others exaggerated the romantic style, glorying in images of melancholy princesses, Arab palaces, enclosed gardens, and nostalgic dreams, using rhythms and rhymes which broke with the traditional meter in Spanish poetry. Poetry was often devoted to the exotic and the extravagant, an idealization of *beauty,* where ideas are replaced by sonorous phrases, so that meaning is obscured and the reader must seek subjective interpretation, a process which served to deconstruct the foundations of the culture this poetry appeared to revere. *Modernismo* advocated radical formal change, with new approaches to poetry and prose writing and a poetic, anti-realist theater. The poetry of Manuel Machado (1874–1946) fused French forms with Spanish folk culture. Eduardo Marquina (1879–1946) and Francisco Villaespesa (1877–1935) contrived an exotic Spanish past, while "*modernismo's* idolization of Form, Art, Beauty—its idealism—and its horror of the normal and exaltation of Experience—its dissidence—led it into an engagement with the world of sensations and sexuality," expressed in Jiménez's early poetry; Valle-Inclán's *Comedias bárbaras* (1907–1922) and early poetry; and the vivid work of Salvador Rueda (1975–1933) (Perriam 55).

In the 1890s other writers in Castilian were less inspired by symbolism and its foreign precursors. These were the moralists and critics who observed the impact of industrialization on Spain (particularly in the Basque country and Catalonia); the influence of positivism and Darwinism, the anti-positivists such as Schopenhauer and Nietzsche, and also anti-clericalism.

Here the *Generation of 1898* emerged (named after the disaster of the War of 1898 in which Spain lost the vestiges of her imperial past), preoccupied with "the problem of Spain." Commentators compared the *Generation*'s serious concerns to *modernismo*'s apparent empty aestheticism. This position has been criticized recently for its reductive and reactionary view of *modernismo*. Moreover, in Onís's 1934 definition there is much overlap between the two movements. In the consensual view, the main proponents of the *Generation of 1898* were Pío Baroja (1872–1956), Azorín (pseudonym of José Martínez Ruíz, 1873–1967), Ramiro de Maetzu (1874–1936), Antonio Machado (1975–1939), Unamumo (1864–1936), Valle-Inclán, and Juan Ramón Jiménez. In general terms, the literary and intellectual foci of both movements centered on spiritual crisis, the need for regeneration, liberalization and modernization in Spain and the restoration of transcendental ideals. A disenchantment with nineteenth-century positivism (and the literary naturalism associated with it), scientific rationalism, the mechanical age versus nature, and the role of the individual as a social being were also common concerns.

Antonio Machado's early poems are self-consciously aesthetic creations, but in his later work he departed from *modernista* formalism towards increasingly personal, ethical and philosophical preoccupations. Machado wrote for Jiménez's literary journal, *Helios,* and it was here that Unamuno published an open letter to Machado. Unamuno's opposition to *modernismo* was well-known, and Machado seems to have taken his views to heart. Machado studied notions of time and intuition in Paris with Henri Bergson: his later poetry would incorporate philosophical concerns with eternal themes. With his brother Manuel, he wrote and translated plays (**Synge** amongst others). As Azorín noted, the *Generation of 1898* loved to de-scribe landscape. Machado's most celebrated work, *Campos de Castilla* (1912, *Fields of Castile*) is a simple yet powerful evocation of the Sorian landscape. Machado laments the Castile filled with decaying aristocracy, pilgrims and beggars, old women in mourning, but he has hope for the Spaniard who fights to live between "one Spain that is dying and another that yawns."

While Machado was an outspoken Republican, Maetzu turned from anti-traditionalism in his treatment of the "problem of Spain," to ultra-conservatism. In *Don Quijote, Don Juan y la Celestina* (1925, *Don Quijote, Don Juan and Celestina*) three characters of Spanish literature are held up to showcase love, power and wisdom: presented as a model for the character and spirit of the Spanish people. Maetzu's examination of the past mirrors the endeavors of other members of the generation (Baroja, Unamuno, Machado, and Azorín) towards a revisionist perspective of Spain's historical past in order to revitalize its future.

Like Machado, Juan Ramón Jiménez turned from *modernismo:* to the extent that he attempted to destroy his early work. His poetry is lauded for its formal innovations, exquisite delicacy of feeling, subtle cadences, and a gentle, lyrical quality. His poems are suffused with melancholy, a musing on solitude and suffering and a platonic notion of beauty. Influenced by the lyrics of **W. B. Yeats,** he incorporated the latter's chief symbols into his work (Young 1980, 136). Jiménez's aim was to strip poetry of its ornaments, to distill rather than to purify. He wished to attain a 'poesía desnuda' (naked poetry), most fully explored in his work between 1916 and 1923. *Platero y yo* (1917, *Platero and I*), a prose poem about a man and a donkey, fuses fantasy and realism to produce something modern. Juan Ramón's lyrical purity and poetic integrity would be hugely influential in poetic movements in Spain.

Miguel de Unamuno (1864–1936) was a poet, novelist, dramatist and essayist. His poetry is often considered anti-poetic, with consciously harsh sounds and unusual metaphors. On the other hand, his *Cristo de Velázquez* (1920, *The Christ of Velázquez*) uses visuals to striking effect. In the essay, *En torno al casticismo* (1902, *On Authentic Tradition*), Unamuno seeks to identify the essence of Spain. *Del sentimiento trágico de la vida* (1913, *The Tragic Sense of Life*) continues the study of Spanish character, but in the context of the spiritual impasse confronting the contemporary individual. Drawing from Kierkegaard, William James, Carlyle, Nietzsche, and other philosophers, Unamuno draws up a personal metaphysics, convinced that the question of existence is the most basic dilemma facing the modern individual. The problem of identity and the search for meaning is central to almost all of Unamuno's creative works. *Niebla* (1914, *Mist*) is existentialist, a labyrinth of shifting appearances, where its protagonist is subject to the whims of fate (a common theme of the '98 writers was the question of free-will and apathy). This "nivola" (Unamuno's personal style of novel) is acutely self-reflexive, with its challenge to the omnipotence of the author (Unamuno appears as a character in the novel) and self-conscious narrative structure. Unamuno's other novels (*Abel Sánchez,* 1917, the reworking of the fratricidal Cain and Abel theme; *San Manuel Bueno, mártir* [1933, *St. Manuel Bueno, Martyr*], which presents in novelistic form Unamuno's religious philosophy) share with the writings of other members of the Generation an appearance of lack of structure, an openendedness, and a contrived anti-realism.

In his early *modernista* works, parodies of romanticism, Ramón María del Valle-Inclán (1866–1936) portrayed his native Galicia in the setting of an idealized past in poetry, and attempted social realism in his theater. But in his later works, Galicia appears as decrepit, rotten and poor. His *Sonatas* (1902–5) employ a self-consciously decadent style to allow the protagonist, the Marqués de Bradomín, a pretentious lothario, to present his life in four stages (seen to correspond to spring, summer, autumn and winter). For his writing for the theater, Valle-Inclán broke with the mimeticism of Spanish theater to develop his own aesthetic style which he named *esperpento* (grotesque tragi-comedy). *Esperpento* is a fairground mirror held up to nature: in this systematic aesthetic distortion, everything appears in its worst possible light. Valle's characters are absurd, exaggerated figures, who are morally degraded, or victims of the social order and of one another—beggars, prostitutes, madmen, and thieves. Valle sees his characters as puppets: their humanity is diminished. Influenced by Nietzsche's *The Birth of Tragedy* (1871), which had a huge impact on Spain in the 1920s, Valle saw the potential of theater for **the masses** to engage with painful experience, but where Greek tragedy had featured gods and heroes, Valle saw the time he lived in as mediocre and debased and thought that theater should reflect this: the characters he depicts are outward manifestations of man's feebleness. Valle-Inclán explores primitive paganism in *Divinas palabras* (1920, *Divine Words*); the anachronistic Spanish honor code in *Los cuernos de Don Friolera* (1925, *Mr. Punch the Cuckold*), and in *Luces de Bohemia* (1924, *Bohemian Lights*), which has been compared to **Joyce's *Ulysses,*** presents a modern odyssey of an anti-hero through an urban landscape: "an absurd, brilliant, and hungry Madrid."

Industrialization and growth since the middle of the nineteenth century had increased the sense of preoccupation with the urban metropolis in Spain as a whole. In Catalonia the growth of the big cities emphasized the way Catalonia was growing apart from the rest of Spain. The Universal Exhibition of 1888 had placed Barcelona on a footing with cities in the rest of Europe and it now turned away from "the stagnation of official Spanish Restoration culture" (Yates 253), and looked towards Europe for inspiration, finding there, "a ferment of modes and styles, shot through with a sense of crisis, the gamut of '-isms' which characterized the turn-of-the-century artistic and literary panorama" (Yates 254). Increasingly, cultural activity was fostered in Catalonia which was separate from the rest of the peninsula, and which promoted the Catalan language: Catalan *modernisme* came to a head between 1892 and 1893 when the journal *L'Avenç* intensified its campaign to modernize the Catalan language and the first *Festa modernista* was held at Sitges under the patronage of the writer and painter Santiago Rusiñol. At this time the poet Joan Maragall began to write for the *Diario de Barcelona,* and Raimon Casellas, later to write the first Catalan *modernista* novel, contributed his first piece of art criticism to *La Vanguardia* (Terry 56).

Catalan *modernisme* was created out of attempts at the fusion of a modern European culture with a regional and local one. A version of late romanticism, questions of aesthetics engaged at every point with the experience of modern society. A different kind of artist was sought to reflect this engagement: one dedicated to the pursuit of his art. The translation of Maeterlinck's *L'Intruse* in 1893 was seen as a symbolic call-to-arms for *modernisme*: there was a renewed faith in the transcendental value of literary creativity. Influenced by Nietzsche, Carlyle, Ruskin, Ibsen, and Wagner, creative activity was eclectic, from the early pure symbolist poetry and later dramatic satire of Rusiñol, to the work of Maragall and Casellas which engaged with the questions of culture and society. In novelistic production from 1900 to 1912 (Casellas, Víctor Català [pseudonym of Caterina Albert], Folch i

Torres, and Pous i Pagès), interest shifted from social relationships to states of mind and the exploration of individual consciousness (Yates 257). Carme Karr i Alfonsetti (1865–1943) wrote a collection of short narratives, *Clixíes: estudis en prosa* (1906, *Snapshots: studies in prose*) in which the unifying metaphor of photography is frequently employed. *Modernisme's* renewal of artistic creation presented a stylization of reality, subject to the fragmented nature of symbolist perception. The theme of the subjective self and individual will confronting an alien reality is plotted in a series of symbolic confrontations and juxtapositions.

Theater too was developing startlingly new scenographic techniques, with important works by Rusiñol, Adrià Gual, Apel les Mestres, Ignasi Iglésias, and Joan Puig i Ferreter. In an atmosphere of enthusiasm for novelty and experimentation, incorporation of international work was accompanied by a return to popular roots (mime, puppetry, pantomime) followed by an interest in mechanical innovations (light-shows, magic lantern slides, Phenakistoscopes, etc.) and ultimately to investigations into the techniques of early cinema (see Yates 258). Independent theater groups and centers for dramatic experimentation were also established at this time: notably Gual's *Teatre Intim* (1898–1907).

Noucentisme, (meaning "of the new century") aimed to go on further in modernity than *modernisme* had done, and, emerging at a time when Catalonia was going through a crisis of national consciousness, it took on a political dimension, becoming an officially sanctioned cultural faction under the semi-devolved government of the conservative Prat de la Riba. *Noucentisme's* focus on the role of Catalan language resulted in rather controlled if polished poetry. The movement's concerns for Catalonia and preoccupation with how cultural activity might best serve political ends were at their height when the first reverberations of **futurism** were felt in Catalonia in 1914. The influence of Apollinaire and **Marinetti** is detected in the first phase of avant-garde writing from 1916 to 1924. The *calligramme,* a vanguard poetic device, was introduced by J. M. Junoy in 1915. "The excitement of the machine age, the flavour of a popular culture referring to the everyday specifics of modern urban life, cubist perspectivism and the new taste for syncopation led to further visual disjunction of poetic etiquette and of conventional syntax" (Yates 263). A new phase began with Breton's *Surrealist Manifesto* of 1924. The Sabadell group (Armand Obiols, Francesc Trabal, and Joan Oliver) cultivated an absurdist streak to challenge literary conventions and to *épater le bourgeoisie.* The Sitges based journal *L'Amic de les Arts* (1926–9) brought J. V. Foix (1893–1987) and Salvador Dalí (1904–1989) into contact. Foix's verse and prose-poetry depicts dreamscapes and magical metamorphoses. This was the start of a surrealist flurry of agitation which would continue into the 1930s.

As *Noucentisme* emerged in Catalonia, the so-called *Generation of 1914* appeared on the Spanish literary scene. Jiménez, Pérez de Ayala, Eugenio d'Ors, Gabriel Miró, Gómez de la Serna, and Benjamín Jarnés all contributed, with José Ortega y Gasset (1883–1955), writer and philosopher, as intellectual leader. What distinguishes the *Generation of 1914*'s concern for Spain from previous times was their return to specific political solutions and to a need to Europeanize Spain, concerns which had been abandoned by the writers of '98. There was also great interest in scientific fields: such as the findings of the histologist Santiago Ramón y Cajal, whose ideas had influenced Edvard Munch's painting *Melancholy (Laura)* in 1900 (Everdell 114). Ortega y Gasset's articles, lectures and essays on philosophical

and political issues contributed to the Spanish intellectual renaissance in the first decades of the twentieth century in Spain, and he is well-known outside Spain as a modernist. *Meditaciones del Quijote* (1914, *Meditations on the Quijote*) elucidates Ortega's phenomenological approach to knowledge. *El tema de nuestro tiempo,* (1923, *The Modern Theme*) presents a perspectival epistemology. *La rebelión de las masas* (1930, *The Revolt of the Masses*) is a reflection on the problems of modern civilization in which he cautions against the destructive influence of mass-minded people, who if not directed by the intellectually and morally-minded superior minority, encourage the rise of totalitarianism. In *La deshumanización del arte* (1925, *The Dehumanization of Art*) he developed an elitist view of culture. Modern art, the archetype of abstraction, was praised by Ortega because it maintains the distinctions between high and low culture. Ortega sought to exclude the masses (themselves a product of modernity) as a potentially threatening, uncultured other. Ortega's theories had a huge impact on Spanish thinking. Works by Pérez de Ayala employed a perspectival method that presents the narration from the points of view of a variety of characters, while the later work of Gabriel Miró stretches languages to its limits in an attempt to capture the nature of time and consciousness. Miró's *Las cerezas del cemeterio* (*The Cherries from the Cemetery*) transgresses the separation between beauty and savagery (in nature), spirituality and carnality, life and death.

Another of the many writers who took up Ortega's theories was Rosa Chacel (1898–1994), whose relationships with other writers ought to place her within the *Generation of 1927,* but she is largely overlooked in accounts of this movement. Jiménez's 1931 book of caricatures, *Españoles de nuestro tiempo* (*Spaniards of Our Time*) refers not to her writing but to her appearance: she is a "niña mayor" (a grown-up girl). Chacel's case serves to highlight the absence of women in the histories of modernist trends—something which needs to be addressed if the history of modernism in Spain is to be fully understood (Mangini). Chacel (like María Zambrano, 1904–1991) counted on the mentorship of Ortega who acted as a protector for the young artists of 1927. She saw Ortega as an "oracle" who advocated a "pure" art, an elite intellectual exercise, a challenge she took up in her first novel, *Estación. Ida y vuelta* (1930, *Round Trip Station*) which is inflected by Joyce's *Portrait of the Artist as a Young Man* and **Proust**'s *Remembrance of Things Past* to depict "quite simply, a man who lives a philosophy." In the prologue to the novel she writes of the "interiority" of her discourse, an anti-realist, multi-perspectivism. Chacel uses irrational personification of objects and employs only pronouns (reminiscent of the "pure" poetry of Jiménez, Salinas, and Jorge Guillén) which banishes representationalism from her work (Mangini 20). Chacel's later work has been likened to that of **Virginia Woolf** in its stream-of-consciousness narrative style and sexually ambiguous characters (see **Androgyny**). The novel for Chacel, as for her modernist counterparts abroad, is a continuous aesthetic quest.

The brilliant poets and writers of the *Generation of 1927* flourished during the 20s and 30s. Jorge Guillén (1893–1984), Pedro Salinas (1891–1951), Rafael Alberti (1902–1999), Vicente Aleixandre (1898–1984), Luis Cernuda (1904–1962), José María Hinojosa (1904–1936), and Federico García Lorca (1898–1936) among others could arguably be described as modernists in their incorporation of the frenetics of the avant-garde into their refashioning of symbolism based on the "pure poetry" borrowed from Paul Valéry which often used **Freud**'s tenets on the workings of the psyche. Aleixandre's poems are hallucinations: fragmented evocations of a surrealist universe where, "glass hair and metal butterflies exist in their own right, not just as metaphors" (Harris 233). The arrival of the avant-garde in Spain is represented by two essays by Ramón Gómez de la Serna (1888–1967), whose *greguerías* beginning in 1910 rework fragments of city life in a process of defamiliarization caused by linguistic disruption; he is credited with spearheading the interest in the avant-garde shown in Spain. While **surrealism** was elitist, the avant-gardists' recuperation of folk traditions forged links between high and low art. Vanguard dramatists experimented with the playful combination of categories: they recast the elements of popular song, **dance,** and farce by linking them to intellectual themes. They adapted circus and *commedia dell'arte* traditions, experimented with startling cinematic effects and worked with musicians, composers, and painters to push boundaries and forge the new. Federico García Lorca gave performances of his poetry and plays (which drew variously on folk and popular traditions and avant-garde elements) to educated audiences, but with his touring group *La Barraca,* he took the Spanish classics ("high art") to the rural communities. While his later works are "rural dramas," earlier he treated the theme of the dehumanizing quality of modern urbanity with a heightened perception of the disordering force of psychological pain in his avant-garde poetics, *Poeta en Nueva York* (1929–30, *Poet in New York*) which Young (1998) compares to **Eliot**'s *The Waste Land* in its chaos of fragmented, broken images, the "bits and pieces" characteristic of modernism. In *Poeta en Nueva York* there is an emphasis on uncannily disconnected limbs, reminiscent of Luis Buñuel (1900–1983) and Salvador Dalí's 1929 film *Un chien andalou.* Graham and

Labanyi (14) describe Lorca as "the paradigmatic modernist: because of the ambivalence of his response to modernity, because of his inability to translate his political sympathies into direct political action, and because neither of these things prevented him from becoming a Republican martyr." While a *Generation of 1936* succeeded the poetic movements of *ultraísmo* and *creacionismo,* by the end of the Spanish Civil War many writers were forced into exile, while others had been killed. Those that remained were concerned with the reeling shock of fratricidal conflict. It would take some time for modernist endeavor in Spain to recuperate.

The confines of this article do not allow for a full exploration of the widely diverse "bits and pieces" (Everdell 28) which make up the story of modernism in Spain. Certain elements, such as the role played by female modernists, have yet to be written into the canon of the old histories. Certain links and connections are surely masked by the imposition of definitions and by our attempts to mark evolutionary processes through history. Spanish modernism is no simple, streamlined movement. It is a rich and vivid area in which further exploration is profoundly rewarding. Rather than a movement, Spanish modernism was a process, a collage of semi-collective challenges, ventures, and readjustments, an aesthetic and reflective response to the "dislocating forces" of the turn of the last century.

Sarah Wright

Selected Bibliography

Anderson, Perry. *The Origins of Postmodernity.* London: Verso, 1998.

———. *The Origins of Postmodernity.* London: Verso, 1998.

Bretz, Mary Lee. *Encounters Across Borders: The Changing Visions of Spanish Modernism, 1890–1930.* Lewisburg: Bucknell University Press, 2001.

Butt, John. "Rage and Idea: Renewal and the Generation of '98." *Times Literary Supplement* (August 7 1998): 4–5.

Davison, Ned J. *The Concept of Modernism in Hispanic Criticism.* Boulder, Colorado: Pruett Press, 1966.

Everdell, William. J. *The First Moderns: Profiles in the Origins of Twentieth-Century Thought.* Chicago: University of Chicago Press, 1997.

Graham, Helen and Jo Labanyi. *Spanish Cultural Studies: An Introduction. The Struggle for Modernity.* Oxford: Oxford UP, 1995.

Harris, Derek. *Metal Butterflies and Poisonous Lights: The Language of Surrealism in Lorca, Alberti, Cernuda and Aleixandre.* Anstruther, Scotland: La Sirena, 1998.

Hart, Stephen. *Spanish, Catalan and Spanish-American Poetry From* Modernismo *to the Spanish Civil War.* Lampeter: The Edwin Mellen Press, 1990.

Jencks, Charles. [Letter]. *The Times Literary Supplement* (12 March 1993): 15.

Labanyi, Jo. *Galdós.* Harlow, Essex: Longman, 1993.

Mangini, Shirley. "Women and Spanish Modernism: The Case of Rosa Chacel." *Anales de la Literatura Española Contemporánea* 12 (1987): 17–28.

Miller, Stephen. "Modernism." *Dictionary of the Iberian Peninsula,* 2 vols. Ed. Germán Bleiberg, Maureen Ihrie and Janet Pérez. Westport, Conn.: Greenwood Press, 1993. 1105–6.

de Onís, Federico. *Antología de la poesía española e hispanoamericana (1882–1932).* Madrid: Centro de Estudios Históricos, 1934.

Perriam, Chris. "Literary *Modernismo* in Castilian: The Creation of a Dissident Cultural Elite." In Graham and Labanyi, 53–55.

Sieburth, Stephanie. *Inventing High and Low: Literature, Mass Culture and Uneven Modernity in Spain.* Durham and London: Duke UP, 1994.

Terry, Arthur. "Catalan Literary *Modernisme* and *Noucentisme:* From Dissidence to Order." In Graham and Labanyi, 55–57.

Williams, Raymond. "When was modernism?" *The Politics of Modernism.* Ed. Tony Pinkney. London: Verso, 1989.

Yates, Alan. "Catalan Literature between *Modernisme* and *Noucentisme.*" *Homage to Barcelona: The City and its Art, 1888–1936.* Ed. M. McCully. London: Arts Council, 1985. 253–63.

Young, Howard T. *The Line in the Margin: Juan Ramón Jiménez and His Readings in Blake, Shelley, and Yeats.* Wisconsin: University of Wisconsin Press, 1980.

———. "Broken Images: Eliot, Lorca, Neruda and the Discontinuity of Modernism." *Exemplaria* 2.1 (1998): 1–14.

Spatial Reading

The concept of "spatial reading" was expounded in an essay by Joseph Frank, developing from an idea of Wylie Sypher's that modern art is pervaded by a philosophical formalism that amounts to a *style* (opposed to nineteenth-century *stylization*) which requires the reader to be more active and also highly self-conscious. This is mainly because of the modernist text's complex construction, which militates against drawing conclusions from any part of the book before its conclusion is reached. A parallel example is with land surveying, which is impossible from the flat ground and needs to take place from an elevated position from which all of a landscape can be seen at one time. The idea of spatial reading largely derives from **cubism,** which argues that a three-dimensional object or event needs to be analyzed from all angles and not just one. So, to take an example from modernist fiction, in **Ford Madox Ford**'s *The Good Soldier* the narrator John Dowell returns again and again to relate the same events from different angles. Modernist approaches also mean that the reader often cannot fully understand events when first encountering them. For example, there are many references to "the girl" early on in *The Good Soldier* but it is only much later that the reader finds out that this is Nancy Rufford. Ford also employs this technique because Dowell is trying to record how events struck him at particular times, when he was often only in partial possession of the facts, and therefore additionally unreliable. Through this technique Ford stresses the point in the novel that we can never fully know other people. All we see is their external show. In the story, Dowell says: "it is very difficult to give an all-round impression of any man. I wonder how far I have succeeded with Edward Ashburnham." His attempt is to lay out all the sides to his "good soldier" so that when readers finish the text they can see the whole character (this similarly applies to **Woolf**'s *Mrs. Dalloway*). Spatial reading also addresses the problem of linearity in fiction: Dowell knows that events are really too multi-dimensional to be told in one straight line, moving from clue to clue like a simple detective story, even though writing automatically gives temporal precedence to whatever is narrated first in a number of synchronous events. Dowell says at one point: "it is so difficult to keep all these people going. I tell you about Leonora and bring her up to date; then about Edward, who has fallen behind. And then the girl gets hopelessly left behind." When the story is narrated in such a cubist or many-sided way, where every statement is provisional and partial, the reader is required to adopt a spatial reading of the text in order to survey any part of it adequately.

Peter Childs

Selected Bibliography
Frank, Joseph. "Spatial form in Modern Literature." In his *The Widening Gyre: Crisis and Mastery in Modern Literature.* Prentice-Hall: New Brunswick, NJ, 1963.
Sypher, Wylie. *Rococo to Cubism in Art and Literature.* New York: Harper and Row, 1960.

Stein, Gertrude (1874–1946)

American writer, educated at Radcliffe College, where she took courses with William James. After giving up her studies at Johns Hopkins Medical School she moved to Paris in 1903 with her brother Leo, and lived there till her death. Their home in Rue de Fleurus, on the Rive Gauche, soon became a famous literary salon, attended by both European and American artists (among others, Roger Fry, **Ford Madox Ford, Ernest Hemingway,** and **Sherwood**

Anderson), who could there admire the Steins' outstanding collection of modern paintings, including works by Cézanne, Renoir, Matisse, Braque, and Picasso. Picasso became one of Stein's closest friends and painted a famous portrait of her. After Leo's departure in 1913 Stein shared her home with her lifelong companion Alice B. Toklas, through whose point of view she was to write her own autobiography (*The Autobiography of Alice B. Toklas,* 1933).

Stein was an extremely prolific writer, whose production ranged across prose (*Three Lives,* 1909; *The Making of Americans,* 1925), poetry (*Tender Buttons,* 1914), essays (*Composition as Explanation,* 1926; *How to Write,* 1931) and lyric drama (*Four Saints in Three Acts,* 1934) to memoirs (*Paris France,* 1939; *Wars I Have Seen,* 1945), all reflecting her fascination with the avant-garde and her enduring interest in **formal experimentation.**

Stein's first published work was the collection *Three Lives,* after the model of Flaubert's *Trois Comptes.* The three stories which make up the volume deal with ordinary, lower-class women—one a servant, one an immigrant of German origins, one a young African American—who lead uneventful lives and die unspectacular deaths. Apart from the scanty plots, the real focus of the narration is on the difficulties the three characters encounter in mastering language—the English language, in particular, since two of them are first-generation German immigrants—and on the ensuing problems of communication. In "Melanctha"—the second and most famous story—Stein rewrites in a heterosexual key the autobiographic, lesbian experiences she had put at the center of her first, unpublished work, *Q.E.D.,* dramatizing the impossible union between Jeff, a young black doctor who believes in the power of language to reveal others, and his beloved Melanctha, whose rich and complex inner life baffles all his attempts to define it once and for all. The three stories anticipate features of a style which will become the distinctive mark of Stein's later and more radically experimental production, notably her idiosyncratic use of repetition. Following what she takes to be Cézanne's lesson, Stein refuses the idea that prose is characterized by a central, structuring element—the linear development of plot—to which every other element must be subordinated. Advocating a non-hierarchical principle of composition, she reverts to the repetition of narrative blocks, which mostly ignore the laws of cause and effect and chronological progression. "I believe in repetition."—she writes—"Yes. Always and always. Must write the eternal hymn of repetition."

The Making of Americans, a *roman-fleuve* in which Stein tries to recapture the complexity of American history through the events of a specific group of characters, was meant to be precisely such a hymn. In its more than a thousand pages, its plot never moves forward, but circles around the obsessive repetition of words, phrases, narrative sequences, doing away with chronology, character development, even with the traditional rules of grammar and syntax.

The radical nature of Stein's experiments with language becomes more and more evident in her later production, from the series of "portraits" devoted to artists, friends, people she simply happened to meet (collected in *Portraits and Prayers,* 1934), to her most experimental work, *Tender Buttons,* a volume of prose poems which Stein defined as "verbal still lives," or "portraits of things," in which she subverted all traditional orders of discourse, applying to writing the lesson of Picasso's **cubism.** Here, Stein plays with words, with their meanings, their sounds, their rhythms, putting them together in long verbal chains ("A rose is a rose is a rose is a rose" remains the best-known one, although by no means the most experimental), using nouns as verbs, creating puns, ultimately shaping a verbal surface in which the most common words acquire a new value and a new—if often startling—life. With her highly experimental writing, Stein questions and redefines the whole enterprise of representation, which to her can no longer aim at an ideal "transparency" effacing the medium that makes it possible. On the contrary, her texts—exactly like the canvases of her beloved Cézanne and Picasso—draw the reader's attention to their constituents, to the materiality of language, and bear the marks of the efforts to come to grips with the world.

If most of Stein's production baffled the average reader, she enjoyed popular success with *The Autobiography of Alice B. Toklas,* written in an easy style which recaptured with great vivacity the main characters and events that characterized her stay in **France,** from the early days in the company of her brother Leo, through her involvement in the First World War, when she drove her car through the French countryside as a member of the American Fund for French Wounded, to her trips to the South in the company of Alice B. Toklas in the post-war years.

Carla Pomaré

Selected Bibliography

Benstock, Shari. *Women of the Left Bank: Paris, 1900–1940.* Austin: U of Texas P, 1986

Bowers, Jane Palatini. *Gertrude Stein.* New York: St. Martin's Press, 1993.

Mellow James R. *Charmed Circle: Gertrude Stein and Company.* New York: Praeger Publishers, 1974.

Neuman, Shirley and Ira B. Nadel, eds. *Gertrude Stein and the Making of Literature.* Northeastern UP, 1988.

Steiner, Wendy. *Exact Resemblance to Exact Resemblance: The Literary Portraiture of Gertrude Stein.* New Haven, Conn.: Yale UP, 1978.

Walker, Jayne L. *The Making of a Modernist: Gertrude Stein from Three Lives to Tender Buttons.* Amherst: U of Massachusetts P, 1984.

Stevens, Wallace (1879–1955)

American poet, educated at Harvard.

After a failed attempt at journalism in New York City, he trained as a lawyer and, in spite of his literary inclinations (he had poems published in little magazines since 1914), he made up his mind to pursue a career outside the world of letters. In 1916 he moved with his wife and daughter to Hartford, Connecticut, where he spent the rest of his life, working full-time for an insurance company, of which he became Vice-President in 1934. Writing poetry on his way to work and after his office-hours, Stevens published his first collection of poetry, *Harmonium,* at the age of forty-four, in 1923, and then almost ceased his literary activity for the next six years. His major volumes of poetry include *Ideas of Order* (1935), *The Man with the Blue Guitar* (1937), *Notes Toward a Supreme Fiction* (1942), and *The Auroras of Autumn* (1950). *The Collected Poems of Wallace Stevens* were first published in 1954. *Opus Posthumous,* gathering as yet unpublished material, came out in 1957. His daughter Holly edited *The Letters of Wallace Stevens* in 1966.

Since his death in 1955 Stevens has enjoyed a steadily growing reputation and he is now recognized as one of the major voices—if not *the* major voice—of American modernism. Probably because of his double career as a poet *and* a businessman, he was a rather isolated figure, always keeping in touch, mainly through his correspondence, with fellow poets and artists, but never really belonging to any schools or groups. Unlike most of his contemporaries, he never visited Europe, and cherished instead in his poems a "Europe of the mind" made up of books, postcards, paintings, artifacts that friends and correspondents sent him from the other side of the Atlantic. Such an attitude extends as well to his poetry, which combines a strong urge to bring about a Wordsworthian marriage between the mind of the poet and the world, with an almost postmodern consciousness of the unbridgeable gap between subject and object, the language of art and the world of facts.

The hermetic yet playful strain of Stevens' first production, influenced by contemporary developments in the visual arts, gives way in his later phase to a more somber and meditative—at times almost "philosophical"—poetry. Here, as well as in the essays collected in the volume *The Necessary Angel* (1951), Stevens addresses questions such as the nature and role of the imagination, the process of perception and the scope of poetry, which define him as an heir to the romantic tradition of Wordsworth and Emerson.

As far back as 1915, in his first published masterpiece, "Sunday Morning," and then later in "The Man with the Blue Guitar," he had voiced the need, typical of the modern age, for secular beliefs that could fill the void of "empty heaven and its hymns." For the mature Stevens, the first and ultimate belief is the belief in "a supreme fiction, recognized as fiction, in which men could propose to themselves a fulfillment"—a fiction that is no ultimate revelation of truth, but a human construct. If, echoing Shelley's *Defense of Poetry,* Stevens charges poetry with the task of providing a version of reality which is free from the layers of interpretations that culture has piled on it, he takes pains to stress that there is no way out of the world of representations. The fictive veil covering *the truth* can not be lifted, but can, and must, be substituted by new veils, that is by new interpretations, to keep abreast with the principle of metamorphosis which to him is life.

Thus, in the language of the "Notes Toward a Supreme Fiction"—his major longer poem—Stevens urges his imaginary poet to get to the core of reality, to its "first idea" or "immaculate beginning," to what both romantics and symbolists had defined as "pure vision," but warns him that there will never be a naked "bride." Significantly, Stevens' man with the blue guitar (both a homage to Picasso and a personal variation on the figure of the poet, blue being the color that identifies imagination in his poetry) when asked to play things "as they are," had replied that these "Are changed upon the blue guitar."

While carrying on his personal meditation on poetry, Stevens creates a world made of colors and sounds, peopled by the characters of his personal mythology, either taken from tradition or created *ex novo*—from the highly idiosyncratic Crispin of the early "The Comedian as the Letter C" to the Shelleyan Ozymandias of the "Notes." Stevens' characters speak—and are spoken about—using Stevens' peculiar idiom, no doubt a difficult language. If it is true that Stevens mostly keeps within the bounds of traditional versification (with a marked preference for iambic pentameters), he exploits all the resources of its medium, combining extended metaphors, repetitions, archaisms, foreign words, neologisms, and bizarre expressions with a massive recourse to irony and self-mockery, and suggesting—as **Marianne Moore** (Stevens' friend and admirer) has noted—a linguist creating multiple languages within a single idiom.

Carla Pomaré

Selected Bibliography

Bates, Milton J. *Wallace Stevens: A Mythology of Self.* Berkeley: U of California P, 1985.

Bloom, Harold. *The Poems of Our Climate.* Ithaca: Cornell UP, 1976.

Doggett, Frank and Robert Buttel, eds. *Wallace Stevens: A Celebration.* Princeton: Princeton UP, 1980.

Filreis, Alan. *Wallace Stevens and the Actual World.* Princeton: Princeton UP, 1991

Perloff, Marjorie. "Pound/Stevens: Whose Era?" *New Literary History* 13 (1982): 485–514.

Schaum, Melita and John N. Serio, eds. *Wallace Stevens and the Critical Schools.* U of Alabama P, 1988.

Vendler, Helen. *Word Chosen Out of Desire.* Cambridge, Mass.: Harvard UP, 1986.

Stravinsky, Igor: *The Rite of Spring*

For many, the most important date of twentieth-century **music** is May 29, 1913. That day saw the premiere of Igor Stravinsky's ballet score, *Le Sacre du Printemps—The Rite of Spring* at the Theatre des Champs Elysees in Paris (see **Dance**). It provoked the most famous riot in musical history. According to Stravinsky, protests were underway about the music even before the curtain rose and these exploded into uproar when the ballet itself started. In a fury, Stravinsky stormed backstage to discover the choreographer Nijinsky standing on a chair and shouting numbers to the dancers who could not hear the music over the din. Nijinsky was so upset that Stravinsky had to hang onto his coat-tails to prevent him from running onto the stage and remonstrating with the audience. The head of the company, Serge Diaghilev was engaged in switching the house lights on and off in an endeavor to distract the audience but also to assist the police in identifying and ejecting the troublemakers. The conductor Pierre Monteux was continuing imperturbably with the music.

Meanwhile, in the audience things were getting out of hand. Two men were making arrangements for a duel, after the woman friend of one of them had slapped the other's face for spitting at the performers. One eye-witness—and it had to be an eye-witness because no one could hear anything—later recounted that he began to feel a throbbing in his temples that he first put down to the hectic urgency of the music: it was only on looking around that he realized the person behind him was pounding out Stravinsky's rhythms on the top of his head. It was quite an occasion. **Gertrude Stein** was there; so was Apollinaire who later complained that he had not heard a note of music because of the racket (or *was* that the music?); so was Debussy, covering his ears, it is said, with his hands.

Where had this music come from? Why did it have this effect? What influence was it to have on other modern arts?

Prior to *The Rite of Spring,* Stravinsky had had enormous success with two ballet scores for Diaghilev's Les Ballets Russes company, *The Firebird* (1910) and *Petrushka* (1911), with Nijinsky unforgettably dancing the title role. The idea for the *Rite* had come to him one day in 1910, he said, as if in a dream. He had a vision of a solemn pagan rite in which a young girl dances herself to death to propitiate the gods of spring, watched over by sage elders sitting in a circle. He worked out a scenario with the painter Nicholas Roerig, but his collaboration on the choreography with Nijinsky soon ran into difficulties. For one thing, Nijinsky knew nothing about music, while Stravinsky realized his new score was so complicated that, while he could hear it in his head, at first he did not know how to write it down. There were 120 rehearsals, with Nijinsky being assisted by Marie Rambert. However, Stravinsky was never happy with what was achieved; and the sight in performance of what he was to call in his autobiography "a group of knock-kneed and long-braided Lolitas jumping up and down" no doubt added to the first night audience's antagonism.

But it was the music that staggered them. Nothing quite like it had been heard before: dissonant, unharmonic, barbaric, music whose sharp and irregular rhythms overrode any discernible melodic line. "From the first to the last bar," wrote the music critic of *Le Figaro,* "there is not a note one expects, unless . . . the one that shouldn't be there." Small wonder that the reviews of the premiere referred punningly to *Le Massacre du Printemps.* For this was not like Spring as seen by romantic composers, a musical tone-poem of rustling leaves, gentle breezes and trilling birdsong. This was instead the kind of Spring that Stravinsky remembered from his Russian childhood, when the new season announced itself by the sound of the cracking of the ice. This was Spring as seen from beneath the earth, loudly and violently asserting its rebirth. The music had none of the grace and fluidity of composer-impressionists like Debussy and Ravel. It was hard and mechanical.

Yet in no time at all Stravinsky's score had moved from being a source of scandal to the status of acknowledged classic. "Make it new," was **Ezra Pound**'s dictum for the aspiring modernist, and this was the music the modernists had been waiting for: more than Schoenberg (whom Stravinsky was to describe as a romantic at heart trying to renounce romanticism), this score represented a real break from the past. It was music that belonged to the new age. The American critic Paul Rosenfeld could not listen to it without thinking of machinery, steel and the vibrations of the twentieth-century world. Writing of the work in 1921, **T. S.** **Eliot** also said he heard in it the sounds of the new century—the motor horn, the beating of metal, the roar of engines—but felt Stravinsky had "transformed these despairing noises into music." The composer demonstrated that it was possible to make art out of the chaos and cacophony of modernity: in a slightly different context, Eliot was later to make the same claim for **James Joyce**'s *Ulysses.*

Indeed, critics were quick to liken what Stravinsky was doing in music with the work of other artistic innovators. The comparison with Picasso's **cubism** suggested itself: a dry, conceptual, intellectual, even mathematical more than sensual or emotional approach to art seemed common to them both. Similarly the work's rigorous objectivity and anti-romanticism was to find an echo in the poetry of T. S. Eliot, particularly in *The Waste Land,* whose underlying theme of sacrifice and rebirth had striking connections with *The Rite of Spring.* Like Eliot, Stravinsky turned away from the idea of art as an in-

dividualist, emotional outpouring: he would only say of his score that he heard it, wrote down what he heard, and was the vessel through which it passed. Also like Eliot, and other modernists like Joyce and **Henry James,** he put no store by any humanist or moralist approach to art, feeling that a work of art was its own justification. "A masterpiece is all that counts," he would say: a modernist credo if ever there was one.

Was the unbridled barbarism of the score, written on the eve of world **war,** consciously or unconsciously prophetic? It would be far too simple to see a direct link between Stravinskian savagery and the descent into violence and horror that was soon to engulf society. Nevertheless, the ballet's strange subject-matter—such a defiant challenge to the "refined" themes of Western culture—strikes an oddly familiar chord. A text that was a key influence on *The Waste Land,* Sir James Frazer's *The Golden Bough* (1890), had dealt with myths and superstitions in ancient religions of sacrifice and rebirth. **Joseph Conrad**'s *Heart of Darkness* (1902) disclosed degenerate **primitivism** lurking beneath a veneer of culture and civilization; and even the most Apollonian of heroes, **Thomas Mann**'s Aschenbach (a surrogate of **Gustav Mahler**) in *Death in Venice* finds himself shockingly yielding to Dionysiac forces in his subconscious that undermine his sense of identity and rationality. These are either disturbing stirrings of discontent and repression beneath the surface of civilization that must eventually erupt into savagery; or they are the attempt of man, and woman, to get more in touch with their natural, instinctual self, which urban modern life has atrophied to the point of neurosis. One thinks here of the pregnant Anna's dance in **D. H. Lawrence**'s *The Rainbow* (1915), as if she is seeking some kind of mystical experience or release—a desire to feel life in the body more than the mind. It might be seen as a Stravinskian dance of life. Anna's husband looks on, bemused and appalled, like the audience on Stravinsky's opening night, but viewed from another perspective, it could appear beautiful, different, liberating.

Stravinsky's score pulsated with the pressure of modern experience and was quickly acknowledged not as an affront to modernity but as the epitome of it. By 1929, Siegfried Sassoon could write a poem "Concert-Interpretation" in which he talks of attending a performance of *Le Sacre* in the hope of another riot and being disappointed by the audience's placidity. "No tremor alarms," he wrote, disconsolately: the music could have been written by somebody dead, "like Brahms." But for anyone hearing it for the first time, the music's pounding rhythm, its barbaric energy, its shredding of romantic harmony, still has the shock of the new. If the origins of literary modernism are difficult to date, musicologists have no such problems. On that May night in Paris in 1913, musical modernism was born.

Neil Sinyard

Selected Bibliography

Boulez, Pierre. *Orientations.* London: Faber & Faber, 1986.
Butler, Christopher. *Early Modernism.* Oxford: Clarendon Press, 1994.
Eksteins, Modris. *Rites of Spring.* London: Bantam Press, 1989.
Eliot, T. S. "London Letter." *The Dial* 71.4 (1921): 452–3.
Rosenfeld, Paul. *Musical Impressions.* London: Allen & Unwin, 1970.
Stravinsky, Igor. *An Autobiography.* London: Calder & Boyars, 1975.

Surrealism

Surrealism flourished in **France** between 1924 and 1939; its "heroic period" of 1924–1929 was bracketed by André Breton's First and Second Manifestoes. Surrealism sprang from the more violently anarchic **dada,** which was born in Zurich in 1916 and expired in Paris in 1922; Tristan Tzara was the connecting link. Dada did not stand *for* anything: it was a "lifestyle" (Richard Huelsenbeck) or a "mental attitude" (Max Ernst), a protest movement that staged "happenings" and experimented with poster art and typography. Its more disciplined successor was inspired and led by André Breton (1896–1966), in close alliance with fellow-poets Louis Aragon, René Crevel, Robert Desnos, Paul Eluard, Benjamin Perét, and Philippe Soupault. Their revolutionary aims were "to transform the world, change life, remake from scratch human understanding" (Breton).

The term "surrealist" was first used by Guillaume Apollinaire in his notes for the Diaghilev ballet *Parade* (1917). Launching the movement, Breton offered two succinct definitions:

> SURREALISM, *n.* Psychic automatism in its pure state, by which one proposes to express—verbally, by means of the written word, or in any other manner— the actual functioning of thought. Dictated by thought, in the absence of any control exercised by reason. . . .

> ENCYCLOPEDIA. *Philosophy.* Surrealism is based on the belief in the superior reality of certain forms of previously neglected associations, in the omnipotence of dream, in the disinterested play of thought. . . . (*Manifestoes* 26)

Breton named Apollinaire, Lautréamont (Isidore Ducasse), Arthur Rimbaud, Alfred Jarry, and Giorgio de Chirico as forerunners. As inheritors of Baudelaire's "artificial paradises," surrealists aimed to disrupt the rule of reason and sponsor "the miraculous, the surprising, insanity, dream, the unconscious, and hallucination" (Schneede 23).

Surrealism was a program of subversive creativity rather than a philosophy. "Surrealism plunges its roots into life," said Breton, and "relives with glowing excitement the best part of its childhood" (*Manifestoes* 124, 39). At the outset, the key was "pure psychic automatism," writing or drawing in a state of trance, without any attempt to control imagery. Breton, who had worked in a psychiatric unit during **World War I,** had studied **Freud,** but the surrealists wanted to stimulate, rather than control, the unconscious and Breton was not content to follow Freudian pathology. He "believ[ed] that if [a person had] any *artistic gift,* he [could], rather than transform his dreams into symptoms, transform them into artistic creations" (*Manifestoes* 160). Breton and Desnos practiced automatic writing which gave mixed results: flashes of brilliance amid masses of mediocrity. The positive effect was to loosen up the flow of imagery, which could then be slightly modified while retaining its spontaneous inspiration. Breton's *Soluble Fish* (1924) is a lucid example. Despite desertions, excommunications, and troubled relations with the French Communist Party, Breton managed to keep the movement alive until 1940, when many surrealists and other artists fled to New York. In the postwar climate of existentialism, surrealism lost its hegemony, but surrealist principles entered into the mainstream of modern art and literature.

Surrealist aesthetics depend on incongruity, combination, and startling conjunction. Incompatible entities are combined through metaphor, which conjures the marvelous out of the real. In the *First Manifesto,* Breton quoted Pierre Reverdy (1918) on the dynamics of the poetic image:

The image is a pure creation of the mind.
    It cannot be born from a comparison but from a juxtaposition of two more or less distant realities.
    The more the relationship between the two juxtaposed realities is distant and

true, the stronger the image will be—the greater its emotional power and poetic reality. . . .

Breton believed in the "alchemy of the word" and its "marvelous instrument," **metaphor;** he longed to "[get his] hands on the prime matter (in the alchemical sense) of language" (*Manifestoes* 299). In his *Second Manifesto,* he reiterates the role of the unconscious—"surrealism aims quite simply at the total recovery of our psychic force by a means which is nothing other than the dizzying descent into ourselves, the systematic illumination of hidden places" (136–37)—but he also de-emphasizes automatism and gives more play to selection and combination.

Breton proposed a neo-Hegelian dialectics whose synthesis would be a state of *surreality:* "Everything tends to make us believe that there exists a certain point of mind at which life and death, the real and the imagined, past and future, the communicable and the incommunicable, high and low, cease to be perceived as contradictions" (123). Surrealism wants to break down antinomies: it aims at "that point where construction and destruction can no longer be brandished one against the other" and "at the annihilation of the being into a diamond, all blind and interior, which is no more the soul of ice than that of fire" (124). After Rimbaud, the poet is to be magician and seer.

Surrealism, the "prehensile tail" of romanticism, sprang from an all-encompassing notion of poetry. Breton rebelled against the restraints of syntax and wanted "to put language 'in a state of effervescence'" (qtd. Balakian 142). Images replace "ideas" and words can make the reader see. Eluard affirms visualization: "Images think for me;" Salvador Dali calls for "meteors of imagination;" and Breton makes words "explode in a dynamic image" (Balakian 143). Surrealist images, fusing disparate entities, "come to [the poet] spontaneously, despotically" (Baudelaire). "It is," Breton says, "from the fortuitous juxtaposition of the two terms that a particular light has sprung, *the light of the image . . .* " (*Manifestoes* 37). The "incandescent flash" of the surrealist image combines the concrete with the impossible in a "lucid madness."

Surrealism was dedicated to exploring the latent powers of the mind. Man is "the inveterate dreamer" and the rhythms of dream, its freedom, its startling combinations are different from those of waking consciousness. Creative hallucination combines heterogeneous images or substitutes one object for another. Rimbaud "[saw] quite frankly a mosque in place of a factory, a school of drummers made up of angels, carriages on roads in the sky, a parlor at the bottom of a lake, etc" (see Balakian 192). Surrealism asserts the free activity of mind in relation to objects and, far from accepting habitual orders of perception, adopts Rimbaud's "derangement of all the senses." It creates its own imaginative reality and revels in the rapidity and daring with which it connects images. Breton evolved the concept of *the Marvelous* as a spiritual necessity and asserted: "Beauty must be convulsive, or it is not beauty." Surreal imagery is often grotesque or macabre. Techniques of incongruous combination, transposition, and parody give visual shape to metamorphosis and ambiguity. Breton, who published an *Anthology of Black Humor* (1939–40), reveled in the Gothic: "Fear, the attraction of the unusual, chance, the taste for things extravagant" (*Manifestoes* 16). Such tastes stimulated tactics of disruption and disorientation, as in Breton's novel, *Nadja* (1928), where coincidences transgress the boundaries of reality and dream.

The movement engendered close relations between literature and painting. Surrealists cultivated "objective hazard," on the model of Lautréamont's bizarre image: "Beautiful like the chance meeting, on a dissection table, of a sewing machine and an umbrella" (*Les Chants de Maldoror*). This illogical conjunction inspired various techniques, such as *collage* and *montage.* The paintings of Max Ernst (1891–1976) and René Magritte (1898–1976) offer surreal combinations: organic and inorganic may be fused, as in Ernst's *Elephant of Celebes* or Picasso's *Bathers Playing Ball* (1932), forming hybrid or monstrous figures. Major surrealist painters are Ernst, Magritte, André Masson (1896–1987), Yves Tanguy (1900–55), Joan Miró (1893–1983), and Salvador Dalí (1904–89), with Giorgio de Chirico (1888–1978) as an influential forerunner. De Chirico's painting derived its theatricality from Renaissance art and its eerie loneliness from images of deserted arcades and city squares exposed to perspectival distortion. De Chirico drew on childhood obsessions and unconscious imagery to construct symbolic stage sets. Rubin has shown that "multiple vanishing points" make his picture space seem illusory, like "space that one has dreamed or imagined" (134). This virtual space is haunted by paralysis, silence, and enigma.

Max Ernst's volatile imagination conjured up surreal imagery in a variety of genres. As Balakian notes, "Ernst's landscapes are based on a subjective reorganization of the animal, vegetable, and mineral kingdoms" (204). One rainy day at an inn, Ernst made his first *frottage,* by rubbing black lead on a paper dropped on the floorboards. The resulting striations suggested embryonic shapes, which Ernst elaborated according to fantasy and personal obsession. This technique stimulated unconscious imagery and allowed him to combine chance and automatism with invention and design, in paintings such as *To 100,000 Doves* (1925) or *The Great Forest* (1927). Ernst also devised a series of ingenious collage novels, including *Histoire naturelle* (1925), the punning *La femme 100 têtes* (1929), and *Une semaine de bonté* (1934).

André Masson used objective chance in his "sand pictures," pouring glue on burlap, scattering sand on it, then rubbing off the residue. From the shapes that emerged, he developed violent or erotic images, often using paint straight from the tube, as in *Battle of Fish* (1927). His animistic compositions exploit the "interplay between accident and intention" (Schneede 86). Joan Miró describes how, in his own semi-automatic compositions, "the picture begins to assert itself, or suggest itself under my brush. The form becomes a sign for a woman or a bird . . . " (qtd. Rubin 156). The first "free, unconscious" stage of a painting like Miró's *The Birth of the World* (1925) involved the random spreading of colors; the second "carefully calculated" stage saw flowing lines emanate from color masses. Yves Tanguy, in a distinctive style, created strange, luminous undersea worlds of biomorphic shapes, noted for their "deep spatial illusionism" (Rubin 194).

As if "attempt[ing] to make thought visible" (Schneede 11), René Magritte produced some of the most striking surrealist images. In *The Human Condition I* (1934), he superimposes an easel painting of woods and fields over an equivalent space outside a window. The easel image is foregrounded in a spatial *mise en abyme* that makes inside oscillate with outside. Magritte's meta-pictorial painting, with its flat, veristic technique, foregrounds the logic of illusion. *The Use of Words I* (1928–29), which bears the inscribed legend "Ceci n'est pas une pipe," forces one to distinguish between words, images, and objects. *The Red Model* (1935), in which boots taper off into toes, illustrates metamorphosis through surreal conjunction. *Ready-Made Bouquet* (1957) superimposes a figure from Botticelli's *Primavera* on the back of a bowler-hatted businessman, flaunting the artifice of pictorial composition. Magritte's bizarre concatenations raise questions of illusion and per-

ception. *Evening Falls* (1964) depicts a shattered window, with the red ball of the sun seen above hills and a castle; shards of glass, propped against the inside of the window, retain fractured images of the scene. The painted imprints on glass remind the viewer that the countryside beyond the window-frame must also be painted on an opaque surface. *Evening Falls* deconstructs itself by demonstrating how painting combines materiality with illusion; at the same time, it pushes illusion to the point of surreality.

Salvador Dalí's virtuosity enabled him to apply a flawless Renaissance technique to personal oneiric fantasies. He cultivated his "paranoiac critical method" of bringing delusional imagery and sexual fetishes to the canvas, consciously exploiting such obsessions, rather than employing images spontaneously. The "lucid madness" of Dalí's surrealist inventions, such as the limp wrist-watches in *The Persistence of Memory* (1931), combined with his personal showmanship, made him a huge success with the public, but tended to obscure the aims of surrealism.

Discovery, invention, and recombination are keys to surrealism, reflected in a wide variety of techniques. Max Ernst often combined *frottage* with *grattage* (scraping off a surface to form linear patterns), as in *Snow Flowers* (1927). Oscar Dominguez invented *decalcomania*, in which paint is poured on sheets that are then folded together; the shapes that emerge can be touched up to form strange or beautiful figures. Wolfgang Paalen devised the parallel technique of *fumage*, exploiting smoke patterns made by a candle. "Incongruous combination" is seen to effect in surrealist *collage*, which Ernst defines as "an alchemical composite of two or more heterogeneous elements," and in *montage*, where separate things are assembled to form imaginary objects.

The surrealist object is a composite of "perception and representation:" from

Breton's neo-Hegelian standpoint, it is the dialectical fusion of matter and thought. Surrealists constructed hybrid objects that gave concrete form to oneiric fantasy. The most famous of such objects are Méret Oppenheim's *Fur-Covered Cup, Saucer, and Spoon* (1936) and Hans Bellmer's *Dolls* (1936), with their grotesque and erotic anatomical distortions. Alberto Giacometti's sculptural abstractions, such as *Suspended Ball* (1930–31) or *Caught Hand* (1932) are menacing symbolic objects, while Marcel Duchamp's *Chocolate Grinder* (1913) and *The Bride Stripped Bare by her Bachelors, Even* (1915–23) are elaborate erotic "machines." Breton's principles of "objective humor" and "objective chance" come into play in the game of *exquisite corpse,* in which each player draws on a piece of paper, folds it, then passes it on, producing ludicrous composite images.

Surrealism is an interarts movement. Apollinaire's friendship with painters set the pattern for closer interactions within the avant-garde. Breton's *Surrealism and Painting* (1928) and the *Collected Works of Lautréamont* (1938)—illustrated by Brauner, Dominguez, Ernst, Magritte, Man Ray, Masson, Matta, Miró, Paalen, Seligmann, and Tanguy—spread the interarts doctrine. Miró saw "no difference between painting and poetry;" Magritte narrowed the gap between painting and philosophy; Ernst composed collage novels and paintings; Breton made surrealist objects; Masson read widely in proto-surrealist authors. Surrealist films aimed to shock, as did Luis Buñuel and Salvador Dalí's *Un Chien Andalou* (1929), with its notorious eye-cutting scene, and *L'Age d'or* (1930), in which a couple are buried in sand and devoured by ants. Antoni Gaudí's architectural extravaganzas in Barcelona replace rectilinear with curvilinear, spiral, or arabesque lines. While purely surrealist writing remains "esoteric," surrealist elements appear in the work of numerous Anglo-American novelists such as **James Joyce, Virginia Woolf, Djuna Barnes,** Anaïs Nin, Henry Miller, Nathanael West, and John Hawkes, while surrealist metaphor has been absorbed into the matrix of modern poetry. Surrealism made a major contribution to modernism and continues as a strong undercurrent in all the arts.

Jack Stewart

Selected Bibliography

Alexandrian, Sarane. *Surrealist Art.* Trans. Gordon Clough. New York: Praeger, 1970.

Balakian, Anna. *Surrealism: The Road to the Absolute.* Rev. ed. New York: Dutton, 1970.

Breton, André. *Manifestoes of Surrealism.* Trans. Richard Seaver and Helen R. Lane. Ann Arbor: U of Michigan P, 1972.

———. *Surrealism and Painting.* Trans. Simon Watson Taylor. New York: Harper, 1972.

Carrouges, Michel. *André Breton and the Basic Concepts of Surrealism.* Trans. Maura Prendergast. N.p.: U of Alabama P, 1974.

Dupin, Jacques. *Miró: Life and Work.* New York: Abrams, n.d.

Erben, Walter. *Joan Miró 1893–1983: The Man and His Work.* Cologne: Benedikt, 1993.

Gablik, Suzi. *Magritte.* Boston: New York Graphic Soc., 1976.

Hammacher, A. M. *René Magritte.* Trans. James Brockway. New York: Abrams, n.d.

Lippard, Lucy R. *Surrealists on Art.* Englewood Cliffs, NJ: Prentice-Hall, 1970.

Matthews, J. H. *The Imagery of Surrealism.* Syracuse: Syracuse UP, 1977.

———. *Toward the Poetics of Surrealism.* Syracuse, NY: Syracuse UP, 1976.

———. *An Introduction to Surrealism.* University Park, Penn.: Pennsylvania State UP, 1965.

Quinn, Edward. *Max Ernst.* Boston: New York Graphic Soc., 1977.

Rubin, William S. *Dada and Surrealist Art.* New York: Abrams, n.d.

Schneede, Uwe M. *Surrealism.* Trans. Maria Pelikan. New York: Abrams, n.d.

Svevo, Italo (1861–1928)

Pseudonym of Ettore Schmitz: novelist, short story writer, essayist, and playwright.

Svevo was born into a wealthy Jewish family in the cosmopolitan port of Trieste, then part of the Austro-Hungarian Empire. His father's family was German, his mother's Italian, and he was sent to school in Bavaria. On his return to Trieste he intermittently studied law and medicine, but abandoned his studies in 1880 due to his father's financial difficulties and failing health. He took a job as a bank clerk, submitting essays and reviews to the newspaper *L'indipendente,* which published his first piece of fiction in 1890. The experience of working as a bank clerk was drawn upon for his first novel, *Una vita* (1892, *A Life*). This novel and his second, *Senilità* (1898, *As a Man Grows Older*), were published at Svevo's own expense and virtually ignored by reviewers. In disgust, Svevo published nothing else for 25 years, turning instead to his parents-in-law's marine paint business, by which he accumulated much wealth during **the war**.

In 1907, searching for an English tutor in Trieste, he met **James Joyce**, who admired Svevo's work (especially *Senilità*) and encouraged his writing. Shortly afterwards, he became acquainted with the work of **Freud** and, partly under his influence, returned afresh to his writing. His next novel, *La coscienza di Zeno* (1923, *Confessions of Zeno*), initially went unnoticed in **Italy,** but, with Joyce's help and once translated into French, it was soon heralded as a major achievement, and is today considered a masterpiece of modern literature. He went on to write a series of short stories, the most famous of which are *Una burla riuscita* (*The Hoax*), *La novella del buon vecchio e della bella fanciulla* (*The Nice Man and the Pretty Girl*), and *Corto viaggio sentimentale* (*Short Sentimental Journey*). Only one of his plays was performed in his lifetime: *Terzetto spezzato* (1925, *Broken Terzetto*).

Though estimates of his work varied widely for several decades after his death in a car crash in 1928, Svevo is now credited with having pioneered the use of **interior monologue** and the stream-of-

consciousness technique. His concern with the ways in which language can transform experience, together with his thematic interest in the connections between guilt and disease, love and jealousy, and death and time, have invoked comparisons to **Proust** (he was once considered "the Italian Proust"). Svevo is frequently cited as the father of the modern Italian novel.

Andrew Harrison

Selected Bibliography

In Italy Svevo's works are published in a standard edition by Dall'Oglio of Milan. English translations of his works have been published in England by Secker and Warburg (London). A bibliography of his works is contained in Weiss (1987).

Furbank, P. N. *Italo Svevo: The Man and the Writer.* London: Secker and Warburg, 1966.

Gatt-Rutter, John. *Italo Svevo: A Double Life.* Oxford: Clarendon Press, 1988.

Weiss, Beno. *Italo Svevo.* Boston: Twayne Publishers, 1987.

Synge, John Millington (1871–1909)

The leading playwright of the Irish literary revival.

Born in Dublin on April 16, 1871 to John Hatch and Kathleen Synge, his family hailed from an Anglo-Irish background, whose landholdings, though in decline, were still substantial enough to keep the Synges in the ascendancy class. Synge's father died when the playwright was an infant and his childhood was deeply colored by his mother's evangelical protestantism. He was later to abandon his religious faith, a process set in motion by his teenage fascination with natural history and his encounter with the writings of Charles Darwin. Spurning his family background and religion gave him autonomy as an artist, but it was also a traumatic experience and led to a dissonance in sensibility that he never fully overcame. It imbued in him a strong and abiding sense of isolation that would later be reinforced by his sense of being an outsider among the Irish peasantry. All his plays are about outsiders of some sort, tramps or misfits whose poetic ebullience sets them apart from their emotionally impoverished communities. It is in the ensuing impression of physical and historical dislocation that a modernist alienation can be felt.

He enrolled in the Faculty of Divinity in Trinity College Dublin in 1889 and, more interested in pursuing his interest in **music** and the Irish language, left with only a pass degree in 1892. During 1893–94, he went to **Germany** with the intention of becoming a musician. Opting in the end for a career as a critic and writer, he went to Paris in 1895, where he studied at the Sorbonne under Anatole de Braz and Henri d'Arbois de Jubainville. Many of Synge's influences were picked up in Paris and he made periodic returns over the next several years. In Paris he met a number of Irish expatriates including **W. B. Yeats,** who famously encouraged him to go to the Aran Islands off the west coast of **Ireland** to find an artistic purpose. Between 1898 and 1902 he made five visits to Aran, which led to his travel work, *The Aran Islands,* eventually published in 1907. Importantly, Aran helped Synge perfect the Hiberno-English idiom (English as spoken by the Irish) that he would put to such effective poetic use in his mature drama.

He wrote three of his most famous plays in 1902, following his fifth and last visit to Aran and following the abortive escapism of his "Big House" play, *When the Moon has Set* (written 1900–1), which shows heavy traces of his reading of Nietzsche. His one-act play, *In the Shadow of the Glen* (1903), set the tone for Synge's bumpy reception amongst certain sections of Irish nationalist opinion through its comic portrayal of an unhappy marriage, and a sexually adventurous younger wife. *The Tinkers Wedding,* a comedy also set in Wicklow, was begun

in 1902 but not performed until its 1909 London production. The one act tragedy *Riders to the Sea* was produced at the Abbey Theatre in 1904. Set in the Aran Islands, this play tells the story of Maurya who has lost her fisherman husband and all but one of her six sons to the sea. Despite her entreaties, her last son Bartley insists on going on a trading mission to the mainland. In the closing moments of the play Bartley's corpse is carried on stage, leading to Maurya's final, powerful speech in which she confronts her loss with stoicism and tragic dignity: "No man at all can be living for ever and we must be satisfied."

In 1905 Synge went on an investigative tour of living conditions in Mayo with the painter and illustrator Jack B. Yeats (the poet's brother), which resulted in twelve articles on the "Congested Districts Board" for the *Manchester Guardian.* In the same year *The Well of the Saints* was produced at the Abbey. A suggestive and ambivalent treatment of the imagination as both liberating and delusory, this play tells the story of a pair of blind, old beggars, Martin and Mary Doul who are convinced that they are beautiful. When they have their sight restored by a visiting "saint" these delusions are painfully dispelled and they are forced to put up with the mocking of the villagers, while Martin must tolerate the drudgery of work in the blacksmith's forge. When their blindness returns, Martin upsets the saint's attempts to cure them a second time by knocking the holy water from his hand. Spurned by an angry community, the Douls head off on the open roads, deluding each other, once again, about their handsomeness.

The Playboy of the Western World, first staged at the Abbey on January 26, 1907, is often regarded as Synge's masterpiece. This play carries allusion to both Oedipus and Christ and is sometimes read as a national allegory. It tells of Christy

Mahon, who arrives in a Mayo shebeen (country pub) claiming to have killed his domineering father. This story of violence wins him the respect and awe of the local girls, particularly Pegeen Mike, the daughter of the hostelry owner. Lured by Christy's fine words, she spurns her fiancé, the timid and priest-fearing Shawn Keogh. Invigorated by his status in the community, Christy wins all the sporting competitions in the village and all seems to be going well, until his supposedly murdered father, Old Mahon, stumbles into the shebeen, seeking vengeance on his son. Old Mahon remembers Christy as an ineffectual and effeminate boy, but Christy can now defend himself and, it seems, slays his "Da" a second time. Finding that there is a "great gap between a gallous story and a dirty deed," Pegeen Mike and all the other villagers turn on Christy and try to hand him over to the police. When Old Mahon rouses himself again, he and a dignified Christy head off together, to "romp through a romancing lifetime," leaving Pegeen Mike to grieve her loss of "the only playboy of the western world."

This play scandalized a large section of nationalist opinion, angry at the depiction of the Mayo villagers as craven, impious, and bloodthirsty and, in particular, at the licentiousness of the Mayo women. Riots were a nightly accompaniment for its full week's run at the Abbey. Similar scenes occurred four years on, when the play went to America. The fracas can be partly understood in terms of a conflict between public expectations of **naturalism** and verisimilitude in drama and a play edging towards a non-realist, modernist aesthetic. Notwithstanding Synge's justification of *Playboy* precisely in terms of its fidelity to the spoken language of the Irish peasantry, this is a drama of conflicting modes and a self-conscious gap between heightened poetry and dismal reality.

The role of Pegeen Mike was played by Synge's fiancé, the Abbey actress Molly Allgood. But Synge, who had long suffered from recurring bouts of ill health, developed Hodgkin's disease in late 1907 and the marriage was postponed. His own sense of mortality haunts his final, unfinished play *Deirdre of the Sorrows*, a dramatic departure for him in that it deals with a story from Irish mythology, usually the province of other revivalist dramatists like Yeats, Lady Gregory, and "AE" (G. W. Russell). In Synge's version the Hiberno-English dialect of his other plays is transported to the ancient setting, despite his fears that the "Saga people" might loosen his "grip on reality." He did not live to see the play performed for he died on March 24, 1909. He was thirty seven.

Though sometimes seen as a straight naturalist, there are nascent modernist energies in Synge's work. To be sure, his plays are energized by the particular—by the sounds, tastes, smells and textures of rural Ireland—but they are far more elliptical, abstract pieces than is sometimes allowed. The sensuous immediacy of their setting and the colloquial veracity of the Hiberno-English idiom suggest a literal or realist drama, but the plays brim with fertile tensions and multifaceted contradictions. Like **Joyce,** Synge often finds the archetypal in the mundane. Moreover his work at once luxuriates in the everyday *and* holds it at arm's length. The language foregrounds the unusual, the exotic and the gorgeous, even as it treats the dull, the squalid and the violent. His repeatedly avowed mission was to create art of joy mingled with **realism** and this opposition often generates a distance between his extravagant language and the recalcitrant materiality of the stage. This opposition between language and reality was to become the hallmark of Irish drama, as the work of playwrights from **Sean O'Casey** to Brian Friel makes clear.

Ronan McDonald

Selected Bibliography

Gonzalez, Alexander G., ed. *Assessing the Achievement of J. M. Synge.* Westport: Greenwood Press, 1996.

Grene, Nicholas. *The Politics of Irish Drama: Plays in Context from Boucicault to Friel.* Cambridge: Cambridge UP, 1999.

Kiberd, Declan. *Synge and the Irish Language.* 2nd ed. Dublin: Gill and Macmillan, 1993.

King, Mary C. *The Drama of J. M. Synge.* London: Fourth Estate, 1985.

Kopper, Edward A. Jr. *A J. M. Synge Literary Companion.* Westport: Greenwood Press, 1988.

McCormack, W. J. *Fool of the Family: A Life of J. M. Synge.* London: Weidenfeld and Nicolson, 2000.

Skelton, Robin, gen. ed. *The Collected Works.* 4 vols. London: Oxford UP, 1962–68.

Watson, George. *Irish Identity and the Literary Revival.* 2nd ed. Washington D.C.: The Catholic U of America P, 1994.

T

Technology and Mechanization 1890–1939

Modernist literary experimentation is closely linked to scientific and technological development. In the last decades of the nineteenth century the process of industrialization (with its radical transformation of the landscape, intense urbanization, mechanization of labor, mass production, gradual globalization), which had been pioneered by Great Britain, was quickly spreading through Europe, as was witnessed by the opening of the Paris Exposition in 1889 (a more sophisticated "replica" of the Crystal Palace Exhibition in 1851), followed by the one in Turin (1902) and by the Deutscher Werkbund Exhibition in 1914. New technological inventions like the telegraph, telephone, and typewriter, photography and the **cinema,** the bicycle, car, and airplane, along with the widespread use of electricity, completely changed the quality of life and human communication, as well as traditional concepts of space, time, distance, and speed.

One of the great, central symbols of modern industrialization was the Eiffel Tower, which in 1913 transmitted the first time signal to the rest of the world, and which found an echo in one of the most radical modernist poetic experiments, Apollinaire's *Lettre-Océan.* The modern industrial metropolis and the multiplicity of its intricate labyrinths, its disorienting

discontinuity, its cacophony of different languages and sounds, became a protagonist in **Joyce's** *Ulysses* (especially in "Aeolus" and "Wandering Rocks"); its overwhelming but also disturbing impressions on the individual were analyzed in the account of an imaginary plane ride in "Flying over London" by **Woolf.** The new worlds opened up by the machine and its multiple applications were celebrated by **Italian futurism** as the key to innovation, the essence of an art which, freed from the obsolete forms of the past, expressed the impetus and convulsive dynamism of modern life. **Futurism** exerted a profound influence on some English and American artists (such as **Lewis, Pound,** and **Lawrence**) who, however, as fierce enemies of the effects of industrialization, could not fully and uncritically embrace **Marinetti's** cult of the machine.

Indeed, in modernist literature (and in modernist films like Fritz Lang's *Metropolis*) the machine is also typically seen as the expression of man's willful desire to dominate nature, and as a dehumanizing force that reduces the individual to a mere mechanism, a type of robot (the word was first coined in 1921). In many modernist works, therefore, there is a close link between technological determinism and cultural pessimism, the apparent promise of technology being represented as a dangerous illusion opening the way to the sort of mass destruction seen in **World War I** and in the even more destructive war which was to follow.

Stefania Michelucci

Selected Bibliography
Kern, Stephen. *The Culture of Time and Space 1880–1918.* Cambridge: Harvard UP, 1983.

Shattuck, Roger. *The Innocent Eye. On Modern Literature and the Arts.* New York: Farrar Straus Giroux, 1984.

Williams, Raymond. *The Politics of Modernism: Against the New Conformists.* London: Verso, 1989.

Thomas, Dylan (1914–1953)

Anglo-Welsh poet, short story writer, and playwright. Born in Swansea to Welsh-speaking parents from rural Carmarthenshire, Thomas was nevertheless brought up in an English-speaking household. His father was English master at Swansea Grammar School, which Thomas himself attended, without distinguishing himself academically. He later became a cub reporter with the *South Wales Daily Post* for a brief period before leaving for London and a precarious career as a full-time writer. He began writing poetry at an early age, and the notebooks he filled in his late teens were to provide material for many of the later published collections of verse. The precocious maturity of *18 Poems* (1934) and *Twenty-five Poems* (1936) immediately established his reputation; his was hailed as a distinctive and unusual voice.

Unlike many of his English peers at the time, Thomas was a writer who did not seem overtly concerned either with politics or society, but rather with elemental human processes, such as conception, birth, and death, and with the human being's relationship with the natural world. Nevertheless, Thomas's "nature" poetry, if it can be thus termed, eschewed the pastoral and the descriptive, choosing instead to focus on vivid and often grotesque images of the hidden workings of the universe and the human body. Similarly, his early stories, such as those included in the mixed poetry and prose collection *The Map of Love* (1939) contain grotesque imagery and exhibit a Gothic concern with extremes: nightmares, witches, torture, and death. Both poems and stories exhibit a Freudian concern with sexuality and its imperatives, as well as with the revelation of hidden, dark impulses. Parallels with **D. H. Lawrence** suggest themselves, particularly in view of the fact that both writers were accused of obscenity. Yet Thomas usually managed to avoid **censorship** because his early work was regarded as so convoluted, even hermetic, that charges of obscenity were difficult to prove. Moreover, unlike Lawrence, Thomas seems to be more concerned with creating linguistic frissons than with telling a story or relaying a message. Some critics discern a surrealist element in his earlier work, though Thomas himself repudiated this connection, perhaps because he associated **surrealism** with automatic writing, which he vehemently denied ever attempting. Indeed, Thomas lays great emphasis on the *craft* of the poet, on the actual physical presence of words on the page and in the mouth, on the sound of poetry, and on its tactile and sensual qualities. Like Mallarmé, Thomas believed that poems were made of words, not ideas. Dedicated from an early age to the life of an artist, Thomas can be seen in retrospect as a poet who created a self-contained, sacramental tower of words on which to perch above the pressing mundane concerns of his native, provincial city, Swansea. Nevertheless, the characters and ambience of the city, as well as aspects of rural Carmarthenshire, where the Thomas family had its roots, find their way into Thomas's work in fictionalized and elaborated form.

In 1938 Thomas moved to Laugharne in rural Carmarthenshire, which was to be his main home for the rest of his life and which provided the inspiration for a number of his major works, such as the radio play *Under Milk Wood* and such poems as "Over Sir John's Hill" and "Poem in October." Generally the poems and stories of the 1940s are more accessible and more lyrical than the early so called "process" poems and the Gothic stories. The autobiographical stories in the collection *Portrait of the Artist as a Young Dog* (1940) reveal Thomas's adroitness both at capturing the voice of a child narrator and at creating moods of nostalgia and poignancy. Thomas's linguistic inventiveness and exuberance are also still in evidence but, on the whole, these later works are less easily labelled "modernist" than his earlier, more experimental work. In the prose broadcasts which Thomas made in the mid-1940s, such as "A Child's Christmas in Wales" and "Holiday Memory," he effects a nostalgic return to childhood. It is an escape which perhaps many adults would like to enact, which may explain these later broadcasts' continuing wide popularity. Similarly, the posthumously published play for voices *Under Milk Wood* (1954) remains Thomas's most enduringly popular work perhaps because of the lyrical and evocative accessibility of the language and the universal theme of the irrepressible burgeoning of sexuality, despite attempts at repression. The 1946 poetry volume, *Deaths and Entrances,* contains many of the poet's most justly acclaimed lyric poems, including "Fern Hill" but it is questionable whether such a poem can actually be regarded as in any sense modernist, since it appears to embrace rather the neoromantic mode, celebratory and quasireligious, which was to characterize most of Thomas's later work.

The modernist Thomas is the poet and short story writer of the 1930s, then; his brief later life and career was largely responsible for creating the enduring Thomas myth of the doomed, self-destructive genius, but it certainly revealed him moving further and further away artistically from his modernist origins. Between 1950 and 1953 Thomas undertook four lengthy reading tours of the United States which were lucrative but exhausting; it was during one of these tours that he collapsed and died in New York in November, 1953. According to legend, the cause of death was alcohol poisoning, memorably though perhaps apocryphally described by the doctor who examined him as "an insult to the brain." Though this fact has been questioned by latter-day biographers, there is no doubt that Thomas's colorful addiction to alcohol during the later years has contributed immeasurably to the legend of the brilliant poet and raconteur destroyed by his own life of excess.

Katie Gramich

Selected Bibliography

Ackerman, John. *Welsh Dylan.* Cardiff: John Jones, 1979.

Bold, Alan, ed. *Dylan Thomas: Craft or Sullen Art.* London: Vision, 1970.

Conran, Tony. "After the Funeral: The Praise Poetry of Dylan Thomas." In *The Cost of Strangeness: Essays on the English Poets of Wales.* Llandysul: Gomer Press, 1982.

Davies, James A. *A Reference Companion to Dylan Thomas.* London, Westport: Greenwood Press, 1998.

Davies, Walford. *Dylan Thomas.* Cardiff: University of Wales Press, 1990.

———, ed. *Dylan Thomas: New Critical Essays.* London: Dent, 1972.

Ferris, Paul. *Dylan Thomas.* London: Hodder & Stoughton, 1977. New edition 1998.

———, ed. *Dylan Thomas: Collected Letters.* London: Dent, 1985.

Stanford, Derek. *Dylan Thomas: A Literary Study.* London: Spearman, 1954.

Talfan Davies, Aneirin. *Dylan: Druid of the Broken Body.* London: Dent, 1964.

Thought, Language, Aesthetics and Being 1900–1940

Thought

Modernist writers were strongly affected by the thought of their time and one manifestation of this was a suspicion of *thought* as such. In his last letter before his death, **W. B. Yeats** declared "Man can embody truth, but he cannot know it" and **T. S. Eliot**'s obituary compliment to **Henry James** that he "had a mind so fine that no idea could violate it" (*Egoist,* April 1918, 2) encapsulates a widespread modernist skepticism about ideas. For he did not mean that James was too intelligent to be passed off with a dud idea, he meant that James's mind did not function in terms of ideas at all. Although Eliot himself was influentially inclined to philosophical and cultural-historical speculation, he also deprecated this tendency, even in himself, and could therefore recognize with special acuteness that James's intelligence manifested itself in his well-nigh complete assimilation of philosophical concerns into a highly self-conscious, infinitely flexible, scrutiny of experience, and more particularly of language. Such a spirit is variously echoed in James's brother William, the American pragmatist philosopher, and in Wittgenstein. Eliot was most importantly a poet, while Wittgenstein several times gave up philosophy and advised promising students to find an honest manual trade.

This skepticism towards ideas as such has a variety of sources. When **Joyce**'s Stephen Dedalus, for example, speaks to Mr. Deasy in *Ulysses* of those "big words that make us so unhappy" he suggests an epochal and generational rejection of inherited values invested in prestigious conceptions such as religion and nationhood. But there are more specifically philosophical sources of this skepticism, several of which will be discussed here. A significant general context is the collapse, by the early part of the twentieth century, of philosophical idealism.

Various kinds of idealism had been in academic ascendancy almost since the time of Immanuel Kant. Kant's *Critique of Pure Reason* (1781) was a foundational text of modern thought. It overcame the

dualism of Descartes, and the skepticism of David Hume, by indicating how the world is known only through necessary categories of thought, so that the structure of thought is the structure of the world. When he described his philosophical enterprise as "transcendental," therefore, he did not mean that it referred to some realm *beyond* the phenomenal world, but that it sought to establish the conditions of possibility for *experiencing* it. The philosopher J. W. Fichte, however, in his lectures at the University of Jena in the seventeen nineties, helped to create a German idealist school by giving this philosophy a subjective inflection. He interpreted Kant, in effect, as saying that world is an aspect of mind. Fichte's one-time disciple, F. W. Schelling, reacted in turn by claiming that the mind is an aspect of the world; and it was primarily from Schelling that Coleridge found confirmation of the idealism by which he influenced the English tradition specifically in relation to imaginative literature. But it was G. W. F. Hegel who developed idealism into its consummate form whereby the whole of human history, including its future, became an intelligible, and even inevitable, manifestation of the human spirit. There were radically dissenting voices in the nineteenth century, most notably Marx's materialist alternative to Hegel's dialectic of the spirit, and Nietzsche's radical deconstruction of almost all cultural values including the traditional pursuit of truth. But it was only in the early twentieth century that forms of idealism ceased to be central to philosophical activity within the academy. There is an emblematic value in T. S. Eliot's writing a Ph.D. thesis on the "objective" idealist F. H. Bradley and then claiming, later in life, that he no longer understood it. The thought of Nietzsche (1844–1900), Heidegger (1889–1976), and Wittgenstein (1889–1951) represented a turn not just against idealism, but against metaphysics as such. The later world no longer believed in the questions, let alone agreed with the answers, of the earlier one. In the Anglo-American context, the demise of idealism can be seen in William James's pragmatism, Bertrand Russell's mathematical logic, and Wittgenstein's restriction of the philosophical enterprise to an analysis of language use. Wittgenstein was like Joyce in being profoundly superficial, in understanding the limits of what could be said.

As the inclusion of Russell, the archetypal intellectual depicted in **D. H. Lawrence**'s *Women in Love* as Sir Joshua Malleson, indicates, the turn against idealism did not always entail a turn against ideas and a more closely significant context was the internal questioning of science. Through much of the nineteenth century natural science had been the most prestigious form of truth statement; as was evident in the way the narrative fiction of the period constantly modeled itself, whether literally or metaphorically, on the methods of science. Zola's **naturalism,** theorized in *The Experimental Novel* (1880), was the culminating example. But well before the turn of the century science had begun to lose some of its epistemological self-evidence. Einstein's relativity theory was to catch the headlines and, like Heisenberg's later "indeterminacy" principle, it seemed to have an analogical application to other, non-scientific spheres. But such analogies must be approached with care. Einstein did not so much bring relativity into the world as find a way of handling it.

Two books written for educated lay readers usefully bracket the period of high modernism: Karl Pearson's *The Grammar of Science* (1892) and Arthur Eddington's *The Nature of the Physical World* (1928). In the middle of the nineteenth century the advance of physical science still seemed an irrefragably demonstrable structure built on the testable foundation of empirical observation. And in the layman's conception this remained the case. But as scientific enquiry addressed itself particularly to astronomical and sub-atomic scales the underlying notion of observation became increasingly problematic. It was evident that the universe at these levels behaved in a different way from the common-sense world of everyday experience, while the necessary questions could only be asked through experiments which were themselves based on highly speculative theory. The last decade of the century, for example, saw a running controversy as to whether the basic material of the universe behaved like waves or particles; a controversy for which there was no direct observation. Pearson expressed the epistemological implications of the new science for a general public by saying that science does not "explain" the workings of the universe, it merely describes what happens in given conditions. Of course, this recognition of epistemological limitation did not impede the progress of science, indeed it reinforced the creative need to think outside common-sense or inherited terms, and it has long been absorbed into scientific consciousness. Nonetheless, it brought home the recognition that science is a construction of the human mind before it is a reflection of the world; a recognition that brought science closer to other creative activities such as imaginative literature.

And for those who had doubts concerning the growing hegemony of scientific methods and criteria in the culture at large this recognition supported a philosophical case for limiting and relativizing their value. Nietzsche, who was well read in contemporary science, remarked in *The Birth of Tragedy* (1872), "great men . . . have contrived, with an incredible amount of thought, to make use of the paraphernalia of science itself, to point out the limits and relativity of knowledge generally, and thus to deny decisively the claim of science to universal validity and universal aims" (112). Likewise, several modern writers deliberately used science as just one possible order of understanding rather than as the ultimate form of truth statement. The point here is not to impugn the objectivity of science as such but to question the increasing assumption in the culture that only scientific criteria are of consequence. The narrative voice of the "Ithaca" episode of *Ulysses* (1922) is a parodic series of "scientific" questions and answers; the first part of **Thomas Mann**'s *The Magic Mountain* (1924) shows Hans Castorp's abortive attempts to understand the mystery of life biologically; Lawrence's essays *Psychoanalysis and the Unconscious* (1921) and *Fantasia of the Unconscious* (1922) question not just the content of **Freud**'s theories but their claims to scientific authority, and indeed the relevance of science in the realm of psychology.

Eddington, looking back on the period, opens with a homely but telling image. The modern physicist, he says, lives in two worlds at once. He uses the same solid plane surface of the writing table as anyone else but he also knows that the table is "really" a mass of moving particles through which, given the appropriate technique, it would be possible to penetrate without disturbance. The X ray, invented by Röntgen in 1895, was pregnantly used in *The Magic Mountain* when Castorp was of the first generation in history to see his own skeleton; in his case the scientific machine designed to save life produces a kind of *memento mori*. The X ray remains a suggestive image for modernism at large. Eddington intimates that the modern physicist continues to live in the Newtonian world of the layman while "seeing through" its limited, almost illusory, character. The common-sense table continues to exist but only as perceived within a human scale of reference. Several of the greatest works of modern literature are characterized by such a double awareness. They use realist representation, indeed they often use it con-

summately, yet with an X ray awareness of its constructed, or purely human, character. Various modernist movements, across all of the arts, shared a radical departure from representational verisimilitude. The terms "**realism**" and "verisimilitude," however problematic they may be, inevitably suggest some truth value in their mode of imitation and the general shift is part of an epistemological change for which contemporary science provides the clearest focus.

The modernist decades were a time of epochal shift, like that of **Shakespeare** and Cervantes, and the most summative works of the period were frequently those which, like them, owned a dual loyalty. Different world conceptions are held together in a mutually testing relation. The past is criticized yet it is also preserved on a new basis. A consequence of this recognition of radical world making is that it came to seem necessary, for a philosopher such as Martin Heidegger, to speak not of *the* world so much as of "world." Lecturing in 1938, Heidegger defined modernity as the "Age of the World Picture":

> The expressions "world picture of the modern age" and "modern world picture" . . . assume something that never could have been before, namely, a medieval world picture and an ancient world picture. The world picture does not change from an earlier medieval one into a modern one, but rather the fact that the world becomes picture at all is what distinguishes the essence of the modern age. (*The Question Concerning Technology* 130)

Heidegger sees this relativistic consciousness as a defining characteristic of modernity, and he goes on to cite both modern humanism and the rise of **anthropology** as aspects of this. Anthropology suggests the growing awareness of human cultural relativity, although the actual practice of anthropology in the early twentieth century was still often at a pre-scientific, or pseudo-scientific, stage in which the beliefs and customs of tribal peoples were studied as evidence of a universal primitive mind such as Lévy-Bruhl articulated in *How Natives Think* (1923). Nonetheless, writers like **Joseph Conrad** in *Heart of Darkness* (1902) and D. H. Lawrence in the "Africa" theme of *The Rainbow* (1915) and *Women in Love* (1920) were already showing how an awareness of these radically other forms of life would rather unsettle than confirm the home civilization.

Heidegger's reference to modern humanism suggests an even more radical kind of relativism. The impact of Darwinism, and the nineteenth-century recognition of the sheer span of time in which humanity had evolved, threw into question not just the centrality of European civilization but of the human as such. This raises another way of looking at the dual vision produced by science. Even apart from the epistemological question, or the problem of knowledge, there was a question of value. Human values are not inherent in the world but are imported into it by the human. Joyce's *Ulysses* is the classic expression of the separation of fact, the observed world of Dublin, from value, the organization of meaning in the text. In this respect the parodic scientism of the "Ithaca" episode embodies a genuinely impersonal, trans-human viewpoint. The awareness of living simultaneously on a human and a non-human plane is made explicit in Lawrence's comments on the work which was to become *The Rainbow* and *Women in Love.* In a letter of 1914 he rejected the "old stable ego" of humanist ethical characterization because he only cared "about what the woman *is*—what she *is*—inhumanly, physiologically, materially— . . . what she *is* as a phenomenon (or as representing some greater, inhuman will), instead of what she feels according to the human conception" (*Letters* i, Cambridge 1981: 183). Yet of course he was equally interested in what his characters

felt as human individuals and the category of the individual retained a crucial importance for him. In the same letter, therefore, he criticizes the Italian futurist **Marinetti** for seeking a purely scientific or technological vision when a human being was in question. This precisely epitomizes the modernist synthesis as outlined above. Marinetti's **futurism,** with its celebration of the machine, represented a debunking of humanism whereas Lawrence was incorporating something of Marinetti's spirit into an enlarged conception of the human. In this he was one with Joyce and Thomas Mann.

In this way, many writers "saved the appearances" of humanism and a traditional order by recognizing that in this area only appearances, viewpoints, are in question anyway although for human beings this viewpoint is the one that matters; or is the only one they can have. The recognition that the world itself does not privilege the human, which was a matter of shock to Thomas Hardy and other Victorian agnostics, was incorporated into a more self-standing humanist conception. In **Virginia Woolf**'s Mr. Ramsey, partly a portrait of her father, the Victorian critic, Leslie Stephen, a note of absurdity begins to surround the figure of the earnest agnostic. To read these modernists either humanistically or anti-humanistically, therefore, is to miss the point since humanism, the necessary human standpoint, is acknowledged in its ultimate groundlessness. *Ulysses,* by re-enacting an ancient tale of homecoming in contemporary terms as a burlesque jostling of cultural structures, myths, discourses, and intellectual disciplines, expresses a modern sense of what the human home is: a construction within a void. The recognition of the self-grounding character of the human world is the truest meaning of the modernist use of myth. **Myth** could be many things, including nostalgia for a lost unity, a fascistic regression, or a literary structure, but its most important meaning was as an emblem of the human world as self-created. Of course, Joyce's comedic inflection of this was not the only possibility. Apart from futurist anti-humanism, the anguish of **Kafka**'s fiction, whatever its other causes or implications, comes from a desire still to *find*, rather than *create*, a meaning.

Language

The human creation of meaning is also focused in the period's interest in language; an interest whose cardinal significance is now sometimes referred to as the "linguistic turn." The pervasive concern with the construction of meaning helps explain the emphasis in all the modernist arts on the nature of their own medium; and in the case of literature this means, as well as literary genres and forms, language itself. By the early teens of the century, it was becoming possible to see language no longer as merely describing or reflecting the world, but actually forming it as world; a viewpoint that was later to be developed by the American linguist Benjamin Lee Whorf. A key turning point was the work of the Swiss linguist Ferdinand de Saussure. Whereas nineteenth-century study of language was predominantly historical, concerned with origins and development, de Saussure's *Course in General Linguistics,* published in 1916 after his death, emphasized the synchronic and structural dimension. He showed how the linguistic sign stands in an arbitrary relation to its external referent while meaning is created relationally within the system of language itself. Whereas Adam in Eden gave names to all the existing objects, on this model we only *have* recognizable objects by creating names for them. Wittgenstein in the *Tractatus Logico-Philosophicus* (1921) was to develop a related point: "The limits of my language mean the limits of my world." Stephen Dedalus's philosophical ruminations while walking the beach in the

"Proteus" episode of *Ulysses* begin with a cognate thought borrowed from Jacob Boehme: "Signatures of all things I am here to read."

What Wittgenstein shares with Stephen's phrase is a sense of mystery. Wittgenstein was to be mistakenly associated with later British movements of linguistic philosophy and logical positivism whose most reductive aspect was expressed in A. J. Ayer's *Language, Truth and Logic* (1936). The powerful destruction of metaphysics argued in Nietzsche and Heidegger has a faint, if not parodic, echo in Ayer's argument that whatever falls outside the knowable in a nearly scientific sense, has no truth value. The richest value of the linguistic focus in British and American philosophy, as in its literary criticism, was in the close scrutiny of language which was to produce works like J. L. Austin's *How to do Things with Words* (1962). The modernist sense of the enigma of language is important for, as the century went by, an ambiguity opened up in the significance of the linguistic turn. The modernist generation were not just its conscious contemporaries, they are an important watershed in its interpretation.

Once again, a literary example helps to clarify the divergent possibilities. The episode of *Ulysses* which is specifically devoted to language, "Oxen of the Sun," creates a running parallel between the development of a fetus and the growth of the English language as represented by a succession of parodic literary prose styles. Nineteenth-century historical thinking about language had been strongly influenced by organicist conceptions and saw language as the manifestation of a particular national character. Such a legacy was of special interest to Joyce as an Irishman whose "mother" tongue was English. On the face of it this episode seems to celebrate the language on this most organic of analogies, yet the parallel with fetal development occurs in a spirit of burlesque which might alert the reader against any too simple interpretation. Joyce is treading a watershed between different views of language. On the one hand, the organic evolution of language is perhaps only a parodic, rather than a real, parallel of fetal development since the episode is after all demonstrating that these historical and personal styles are themselves subsystems within the language which can be individually reproduced. Dickens used to refer to himself as the "Inimitable" yet his stylistic characteristics can be anatomized and reproduced. This is not quite to say that *he* can be reproduced but to the extent that the "style is the man" this episode adumbrates the questioning of identity which goes on in various ways throughout the text. At the same time the episode plays with, and within, language as if in a sea of possibility so that, behind the particular styles, language itself is enjoyed as a protean second nature. The overall effect is that, while the parodic tone hints at the literal absurdity of the biological analogy, it also highlights its metaphorical appropriateness. Joyce admits of opposite readings with equal plausibility as if he had deliberately built into his work the revelatory ambiguity of an epochal shift.

The recognition that language in some sense determines world has continued to generate radically different schools of thought over the rest of the century. Contemporaneously with the writing of *Ulysses,* Eliot, **Pound,** and Lawrence were thinking about language as the vehicle of cultural tradition. Without being sentimentally organicist, they all recognized, in their different ways, the complexity of language as the fundamental medium of culture in its historical, creative and unconscious dimensions. Eliot and Pound had a crusading interest in precision of language as the means of cultural health. The difficulty here lies in the extent to which the forms of language are thought to be coterminous with the forms of life.

When Wittgenstein, in the *Philosophical Investigations* (1953), saw language as embodying a "form of life" (88), he was insisting that it is only part of a constitutive and unconscious whole which cannot be brought into a fully conscious or conceptual focus *within* language. His invoking of a whole life form was an implicit warning against the assumption that a critique of language could encompass the totality of the form of life it reflects, and Wittgenstein himself refrained, notoriously, from developing a positive overall conception or theory. His work consists of brilliant local insights, often couched in the form of questions or puzzles rather than answers. The most philosophically magisterial development of the view of language as the collective, creative medium of culture which, because its processes are largely beyond conscious conceptualization, is resistant to technical analysis, was to be provided by Martin Heidegger. He was unknown to the British modernist writers although the English literary critic, F. R. Leavis, developed a comparable view out of his own critical thought about language; a view most summatively argued much later in *The Living Principle* (1975). Lawrence, the novelist who became a crucial author for Leavis, and **Rainer Maria Rilke,** one of the poets adduced by Heidegger, are among the most telling literary embodiments of this understanding. All these writers saw some principle of living mystery not just beyond but within language. This may be why they remained more influential toward the mid century than did Henri Bergson who had an immense vogue in the early decades. Bergson's awareness of time, as in his *Creative Evolution* (1907), had a clear epochal relation to the modernists' near obsession with this theme, as was critically pointed out in **Wyndham Lewis**'s *Time and Western Man* (1927). Bergson argued a form of creative vitalism, in some ways comparable to Heidegger's, in which the conceptual and controlling functions of the mind were less central. Bergson's mode of discourse, however, while having its own rhetorical élan, was itself rather abstract and conceptual to some tastes. Lawrence, a more full-blooded vitalist, found him "a bit thin" (*Letters* i, Cambridge 1979: 544). Yet if Bergson's mode of reflection was somewhat disembodied it corresponded to a comparable aspect of **Proust** and Woolf and his subsequent eclipse increases his significance as an epochal manifestation.

The other way of taking the recognition that language governs culture, however, is precisely to attack mystery as mere mystification and to use the analysis of language, particularly in the exposure of ideology, to give a complete, or at least a sufficient, critical insight into a collective culture or individual worldview. Thus, if language is the index, and perhaps even the creating structure, of the human world, then it provides a total critical insight into that world. This view has become academically widespread in the latter half of the century in the form of what Paul Ricoeur has called "the hermeneutics of suspicion" (*The Rule of Metaphor,* London 1975, 285). Saussure is often appealed to as justifying the position here, as in Roland Barthes's *Mythologies* (1957), but it is noteworthy that Saussure became an important influence outside linguistics only in the latter part of the century when his analysis of linguistic structure, as based on the arbitrariness of the sign, began to be accorded a quasi-metaphysical significance as if he were saying that meaning itself is arbitrary.

As modernist poets, as well as cultural critics, Eliot and Pound were somewhere between these positions of participating in creative mystery or engaging in ideological exposure. On the one hand they saw that civilization depends on words and it is the function of the poet and the critic to keep words accurate. Eliot, as in his sense of the workings of tradition, recognized an

unconscious and implicit dimension in this. It would be neither possible nor desirable to bring the whole form of life implicit in language into consciousness. In this aspect he was closer to Heidegger. Pound had the more aggressive self-confidence of the ideological critic for whom ideological exposure encompasses the whole life form in question. Yet taken together they indicate two wings of the modernist moment in which language, like the female moons in Joyce's "Ithaca" episode and Lawrence's "Moony" chapter of *Women in Love,* is rather an inscrutable surface sustained by an invisible body whose dark side cannot be known.

The intensive focus on language, and the difficulty of establishing an analytical purchase on it, may be understood by a further epochal feature. What we look back on as cultural *periods* are often defined as such by dominant metaphors through which many areas of life are understood such as the medieval and renaissance great chain of being, the eighteenth-century clock or machine, or the nineteenth-century organism. What makes it, in retrospect, a period is that the metaphor itself is not questioned; radical questioning of the metaphor is what denotes the beginning of a new cultural phase. In the twentieth century, language itself became a pervasive metaphor reflecting the awareness of cultural formation in many domains. By the same token, however, this suggests why it may be difficult to *see around* the medium of language. The modernist period typically combined the two rival emphases which subsequently emerged as opposed. The critical and ideological insight attained by scrutiny of language was balanced by a respect for its unconscious or tacit dimension. Once again, in this respect as in others, modernism seems to sit on the cusp of a transition in world views. A further, and more explicit, awareness of such a philosophical shift can be focused in a new attention to Being.

Aesthetics and Being

An important strain of German philosophy in the period, even when unknown to modernist writers in English, often provides the pertinent articulation of their outlook and recognitions. The reaction against conceptual modes of knowledge had its most radical form in Heidegger's analysis of the progress of thought and civilization as a progressive forgetfulness of "Being," a term usually capitalized in translation to render its special Heideggerean inflection as in *Being and Time* (1927). He endorsed Nietzsche's exposure of the whole tradition of metaphysics from Plato onwards as an enormous falsehood and psychological deceit. In particular, the centrality of epistemology, the problem of knowledge, had grown, as they both thought, from an unwitting reification of consciousness and world into separate entities, the subjective and objective. On this analysis, Descartes' problem of the dualism of mind and world is not the foundational starting point he had claimed but the product of a highly evolved error in our very notion of thinking. Nietzsche proposed instead that the question of value was more primary than that of knowledge: we know, or question, what is of interest to us as living beings. Even the ideals of academic and scientific disinterestedness fall ultimately within this general truth. Heidegger approved all this but went on to argue that Nietzsche was not the end of metaphysics, as he had claimed, because the question of Being was more primary again than that of value. Heidegger's concern was not with individual beings but with the sheer mystery of Being; the sense of wonder that anything should be there at all. Our everyday instrumental dealing with individual beings deadens us to Being; and philosophical activity, as traditionally practiced, only reinforces this. For Heidegger this loss, or forgetting, of Being had set in since pre-Socratic times. Quite independently, Lawrence and Pound had the same conviction, partly derived from reading John Burnet's *Early Greek Philosophy* (1892), and they invoked the supposedly pre-dualistic sensibility of archaic man to define his mythopoeic relation to the world. This helps to explain a central paradox of modernism: the most sophisticated achievement of the present is a return to, or a new appreciation of, the archaic and the mythic. As Thomas Mann put it in his lecture on Freud in 1936, "in the life of humanity the mythic is indeed an early and primitive stage but in the life of the individual it is a late and mature one" (*Essays of Three Decades,* London 1947, 422).

Such a turn to the mythic and the archaic may have many meanings and motives including sentimental nostalgia, cultural despair, and political regression. In the defining cases such as Yeats, Joyce, Lawrence, or Rilke, however, it was not a simple motif of return but the search for a sophisticated contemporary equivalent for the archaic wholeness and relatedness. The modernists in many ways achieved the ambition of the German romantic thinkers, Friedrich Schlegel and F. W. Schelling, who both argued in 1800 the need for modernity to create a "new mythology." They were thinking in the context of a contemporary poetic need: a true poetry required a mythology. The modernists, rather, recognized that poetry, in its fullest sense, *was* the modern equivalent of myth. That is why Nietzsche's and Heidegger's emphasis on value and Being as opposed to the truth question—and especially when the traditional concern for truth seems to distort these other emphases—gave a new importance to the category of the aesthetic which had effectively grown up only since the mid-eighteenth century. A number of modernist writers were powerfully influenced by the aestheticist movement of the late nineteenth century but with a critical attitude which radically transposed its meaning. Modernism is not typically aesthet*icist,* it is a turn against the previous generation's aestheticism, but it uses highly self-conscious aesthetic means to do so and Edmund Wilson had good reason to see the period, in *Axel's Castle* (1931), as a continuation of aestheticism. Wilson's interpretation implies a measure of withdrawal from historical commitment and a comparable charge was made in Wyndham Lewis's *Time and Western Man.* He attacked the pervasive preoccupation with time in this period extending from Bergson, Einstein, and A. N. Whitehead in philosophy and science through to Joyce and Proust in literature. Lewis saw time as a less real dimension than space since, apart from the fleeting present, experience in time is known only in the imaginative mode of memory and anticipation. Hence this whole preoccupation with time was an indulgent withdrawal in keeping with Edmund Wilson's aestheticist interpretation. But the category of the "aesthetic" is like what Nietzsche defined as the "superhistorical" spirit, the ability to stand mentally outside the beliefs and urgencies of contemporary history (*Untimely Meditations* 64–5). In this regard it is deeply ambivalent and it went through a crucial transformation in the period which can be understood through Nietzsche's parallel transformation of Schopenhauer's thought on this subject. For Nietszche stands to modernism as Schopenhauer stands to the nineteenth-century symbolist and aesthetic movements.

Schopenhauer's pessimistic philosophy in *The World as Will and Idea* (1818) saw human consciousness as evolved by nature to achieve its own blind "purpose," in the same way that wings or claws have been evolved. But the irony of consciousness is that it works by imagining itself to be independently purposive rather than merely reflecting the great process, or Will, of nature. For him, all human purposes are an illusion. Given this under-

standing of things, the only dignified posture for the individual intelligence is mental withdrawal from the whole process and, adapting Kant's definition of the artistic realm in the *Critique of Judgment* (1790) as "purposiveness without purpose," Schopenhauer saw artistic experience as the principal means to this end. Art gives intensity with detachment. Nietzsche was strongly influenced by Schopenhauer, and always accepted his underlying analysis, but he gradually turned the nihilistic implication of Schopenhauer's thought on its head to serve a vitalistic affirmation. This inversion can be seen in the early *The Birth of Tragedy out of the Spirit of Music* (1872) and the late *Twilight of the Idols* (1888). In the first, he adapts Schopenhauer's metaphysic of illusion to affirm the dream itself: "It is a dream. I will dream on" for only as a conscious dream, or as an "*aesthetic phenomenon*" are "human existence and the world eternally *justified*" (44, 52; Nietzsche's emphases). In the later work, however, he turns more critically against Schopenhauer for the sake of what seems at first glance to be a simpler vitalism. Artistic beauty, instead of standing in opposition to natural impulse, is now merged with the attraction of sexuality as part of a procreative affirmation: "nothing is beautiful only man: on this piece of naivety rests all aesthetics; it is the *first* truth of aesthetics. Let us immediately add its second: nothing is ugly but *degenerate* man—and the domain of aesthetic judgment is therewith defined" (90). Nietzsche did not abandon the category of the aesthetic, he made it coterminous with all experience. Life itself, like art, is now a "purposiveness without purpose;" it is lived for its intrinsic value rather than for some transcendental end. Whereas aestheticism saw life in opposition to art, Nietzsche now saw art as the most telling image for the "joyful and trusting fatalism" (*Twilight of the Idols* 114) with which life should be accepted; as indeed it is in Yeats, Joyce, and Lawrence who strongly assimilated the Nietzschean spirit.

When Nietzsche saw the aesthetic as a "justification" of human existence, as a constatation of values in life, he opened the way to Heidegger's account of art as an intuition of Being. For just as Heidegger saw the question of Being as more primordial than that of value, so he saw the function of art as pre-eminently the unveiling of Being. "Purposiveness without purpose" now suggested freedom from the instrumental relation to individual beings which commonly occludes Being. A favorite quotation of his was Hölderlin's "poetically man dwells upon the earth" (*Poetry, Language, Thought* 213). Art lets us know what it is to "be." Such an Heideggerean dimension is evident in Lawrence and Rilke just as it is tragically absent in Kafka and **Beckett.** Once again, the aesthetic, instead of having a separatist implication, becomes both the philosophical model and the practical means of a supremely concentrated awareness of living value.

It is helpful to draw on philosophical parallels in this German tradition as modernist literature, despite its frequent foregrounding of its own artistic processes, did not wear its metaphysical meaning on its sleeve. Once again, the resistance to conceptualization, the desire to make the reader attend rather than "know," is embodied, as Yeats might say, in the nature of the work. That helps explain another phenomenon of the period: the changing significance of literary criticism. The leading modernist writers were remarkable and original critics, and would perhaps not be so comprehensible, let alone influential, without their criticism. Furthermore, what has been said about the world-forming mythopoeic and aesthetic conceptions invested in imaginative literature suggests that an especially primor-

dial philosophical burden now falls upon it. Yet by the same token, the literature must not declare such significance too explicitly or conceptually; if it does so it ceases to be, or truly to reveal, the experience in question. Thomas Mann, for example, is often a brilliant orchestrator of cultural themes rather than truly an artist in this sense. The corresponding importance of literary criticism was in directing attention to primordial significances implicit within literary texts, just as the concern for "tradition" affirmed the larger, collective cultural formation to which individual texts and authors contributed. Matthew Arnold's sense of literature as the modern substitute for religion was increasingly realized not, as the classicist Arnold had thought, as a source of transmitted wisdom, "the best that is known and thought in the world," but rather as the active means of questioning and discovering fundamental values, truths, and understandings for which there was no alternative grounding. The central *philosophical* feature of modernism, reworking a strain of romantic thought, is its claim for literature itself as a supreme and irreplaceable form of understanding.

Perhaps the most significant step within the period toward the breaking up of this modernist holism and romantic primordiality was the activity of the German, largely Jewish, group of Marxist critics based at the School of Social Thought in Frankfurt, and which was to become increasingly influential from the 1930s onwards. As the forces of fascism closed in around them, this group, including Theodor Adorno, Walter Benjamin, and Herbert Marcuse, combined Marxist ideological critique of capitalist and bourgeois culture with a post-Nietzschean emphasis on the importance of the aesthetic. Whereas vulgar Marxist critique was suspicious of the aesthetic as a bourgeois indulgence and self-deception, and typically assimilated it to the social and moral efficacy of art, the Frankfurt school privileged the aesthetic as a unique means of cultural insight, and not just symptomatically so. This was a powerful but intrinsically unstable combination of commitments. In Marcuse the outcome was typically a broad brush critique as in *Eros and Civilization* (1955) and *One Dimensional Man* (1964), or his ultimately Schillerian defense of the aesthetic in *The Aesthetic Dimension* (1979). Walter Benjamin's brilliant and haunting essays typically meditated on the nature of modernity through its specific cultural products so that his speculative insights were always rooted in concrete occasions. Adorno, by contrast, pushed to paradoxical, and perhaps ultimately stultifying, extremes the competing logic of an ideologically critical aestheticism raised to the level of general theory. This was focused in his *Negative Dialectics* (1966) in which the modernist aesthetic is seen as an imaginative challenge to the hegemonic ideology. More darkly, in *Dialectic of Enlightenment* (1944) co-written with Max Horkheimer, as the perennial struggle of enlightenment against myth meets the ever resourceful power of myth to colonize enlightenment itself, the result is an unresolvable conflict of mutually suspicious ideological formations. These authors' view of myth as hostile to enlightenment contrasts with the attempts of Thomas Mann and the Jewish anthropologist, Karl Kerenyi, over the same period to maintain its humanist value as embodied in so much modernist mythopoeia. Yet Adorno and Mann, who knew each other personally during their wartime exile in California, even while they disagreed on the significance or value of myth, shared a Nietzschean model of culture as myth. Part of the difference is that while Mann sought to resolve contradictions in transcendent irony, the restless strains in Adorno's thought anticipate how the elements of ideological critique, post-

modern relativism, and a renewed aestheticism have all become separate, rival strains in later twentieth-century art and criticism.

Michael Bell

Selected Bibliography

Adorno, Theodor and Max Horkheimer. *Dialectic of Enlightenment.* Trans. John Cumming. London and New York: Verso, 1986.

Berman, Marshall. *All That is Solid Melts into Air.* New York: Simon and Schuster, 1982.

Bradbury, Malcolm, and James McFarlane, eds. *Modernism 1890–1930.* Harmondsworth: Penguin, 1976.

Butler, Christopher. *Early Modernism: Literature, Music and Painting in Europe, 1900–1916.* Oxford: Clarendon Press, 1994.

Ellman, Richard, and Charles Feidelson, eds. *The Modern Tradition: Backgrounds of Modern Literature.* New York: Oxford UP, 1965.

Heidegger, Martin. *The Question Concerning Technology and Other Essays.* Trans. William Lovitt. New York: Harper and Row, 1977.

———. *Poetry, Language, Thought.* Trans. Albert Hofstadter. New York: Harper and Row, 1971.

Longenbach, James. *Modernist Poetics of History: Pound, Eliot and the Sense of the Past.* Princeton NJ: Princeton UP, 1988.

Megill, Alan. *Prophets of Extremity: Nietzsche, Heidegger, Foucault, Derrida.* Berkeley and London: U of California P, 1985.

Nicholls, Peter. *Modernisms: A Literary Guide.* London: Macmillan, 1995.

Nietzsche, Friedrich. *The Birth of Tragedy out of the Spirit of Music.* Trans. Walter Kaufmann. New York: Random House, 1967.

———. *Twilight of the Idols.* Trans. R. J. Hollingdale. Harmondsworth: Penguin, 1990.

———. *Untimely Meditations.* Trans. R. J. Hollingdale. Cambridge: Cambridge UP, 1983.

Pippin, Robert. *Modernism as a Philosophical Problem.* Oxford: Blackwell, 1991.

Reiss, Timothy, J. *The Discourse of Modernism.* Ithaca and London: Cornell UP, 1982.

Schwartz, Sanford. *The Matrix of Modernism: Pound, Eliot and Early Twentieth-Century Thought.* Princeton NJ: Princeton UP, 1985.

Sloterdijk, Peter. *Critique of Cynical Reason.* Trans. Michael Eldred. London and New York: Verso, 1988.

Wilson, Edmund. *Axel's Castle.* New York, Scribners, 1931.

Wittgenstein, Ludwig. *Philosophical Investigations.* Trans. G. E. M. Anscombe. Oxford, Blackwell, 1953.

Toller, Ernst (1893–1939)

Toller's art feeds off his experiences as an Independent socialist and elected president of the Central Committee of the Bavarian Soviet Republic, founded and suppressed in 1919. He utilized the visionary strain of **expressionism** to imagine an alternative political and ideological reality in his plays.

In *Die Wandlung* (1919, *The Transformation*), his first important play, Toller dialectically interacts the dream scenes in which his hero Friedrich develops his consciousness of the suffering in his society, with the "real" scenes where Friedrich attempts to apply his insights to reality. Unfortunately the shifts between the two types of scenes are so stark that they become disconnected and, in particular, the dreams are often too sensational to relate clearly to reality, which disrupts narrative continuity of the whole. In his next play *Masse-Mensch* (1920, *Masses and Man*), written in prison after the failure of the Bavarian Soviet Republic, Toller learned to counterpoint his scenes with greater subtlety, realizing that the realistic ones ultimately had no greater ontological validity than the dreams. The play is a meditation on revolution, with a female protagonist who struggles with the dilemma of causing murder through revolution for the freedom of the workers, and with the competing demands of freedom and necessity, personal and social love, individual survival and the welfare of **the masses.**

Toller's later plays of the twenties, such as *Feuer aus den Kesseln* (1930, *Fire from the Kettle*), gradually became more characterized by New Objectivity than by expressionism. This transition partly reflected his dwindling belief in social change in the face of the rise of fascism. He went into exile to America in 1933, where he later committed suicide.

Carl Krockel

Selected Bibliography

Toller's works are available in Carl Hanser Verlag, Wemding, and The Bodley Head, London.

Davies, Cecil. *The Plays of Ernst Toller.* Amsterdam: Harwood Academic Publishers, 1996.

Dove, Richard. *He was a German.* London: Libris, 1990.

Ossar, Michael. *Anarchism in the Dramas of Ernst Toller: The Realm of Necessity and the Realm of Freedom.* New York: State Univeristy of New York Press, 1980.

Trakl, Georg (1887–1914)

Trakl described the essence of his poetry, and of **German expressionism:** "Feeling in the moments of deathlike existence: All human beings are worthy of love. Waking, you feel the world's bitterness; in this lies your unredeemed guilt; your poem an incomplete atonement." Born in Salzburg, he attempted to redeem his age by embracing its decay and sin in his visionary poetry. Trakl's writing was supported anonymously by Ludwig Wittgenstein. He published the collections *Gedichte* (1913, *Poetry*), and posthumously, *Sebastian im Traum* (1915, *Sebastian in a Dream*).

His poetry up to 1909, such as "Die drei Teiche in Hellbrunn" ("The Three Ponds in Hellbrunn"), was derivative from the first person subjectivity of the German romantic tradition, but already carried his later thematic polarity between juxtaposed positive and negative images. In his next phase, which included "Die schöne Stadt" (1909–1910, "The Beautiful City"), he developed an urban poetry of objective images in flux, whose precarious unity was dependent on the setting of the city, not on the earlier sentimentality of his vision.

In "Helian" (1912–1913), Trakl achieved maturity in his free verse through the dynamism of syntax, meter, and line length, and a corresponding flexibility of the personal and omniscient, realistic and visionary, idyllic and grotesque. In his remaining compositions he attempted to consolidate this style. The First World War

offered experiences which he was powerless to counter, as a solitary nurse for
ninety badly wounded soldiers from the
Battle of Grodek and helpless observer of
deserters being hanged outside, or in his
role as a poet. His last poem "Grodek"
(1914) was drafted during this period;
Trakl unconvincingly attempts to redeem
the brutal imagery of "broken mouths" and
"bleeding heads" with a Teutonic celebration of the "spirits of heroes," and then
pacifist concern for the "unborn children."
Weeks later, he died from an overdose of
cocaine.

Carl Krockel

Selected Bibliography

Trakl's works are available in Otto Müller Verlag,
  Salzburg, and in English in Carcanet Press,
  London.
Detsch, Richard. *George Trakl's Poetry: Toward a
  Union of Opposites.* University Park: Pennsyl-
  vania State UP, 1983.
Kudszus, W. G. *Poetic Process.* Lincoln: University
  of Nebraska Press, 1995.
Leiva-Merikakis, Erasmo. *The Blossoming Thorn:
  Georg Trakl's Poetry of Atonement.* Cranbury:
  Associated UP, 1987.

Tranström̈er, Tomas (b. 1931)

Swedish poet.

The central poetic device in Tran-
ström̈er's poetry is the metaphor. His poetic language is distinguished by a high
degree of concentration and it is generally
exact and concrete. Tranström̈er shows affinities with the imagist and surrealist
mainstream of modernism though his rigorous imagery is uniquely his own. In
Tranström̈er's poetic universe one also recognizes elements from a mystical tradition. In his first collection *17 dikter* (1954,
17 Poems) Tranström̈er's poetic language
is already fully matured and developed.
Hemligheter på vägen (1958, *Secrets
Along the Way*) is infused with a mystical
view of life and a wish to capture realities
behind what is seen. Several poems in *Den

halvfärdiga himlen (1962, *The Half-
Finished Heaven*) bear witness to the
fundamental importance of **music** and musical inspiration in Tranström̈er's oeuvre.
Through *Klanger och spår* (1966, *Sounds
and Tracks*); *Mörkerseende* (1970, *Night
Vision*), where he also attempts the prose
poem; and *Stigar* (1973, *Paths*), Tran-
ström̈er's characteristic diction remains
relatively unchanged. *Östersjöar* (1974,
Baltics) marks a change and a renewal: a
long poem in six parts where the poet
speaks in his own voice and in an ordinary
conversational tone. In *Sanningsbarriären*
(1978, Eng. tr. *Truth Barriers,* 1980) anonymity is cast off and in one of the central
poems the lyrical speaker confronts the
problem of identity, his own and that of
others. The prose poem becomes a prominent form in Tranström̈er's later writing,
as in *Det vilda torget* (1983, *The Wild
Market-Square*) and *För levande och döda*
(1989, *For the Living and the Dead*). This
form is also cultivated in *Sorgegondolen*
(1996, *The Sorrow Gondola*) where Tran-
ström̈er furthermore attempts the concentrated haiku form of poetry. He has also
published an autobiographical essay, *Min-
nena ser mig* (1993, *The Memories See
Me*). Tranström̈er is a poet of international
stature and one of the leading poetic modernists of his time. Translations into foreign languages are numerous. Among the
many translations of Tranström̈er into English are Robin Fulton's of *Selected Poems*
(1981) and *Collected Poems* (1987). There
is also an edition of Tranström̈er's *Selected
Poems 1954–1986* (1987) translated by
Robert Bly, Robin Fulton, May Swenson
and others.

Mats Jansson

Selected Bibliography

Espmark, Kjell. Resans formler. *En studie i Tomas
  Tranströmers poesi.* Stockholm: Norstedts,
  1983.
Schiöler, Niklas. Koncentrationens konst. *Tomas
  Tranströmers senare poesi.* Stockholm: Bon-
  niers, 1999.

Tunneling

In her diaries, during the writing of *Mrs. Dalloway,* **Woolf** called her technique of constructing character "tunneling." By this she meant she would burrow into the character's past in order to unearth a history.

Her characters are then revealed to the reader as split beings who are living in the past and present. It is their current thoughts that tell us who they are, but only their memories of the past that explain them—why they are who they are.

Peter Childs

U

Ulysses (1922)

James Joyce's epic novel, published in 1922, celebrates the events of one day in Dublin, June 16, 1904, in the lives of its three central characters: Leopold Bloom, his wife Molly Bloom, and Stephen Dedalus. The book is modeled on episodes in Homer's *Odyssey,* with Bloom corresponding to Odysseus, Molly to Penelope, and Stephen Dedalus to Telemachus. The Homeric analogies work not only on the level of characterization but also in the settings and occasionally even in minute details. *Ulysses* is among the foremost works of twentieth-century literature and represents a watershed in the history of the novel. Next to **Finnegans Wake** it is Joyce's most innovative creative achievement.

Joyce began writing *Ulysses* in late 1914 or early 1915, although his original idea for a story with that title dates back to 1906 and was conceived as another story for **Dubliners.** It was to feature a Mr. Hunter, a Dubliner who had actually rescued Joyce after he had been knocked down in the street. Joyce believed Hunter to be Jewish, which suited his artistic purpose, because it set him apart from the catholic-nationalist/Anglo-Irish literary debate of the day. However, that story "never got any forrader than the title" Joyce told his brother Stanislaus in a letter of 1907. Yet the idea stayed with Joyce, and by June 1915, it had taken a radically

new shape as the outline of the novel and the first completed chapter show. Through the good offices of **Ezra Pound,** *Ulysses* began to appear serially in the American journal *The Little Review* from March 1918 through December 1920. It was also thanks to Pound that portions of *Ulysses* were published in Harriet Shaw Weaver's London periodical, *The Egoist.*

If during the eight-year gestation of *Ulysses* Joyce kept revising and expanding parts, Pound and *The Little Review's* editor made unauthorized deletions fearing legal problems. Even so, four issues of *The Little Review* were seized and burned by the United States Post Office. In February 1921, the co-editors of *The Little Review* were found guilty of publishing obscenity; they were fined and prohibited from issuing any further episodes of *Ulysses.*

Joyce had great difficulty finding a publisher and was close to giving up when Sylvia Beach offered to publish *Ulysses* under the imprint of her Paris bookstore, Shakespeare and Company, in 1921. She financed the project by enlisting subscribers, and Maurice Darrantiere, a printer in Dijon, agreed to print the work as it stood. He provided Joyce with multiple galley proofs which were used for revisions and expansions almost to the day of the novel's publication.

Ulysses is based on an elaborate framework. For the benefit of some early critics Joyce produced schemas outlining Homeric correspondences and "symbols" such as colors, arts, or body organs for each chapter, but he refused to have them included in the novel. Nor do the titles of the episodes which Joyce used during composition, and which critics still employ for easy reference, appear in the published text. *Ulysses* is divided into three major parts indicated by Roman numerals, the Telemachiad (episodes 1–3: Telemachus, Nestor, Proteus), The Wanderings of Ulysses (episodes 4–15: Calypso, Lotuseaters, Hades, Aeolus, Lestrygonians, Scylla and Charybdis, Wandering Rocks, Sirens, Cyclops, Nausicaa, Oxen of the Sun, Circe) and Nostos (episodes 16–18: Eumaeus, Ithaca, Penelope).

Ulysses combines intense psychological **realism** with an encyclopedic view of Dublin and its inhabitants. It begins in the modernist tradition following the consciousness of one character, Stephen Dedalus, in the Telemachiad. But with the fourth episode, the novel seems to begin anew as protagonists and locale are changed and the clock is set back to the time of the opening. Throughout the rest of the book the narrative focus shifts frequently among various characters whose consciousnesses are foregrounded, with resulting contradictions. *Ulysses* is polyphonic in its plurality of idiolectal and sociolectal voices and consciousnesses; it is also thoroughly dialogical as no authoritarian authorial voice prevails over the diverse languages and ideologies of its protagonists. Readers are unusually challenged as Joyce would not submit to artistic limitations of any kind. As his friend, the painter Frank Budgen, put it: "The multiplicity of technical devices in *Ulysses* is proof that Joyce subscribed to no limiting aesthetic creed, and proof also that he was willing to use any available instrument that might serve his purpose" (198). The themes, like the techniques, are multiple. In the course of the novel the apparently mundane events of June 16–17 1904 acquire universal significance. It is fair to claim that Joyce transformed a day in the life of Dublin into art, making the local cosmopolitan. The all-round character Leopold Bloom is caring and kind, adaptable yet prudent, and belongs to no one racial or national tradition. He is a surprisingly convincing modern-day incarnation of Homer's versatile Odysseus.

Ulysses opens with Stephen Dedalus, the hero of *A Portrait of the Artist,* recently returned from Paris for his mother's death and funeral. It is early morning on a fine summer's day, and, in the Martello Tower in Sandycove, Stephen and Malachi 'Buck' Mulligan have just arisen. Stephen, who is estranged from his family and dissatisfied with his artistic progress, becomes increasingly impatient with Mulligan's insincerity. Although he is distrustful of him, Stephen hands Mulligan the key of the tower when prompted to do so (Telemachus) and goes to teach at Mr. Deasy's preparatory school in Dalkey. His attitude to a weak student is unusually empathetic. After a vexing conversation with the headmaster he accepts payment for his services (Nestor). Stephen considers his position as he walks along Sandymount Strand and reflects on problems of perception, identity, and art (Proteus). We lose sight of Stephen in episode four (Calypso) as Leopold Bloom enters to dominate our attention. With Bloom the narrative focus moves from the concerns of a youthful, self-absorbed, iconoclastic artist to those of a mature, caring, middlebrow family man.

We read how Bloom prepares breakfast for his wife Molly in their house in Eccles Street. She tells him that Boylan, the manager of her concert tour, will be visiting in the afternoon. Only retrospectively do we realize that the couple's silences are as meaningful as their conversations. Bloom walks across the city to collect a letter from a woman correspondent addressed to his pseudonym, Henry Flower. He attends a sodality mass in All Hallows Church before visiting the Turkish Baths (Lotus Eaters). He travels to Paddy Dignam's funeral in Glasnevin with Stephen's father Simon Dedalus and a few others, and his thoughts turn to religion, social customs and death (Hades). He then visits the offices of the *Freeman's Journal* to get an advertisement renewed and notices Stephen who is handing in a letter on behalf of Mr. Deasy (Aeolus). Bloom feels hungry and calls into Davy Byrne's pub for a Gorgonzola sandwich and a glass of Burgundy. His mind is preoccupied with food and the sensual (Lestrygonians). He goes to look up an advertisement in the National Library where Stephen is expounding his Shakespeare theory to an intellectual audience maintaining that art is a sublimation of personal experience.

Both Bloom and Stephen wander about town (Wandering Rocks). Bloom finds himself in the Ormond Hotel where he has a meal. Listening to Simon Dedalus and Ben Dollard singing in the Bar, he answers his pen-pal's letter and observes Boylan delaying in the Bar before departing for his assignation with Molly (Sirens). Bloom proceeds to Barney Kiernan's pub to meet Cunningham in connection with the Dignam family. Forgetting his usual prudence he is drawn into a hostile argument with an intransigent nationalist. He adopts a pacifist stand and asserts his own Irish nationality while defending the Jews (Cyclops). Before calling to the Dignam's house to make insurance arrangements, Bloom spends some time on Sandymount Strand as night falls. He watches young Gerty MacDowell exposing herself and masturbates (Nausicaa). His thoughts that have been troubled all day by reminders of Boylan and Molly now seem relaxed.

Stephen and Bloom only meet in the fourteenth episode (Oxen of the Sun) in Holles St National Maternity Hospital where Bloom, inquiring about a friend in labor, finds Stephen drinking with medical students. Bloom follows Stephen to Nighttown, Dublin's red-light district. In Bella

Cohen's brothel Stephen has a ghoulish hallucination of his mother whose dying wishes he failed to fulfill. While trying to dispel the hallucination he smashes a chandelier and runs away. Shortly afterwards in the street outside he is knocked to the ground by a British soldier in a street brawl (Circe). Both times Bloom intervenes on Stephen's behalf. He takes him to his own home in 7 Eccles Street via the Cabman's Shelter where he treats him to a cup of coffee and a bun (Eumaeus). In Bloom's kitchen the two have a meandering conversation over a cup of cocoa before Stephen leaves declining an offer of lodgings and Bloom goes up to his wife and bed (Ithaca). The novel closes with Molly's rambling **interior monologue** as she lies awake in bed (Penelope). She muses over her life with Bloom, her childhood in Gibraltar, her adulterous relationship and her plans for the future. Though Molly's soliloquy ends with an affirming "Yes," the novel closes without imparting any sense of resolution.

Ulysses, replete with historical, social, literary, musical and geographical allusions, permits a wide variety of approaches, from conventional ones which concentrate on character and plot, to psychoanalytic, cultural materialist, and postcolonial readings. And yet, no single reading comes close to "explaining" the book.

Note on Editions of *Ulysses*

Because of "unusual circumstances," Joyce's working procedures and the pressures of a deadline, the Shakespeare & Company edition of *Ulysses* of 1922 was seriously flawed, and so were all subsequent editions derived from it. Hans Walter Gabler with Wolfhard Steppe and Claus Melchior set out to establish a text based on a "continuous manuscript," the *Critical and Synoptic Edition* of 1984 in three volumes, and a one volume "Reading Text." This edition was exposed to acrimonious criticism.

For a succint account of the publication history of *Ulysses* and the debates about editions, see Jeri Johnson's "Composition and Publication History" in her World's Classics edition of the novel (Oxford UP, 1993: xxxviii–lvi). The most recent edition of *Ulysses,* again controversial, is Danis Rose's for Picador, London, 1997. Rose's unusual approach claims to remove obstructions between writer and reader.

Christine O'Neill

Selected Bibliography

Blamires, Harry. *The New Bloomsday Book: A Guide through Ulysses.* 3rd ed. London and New York: Routledge, 1996.

Budgen, Frank. *James Joyce and the Making of Ulysses and Other Writings.* Oxford: Oxford UP, 1989.

Gifford, Don and Robert J. Seidman. *Ulysses Annotated: Notes for James Joyce's Ulysses.* 2nd rev. and enlarged ed. Berkeley: U of California P, 1988.

Groden, Michael. *Ulysses in Progress.* Princeton: Princeton UP, 1977.

Hart, Clive and David Hayman, eds. *Ulysses.* Berkeley and Los Angeles: U of California P, 1974.

Kenner, Hugh. *Ulysses.* London: George Allen & Unwin, 1980.

Lawrence, Karen. *The Odyssey of Style in Ulysses.* Princeton, N.J.: Princeton UP, 1981.

Osteen, Mark. *The Economy of Ulysses: Making Both Ends Meet.* Syracuse, New York: Syracuse UP, 1995.

Senn, Fritz. *Inductive Scrutinies: Focus on Joyce.* Ed. Christine O'Neill. Dublin: Lilliput Press, 1995.

———. *Joyce's Dislocutions: Essays on Reading as Translation.* Ed. Jean Paul Riquelme. Baltimore: Johns Hopkins UP, 1984.

Sherry, Vincent. *Joyce: Ulysses.* Cambridge: Cambridge UP, 1994.

Staley, Thomas F. and Bernard Benstock, eds. *Approaches to Ulysses: Ten Essays.* Pittsburgh: U of Pittsburgh P, 1970.

Thornton, Weldon. *Allusions in Ulysses: A Line-by-Line Reference to Joyce's Complex Symbolism.* The U of North Carolina P: Simon and Schuster, 1973.

Ungaretti, Giuseppe (1888–1970)

Ungaretti, who is often deemed to be the father of modern Italian poetry, was also an essayist and translator. He was born in Alexandria, Egypt, of Tuscan parents, and educated in a French school. At the age of twenty-four he went to Paris to study at the Collège de France and, later, at the Sorbonne under Henri Bergson. In Paris he moved among a wealth of experimental writers and artists including Apollinaire, Picasso, Modigliani, and a number of the Italian futurists. After the war he worked as a correspondent and journalist, first for Mussolini's *Popolo d'Italia,* and then for the *Gazzetta del popolo.* From 1936, when he was awarded the Chair of Italian at the University of Sao Paolo, Ungaretti occupied a number of prestigious academic posts and won numerous literary awards and honors for his work. He was nominated to the Italian Academy in 1942, and also became professor at the Universities of Rome and Columbia (USA).

The vision which informs Ungaretti's poetry is of a universal life-force from which mankind has become fatally estranged. His poetry strives to restore the connection by rejecting rhetoric and logic in favor of a pared-down and minimalist but nonetheless sensuous, evocative use of language. His evocation of complex interior states, and his desire to create a verbal form of **music** in his poetry, invites comparison to Mallarmé and the symbolists, and his rejection of punctuation and logic reflects trends associated with Italian futurist poetry, but his poetry is also intensely personal. Ungaretti was, in his own time, labelled an "hermeticist" because his connotative style was considered deliberately obscure and impenetrable (a charge which the poet vigorously denied). His collections of poetry are entitled *Allegria dei naufragi* (1919, *The Joy of Shipwrecks*), *Sentimento del tempo* (1933, *Sentiment of Time*), *Il Dolore* (1947, *The Grief*), *La Terra promessa* (1950, *The Promised Land*), and *Un grido e paesaggi* (1952, *A Cry and Landscapes*). He gave his anthology of collected poems the title *La Vita d'un uomo* (1947, *Life of a Man*). He also produced three major books of translation: *40 Sonetti di Shakespeare* (1946, *Forty Sonnets by Shakespeare*), *Da Góngora a Mallarmé* (1948, *From Góngora to Mallarmé*), and *Fedra di Jean Racine* (1950, *Phaedre by Jean Racine*).

Andrew Harrison

Selected Bibliography

Ungaretti's works are published in Italy by Mondadori. English translations are available through various publishing houses. A bibliography of his writings may be found in *Contemporary Authors* 19–20 (1968): 437–439.

Cambon, Glauco. *Giuseppe Ungaretti*. New York and London: Columbia UP, 1967.

Wells, W. "Ezra Pound and Giuseppe Ungaretti: A Resonating Silence." *Paideuma* 24.2–3 (1995): 69–77.

V

Verga, Giovanni (1840–1922)

Novelist, short story writer, and playwright, Verga's innovations in the writing of realist narrative gesture towards the modernist techniques of narrated **interior monologue** and stream of consciousness.

He was born into an upper-class family in Catania, Sicily. Later, living in Florence and Milan, he was exposed to French fiction and became the close friend of his fellow Sicilian Luigi Capuana, founder of the "Versimo" movement (an Italian version of Zola's French naturalist school). Although he has become firmly associated with this movement, Verga's work is not bound by it. He began by writing popular romance novels about the lives of the wealthy, but his major fiction charts the desperate lives of Sicilian peasants. His major undertaking was the plan to write a series of five novels tracing the struggle for existence at every level of society: the project was entitled *I Vinti* (*The Vanquished*). Two of the novels in the projected series were completed—*I Malavoglia* (1881, *The House by the Medlar Tree*) and *Mastro-don Gesualdo* (1888, *Mastro-Don Gesualdo*)—while one—*La Duchessa di Leyra* (*The Duchess of Leyra*)—remained incomplete at the time of his death.

Verga sought to remove the authorial voice from his fiction by deriving the content and language of each of his works from the social class depicted. In this way he attempted to describe the fictional environment from within and to access the personal psychologies of his characters. In addition to his novels, he wrote a number of short stories, from which he derived several plays. **D. H. Lawrence** translated one of his novels and two collections of his shorter fiction: *Mastro-Don Gesualdo* (USA 1923, England 1925), *Cavalleria Rusticana and Other Stories* (1928), and *Little Novels of Sicily* (1925).

Andrew Harrison

Selected Bibliography
Verga's works are published in Italy by Mondadori. Recent editions of D. H. Lawrence's translations have been published in England by Penguin (London) and in America by Greenwood Press (Connecticut). A bibliography of Verga's works is contained in Cecchetti (1978).

Cecchetti, Giovanni. *Giovanni Verga.* Boston: Twayne Publishers, 1978.

Hyde, G. M. *D. H. Lawrence and the Art of Translation.* London: Macmillan, 1981.

Lucente, Gregory. *The Narrative of Realism and Myth: Verga, Lawrence, Faulkner, Pavese.* Baltimore: Johns Hopkins UP, 1979.

Woolf, David. *The Art of Verga: A Study in Objectivity.* Sydney: Sydney UP, 1977.

Vittorini, Elio (1908–1966)

As novelist, short story writer, essayist, editor, and translator, Vittorini is often credited with having opened up Italian literature to foreign influences. He was born in Sicily, where his father worked on the railroads. On leaving home he worked for a time building roads and bridges, and was to have become an accountant—but his interests were literary. In 1929 he moved to Florence, where he worked for the journal *Solaria* as a proofreader and journalist. In 1936 he went to Milan, where he began to translate English and American writers, among them **D. H. Lawrence, Faulkner,** and **Hemingway.** He also undertook editorial work, rising to become an editor for Bompiani, Einaudi, and Mondadori. During his lifetime Vittorini founded and directed a number of periodicals, overseeing the publication of (among other writers) the young Italo Calvino and Roland Barthes. Politically, Vittorini was strongly anti-fascist before the war; he flirted with communism after it; and he finally settled on a liberal socialist outlook. The subject matters and styles of his fiction draw upon his political leanings. The existential atmosphere of his fiction reflects his fascination with American writers, and his highly poetic prose style shows the influence of the major European modernists, but both are used to undermine an oppressive world order that can be directly related to the author's experience of fascism.

Vittorini's published works are as follows: *Piccola borghesia* (1931, *Petty Bourgeoisie*), *Il garofano rosso* (written 1933, published 1948, *The Red Carnation*), *Nei Morlacchi—Viaggio in Sardegna* (1936, *In the Morlacchi—Voyage to Sardinia*), *Conversazione in Sicilia* (1941, *Conversation in Sicily*), *Uomini e no* (1945, *Men and Non-Men*), *Il sempione strizza l'occhio al Fréjus* (1947, *The Twilight of the Elephant*), *Le Donne di Messina* (1949, *Women of Messina*), *La Garibaldina* (1950, *The Garibaldina*), and *Erica e i suoi fratelli* and *La Garibaldina* (1956, published together and translated as *The Dark and the Light*). One book of nonfiction was published during his lifetime: *Diario in pubblico* (1957, *Public Diary*). Other sketches and fragments were col-lected posthumously in three volumes: *Le due tensioni* (1967, *Two Tensions*), *Le città del mondo* (1969, *Cities of the World*), and *Nome e lagrime* (1972, *Tears and a Name*).

Andrew Harrison

Selected Bibliography
Vittorini's collected works are published in Italy by Mondadori. English translations of his works have been published in America by New Directions (New York). A bibliography of his works is contained in Potter (1979).
Pacifici, Sergio. "Elio Vittorini." In his *A Guide to Contemporary Italian Literature: From Futurism to Neorealism.* Carbondale and Edwardsville: Southern Illinois UP, 1962. 87–113.
Potter, Joy Hambuechen. *Elio Vittorini.* Boston: Twayne Publishers, 1979.

Vorticism

A British modernist movement in art and literature, vorticism took root from **Wyndham Lewis**'s 1913 quarrel with Roger Fry and his exit from the Omega Workshops to form the Rebel Art Centre. The center was in operation from April to June 1914, and was run by Lewis and Kate Lechmere, attracting the attention of artists like Frederick Etchells, Henri Gaudier-Brzeska, and Jacob Epstein; it also attracted to it the literary figures **Ford Madox Ford, T. E. Hulme,** and **Ezra Pound,** who had recently left his own imagist movement. In summer 1914, the group, in publicly dissociating themselves from the Italian futurists during one of **Marinetti**'s lecturing visits to London, formed the vorticist movement. The main vehicle for the promotion of vorticist ideas was the journal *Blast: The Review of the Great English Vortex,* published in summer 1914, with *Blast II* appearing during 1915. The vorticists promoted an anti-romantic emphasis in literature, and static, austere, mechanical form in the visual arts, criticizing the futurists for their concentration on movement. Among the major achievements of vorticism and the vorticist atmosphere are Lewis' *Timon of Athens* drawings, Epstein's sculpture entitled *Rock Drill,* and Gaudier-Brzeska's sculpture *Hieratic Head of Ezra Pound.* The publication of *Blast II* brought the movement to an end.

Andrew Harrison

Selected Bibliography

Dasenbrock, Reed Way. *The Literary Vorticism of Ezra Pound and Wyndham Lewis: Towards the Condition of Painting.* Baltimore and London: Johns Hopkins UP, 1985.

Ferrall, Charles. "'Melodramas of Modernity': The Interaction of Vorticism and Futurism before the Great War." *University of Toronto Quarterly* 63.2 (1993/4): 347–368.

Wees, William C. *Vorticism and the English Avant-Garde.* Manchester: Manchester UP, 1972.

W

Wales

Modernism in Wales took notably distinct forms in Welsh- and English-language culture. In the Welsh language, one of the predominant literary figures at the turn of the century was the poet T. Gwynn Jones, who occupies a place in the Welsh literary canon analogous to that occupied by **Yeats** in the Irish. Jones began his poetic career as an imaginatively lush symbolist, drawing heavily on Welsh mythology for his subject-matter. In later years, however, his work becomes increasingly satirical in tone, eschewing mellifluousness in favor of a deliberate harshness, indicating a loss of belief and even an existential despair which is not unreminiscent of the early **Eliot.** Two other major poets of the early decades of the twentieth century who broke away from the dominant, and somewhat turgid, romantic mode of nineteenth-century Welsh verse were T. H. Parry Williams and his cousin, R. Williams Parry. Neither of these two undoubtedly great poets can be identified as modernist in terms of their use of form or language; indeed, both excelled in the sonnet form which, though unusual in the Welsh tradition, can hardly be regarded as iconoclastic. Only the philosophical uncertainty and the often ambivalent attitudes displayed in their work mark them out as modern sensibilities.

Saunders Lewis and John Gwilym Jones are more immediately recognizable as modernist artists. Lewis was perhaps the most influential and certainly the most formidable Welsh literary talent of the century. As poet and playwright, Lewis forged a bold and distinctive style which commandeered traditional elements, such as myth and strict meter, to a fierce political purpose and a synthesizing catholic vision. John Gwilym Jones was a playwright of a quite different kind: the first to experiment with Brechtian alienation techniques in Welsh and the first to abandon naturalistic staging completely. His plays *Hanes Rhyw Gymro* (1964, *The Story of a Welshman*), *Ac Eto Nid Myfi* (1976, *And Yet Not Me*) and *Yr Adduned* (1979, *The Promise*) are considered to be his masterpieces; though these are clearly of fairly recent date, his first plays appeared as early as the 1930s. Jones was also a notable prose writer; his volume of stories entitled *Y Goeden Eirin* (1946, *The Plum Tree*) is generally regarded as the first example of the stream of consciousness technique in Welsh. Perhaps the most iconoclastic of all Welsh-language authors of the period, though, was Caradog Prichard, whose poetry began to appear in the 1920s but whose masterpiece, the novel *Un Nos Ola' Leuad* (*One Moonlit Night*) was not published until 1961. Linguistically experimental, fragmented, poetic, dealing with taboo subjects such as madness, sexual abuse, and murder, this novel occupies a place in Welsh literature which can only be compared with that of **Joyce's *Ulysses*** in English-language literature. It is a text which retains the power to disturb and mesmerize; sadly, but perhaps inevitably, Prichard's novel has had no progeny in the Welsh literary tradition.

Although modern Welsh writing in English may be said to have been initiated by the *fin de siècle* female novelist, Allen Raine, her work is firmly late Victorian in style. That of **Caradoc Evans,** conversely, is strikingly innovative, both linguistically and ideologically. His notorious collection of short stories *My People* (1915) shows some naturalist influence but is fundamentally a modernist text with grotesque distortions in language and characterization. Indeed, there are some elements of the unmistakeable Evans style which might even be termed surrealistic. Similar elements are to be found in the early prose work of Glyn Jones and **Dylan Thomas,** though the work of the latter two writers generally lacks the mordant satire which endows Caradoc Evans's work with its vehement energy. Nevertheless, grotesquerie is plentiful in the early stories of Dylan Thomas, such as "The Lemon" and "The School for Witches" (both 1936) which contain Gothic imagery and nightmarish visions. The stories of Glyn Jones's *The Blue Bed* (1937) are an odd combination of the poetically ebullient and the disturbingly grotesque. Meanwhile, Dorothy Edwards's single volume of short stories, *Rhapsody* (1927) reveals a unique voice in the Anglo-Welsh context, a voice reminiscent of the exquisite subtleties of style in the work of contemporary English modernists, such as **Virginia Woolf** or **Dorothy Richardson.**

Dylan Thomas's *18 Poems* (1934) and *Twenty-five Poems* (1936) and Glyn Jones's *Poems* (1939) display the work of poets fascinated with the sonorous and tactile qualities of words themselves and, some would argue, display the daring experimentalism of poets for whom English itself was not an ancestral language but a

new and challenging one. Certainly both poets betray a distinctively Welsh preoccupation with metrical form, structure and alliteration, though this may also owe something to the influence of Hopkins. Be that as it may, both poets sounded a distinctively Welsh modernist note at a time when the more restrained English voices of **W. H. Auden** and the later Eliot were in the ascendant. Another important Anglo-Welsh poet of the time was Lynette Roberts, whose 1944 volume *Poems* was published and championed by T. S. Eliot. Roberts was a poet far removed from the exuberance of Dylan Thomas; her work is more reminiscent of that of **David Jones,** with its reference to Welsh **myth,** its apparent hermeticism, and its experimentation with prose-poetry. She also, like Jones, attempted to write epic-length verse in the form of her bizarre war poem *Gods with Stainless Ears* (1951).

Despite the achievements of these Welsh modernists it should be borne in mind that **realism** continued to be a dominant mode of writing in Wales in both languages throughout the first half of the twentieth century. The pre-eminent Welsh prose writer of the period was Kate Roberts, whose short stories (in collections such as *Rhigolau Bywyd* [1929, *The Ruts of Life*] and novels (such as *Traed mewn Cyffion* [1936, *Feet in Chains*]) are masterpieces of bleak yet immensely compassionate realism. Similarly, the English-language industrial novel of the 1930s tended to employ a pseudo-documentary realism in its portrayal of the hardships of working-class life in the South Wales coalfield. Among the best examples are *Cwmardy* (1937) by Lewis Jones and *These Poor Hands* (1939) by Bert Coombes. It might be suggested that the overwhelming poverty of the majority of the population of Wales during the early decades of the century militated against the development of an urbane modernist literature; economic and social circumstances were such that they perhaps required a more direct expression of reality than modernist techniques were able to offer.

Katie Gramich

Selected Bibliography

Adams, Sam and Gwilym Rhys Hughes, eds. *Triskel One: Essays on Welsh and Anglo-Welsh Literature.* Swansea: Christopher Davies, 1971. Also: *Triskel Two,* 1973.

Conran, Tony. *The Cost of Strangeness: Essays on the English Poets of Wales.* Llandysul: Gomer Press, 1982.

Garlick, Raymond. *An Introduction to Anglo-Welsh Literature.* Cardiff: University of Wales Press, 1972.

Johnston, Dafydd. *The Literature of Wales: A Pocket Guide.* Cardiff: University of Wales Press, 1994.

———, ed. *A Guide to Welsh Literature c. 1900–1996.* Volume 6. Cardiff: University of Wales Press, 1998.

Jones, Glyn. *The Dragon has Two Tongues.* London: Dent, 1968.

Jones, Gwyn. *The First Forty Years: Some Notes on Anglo-Welsh Literature.* Cardiff: University of Wales Press, 1957.

Mathias, Roland. *A Ride Through the Wood: Essays on Anglo-Welsh Literature.* Bridgend: Poetry Wales Press, 1985.

Prichard, Caradog. *One Moonlit Night.* Trans. Philip Mitchell. Edinburgh: Canongate, 1995. Also a parallel text edition, trans. Mitchell, intro. Menna Baines, London: Penguin, 1999.

Rowlands, John. *Ysgrifau ar y Nofel.* Cardiff: University of Wales Press, 1992.

———, ed. *Sglefrio ar Eiriau.* Llandysul: Gomer Press, 1992.

Stephens, Meic, ed. *The New Companion to the Literature of Wales.* Cardiff: University of Wales Press, 1998.

Thomas, M. Wynn. *Internal Difference: Literature in Twentieth-Century Wales.* Cardiff: University of Wales Press, 1992.

Williams, Gwyn. *An Introduction to Welsh Literature.* Cardiff: University of Wales Press, 1978; reprinted 1992.

The War

On June 28, 1914 a Serbian student, Gavrilo Princip, shot and killed the Archduke Franz Ferdinand of Austria and his wife. It was the latest and most outrageous action in an aggressive terrorist campaign conducted by Balkan nationalists against Austrian rule. This assassination was the immediate cause of what the chief participants styled the "First World War."

The Austrians alleged that the Serbian government had instigated the plot and Austria-Hungary declared war on Serbia on July 28. **Russia** mobilized along the German and Austrian frontiers on July 29; **Germany** declared war on Russia on August 1 and on **France** on August 3, invading Belgium also on that day. Britain declared war on Germany on August 4. Turkey (from whom Austria-Hungary had taken Serbia in 1908–9) joined Germany and Austria-Hungary in November followed by Bulgaria in October 1915. Japan joined the original allies Britain and France in August 1914; **Italy** joined them in May 1915 and the United States in April 1917.

Fighting continued on several fronts until November 11, 1918 when an armistice was signed. Ten weeks later a Peace Conference opened with the object of settling the new Europe. On June 28, 1919 the Treaty of Versailles was signed. Germany protested against the harshness of its conditions; sections of public opinion in Britain and France complained of the leniency of the conditions; the United States Congress refused to ratify the treaty. Amongst its other effects the conditions imposed by the treaty helped to provoke further hostilities in 1939.

In treaties of 1919 and 1920 the Austrian Empire was formally broken up and thus began the end of Empires and the military-aristocratic social order that they had maintained and encouraged.

Britain in 1914

The traditional military structure in Britain was part of a traditional social structure; the one could not have been questioned without calling the other into question, and this is indeed what happened. The first stirrings of discontent against the capacity of the traditional military hierarchy to conduct war had occurred during the Crimean War. The conduct of that war had provoked such protests as the "Administrative Reform Association" of which Charles Dickens was a prominent member. These murmurings were not influential however and it was not until the excesses of Passchendaele and the Somme that public opinion started to move decisively against the old order.

The nature of that order cannot be simply summarized. In Britain as a whole it had to do with the primacy of England in maintaining, briefly enough, a United Kingdom of the British Isles; in England it had to do with a conviction that though the upper classes may lose their way and the lower may mutiny, middle England remained stable and could keep its head. That stability, however, had to incorporate the radicalism of Blake and Godwin and the rationality of Bentham, Mill, **Shaw,** John Maynard Keynes, and others after them. It was able to do this and to tolerate the waywardness of the upper classes for much longer than the same forces had been able to in France but eventually the tension was too much to maintain. Cautious and piecemeal reform had prolonged the birth of a new order; perhaps it had eased it; perhaps it had postponed it; perhaps it was mere procrastination. Whatever view can be taken it is clear that Britain in 1918 could not be what Britain in 1914 had been.

Modernity, like the First World War, was a European crisis. It was the result of the technological and economic development in Europe itself; in the parts of the world under European control; and in the parts of the world affected by European expansion. That technological and economic development had acquired a momentum that took it beyond moral, cultural, or spiritual direction. Relationships that had been based upon the land and its cycles and requirements were now based upon markets and their cycles and requirements.

This process had begun in the late Middle Ages but it was only when the old ruling order showed itself utterly incapable of rising to the occasion that the crisis became manifest. The First World War seemed to make that incapacity clear. It was at once the finest appearance of the loyalties that united classes of English men and the last time that those loyalties could be relied upon.

Literary Culture in Pre-War Britain

E. M. Forster (1879–1970) wrote of his childhood and youth in an age "the cloud on whose horizon was no bigger than a man's hand" ("The Challenge of Our Time"). Late-Victorian Britain could well have seemed remarkably untroubled to many of its inhabitants. The complex of alliances that had turned Europe into an armed camp in an effort to police the burgeoning rivalry produced by forces quite out of any nation's control was something of which many late Victorians were blissfully unaware. Forster comments "In came the nice fat dividends, up rose the lofty thoughts, and we did not realize that all the time we were exploiting the poor of our own country and the backward races abroad, and getting bigger profits from our investments than we should."

Literary culture reflected this state of ignorance; late Victorian writing was heavily influenced by romantic traditions and the work of Robert Louis Stevenson was not only popular but attracted intelligent interest. Stevenson and **Henry James** became close literary friends and Stevenson's influence can be traced in **Joseph Conrad.** Stevenson's influence can also be traced in the work of Sir Arthur Quiller-Couch (1863–1944), known by his pseudonym "Q," who was not only a best-selling novelist but became King Edward VII Professor of English at the University of Cambridge in 1912.

The poets of the nineties (**W. B. Yeats**'s "companions of the Cheshire Cheese") constituted an *avant-garde* as Tennyson had given way to Swinburne and the influence of Pater had grown. At the same time the tradition of Thackeray, Trollope, and George Eliot continued in Galsworthy, Bennett, and H. G. Wells. Thomas Hardy, as a novelist until 1896 and thereafter as a poet, is a major literary figure until his death in 1928.

Bloomsbury took over from the Cheshire Cheese and **Virginia Woolf** could even claim that the Modern Age had begun "in or around December 1910," in which month her brother had helped to organize an exhibition of post-impressionist works in London. Edward Marsh issued his first *Georgian Poets* anthology in 1912; John Masefield (1878–1967), James Stephens (1882–1950), Robert Graves (1895–1985), Edmund Blunden (1896–1974), Walter de la Mare (1873–1956), and John Drinkwater (1882–1937), were all included at one time or another in these anthologies that continued annually until 1922. G. K. Chesterton (1874–1936) and Rudyard Kipling (1865–1936) also represent something of the complex literary culture of this time and must be thought of at the same time as *Les Imagistes,* for example, who featured in *Des Imagistes* (1914) anonymously edited by **Ezra Pound,** and in *Some Imagist Poets,* edited by Amy Lowell, in 1915 and again in 1916 (a third volume was published in 1917 but not distributed in Britain). It is salutary to remember that Q had included two early poems by Ezra Pound in his *Oxford Book of Victorian Verse* (1912).

Modernists such as **T. E. Hulme, T. S. Eliot** and Ezra Pound in Britain thought that they could successfully break with the immediate past, the Victorians and the romantics before them, in the light of a new consciousness provoked by modernity. The tradition proved in the event to be harder to break than they thought it would be.

Literary Culture in Britain, 1914–1918

The war poets themselves always were in need of close critical attention; the danger was that approval of the sentiments would overtake critical judgment of the work. Their achievements are very varied and their relationships to modernist currents differ widely. Isaac Rosenberg (1890–1918) is the true modernist, reaching a declamatory style that echoes the futurists' or the constructivists' efforts to find archetypal figures of human endeavor. Rosenberg's female figure in "Girl to Soldier on Leave" is no social-realist heroine but a mythical figure striding a huge stage. "Dead Man's Dump" is impressive, but the studied irony of "Break of Day in the Trenches" is even more satisfying and "Returning, We Hear Larks" is simply one of the finest modernist poems of its kind. The deliberately stilted utterances invoke a mind genuinely reaching beyond the immediate experience to touch an imagined realm. On the other side of the conflict Ludwig Wittgenstein was composing his *Tractatus Logico-Philosophicus.* In that work a remarkable world is glimpsed, a world of crystalline purity, a world of logical clarity. Rosenberg's poem conjures up the kind of being who might be able to live in such a world. His poems were edited by two men whose allegiances cross the divide of this time; Gordon Bottomley (1874–1948) whose "To Iron-Founders and Others" was one of the later poems Q admitted into his second edition of *The Oxford Book of English Verse,* and D. W. Harding, whose essay in *Scrutiny* reviewing "Burnt Norton" on its appearance in 1936 remains one of the best essays written on that poem. This conjunction of the old and the new is typical of the moment.

Edmund Blunden offers a different kind of vision of clarity in some of his work. In many of his finest poems of the war years Blunden contrasts the world he knew best, the English countryside and English poetry, sharply and with a poignant but clear-sighted irony, with the world he saw taking shape around him, which he knew to be the ruin of the world he loved. Blunden uses technically traditional approaches to contrast with the world he sees; "Report on Experience" and "Passing the Chateau: Vlamertinghe" are good examples. "The Zillebeke Brook" is a very fine poem indeed. "The Zonnebeke Road" needs to be read with Rosenberg fresh in the memory: this is what the effort to transcend looks like from the point of view of one who sees what will be lost in the process.

Siegfried Sassoon (1886–1967) is a much more interesting poet than the best-known poems would suggest. *Counterattack* (1918) has a fine spirit and some of the poems are not without poetic interest, though they are mainly interesting and impressive as the sharply etched satires he wanted them to be. Poems such as "The Death-Bed" are moving and subtle at several points but most interesting are poems such as "Concert Party" where the almost surreal world he conjured up in some of his descriptions in *Memoirs of an Infantry Officer* takes his imagination over and edges out the righteous indignation.

Wilfred Owen (1893–1918) is still the best-known poet of the war, if only for the poignancy and bravery of his determination to return to the front where he was killed at last in 1918. T. S. Eliot admired "Strange Meeting" (and used it in "Little Gidding") and the poem does have many striking moments; Owen's experimentation with rhyme is sometimes highly valued but on the whole he rarely rose above impassioned protest, valuable for what it is, but not to be mistaken for any thing other than it is.

W. B. Yeats rejected poems of the war for his edition of the *Oxford Book of Modern Verse* (1936) on the grounds that "passive suffering is not a theme for poetry." He objected to Owen's poetry as "all blood, dirt and sucked sugar stick" (Letter to Dorothy Wellesley, December 21, 1936). The grounds for the objection are as impeccably modernist as T. S. Eliot's observation that there is a sentimentality of the sordid—"Another variety of the pleasant, by the way, is the unpleasant (*sc.* Rupert Brooke on sea-sickness, and Masefield on various subjects)" ("Verse Pleasant and Unpleasant"). Nor can modernist objections be dismissed out of hand though they sound a little precious and a little pompous after all these years. Many of the most well known poems are sentimental, but the most interesting poems do not at all take passive suffering for their theme.

W. W. Gibson's (1878–1962) "The Dancers" is illustrative of a tendency among traditional poets to combine a frequently very straightforward moral view with a disturbing aesthetic detachment. The poem offers an image of dragon-flies ("demoiselles"—"young ladies") dancing "above the dreamless dead." This is not very far from the world that Baudelaire conjures up in "*La Corse,*" for example. The modern world affected even those who did not feel that they could embrace it, or that they could develop a technique to address it.

These themes can be gathered together in the career of Edward Thomas (1878–1817). He begins as a prose writer of the English countryside, much in the manner of Richard Jefferies, whose biographer he was, and as a *laudator temporis acti* by default, as such writing tends to celebrate an England that was rapidly disappearing and certainly had no connection with the world of the industrial Midlands, Clydeside, Tyneside, or the Welsh valleys. On the other hand it must be noted that English culture had not completely made the adjustment to emerging industrialism.

A good example of this unwillingness to adjust is offered by Q's *Oxford Book of English Verse*. It had first been published in 1900 and had not then, of course, been affected at all by modernist developments. However, when he came to re-edit the book in 1939, after those developments had been well established for some years, he still took no notice of those developments. It would be a great mistake to imagine that what he represented was merely seen off by a modernist revolution. Ralph Vaughan Williams (1872–1958), Gerald Finzi (1901–1956) and Edmund Rubbra (1901–1986) were writing **music** in an English pastoral tradition into the 1950s; Walter de la Mare was publishing and selling up to his death in 1956; Thomas Hardy published a volume, *Late Lyrics and Earlier,* for the traditional nature of which he apologized in the "Afterword," in 1922, the same year as *The Waste Land* was published.

Thomas's verse is the point. He saw, perhaps earlier than any other English poet, that verse had to be conceived of differently and he spoke of writing in "paragraphs" rather than in lines. Several of his greatest poems will not yield to scansion at all, and some of his greatest effects are achieved by a modulation that approaches, and even becomes at times, prose. One of his greatest achievements, "As the Team's Head Brass" illustrates this point perfectly and can be usefully compared with Thomas Hardy's magnificent achievement of compression "In Time of the Breaking of Nations." Both are war poems and resonate with the feeling of a world changed beyond repair; Hardy's is impeccably traditional in form and Thomas's by contrast meanders thoughtfully until a recognizable verse pattern emerges in the final line to enact the finality of the poem's conclusion. Thomas enlisted in 1915 at the age of 37 and died at Arras in 1917. His entire verse output was composed in two and a half

years before his death. C. H. Sisson has commented "his death, very likely, was what he wanted." When Walter de la Mare reviewed *Poems* (1917) for *The Times Literary Supplement,* he wrote prophetically of Thomas's work "taking the aspect of the past on the eve of a long farewell."

Literary Culture in Post–War Britain

The effect of the First World War on literature can be traced in R. C. Sherriff's (1896–1975) hugely successful and moving play *Journey's End* (1929) but it is also clearly expressed in **D. H. Lawrence**'s novel *Kangaroo* (1923). Sheriff is working within the same theatrical traditions as, say, John Galsworthy, whose *Strike,* for example, offers very similar pictures of ordinary people rising to some dignity and resoluteness under stress; Lawrence is not. Lawrence's rambling, fantastic, quasi-autobiographical composition looks forward in at least one respect—small enough it may be—to postmodernist fictions; its teasing identification of its central character, Richard Lovatt Somers, by his initials is a bizarre anachronism: "RLS" was the literary *soubriquet* of Robert Louis Stevenson. Such playing with time moves quickly away from Galsworthy and Sherriff.

Otherwise the war surfaces in odd survivals. F. R. Leavis, the champion at Cambridge of T. S. Eliot in the face of Q and his *Oxford Book of English Verse,* served as an ambulance orderly during the war and never spoke about it. C. S. Lewis (1898–1963), who wrote his *Preface to Paradise Lost* as a deliberate rebuttal of Leavis's and Eliot's attacks on Milton in the name of a new view of English poetry, wrote of his war years as the happiest years of his life (see, for example, *Mere Christianity* or *Surprised by Joy*). Lewis's friend J. R. R. Tolkien (1892–1973) drew on his memories of No Man's Land when he came to describe the cursed land of Mordor in *The Lord of the Rings.* The disaster that the war was for so many cannot easily be expressed.

The American poet Alan Seeger died in 1916; the Canadian John McRae in 1918; the English composer, George Butterworth, died in 1916; T. E. Hulme who was in many ways the father of English modernism, died in 1917 leaving two dozen poems and the essays in *Speculations* (1924); Antonio Sant'Elia, the futurist architect, died on the front line in 1916, the year after he had enlisted; the sculptor Henri Gaudier-Brzeska died in 1915; poet and composer Ivor Gurney descended into madness after the war; D. H. Lawrence's friend Harry Crosby killed himself in 1929 unable to live with his experiences. Some of the finest poems that were written in the post-war period are expressions of lost innocence and confused guilt (see Edmund Blunden's "1916 Seen from 1921," or Siegfried Sassoon's "Repression of War Experience").

In many ways the American experience is the bleakest. **Gertrude Stein** wrote "After the war, we had the twentieth century." The burial of the "Unknown Soldier" at Arlington on November 11, 1921 seemed to many a cynical and duplicitous exercise in which sentimentality once more obscured ugly political realities. **John Dos Passos** got through the war and wrote about it in *One Man's Initiation* (1920) and *Three Soldiers* (1921); **Hemingway** wrote his *A Farewell to Arms* a few years later in 1925. **E. E. Cummings**'s *The Enormous Room* (1922) is a black farce based upon his experiences after he was arrested for "treasonable correspondence" and imprisoned in a French concentration camp.

On the other side of the conflict, the pianist Paul Wittgenstein, brother of the philosopher, Ludwig, lost his right hand. Many composers wrote concertos for the left hand for piano and orchestra for him but it could be little consolation (though he liked Britten's).

On a more positive note, it became very difficult to tell

> with such high zest,
> To children ardent for some desperate
>   glory,
> The old lie, *Dulce et decorum est*
> *Pro patria mori*

at least partly because some of the children had become much wiser than their fathers were, and much sadder.

The poetry of the Spanish Civil War (1936–1939) and of the Second World War (1939–1945) shows little recrudescence of the passionate youthful cry of pain and dismay that marks so many of the poems of the First World War. That may have been the sound of the coming of age of modernism in the countries affected by the First World War.

Nicholas Potter

Selected Bibliography

"Apteryx" (T. S. Eliot). "Verse Pleasant and Unpleasant." [Review of *Georgian Poetry, 1916–1917*]. *The Egoist* 5:3 (March 1918): 43.

Forster, E. M.. "The Challenge of Our Time." In his *Two Cheers for Democracy*. Harmondsworth: Penguin, 1965.

Sisson, C. H. *English Poetry, 1900–1950: An Assessment*. London: Rupert Hart-Davis, 1971.

Yeats, W. B. *The Letters of W. B. Yeats*. Ed. Allan Wade. London: Rupert Hart-Davis, 1954.

(See also general selected bibliography under Cardinal, Izenberg, Oudit, A. K. Smith, and Tate.)

Wedekind, Frank (1864–1918)

Wedekind's achievement lies in his development of an alternative to **Hauptmann**'s naturalist theater in the 1890s. Experiences as the secretary of a Parisian circus and of the art forger Willy Grétor, and as a performer at night-clubs in Munich and Berlin, all introduced Wedekind to sections of society which would inspire the anarchism of his work. In his plays he eschewed philosophical and aesthetic sophistication, in favor of an extravagant and exaggerated style. His characters' absurd behavior and monologues communicate their libidinal impulses, often directly to the audience—impulses that Wedekind believed could ultimately transform society. Apart from composing plays, he was also a senior editor and dominant voice of the satirical magazine *Simplizissimus* in the 1890s.

In *Frühlings Erwachen* (1891, *Spring Awakening*) Wedekind satirizes the hypocrisy of teachers and parents who compel the adolescent characters to succeed academically and to control their sexuality. Melchior's philosophical dilemma between suicide or facing expulsion from his family and school after writing a thesis on sex, is comically reduced to farce. He rejects his dead friend Moritz, who holds his head under his arm, for the "muffled gentleman" who reassures him that "with a hot supper in your belly, you can laugh at it."

In Wedekind's most influential achievement, the "Lulu" plays *Erdgeist* (1895, *Earth Spirit*) and *Die Büchse der Pandora* (1904, *Pandora's Box*), he envisaged "the joyful woman," his revision of Nietzsche's "superman," who embodies **Freud**'s "pleasure principle." Lulu destroys an old businessman, an artist, her father-figure Dr. Schön, his son Alwa, as well as other male figures, who attempt to project their feminine ideal upon her from their desire to possess her sexually. Finally, she is reduced to prostitution and murdered by Jack the Ripper. This play exerted a fascination on later artists for its depiction of a woman who heroically undermines male, bourgeois morality by following her libidinal instincts. Alban Berg compressed these two plays into his opera *Lulu* (1937).

Wedekind became a cult figure for the German avant-garde during the Weimar period, having endured public denunciations and prosecution during his lifetime. The expressionist playwrights and **Bertolt**

Brecht elaborated from his use of monologue, his treatment of characters as puppets without inner psychological tensions, and from his acting which excluded psychological consistency. Also, in 1916 the dadaist Café Voltaire opened with a program of his songs.

Carl Krockel

Selected Bibliography
Wedekind's works are available in Georg Müller Verlag, Munich, and Methuen, London.
Best, Alan. *Frank Wedekind.* London: Oswald Wolff, 1975.
Gittleman, Sol. *Frank Wedekind.* New York: Frederick Ungar 1969.

Werfel, Franz (1890–1945)

A Jew, Werfel was born in Prague, where he developed a friendship with **Franz Kafka;** he moved to Vienna in 1918. His early literary career was as an expressionist poet, which included the collections *Der Weltfreund* (1910, *The World's Friend*) and *Einander* (1915, *Each Other*). Unlike his contemporaries, he optimistically anticipated a spiritual regeneration, and was later satirized by **Musil** in *Der Mann ohne Eigenschaften* through the character of Feuermaul—literally, "fire-mouth." "Am Abend" ("At Evening"), from *Der Weltfreund,* describes how the narrator overcomes his sense of alienation through a mystical union with a deformed girl packing cheese, achieved simply by meeting her gaze.

From the 1920s Werfel concentrated on writing novels and plays, moving towards a realistic style which followed the trend of New Objectivity in the German arts, which rejected the visionary imagination of **expressionism**. His subjects vary from *Verdi, Roman der Opera* (1924, *Verdi, a Novel of the Opera*), on the Italian composer's struggle to overcome his sense of inferiority to Wagner, to *Barbara oder Die Frömmigkeit* (1929, *Barbara or Pi-*

ety), about the 1918 Revolution in Vienna. In Werfel's most famous novel *Die vierzig Tage des Musa Dagh* (1933, *The Forty Days of Musa Dagh*), he depicted the Turkish genocide of Armenians. He was attempting to warn of the consequences of Nazism, despite his own naïve response to it in signing a declaration of loyalty to the regime in 1933. He painstakingly researched the novel from 1930 onwards to record with accuracy the miraculous survival of a group of Armenians who fought against the Turks. He also gives his history a timeless poignancy by reintroducing the mysticism of his expressionist period with the hero Gabriel finding in the crippled Iskuhi his racial origins, "not the wish to be joined in future, but the utter certainty of having been so in the past."

Werfel emigrated to the United States in 1940, where he enjoyed greater success than any of his compatriots. *Das Lied von Bernadette* (*The Song of Bernadette,* 1941), on the founder of Lourdes, was adapted into a successful **film.** His play *Jacobowsky und der Oberst* (1944, *Jacobowsky and the Colonel*), which depicts a flight from Paris during the Nazi occupation, was staged, and first published as a college text.

Carl Krockel

Selected Bibliography

Werfel's works are available in S. Fischer Verlag, Frankfurt am Main, and Hamish Hamilton, London.

Foltin, Lore B., ed. *Franz Werfel: 1890–1945.* Pittsburgh: University of Pittsburgh Press, 1961.

Huber, Lothar, ed. *Franz Werfel: An Austrian Writer Reassessed.* New York: Berg Publishers, 1989.

West, Rebecca (pseudonym of Cicely Isabel Fairfield) (1892–1983)

Although Rebecca West's career spanned the modernist era—she began publishing journalism in 1911 and kept writing until her death in 1983—only a fraction of her works falls within traditional definitions of literary modernism. Rather, West is an important figure for reinterpreting this era and the conventional categories of literary modernism, primarily because of her ongoing engagement with political thought, as well as her literary experimentation in prose evidenced by the wide range of genres in which she worked. Eleven novels by West have been published, six books of literary criticism, a psychobiography of St. Augustine, short stories, several studies of treason, virtually innumerable reviews, articles, and reports, and a massive travelogue-history of Yugoslavia that indirectly influenced United States foreign policy in the Balkans into the 1990s (Hall 83). Throughout the decades in which she wrote these works, West's political point of view slid from left to right, from socialist and suffragist to anti-communist and advocate of the "Rule of Law." At the same time, West designated herself a feminist throughout her life, despite these changing views, and her conceptions of gender greatly influenced her individual brand of modernism. In an early review she wrote, "I myself have never been able to find out precisely what feminism is: I only know that people call me a feminist whenever I express sentiments that differentiate me from a doormat or a prostitute" ("Mr. Chesterton" 219). While West believed strongly in the significance of art for human life, and her many theater and book reviews demonstrate her commitment to its promotion, one of her contributions to the modernist era was her ability to probe, through multiple genres, the ways in which the imaginative life of art and the practical life of politics are intertwined. West wrote about major struggles of the century—two world wars, nationalism, imperialism, socialism, fascism, **feminism,** the cold war, the possibility of religious belief, the position of women in modernity. Her witty and erudite engagement with these issues made her a significant contributor to literary developments and a shaper of public opinion in the modernist era and beyond.

West was born Cicely Isabel Fairfield in London in 1892, the youngest of three sisters. Her father, Charles Fairfield, descended from the protestant gentry of County Kerry, **Ireland.** He became an adventurer of the intellect as well as of the British empire. He traveled, among other places, to **Canada,** Colorado, and Australia, making his way by his wits and his writing, and eventually becoming a journalist for the Melbourne *Argus,* the Glasgow *Herald* and other publications. His opinions were passionate, controversial, conservative. He positioned himself against socialism and women's suffrage, preferring the power of the individual and the governing class to democratic rule. His heroes included Edmund Burke and Herbert Spencer, to whom West was exposed when very young (Glendinning *Rebecca* 18–19). She later claimed, "I cannot remember a time when I had not a rough idea of what was meant by capitalism, socialism, individualism, anarchism, liberalism, and conservatism" ("My Father"). Her father abandoned the family to move to **Africa** when West was eight; he died a pauper in Liverpool when she was fourteen. She claimed later in life: "I had a glorious father, I had no father at all," and she wrote numerous accounts of him which suggest the depth of his influence on her (Glendinning *Rebecca* 23).

West's Scottish mother Isabella Mackenzie returned to Edinburgh with her daughters after her husband left. She was a talented pianist, but as a woman had received few opportunities for a musical career. Through self-sacrifice and a series of scholarships, Isabella educated her daughters, encouraged in them a love of the arts, and kept them from the depths of poverty. The three daughters in this household understandably gravitated toward the suf-

frage movement and participated in its activities in Edinburgh; Rebecca West's first published piece of writing, at fourteen, was a letter to *The Scotsman* defending "Women's Electoral Claims" (Glendinning *Rebecca* 31). This phase of West's life contributed to the setting and plot of *The Judge* (1922), a rather turgid novel of deep psychological insight, with the disturbing epigraph: "Every mother is a judge who sentences the children for the sins of the father." In addition to multiple autobiographical pieces such as *Family Memories* (1987), West fictionalized her childhood in the neo-Victorian novel *The Fountain Overflows* (1956), a bestseller in the mid-1950s. This work was the first volume of an unfinished tetralogy, of which two more were published posthumously, *This Real Night* (1984) and *Cousin Rosamund* (1985). West conceived the volumes as a "saga of the century," following a family from the 1890s into the 1950s, and incorporating the effects of two world wars on their lives. Themes of these novels tend to be structured on binary oppositions—West was deeply interested in Manicheanism, and tended to view struggles in dualistic terms—good vs. evil, earthly art vs. spiritual truth, justice vs. injustice (Glendinning "Afterword" 295). As fiction about the maturation of women under the conditions of modernity, the books bear comparison to **Woolf**'s *The Years.*

After briefly attending the Academy of Dramatic Art in London, Cicely Fairfield jettisoned her too-polite name for that of the tragic heroine of Ibsen's *Rosmersholm.* She burst into the pages of the newly founded *The Freewoman* with a review of *The Position of Women in Indian Life* which began, "There are two kinds of imperialists—imperialists and bloody imperialists" (12). This review set the provocative tone of West's journalism, and initiated her voluminous writing about empire as well as about the differences among women due to class, education, and political position. At this early point in her career, West advocated socialism as well as feminism: woman must "capture the commanding fortresses of industry, from which she can dictate the conditions of her own labor," she claimed (13).

West introduced **Ezra Pound** to the staff of *The New Freewoman,* a journal originally dedicated to considering feminism as a movement wider than suffrage, and he became the literary editor. When *The Egoist* was born from its ashes in 1913, West briefly worked as its literary editor, but quarreled with Pound over his goal of replacing the feminist nature of the journal with more purely "literary" content (Marcus "Editor's" 8). She left *The Egoist* to write for more directly political journals such as the socialist *The Clarion.* Such choices allowed West to negotiate her commitments to both politics and literature, but by distancing herself from Pound, **Joyce, Eliot,** and others, West moved away from what would become the male center of aesthetically oriented high modernism.

During these years West was also developing friendships with the Fabian socialists and literary figures in London including **George Bernard Shaw,** Violet Hunt, **Ford Madox Ford,** and H. G. Wells. West had written an irreverent review of Wells' novel *Marriage* which attracted his attention and began their decade-long liasion. Their affair produced a son, Anthony, whose out-of-wedlock birth she tried to keep from the public eye as late as 1947. Her experiences as a single mother deepened her commitment to feminism.

While somewhat critical of the fiction of Wells and Arnold Bennett in reviews, particularly of their representations of women, West evinced interest in realist and naturalist literary forms.

She wrote a mixed tribute to Bennett upon his death in 1931, praising his fiction for showing that even linendrapers are "tragic and glorious" (17). At the same time, West championed diverse modernist

writers. Her first extensive work of literary criticism was a study of **Henry James,** at once reverential and critical (1916). West praised James' "masterly use of technical resource" (58) and his ability to "dive down serenely . . . into the twilit depths of the heart to seize his secrets" (99) while she complained about his stylistic excesses and his "persistent presentation of woman not as a human but as a sexual being" (53). In reviews in many periodicals, including *The Bookman, The New York Herald Tribune, The New Statesman, The Daily Telegraph,* and the feminist weekly *Time and Tide,* West analyzed and often applauded the work of May Sinclair, Rose Macaulay, **Katherine Mansfield, W. B. Yeats, Wyndham Lewis,** Storm Jameson, Lytton Strachey and others. She wrote with particular enthusiasm about the works of Virginia Woolf, for example calling *Orlando* "a poetic masterpiece of the first rank" (1). West defended **D. H. Lawrence**'s works with vigor, all the way to the obscenity trial of *Lady Chatterley's Lover* in 1960, finding in them a commitment to the principle of life that she believed was sorely missing in modernity. West called Joyce "sentimental" in her long and associative, but generally appreciative, critique of *Ulysses* in *The Strange Necessity* which elicited responses from Joyce (see Halper) and **Beckett** (248). This essay, which argues for the "strange necessity"of art to human life, can be read as a powerful modernist manifesto. Her later *The Court and the Castle* (1958) examines the interplay of religious ideas, changes in political systems, and literary forms from **Shakespeare** to **Kafka.**

West's own early fiction demonstrates a fascination with psychology and consistent attention to the conflicts of gender in modernity. In the first edition of *Blast* in 1914, Wyndham Lewis published "Indissoluble Matrimony," a story that pits a strong, sensual, politically outspoken heroine against her weak, nerve-addled husband, versions of which would appear in West's work through many decades. Her comment "I am an old-fashioned feminist. I believe in the sex war" sums up West's belief in what she and others of the era called "sex antagonism" ("Nagging" 1052). **World War I** also figured as a field of sexual as well as national antagonism for West; her Conradian *The Return of the Soldier* (1918) was the first British novel to fictionalize the effects of shell shock, but the story takes place on the feminized ground of the home front. The tale is narrated by Jenny, the soldier's cousin, and emphasizes the internal violence of war and class relations rather than the external violence of the battlefield through psychological and narrative complexity. This book establishes that West was aware of **Freud**'s theories relatively early, and joined other modernists in popularizing psychoanalytic insights. During her own **psychoanalysis** in the 1920s, West wrote but never completed a semi-autobiographical, rather Lawrentian novel of a talented, professional woman searching for a "primitive" man. It was published posthumously as *Sunflower* in 1986. *Harriet Hume* (1929) remains another of West's modernist fictional experiments; this "London fantasy" about a pianist with mindreading abilities sets masculine against feminine in what Jane Marcus calls a "feminist fantasy novel" of the 1920s. Like Woolf in *Orlando,* West uses fantasy to criticize patriarchal political structures such as British imperialism. Her fiction of the 1930s turns back toward **realism,** with the stories of *The Harsh Voice* (1935) and the novel *The Thinking Reed* (1936) examining the place of women within the sexual and financial economies of the interwar period.

West's greatest and most famous work is the encyclopedic *Black Lamb and Grey Falcon,* a history-travelogue of Yugoslavia, a country she visited several times in the late 1930s. West forged a literary form that allowed her to join political analysis,

history, reflections on literature, the arts, and much else by mixing her talents as a novelist with her talents as a journalist. This highly imaginative, politically engaged book owes much of its looping narrative form to modernist techniques, but the direct treatment of political matters moves modernism in a different direction. The "Epilogue" of *Black Lamb and Grey Falcon* is a stirring call to arms directed toward England in the early days of World War II. Throughout this work, West invokes Freudian dualisms of Eros and Thanatos, a life-wish and a death-wish that she believes inform human actions throughout history.

In the post–World War II era, West's politics became more conservative, and she spoke out vociferously against communism, having developed a skepticism of the Soviet project not long after the Russian Revolution. Much of her next several decades of political journalism reported on legal trials: of murderers, political traitors, and the Nazis at Nuremberg. Many of these pieces appeared in *The New Yorker* and elsewhere, and some were later collected in *A Train of Powder* (1955). West expanded her reports on traitors with meditations on loyalty, betrayal, and the law to comprise the volumes *The Meaning of Treason* (1947) and *The New Meaning of Treason* (1964). Her novel *The Birds Fall Down* is a fictional treatment of these themes, and reads much like a feminist rewriting of **Conrad**'s *Under Western Eyes,* a novel of spies and intrigue told from the point of view of a young woman. West's work earned her the honor of becoming a Dame of the British Empire in 1958.

West's reputation among literary and cultural critics has been varied. West was the only contemporary writer mentioned in *A Room of One's Own;* Virginia Woolf characterized her as an "arrant feminist" in the eyes of one of her angry male characters. Woolf's synechdochic use of West illustrates her notoriety during the modernist era. Second-wave feminists redis-covered this feminist figure and have tended to praise her early, bold, socialist-feminist works and experimental fiction. Other critics, many of them men, prefer the works of West's mature years, begin-ning with *Black Lamb and Grey Falcon* and including the political journalism and neo-realist fiction that reached audiences on both sides of the Atlantic. Throughout her many works, West advocated a social contract that would be fair for all citizens, especially women, but doubted its possi-bility due to human drives for masochistic self-sacrifice, for the "disagreeable over the agreeable," for communal as well as personal death. Just as West pioneered the genre of psychobiography with her study *St. Augustine* (1933), she helped to de-velop the psychological interpretation of history throughout her works. Like many modernists, West championed the creative forces of art as an antidote to the death-wish she found so prominent in modernity.

Loretta Stec

Selected Bibliography

Beckett, Samuel. "Dante . . . Bruno. Vico . . . Joyce." *Transition* (June 1929): 242–253.

Glendinning, Victoria. "Afterword." *Cousin Rosa-mund.* New York and Harmondsworth: Pen-guin, 1986. 287–295.

———. *Rebecca West: A Life.* New York: Alfred A. Knopf, 1987.

Hall, Brian. "Rebecca West's War." *The New Yorker* (15 April 1996): 74–83.

Halper, Nathan. "James Joyce and Rebecca West." *Studies in Joyce.* Ann Arbor: UMI Research Press, 1983. 51–53

Marcus, Jane. *The Young Rebecca.* Bloomington/In-dianapolis: Indiana UP, 1982.

———. "Editor's Introduction." Marcus, *Young Re-becca* 3–11.

———. "A Wilderness of Her Own: Feminist Fan-tasy Novels of the 1920s"

Rollyson, Carl. *Rebecca West: A Saga of the Cen-tury.* London: Hodder and Stoughton, 1995.

Stetz, Margaret. "Rebecca West's Criticism: Alli-ance, Tradition and Modernism." *Rereading Modernism: New Directions in Feminist Criti-cism.* New York and London: Garland, 1994. 41–66.

West, Rebecca. *Arnold Bennett Himself.* New York: John Day, 1931.

———. *Henry James.* 1916. New York: Haskell House, 1974.

———. "High Fountain of Genius." Rev. of Vir-ginia Woolf, *Orlando. New York Herald Tri-bune Books* 21 Oct 1928. 1, 6.

———. "Mr Chesterton in Hysterics: A Study in Prejudice." *The Clarion* 14 November 1913. Rpt. in Marcus, *Young Rebecca* 218–222.

———. "My Father." *The Sunday Telegraph* (30 December 1962): 4.

———. "On a Form of Nagging." *Time and Tide* (31 October 1924): 1052–1053.

———. "The Position of Women in Indian Life." *The Freewoman.* 30 November 1911. Rpt. in Marcus, *Young Rebecca* 12–14.

Whitman, Walt (1819–1892)

Whitman was a crucial figure underlying the development of modernist literature both in America and beyond. In his pio-neering essay "Walt Whitman: Precipitant of the Modern," Alan Trachtenberg goes so far as to assert that "modernism emerged in America and shaped itself at least in part as a diverse collective re-sponse to Whitman's call, an answer to the Answerer" (Trachtenberg 197). He identi-fies key figures in the fields of architecture, painting, **dance,** prose-writing, and poetry in order to indicate the extent of Whit-man's impact.

Certainly, the poets **Ezra Pound, Wil-liam Carlos Williams,** and Hart Crane felt an instinctive affinity with Whitman, and believed their subsequent writing to have been "shaped" to some inevitable degree by their precursor. Pound defined himself as a latter-day, bourgeois version of Whit-man, asserting that "Mentally I am a Walt Whitman who has learned to wear a collar and a dress shirt (although at times inim-ical to both)" (Pound 145). Crane, in his almost overwhelming admiration for Whitman, wrote in March 1923: "I begin to feel myself directly connected with Whitman. I feel myself in currents that are positively awesome in their extent and possibilities" (Weber 128). Williams similarly expressed his driving need to establish some contact with Whitman, indicating simultaneously a degree of bewilderment at the extent of identification: "I don't know why I had that instinctive drive to get in touch with Whitman" (Sutton 312).

These key literary figures—and many others—identified in Whitman an almost prophetic figure whose poems revealed a new outlook on experience, at a time of radical change. Whitman's writing is characterized by energy, freshness, worldliness, directness, and simplicity: it embodies a spontaneous and invigorating response to America and its people which advocates democracy and the "oneness" of universal brotherhood. It is liberating also in terms of its acceptance of emotion, and its unrestrained emphasis on the beauty of physicality and eroticism, such as when Whitman is "singing the phallus, / Singing the song of procreation" (Whitman 91). The poem "I Sing the Body Electric" in its entirety exemplifies Whitman's celebration of the human body through erotic writing. In the "Calmus" poems the erotic writing is at times explicitly homosexual: a crucial element of Whitman's writing which led to his reputation as a pioneer who openly subverted bourgeois convention and the repression of feeling. In his championing of "manly love" he not only challenged conventional prejudices regarding homosexuality; he also attempted to redress stereotypical views of masculinity, by asserting that emotionality and sensitivity are appropriate aspects of the male psyche and persona.

In order to articulate the radical and challenging views that served to delight some of his contemporary readers while shocking and alienating others, Whitman adopted a free-verse method that allowed him the ultimate flexibility. Trachtenberg describes the way in which this mode of writing is distinctive, and recognizable either as the work of Whitman or a disciple:

"Whitmanesquerie can be recognized by its favoring of a long, engorged, fragmented, and shapeless line of unmetered verse" (Trachtenberg 199). This description indicates an extreme formlessness which seems antithetical to the modernists' intense preoccupation with aesthetic shaping of art. Yet Pound referred to specific patterns within Whitman's writing which were not only identifiable but addictive: "when I write of certain things I find myself using his rhythms" (Pound 145).

D. H. Lawrence was more overtly enthusiastic about the Whitmanesque free-verse, claiming in his essay "Poetry of the Present" that Whitman had found the true modern poetic voice: "This is the unrestful, ungraspable poetry of the sheer present, poetry whose very permanency lies in its wind-like transit. Whitman's is the best poetry of this kind" (183). In addition, in the first draft of his "Whitman" essay (published in revised form in *Studies of Classic American Literature* in 1923), Lawrence asserted that he owed the "last strides into freedom" to Whitman, and ranked his precursor in status beside Dante and **Shakespeare.** Lawrence adopted Whitman's free-verse as a model for his poetry and always adhered to it—in spite of the "quarrel" that led him to reject many other aspects of Whitman's ideology. It is interesting that while Lawrence chose to adopt Whitman's form and reject much of his philosophy, Williams believed that in order to achieve Whitman's status it was necessary to divert onto another track: "The only way to be like Whitman is to write *unlike* Whitman" (Williams 31).

The response of many crucial modernist writers to Whitman was split between admiration and antipathy: a sense that emulation may be appropriate but only to a certain extent. Pound referred to the "acute pain" caused by reading Whitman; Williams suggested that the later Whitman was a "magnificent failure" revealing all

Wilde, Oscar (1854–1900) 457

the defects of his method; while D. H. Lawrence emphatically referred to Whitman's "Post-mortem effects" and dismissed "Allness" (involving loss of self and indiscriminate merging) as "an addled egg." Crane, too, doubted the applicability of Whitman's vision, in which he becomes a "Saunterer on the free ways still ahead!" to the noisy, thronging modern world. Many resented the egocentricity of a man whose trademark was the poem "Song of Myself."

However, these negative responses are symptomatic of the way in which developing poets must react against and dismiss precursors who have been most profoundly influential, in order to find an individual voice. Modernist poets recognized in Whitman the greatness of a true innovator who would inspire his aesthetic successors: "Whitman, the one man breaking a way ahead. Whitman, the one pioneer. And only Whitman. No English pioneers, no French . . . Ahead of Whitman, nothing . . . And lots of new little poets camping on Whitman's camping ground now" (D. H. Lawrence, *Studies* 179). Modernist poetry, particularly in America, was largely an attempt to find a pitch on Whitman's camping ground, and to look for suitable ways out onto the open road beyond.

Bethan Jones

Selected Bibliography

Lawrence, D. H. "Poetry of the Present." *The Complete Poems.* Ed. Vivian de Sola Pinto and Warren Roberts. London: Penguin, 1993.
———. *Studies in Classic American Literature.* London: Penguin, 1971.
Pound, Ezra. *Selected Prose: 1909–1963.* New York: New Directions, 1973.
Sutton, Walter. "A Visit with William Carlos Williams." *The Minnesota Review* I (April 1961).
Trachtenberg, Alan. "Walt Whitman: Precipitant of the Modern." *Walt Whitman.* Ed. Ezra Greenspan. Cambridge: Cambridge UP, 1995.
Weber, Brom, ed. *The Letters of Hart Crane.* Berkeley: University of California Press, 1952.

Whitman, Walt. *Leaves of Grass.* Ed. Sculley Bradley and Harold W. Blodgett. New York and London: W.W. Norton & Co., 1973.

Wilde, Oscar (1854–1900)

Writing in "The Critic as Artist," an essay first published in 1890, Oscar Wilde stated: "It is enough that our fathers believed. They have exhausted the faith-faculty of the species. Their legacy to us is the skepticism of which they were afraid." Beyond the biting wit, or the much written about details of his life as a homosexual in late nineteenth-century England, it is, perhaps, this embracing of doubt, relativism, uncertainty, and paradox, which makes Wilde the "modern man" he styled himself in this and other writings.

Wilde was born in Dublin in 1854. His father was Sir William Wilde, a distinguished surgeon; his mother, Lady Jane, wrote for the Irish nationalist cause as "Sperenza," and on women's rights. After Trinity College Dublin, Wilde fell under the spell of Pater at Oxford, and began to cultivate the aestheticism and conversational wit for which he became (in)famous. He was a public figure before he was a published writer.

Wilde's first play *Vera* was produced in New York in 1882: a melodramatic story of Russian nihilism, it is not typical of the plays on which his fame is secured; but, in its use of "place symbolism" (Worth 37) it does anticipate some of the techniques of the later plays. Wilde's interest in symbolism was confirmed by the first of many trips to Paris in 1883, where he met Hugo, Mallarmé, Verlaine and others. Its use is seen most significantly in *Salomé,* a dramatic retelling of the Biblical story, with the Wildean twists that Salomé is driven by physical desire for the John the Baptist figure, Iakanaan's (dead) body rather than by his spirituality, and that her dance exists independently of Herod's granting of her wish, suggesting the amorality of art. Written originally in French, the play, first published in 1893, is now seen as central to Wilde's work (see Tydeman and Price). It influenced **Yeats,** who reworked it at least twice (*The King of the Great Clock Tower* (1934) and *The Full Moon in March* [1935]), and, as Worth argues "it has haunted the European imagination ever since" (7): it was first performed by the Théâtre de l'Oeuvre in 1896, the year they also staged Jarry's *Ubu Roi;* and it was a cornerstone of modernist theater in **Germany, Russia** and Eastern Europe.

Wilde married Constance Lloyd in 1884, and made his living as a journalist. Notably, foreshadowing the extent to which the radical sympathies in his later plays often centered on the lot of a woman (see Eltis), he took over the editorship of *Ladies' World* in 1887, pointedly changing its title to *Woman's World,* and commissioning articles on women's suffrage. A Max Beerbohm cartoon of the early nineties captures an interesting view of Wilde: he is led by two female figures, one labelled "Fashion," the other "Women's Rights."

In 1888 Wilde published a volume of fairy tales, *The* Happy *Prince and Other Tales.* Although originating in stories told to his children, these tales exhibit what one critic has called a "fracture between plot and discourse" (Raby 103) familiar in later twentieth-century retellings of the fairy tale. Their success was repeated in *The House of Pomegranates* in 1891; and it was in this year that Wilde was able to give up journalism with the publication of the novel *The Picture of Dorian Gray* and the collection of essays *Intentions,* which included "The Critic as Artist," "The Decay of Lying," "The Truth of Masks," and the satirical biography of a forger "Pen, Pencil, and Poison."

Dorian Gray, a portrayal of the sinister double life of the eponymous hero who remains young while his portrait ages, and of the aesthete Lord Henry Wotton, can be seen to reflect Victorian rather than modern anxieties; Ellmann calls it "the tragedy of aestheticism" (297). Yet, many of its most memorable phrases—"No artist desires to prove anything," "No artist has ethical sympathies," "The artist can express everything"—are arguably forward looking. Its "Preface" is, for example, a model for the vorticist manifesto of **Wyndham Lewis.** It also echoes many of the sentiments Wilde was producing in the essays written at this time, which can be read as more than a collection of confrontational aphorisms. Indeed, Northrop Frye sees *Intentions,* and the companion essay "The Soul of Man Under Socialism" (1891), as "the herald of a new age of literature." In these essays Wilde notes the importance of the machine as both threatening and liberating; argues for the mutability of human nature—"The only thing that one really knows about human nature is that it changes"—and for a relativism which arguably goes beyond aestheticism—"For in art there is no such thing as a universal truth. A truth in art is that whose contradictory is also true." The most striking feature of *Intentions* is to suggest that language is not dependent upon a pre-linguistic "truth," and that words, in some sense, construct the world (see Longxi). In an idea which is echoed in **Joyce's** *Ulysses,* Wilde writes in "The Decay of Lying" of the "mirror of art" as "a cracked mirror" which can reflect multiple images rather than a static truth.

In 1891 Wilde also met Lord Alfred Douglas and began the relationship which was to lead to his eventual trial for homosexual practices and imprisonment for two years in 1895. Between these two dates he produced the series of social comedies, or plays of modern life, on which his reputation still largely rests: *Lady Windemere's Fan* (1892), *A Woman of No Importance* (1893), *An Ideal Husband*

(1895), and what is still considered his masterpiece, *The Importance of Being Earnest* (1895). These can be seen in the long tradition of the well-made play, and as opportunities for Wilde to indulge his wit. Yet, they might also be seen as dramas which knowingly play with the conventions of melodrama and social comedy; Worth finds an anticipation of the Absurd and of **Beckett** in their stylization of social rituals (84, 99). Wilde himself called Act I of *A Woman of No Importance* "perfect" because nothing happens during it. Similarly, beneath its sparkle and famous one-liners, *Earnest* can be seen to anticipate the sense of meaninglessness of **T. S. Eliot**'s *Waste Land,* or the materialist ennui of **Fitzgerald**'s *The Great Gatsby,* in its repeated question "What shall we do?" at the end of Act I. When **Auden** called the play "the only purely verbal opera in English" he was thinking primarily of its linguistic playfulness, but his judgment might also be read as an indication of the extent to which Wilde saw the world as dependent upon precarious human constructs rather than the earnest (Wilde intended the pun) and exhausted values of Victorian society.

Released from prison in 1897, where he wrote a letter to Douglas, published as *De Profundis* (1905; full text 1965) and *The Ballad of Reading Gaol* (1898), Wilde spent the remainder of his life abroad. He wrote in prison: "I was a man who stood in symbolic relation to the art and culture of my age." Having been received into the Catholic Church, he died in 1900; with an irony he would have appreciated, he was on the verge of a new century and a new age, many of the concerns of which he equally stood in relation to.

Paul Wright

Selected Bibliography

Ellmann, Richard. *Oscar Wilde.* London: Hamish Hamilton, 1987.

Eltis, Sos. *Revising Wilde.* Oxford: Clarendon Press 1996.

Hart-Davis, Rupert. *The Letters of Oscar Wilde.* London: Hart-Davis, 1962.

———. *More Letters of Oscar Wilde.* London: John Murray, 1985.

Holland, Merlin, ed. *The Complete Works of Oscar Wilde.* London: Collins, 1994.

Longxi, Zhang. "The Critical Legacy of Oscar Wilde." *Texas Studies in Literature and Language* 30 (1988): 87–103.

Raby, Peter, ed. *The Cambridge Companion to Oscar Wilde.* Cambridge: CUP, 1997.

Tydeman, William, and Steven Price. *Salomé.* Cambridge: CUP 1997.

Worth, Katherine. *Oscar Wilde.* London: Macmillan, 1987.

Williams, William Carlos (1883–1963)

American poet.

Son of an Englishman brought up in the West Indies and of a Puertorican, he graduated from the Medical School of the University of Pennsylvania (where he met **Ezra Pound, Hilda Doolittle** and the painter Charles Demuth). After a one-year stay in Europe (1909–1910), where he trained as a pediatrician in Leipzig, he settled with his family in his native town, Rutherford, New Jersey, working at the local hospital. Managing to combine his profession with his interest in poetry, he never lost touch with the avant-garde artists then active in the New York area (among others, Marcel Duchamp, **Marianne Moore, Wallace Stevens,** the photographer Alfred Stieglitz, the painter Stuart Davies, the art patron Walter Arensberg), and came to be recognized as one of the leading exponents of American modernism.

Williams privately published his first volume of poetry (*Poems*) in 1909, followed in 1913 by *The Tempers,* which was prefaced by Pound. Both volumes still reflect the influence of traditional models (**Shakespeare,** the Romantics, Browning), and it is only with his third volume, *Al Que Quiere!* (1917), that Williams started to develop a personal poetic voice. His poems of this period are often short lyrics—

bearing the imprint of **imagism** in their verbal economy—devoted to the observation of apparently minor, even trivial details of life ("The Red Wheelbarrow" is the most famous example), taken either from the natural world or from the degraded reality of industrial America. With their objectivism they anticipate Williams' later theoretical imperative "no ideas but in things," with which he advocated an anti-intellectual poetry capable of bringing man in touch with the concrete elements of everyday experience.

The experimental strain of Williams' literary production reached its climax in the twenties, with works such as *Kora in Hell* (1920) and *Spring and All* (1923), where he alternated reflections on art, his medical profession and the external world in an elliptical and fragmented style, combining poetry and prose, which recalled surrealist and dadaist techniques as well as the lesson of **cubism.** In 1922 Williams reacted negatively to the publication of **Eliot**'s *Waste Land,* and increasingly defined his poetry in opposition to Eliot's model (in 1939 he wrote to Pound: "I'm glad you like Eliot's verse, but I'm warning you, the only reason it doesn't smell is that it is synthetic"). Following **Whitman**'s lead, Williams stressed the necessity of a vital link with the American soil, the American experience and the American idiom (which he accused Eliot of having forsaken). Such an urge underscores *In the American Grain* (1925), a prose work in which Williams revisited the course of American history from its origins to the Civil War, focusing his narration on a series of characters, from the mythic Eric the Red to Abraham Lincoln, whose personal histories he recaptured through a highly personal collage of documents and fiction. In his gallery of men who have made the history of America, Williams' emphasis is on the relationship each of them entertains with the American continent, the dividing line between positive and negative char-

acters being precisely their willingness to interact with the New World and its inhabitants. Hence Williams' attack on the Puritans, whom he accuses of having withdrawn to the sterile citadel of their faith, negatively conditioning the development of American culture.

After trying his hand at both short stories (later collected in *The Farmer's Daughter,* 1961) and the novel (*White Mule,* 1937; *In the Money,* 1940) in the late thirties Williams started writing the work for which he is now best known, the long poem *Paterson* (published 1946–1958), which occupied him for more than a decade. In its five books Williams mixed his own poetry with historical documents, passages from private letters, newspaper clippings, in an attempt to give voice to the past and present dimension of the industrial city of Paterson, New Jersey. The accent is on the city's—and its inhabitants'—degraded state, which Williams blames on the process of industrial development but also on a more subtle, romantic malaise: the divorce between Paterson (both the city and a mythic giant bearing the same name) and its people, between man and woman, between the mind and language. "Divorce is the symbol of knowledge in our times," Williams writes, and *Paterson* suggests that such a condition can be healed only by finding a new language—intended both as an act of communication and as an instrument for the knowledge of reality—to bridge the gap between humanity and its world. To Williams a new language means first of all a new line, no longer based on the traditional rules of versification but on the rhythms, the pauses, the natural beats of the spoken voice.

In his last volumes *Desert Music* (1954) and *Pictures from Brueghel* (1962) (posthumously awarded the Pulitzer Prize in 1963), Williams continued his experiments with poetic form, further developing the triadic line he had been working on since *Paterson*. His results were highly influential with younger poets, notably with Charles Olson and his notion of projective verse, with Robert Creeley, Denise Levertov, and Allen Ginsberg.

Carla Pomaré

Selected Bibliography

Ahearn, Barry. *William Carlos Williams and Alterity*. Cambridge: Cambridge UP, 1994.

Dijkstra, Bram. *Cubism, Stieglitz, and the Early Poetry of William Carlos Williams*. Princeton: Princeton UP, 1988.

Doyle, Charles, ed. *William Carlos Williams: The Critical Heritage*. London: Routledge and Kegan Paul, 1980.

Laughlin, James. *Remembering William Carlos Williams*. New York: New Directions, 1995.

Mariani, Paul. *William Carlos Williams: A New World Naked*. New York: Norton, 1981.

Riddel, Joseph N. *The Inverted Bell: Modernism and the Counterpoetics of William Carlos Williams*. Baton Rouge: Louisiana State UP, 1974.

Winnicott, Donald (1896–1971)

English pediatrician and psychoanalyst.

See under **Psychoanalysis.**

Woolf, Virginia (1882–1941)

Scholars outside Britain sometimes mistakenly describe the family background of Virginia Woolf as "aristocratic." It is an understandable misinterpretation, since both her father and grandfather were awarded knighthoods—a non-hereditary title—as a kind of longservice medal at the end of their distinguished careers. But the nineteenth-century Stephens themselves are more accurately described as patricians: part of that impressive network of upper-middle-class families whose record—sustained over several generations—of high ethical principles, high intelligence, and very hard work lies behind most of nineteenth-century Britain's more enlightened achievements. In this they may be compared to those New England patrician families to whom the United States is similarly indebted. And in fact the two communities were linked: James Russell Lowell and Charles Eliot Norton were friends of the Stephens, and Virginia's affectionate godfather, who spent much time in London, was Oliver Wendell Holmes.

In several respects Virginia Woolf's own career echoes and repeats, in her own terms, patterns set by previous generations of Stephens. Her great-grandfather worked hard and long for the abolition of the slave trade. (His second wife was in fact a sister of William Wilberforce, the great antislavery campaigner.) And even after Britain had abolished the trade in slaves, his son James continued the work. So far only the trade and not the institution of slavery itself had been abolished in Britain's colonies, where the treatment of the indigenous population, even when "free," was also often unjust. Recognizing this, Stephen gave up a very lucrative private legal practice to become a civil servant, and secured a key position in the Colonial Office. From this base, almost singlehanded, he gradually forced through many reforms and himself wrote the Act of Parliament that made slavery illegal in the British Empire. But the enormous workload and the constant strain of public controversy took their toll. Though he never gave up, even starting a new career as a Cambridge professor after retirement, he suffered for years from nerve problems very suggestive of some of those that later affected his granddaughter, though less intense.

The same blend of overwork, high principles, and nerve problems recurs again in his son Leslie, Virginia's father. Leslie Stephen had given up a prestigious career as a Fellow of a Cambridge college because he refused to pretend—as the University then required—that he was still a Christian. As a freelance cultural journalist and editor in London, he wrote powerfully in support of the cause of the emancipationist North in the American Civil War, then went on to produce a wide range of often still attractively readable works. The massive multi-volume *Dictionary of National Biography,* which he essentially created, must be the only unrevised Victorian reference work still in active use today: an astonishing achievement. But again unrelenting strain gradually turned this intelligent, well-meaning, but emotionally naive man into the classic Victorian domestic tyrant, preying psychologically on his helpless womenfolk.

So much of this can be seen again in Virginia Woolf's own career (though in her own marriage it was the male spouse whose life and career was often uncomplainingly sacrificed). Again we find the same workaholism, and the emancipationist drive. Women were for her the slave class now most needing to be freed; but there was much else to be done too. Considering the time her recurring nervous illnesses compelled her to waste—illness clearly worsened, as with her forbears, by the very intensity she put into her activities—the amount of work she got through is staggering. Her books alone would represent a creditable life's work; but they were accompanied by a cascade of literally hundreds of reviews, articles, and essays. In addition there are her countless brilliant letters, and voluminous diaries and notebooks: a literary achievement in their own right. And on top of this she and her husband also built up a successful publishing house, at first doing most of the practical physical work involved themselves.

Her mind had all the characteristic Stephen fertility and many-sidedness. Most of the Stephens seem to have sustained at least two careers, and even as a novelist Virginia Woolf herself seems to be at least two people: a relatively traditional realist in *Night and Day* (1919), *The Pargiters* (unpublished until 1978), and in *The Years* (1937); but an untiringly inventive modernist in *Jacob's Room* (1922), *Mrs.*

Dalloway (1925), *To the Lighthouse* (1927), *Orlando* (1928), *The Waves* (1931), and *Between the Acts* (1941). In these latter works she effectively "changes the rules of the fictional game" (as the best of her biographers puts it) in every book: a striking feat.—All this in addition to her volumes of literary criticism, two powerful feminist polemics: *A Room of One's Own* (1929), and *Three Guineas* (1938), plus a biography of Roger Fry.

Her Stephen heritage shows again—though of course the particular targets shift with the changing generations—in her self-confident disrespect for the received pieties of establishment thinking. Just as her father had no time for Victorian institutionalized Christianity and jingo patriotism, so Virginia is equally impatient of sexual cant, and of the social shibboleths by which men keep society militaristic and women in their place. And behind father and daughter alike can be heard the voice of old Sir James, politely but firmly enlightening the Colonial Office (and indeed the voices of other, earlier Stephens too). Unique as both the achievements and the problems of her own life were, his granddaughter had her place in a lineage, a tradition of independent thought, and she knew it. It was an awareness that gave her a greater basic confidence in her own identity, a greater sense of direction, than the more indignant modern feminist hagiographers of Poor Young Virginia sometimes allow.

Nowhere is this uniqueness-within-continuity more evident than in the sphere of religion. Virginia's great-grandfather the antislavery campaigner had had a strong religious faith which led him to make his friends among the so-called Clapham Sect: a loose grouping of deeply pious but practical-minded middle-class Londoners, who were a great force for good in early nineteenth-century Britain. His son, Virginia's grandfather—equally religious and deeply puritanical—actually married the daughter of the clergyman who was the Sect's informal leader. In time, perhaps not surprisingly, all their children reacted against the rather strenuous devoutness of the family home, and lost their Anglican faith. But that did not mean that religious issues necessarily ceased to engage their minds: Virginia's Aunt Caroline went on to become a Quaker, and to teach her own form of religious mysticism. And *An Agnostic's Apology,* published fairly late in his life, was not the least well known of Leslie Stephen's own books. A decade earlier his *The Science of Ethics* had also tackled religious questions from his own standpoint.

Once again here is an aspect of her family background of which Virginia Woolf was well aware, and which fed into, and colored, her own thought. She fully shared her parents' agnosticism. She scorned the pomps of the Established Church, and had a general disdain for revealed religion. **T. S. Eliot**'s conversion to anglo-catholicism really shocked her. Yet there was a part of her being for which this was never enough, as many of her comments show (see the complaint in her essay "The Narrow Bridge Of Art" that "science and religion *have destroyed belief*"). To a degree, this merely meant that she was part of the world she lived in. "We were all of us feeling about for a replacement for Christianity in those days," a friend of hers once said to the present writer, speaking of the early 1920s. "It seemed so obvious that there was so much that the Victorian version of it just couldn't account for. And yet religion had always been there. Even for skeptics, it was almost impossible to imagine a world that simply did without it, without anything filling its place."

What did fill its place in Virginia Woolf's case was an interesting combination of several strains of thought. One of them was a continuing internal mental dialogue with the image of her loved, admired, yet hopelessly exasperating father,

the celebrated Agnostic. In *Mrs. Dalloway,* for instance, a description of the illusory figure of a great mother-goddess, a "spectral presence . . . made of branches and sky" seen at dusk by "the solitary traveller" walking in a wood, is followed by a curious tentative aside: "*But if he can conceive of her, then in some sort she exists . . .* " But Sir Leslie was no longer there to respond to the implicit challenge.

It is typical both of Virginia Woolf herself and of her times that this imagined figure should have been female. Hers was the generation that saw the development of both comparative religious studies and the anthropological study of religion and **myth**. (Here lay the intellectual stimulus, of course, that helped make a new use of myth so integral a part of the modernist movement in literature.) And the attempt to reach back behind theology to the original roots and meaning of religion had led further to a widespread belief that the original primal deity had not been male, but female: a mother- or fertility-goddess. Of course this would have been a very welcome idea to a lifelong enemy of male domination like Virginia Woolf anyway; but in the dying years of the romantic movement the thought was also congenial for other reasons. For one thing, it sorted so well with that deep vein of pantheism in the English romantic poetry with which Virginia Woolf was well familiar. From the age of twelve at least, her poetry reading was already accustoming her to the idea of a universal life-force in nature, sacred, eternal, pure—and ruthless: a concept that required neither the apparatus of formalized religion nor any belief in a personalized deity. Yet, if one *did* wish to personify it—and for an essentially poetic novelist it was not unnatural at times to do so—the fecund primal earth-mother of modern **anthropology** afforded a better image than any invocation of a grimly punitive God-the-Father.

Thus on one occasion in her twenties Virginia, who had problems with physical sex, slightly puzzled her circle by choosing to go to a fancy-dress party as Cleopatra— a queen whose qualities, as her friend Ottoline Morrell delicately put it, "were just those that Virginia did not possess." But the choice of role was not illogical. Cleopatra is associated with the goddess Isis, whose headdress she bears in the best-known antique picture of her. And Isis is an embodiment of the primal Earth-Mother: that is to say, of that eternal living power in the universe which the recurrent mystical strain in Virginia Woolf's writing constantly reaches out towards—and of which human copulation is only one facet. She would not have seen herself as any less entitled than Cleopatra to show allegiance to what such a deity emblematized. At the end of her career she in fact uses exactly this same cluster of ideas—Isis, Cleopatra, the stream of life through time—to form the backbone of her final novel *Between the Acts,* while a related conception equally underlies the structure of *Mrs. Dalloway.* Both the progressive revolt of the young Virginia Woolf's own circle of friends—the so-called **Bloomsbury** Group—against Victorian sexual prudery, and the interest of the same circle in the new theories of Freudian psychology, fused well enough with this deeply instinctive feeling on Virginia Woolf's part for what may be called (though the terminology is not her own) the holiness of the eternal creative life force.

Such a way of thinking fitted well with other aspects of her mind too. She had lost her mother at 13, and the half-sister who took over the running of the family home died two years later, leaving her largely in the hands—in the latter case, perhaps a little too literally—of her psychologically inept father, and an even more inept and sexually naive half-brother. (She was never sent to school.) For an intelligent, shy, sensitive, and nervously-disposed adolescent this disaster was soon worsened by the half-brother's clumsy attempt to launch

her, along with her sister Vanessa, into the rigid world of Victorian fashionable society. Social fiasco after fiasco followed, with little escape possible save into the emotional falsities of home life. Nothing could have been better calculated to induce in her a passionate sense of alienation from the values of Victorian bourgeois society, a conviction that the real world around her was a kind of delusory theater that all were conspiring to enact—that true reality lurked somewhere behind this false facade, difficult to focus upon and fully knowable only in brief "moments of being." In short she had glimpsed, a Sartrean existentialist might perhaps say, the Authentic. Wordsworth would rather have said that she had glimpsed the realm of which he had tried to speak in his greatest poems. But Plato is here, too, of course; reaching her both indirectly through romantic pantheism and through her own reading.

Phrase it how one may, it is this delighted vision that all her modernist works essentially pursue. Yet all her life some part of Virginia Woolf's mind was also infected with a latent death-wish, if for long periods gallantly suppressed. It is not only that a few not always too serious suicide attempts fleck her career. Ultimately more sinister, viewed over the years, are the seemingly casual references to drowning that recur rather too often in the writings of a woman who was eventually to end her life by that method. This shadow across her life is not something that the stresses of her adolescence really account for. At bottom, it seems rather to have been genetic, pathological. (When sick with a high fever during his teens her solid-seeming brother Thoby also suddenly tried to throw himself out of a window.) But tragic though it was, it must be admitted that this darker strain in Virginia Woolf also works to the benefit of her modernist fictions, tending to give them a texture, sometimes even a dramatic dimension, that they would otherwise lack. The ruthless juxtaposition of the mad, doomed Septimus with the life-delighting Clarissa in *Mrs. Dalloway* is a particularly clear-cut instance.

As a consciously "modern" writer, then, (her friend Lytton Strachey explicitly praised her fluidly-written early short story "The Mark On The Wall" for suggesting *the modern point of view* so well) Virginia Woolf had multiple yet harmonious aims. She wished to develop a new mode of writing that would enable her to break through the materialistic surface of the "real" world, and the conventional nineteenth-century realistic fiction that was its expression, in order to convey her experience of the truer reality that lay behind it. Since that experience was mediated only through "myriads of impressions," quite irreducible to clear-cut propositions, she was setting herself a strikingly difficult goal. But if widely enough shared, such a shift in perceptions, she felt, would in itself help collapse the false Victorian scheme of things. And the very difficulty of the task was an attraction in itself: she always thought much about questions of technique, exploring foreign authors with a fellow-professional's eye.

Not least Dostoyevsky, Chekhov, and particularly **Proust,** elated her when they showed her possibilities as yet unexplored in English writing. In her essay "More Dostoevsky" she lauds his gift for suggesting "the dim and populous undergrowth of the mind's consciousness where desires and impulses are moving blindly beneath the sod." She more than once praises Chekhov for his Russian willingness to end on a question rather than a conclusion. But she was equally willing to learn from painters and art critics, exchanging ideas with her sister, the painter Vanessa Bell, all her life. Clive Bell's theory of "significant form" (the quality in his view most essential to a work of art, and independent of the work's overt sub-

ject) had obvious interest for a novelist who never placed her main focus on plot, as did also his view that contemplation of artistic form mediates a sense of ultimate reality. Discussions with Roger Fry, who led the Bloomsbury group in their successful effort to wake up the English to post-impressionist art, stimulated and clarified her mind. Even on the simplest level, his disdain for the photographic **realism** of late Victorian painting reassuringly matched her own doubts about realist fiction. And of course she learned from the work of her colleagues too, not least from **Joyce's *Ulysses.*** T. S. Eliot taught her something about the elision of redundant transitions in writing. And before her own too-early death **Katherine Mansfield** had become a worryingly close competitor, sharing many of the same ideals. (It is instructive, for example, to compare *Mrs. Dalloway* with Mansfield's "The Garden Party.")

When all that has been said, the fact remains that any relatively brief account of a volatile and active-minded woman whose adult career covered some four decades in a rapidly changing world must necessarily be selective. Many would say, for instance, that when rejecting the world of the conventional realistic novel Virginia Woolf effectively moves not in one but *two* directions: towards the transcendental certainly, but down into the world of the subconscious as well. That there is point to such a comment can be seen from her remark about Dostoyevsky quoted above; but since for her the road to the transcendental runs *through* the unconscious, the distinction does not seem worth laboring in an account of this kind. Nor has full justice been done here to her frequent ambivalence. (If she is hostile to many of the values of the upper-middle-class world of the Victorian/Edwardian era, for example, she clearly felt its glamour too; while for a convinced feminist she took oddly little interest in Women's Suffrage.) On literary matters her expressed aims and ideals fluctuate, and can diverge from her actual practice. It is never helpful to try to make just one or two of her essays into a simplistic key to her creative work, in the way that "Modern Fiction" and "Mr. Bennett and Mrs. Brown" have been so often overused. A look at the diversity of her major modernist fictions may help to make this clearer.

Jacob's Room

Jacob's Room, a small literary masterpiece whose stature grows ever larger in retrospect, perfectly exemplifies Virginia Woolf's gift for fusing her autobiographical concerns with her technical preoccupations. On the personal level it is a quietly moving expression of grief for her lost elder brother Thoby, who died of typhoid when she was 24. (In the novel, however, Jacob's life is cut short by **World War I,** an expression also of quiet anger at the waste of so many other young lives.) Thoby was forceful-seeming but very reserved, a rather conventional young man, though with a certain dreaminess. When he died at 26 his identity still did not seem fully formed: what direction his life might have taken was still an open question. And much of the life that he had had—away at boarding-school and university, or in London—was also largely unknowable to his sister. She knew she loved him; his being—his manner, the flavor of his personality—remained real to her, and these could be conveyed. Yet who, or what, was it that she loved? So often, there could be only question marks. Informed or creative guesswork could invent little scenes or episodes that filled a little of the void of not-knowing; but the central enigma remained.

This is what the book tells or shows us. It is about "Jacob's room" in the sense that it is about the changing contents of the space that encloses Jacob as he moves through his short life—the shifting backdrops, people, objects, incidents. By the novel's end the room has been furnished and Jacob, his enigma intact, has in effect been defined as the shape of the hole in the middle of the picture. We feel we know him by knowing what it is *not* to know him fully. The women who pass through Jacob's room, their lives undercut by lack of the financial, educational, and social male privileges he takes for granted, add further perspective.

This densely personal tour de force well illustrates Virginia Woolf's grounds for deep skepticism about traditional literary biography, and the in-depth character-drawing and analyses of traditional serious fiction. The novelist Lawrence Durrell once wrote that after Freud the problem of character for a novelist was that of "trying to put a lid on a box that no longer has any sides." Decades earlier, working less from Freud than from personal introspection and her reading of the Russians, Virginia Woolf had already seen the point and found in *Jacob's Room* a brilliantly original answer.

Mrs. Dalloway

Mrs. Dalloway, Virginia Woolf's next and perhaps best-loved novel, however evades the "Durrell problem"—as so often in modernist fiction—by the use of essentially "flat" (though far from lifeless) characters. Even the presentation of Clarissa herself, if not strictly "flat" in **E. M. Forster**'s terms, is certainly somewhat flattened. The novel is written largely as a kind of multiple stream-of-consciousness, already in full flow when the book begins and still pouring unstoppably on when it ends. Nevertheless by the closing pages the two central stories have been neatly linked and completed. The action occupies only one June day, as we follow the thoughts of various people going about their affairs in London's West End. (The echoes of Joyce's *Ulysses* are not accidental.) At the day's end most of them, and others we have met in their thoughts, will gather at a grand party given by Clarissa Dalloway, the charming fashionable middle-aged wife of a prosperous politician. Also brought to her party is the news of the suicide of Septimus Warren Smith, a young man she did not know, whose mind had been unbalanced by his wartime experiences.

Clarissa loves and responds to life intensely, but many see her as frittering it away on trivial amusement. She would disagree, feeling her parties are somehow important and describing them as "an offering"—which indeed they are, to that primal life force of which she herself is in effect a priestess. Clarissa's love of life is however so intense that the thought that she must eventually lose it has become unbearable—so much so that the idea of death seems paradoxically to have become almost attractive to her, presumably as a way of escaping this strain. Two things mainly seem to save her. One is the sight of an old woman, apparently living alone, calmly preparing for the night in a house across the street. The other is the news of Septimus's suicide, a young man defiantly (as she thinks) throwing away life. Both somehow put into her mind the thought that perhaps death is not something to make such a fuss about after all—and her neurosis is relieved, perhaps healed.

This is the account normally given of *Mrs. Dalloway,* but it omits a vital dimension of the book. One-seventh of the text is not in stream-of-consciousness at all, but written in a curious vatic tone. The pointers richly supplied by these passages make it clear that the book is also to be read as a pagan midsummer festival, with Clarissa as its priestess and Septimus as the necessary human sacrifice. The old Celtic gods of the Ancient Britons—not least the *Mor Rigan* or Great Mother—have their avatars in many of the characters, sometimes anonymous, sometimes given Celtic surnames. (On another level, though, the novel may also be seen as an

attempt, as original as *Jacob's Room,* to offer an image not of a person but of London: viewed as a collection of consciousnesses rather than buildings, and as simultaneously a focus of light and of darkness.)

To the Lighthouse

To the Lighthouse has often been judged Virginia Woolf's greatest novel. Be that as it may, it is certainly—irrespective of page-counts—a larger achievement than either *Jacob's Room* or *Mrs. Dalloway,* combining and taking further themes and concerns from both the previous books.

Virginia Woolf's lifelong problems with the memory of her father have been noted earlier. But the image of her mother also haunted her until she had written this novel. Julia Stephen was a beautiful, high-minded woman, attractive to men, socially conventional, but intelligent and with considerable spirit, despite her life of endless self-sacrifice. Unfortunately, her Victorian devotion to "good works" (which included endlessly spoiling a self-pitying husband) became so obsessive that she literally worked herself into an early grave. While she lived, it also made her too busy to respond fully to her children's emotional needs.

The confusion that this left in the mind of her daughter is very understandable: love, anger, admiration, irritation, affectionate amusement, bewilderment. How could Julia have seemed so contented in her marriage to a man who was helping suck the life out of her? Under their idiosyncrasies, did their parents at bottom have the right values in life? What *is* the purpose of life?

As material for a novel, all this was enriched by a halo of Cornish sunlight. The Stephen family had spent the summer months of every year in a large shabby house in a pleasant garden, idyllically situated on the Cornish coast (with a distant lighthouse). For a child like Virginia, this was paradise, and her intense response to the beauty of the landscape and seascapes around her gave her first intuitions of a transcendental reality beyond the mundane world. But all ended with Julia's death. *To the Lighthouse* transfers this entire setting to an island in the Hebrides.

The first of the novel's three parts presents a day before the First World War. Mr. and Mrs. Ramsay are sympathetic but clear-sighted depictions of the Stephen parents and their mutual relationship. The Ramsays' children more diffusely reflect the real Stephens, and there are a number of guests, including the unmarried Lily Briscoe, an amateur painter bedazzled like the others by Mrs. Ramsay. James, the youngest of the Ramsay's sons has set his heart on visiting the distant lighthouse; but is resentfully disappointed. In the second, much shorter section, we see the house deserted during the war; and on the edge of sliding into irrecoverable decay. But the family and their friends return at last; though meanwhile, offstage, Mrs. Ramsay and two of her children have died. Through peace and war the beam of the lighthouse continues to probe at the windows, pregnant with a sense of wordless meaning. Yet while she lived Mrs. Ramsay was in her way a lighthouse too.

In the final section Mr. Ramsay finally leads a family expedition on a sailing trip out to the lighthouse. He emerges for a moment from his endless self-absorption to praise James' handling of the boat; and his children, in surprised pleasure, at last forget their resentments and see his positive qualities. "It is finished" says Lily Briscoe, far off in the house garden, and the echo (John XIX, 30) is very clear. Yet Lily is actually referring to her own painting, and has become the author's representative in the book. For at bottom she, too, is not merely attempting to depict "Mrs. Ramsay's" world and its setting, but to utilize this raw material to create an autono-

mous work of art that, like the painting, will mediate through aesthetic form that flickering sense of the transcendental of which the beams of the lighthouse are somehow an analog. Thus described, *To the Lighthouse* may sound like a traditional novel; where it differs, is partly in substituting a quasi-musical **rhythm** and orchestration of mood, voices, and echoing visual effects, for the usual plot-structure. But it also largely replaces conventional characterization by a trick of letting us listen to her characters' reveries—sometimes interwoven, sometimes not—until we can identify them much as we do living people.

Orlando

Orlando, which the author herself described as an "escapade," is an exuberantly-written biography of a charming and ornamental young Elizabethan nobleman who somehow never dies but lives on, ever young, on a kind of Heritage tour of some of the more picturesque parts of English history up to modern times. In mid-career he finds he has turned into a woman, which gives rise to the natural ironies; and there is also some light satire on literary critics, and inevitable mockery of serious biographers. On a private level, the book is an offering of love and admiration to the openly bisexual writer Vita Sackville-West—and by the same token it questions, lightly, gently, assumptions about gender difference at a time when most readers regarded lesbianism as taboo.

The Waves

The Waves moves farther from the conventions and assumptions of the conventional realistic novel than any of Virginia Woolf's other books. It is an extreme embodiment of her characteristically modernist belief in the power of art to capture, or at least to reach through to, a mystical, more "true" reality beyond the details of daily living. Yet even when, as here, these practical details are played down to a near-minimum, the paradox remains for a novelist that this unworldly art must still be created precisely *by writing about more-or-less ordinary people living more-or-less ordinary lives:* thus creating a double perspective.

The Waves is made up of sets of soliloquies, "spoken" by six characters at successive stages in their life, from schooldays onwards, interleaved with much briefer, beautifully-written passages describing the Sun at successive points in its movement through the day. The soliloquies give only a minimum of practical information, being rather the voice of an inner self observing the experiences of an outer self. Towards the end of the book the voice of one character, Bernard, comes to dominate; yet even in his case we never learn his job or the least detail about his wife and children. Nearer poem than novel, there is also a profoundly musical, orchestrated quality to this near-plotless work, though it shows also an intense visual sensitivity. "To me," wrote her sister, "painting a floor covered with toys and keeping them all in relation to each other and the figures and the space of the floor and the light on it means something of the same sort that you seem to me to mean." *The Waves* in fact seeks to "mean" more than that, but it is a perceptive judgment.

Between the Acts

Between the Acts was published shortly after Virginia Woolf's death. In an oddly mannered, slightly staccato way, at times lightly sardonic, at times overtly poetical, we are taken through a day—the day of the village pageant—in June 1939. In short we are at the end of the interval between Act I (1914–18) and Act II (1939–45) of the World War. The novel perfectly encapsulates the haunting "feel" of that summer: prosperity returning, peaceful weather, the countryside at its most beautiful; and yet with everyone's sense of the long traditions that had built

up this beauty painfully sharpened by expectation of its coming airborne destruction. This feeling clearly connects with the subject of the pageant (cameos from successive periods of English history).

But we are Between the Acts in other senses too. The pageant's author and director, Miss La Trobe, is again an embodiment of the author's beliefs as to the situation and almost sacred role of the artist. Her pageant halts the normal action of life for a day, hopefully to unify the community and to deepen its consciousness (the audience are for example disconcerted to be shown themselves in mirrors) before their daily acts are resumed. The performance is staged in an open-air setting that involves the natural world too in this human production. This makes a smooth transition into a yet deeper stratum of veiled reference in the novel: to the eternal fructifying life-force that is emblematized in the legend of Isis and her mate—of whom the brother and sister who own the estate where the pageant is staged are clearly avatars. The book is rich in oblique reference to the Egyptian myth. As night falls, the most powerfully sexual couple in the play move towards a sexual union of which it is hinted a child may be born. For the Great Mother the next act is beginning.

(Virginia Woolf's realistic novels, though nowadays of increasing interest to feminists, are otherwise outside the province of a survey of twentieth-century modernism.)

Keith Brown

Selected Bibliography

The catalogue of the Bodleian Library now contains at least 383 entries under "Virginia Woolf" (the number rises continually), most of which have been published in the last 25–30 years. Differing factions within the field of Virginia Woolf studies would disagree totally about the value of many of these books. Thus, these are only a few starting suggestions.

Beer, Gillian. *Virginia Woolf: the common ground.* Edinburgh: Edinburgh UP, 1996. (Worthwhile collections of essays and papers on Woolf's fiction are so numerous that any choice must be invidious, but this book can be safely recommended.)

Brown, Keith. "Mrs. Dalloway on Mt. Caburn." *The Cambridge Review* (29 January 1982) (See comment under Mepham below.)

Lee, Hermione. *Virginia Woolf.* London: Chatto & Windus, 1996. (The definitive biography, packed with useful and interesting detail.)

Mepham, John. *Virginia Woolf: a literary life.* London: Macmillan, 1991. (Incomparably the best book ever written on Woolf's literary career. Startlingly clear-headed, Mepham disposes of many persistent misconceptions. He seems however not fully aware of the *specificity* of the veiled mythological allusions in some of Woolf's books. To fill this gap, see Maika and Brown.)

Maika, Patricia. *Virginia Woolf's "Between the Acts" and Jane Harrison's Conspiracy.* Studies in Modern Literature No.78. Ann Arbor/London: UMI Research Press, 1984/87.

Marler, Regina. *Bloomsbury Pie.* New York: Henry Holt; London: Virago, 1997. (Conversational, even gossipy, in tone, but still a helpful read before plunging into the confusing forest of publications that has grown from the cults of Virgiania Woolf and "Bloomsbury," and the feminist controversies of the past thirty years.)

Rosenberg, Beth Carole, and Dubino, Jeanne, eds. *Virginia Woolf and the Essay.* New York: St. Martin's Press, 1997. (Offers a useful shift of focus away from the novels.)

World War One

See under **The War.**

Y

Yeats, W. B. (1865–1939)

In an 1883–4 poem unpublished in his life-time, "The Veiled Voices and the Questions of the Dark," Yeats meditates upon the anonymity of urban existence as he is whisked through the night in a tram car. Retrospectively, it is an uncharacteristic moment in the early Yeatsian oeuvre, the concerns of which tend to be rural and folkloric rather than metropolitan, its dominant the Celticism he adopted and adapted from Standish O'Grady, George Sigerson, and Douglas Hyde. That said, the poem strikes a typically Yeatsian note in its dismissive response to the modernity personified in the tram's monadic passengers—a convulsive reaction that will find many targets in Yeats's work, from Victorian materialism to the ideology of the Irish Free State. Anachronistically embodied in the figure of St. Patrick in *The Wanderings of Oisin* (1889), against whom the eponymous pagan Fenian is pitted, the "filthy modern tide" will be stridently denounced in "The Statues" (1938), and polemically disparaged in the self-conscious histrionics of the late prose jeremiad *On the Boiler* (1938).

In this reactionary cast to Yeats's imagination lies his affinity with a number of early modernists, such as **T. S. Eliot** and **Wyndham Lewis;** but he belonged to an older generation than theirs, and the formative influence of the literary movements of the *fin de siècle* is crucial to his poetics.

In his first essay at a collected poems, the 1895 *Poems,* Yeats grouped a selection of early work drawn from two previous collections—*The Wanderings of Oisin and Other Poems* (1889) and *The Countess Cathleen and Various Legends and Lyrics* (1892)—under the title "Crossways," his brief preface to the volume arguing that "in them he tried many pathways." Yeats's early poetic forays led him not only to Celtic materials, but also to symbolism, as evinced in the occult hermeticism of those poems he chose to include in "The Rose" subdivision of *Poems.* The volume's young Irish author, we should recall, was at the heart of English aestheticism at this date, publishing in *The Dome, The Savoy,* and *The Yellow Book:* the Celticism of his collection of Irish folklore, *The Celtic Twilight* (1893), at one with the Decadent pre-occupations and Paterian style of his short stories, *The Secret Rose* (1897), "The Tables of the Law," and "Rosa Alchemica" (1897). Yeats's aestheticism, like his Celticism, was fueled by his antipathy towards aspects of late Victorian Britain, its materialism, utilitarianism, and imperialism. As Terence Brown observes, in Yeats's mind "aestheticism . . . represented a credible alternative to the meaningless, vulgarizing rhythms of modernity" (58) the sickening progress of the *fin de siècle's* tram car. Yeats's poetic of the 1890s is thus one transitional to modernism—or, more precisely, to that variety of modernism into which late nineteenth-century aestheticism leaches, a strain which includes the poetry of Eliot, **Wallace Stevens,** and the early **Ezra Pound.**

It is in the context of Yeats's aestheticism that his cultural nationalism is most profitably viewed. John Wilson Foster rightly identifies the modernist (and aestheticist) characteristics of the Irish Literary Revival as "mysticism, symbolism, millenarianism and anti-modernization," but erroneously goes on to argue that "it would be difficult to regard as modernist" the "obstinate nativism" of the revivalist poets and dramatists (55, 46). Nationalism, however, was central to much modernism prior to the First World War, as is seen in the stridently jingoistic posturing of **Italian futurism,** to take just one example. In the case of **Ireland,** Celticism and romantic nationalism can be seen as related to, and indeed preceding that of other modernist appeals to "Tradition" in the face of a degraded modernity. In the later terminology of T. S. Eliot, the individual talents of the Revival appeal to the "monuments" of an Irish cultural tradition which their texts consequently recover for a culturally denuded present. Such a recuperative backward look allowed Yeats and others to perceive in their work a social and political relevance to what otherwise might appear a disinterested concern with the nation's past. In his 1892 essay "The Rhymers' Club" Yeats wrote of fellow Rhymer and Irishman, John Todhunter, that the latter's Celticism was a "road" that "leads where there is no lack of subjects, for the literature of Ireland is still young, and on all sides of this road is Celtic tradition and Celtic passion crying for singers to give them voice. England is old and her poets must scrape up the crumbs of an almost finished banquet, but Ireland has still full tables." In a slightly later essay, "What is Popular Poetry?" (1901), Yeats implicitly defends the esoteric symbolism of his poetry at the turn of the century—over a third of *The Wind Among the Reeds* (1899)

had been devoted to explanatory notes, prefiguring Eliot's practice in *The Waste Land*—speciously arguing that "There is only one kind of good poetry, for the poetry of the coteries [such as the Rhymers' Club], which presupposes the written tradition, does not differ in kind from the true poetry of the people, which presupposes the unwritten tradition. Both are alike strange and obscure, and unreal to all who have not understanding." Though the Rhymers' Club had dispersed and English Decadence effectively come to an end by the date of this essay, one senses in Yeats's remarks an anxiety that the aestheticism of his 1890s poetry and prose had little bearing on the world outside the upstairs' room at the Cheshire Cheese, where the Rhymers had convened. It is an anxiety that Yeats, in his 1922 autobiography, *The Trembling of the Veil,* would project onto those of his contemporaries, some associated with the Rhymers' Club, whom he memorably dubbed "The Tragic Generation"—Ernest Dowson, Lionel Johnson, Arthur Symons, and **Oscar Wilde,** writers whose lives were wrecked through dissipation, mental breakdown or Victorian homophobia. The fate of these tragedians arguably figures forth Yeats's fear that the late Victorian poet—in marked contrast to the thesis held by his beloved Shelley—is not so much the "unacknowledged legislator" for his or her society as simply unacknowledged, *tout court.*

Yeats's unease registers the symbolist absention from the social as developed, in French poetry, from Charles Baudelaire to Stéphane Mallarmé and Paul Valéry. His rich combination of Celticism and symbolism (and occultism) finds a chime in fellow revivalists' various formal experiments, including, in the field of drama, **J. M. Synge**'s synthetic Hiberno-English and Lady Gregory's Kiltarnese, which can equally be viewed as paleo-modernist in their highly self-reflexive quality. This is not to downplay the importance of the Literary Revival's political agenda—its cultural nationalism, especially through the medium of the Abbey Theatre, may well have been formative in the politicizing of some of its audience. But Yeats's later argument—in his 1923 lecture to the Royal Academy of Sweden, "The Irish Dramatic Movement"—that the Revival had "conceived" the Easter Rising of 1916 is somewhat reductive, and reveals a strong desire on Yeats's part of being seen, in R. F. Foster's words, "at the centre of Irish history" (229).

In the light of the foregoing, one must question Stan Smith's claim that Yeats's modernism dates from *The Green Helmet* (1910), "which mark[s] a major breakthrough in his style, heralding a new, tough, argumentative dialogism . . . rather than retreating to the twilight's glimmer" (208). Smith is here correctly contesting the common assumption that Pound's friendship with Yeats resulted in the latter somehow "becoming" a modernist with the poems collected in *Responsibilities* (1914). However, a more capacious—indeed, more dialogic—conception of modernism would see *The Green Helmet* as signaling a change in a poetic already colored by modernism in its symbolist form.

The Yeats of the 1920s and '30s is fully conscious that an autotelic poetry courts accusations of historical irrelevance. The posturingly arrogant claims made on behalf of the imagination in the third part of the title poem to *The Tower* (1928)—"Death and life were not" till man created these from his "bitter soul"—constitute an attempt to turn the tables on such accusations; but as such they are simply the flip side of Yeats's self-doubts, those expressed in the poet's moving recognition of the gulf that separates his literary activity from the lives of the combatants in "The Road at my Door," one of the "Meditations in Time of Civil War:" trying to silence the envy in his thought, the poet turns towards his cham-

ber, caught "In the cold snows of a dream." Such thoughts gnaw at the vitals of Yeats's work, long outlasting his *symboliste* phase, and inform the self-interrogative mood of his late poem "Man and the Echo." In the course of that poem, Yeats famously asks if his play sent out "Certain men the English shot?," and it is difficult to determine whether an answer in the negative would not disturb the speaker more than a positive reply. The play in question, the nationalist allegory *Cathleen ni Houlihan* (co-authored with Lady Gregory), illustrates well the Literary Revival's modernism, undermining realist theatrical conventions, not, as in Yeats's later Noh-inspired drama, by rejecting them, but by the introduction of the symbolic figure of Cathleen into a representational drama set in Mayo, 1798, on the eve of rebellion. "Man and the Echo" questions the political efficacy of the play's modernist form and, by extension, the entire Revival's contribution to the nationalist cause in the run-up to the 1916 Rising and the Anglo-Irish War.

Thus, if the cultural nationalism of Yeats and other revivalists is informed by a desire to *re-present* Ireland to itself in literary form, the "Ireland" constructed to this end took on its own autonomous existence. Hence the antipathy it generated in later writers, several of whom tended to conflate the revival's representation of Ireland with the more obviously ideological national self-images promoted by Irish Ireland and Éamon de Valera. The older Yeats admits to the free-floating nature of the Revival's Ireland in several contexts: in "The Municipal Gallery Re-visited" the portraits among which the speaker stands, "the images of thirty years," have precisely that property of "*non-realist* representation" which Terry Eagleton has identified in the Revival's modernism: "art faithful to an action which is itself realistically improbable, or one which represents it in a non-realist way" (305). This is not, Yeats's persona declares, the dead Ireland of his youth, but one "The poets have imagined, terrible and gay." Likewise, in "The Circus Animals' Desertion" Yeats confesses that "Players and painted stage took all my love," not the things they represented. Partially unhinged from its referent, Yeats's Ireland, "terrible and gay," is an *emblematic* Ireland; that is, it relates to its horizon of production in the manner of an "emblem" or moral fable. The autonomy of these images is that of the high modernist artwork, which can never attain the closeness to lived experience enjoyed by the folkloric artefact.

Paul de Man argues that as early as *The Countess Cathleen and Various Legends and Lyrics* the emblem figures in Yeats's work as the contrary to the natural image; emblems, as opposed to images, "have no mimetic referent whatever. . . . They are taken from the literary tradition and receive their meaning from traditional or personal, but not from natural associations." For de Man the appearance of the emblem in Yeats signals the difference between his poetry and that of European romanticism in general (within which he overhastily places French symbolism), which still insists on "the ontological priority of natural things." The "unresolved conflict between image and emblem" de Man reads out of Yeats's career has been recast by David Lloyd in terms of Yeats's earlier cultural nationalism, and its symbolist poetic, and his later, allegorical or emblematic work, the non-mimetic quality of which reflects Yeats's increasingly tangential relationship to Ireland after independence (165, 168, 177). Both de Man's and Lloyd's approaches to Yeats can be seen, in the present context, as illustrating the problematic interface between nationalist politics and modernism in the Literary Revival, and its consequences for the later poetry of Yeats. Lloyd draws attention to Yeats's complex allusion to "the Homeric epic tradition" at the end of "Coole

and Ballylee, 1931," in *The Winding Stair and Other Poems* (1933), and to the poet's tacit admission that he, and the other revivalists, failed to create "The book of the people." Lloyd contends that the poem's emblem-making ("Another emblem there!" cries the persona on observing a "mounting swan" by the lakeside at Coole) signifies a resistance to a mimetic poetics, which would entail an organic connection between poet and his environment, and this foregrounds the "radical dislocation" of the poet, not only from the poem's Galway setting, but from independent Ireland. The signature of Yeats's poetry at this date is that, paradoxically, it is in and through his alienated condition that the poet "finds the sources of his power" in the autonomous reaches of his poetic language (68). Yet it is useful to add the mild caveat that the "dislocation" Lloyd analyses in *The Winding Stair and Other Poems* can be sensed, albeit in a restrained vein, in the symbolism of Yeats's early poetry. As the example of French symbolism suggests, Yeats's early poetic is not fully reducible to the symbolism that informs cultural nationalism, in which, Lloyd contends, there is an "organic continuity between the symbol and what it represents" (71). Yeats's symbolism is modernist, rather than late romantic. Rainer Emig has pointed out the "suspicion" in several of Yeats's early poems, such as "The Man who dreamed of Faeryland," "that the escapism of a hermetic symbolism is eventually unsatisfactory;" an unease Emig links to "the closed internalizing nature of modernist techniques" which produces "texts [that] can only imagine their outside to be like their own texture" (50, 40). Emig's understanding of modernism, for all its sophistication, is a definition of the high modernism suffused by the aestheticism of the 1890s. His argument would find little purchase on the writings of, say, **Gertrude Stein** or Louis Zukofsky (neither of whom he mentions in the course of his argument); and, for precisely this reason, his thesis usefully brings into focus Yeats's particular form of modernism. It is a poetic that the Irish poet Austin Clarke harshly imagined, in "A.E.," as a purgatory Yeats "had ghosted from hatred," incessant repetition "systematised by metaphysics. . . ."

Alex Davis

Selected Bibliography

Brown, Terence. *W. B. Yeats: A Critical Biography.* Dublin: Gill and Macmillan, 1999.

de Man, Paul. *The Rhetoric of Romanticism.* New York: Columbia UP, 1984.

Donoghue, Denis. *Yeats.* London: Fontana, 1971.

Eagleton, Terry. *Heathcliff and the Great Hunger: Studies in Irish Culture.* London: Verso, 1995.

Ellman, Richard. *The Identity of Yeats.* 2nd ed. New York: Oxford UP, 1964.

Emig, Rainer. *Modernism in Poetry: Motivations, Structures and Limits.* London: Longman, 1995.

Engleberg, Edward. *The Vast Design: Patterns in W. B. Yeats's Aesthetic.* 2nd ed. Washington, DC: Catholic University of America Press, 1988.

Foster, John Wilson. *Colonial Consequences: Essays in Irish Literature and Culture.* Dublin: Lilliput, 1991.

Foster, R. F. *Paddy & Mr Punch: Connections in Irish and English History.* London: Allen Lane, 1993.

———. *W. B. Yeats: A Life.* Vol 1. *The Apprentice Mage.* Oxford: Oxford UP, 1997.

Kermode, Frank. *Romantic Image.* London: Routledge & Kegan Paul, 1957.

Lloyd, David. *Anomalous States: Irish Writing and the Post-Colonial Moment.* Dublin: Lilliput, 1993.

Logenbach, James. *Stone Cottage: Pound, Yeats and Modernism.* New York: Oxford UP, 1988.

Smith, Stan. *The Origins of Modernism: Eliot, Pound, Yeats and the Rhetorics of Renewal.* Hemel Hempsead: Harvester, 1994.

Selected Bibliography

Adorno, Theodor, and Max Horkheimer. *Dialectic of Enlightenment*. Trans. John Cumming. London: Allen Lane, 1972.

Albright, Daniel. *Untwisting the Serpent: Modernism in Music, Literature and Other Arts*. Chicago: U of Chicago P, 2000.

Baker, Houston A. *Modernism and the Harlem Renaissance*. Chicago: Chicago UP, 1987.

Banfield, Anne. *The Phantom Table: Woolf, Fry, Russell and the Epistemology of Modernism*. Cambridge: Cambridge UP, 1999.

Baudelaire, Charles. *The Painter of Modern Life and Other Essays*. Trans. and Ed. Jonathan Mayne. London: Phaidon, 1964.

Beebe, Maurice. "What Modernism Was." *Journal of Modern Literature* 3 (1974): 7–38.

Bell, Michael, ed. *The Context of English Literature: 1900–1930*. London: Methuen, 1980.

———. *Literature, Modernism and Myth*. Cambridge: Cambridge UP, 1997.

Benjamin, Andrew, ed. *The Problems of Modernity: Adorno and Benjamin*. London: Routledge, 1989.

Benjamin, Walter. *Illuminations*. Ed. Hannah Arendt. London: Collins, 1973.

———. *Charles Baudelaire: A Lyric Poet in the Era of High Capitalism*. Trans. Harry Zohn. London: New Left, 1973.

Benstock, Shari. *Women of the Left Bank, Paris 1900–1940*. London: Virago, 1987.

Bergonzi, Bernard, ed. *The Twentieth Century*. London: Barrie, 1970.

———. *The Myth of Modernism and Twentieth-Century English Literature*. Brighton: Harvester, 1986.

Berman, Marshall. *All That Is Solid Melts into Air. The Experience of Modernity*. New York: Simon and Schuster, 1982.

Bernstein, Richard J., ed. *Habermas and Modernity*. Cambridge: Polity, 1985.

Bloom, Clive, ed. *Literature and Culture in Modern Britain, Volume 1: 1900–1929*. London: Longman, 1993.

Booth, Howard J. and Nigel Rigby, eds. *Modernism and Empire*. Manchester: Manchester UP, 2000.

Bornstein, George, ed. *Representing Modernist Texts: Editing as Interpretation*. Ann Arbor: U of Michigan P, 1991.

Bradbury, Malcolm. *The Social Context of Modern English Literature*. Oxford: Blackwell, 1971.

———. *The Modern World: Ten Great Writers*. London: Secker, 1988.

———. "Modernisms/Postmodernisms." *Innovation/Renovation: New Perspectives on the Humanities*. Ed. Ihab Hassan and Sally Hassan. Madison: U of Wisconsin P, 1983. 311–328.

Bradbury, Malcolm, and James McFarlane, eds. *Modernism: 1890–1930*. Harmondsworth: Penguin, 1976. Rptd with new preface, 1991.

Brooker, Peter, ed. *Modernism/Postmodernism*. London: Longman, 1992.

Brown, Dennis. *The Modernist Self in Twentieth-Century English Literature*. London: Macmillan, 1989.

Bürger, Peter. *The Theory of the Avant-Garde*. Trans. M. Shaw. Manchester: Manchester UP, 1984.

———. *The Decline of Modernism*. Trans. Nicholas Walker. Cambridge: Polity, 1992.

Butler, Christopher. *Early Modernism: Literature, Music and Painting in Europe 1900–16*. Oxford: Oxford UP, 1994.

Cahoone, Lawrence, ed. *From Modernism to Postmodernism: An Anthology*. Oxford: Blackwell, 1996.

Calinescu, Matei. *Five Faces of Modernity: Modernism, Avant-Garde, Decadence, Kitsch, Postmodernism*. Durham: Duke UP, 1987.

Cantor, Norman. *Twentieth Century Culture: Modernism to Deconstruction*. New York: Lang, 1988.

Cardinal, Agnes et al., eds. *Women's Writing on the First World War*. Oxford: Oxford UP, 1999.

Carey, John. *The Intellectuals and the Masses: Pride and Prejudice Among the Literary Intelligentsia, 1880–1939*. London: Faber, 1992.

Chapple, I. A. V. *Documentary and Imaginative Literature 1880–1920*. London: Blandford, 1970.

Chiari, Joseph. *The Aesthetics of Modernism*. London: Vision, 1970.

Childs, Peter. *Modernism*. London: Routledge, 2000. (New Critical Idiom series.)

———. *The Twentieth Century in Poetry*. London: Routledge, 1999.

Clark, Suzanne. *Sentimental Modernism*. Indianapolis: Indiana UP, 1991.

Collier, Peter, and Judy Davies, eds. *Modernism and the European Unconscious*. Cambridge: Polity, 1990.

Craig, David. *The Real Foundations: Literature and Social Change*. London: Chatto, 1973.

Davies, Alistair. *An Annotated Critical Bibliography of Modernism*. Brighton: Harvester, 1982.

De Jongh, James. *Vicious Modernism: Black Harlem and the Literary Imagination*. Cambridge: Cambridge UP, 1990.

Docherty, Thomas, ed. *Postmodernism: A Reader*. Hemel Hempstead: Harvester, 1982.

Donald, James, Anne Friedberg, and Laura Marcus, eds. *Close Up 1927–1933: Cinema and Modernism*. London: Cassell, 1998.

Edel, Leon. *The Psychological Novel 1900–1950*. London: Hart-Davies, 1955.

Eliot, T. S. *Selected Prose*. Ed. Frank Kermode. London: Faber, 1975.

Ellman, Richard, and Charles Fiedelson, Jr., eds. *The Modern Tradition: Backgrounds of Modern Literature*. London: Oxford UP, 1965.

"The Fate of Modernity." Spec. issue of *Theory, Culture and Society* 2:3 (1985).

Faulkner, Peter. *Modernism*. London: Methuen, 1977. (Critical Idiom Series).

———. *A Modernist Reader: Modernism in England 1910–30*. London: Batsford, 1986.

Felski, Rita. *The Gender of Modernity*. Cambridge: Harvard UP, 1996.

Ford, Boris, ed. *The New Pelican Guide to English Literature, Volume 7: From James to Eliot*. Harmondsworth: Penguin, 1983.

Frank, Joseph. *The Widening Gyre: Crisis and Mastery in Modern Literature*. New Brunswick: Prentice-Hall, 1963.

Frascina, Francis, and Charles Harrison, eds. *Modern Art and Modernism. A Critical Anthology*. London: Open U, 1982.

Friedman, Alan. *The Turn of the Novel*. New York: Oxford UP, 1966.

"From Modernism to Postmodernism." Spec. issue of *Journal of Modern Literature* 3:5 (1974).

Furbank, P. N., and Arnold Kettle, eds. *Modernism and Its Origins*. Milton Keynes: Open U, 1973.

Gamache, Lawrence B., and Ian S. MacNiven, eds. *The Modernists: Studies in a Literary Phenomenon; Essays in Honour of Harry T Moore*. London: Associated UP, 1987.

Gambrell, Alice. *Women Intellectuals, Modernism, and Difference: Transatlantic Culture, 1919–1945*. Cambridge: Cambridge UP, 1997.

Giddens, Anthony. *The Consequences of Modernity*. Cambridge: Polity, 1991.

Gilbert, Sandra, and Susan Gubar. *No Man's. Land: The Place of the Woman Writer in the Twentieth Century*. 3 vols. New Haven: Yale UP, 1988–94.

Giles, Steve, ed. *Theorizing Modernisms: Essays in Critical Theory*. London: Routledge, 1993.

Gilroy, Paul. *The Black Atlantic: Modernity and Double Consciousness*. London: Verso, 1993.

Habermas, Jürgen. *The Philosophical Discourse of Modernity: Twelve Lectures*. Trans. Frederick Lawrence. Cambridge: Polity, 1987.

Hanscombe, Gillian and Virginia L. Smyers. *Writing for their Lives: The Modernist Women 1910–40*. London: Women's, 1987.

Harding, Jason. *The Criterion—Cultural Politics and Periodical Networks in Inter-War Britain*. Oxford: Oxford UP, 2002.

Howe, Irving, ed. *Literary Modernism*. Greenwich: Fawcett, 1967.

———. *The Decline of the New*. London: Gollancz, 1971.

Hughes, H. Stuart. *Consciousness and Society: The Reorientation of European Social Thought: 1890–1930*. Brighton: Harvester, 1979.

Hughes, Robert. *The Shock of the New: Art and the Century of Change*. London: Thames, 1980.

Hulme, T. E. *Speculations*. 1924. London: Routledge, 1936.

Huyssen, Andreas. *After the Great Divide: Modernism, Mass Culture, Postmodernism*. London: Macmillan, 1988.

Izenberg, Gerald, N. *Modernism and Masculinity: Mann, Wedekind, Kandinsky through World War I*. Chicago: U of Chicago P, 2000.

Jackson, Holbrook. *The Eighteen-Nineties: A Review of Art and Ideas at the Close of the Nineteenth Century*. 1913. Harmondsworth: Penguin, 1931.

James, Henry. *The Art of the Novel*. New York: Scribner's, 1934.

———. *Henry James: Selected Literary Criticism*. Ed, Morris Shapira. London: Heinemann, 1963.

Jameson, Fredric. *The Political Unconscious: Narrative as a Socially 5ymbolic Act*. London: Routledge, 1989.

———. "Postmodernism, or the Cultural Logic of Late Capitalism." *New Left Review* 146 (1984): 53–93.

———. *Fables of Aggression: Wyndham Lewis, the Modernist as Fascist.* Berkeley: U of California P, 1979.

Jay, Mike, and Michael Neve, eds. *1900: A Fin-de-Siècle Reader.* Harmondsworth: Penguin, 1999.

Josopovici, Gabriel. *The Lessons of Modernism and Other Essays.* London: Macmillan, 1977.

Kampf, Louis. *On Modernism: The Prospects for Literature and Freedom.* Cambridge: MIT, 1967.

Kazin, Alfred. "On Modernism." *New Republic* (17 January 1976): 29–31.

Kelly, Mary. "Re-viewing Modernist Criticism." *Screen* 22:3 (1981): 41–62.

Kenner, Hugh. *The Pound Era.* London: Faber, 1972.

Kermode, Frank. *The Sense of an Ending: Studies in the Theory of Fiction.* London: Oxford UP, 1967.

———. *Continuities.* London: Routledge, 1968.

Kiely, Robert, and John Hildebidle, eds. *Modernism Reconsidered.* Cambridge: Harvard UP, 1983.

Kolocotroni, Vassiliki, Jane Goldman and Olga Taxidou, eds. *Modernism: An Anthology of Sources and Documents.* Edinburgh: Edinburgh UP, 1998.

Korg, Jacob. *Language in Modern Literature: Innovation and Experiment.* Brighton: Harvester, 1979.

Langbaum, Robert. *The Modern Spirit: Essays on the Continuity of Nineteenth- and Twentieth-Century Literature.* London: Chatto, 1970.

Lehmann, A. G. *The Symbolist Aesthetic in France 1885–1895.* Oxford: Blackwell, 1950.

Levenson, Michael H. *A Genealogy of Modernism.* Cambridge: Cambridge UP, 1984.

———. *Modernism and the Fate of Individuality: Character and Novelistic Form from Conrad to Woolf.* Cambridge: Cambridge UP, 1991.

———. *The Cambridge Companion to Modernism.* Cambridge: Cambridge UP, 1999.

Levin, Harry. "What Was Modernism?" In his *Refractions: Essays in Comparative Literature.* New York: Oxford UP, 1966. 271–95.

———. *Memories of the Moderns.* New York: New Directions, 1980.

Lodge, David. *The Modes of Modern Writing: Metaphor, Metonymy and the Typology of Modern Literature.* London: Arnold, 1977.

———. "Modernism, Anti-Modernism, Postmodernism." In his *Working with Structuralism.* London: Routledge, 1981. 3–16.

Lunn, Eugene. *Marxism and Modernism.* London: Verso, 1985.

"Modernism & Postmodernism." Spec. issue of *New Literary History* 3:1 (1971).

"Modernity, Modernism; Postmodernity, Postmodernism." Spec. issue of *Cultural Critique* 5 (Winter 1987).

Nicholls, Peter. *Modernisms: A Literary Guide.* London: Macmillan, 1991.

Ortega y Gasset, José. *The Dehumanization of Art, and Other Writings on Art and Culture.* New York: Doubleday, 1956.

Ouditt, Sharon. *Women Writers of the First World War: An Annotated Bibliography.* London: Routledge, 1999.

Perloff, Marjorie. *The Futurist Moment. Avant-Garde, Avant Guerre, and the Language of Rupture.* Chicago: U of Chicago P, 1986.

Poggioli, Renato. *The Theory of the Avant-Garde.* Trans. G. Fitzgerald. Cambridge: Harvard UP, 1968.

"The Politics of Modernism." Spec. issue of *News from Nowhere* 7 (Winter 1989).

Pound, Ezra. *The Literary Essays of Ezra Pound.* Ed. T. S. Eliot. London: Faber, 1954.

Reiss, Timothy. *The Discourse of Modernism.* Ithaca: Cornell UP, 1982.

Scott, Bonnie Kime. *Refiguring Modernism: Volume 1: The Women of 1928.* Bloomington: Indiana UP, 1995.

———. *Refiguring Modernism: Volume 2: Postmodern Feminist Readings of Woolf, West, and Barnes.* Bloomington: Indiana UP, 1995.

———, ed. *The Gender of Modernism.* Bloomington: Indiana UP, 1990.

Smith, Angela K. *The Second Battlefield: Women, Modernism and the First World War.* Manchester: Manchester UP, 2000.

———, ed. *Women's Writing of the First World War: An Anthology.* Manchester: Manchester UP, 2000.

Smith, Stan. *The Origins of Modernism.* Hemel Hempstead: Harvester, 1987.

Solomon, Robert C. *Continental Philosophy since 1750: The Rise and Fall of the Self.* Oxford: Oxford UP, 1988.

Spender, Stephen. *The Struggle of the Modern.* London: Hamilton, 1963.

Stead, C. K. *The New Poetic.* 1964. London: Hutchinson; Harmondsworth: Penguin, 1979.

Stevens, Hugh, and Caroline Howlett, eds. *Modernist Sexualities.* Manchester: Manchester UP, 2000.

Stevenson, Randall. *Modernist Fiction: An Introduction.* London: Harvester, 1992.

Sussman, Henry. *Afterimages of Modernity: Structure and Indifference in Twentieth-Century Literature.* Baltimore: Johns Hopkins UP, 1990.

Svarny, Erik. *"The Men of 1914"*: *T. S. Eliot and Early Modernism*. Milton Keynes: Open UP, 1990.

Symons, Julian. *Makers of the New. The Revolution in Literature 1912–1939*. London: André Deutsch, 1987.

Sypher, Wylie. *Rococo to Cubism in Art and Literature*. New York: Harper, 1960.

Tate, Trudi. *Modernism, History and the First World War*. Manchester: Manchester UP, 1998.

Tillyard, S. K. *The Impact of Modernism. The Visual Arts in Edwardian England*. London: Routledge, 1988.

Timms, Edward, and David Kelley, eds. *Unreal City: Urban Experience in Modern European Literature and Art*. New York: St. Martin's, 1985.

Timms, Edward, and Peter Collier, eds. *Visions and Blueprints. Avant-Garde Culture and Radical Politics in Early Twentieth-Century Europe*. New York: St. Martin's, 1988.

Trotter, David. *The English Novel in History: 1895–1920*. London: Routledge, 1993.

Vargish, Thomas and Delo E. Mook. *Inside Modernism. Relativity Theory, Cubism, Narrative*. New Haven: Yale UP, 1999.

Waugh, Patricia. *Practising Postmodernism: Reading Modernism*. London: Arnold, 1992.

———, ed. *Postmodernism: A Reader*. London: Arnold, 1992.

Weightman, John. *The Concept of the Avant-Garde*. Toronto: U of Toronto P, 1972.

White, Allon. *The Uses of Obscurity: The Fiction of Early Modernism*. London: Routledge, 1981.

White, John L. *Literary Futurism. Aspects of the First Avant-Garde*. Oxford: Clarendon, 1990.

Wilde, Alan. *Horizons of Assent: Modernism, Postmodernism and the Ironic Imagination*. Baltimore: Johns Hopkins UP, 1981.

Williams, Raymond. *Culture and Society: 1780–1950*. Harmondsworth: Penguin, 1961.

———. *The Long Revolution*. Harmondsworth: Penguin, 1965.

———. *The English Novel from Dickens to Lawrence*. London: Chatto, 1970.

———. *Keywords: A Vocabulary of Culture and Society*. 2nd edition. London: Fontana, 1983.

———. *The Politics of Modernism: Against the New Conformists*. Ed. Tony Pinkney. London: Verso, 1989.

Willison, Ian et al., eds. *Modernist Writers and the Marketplace*. London: Macmillan, 1996.

Wilson, Edmund. *Axel's Castle: A Study in the Imaginative Literature of 1870–1930*. New York: Scribner's, 1931.

Woolf, Virginia. *Collected Essays*. London: Hogarth, 1971.

Young, Allan. *Dada and After: Extremist Modernism and English Literature*. Manchester: Manchester UP, 1981.

Index

List of Contributors

The editor of this volume, PAUL POPLAWSKI, is director of studies at Vaughan College, University of Leicester. He has taught widely in nineteenth- and twentieth-century literature and specializes in D. H. Lawrence, modernism, and Jane Austen. His most recent books include his revised third edition of the late Warren Roberts' *A Bibliography of D. H. Lawrence* (2001) and, as editor, *Writing The Body in D. H. Lawrence: Essays on Language, Representation and Sexuality* (Greenwood 2001). His *D. H. Lawrence: A Reference Companion* (Greenwood 1996) has recently been published in a Japanese translation (2002), and he is currently working, as contributing editor, on a major new textbook, *Literature in Context*.

WASSIL BALEWSKY is a researcher in Bulgarian and Slavic studies at the Institute of Literature in the Bulgarian Academy of Sciences in Sofia.

MARIA BALSHAW is research fellow in American literature at the University of Birmingham. She is the author of *Looking For Harlem: Urban Aesthetics in African-American Literature* (2000), co-editor, with Liam Kennedy, of *Urban Space and Representation* (1999) and *City Sites: an Electronic Book:* www.citysites. org.uk (2000).

MICHAEL BELL is professor of English and Comparative Literary Studies at the University of Warwick. He writes mainly on modernism, on fiction since Cervantes, and on topics in philosophy and literature. Recent books include: *Gabriel Garcia Marquez: Solitude and Solidarity* (1993), *D. H. Lawrence: Language and Being* (1992), *Literature, Modernism and Myth* (1997), *Sentimentalism, Ethics and the Culture of Feeling* (2000).

NATHALIE BLONDEL is a freelance writer, editor and lecturer living in Bristol, England. She is the world authority on Mary Butts and her works include *Mary Butts: Scenes from the Life* (1998) and *The Journals of Mary Butts* (2002).

KEITH BROWN is a professor of British literature at Oslo University. His professional interests, and publications, are divided between the English Renaissance (Hobbes, Shakespeare, theater history) and early-to-mid-twentieth century British fiction. He has been a frequent contributor to the *Times Literary Supplement*.

CLAIRE BRUYÈRE is a professor emerita of American literature at the University of Paris VII, Denis Diderot. She has published two books on Sherwood Anderson and her other interests and publications are in American book history and American publishing.

MICHAEL CHAPMAN is professor of English and dean of the Faculty of Human Sciences at the University of Natal, Durban, South Africa. His numerous publications include the literary history *Southern African Literatures* (1996) and, most recently, the anthology *The New Century of South African Poetry* (2002).

PETER CHILDS is principal lecturer in English at the University of Gloucestershire. He is the author of, among other books, *Modernism* (2000) and *Reading Fiction: Opening the Text* (2001).

GIOVANNI CIANCI is professor of English literature at the University of Milan. His research specialism is in twentieth-century literature and modernism. He has published on the Cambridge School of Criticism, Joyce, D. H. Lawrence, and Wyndham Lewis. His most recent publications are *John Ruskin and Modernism*, co-edited with Peter Nicholls (2001) and *Il Cézanne degli Scrittori, dei Poeti e dei Filosofi* (2001).

PATRICK CROTTY is professor of Irish and Scottish Literary History at the Academy for Irish Cultural Heritages, University of Ulster. He has published widely on Irish, Scottish, and Anglo-Welsh writing, and is currently editing the *New Penguin Book of Irish Verse* and—with Alan Riach—the three volume, annotated *Complete Collected Poems of Hugh MacDiarmid*.

CORNELIUS CROWLEY is a professor in the English Department at Nanterre University, Paris. His Ph.D. thesis (University College Dublin) was on Henry James and the logic of representation. He has published a number of articles in French academic reviews. His recently published work has been on relations between literature and philosophy, on D. H. Lawrence, on David Hume, and on modern conceptions of the infinite.

JAMES CUNNINGHAM has taught widely in the field of English literature and his major research specialism is in Shakespearean studies. He is the author of *Shakespeare's Tragedies and Modern Critical Theory* (1997).

KEITH CUSHMAN is professor of English at the University of North Carolina at Greensboro. The author or editor of five books about D. H. Lawrence, he regularly teaches Cummings in his modern poetry courses.

ALEX DAVIS lectures in English at University College, Cork. He is the author of *A Broken Line: Denis Devlin and Irish Poetic Modernism* (2000), and co-editor of two collections of essays, *Modernism and Ireland: The Poetry of the 1930s* (1995) and *Locations of Literary Modernism: Region and Nation in British and American Modernist Poetry* (2000).

TIMOTHY DOBSON is an associate lecturer for the Open University.

KETAKI KUSHARI DYSON, an England-based writer of the Indian diaspora, is the author of many titles in Bengali and English, covering poetry, fiction, drama, essays, literary translation, and academic work. She has translated the poetry of Tagore and, more recently, of Buddhadeva Bose, a major post-Tagore poet.

CAROLINE FRANKLIN is reader in English at the University of Wales Swansea. She is author of *Byron's Heroines* (1992) and *Byron: A Literary Life* (2000), and has edited several reprint editions of eighteenth- and nineteenth-century women's writing. She is currently editing a reprint edition of Harriet Martineau's *Illustrations of Political Economy*.

JAY A. GERTZMAN is author of *A Descriptive Bibliography of Lady Chatterley's Lover* (1989) and *Bookleggers and Smuthounds: The Trade in Erotica, 1920–1940* (1999). He is professor emeritus from Mansfield University of Pennsylvania and living near New York City, where he does volunteer work for the National Coalition Against Censorship and where he is researching changes in the distribution of erotica in the second half of the twentieth century.

JOHN GOODBY is director of postgraduate studies at the Department of English, University of Wales Swansea, and a specialist in Irish writing, diaspora culture, and twentieth-century poetics. His publications include *Irish Poetry since 1950* (2000) and *Under the Spelling Wall: the Critical Fates of Dylan Thomas* (2003). He is the editor of *Irish Studies: The Essential Glossary* (2003) and co-editor of *Dylan Thomas: The New Casebook* (2001). He is currently completing a study of the poetry of Paul Muldoon (2004).

KATIE GRAMICH is based in Bristol as staff tutor in literature with the Open University. She teaches nineteenth- and twentieth-century literature, and has published extensively on Welsh writing and culture, women's writing, modern poetry, and post-colonialism. She co-edited the essay collection, *Dangerous Diversity: The Changing Faces of Wales* (1998), and has edited a reprint edition of *Queen of the Rushes* by Allen Raine (1998).

FIONA M. GREEN is lecturer in the English Faculty, University of Cambridge and a fellow of Jesus College. She has published articles on Marianne Moore, Elizabeth Bishop, and Susan Howe.

ROBERT C. HANSEN is professor of theater at the University of North Carolina at Greensboro where he teaches theater history, dramatic literature, and stage design.

JASON HARDING currently teaches at the National Chi Nan University in Taiwan. His study of inter-war literary journalism, *The Criterion—Cultural Politics and Periodical Networks in Inter-War Britain,* was published by Oxford University Press in 2002. He has contributed to the *Times Literary Supplement, London Review of Books,* and *Cambridge Quarterly*.

ANDREW HARRISON has published several essays on the modernist context of the writings of D. H. Lawrence and he has recently published *D. H. Lawrence and Italian Futurism: A Study of Influence* (2003). He has taught at the Universities of East Anglia, Warwick, and Nottingham.

ANDREW HISCOCK is a lecturer in English literature at the University of Wales Bangor. His research specialisms are Renaissance and Canadian literature. Publications include *Authority and Desire: Crises of Interpretation in Shakespeare and Racine* (1996) and, co-edited with Katie Gramich, *Dangerous Diversity: The Changing Faces of Wales* (1998). He is at present preparing a study on the post-war Canadian short story.

ANN HURFORD works for the School of Continuing Education at Nottingham University. She also teaches at the Nottingham Trent University where her area of interest is American literature. She is currently working on a doctoral thesis on the contemporary novelist Anne Tyler.

GEORGE HYDE is professor of English and Comparative Literature at Kyoto Women's University, Japan, and senior research fellow in the School of English and American Studies of the University of East Anglia, Norwich. He has published on Nabokov and Lawrence and is researching the life and work of George Borrow. His most recent publication is a translation of Krzysztof Mikłaszewski's book on Tadeusz Kantor (2002).

MATS JANSSON is associate professor of Comparative Literature at the University of Gothenburg. His books include *Tradition och fornyelse* (1991), on the introduction of T. S. Eliot in Sweden, and *Kritisk tidsspegel* (1998), on the Swedish modernist breakthrough in the 1940s. He has co-edited *English and Nordic Modernisms* (2002) and he has also published *Om kritik* (2002), a selection and translation of Eliot's literary criticism.

LEE JENKINS received her Ph.D. from Cambridge and is lecturer in English at University College Cork. Her main publications are *Wallace Stevens: Rage For Order* (1999) and, as co-editor, *Locations of Literary Modernism: Region and Nation in British and American Modernist Poetry* (2000).

BETHAN JONES is lecturer in English at the University of Hull. Her research interests include modernism, the works of Margaret Atwood and the interrelations between literary texts and music. She has published widely on the works of D. H. Lawrence and she is currently co-editing a volume of his short fiction, *The Escaped Cock and Other Stories,* for Cambridge University Press. She is editor of *The Journal of the D. H. Lawrence Society* and contributes regularly to *Etudes Lawrenciennes.*

COLBERT KEARNEY has taught and written widely on Irish literature. His most recent book is *The Glamour of Grammar,* a study of O'Casey's language, published by Greenwood. He is professor of Modern English at University College Cork.

ROBERT V. KENNY is director of French Studies in the School of Modern Languages at the University of Leicester. His research interests include twentieth-century poetry and he has a number of publications on Pierre Reverdy. He

has also published articles on the *comédies-ballets* of Molière and Lully and he is currently working on itinerant French theater companies in the early eighteenth century and the *théâtre de la foire.*

CARL KROCKEL studied English and Related Literature at the University of York and received an MA in modernism at the University of East Anglia, where he also taught while completing his Ph.D. on D. H. Lawrence and German Culture.

ROBIN MacKENZIE is lecturer in French at the University of Wales Swansea. His research interests lie in French fiction from romanticism to modernism; he has published a monograph and various articles on the work of Marcel Proust.

MARIA MARGARONI is assistant professor in the Department of Foreign Languages and Literatures at the University of Cyprus. Her main publications are in the areas of British working-class fiction and drama, literary theory, postmodern philosophy, and feminism. Her current research projects include a book on Julia Kristeva and an edited collection of essays on *The Politics of Metaphoricity.*

FERNANDO CABRAL MARTINS is professor of Modern Portuguese Literature at Universidade Nova de Lisboa. He is the author of two essays, on Cesário Verde (1986) and Mário de Sá-Carneiro (1994), and a collection of critical studies, *O Trabalho das Imagens* (2000).

RONAN McDONALD is a lecturer in English at the University of Reading. He is co-editor of *Bullan: An Irish Studies Journal* and has published many articles and reviews on Irish literature. *Tragedy and Irish Writing: Synge, O'Casey, Beckett* is forthcoming with Macmillan.

RUTH McELROY is lecturer in English and leader of the media and cultural studies course at University College Worcester. She is currently working on Anglo-Indian fiction of the early twentieth century and, with Jill Terry, is writing *Beginning Cultural Studies.*

TERRI MESTER is currently a visiting associate professor in film at Case Western Reserve University in Cleveland, Ohio. Her most recent publication is *Movement and Modernism: Yeats, Eliot, Lawrence, Williams and Early Twentieth-Century Dance.*

STEFANIA MICHELUCCI is assistant professor in English studies at the University of Udine (Italy). She has published numerous articles on nineteenth- and twentieth-century British authors and has a special interest in the relationship between literature and the visual arts. Her publications include *Space and Place in the Works of D. H. Lawrence* (2002), and, as editor, the Cambridge edition of Lawrence's *Twilight in Italy and Other Essays* (1997). Forthcoming publications include a book on the poetry of Thom Gunn.

NIGEL MORRIS is senior lecturer in media theory at the University of Lincoln. He has published articles on aspects of American, British, and German cinema, and contributed sections on film to Paul Poplawski's *D. H. Lawrence: A Reference Companion* (Greenwood 1996). He is currently completing a book for Wallflower Press on the films of Steven Spielberg in relation to critical theory.

CHRISTINE O'NEILL is a writer and critic in Dublin. Her research specialism is the work of James Joyce, and she has published on Joyce, stylistics and discourse analysis. She has edited a collection of Fritz Senn's essays, *Inductive Scrutinies: Focus on Joyce* (1995).

HELEN OAKLEY received her Ph.D. from Nottingham University. She has lectured in American literature at Aberystwyth University in Wales and has recently published *The Recontextualization of William Faulkner in Latin American Fiction and Culture* (2002).

JUAN PELLICER was born in México, D.F., but now teaches at the University of Oslo in Norway where he has been associate professor and chair of the Spanish and Portuguese department. His books include *El placer de la ironía. Leyendo a García Ponce.* (1999) and he has published extensively in Colombian, Spanish, English and Mexican books and literary journals on writers such as León Felipe, José Gorostiza, Octavio Paz, Carlos Pellicer, Elena Poniatowska, María Luisa Puga, among many others. He also writes regularly on Mexican politics and culture.

CARLA POMARÉ is associate professor of English literature at the University of Piemonte Orientale, Vercelli, Italy. Her publications include a study of Wallace Stevens and W. B. Yeats (*La visione e la voce. Percorsi paralleli dai romantici ai moderni,* 1993), as well as essays on Stevens' debt to Ruskin, and on Stein's appreciation of Cézanne.

NICHOLAS POTTER teaches English at Swansea Institute of Higher Education; he has published on Shakespeare and on writers of the modern period such as T. S. Eliot, Edmund Blunden and E. M. Forster.

LYNDA PRESCOTT has taught at the universities of Nottingham and Bradford, and is currently a staff tutor in arts and lecturer in literature at the Open University. Her research interests center on twentieth-century prose writing, and she has contributed chapters on Conrad and Kipling to recent Open University coursebooks.

PETER PRESTON is acting head of the School of Continuing Education and joint director of the D. H. Lawrence Research Centre at the University of Nottingham. He has published widely on Lawrence and Arnold Bennett, and has recently produced annotated paperback editions of Dickens's *The Old Curiosity Shop* and *Little Dorrit.*

RICHARD PRICE is a curator of Modern British Collections at the British Library, London. His books include *The Fabulous Matter of Fact: the Poetics of Neil M. Gunn;* as co-editor, *La Nouvelle Alliance* (French influences on Scottish modern literature), *César Vallejo: Translations, Transformations, Tributes,* and *The Star You Steer By: Essays on Basil Bunting;* as co-author, *Eftirs/Afters* (translations of French modernist poetry); and the poetry collections *Hand Held, Perfume and Petrol Fumes,* and *Frosted, Melted.*

ALAN RIACH, formerly associate professor of English at the University of Waikato, New Zealand, is currently reader in Scottish Literature at the University of Glasgow. General editor of the 16-volume *Collected Works of Hugh MacDiarmid,* he is also a poet whose books include *First & Last Songs* (1995) and *Clearances* (2001).

CHRISTOPHER ROLFE is senior lecturer in French and director of the Centre for Quebec Studies at the University of Leicester. He has published on a wide range of Quebec-related subjects but his research is now focused on contemporary print-making in Quebec. He is a former President of the British Association for Canadian Studies.

SIMON J. ROSS teaches at Bretton Hall College at the University of Leeds. He specializes in modernism and post-colonial studies, and has published on the relationship between empire, modernism, and negritude with Africa World Press. He is currently working on the relationship between modernism, nationalism, and subjectivity in the long poems of Aimé Césaire and Hugh MacDiarmid.

ANDREW ROTHWELL is professor of French at the University of Wales Swansea. His research interests focus on modern and contemporary French poetry, particularly its interaction with the visual arts, and translation. His publications include a monograph on Pierre Reverdy and articles on other writers of the early avant-garde, Dada and surrealism, and the poetry and art criticism of Bernard Noël.

STEFANA ROUSSENOVA teaches English literature of the nineteenth and twentieth century in the Department of English and American Studies at Sofia University, Bulgaria.

MAX SAUNDERS, professor of English at King's College, London, is the author of *Ford Madox Ford: A Dual Life,* 2 volumes (1996) and has edited Ford's *Selected Poems* (1997), *War Prose* (1999), and (with Richard Stang) *Critical Essays* (2002).

NEIL SINYARD is senior lecturer in film studies at the University of Hull. His books include *Filming Literature* (1986) and studies of directors such as Wilder, Hitchcock, Woody Allen, Nicolas Roeg and Jack Clayton; and he has a particular interest in the interrelationship between the arts in the years immediately preceding the First World War.

SEBASTIAN SKEAPING is currently working on his Ph.D. on Paul Bowles at Clare Hall, Cambridge, and hopes to write about the great German conductor Wilhelm Furtwängler.

MARIA IRENE RAMALHO DE SOUSA SANTOS is professor of English and American Studies at the University of Coimbra, Portugal. She has been visiting faculty at the University of Wisconsin-Madison, Department of Comparative Literature, every fall for the past 12 years. Her major fields of research are poetry and comparative poetics and feminist criticism. Her most recent book is *Atlantic Poets: Fernando Pessoa's Turn in Anglo-American Modernism* (2002), and she has contributed a section on American modernist poets, "Poetry in the Machine Age," to the 5th volume of *the Cambridge History of American Literature* (2003).

LORETTA STEC teaches twentieth-century British literature and postcolonial literature at San Francisco State University. She has published articles on Virginia Woolf, Rebecca West, Katharine Burdekin, and Bessie Head, among others, and is researching women journalists of the modernist era.

JACK STEWART, professor emeritus, University of British Columbia, is the author of *The Vital Art of D. H. Lawrence: Vision and Expression* (1999) and of numerous articles tracing interrelations of literature and painting in the writings of Lawrence, Woolf, and Durrell.

IIDA TAKEO is professor of English at Kurume University, Japan. His articles on D. H. Law-rence have appeared in international journals and his publications include, as editor, *The Reception of D. H. Lawrence Around the World* (1999). He has also written two books on Lawrence in Japanese.

JOHN TURNER is senior lecturer in English at the University of Wales Swansea. He has written books on Wordsworth and Shakespeare, and is currently writing a book on D. H. Lawrence and the history of the psychoanalytic movement. In addition to many articles on Lawrence, he has also edited the Otto Gross–Frieda Weekley Correspondence, and, most recently, the Wilkinson Diaries, for the *D. H. Lawrence Review.*

EIBHEAR WALSHE lectures at the Department of English at University College Cork where he teaches courses on Wilde, on modern Irish fiction and on Irish lesbian and gay writing. He has edited *Ordinary People Dancing: Essays on Kate O'Brien* (1993), *Sex, Nation, and Dissent in Irish Writing* (1997) and *Elizabeth Bowen Remembered* (1999). He is working on a study of Oscar Wilde and Ireland.

STEPHEN WILSON teaches at the University of Coimbra, Portugal, and his main research interest is in the work of Ezra Pound.

SUE WILSON completed her Ph.D. on the plays and prose of Samuel Beckett at the University of Nottingham in 1998. She is now lecturer in drama at Anglia Polytechnic University, Cambridge.

JOHN WORTHEN recently retired as professor of D. H. Lawrence studies at the University of Nottingham. His books on Lawrence include the biography *D. H. Lawrence: The Early Years,* and he has been responsible for several editions of Lawrence for Cambridge University Press; he is also author of *The Gang: Coleridge, the Wordsworths and the Hutchinsons in 1802.*

PAUL WRIGHT is a lecturer in English and creative writing at Trinity College, Carmarthen. His main research interest is British romanticism. He has published work on Keats, Wordsworth and Milton, and is currently working on an edition of Byron's poems.

SARAH WRIGHT completed her doctorate at Clare Hall, Cambridge, and currently works as lecturer in the Department of Hispanic Studies at the University of Hull. She is the author of *The Trickster-Function in the Theatre of García Lorca* (2000).

CAROLINE ZILBOORG was a member of the Faculty of English at Cambridge University and is a Life Member of Clare Hall. She is now based in Brittany, France. She has edited two volumes of correspondence between Richard Aldington and H.D., and these have been recently published in an expanded and revised single-volume paperback edition (2003). Her most recent book is *Mary Renault: A Literary Biography* (2001); she has a special interest in biography and in women's writing.